Lecture Notes in Computer Science

Edited by G. Goos and J. Hartmanis

405

C.E. Veni Madhavan (Ed.)

FST and TCS 9

Foundations of Software Technology and Theoretical Computer Science

Ninth Conference, Bangalore, India
December 19–21, 1989
Proceedings

Springer-Verlag
Berlin Heidelberg New York London Paris Tokyo Hong Kong

Editor

C. E. Veni Madhavan
Department of Computer Science and Automation
Indian Institute of Science
Bangalore 560 012, India

CR Subject Classification (1987): C.2.4, D.1–2, E.1, F.1.3, G.2.2, I.1.2, I.2.3, I.3.5

ISBN 3-540-52048-1 Springer-Verlag Berlin Heidelberg New York
ISBN 0-387-52048-1 Springer-Verlag New York Berlin Heidelberg

Printing and binding: Druckhaus Beltz, Hemsbach/Bergstr.
2145/3140-543210 – Printed on acid-free paper

Preface

The annual FST&TCS conference has been an important forum in India, for the presentation of new results on topics of current research interest, and for the interaction between various research groups from all over the world. The ninth conference attracted 116 contributions from 13 countries. A panel of over 250 referees was used in identifying 3 referees for each paper. Twenty-five of these papers were selected for presentation and inclusion in the conference proceedings.

The high quality of submitted papers, the careful reviews, and the deliberation of the Programme Committee have helped in putting up an interesting programme. The focus of the conference has been on the theoretical and foundational issues in algorithms, programming, systems and software engineering.

The conference organizers thank all those who submitted papers, all the reviewers, the sponsoring organizations for their support, and the many helpful students, academic and professional colleagues within the country for the success of this conference. Our special thanks go to invited speakers, G Rozenberg, M Hennessy, M Joseph and L Guibas.

The Conference Secretariat at TRDDC, Pune provided an admirable infrastructural support. Students and faculty of the Department of Computer Science and Automation, IISc, Bangalore, provided immense help for local arrangements.

C E Veni Madhavan

Conference Advisory Committee

D Bjorner (Denmark)
A Chandra (IBM Research)
S Crespi Reghizzi (Milan)
Z Galil (Columbia)
D Gries (Cornell)
M Joseph (Warwick)
A Joshi (Pennsylvania)
U Montanari (Pisa)
R Narasimhan (TIFR)
M Nivat (Paris)
R Parikh (New York)
S Rao Kosaraju (Johns Hopkins)
S Sahni (Minnesota)
W A Wulf (Virginia)

Technical Programme Comittee

G P Bhattacharjee (IIT Kharagpur)
S Biswas (IIT Kanpur)
A Kumar (IIT Delhi)
S Kumar (TRDDC Pune)
C R Muthukrishnan (IIT Madras)
K V Nori (TRDDC Pune)
L M Patnaik (IISc Bangalore)
H V Sahasrabuddhe (Poona University)
R Sangal (IIT Kanpur)
R K Shyamsunder (TIFR Bombay)
P S Thiagarajan (Matscience Madras)
C E Veni Madhavan (IISc Bangalore)
G Venkatesh (IIT Bombay)

List of Reviewers

K Abrahamson, Wash State Univ
M Ahuja, Ohio State Univ
S A Andresson, Chalmers Univ
V Arvind, IIT Delhi
B R Badrinath, IBM
K K Bagchi, Aalborg Univ
C Bajaj, Purdue Univ
D Beauquier, France
A Beauvieux, IBM
S Bettayeb, Lousiana State Univ
E Bevers, Univ of Leuven
G P Bhattacharje, IIT Kharagpur
B Bhattacharya, ISI, Calcutta
S Biswas, IIT Kanpur
D Bjorner, Tech Univ of Denmark
J R S Blair, Univ of Tennesse
P Boehm, Tech Univ of Berlin
R Brieler, Univ of Munchen
S Browne, Purdue Univ
B Bruckner, Univ of Bremen
D R Bush, Linkoping Univ
D L Carvar, Lousiana State Univ
D Chan, Memphis State Univ
V Chandru, IISc, Bangalore
N S Chaudhari, Univ of Indore
A Cheese, ECRC, Munchen
J Chen, Columbia Univ
P Clote, Univ of Luminy
D Coppersmith, IBM
A Corradi, Univ of Bologna
B Courcelle, France
M Crochemore, Univ of Paris
R K DeBry, IBM
S K Debray, Univ of Arizona
A H Dekker, Univ of Tasmania
B Demoen, Univ of Lueven
K Y Deshpande, TCS
P Minh Dung, AIT, Bangkok
M Dutta, Univ of Guvahati
H Ehrig, Univ of Berlin
J Fiadeiro, Imperial College
S Fortune, AT&T Bell Labs
H Fujita, I-COT
K Furukawa, I-COT
D Gangopadhyay, IBM
M Garzon, Memphis State Univ
E Van Gestel, Univ of Lueven
N S Gopalakrishnan, Univ of Pune
A K Goswami, Warwick Univ
D Gries, Cornell Univ
M Hansen, Tech Univ of Denmark
A Hoppe, Lousiana State Univ
R Janardan, Univ of Minnesota
J M Janas, Univ of Munich
M Joseph, Warwick Univ
J Kamper, Univ of Oldenberg
K Kanchanasut, Melbourne Univ
R Kannan, CMU
D Kapur, SUNY Albany
H Karnick, IIT Kanpur
C Kenyon, Princeton Univ
S Khuller, Cornell Univ
S M Kim, Univ of Oklohoma
C M R Kintala, AT&T Bell Labs
W Kirchher, San Jose State Univ
N Klarlund, Cornell Univ
K Krithivasan, IIT Madras
G Kulkarni, TCS
A Kumar, IIT Delhi
P S Kumar, IISc Bangalore
S Arun Kumar, Univ of Sussex
S Ashok Kumar, C-DOT, Bangalore
S Kumar, TRDDC
V Kumar, Univ of Missouri
S Lakshmivarahan, Oklohoma
G Lausen, Univ of Mannheim
D LeDetayer, IRISA
K Lodaya, Matscience, Madras

H H Lovengreen, Univ of Denmark
J Lu, Univ of New Castle, Tyne
S Rao Maddila, Univ of Illinois
S N Maheshwari, IIT, Delhi
V M Malhotra, AIT, Bangkok
F M Malvestuto, STUDI-DOC, Rome
M Mata, Univ of Victoria
G M Megson, Univ of New Castle
A Mirzaian, York Univ
R P Mody, Poona Univ
B M E Moret, Univ of New Mexico
A Mukhopadhyay, IIT Kanpur
M Mukund, Matscience Madras
J Ian Munro, Univ of Waterloo
P V R Murthy, IISc, Bangalore
K N R Nair, Poona Univ
A Nakamura, Hiroshima Univ
N K Nanda, AIT, Bangkok
Y Narahari, IISc, Bangalore
K Narayana, Penn State Univ
M Nielsen, Univ of Aarhus
N Nirmal, MCC, Madras
K V Nori, TRDDC
S P Pal, IISc, Bangalore
C Pandu Rangan, IIT, Madras
L M Patnaik, IISc, Bangalore
R Paturi, Univ of San Diago
C Patvardhan, IISc, Bangalore
M Pavan Kumar, TRDDC
B Plateau, Univ of Paris
A Proskurowski, Univ of Oregon
M Protasi, Univ of Rome
G Pucci, Univ of New Castle
V Radhakrishna, Carleton Univ
S Ramakrishnan, Bowling Green
R Ramanujam, Matscience, Madras
S Ramesh, TIFR
M R K Krishna Rao, TIFR
S S Ravi, SUNY Albany
B Ravikumar, Univ of Rh Island
D Rine, George Mason Univ
J Rolim, Odense Univ
G Rolli, CSO Svizerra
H V Sahasrabuddhe, Poona Univ
R Sangal, IIT, Kanpur
P Sankar, IISc, Bangalore
S Sankar, Stanford Univ
M Santha, Univ of Paris
V Sarkar, IBM
S R Sataluri, AT&T Bell Labs
T Sato, ICOT
S Saxena, IIT, Kanpur
R K Shyamsunder, TIFR
H Ulrich Simon, Univ of Dortmund
K P Smith, Univ of Illinois
A K Somani, Wash State Univ
N Soundarajan, Ohio State Univ
D M Spresser, James Madison Univ
Y N Srikant, IISc, Bangalore
P K Srimani, Southern Ill. Univ
G Srinivasaraghavan, IIT Delhi
I A Stewart, Univ of New Castle
V Subrahmanian, Univ of Maryland
M Subramaniam, TRDDC
K G Subramanian, MCC, Madras
S Sur-Kolay, ISI, Calcutta
M Takahashi, Hiroshima Univ
T Takaoka, Univ of Ibaraki
J Tang, Univ of Newfoundland
P S Thiagarajan, Matscience
S K Tripathi, Univ of Maryland
G Turan, Univ of Illinois
P M Vaidya, AT&T Bell Labs
C E Veni Madhavan, IISc Bangalore
G Venkatesh, IIT Bombay
H Venkateswaran, IISc, Bangalore
K Vidyasankar, Newfoundland Univ
V Vinay, IISc, Bangalore
P Weil, Univ of Paris
M Winslett, Univ of Illinois
Jia-Huai You, Univ of Alberta
O Zajicek, Courant Institute

TABLE OF CONTENTS

A linear-time recognition algorithm for P_4-reducible graphs

B. Jamison, S. Olariu

Department of Computer Science
Old Dominion University
Norfolk, Virginia 23529
U.S.A.

Abstract

P_4-reducible graphs are precisely the graphs none of whose vertices belong to more than one chordless path with three edges. As it turns out, the class of P_4-reducible graphs strictly contains the well-known class of cographs. A remarkable property of P_4-reducible graphs is their unique tree representation up to isomorphism. In this paper we present a linear-time algorithm to recognize P_4-reducible graphs and to construct their corresponding tree representation.

1. Introduction

The class of cographs, or complement-reducible graphs, arises naturally in many different areas of applied mathematics and computer science. In the literature the cographs are also known as P_4-restricted graphs, D^*-graphs (Jung[6]), HD-graphs (Sumner[11]), CU-graphs (Corneil and Kirkpatrick[2]). It comes as no surprise that the class of cographs has been studied extensively from both the theoretical and algorithmic points of view [2], [3], [4], [6], [7], [8], [9], [10]. An early characterization by Lerchs[7], asserts that cographs are precisely the graphs which contain no induced subgraph isomorphic to the P_4 (defined as the chordless path with four vertices and three edges). Lerchs[7] also proved that the cographs admit a unique tree representation up to isomorphism.

The first effort by Stewart[10] to recognize cographs resulted in an $O(n^2)$ algorithm. Later, Corneil et al[4] reduced the complexity to linear. Their algorithm can be exploited for the purpose of optimizing this class of graphs: given a cograph G, this involves finding the largest size $\omega(G)$ of a clique, the largest size $\alpha(G)$ of a stable set, the smallest number $\chi(G)$ of colours such that adjacent vertices receive distinct colours, and the smallest number $\theta(G)$ of cliques that cover all the vertices of G. In addition, the recognition algorithm of Corneil et al[4] can be used to find efficient solutions to many other algorithmic problems [2], [3].

Quite often, practical applications suggest the study of graphs that are unlikely to have more than a few induced P_4's. Examples include examination scheduling and semantic clustering of index terms (see [4]). In examination scheduling, a *conflict graph* is readily constructed: the vertices represent different courses offered, while courses x and y are linked by an edge if, and only if, some student takes both of them. (In the weighted version, the weight of edge xy stands for the number of students taking both x and y). Clearly, in any coloring of the conflict graph, vertices that are assigned the same color correspond to courses whose examinations can be held concurrently. It is usually anticipated that very few paths of length three will occur in the conflict graph. In the second application, we construct a graph whose vertices are the index terms; an edge occurs between two index terms to denote self-referencing or semantic proximity. Again, very few P_4 are expected to occur.

These applications have motivated Jamison and Olariu[5] to introduce the notion of a P_4–reducible graph: this is a graph none of whose vertices belongs to more than one P_4. Clearly, P_4–reducible graphs strictly contain the class of cographs. As it turns out, a remarkable property of the P_4–reducible graphs is their unique tree representaion up to (labelled) tree isomorphism.

The purpose of this paper is to present a linear-time incremental algorithm to recognize P_4–reducible graphs. As a by-product of our algorithm we obtain, for a P_4–reducible graph G, in linear time, the largest induced cograph of G. Furthermore, our recognition algorithm is subsequently used for the purpose of obtaining the unique tree associated with a P_4–reducible graph.

The paper is organized as follows: Section 2 introduces the terminology and gives background information about cographs and P_4–reducible graphs; Section 3 gives the main theorem which is at the heart of our linear-time recognition for P_4–reducible graphs; Section 4 spells out the details of the algorithm and addresses the time complexity analysis; finally, Section 5 shows how to use the canonical cotree of a P_4–reducible graph G in order to obtain in linear time the corresponding pr-tree.

2. Background and terminology

All the graphs in this work are finite, with no loops nor multiple edges. In addition to standard graph-theoretical terminology compatible with Berge[1], we use some new terms that we are about to define.

For a vertex x of a graph G, $N_G(x)$ will denote the set of all the vertices of G which are adjacent to x: since we assume adjacency to be non-reflexive, $x \notin N_G(x)$. We let $d_G(x)$ stand for $|N_G(x)|$.

To simplify the notation, a P_4 with vertices a, b, c, d and edges ab, bc, cd will be denoted by abcd. In this context, the vertices a and d are referred to as *endpoints* while b and c are termed *midpoints* of the P_4. Consider a P_4 in G induced by A = {a,b,c,d}. A vertex x outside A is said to have a *partner* in A if x together with three vertices in A induces a P_4 in G. Given an induced subgraph H of G and a vertex x outside H, we say that x is *neutral* with respect to H if x has a partner in no P_4 in H. In the remaining part of this work we shall often associate, in some way, rooted trees with graphs. In this context, we shall refer to the vertices of trees as *nodes*. For a node w in a tree T, we let p(w) stand for the parent of w in T.

To make this paper self-contained, we shall review some of the properties of cographs and P_4–reducible graphs.

To begin, Lerchs[7] showed how to associate with every cograph G a unique tree T(G) called the *cotree* of G, and defined as follows.

- every internal node, except possibly for the root, has at least two children.
- the internal nodes are labeled by either 0 (0-nodes) or 1 (1-nodes) in such a way that the root is always a 1-node, and such that 1-nodes and 0-nodes alternate along every path in T(G) starting at the root;
- the leaves of T(G) are precisely the vertices of G, such that vertices x and y are adjacent in G if, and only if, the lowest common ancestor of x and y in T(G) is a 1-node.

Lerchs[8] proved that the cographs are precisely the graphs obtained from single-vertex graphs by a finite sequence of

$\textcircled{0}$ and $\textcircled{1}$ operations defined as follows. Let $G_1=(V_1,E_1)$ and $G_2=(V_2,E_2)$ be arbitrary graphs with $V_1 \cap V_2 = \emptyset$. Now,

- $G_1 \textcircled{0} G_2 = (V_1 \cup V_2, E_1 \cup E_2)$;
- $G_1 \textcircled{1} G_2 = (V_1 \cup V_2, E_1 \cup E_2 \cup \{xy \mid x \in V_1, y \in V_2\})$;

Next, Jamison and Olariu[5] prove the following fundamental result which is at the heart of a constructive characterization of P_4–reducible graphs.

Proposition 1. (Theorem 1 in [5]) A graph G is P_4–reducible if, and only if, for every induced subgraph H of G exactly one of the following conditions are satisfied:

(i) H is disconnected;

(ii) $\overline{H}$ is disconnected;

(iii) there exists a unique P_4 abcd in H such that every vertex of H outside $\{a,b,c,d\}$ is adjacent to both b and c and non-adjacent to both a and d. □

For the purpose of constructing the P_4–reducible graphs, Jamison and Olariu[5] defined yet another graph operation as follows. Let the graphs $G_1=(V_1,E_1)$ and $G_2=(V_2,E_2)$ ($V_1 \cap V_2 = \emptyset$) be such that $V_1 = \{a,d\}$, $E_1 = \emptyset$, and some adjacent vertices b, c in V_2 are adjacent to all the remaining vertices in V_2. Now

$$G_1 \textcircled{2} G_2 = (V_1 \cup V_2, \{ab,cd\} \cup E_2) \qquad (*)$$

Proposition 2. (Theorem 2 in [5]) G is a P_4-reducible graph if, and only if, G is obtained from single-vertex graphs by a finite sequence of operations $\textcircled{0}, \textcircled{1}, \textcircled{2}$. □

The following natural observation follows directly from Proposition 2.

Observation 0. *Let G be a P_4-reducible graph. If G ($\overline{G}$) is disconnected with components $G_1, G_2, \ldots, G_p$ ($p \geq 2$), then we can write $G=G_1 \textcircled{0}(\textcircled{1}) G_2 \textcircled{0}(\textcircled{1}) .. \textcircled{0}(\textcircled{1}) G_p$.* □

[Follows from Proposition 2 by a trivial inductive argument.]

(To make the notation used in Observation 0 more precise, note that operation $\textcircled{0}$ is used throughout in case G is disconnected, while operation $\textcircled{1}$ is used throughout in case $\overline{G}$ is disconnected.)

Proposition 1, Proposition 2, and Observation 0 combined suggest a natural way of associating with every P_4–reducible graph G a tree T(G) (called the *pr-tree* of G), as described by the following recursive procedure.

Procedure Build_tree(G);
{Input: a P_4–reducible graph G=(V,E);
Output: the pr-tree T(G) corresponding to G.}
begin
  if $|V| = 1$ **then**
    return the tree T(G) consisting of the unique vertex of G;
  if G ($\overline{G}$) is disconnected **then begin**
    let $G_1, G_2, \ldots, G_p$ ($p \geq 2$) be the components of G ($\overline{G}$);
    let $T_1, T_2, \ldots, T_p$ be the corresponding pr-trees rooted at $r_1, r_2, \ldots, r_p$;
    return the tree T(G) obtained by adding $r_1, r_2, \ldots, r_p$ as children of a node labelled 0 (1);
    end
  else begin {now both G and $\overline{G}$ are connected}
    write $G = G_1 \textcircled{2} G_2$ as in (*);
    let T_1, T_2 be the corresponding pr-trees rooted at r_1 and r_2;
    return the tree T(G) obtained by adding r_1, r_2 as children of a node labelled 2
    end
end; {Build_tree}

As it turns out (see [5]) the pr-tree of a P_4–reducible graph G is unique up to isomorphism. Let G=(V,E) be a P_4–reducible graph. The *canonical cograph* C(G) associated with G is the induced subgraph of G obtained by the following procedure.

Procedure Greedy(G);
{ Input: a P_4–reducible graph G;
Output: the canonical cograph C(G) }

```
begin
  H ← G;
  while there exist P4's in H do begin
    pick a P4 uvxy in H;
    pick z at random in {u,y};
    H ← H - {z}
  end;
  return(H)
end;
```

It is clear that procedure Greedy removes *precisely* one endpoint of every P_4 in G. The fact that the graph C(G) returned by Greedy is a cograph follows directly from the definition of P_4–reducible graphs; the uniqueness implied by the definition of the canonical cograph is justified by the following result.

Proposition 3. (Theorem 3 in [5]) The canonical cograph of a P_4-reducible graph is unique up to isomorphism. □

3. Algorithms - a preview

We propose to develop a linear-time incremental algorithm to recognize P_4–reducible graphs. In the process, we shall build a cograph which turns out to be the canonical cograph of the P_4–reducible graph (in case the algorithm is successful).

To outline our recognition algorithm for P_4–reducible graphs, consider an arbitrary graph G. We assume that we have already processed a non-empty induced P_4–reducible subgraph H of G. (Note that such a subgraph H can always be found: in fact, the subgraph induced by a subset of at most four vertices in G is a P_4–reducible graph.)

The relevant information about H is stored in the tuple (T(H),L(H)): T(H) is the cotree associated with the canonical cograph C(H) of H (we shall refer to T(H) as the *canonical cotree* of H); L(H) contains precisely one endpoint of every P_4 in H. In addition, for the purpose of checking that no vertex belongs to more than one P_4, those vertices that are known to belong to some P_4 in H are "flagged".

To process a new vertex x we need to verify the following conditions:

- x is neutral with respect to H;
- x belongs to at most one P_4 in H+x; furthermore, this P_4 involves no "flagged" vertex;

Trivially, if either of these conditions fails, then H+x cannot be a P_4–reducible graph and the algorithm terminates. If, on the other hand, both conditions are satisfied, then H+x is a P_4–reducible subgraph of G and we proceed to update the tuple (T(H),L(H)). This involves the following operations:

- if x belongs to no P_4 in H+x then, as we are about to see, x is added as a leaf in T(H), and L(H) is unchanged;
- if x is an endpoint of a P_4 in H+x, then T(H) is unchanged, and x is added to L(H) and flagged;
- if x is a midpoint of a P_4 in H+x, then with y standing for an endpoint of this P_4, we do the following: y is removed from T(H) and added to L(H); x is added as a leaf in T(H-y).

Our recognition algorithm for P_4–reducible graphs relies, in part, on a marking scheme similar to that developed by Corneil et al[4]. For convenience, we borrow their notation relevant to the marking scheme.

For a vertex u in the canonical cotree T(H), rooted at R, we let d(u) stand for the number of children of u; md(u) represents the current number of marked, and subsequently unmarked children of u. (Initially, md(u) is 0 for all the nodes u in T(H); when u is unmarked, md(u) is reset to 0.) A marked 1-node of T(H) is said to be *properly marked* whenever md(u) = d(u) - 1; otherwise it will be termed *improperly marked.*

The procedure Mark using the adjacency information of a new vertex x performs the following actions:

- marks, and subsequently unmarks, as appropriate, certain nodes of T(H);
- builds up a linked list Π(x) of P_4's in H containing vertices adjacent to x;

• adds marked but not subsequently unmarked nodes of T(H) to one or the other of the linked lists M_0 (containing marked 0-nodes), M_1 (containing improperly marked 1-nodes) or M_2 (containing properly marked 1-nodes).

Procedure Mark(x);
```
0.  begin
1.    M₀ ← M₁ ← M₂ ← ∅; c₀ ← c₁ ← c₂ ← 0; Π(x) ← ∅;
2.    for each v in N_G(x) do
3.      if (v is a leaf in T(H)) or (v∈L(H)) then begin
4.        Π(x) ← Π(x) ∪ {P₄ in H containing v};
5.        mark v unless v∈L(H)
6.      end;
7.    for each marked node u in T(H) do
8.      if d(u) = md(u) then begin
9.        unmark u;
10.       md(u) ←0;
11.       if u ≠ R then begin
12.         w ← p(u);
13.         mark w;
14.         md(w) ← md(w)+1;
15.         add u to the list of marked and subsequently unmarked children of w
16.       end
17.     end
18.     else {now d(u) ≠ md(u), and so u is marked but not unmarked}
19.       case label (u) of
20.         0:    begin {u is a marked 0-node}
21.                 c₀ ← c₀+1;
22.                 M₀ ← M₀ ∪ {u}
23.               end;
24.         1:    begin
25.                 if md(u) ≠ d(u)-1 then begin {u is improperly marked}
26.                   c₁ ← c₁+1;
27.                   M₁ ← M₁ ∪ {u}
28.                 end
29.                 else begin {now u is a properly marked 1-node}
30.                   c₂ ← c₂+1;
31.                   M₂ ← M₂ ∪ {u}
32.                 end
33.               end
34.       endcase;
35.   if (c₀ + c₁ + c₂ > 0) and d(R)=1 then mark R
36. end; {Mark}
```

In the remainder of this paper a node w of T(H) will be referred to as *marked* only if w remains marked at the end of procedure Mark (i.e. w is marked but not subsequently unmarked). For a node w in T(H), T(w) will denote the subtree of T(H) rooted at w. For later reference, we make note of the following simple observations.

Observation 1. *Let w be a marked node in T(H). There must exist a child w' of w such that all the leaves in T(w') are adjacent to x.* □

[Otherwise, the node w could not possibly be marked.]

Observation 2. *Let w be a node of T(H) that was never unmarked. There must exist a descendant w'' of w in T(w) such that all the leaves in T(w'') are non-adjacent to x.* □

[Otherwise, w would have been marked and subsequently unmarked.]

Let w be an arbitrary node of T(H) and let I(w) stand for the set of children of w which have a marked (and not subsequently unmarked) descendant in T(H). Let T'(w) stand for the subtree of T(w) defined by

$$T'(w) = T(w) - \bigcup_{u \in I(w)} T(u)$$

Partition of the leaves of T'(w) into non-empty, disjoint sets A(w) and B(w), in such a way that x is adjacent to all the leaves in A(w) and adjacent to no leaf in B(w).

Observation 3. *w is the lowest common ancestor of any leaves a in A(w) and b in B(w).* □

[To see this, note that every descendant w' of w in T'(w) is such that T(w') contains leaves from A(w) or B(w) only, for otherwise with u standing for a counterexample with the lowest level in T'(w), u must be marked, a contradiction.]

If T(H) contains marked nodes, then the marked node with the lowest level in T(H), denoted $\alpha(x)$ (or simply α, if no confusion is possible) plays a distinguished role in our algorithm. (If several marked nodes are at the same level, pick one at random.)

Let

$$(P) \quad R = w_1, w_2, ..., w_p = \alpha(x) \quad (p \geq 1) \tag{1}$$

stand for the unique path in T(H) joining R and α. The path (P) is referred to as *complete* if no marked vertex in T(H) lies outside (P).

For nodes w_j with $1 \leq j \leq p-1$ of a complete path (P), the subtree $T(w_j) - T(w_{j+1})$ contains no marked node (with the possible exception of w_j itself): as before, we let

- $A(w_j)$ stand for the set of leaves in $T(w_j) - T(w_{j+1})$ which are adjacent to x;
- $B(w_j)$ stand for the set of leaves in $T(w_j) - T(w_{j+1})$ which are not adjacent to x.

For w_p (= $\alpha(x)$), denote by

- $A(w_p)$ the set of all the leaves in $T(w_p)$ which are adjacent to x;
- $B(w_p)$ the set of all the remaining leaves in $T(w_p)$.

Observation 4. *No w_k $(1 \leq k \leq p)$ on the path (P) is marked and subsequently unmarked.* □

[This is obvious, by definition, for α; let j be the largest subscript for which w_j is a counterexample. However, since w_j was both marked and unmarked, it follows, in particular, that so was w_{j+1}, a contradiction.]

Observation 5. *Let w be an arbitrary unmarked node, or an improperly marked 1-node in P. There exists a non-empty set S of leaves of T(w), such that x is non-adjacent to all the leaves in S.* □

[By Observation 4, any unmarked node in (P) cannot have been both marked and then, unmarked. Now the conclusion follows instantly from Observation 2.]

Observation 6. *If d(R) = 1 and R is marked, then R is properly marked.* □

[This follows easily from the marking scheme: if d(R)=1 and R is marked, but not unmarked then, trivially, md(R)=0 and so d(R) = md(R)+1, implying that R is properly marked.]

Call a node w_j $(1 \leq j \leq p-1)$ of (P) *regular* if w_j is either a properly marked 1-node or else an unmarked 0-node. Otherwise, w_j is termed *special.*

The path (P) is said to be *admissible* if the following conditions are satisfied.

(a1) (P) is complete;

(a2) there is at most one subscript k $(1 \leq k \leq p-1)$ such that the node w_k is special. Furthermore, if a special node exists, then the following conditions must be true

(a2.1) k = p-2 or k = p-1;

(a2.2) if k = p-1 then $|A(w_p)| = |B(w_p)| = 1$ with both vertices in $A(w_p)$ and $B(w_p)$ unflagged; furthermore, $|B(w_k)| = 1$ and the vertex in $B(w_k)$ is unflagged whenever w_p is a 0-node; and $|A(w_k)| = 1$ and the vertex in $A(w_k)$ is unflagged whenever w_p is a 1-node.

(a2.3) if k = p-2 then $|B(w_p)| = |A(w_{p-1})| = |A(w_k)| = 1$ with none of the vertices in $B(w_p)$, $A(w_{p-1})$, $A(w_k)$ flagged and $B(w_{p-1}) = \emptyset$ whenever w_p is a 0-node; $|A(w_p)| = |B(w_{p-1})| = |B(w_k)| = 1$ with none of the vertices in $A(w_p)$, $B(w_{p-1})$, $B(w_k)$ flagged and $A(w_{p-1}) = \emptyset$ whenever w_p is a 1-node;

Note that, if T(H) contains no marked nodes, then the path (P) is, trivially, empty and hence vacuously admissible.

Now in our notation, Theorem 1 in Corneil et al[4] can be formulated as follows.

Proposition 4.(Corneil et al[4]) *If H is a cograph, then H+x is a cograph if, and only if, the path in T(H) joining the root and $\alpha(x)$ is admissible and contains no special nodes.* □

We are now ready to state a result which provides the theoretical basis for our recognition algorithm for P_4–reducible graphs. We assume the existence of an underlying graph G=(V,E) which is in the process of being investigated by the recognition algorithm.

THEOREM 1. *If H is a P_4-reducible graph, then H+x is a P_4-reducible graph if, and only if, x is neutral with respect to H and the path joining the root of T(H) and $\alpha(x)$ is admissible.*

PROOF OF THEOREM 1. Let $H=(V_H,E_H)$ be a P_4–reducible graph described by the tuple (T(H),L(H)), where T(H) is the cotree associated with the canonical cograph C(H). Assume that the vertex x is neutral with respect to H. If T(H) contains no marked nodes, or if the path in T(H) joining R and $\alpha(x)$ is admissible and contains no special nodes, then by Proposition 4 C(H)+x is a cograph and, hence, no P_4 in H+x contains x. It follows that H+x is a P_4–reducible graph.

Now we may assume that the path (P) joining R and $\alpha(x)$ is admissible and contains a special node. In this case, a straightforward argument, which is left to the reader, shows that x is contained in precisely one P_4 in H+x.

Conversely, assume that H+x is a P_4–reducible graph. In particular, x must be neutral with respect to H. We only need prove that in the presence of special nodes, the path (P) joining R and $\alpha(x)$ is admissible.

Our proof relies on the following intermediate results that we present as facts. Write (P) as in (1).

FACT 1. *(P) is complete.*

Proof. Suppose not; let γ stand for the lowest marked node in T(H) which does not belong to (P), and let w_i stand for the lowest common ancestor of α and γ in T(H). We claim that

$$\gamma \text{ and } w_i \text{ are either both 0–nodes or both 1–nodes.} \tag{2}$$

[Suppose not; symmetry allows us to assume that γ is a 0-node and that w_i is a 1-node. By Observation 1, Observation 2, and Observation 3 combined, we find leaves a, b, c, d in $A(\alpha)$, $B(\alpha)$, $A(\gamma)$, $B(\gamma)$ respectively. Since w_i is a 1-node, we have ad, bc, bd $\in$ E. Since γ is a 0-node, cd$\notin$E. It follows that xcbd is a P_4. Now α must be a 1-node, for otherwise ab$\notin$E and so xadb would be a second P_4 containing x. Clearly, our choice of α implies that α and w_i are distinct nodes of T(H). Since they are both 1-nodes, we find a 0-node w_j on the path from α to w_i. Let t be an arbitrary leaf in $T(w_j)$ - $T(w_{j+1})$. Clearly, ta, tb$\notin$E and tc, td $\in$E. We must have xt$\in$E, or else xctd is a P_4, implying that x belongs to two distinct P_4's. However, now txab is a P_4, contradicting that H+x is P_4–reducible.]

Now (2) allows us to assume, without loss of generality that

$$\text{both } \gamma \text{ and } w_i \text{ are 0–nodes.}$$

(the case where γ and w_i are both 1-nodes is perfectly symmetric)

As before, by Observation 1, Observation 2 and Observation 3 combined we find leaves a, b, c, d in $A(\alpha)$, $B(\alpha)$, $A(\gamma)$, $B(\gamma)$ respectively. Since, by assumption, w_i and γ are distinct 0-nodes, we find a 1-node θ on the path in T(H) from γ to w_i.

Let t be an arbitrary leaf in $T(\theta)$ - $T(c(\theta))$ (here, $c(\theta)$ is the child of θ which lies on the path from γ to θ). Obviously, we have at, bt$\notin$E and tc, td$\in$E.

Observe that xt$\in$E, for otherwise {a,x,c,t,d} induces two distinct P_4's. Now axtd is a P_4 in H+x. Furthermore, note that α must be a 0-node, else baxt is a second P_4 containing x. Since α and w_i are distinct 0-nodes, we find a 1-node w_j on the path from α to w_i.

Let t' be a leaf in $T(w_j)$ -$T(w_{j+1})$. We have t'a, t'b$\in$E, t'c, t'd$\notin$E. But now either bt'xc or xat'b is a P_4 depending on whether or not xt'$\in$E. Either case leads to a contradiction, and the proof of Fact 1 is complete. □

FACT 2. *If w_k $(1 \le k < p)$ is an improperly marked 1-node or an unmarked 1-node, then $k=p-1$ or $k=p-2$, depending on whether or not $\alpha(x)$ is a 0-node. Furthermore, if $k=p-2$, then w_{p-1} is unmarked.*

Proof. To begin, we claim that

$$d(w_k) \ge 2. \tag{3}$$

[This follows from the definition of the cotree, combined with Observation 6.]

Clearly, (3) implies that $T(w_k) - T(w_{k+1}) \ne \emptyset$. By Observation 4, w_{k+1} cannot be marked and subsequently unmarked, and so $d(w_k) \ge md(w_k) + 1$. Since this inequality must, in fact, be strict, there exists a leaf d in $T(w_k) - T(w_{k+1})$ with $dx \notin E$.

We let, as usual, a, b stand for arbitrary leaves in $A(\alpha)$, $B(\alpha)$ respectively. Obviously, since w_k is a 1-node, we have ad, bd$\in$E. It is easy to see that

if the statement is false, then we find distinct subscripts i, j

$(k < i < j \le p)$ such that both w_i and w_j are 0–nodes.

[To justify this observation, note that in case w_p is a 0-node we set $j \leftarrow p$ and since $k<p-1$ we set $i \leftarrow p-2$; in case w_p is a 1-node, we set $j \leftarrow p-1$ and $i \leftarrow k+1$.]

Let t be an arbitrary leaf in $T(w_i) - T(w_{i+1})$. Since w_i is a 0-node, ta, tb$\notin$E; since w_k is a 1-node, ad, bd, td$\in$E. If w_p is a 0-node, then xadb is a P_4; in addition, either bdtx or xadt is a P_4 depending on whether or not xt$\in$E.

We shall, therefore, assume that w_p is a 1-node. Let t' be an arbitrary leaf in $T(w_j) - T(w_{j+1})$. Note that tt', t'a, t'b $\notin$E and t'd$\in$E; since w_p is a 1-node we have ab$\in$E. But now, {a,b,x,t,t',d} induces at least two distinct P_4's containing x. [To see that this is the case, note that xt, xt'$\notin$E, else baxz, xzdb are P_4's with z=t or z=t' such that xz$\in$E. However, now xadt and xadt' are distinct P_4's containing x, contrary to our assumption.]

Finally, we claim that

if $k=p-2$, then w_{p-1} is unmarked.

[If w_{p-1} were marked, then by Observation 1 we find a vertex c in $T(w_{p-1}) - T(w_p)$ with xc$\in$E. Since w_{p-1} is a 0-node ac, bc$\notin$E; since w_k is a 1-node, cd$\in$E. But now, the set {a,b,c,d,x} induces two distinct P_4's containing x (namely baxc and bdcx), a contradiction.]

This completes the proof of Fact 2. □

FACT 3. *If w_k $(1 \le k < p)$ is a marked 0-node, then $k=p-1$ or $k=p-2$, depending on whether or not $\alpha(x)$ is a 1-node. Furthermore, if $k=p-2$, then w_{p-1} is properly marked.*

Proof. Trivially, $w_k \ne R$. By Observation 1, and Observation 4 combined, there exists a leaf c in $T(w_k) - T(w_{k+1})$ such that xc$\in$E. We claim that

if the statement is false, then we find distinct subscripts i, j

$(k < i < j \le p)$ such that both w_i and w_j are 1–nodes.

[To justify this observation, note that if w_p is a 0-node, then since $k<p-2$ we set $j \leftarrow p-1$ and $i \leftarrow k+1$; if w_p is a 1-node, then set $j \leftarrow p$ and since $k<p-1$, we set $i \leftarrow k+1$.]

As usual, we let a, b stand for arbitrary leaves in $A(\alpha)$, $B(\alpha)$, respectively. Let t be an arbitrary leaf in $T(w_i) - T(w_{i+1})$. Since w_i is a 1-node, we have at, bt$\in$E; since w_k is a 0-node, we have ac, bc, tc$\notin$E. We note that

$$w_p \text{ is a 0–node.} \tag{4}$$

[Otherwise, baxc is a P_4, and either taxc or btxc is a P_4 depending on whether or not xt$\notin$E.]

By (4), $j \ne p$; let t' be an arbitrary leaf in $T(w_j) - T(w_{j+1})$. Note that since w_p is a 0-node ab$\notin$E; now xt, xt'$\in$E, or else {b,z,a,x,c} induces two distinct P_4's with z=t or z=t'. But now, btxc, bt'xc are distinct P_4's containing x, contrary to our assumption.

Finally, we claim that

if k=p-2, then w_{p-1} is properly marked.

[Suppose not; now by Observation 5, $T(w_{p-1})$ - $T(w_p)$ contains a leaf d with $xd \notin E$. However, with c as above, {c,x,a,d,b} induces two distinct P_4's in H+x, a contradiction.]

This completes the proof of Fact 3. □

FACT 4. *The path (P) contains at most one special node.*

Proof. To begin, note that by Fact 2 and Fact 3 combined, (P) cannot contain two distinct special nodes of the same kind (both 0-nodes or both 1-nodes). We let w_k ($1 \le k < p$) be a special 1-node and w_r ($1 < r < p$) be a special 0-node in (P).

If w_p is a 0-node, then by Fact 2, k=p-1. By Fact 3, r=p-2 and w_{p-1} must be properly marked, a contradiction.

Thus w_p must be a 1-node. By Fact 3, r=p-1. By Fact 2, k=p-2 and w_{p-1} must be unmarked, a contradiction. □

To complete the proof of Theorem 1, we only need prove that the conditions (a2.2) and (a2.3) in the definition of the admissible path are satisfied. For this purpose, we distinguish between the following two cases.

Case 1. w_p is a 0-node.

If w_k is an improperly marked 1-node or an unmarked 1-node, then, by Fact 2, k=p-1. For every choice of a leaf a in $A(w_p)$, b in $B(w_p)$, and d in $B(w_k)$, xadb is a P_4. It follows that

$$|A(w_p)| = |B(w_p)| = |B(w_k)| = 1$$

and that none of the vertices a, d, b can be "flagged": any such flagged vertex would belong to two distinct P_4's in H+x, a contradiction.

Furthermore, if w_k is a marked 0-node, Fact 3 implies that k=p-2 and that w_{p-1} is properly marked. This implies that $B(w_{p-1}) = \emptyset$. Now for every choice of b in $B(w_p)$, t in $A(w_{p-1})$, and c in $A(w_k)$ we have btxc a P_4. It follows that

$$|B(w_p)| = |A(w_{p-1})| = |A(w_k)| = 1$$

with none of the vertices b, t, c "flagged".

Case 2. w_p is a 1-node.

If w_k is a marked 0-node then, by Fact 3, we have k=p-1. Note that for every choice of a in $A(w_p)$, b in $B(w_p)$, and c in $A(w_k)$, baxc is a P_4, implying that

$$|A(w_p)| = |B(w_p)| = |A(w_k)| = 1$$

with none of the vertices a, b, c "flagged".

If w_k is an improperly marked 1-node or an unmarked 1-node then, by Fact 2, k=p-2 and w_{p-1} is unmarked. By Observation 1, $A(w_{p-1}) = \emptyset$. Furthermore, for every choice of a in $A(w_p)$, d in $B(w_k)$ and t in $B(w_{p-1})$, xadt is a P_4, and so

$$|A(w_p)| = |B(w_{p-1})| = |B(w_k)| = 1$$

with none of the vertices a, d, t "flagged".

This completes the proof of the theorem. □

Corollary 1. *If* $|M_0 \cup M_1| > 2$, *then H+x is not a P_4-reducible graph.*

Proof. If $c_0 + c_1 > 2$ then the path (P) joining α and R cannot be admissible. The conclusion follows by Theorem 1. □

4. Algorithms - the details

As previously mentioned, our recognition algorithm for P_4–reducible graphs is incremental. Given a graph G=(V,E), whose vertices are enumerated as $v_1, v_2, ..., v_n$, we proceed in the following two stages.

Algorithm Recognize(G);
Stage 1. [Initialization]
set all the vertices in G "unflagged";

$H \leftarrow \{v_1, v_2\}$;
construct the cotree T(H) rooted at R;
$L(H) \leftarrow \emptyset$;

Stage 2. [Incrementaly process the remaining vertices in G - H, as follows]
    Step 2.0   pick x in G - H; Mark(x);
    Step 2.1   if x is not neutral with respect to H then return("no");
    Step 2.2   if x belongs to more than one P_4 or if x belongs to a P_4 involving a "flagged" vertex in H+x then return("no");
    Step 2.3 $H \leftarrow H + x$; update (T(H),L(H)).

We assume that upon executing the statement **return("no")** the entire algorithm terminates: H+x is not a P_4–reducible graph (This will be justified later). Since the details of Step 2.0 have been discussed in Section 3, we shall turn our attention to the remaining steps in Stage 2. For this purpose, we note that Step 2.1 can be implemented by the following procedure.

Procedure Test_Neutral(x);
$\{\Pi(x)$ is a list of $\vec{P_4}$'s created in procedure Mark$\}$
1. **begin**
2.   **while** $\Pi(x) \neq \emptyset$ **do begin**
3.   pick a P_4 in $\Pi(x)$ with endpoints x_0 and x_3 and midpoints x_1 and x_2;
4.   **if** x has a partner in $\{x_0,x_1,x_2,x_3\}$ **then** return("no");
5. $\Pi(x) \leftarrow \Pi(x) - \{x_0,x_1,x_2,x_3\}$
6.   **end**

7. **end**;

Two nodes of T(H) play a distinguished role in Steps 2.2 - 2.3: first, $\alpha(x)$ stands, as before, for a marked node in T(H) with the lowest level (ties being broken arbitrarily); next, $\gamma(x)$ is a candidate for a special node on the path joining α and R. (We shall write, simply, α and γ instead of $\alpha(x)$ and $\gamma(x)$ since no confusion is possible.)

Step 2.2 is further refined into two substeps as follows.

Step 2.2 [if x belongs to more than one P_4 or if x belongs to a P_4 involving a "flagged" vertex in H+x then return("no");
]

Step 2.2.1 Find α;

Step 2.2.2 If the path in T(H) joining R and α is not admissible then return("no");

Step 2.2.1 is implemented by the procedure Find whose details are given below.

Procedure Find;
{returns a node that plays the role of α.}
1. **begin** Find $\leftarrow$ undefined;
2. **if** $c_0 + c_1 + c_2 = 0$ **then** Find $\leftarrow \Lambda$;
3. **case** $c_0 + c_1$ **of**
4.   0   :**if** p(p(z)) is an unmarked node of T(H) for some z in M_2 **then**
5.   Find $\leftarrow$ z
6.   **else begin**
7.   let z be a node in M_2 such that $z \neq p(p(z'))$ for all $z' \in M_2$;
8.   Find $\leftarrow$ z
9.   **end**;
10. 1   :**begin**
11.   let z be the unique node in $M_0 \cup M_1$;
12.   **if** $z=p(z')$ or $z=p(p(z'))$ for some $z' \in M_2$ **then**
13.   Find $\leftarrow$ z'
14.   **else**
15.   Find $\leftarrow$ z
16.   **end**;
17. 2   :**if** for distinct z, z' in $M_0 \cup M_1$, $z' = p(z)$ or $z' = p(p(z))$ **then**
18.   Find $\leftarrow$ z
19. **endcase**

20. **end**; {Find}

The following result shows that H+x is a P_4–reducible graph only if the node returned by the procedure Find can play the role of α. More precisely:

FACT 5. *Let z be the node returned by the function Find. H+x is P_4-reducible, only if the following statements are satisfied:*

5.1) $z = \Lambda$ whenever T(H) contains no marked nodes;

5.2) z and α coincide whenever T(H) contains marked nodes.

Proof. To begin, note that procedure Find returns "undefined" whenever $c_0+c_1>2$. By Corollary 1, H+x cannot be P_4–reducible. Next, line 2 in procedure Find guarantees that $z = \Lambda$ whenever $c_0+c_1+c_2=0$. To show that 5.2 must also be satisfied, we shall rely on the following simple observations.

Observation 7. *Let z be a marked node in T(H) such that the parent of z or the grandparent of z (but not both) is either a marked 0-node or an improperly marked 1-node or an unmarked 1-node. Then H+x is P_4-reducible only if z and α coincide.*

[By assumption, T(H) contains marked nodes. Let, as usual, α stand for a marked node of the lowest level in T(H). If H+x is P_4–reducible, then by Theorem 1, the path (P) in T(H) joining α and R is admissible. Thus z must belong to (P). But now, z must coincide with α, for otherwise we contradict Fact 2 or Fact 3 in the proof of Theorem 1.]

Observation 8. *Let $M_2 \neq \emptyset$ and $M_0 \cup M_1 = \emptyset$; H+x is P_4-reducible only if α is either a node in M_2 whose grandparent is unmarked or, failing this, a node in M_2 which is grandparent of no node in M_2.*

[Clearly, $\alpha \in M_2$; let z be a node in M_2 such that p(p(z)) is unmarked. By Observation 7, z and α must coincide; now we may assume that no such node z exists. It follows that α is a node in M_2 that is grandparent of no node in M_2, as claimed.]

Observation 9. *Let $|M_0 \cup M_1| = 1$; H+x is P_4-reducible only if α is either a node in M_2 whose parent or grandparent is the unique node in $M_0 \cup M_1$ or, failing this, α is the unique node in $M_0 \cup M_1$.*

[Let t stand for the unique node in $M_0 \cup M_1$. If for some node z in M_2, t = p(z) or t = p(p(z)), then by Observation 7, z and α coincide. If no such z exists in M_2, then $\alpha \notin M_2$ or else we contradict Fact 2 or Fact 3. It follows that α and t coincide.]

Observation 10. *Let $|M_0 \cup M_1| = 2$; H+x is P_4-reducible only if α belongs to $M_0 \cup M_1$.*

[If $\alpha \notin M_0 \cup M_1$, then the path in T(H) joining α and R cannot be admissible.]

Now the conclusion follows immediately from Observations 8-11, and the proof of Fact 5 is complete. □

We assume that whenever the **unmark w** statement is executed during Step 2.2 and Step 2.3 of the algorithm Recognize described above, with $w \in M_i$, the following statements are implicitly performed

$$M_i \leftarrow M_i - \{w\};$$

$$c_i \leftarrow c_i - 1;$$

$$md(w) \leftarrow 0;$$

Step 2.2.2 is implemented by the procedure Test_Admissible whose details are spelled out next. As justified by Fact 5, we may use α for the node returned by procedure Find.

```
Procedure Test_Admissible;
{tests the path in T(H) joining α and R for admissibility.}
begin
  if α = undefined then return("no");
     γ ← α; if α = Λ then exit;
  if (p(α)∈M0) or (label(p(α))=1 and p(α)∉M2) then γ ← p(α)
  else if (p(p(α))∈M0) or (label(p(p(α)))=1 and p(p(α))∉M2) then γ ← p(p(α));
  {to begin, check the path between γ and R}
  z ← γ;
  if label(z)=0 then begin
     z ←p(z)
  else z ← p(p(z));
  while z∈T(H) do begin
     if z∉M2 then return("no") else unmark z;
```

```
12.     z ← p(p(z))
13.   end;
      {check whether an appropriate number of nodes remain marked}
14.   if (γ=p(p(α))) and (label(α)=0) then {we know that p(α)∈M2}
15.        unmark p(α);
16.   if (c0+c1+c2>2) or ((c0+c1+c2>1) and (γ not marked)) then return("no");
      {finally, check the conditions 2.2 and 2.3}
17.   case γ of
18.     p(α)    :begin if |A(α)|≠1 or |B(α)|≠1 or one of the vertices in A(α), B(α) is "flagged" then return("no")
                     else flag the vertices in A(α), B(α);
19.                if label(α)=0 and (|B(γ)|≠1 or B(γ) contains a "flagged" vertex) then return("no")
                   else flag the vertex in B(γ);
20.                if label(α)=1 and (|A(γ)|≠1 or A(γ) contains a "flagged" vertex) then return("no")
                   else flag the vertex in A(γ)
21.             end;
22.     p(p(α)) :begin if label(α)=0 and (|B(α)|≠1 or |A(p(α))|≠1 or |A(γ)|≠1 or B(α), A(p(α)), A(γ) contain "flagged" vertices
                              or B(p(α))≠∅) then return("no")
                     else flag the vertices in B(α), A(p(α)), A(γ);
23.                  if label(α)=1 and (|A(α)|≠1 or |B(γ)|≠1 or |B(p(α))|≠1 or A(α), B(γ), B(p(α)) contain "flagged" vertices
                              or A(p(α))≠∅) then return("no")
                     else flag the vertices in A(α), B(γ), B(p(α))
24.             end
25.   endcase;
26    if α≠γ then flag x
27. end; {Test_Admissible}
```

Observation 12. *If γ is chosen in lines 4-5 of Test_Admissible, then exactly one of the following conditions hold true:*

(i) $label(\alpha) = 0\ (1)$, $label(\gamma) = 1\ (0)$, and $\gamma = p(\alpha)$;

(ii) $label(\alpha) = 0\ (1)$, $label(\gamma) = 0\ (1)$, and $\gamma = p(p(\alpha))$; furthermore,

$p(\alpha)$ is properly marked whenever $label(\alpha) = 0$,

$p(\alpha)$ is unmarked whenever $label(\alpha) = 1$.

[Follows trivially from the code for lines 4-5.]

FACT 6. *The path (P) in T(H) from α to R is admissible if, and only if the statement return("no") is not executed in Test_Admissible.*

Proof. To begin, assume that (P) is admissible. If (P) contains no special node then α and γ coincide and we are done. We may therefore assume that (P) contains a special node. By Observation 12, this special node will be correctly determined in lines 4-5.

Next, lines 6-15 will unmark all properly marked 1-nodes in (P) from γ (exclusive) to R (inclusive) and, in case both α and γ are 0-nodes, $p(\alpha)$ which by Fact 3 is a 1-node is also unmarked. It follows that when line 16 is reached $c_0+c_1+c_2 \leq 2$, with equality if α and γ are both marked. Finally, it is easy to see that the admissibility of (P) implies that return("no") will not be executed in lines 17-25.

Conversely, assume that the statement return("no") is not executed in Test_Admissible. We only need prove that if $\alpha \in T(H)$, then the path (P) is admissible.

First, we claim that

(P) is complete.

[Otherwise, line 16 would have detected the presence of a marked node in T(H) outside (P).]

Next, we claim that

(P) contains at most one special node.

[Otherwise we would have executed the return("no") statement in line 11 in case (P) contained an unmarked node or an improperly marked node other than (possibly) γ, or line 16 if (P) contained a marked 0-node other then γ.]

Finally, it is easy to see that since no return("no") was executed in lines 17-25, the conditions (a2.2) and (a2.3) are satisfied, and the path (P) is admissible. □

We note that by virtue of Fact 5 and Fact 6, Theorem 1 can be reformulated as follows.

THEOREM 2. *If H is a P_4-reducible graph, then H+x is a P_4-reducible graph if, and only if, the statement return("no") is not executed in Step 2.1 and Step 2.2.* □

To make our arguments more transparent, we further refine Step 2.3 as follows

Step 2.3 [H ← H + x; update (T(H),L(H))]

        if $\alpha = \gamma$ then

           Update_1

        else

           Update_2;

Here, Update_1 is reminiscent of the way Corneil et al[4] update the cotree once they know that x is contained in no P_4 in H+x. The procedure Update_2 deals with the more general case where the path in T(H), though admissible, is known to contain a special node, namely γ. T(H) is altered to represent the canonical cotree of H+x. The details of these two procedures are spelled out next.

Procedure Update_1;
{x is contained in no P_4 in H+x;
we do: H ← H+x; T(H+x) ← T(H) + x; L(H+x) ← L(H)}
1. begin
2.   if $\alpha = \Lambda$ then
3.   if all nodes in T(H) were marked and subsequently unmarked **then**
4.   add x as a child of R
5.   else {no node in T(H) was marked}
6.   if d(R) =1 then
7.   make x a child of the (only) child of R
8.   else begin
9.   make the old root and x children of a new 0-node θ;
10.   make θ the only son of the new root
11.   end
12.   else {now α is the only marked node in T(H)}
13.   if label(α) = 0 (1) then
14.   if md(α) = 1 (d(α) - md(α) = 1) then begin
15. λ ← unique marked and unmarked (never marked) child of α in T(α);
16.   if λ is a leaf in T(H) then begin
17.   make λ, x children of a new node θ;
18.   make θ a child of α
19.   end
20.   else
21.   make x a child of λ
22.   end
23.   else begin {now md(α) ≠ 1 (d(α) - md(α) ≠ 1)}
24.   add every marked child of α to a new node θ with label(θ)=label(α);
25.   if label(α) = 0 then begin
26.   make x, θ children of a new node θ';
27.   make θ' a child of α
28.   end
29.   else begin
30.   make θ a child of p(α);
31.   make x, α children of a new node θ';
32.   make θ' a child of θ
33.   end
34.   end
35. end; {Update_1}

To specify the details of the procedure Update_2, we shall find it convenient to introduce the following notation:

• write A(α) = {a}, whenever |A(α)| = 1;

• write B(α) = {b}, whenever |B(α)| = 1;

- write $A(\gamma) = \{c\}$, whenever $|A(\gamma)| = 1$;
- write $B(\gamma) = \{d\}$, whenever $|B(\gamma)| = 1$;

if $\gamma \neq p(\alpha)$ then

- write $A(p(\alpha)) = \{t\}$ whenever $|A(p(\alpha))| = 1$;
- write $B(p(\alpha)) = \{t'\}$ whenever $|B(p(\alpha))| = 1$.

For the purpose of justifying our way of updating the tuple (T(H),L(H)) in Step 2.3 we need the following intermediate result.

FACT 7. *x is the endpoint of a unique P_4 in H+x if, and only if, γ is a 1-node.*

Proof. Let γ be a 1-node. If α is a 0-node, then by Fact 2 in the proof of Theorem 1 we have $\gamma = p(\alpha)$; furthermore, (a2.2) in the definition of an admissible path implies that with a, b, d, as above, {x,a,b,d} induces a P_4 in H+x having x as one of its endpoints.

Similarly, if α is a 1-node, then by Fact 2, again, we have $\gamma = p(p(\alpha))$; now by (a2.3) in the definition of an admissible path we note that, in our notation, {x,a,d,t'} induces a P_4 in H+x, having x as an endpoint.

Conversely, suppose that x is endpoint of a P_4 xyzw in H+x. We propose to show that the assumption that γ is a 0-node leads to a contradiction.

If α is a 1-node, then by Fact 3 it must be the case that $\gamma = p(\alpha)$. By (a2.2) baxc is a P_4 distinct from xyzw, a contradiction.

If α is a 0-node, then by Fact 3, again, $\gamma = p(p(\alpha))$. Now (a2.3) guarantees that btxc induces a P_4, contrary to our assumption. □

Procedure Update_2;
{x is contained in precisely one P_4 in H+x;
the procedure performs H ← H + x and updates T(H) and L(H) accordingly}
1. **begin**
2.   **if** label(γ) =1 **then begin**
3.   T(H+x) ← T(H);
4.   L(H+x) ← L(H) ∪ {x};
5.   **end**
6.   **else begin** {now γ is a 0-node}
7.   L(H+x) ← L(H) ∪ {b};
8.   remove b from T(H);
9.   **case** α **of**
10.   1   :**if** $B(\gamma) = \emptyset$ **then begin**
11.   add a as a child of γ;
12.   add x as a child of $p(\gamma)$;
13.   remove α from T(H)
14.   **end**
15.   **else begin**
16.   make a, c children of a new 0-node θ;
17.   make θ, x children of α
18.   **end**;
19.   0   :**begin**
20.   **if** $B(\gamma) = \emptyset$ **then**
21.   add x as a child of $p(\gamma)$
22.   **else begin**
23.   make $p(\alpha)$ and c children of a new 0-node θ;
24.   make θ and x children of a new 1-node θ';
25.   make θ' a child of γ;
26.   **end**;
27.   **if** md(α) = 1 **then begin**
28.   let α' be the marked and subsequently unmarked child of α;
29.   **if** α' is a leaf in T(H) **then**
30.   make α' a child of $p(\alpha)$
31.   **else begin**
32.   make every child of α' a child of $p(\alpha)$;
33.   remove α' from T(H)

```
34.                     end;
35.                   remove α from T(H)
36.                 end;
37.                 unmark α, unless already removed;
38.                 if γ is marked then unmark γ
39.               end
40.     endcase
41. end; {Update}
```

FACT 8. *The cotree $T(H+x)$ returned by Step 2.3 is the canonical cotree of $H+x$.*

Proof. We assume that T(H) was the canonical cotree of H. If x is endpoint of no P_4 in H+x then, by Proposition 4, $\alpha = \gamma$ and hence Update_1 is executed. Now the assumption that T(H) was the canonical cotree of H implies that T(H+x) is the canonical cotree of H+x.

We may, therefore, assume that x belongs to some P_4 in H+x. If x is endpoint of this P_4 then, by Fact 7, γ is a 0-node and lines 2-5 in Update_2 guarantee that x is added to L(H) while T(H+x) coincides with T(H).

If x is midpoint of a unique P_4 in H+x then, by Fact 7, γ is a 0-node. By Proposition 3 we can remove an arbitrary endpoint of this P_4. We consistently remove the unique leaf in $B(\alpha)$, denoted by b from T(H) and insert x into T(H-b), while b is inserted into L(H). The conclusion follows. □

Our next result shows that the iteration consisting of processing $x \in G-H$ takes time proportional to the degree of x.

THEOREM 3. *Given a P_4-reducible graph H described by $(T(H),L(H))$ and a given vertex $x \notin H$, the algorithm Recognize performs in time $O(d_G(x))$ one of the following:*

(i) either determines that $H+x$ is not a P_4-reducible graph, or else

(ii) incorporates x into H, updating T(H) and L(H) accordingly.

PROOF OF THEOREM 3. To begin, we note that Stage 1 of the algorithm takes obviously constant time since only two vertices are processed. To argue about the complexity of Stage 2, we claim that

$$\text{Procedure Mark(x) runs in } O(d_G(x)) \text{ time.} \tag{5}$$

To justify (5), note that since all the internal nodes of T(H), with the possible exception of the root, have at least two children, the number of nodes that are marked (and possibly subsequently unmarked) is bounded by $O(d_G(x))$. Hence, $|M_0 \cup M_1 \cup M_2|$ is bounded by $O(d_G(x))$. It follows that the number of nodes of T(H) that are examined by procedure Mark is also bounded by $O(d_G(x))$. Clearly, every node examined by Mark(x) is processed in constant time.

Furthermore, since x is adjacent to vertices belonging to at most $d_G(x)$ P_4's in H, it follows that $|\Pi(x)|$ is bounded by $O(d_G(x))$. Note that each P_4 in $\Pi(x)$ can be identified in constant time if a suitable data structure is used.

By virtue of (5), Step 2.0 of Stage 2 is performed in time bounded by $O(d_G(x))$.

Next, we claim that

$$\text{Procedure Test\_Neutral(x) runs in } O(d_G(x)) \text{ time.} \tag{6}$$

Trivially, (6) follows from the observation that $|\Pi(x)|$ is bounded by $O(d_G(x))$, together with the fact that each P_4 in $\Pi(x)$ is processed in constant time (line 4).

By virtue of (6), Step 2.1 of Stage 2 takes $O(d_G(x))$ time to run. Further, we claim that

$$\text{Procedure Find runs in } O(d_G(x)) \text{ time.} \tag{7}$$

To see that (7) holds true, note that by a previous observation $|M_2|$ is bounded by $O(d_G(x))$. For each element in M_2 each of the tests in line 4, line 7, and line 12 takes a constant time once a bit-vector representation for M_2 is assumed.

Furthermore, we claim that

$$\text{Procedure Test\_Admissible runs in } O(d_G(x)) \text{ time.} \tag{8}$$

To justify (8), observe that the loop in lines 10-13 is executed at most $O(|M_2|)$ times and that each iteration takes constant time once a bit-vector representation for M_2 is assumed.

The conditions (a2.2) and (a2.3) (lines 18-23) take $O(d_G(x))$ time to check if we are careful to keep the children of each node in T(H) in a bit-vector form.

Now (7) and (8) combined show that Step 2.2 of Stage 2 is performed in time bounded by $O(d_G(x))$.

Further, we claim that

$$\text{Procedure Update\_1 runs in } O(d_G(x)) \text{ time.} \tag{9}$$

To see that this is the case, observe that all the transformations in Update_1 can be carried out in constant time, except for line 24 which involves $O(A(\alpha))$ operations, which is bounded by $O(d_G(x))$, as claimed.

Finally, we claim that

$$\text{Procedure Update\_2 runs in } O(d_G(x)) \text{ time.} \tag{10}$$

To see that this is the case, we note that by Fact 7, in case γ is a 1-node, x is endpoint of a P_4 in H+x and so lines 2-5 take a constant time to execute. Furthermore, if γ is a 0-node, then all the tree transformations entailed by removing b from T(H) and adding x to T(H)-b take a constant time with the exception of line 32 which requires $O(A(\alpha))$ time.

To complete the proof of Theorem 3, note that (9) and (10) combined imply that Step 2.3 is also performed in time bounded by $O(d_G(x))$. □

5. Tree Representation for P_4-reducible graphs.

Let G be a P_4–reducible graph represented by the tuple (T(G),L(G)). We now address the problem of efficiently constructing the pr-tree representation of G. For this purpose we shall use the fact that T(G) is the canonical cotree of G (i.e. the cotree corresponding to the canonical cograph C(G) of G), and that every vertex in L(G) is endpoint of precisely one P_4 in G. Our arguments make use of the following result.

THEOREM 4. *For every $u \in L(G)$ such that uvwz is a P_4 in G with v, w, z in T(G), there exist a unique 0-node $\lambda(u)$ and a 1-node $\lambda'(u)$ in T(G) satisfying*

$$\lambda(u) = p(z);\ \lambda'(u) = p(w) = p(\lambda(u)) \tag{11}$$

Furthermore,

$$\textit{either } \lambda(u) = p(v) \textit{ or else } \lambda''(u) = p(v) \textit{ with } \lambda(u) = p(\lambda''(u)). \tag{12}$$

PROOF OF THEOREM 4. Clearly, it it sufficient to show that if the statement is true for some induced subgraph H of G, then it is also true after incorporating x into H. We may assume that x is contained in some P_4 in H+x, for otherwise there is nothing to prove. We shall distinguish between the folowing two cases.

Case 1. *x is endpoint of a P_4 in H+x.*

By Fact 7, γ is a 1-node in T(H). If α is a 0-node, then the condition (a2.2) guarantees that

$$|A(\alpha)| = |B(\alpha)| = |B(\gamma)| = 1$$

Now writing $A(\alpha)=\{v\}$, $B(\alpha)=\{z\}$, $B(\gamma)=\{w\}$, (11) is satisfied with x standing for u, α in place of λ and γ in place of λ'.

If α is a 1-node, then condition (a2.3) guarantees that

$$|A(\alpha)| = |B(p(\alpha))| = |B(\gamma)| = 1 \text{ and } A(p(\alpha)) = \emptyset.$$

Now writing $A(\alpha)=\{v\}$, $B(p(\alpha))=\{z\}$, $B(\gamma)=\{w\}$, (11) and (12) are satisfied with x standing for u, α in place of λ'', $p(\alpha)$ in place of λ, and γ in place of λ'.

Case 2. *x is midpoint of a P_4 in H+x.*

By Fact 7, γ must be a 0-node. First, if α is a 1-node, then condition (a2.2) translates as

$$|A(\alpha)| = |B(\alpha)| = |A(\gamma)| = 1$$

Now writing $A(\alpha)=\{v\}$, $B(\alpha)=\{u\}$, $A(\gamma)=\{z\}$, after executing lines 10-18 in Update_2, condition (11) is verified with x standing for w, and with either γ and $p(\gamma)$ in place of λ and λ' (in case $B(\gamma)=\emptyset$), or with θ in place of λ and α in place of λ' (in case $B(\gamma)\neq\emptyset$).

Finally, if α is a 0-node, then condition (a2.3) guarantees that

$$|B(\alpha)| = |A(p(\alpha))| = |A(\gamma)| = 1 \text{ and } B(p(\alpha)) = \emptyset.$$

Now writing $B(\alpha)=\{u\}$, $A(p(\alpha))=\{v\}$, $A(\gamma)=\{z\}$, and letting x stand for w, after executing lines 19-35 in Update_2, conditions (11) and (12) hold true with either $p(\alpha)$ in place of λ'', γ in place of λ, and $p(\gamma)$ in place of λ', or else with $p(\alpha)$ standing for λ'', θ standing for λ and θ' standing for λ'.

To complete the proof of the theorem, note that conditions (a2.2) and (a2.3) guarantee, on the one hand the uniquenes of $\lambda(u)$ and, on the other, that no further alteration of T(H+x) can separate λ and λ' or λ'', λ, and λ'. □

Since for every vertex u in L(G) there is a *unique* $\lambda(u)$ with the properties mentioned in Theorem 4, we shall write simply λ, λ', λ'' dropping the reference to u.

To construct the tree representation of a P_4-*reducible* graph G, we need a way of incorporating the vertices of L(G) into the tree structure. For this purpose, a new type of node is needed; this is the 2-node which has precisely two children: a 0-node and a 1-node. Obviously, the 2-node corresponds to the ② operation as in (*). The details of this tree construction are spelled out in the following procedure.

Procedure Build-tree1(G);
{Input: a P_4-*reducible* graph represented as (T(G),L(G))
Output: a tree T1(G), rooted at R;}
1. **begin**
2.   T1(G) ← T(G);
3.   **while** L(G) ≠ ∅ **do begin**
4.   pick an arbitrary vertex u in L(G);
5.   find v,w,z in T1(G) such that uvzw is a P_4 in G;
6. λ ← p(z); λ' ← p(w); λ'' ← p(v);
7.   create a 2-node β;
8.   add u as a child of λ;
9.   **if** $\lambda = \lambda$'' **then begin**
10.   **if** d(λ') ≠ 2 **then begin**
11.   add β as a child of λ';
12.   add λ and a new 1-node τ as children of β;
13.   add v, w as children of τ
14.   **end**
15.   **else begin**
16.   add λ, λ' as children of β;
17.   add β as a child of p(λ');
18.   add v as a child of λ'
19.   **end**
20.   **else begin**
21.   add λ, λ'' as children of β;
22.   add w as a child of λ'';
23.   **if** d(λ') ≠ 2 **then**
24.   add β as a child of λ'
25.   **else begin**
26.   add β as a child of p(λ');
27.   remove λ' from T1(G)
28.   **end**
29.   **end**;
30.   L(G) ← L(G) - {u}
31.   **end**;
32.   **if** d(R) = 1 **then** R ← unique child of R
33. **end**;

The following result argues about the correctness and the running time of procedure Build-tree1. More precisely, we have the following theorem.

THEOREM 5. *The tree T1(G) returned by the procedure Build-tree1 is precisely the pr-tree corresponding to G. Furthermore, T1(G) is constructed in linear time.*

PROOF OF THEOREM 5. We only need prove that the root R of T1(G) satisfies the following three conditions, as they extend easily to subtrees.

(t1) R is a 0-node of degree p whenever G is disconnected having p ($p \geq 2$) distinct components;

(t2) R is a 1-node of degree q whenever $\overline{G}$ is disconnected having q ($q \geq 2$) distinct components;

(t3) R is a 2-node whenever G and $\overline{G}$ are connected.

Our proof relies of the following intermediate results.

FACT 9. *If both G and $\overline{G}$ are connected, then the canonical cograph C(G) induces a disconnected subgraph of $\overline{G}$ with precisely two components, one of them containing a single vertex.*

Proof. Write G=(V,E). By Proposition 1, there exists a P_4 abcd in G such that every vertex in V−{a,b,c,d} is adjacent to both b and c and non-adjacent to both a and d.

Proposition 3 allows us to assume without loss of generality that C(G) contains b, c, and d but not a. Now c is adjacent to all the remaining vertices in V−{a}, implying that C(G) induces a disconnected subgraph of $\overline{G}$ with exactly two components; trivially, {c} is one of them. □

FACT 10. *Let $\overline{G}$ be disconnected; enumerate the components of $\overline{G}$ as $G_1, G_2, \ldots, G_q$ with $q \geq 2$. Let I stand for the set of all the subscripts i ($1 \leq i \leq q$) such that both G_i and $\overline{G}_i$ are connected. Then $\overline{C(G)}$ is disconnected and contains $q + |I|$ components, $|I|$ of them being single vertices.*

Proof. For every $i \in I$, Fact 9 guarantees that $\overline{C(G)}$ is disconnected and contains two components, one of which is a single vertex. The conclusion follows. □

Observe that (t1) is implied by the following result.

FACT 11. *If G is disconnected, then the tree T1(G) is rooted at a 0-node whose degree equals the number of components of G.*

Proof. Enumerate the components of G as $G_1, G_2, \ldots, G_p$ with $p \geq 2$. Trivially, the canonical cograph C(G) is also disconnected with components C(G_1), C(G_2), ..., C(G_p). Hence the canonical cotree T(G) is rooted at a 1-node R' with d(R')=1.

Let w stand for the unique child of R' in T(G). By the previous argument w has precisely p children, corresponding to the components of C(G). Since d(R')=1, it follows that w cannot play the role of λ(u) for any u in L(G). Consequently, when we exit the while loop (lines 3-31), w is left unchanged. Now line 32 guarantees that T1(G) is rooted at w, as claimed. □

Next, note that (t2) is implied by the following result.

FACT 12. *If $\overline{G}$ is disconnected, then the tree T1(G) is rooted at a 1-node whose degree equals the number of components of $\overline{G}$.*

Proof. Enumerate the components of $\overline{G}$ as $G_1, G_2, \ldots, G_q$ with $q \geq 2$. Let I stand for the set of all the subscripts i ($1 \leq i \leq q$) such that both G_i and $\overline{G}_i$ are connected. By Fact 10, the canonical cograph C(G) induces a disconnected subgraph of $\overline{G}$, containing q + |I| components, with |I| of them being single vertices. Consequently, the canonical cotree T(G) is rooted at a 1-node R with d(R) = q + |I|. By Proposition 1, each component G_i of $\overline{G}$ with $i \in I$ contains a unique P_4 $u_1 v_i w_i z_i$. By virtue of Proposition 3, we may assume that C(G_i) contains v_i, w_i, and z_i but not u_i. It follows that $u_i \in$ L(G) for all $i \in I$.

To see that R is the root of T1(G), note that whenever R=λ'(u) for some u in L(G), lines 10 and 23 in Build_tree1 guarantee that the newly created 2-node becomes a child of R.

To see that R has degree q in T1(G) note that the |I| children of R which are leaves in T(G) are precisely the vertices

w_i with $i \in I$. Each of them will be incorporated into a corresponding 2-node, leaving R with exactly q children, as claimed. □

Further, the following result implies (t3).

FACT 13. *If both G and $\overline{G}$ are connected, then the tree T1(G) is rooted at a 2-node.*

Proof. Write G=(V,E). Since both G and $\overline{G}$ are connected, Proposition 1 guarantees the existence of a unique P_4 abcd in G such that every vertex in V−{a,b,c,d} is adjacent to both b and c and non-adjacent to both a and d. We shall assume, without loss of generality, that C(G) contains b, c, and d but not a; we note that c is adjacent to all the vertices in V−{a,c}. Consequently, the canonical cotree T(G) is rooted at a 1-node R of degree 2: c is one of the children of R, the other one being a 0-node τ.

Furthermore, C(G) − {c} is disconnected, containing as components {b} and the subgraph induced by V−{a,b,c}. If G is isomorphic to the P_4, then τ has b and d as children and we are done; otherwise, τ has precisely two children, namely b and a node τ' (which must be a 1-node).

Next, C(G) − {b,c} is disconnected, containing {d} and the subgraph induced by V − {a,b,c,d} as components. But now, since G is a P_4*–reducible* graph, it follows that R plays the role of λ'(u) for a single vertex in L(G), namely a.

Now the test in line 23 fails, and so lines 26-28 will be executed, implying that R will be replaced as a root of T1(G) by a 2-node, as claimed. □.

Finally, to address the complexity of procedure Build-tree1, we note that by the definition of P_4*–reducible* graphs, L(G) contains at most $\lfloor \frac{n}{4} \rfloor$ vertices. Each of them is processed in constant time, and the conclusion follows. This completes the proof of Theorem 5. □

6. References

1. C. Berge, Graphs and Hypergraphs, North-Holland, Amsterdam, 1973.

2. D. G. Corneil and D. G. Kirkpatrick, Families of recursively defined perfect graphs, *Congressus Numerantium*, 39 (1983), 237-246.

3. D. G. Corneil, H. Lerchs, and L. Stewart Burlingham, Complement Reducible Graphs, *Discrete Applied Mathematics*, 3, (1981), 163-174.

4. D. G. Corneil, Y. Perl, and L. K. Stewart, A linear recognition algorithm for cographs, *SIAM J. on Computing*, 14 (1985), 926-934.

5. B. Jamison and S. Olariu P_4*–reducible*-graphs, a class of uniquely tree representable graphs, *Studies in Applied Mathematics, to appear.*

6. H. A. Jung, On a class of posets and the corresponding comparability graphs, *J. Comb. Theory (B)*, 24 (1978), 125-133.

7. H. Lerchs, On cliques and kernels, Dept. of Computer Science, University of Toronto, March 1971.

8. H. Lerchs, On the clique-kernel structure of graphs, Dept. of Computer Science, University of Toronto, October 1972.

9. D. Seinsche, On a property of the class of n-colorable graphs, *J. Comb. Theory (B)*, 16, (1974), 191-193.

10. L. Stewart, Cographs, a class of tree representable graphs, M. Sc. Thesis, dept. of Computer Science, University of Toronto, 1978, TR 126/78.

11. D. P. Sumner, Dacey Graphs, *J. Australian Math. Soc.* 18 (1974), 492-502.

Fast Parallel Approximations of the Maximum Weighted Cut Problem through Derandomization*

Grammati Pantziou[1] *Paul Spirakis*[1,2] *Christos Zaroliagis*[1]

Abstract

Given a graph with positive integer edge weights one may ask whether there exists an edge cut whose weight is bigger than a given number. This problem is NP-Complete. We present here an approximation scheme in NC which provides tight upper bounds to the proportion of edge cuts whose size is bigger than a given number. Our technique is based on the method to convert randomized algorithms into deterministic ones, introduced by [Luby, 85 and 88]. The basic idea of those methods is to replace an exponentially large sample space by one of polynomial size. Our work examines the statistical distance of random variables of the small sample space to corresponding variables of the exponentially large space, which is the space of all edge cuts taken equiprobably.

1 Introduction

The problem of finding the maximum weighted edge cut in a weighted graph of n vertices and m edges is NP-Complete (see [Karp, 72]). The problem remains NP-Complete even if the weights of all the edges of the graph are equal to 1 (SIMPLE MAX CUT, see [Garey, Johnson, Stockmeyer, 76]). Maximum edge cuts are useful in VLSI design. It is clear that the variation of the problem which asks of what is the number (or fraction) of edge cuts whose weight is bigger than a given number, is still NP-hard (in fact it is #P-Complete, since it is the enumeration version of an NP-Complete problem, see e.g. [Valiant, 77] or [Garey, Johnson, 79]).

One may consider the space of all possible edge cuts of a weighted graph (2^n of them, corresponding to the partitions of the vertex set into two pieces). Thus, by forming partitions of the vertex set at random, one may construct fast Monte Carlo algorithms to approximate the MAX CUT problem. Such an approach is, in general, not very successful unless many random partitions are formed and running averages are estimated.

We prove here the surprising result that there is an $O(n)$-sized subset of edge cuts which has the same mean edge cut weight and bigger variance compared with the space of all cuts, taken

*This research was supported in part by the ESPRIT Basic Research Action No. 3075 ALCOM, and in part by the Ministry of Education of Greece.

1. Computer Technology Institute, P.O. Box 1122, 26110, Patras, and Computer Science and Eng Dept, University of Patras, 26500 Patras, Greece.

2. Courant Institute of Mathematical Sciences, NYU, 10012 New York, USA.

equiprobably. Furthermore, this set of cuts can be constructed in NC (in $O(\log n)$ parallel time by using at most $O(n^2 + nm/\log n)$ processors). Thus, this single, easy to construct, set eliminates the need for the Monte Carlo approach and directly provides a tight upper bound on the number (or the fraction) of edge cuts whose weight is bigger than a given number. (This upper bound is tight in the sense that Chebyshev's inequality cannot be made more precise from just the mean and the variance of an otherwise arbitrary distribution.) Thus, we provide here an approximation in NC to the MAX CUT problem.

Our approach is based on the techniques of converting randomized algorithms into deterministic ones, introduced by [Karp, Wigderson, 84] and analyzed in depth by [Luby, 85], [Luby, 88], and [Goldberg, Spencer, 87]. [Alon, Babai, Itai, 86] provide an excellent account of this approach and credit the original ideas to [Joffe, 74] and [Lancaster, 65], also [Bernstein, 45]. These ideas exploit the fact that 2-wise (or d-wise) independence (instead of complete independence) is all one needs in certain probabilistic algorithms, and this remark, in turn, means that exponentially smaller sample spaces suffice compared to what is required for full independence. We were particularly motivated by the so-called simple PROFIT/COST problem of [Luby, 88]. In that work, Luby examined the expected value of a "benefit" function and proved that it stays the same in the smaller space. We examine, in addition, the variance and prove that it increases in the smaller space. Thus the smaller space is a good predictor of extreme values in the large space.

2 The Max Cut Problem, its Variations and Labellings

Given a graph $G = (V, E)$ and integer weights $w(e) > 0$ for each $e \in E$ and a positive integer K, the MAX CUT problem asks whether there is a partition of V into disjoint sets V_1 and V_2, such that the sum of the weights of the edges that have one endpoint in V_1 and the other in V_2 is at least K. The problem is NP-Complete and remains so, even when $w(e) = 1$ for all $e \in E$ (and even when the maximum degree in G is less than or equal to 3). For $|V| = n$ there are 2^n edge cuts (including the cases whether $V_1 = \emptyset$ or $V_2 = \emptyset$). Obviously, the related problem of asking whether the proportion of edge cuts whose weight is at least K is bigger than a given rational number, is still NP-hard and in fact #P-Complete.

Definition 1 *Let $C(V_1, V_2)$ be the set of edges with one endpoint in V_1 and the other in V_2. Let $W(C)$ be the sum of $w(e)$ for $e \in C(V_1, V_2)$.*

There is an one-to-one correspondence between each partition (V_1, V_2) of V and each 0/1 labelling $\hat{l} = \{l_i \in \{0, 1\} : i \in V\}$ in the obvious way (the vertices of V_1 are 0-labelled). Hence, each 0/1 labelling $\hat{l}$ of the graph G define an edge cut $C(\hat{l})$. Consider a probability distribution on labellings $\hat{l}$ such that each label l_v is independently chosen to be 1 or 0 with probability 1/2. In this space, each of the 2^n labellings is equally likely. Let Ω_1 be the corresponding sample space, and (Ω_1, Pr_1) the probability space.

Definition 2 *Consider a function* $COST : V^2 \times \{0,1\}^2 \to Z^+ \cup \{0\}$ *such that, for any two vertices* v,w *and their labels* l_v, l_w *in a labelling* $\hat{l}$*:*

$$COST(v,w,l_v,l_w) = \begin{cases} weight(v,w) & \text{if } l_v \neq l_w \\ 0 & \text{else} \end{cases}$$

where

$$weight(v,w) = \begin{cases} w(e) & \text{if } e = \{v,w\} \in E \\ 0 & \text{else} \end{cases}$$

For ease of notation, we will write $COST(l_v, l_w)$ instead of $COST(v,w,l_v,l_w)$. Clearly then, the weight $W(C)$ of a cut $C(\hat{l})$ is

$$W(C(\hat{l})) = \sum_{\{v,w\}\in E} COST(l_v, l_w)$$

where $l_v, l_w \in \hat{l}$.

Let us define the random variable $\widetilde{W}$ on Ω_1 which is the weight of the edge cut corresponding to a randomly chosen labelling $\hat{l}$ according to the probability distribution defined on Ω_1. In fact, $\widetilde{W}$ is a function of the n independent random variables l_v, $v \in V$. Let $\overline{W}$ and Var_w be the mean value and variance of the variable $\widetilde{W}$. By Chebyshev's inequality then (for any $t > 0$)

$$Prob(\ |\widetilde{W} - \overline{W}| \geq t \cdot \sqrt{Var_w}\ ) \leq \frac{1}{t^2} \quad (1)$$

i.e. by knowing the mean value of the weight of edge cuts and the corresponding variance, we get a (tight) upper bound on the fraction of edge cuts whose weight is greater than $t \cdot \sqrt{Var_w}$. Clearly (1) holds for $\widetilde{W} = \textit{the weight of the maximum cut}$, too.

3 Our Approximation Scheme

Assume now that the random variables l_i ($i \in V$) are defined (as in [Luby,88]) on a specially designed probability space (Ω_2, Pr_2), containing only $\Theta(n)$ sample points ω, such that the l_i are only *pairwise* independent. Then we can compute efficiently in parallel (in NC) the weights of the cuts corresponding to all the sample points $\omega \in \Omega_2$, and compute (in NC) the corresponding mean values, variances and other statistics of the weights. This computation will be meaningful only when the statistics in (Ω_2, Pr_2) can be used to derive statistics for the space Ω_1 (and the corresponding distribution). We use here the (Ω_2, Pr_2) as constructed in [Luby,88] namely: $\Omega_2 = \{0,1\}^{k+1}, k = \lceil \log n \rceil$. For each $\omega \in \Omega_2$ we have $Prob(\omega) = 2^{-(k+1)}$. The random variables $\hat{l} = \{l_i \in \{0,1\} : i \in V\}$ are defined on (Ω_2, Pr_2) as follows: For all $i \in V$ let $< i_1, i_2, \ldots, i_k >$ be the binary expansion of i. For all $\omega \in \Omega_2$, define l_i at ω to be:

$$l_i(\omega) = (\sum_{j=1}^{k}(i_j \cdot \omega_j) + \omega_{k+1}) \bmod 2 \quad (2)$$

With this definition the random variables are uniformly distributed, pairwise and also *three-wise* independent. (For the proof of the three-wise independence see [Pantziou, Spirakis, Zaroliagis, 89].) Furthermore, each label l_i is equally likely to be 0 or 1.

Lemma 1 *The mean value of the weights of edge cuts in the space* (Ω_2, Pr_2) *is the same as in the space* (Ω_1, Pr_1).

Proof: (see also [Luby,88]). Let $\overline{W_1}$ the mean value of the edge cut in (Ω_1, Pr_1) and $\overline{W_2}$ the corresponding value in (Ω_2, Pr_2). We have

$$\overline{W_2} = E[\sum_{\{v,w\}\in E} COST(l_v, l_w)] = \sum_{\{v,w\}\in E} E[COST(l_v, l_w)] \quad (3)$$

where $E[\,]$ is the expected value operator.
Let $e = \{v, w\}$. We then get

$$\overline{W_2} = \sum_{e\in E} w(e)[Prob(l_v = 0 \wedge l_w = 1) + Prob(l_v = 1 \wedge l_w = 0)]$$

$\Rightarrow \overline{W_2} = \frac{1}{2}\sum_{e\in E} w(e)$, because, for example, $Prob(l_v = 0 \wedge l_w = 1) = Prob(l_v = 0) \cdot Prob(l_w = 1)$ due to pairwise independence. Clearly this value of $\overline{W_2}$ is the same as $\overline{W_1}$. ∎

Definition 3 *Let* Var_1, Var_2 *be the variances of the random variable (r.v.)* $\widetilde{W}$ *in the spaces* (Ω_1, Pr_1) *and* (Ω_2, Pr_2) *accordingly.*

We now prove a far more interesting result.

Theorem 1 $Var_2 \geq Var_1$.

Proof: In the sequel, let $e = \{v, w\}$. The variance (in either space) is given by

$$Var = E[(\sum_{e\in E} COST(l_v, l_w))^2] - (\frac{1}{2}\sum_{e\in E} w(e))^2 \quad (4)$$

Now, since $(\sum_{e\in E} COST(l_v, l_w))^2 =$

$$= \sum_{e\in E} COST^2(l_v, l_w) + 2\sum COST(l_v, l_w) \cdot COST(l_u, l_z)$$

(where the second sum runs over all $\{v, w\}, \{u, z\} \in E$ such that $\{v, w\} \neq \{u, z\}$) and since $E[\sum_{e\in E} COST^2(l_v, l_w)] = \frac{1}{2}\sum_{e\in E} w^2(e)$ (in both spaces), we get finally (by (4)) the following result, where $e = \{v, w\}, e' = \{u, z\}$ and $A = \{\{e, e'\} : e \neq e' \wedge e, e' \in E\}$:

$$Var = \frac{1}{4}\sum_{e\in E} w^2(e) - \frac{1}{2}\sum_{\{e,e'\}\in A} w(e) \cdot w(e') + 2\sum_{\{e,e'\}\in A} E[COST(l_v, l_w) \cdot COST(l_u, l_z)] \quad (5)$$

Let $Q = \sum E[COST(l_v, l_w) \cdot COST(l_u, l_z)]$ where $\{v, w\} \in E, \{u, z\} \in E$ and $\{v, w\} \neq \{u, z\}$. Let Q_1, Q_2 be the values of Q in the spaces (Ω_1, Pr_1) and (Ω_2, Pr_2). We now calculate Q in the two spaces.

Space (Ω_1, Pr_1):
To calculate Q_1, we split it into two parts, $Q_1 = P_{11} + P_{12}$ where

$$P_{11} = \sum E[COST(l_v, l_w) \cdot COST(l_u, l_z)]$$

running over all $\{v, w\}$ and $\{u, z\}$ with $v = u$, and P_{12} is a similar sum running over all $\{v, w\}$ and $\{u, z\}$ with distinct v, w, u, z. Clearly,

$E[COST(l_v, l_w) \cdot COST(l_u, l_z)] =$
$= w(e) \cdot w(e') \cdot [Prob(l_v = 0 \wedge l_w = 1 \wedge l_z = 1) + Prob(l_v = 1 \wedge l_w = 0 \wedge l_z = 0)]$
$= w(e) \cdot w(e') \cdot [Prob(l_v = 0) \cdot Prob(l_w = 1) \cdot Prob(l_z = 1)$
$+Prob(l_v = 1) \cdot Prob(l_w = 0) \cdot Prob(l_z = 0)]$
$= \frac{1}{4} w(e) \cdot w(e')$

(because of independence of l_v, l_w, l_z). Thus, $P_{11} = \frac{1}{4} \sum w(e) \cdot w(e')$ over all e, e' with one vertex in common. Similarly, $P_{12} = \frac{1}{4} \sum w(e) \cdot w(e')$ over all e, e' with disjoint vertices.
Space (Ω_2, Pr_2):
Again, we split Q_2 into two sums, $Q_2 = P_{21} + P_{22}$ where P_{21} runs over all pairs of edges with one vertex in common and P_{22} runs over all pairs of edges with disjoint vertices. For the P_{21} we have (for $e = \{v, w\}$ and $e' = \{u, z\}$):

$$P_{21} = \sum w(e) \cdot w(e') \cdot [Prob(l_v = 0 \wedge l_w = 1 \wedge l_z = 1) + Prob(l_v = 1 \wedge l_w = 0 \wedge l_z = 0)]$$

Due to the three-wise independence of l_v, l_w, l_z in the space (Ω_2, Pr_2), we have $Prob(l_v = 0 \wedge l_w = 1 \wedge l_z = 1) = Prob(l_v = 1 \wedge l_w = 0 \wedge l_z = 0) = 1/8$. Thus, $P_{21} = \frac{1}{4} \sum w(e) \cdot w(e')$, *the same value as* P_{11}.

For P_{22} we have:

$$P_{22} = \sum E[E[COST(l_v, l_w)/COST(l_u, l_z)] \cdot COST(l_u, l_z)] \quad (6)$$

where the sum runs over all $\{v, w\}, \{u, z\}$ with distinct v, w, u, z (see e.g. [Papoulis,86]).

In order to find $E[COST(l_v, l_w)/COST(l_u, l_z)]$ it is enough to find the conditional probabilities $Prob(U_1/L_1), Prob(U_1/L_2), Prob(U_2/L_1), Prob(U_2/L_2)$ where $U_1 =$ "$l_v = 0 \wedge l_w = 1$", $U_2 =$ "$l_v = 1 \wedge l_w = 0$", $L_1 =$ "$l_u = 0 \wedge l_z = 1$", $L_2 =$ "$l_u = 1 \wedge l_z = 0$".

Lemma 2 $\frac{1}{4} \leq Prob(U_i/L_j) \leq \frac{1}{2}$ *for* $i = 1, 2$ *and* $j = 1, 2$.

Remark 1: In fact, the above probability either equals 1/4 or equals 1/2.
Proof: By induction for any $n \geq 4$. We prove it here only for $i = 1, j = 1$. The other cases are similar.
Basis: for $n = 4$ it can be easily verified that the assertion of the lemma holds.
Induction hypothesis: suppose that for $n = 2^k$ the assertion of the lemma holds. For the sake of

clarity, we can view the sample space as a $n \times 2n$ matrix A_k of $0, 1$ as follows: the horizontal dimension of the matrix represents the sample points ω while the vertical dimension represents the vertices of the graph. The element in the i-th row and ω-th column of A_k is the r.v. $l_i(\omega)$ which according to formula (2) can be 0 or 1. Therefore, in the sample space A_k we have that $Prob(U_1/L_1) = 1/4$ or $Prob(U_1/L_1) = 1/2$. Let us analyze a little bit more the induction hypothesis. The equation $(l_u, l_z) = (0, 1)$ holds for exactly $n/2$ points of A_k, since $Prob(l_u = 0 \wedge l_z = 1) = 1/4$ (due to pairwise independence). This means that there are: either $n/8$ points of A_k such that $(l_v, l_w) = (0, 1)$ and $n/8$ points such that $(l_v, l_w) = (1, 0)$ (and thus $n/8$ points such that $(l_v, l_w) = (0, 0)$ and $n/8$ points such that $(l_v, l_w) = (1, 1)$), or $n/4$ points of A_k such that $(l_v, l_w) = (0, 1)$ and $n/4$ points such that $(l_v, l_w) = (1, 0)$.

Induction step: we shall prove the assertion of the lemma for $n = 2^{k+1}$, i.e. for the sample space A_{k+1}.

Remark 2: if n is not a power of 2, we can just add dummy vertices to the graph (with no edges among them). This does not affect the algorithm at all.

As it can be easily checked (from [Luby,88]), the new sample space A_{k+1} is constructed from A_k as follows:

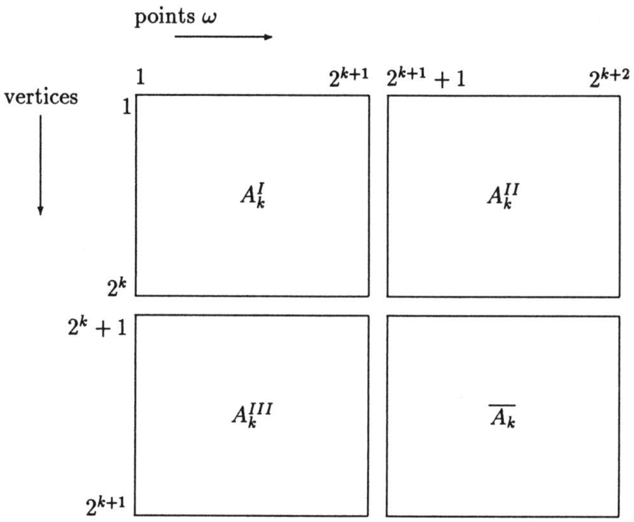

where $A_k^I = A_k^{II} = A_k^{III} = A_k$, due to formula (2). The superscript denotes the different occurrences of A_k. $\overline{A_k}$ is the matrix produced from A_k by taking the complement of each row.

We distinguish among the following cases.

Case 1: Fix two vertices u, z such that $u, z \in [1, 2^k]$.

1.a) $v, w \in [1, 2^k]$. Because of the pairwise independence, we have $(l_u, l_z) = (0, 1)$ in $n/2$ columns (points) of A_{k+1}, where half of them belong to A_k^I and the other half to A_k^{II}. By the induction hypothesis we have $(l_v, l_w) = (0, 1)$ either for $n/16$ or $n/8$ columns for each of A_k^I, A_k^{II}. Thus, for the new space A_{k+1} we have $\frac{n/16+n/16}{n/2} \leq Prob(U_1/L_1) \leq \frac{n/8+n/8}{n/2}$, i.e. the assertion of the lemma holds.

1.b) $v, w \in [2^k + 1, 2^{k+1}]$

1.b.1) $v = 2^k + u, w = 2^k + z$. Then (by the pairwise independence) we have $(l_u, l_z) = (0, 1)$ in $n/2$ columns of A_{k+1} and $(l_v, l_w) = (0, 1)$ in $n/4$ columns (of A_{k+1})which belong solely to A_k^{III}. We cannot have $(l_v, l_w) = (0, 1)$ in $\overline{A_k}$ (while $(l_u, l_z) = (0, 1)$) because of the following fact: suppose that $(l_v, l_w) = (0, 1)$ in column j, $1 \leq j \leq 2^{k+1}$ (i.e. in A_k^{III}). Then in the column $2^{k+1} + j$ (in which $(l_u, l_z) = (0, 1)$) we shall have by the construction of $\overline{A_k}$ $(l_v, l_w) = (1, 0)$. Thus, $Prob(U_1/L_1) = 1/2$ and the assertion holds.

1.b.2) $v \neq 2^k + u, w \neq 2^k + z$. There are $n/2$ columns with $(l_u, l_z) = (0, 1)$, where half of them belong to A_k^I and half of them to A_k^{II}. This is the same if we were restricted: 1) into A_k^I where $v_{new} = v - 2^k$, $w_{new} = w - 2^k$ and looking for $(l_{v_{new}}, l_{w_{new}}) = (0, 1)$ while $(l_u, l_z) = (0, 1)$, and 2) into A_k^{III} where $v_{new} = v - 2^k$, $w_{new} = w - 2^k$ and looking for $(l_{v_{new}}, l_{w_{new}}) = (1, 0)$ while $(l_u, l_z) = (0, 1)$. (This last one happens because of $\overline{A_k}$). The rest of the proof now, is similar to case 1.a.

1.b.3) $v \neq 2^k + u$, $w = 2^k + z$. Consider the first half of w. Then we are in the following case: $u, z, v, w \in A_k^I$, $u \neq v \neq z$, $w = z$. Then, for the row $w = z$ there are $n/4$ 1's. From the pairwise independence, these $n/4$ 1's correspond to $n/8$ 0's and $n/8$ 1's of row v. This means that there are $n/8$ $(l_v, l_w) = (0, 1)$. For the other half of w, there are no pairs $(l_v, l_w) = (0, 1)$. The reason is the construction of $\overline{A_k}$, because in every column where $(l_u, l_z) = (0, 1)$ (i.e. $l_z = 1$) we have $l_w = 0$. Thus $Prob(U_1/L_1) = \frac{n/8}{n/2} = 1/4$ and the lemma holds.

1.b.4) $v = 2^k + u$, $w \neq 2^k + z$. Similar to 1.b.3.

1.c) $v \in [1, 2^k]$, $v \neq u \neq z$, $w \in [2^k + 1, 2^{k+1}]$. Consider the row w. The first half of w, denoted as w_1, belongs to A_k^{III}. This means that we can restricted into A_k^I. Thus, either $n/16$ or $n/8$ columns have $(l_v, l_w) = (0, 1)$ by the induction hypothesis. The second half of w, denoted as w_2, belongs to $\overline{A_k}$. Therefore, we can be restricted into A_k^{II}, but now looking for $(l_v, l_w) = (0, 0)$. This can be done by taking as w_2 the complement of the real w_2. By the induction hypothesis there are either $n/16$ columns with $(l_v, l_w) = (0, 0)$ (corresponding to the case where there are $n/16$ columns having $(l_v, l_w) = (0, 1)$ in A_k^I), or none column with $(l_v, l_w) = (0, 0)$ (corresponding to the case where there are $n/8$ columns having $(l_v, l_w) = (0, 1)$ in A_k^I). Thus, the lemma holds in this case too.

Case 2: Fix two vertices u, z such that $u, z \in [2^k + 1, 2^{k+1}]$. The subcases of case 2 and their proofs are similar to those of case 1.

Case 3: Fix two vertices u, z, such that: either $u \in [1, 2^k]$ and $z \in [2^k+1, 2^{k+1}]$ or $u \in [2^k+1, 2^{k+1}]$ and $z \in [1, 2^k]$. Again the subcases of case 3 and their proofs are similar to the above ones. ∎

Corollary 1 $\frac{1}{4}\sum w(e) \cdot w(e') \leq P_{22} \leq \frac{1}{2}\sum w(e) \cdot w(e')$ *where* $e, e' \in E$ *and have no points in common.*

Proof: From Lemma 2 and formula (6). ∎

Corollary 2 $Q_1 \leq Q_2$.

Proof: $Q_1 = P_{11} + P_{12}, Q_2 = P_{21} + P_{22}$ and we showed that $P_{11} = P_{21}$ and $P_{12} \leq P_{22} \leq 2 \cdot P_{12}$. ∎

Now, by formula (5), we get

$$Var_1 \leq Var_2 \leq Var_1 + \frac{1}{4}\sum w(e) \cdot w(e')$$

This completes the proof of theorem 1. ∎

Theorem 2 *For the r.v.* $\widetilde{W}$ *of* (Ω_1, Pr_1) *we have*

$$Prob(\ |\widetilde{W} - \overline{W_2}| \geq t \cdot \sqrt{Var_2}\ ) \leq \frac{1}{t^2}$$

for any $t > 0$.

Proof: Since $\overline{W_1} = \overline{W_2}$ and $Var_1 \leq Var_2$ we have

$$|\widetilde{W} - \overline{W_2}| \geq t \cdot \sqrt{Var_2} \Rightarrow |\widetilde{W} - \overline{W_1}| \geq t \cdot \sqrt{Var_2} \geq t \cdot \sqrt{Var_1}.$$

Let $EVENT_1$ = "$|\widetilde{W} - \overline{W_1}| \geq t \cdot \sqrt{Var_1}$" and $EVENT_2$ = "$|\widetilde{W} - \overline{W_2}| \geq t \cdot \sqrt{Var_2}$". Then $EVENT_2 \Rightarrow EVENT_1$, thus

$$Prob(EVENT_1 / EVENT_2) = 1 \Rightarrow Prob(EVENT_1) \geq Prob(EVENT_2).$$

But $Prob(EVENT_1) \leq \frac{1}{t^2}$ by Chebyshev's inequality. Thus $Prob(EVENT_2) \leq \frac{1}{t^2}$ also. ∎

4 The NC Approximation Algorithm

The following algorithm computes the mean and the variance of the small space Ω_2 in NC.

```
(1) for all ω ∈ Ω2 pardo
        for all v ∈ V pardo
            compute l_v(ω)
        odpar
    odpar
```

(2) **for all** $\omega \in \Omega_2$ **pardo**

compute $W(C(\hat{l}(\omega)))$

odpar

(3) *compute* $\overline{W_2}$; (* using formula (3) *)

(4) *compute* Var_2 ; (* using formula (4) *)

Theorem 3 *The above algorithm computes the mean and the variance of* Ω_2 *in* $O(\log n)$ *time using* $O(n^2 + nm/\log n)$ *processors and thus provides a (tight) upper bound on the fraction of edge cuts whose weight is greater than a given integer.*

Proof: The correctness of the algorithm is obvious from the previous discussion. Clearly, all the steps of the above algorithm can be computed in $O(\log n)$ time, with at most $O(n^2 + nm/\log n)$ processors, using an optimal parallel prefix sum algorithm (see, e.g. [Cole, Vishkin, 86]). ∎

5 Conclusion and Further Work

We do not have an analogous main lemma (as lemma 2) for higher moments, because the corresponding conditional probability becomes zero for a *small* number of vertices. Thus, the existence of a result like lemma 2 depends now on the weights of the edges of the graph. In the special case where the values of all the weights are almost the same, we can get a similar result to Theorem 1 between the third moments in the two spaces. We conjecture that, when the largest difference between the edge weights is $o(n)$, then Theorem 1 holds for all the higher moments. In such a case, tighter bounds would exist (and the smaller space would approximately *characterize the distribution* of the cut weights of the graph).

It seems that our approximation scheme can be extended to handle a lot of #P-Complete problems (especially graph partitions and weighted path problems) and we are currently working on this direction.

6 Acknowledgements

The first and the third author wish to thank George Moustakides for many helpful discussions.

7 References

[Alon, Babai, Itai, 86] "A fast and simple Randomized parallel Algorithm for the Maximal Independent Set Problem", J. of Algorithms, 7, 567-583, 1986.

[Bernstein, 45] "Theory of Probability", (3rd ed.), GTTI, Moscow, 1945.

[Cole, Vishkin, 86] "Deterministic Coin Tossing with Applications to Optimal Parallel List Ranking", Inform. and Control, Vol.70, N.1, pp. 32-53, July 1986.

[Garey, Johnsn, 79] "Computers and Intractability – A Guide to the Theory of NP-Completeness", Ed. Freeman and Co, San Francisco, 2nd printing, 1979.

[Garey, Johnson, Stockmeyer, 76] "Some Simplified NP-Complete Graph Problems", Theor. Comp. Science 1, 237-267, 1976.

[Goldberg, Spencer, 87] "A new Parallel Algorithm for the Maximal Independent Set Problem", Proc. 28th IEEE FOCS, pp. 161-165, 1987. Also in SIAM J. on Computing, April 1989, pp. 419-427.

[Joffe,74] "On a set of almost deterministic k-independent random variables", Ann. Probability, 2 (1974), 161-162.

[Karp, 72] "Reducibility among Combinatorial Problems", in "Complexity of Computer Computations", Plenum Press, NY, 1972.

[Karp, Wigderson, 84] "A Fast Parallel Algorithm for the Maximal Independent Set Problem", Proc. 16th ACM STOC, pp. 266-272, 1984.

[Lancaster, 65] "Pairwise Statistical Independence", Ann. Math. Stat. 36, (1965), 1313-1317.

[Luby, 85] "A simple Parallel Algorithm for the Maximal Independent Set Problem", Proc. 17th ACM STOC, pp. 1-10, Providence RI, 1985.

[Luby, 88] "Removing Randomness in Parallel Computation without a Processor Penalty", Proc. 29th IEEE FOCS, pp. 162-174, 1988.

[Pantziou, Spirakis, Zaroliagis, 89] "Fast Parallel Approximations of the Maximum Weighted Cut Problem through Derandomization", Techn. Rep. TR–83.04.89, Computer Technology Institute, Patras, 1989.

[Papoulis, 86] "Probability, Random Variables and Stohastic Processes", 2nd edit., McCraw-Hill, 1986.

[Valiant, 77] "The Complexity of enumeration and reliability problems", Report No. CSR-15-77, CS Dept, Univ. of Edinburg, Scottland.

A NEW CLASS OF SEPARATORS AND PLANARITY OF CHORDAL GRAPHS

P.SREENIVASA KUMAR
C.E.VENI MADHAVAN
Department of Computer Science and Automation
Indian Institute of Science
Bangalore, INDIA

ABSTRACT

We introduce a new class of clique separators, called base sets, for chordal graphs. Base sets of a chordal graph closely reflect its structure. We show that the notion of base sets leads to structural characterizations of planar k-trees and planar chordal graphs. Using these characterizations, we develop linear time algorithms for recognizing planar k-trees and planar chordal graphs. These algorithms are extensions of the Lexicographic_Breadth_First_Search algorithm for recognizing chordal graphs and are much simpler than the general planarity checking algorithm. Further, we use the notion of base sets to prove the equivalence of hamiltonian 2-trees and maximal outerplanar graphs.

1. INTRODUCTION

A graph $G = (V,E)$, where V is the vertex set and E is the edge set, is always considered here as being finite, undirected and simple. A graph G is *chordal* if every cycle of length at least four has a chord i.e. an edge joining two non-consecutive vertices of the cycle. A vertex v is said to be *simplicial* in graph G if $adj(v)$, the set of vertices adjacent to v, induces a clique in G. A *perfect elimination ordering* (peo) $\sigma=(v_1,v_2,\ldots,v_n)$, of the vertices of a graph G is an ordering such that v_i is simplicial in the subgraph of G induced by $v_i,\ldots,v_n$. In a graph, a *minimal vertex separator* is one which does not properly contain any other vertex separator. A graph is a *k-tree* if it can be obtained by the following recursive construction rules:

(1) Start with a k-clique; a k-clique is a k-tree.
(2) Choose a k-clique Q in the existing k-tree, add a vertex and make it adjacent to all the vertices in Q.

k-trees form an important subclass of chordal graphs. Of the many characterizations of chordal graphs, the following are of interest to us:

Theorem 1. [G80] *The following are equivalent for a graph G:*
(1) G is chordal.
(2) Every minimal vertex separator of G is a clique.
(3) G has a perfect elimination ordering.

Chordal graphs have applications in relational database design [BFMY83] and solution of sparse linear systems [R70], and have been of current interest [K88,HL89].

In this paper, we introduce a new type of clique separator of a chordal graph, termed base set. We show that the notion of base sets leads to neat structural characterizations of planar k-trees and planar chordal graphs. Using these characterizations, we give linear time algorithms to recognize planar k-trees and planar chordal graphs. These algorithms are extensions of the standard recognition algorithm for chordal graphs and are much simpler to implement compared to the general planarity checking algorithm [HT74]. Using the notion of base sets, we also show that maximal outerplanar graphs are exactly hamiltonian 2-trees.

Now we state the notations and definitions used in the rest of the paper. Let σ be a peo of a chordal graph G and let $v \in V(G)$. We treat σ as a function $\sigma:\{1,2,...,n\} \rightarrow V$. Accordingly, $\sigma(r)$ denotes the rth vertex in the perfect elimination ordering and $\sigma^{-1}(v)$ gives the position of a vertex v in the peo. We denote by $N(v,\sigma)$ the set of neighbours of v which appear later than v in σ i.e., $N(v,\sigma) = \{u \in V(G):(u,v) \in E(G)$ *and* $\sigma^{-1}(u) > \sigma^{-1}(v)\}$. From the definition of a peo, it is clear that $N(v,\sigma)$ induces a clique for any vertex v of G. The chordal graph G can be constructed from an empty graph as follows: add the vertices in the order $\sigma(n),\sigma(n\text{-}1),...,\sigma(1)$ and make each vertex v adjacent to vertices in $N(v,\sigma)$. We call this process *reconstruction* of G wrt peo σ. We denote by $V_i(\sigma)$ $(1 \leq i \leq n)$ the set of vertices numbered i through n wrt σ i.e., the set $\{u \in V(G):\sigma^{-1}(u) \geq i\}$. $G_i(\sigma)$ denotes the subgraph of G induced by $V_i(\sigma)$. Note that $G_1(\sigma)$ is the graph G itself and $G_n(\sigma)$ is the single vertex graph consisting of $\sigma(n)$. When the peo σ is clear from the context, we use G_i and V_i to mean $G_i(\sigma)$ and $V_i(\sigma)$ respectively. The maximum clique size of G is denoted by $\omega(G)$. A *nontrivial* chordal graph is one which has at least two maximal cliques. Throughout the paper the chordal graphs under discussion are assumed to be nontrivial and connected.

In the process of reconstruction of a k-tree G wrt a peo σ, for any vertex v with $\sigma^{-1}(v) < n\text{-}k$, the addition of v introduces a new maximal clique in the graph being built. Whereas in the case of chordal graphs, not every addition of vertices introduces a new maximal clique. The base sets of a chordal graph wrt σ are precisely the $N(v,\sigma)$ sets corresponding to those vertices v whose addition in the reconstruction of G wrt σ increases the number of maximal cliques by one. We ignore the $N(v,\sigma)$ sets of those vertices whose addition increases the size of one of the existing maximal cliques because such additions do not alter the clique structure of the graph being built. Base sets of a chordal graph closely reflect its clique structure.

In Section 2, we define the notion of base sets and prove that they are a unique set of clique separators of a chordal graph. We also prove certain properties of base sets which are used in the later sections.

In Section 3, we develop characterizations for planar k-trees and planar chordal graphs.

In Section 4, we propose linear time algorithms to recognize planar k-trees and planar chordal graphs.

In Section 5, we prove the equivalence of hamiltonian 2-trees and maximal outer-planar graphs.

2. BASE SETS OF CHORDAL GRAPHS

We first define the notion of a base set of a chordal graph with the help of a peo σ. This way of defining is simple and is useful for algorithmic purposes. We later show that any peo of the chordal graph leads to the same set of base sets.

We define a set $B \subseteq V(G)$ to be a *base set* of a chordal graph G wrt a peo σ if there exists a vertex v with $\sigma^{-1}(v)=t$ such that (i) $B=N(v,\sigma)$ and (ii) B is not a maximal clique in $G_{t+1}(\sigma)$. For a base set B, the vertices which satisfy (i) and (ii) above are called its *dependent vertices* wrt σ. We denote this of set of vertices by $D(B,\sigma)$. The size of the set $D(B,\sigma)$ is called the *multiplicity* of the base set B wrt σ and is denoted by $\mu(B,\sigma)$. Figure 1 shows a chordal graph along with one of its peos σ and the set of base sets wrt σ. Note that in the case of a k-tree, for any vertex v with $\sigma^{-1}(v)<n\text{-}k$, $N(v,\sigma)$ is a base set wrt σ.

In the following lemmas we prove certain fundamental properties of base sets.

Lemma 1. *The number of base sets of a chordal graph G wrt peo σ is at most one less than the number of maximal cliques in G.*

Proof. Let m_i and b_i denote the number of maximal cliques and the number of base sets in the subgraph $G_i(\sigma)$ respectively. We need to show that $b_1 \leq m_1$-1. We prove by induction on t that $b_{n-t} \leq m_{n-t}$-1. In the basis case where t=0, the hypothesis is true as m_n=1 and b_n=0. We skip the details of the induction step as they can be easily worked out.□

Lemma 2. *Let B be a base set of a chordal graph G wrt a peo σ and let $t = max\ \{\sigma^{-1}(x) : x \epsilon D(B,\sigma)\}$. Then B is a clique separator of G_j, $1 \leq j \leq t$.*

Proof. We show that B is a separator in G_{t-i} by induction on i. Consider the basis case where $i=0$. Since $\sigma(t) \epsilon D(B,\sigma)$, $\sigma(t)$ is adjacent to all vertices of B. Further since B is not a maximal clique in $G_{t+1}(\sigma)$, there is a vertex $x \epsilon V_{t+1}$ which is adjacent to all vertices of B. Therefore, in the subgraph $G_t(\sigma)$,the removal of B separates $\sigma(t)$ and x. Now we show that if B is a separator in G_{n-j} then it is also a separator in G_{n-j-1}. Suppose B is a separator in G_{t-j} but not a separator in $G_{t-(j+1)}$. Let $\{u\} = V_{t-j-1} - V_{t-j}$. Then $N(u,\sigma)$ must contain at least one vertex from each of the connected components of G_{t-j}-B. Since $N(u,\sigma)$ is a clique, this contradicts the fact that B is a separator in G_{t-j}. Thus B is a separator in $G_{t-(j+1)}$. Hence, by induction, B is a separator in G_j,$1 \leq j \leq t$. Since any $N(v,\sigma)$ is a clique, B is a clique separator.□

We now show that any two different peos α and β of a chordal graph lead to the same set of base sets. Thus the set of base sets is a unique set of separators of a chordal graph. Further, we will also show that a base set has the same multiplicity wrt any peo. To this end we introduce the following definitions and notation.

Let B be a base set of a chordal graph G wrt a peo σ. We call a connected component M of $G(V_i - B)$ a *dependent component* of B in the subgraph $G_i(\sigma)$ if there exists a vertex $x \epsilon V(M)$ such that for all $y \epsilon B$, $(x,y) \epsilon E(G_i(\sigma))$. We denote the number of dependent components of B in the subgraph $G_i(\sigma)$ by $d_i(B,\sigma)$. Note that $d_1(B,\alpha) = d_1(B,\beta)$ for any peo's α and β as $G_1(\alpha) = G_1(\beta) = G$. So, we denote $d_1(B,\alpha)$ by just $d(B)$. In the following lemma we prove the relation between $d(B)$ and the multiplicity of B wrt any peo σ.

Lemma 3. *Let B be a base set of a chordal graph G wrt peo σ. Then $d(B) = \mu(B,\sigma)+1$.*

Proof. Let $t = \max\ \{\sigma^{-1}(x) : x \epsilon D(B,\sigma)\}$. By the definition of t, B is not a base set in $G_{t+1}(\sigma)$. We first show that $d_{t+1}(B,\sigma)=1$. Since $\sigma(t) \epsilon D(B,\sigma)$, B is not a maximal clique in $G_{t+1}(\sigma)$. Let B be contained in a maximal clique Q of $G_{t+1}(\sigma)$. Any vertex in Q-B is adjacent to all vertices in B. Thus $d_{t+1}(B,\sigma) \geq 1$. Suppose $d_{t+1}(B,\sigma) \geq 2$. Let s be an integer ,where $t+1 \leq s \leq n$, such that $d_s(B,\sigma)=2$ but $d_{s+1}(B,\sigma)=1$. Let $\{v\} = V_s - V_{s+1}$. Since $d_s(B,\sigma)=2$, in the process of obtaining $G_s(\sigma)$ from $G_{s+1}(\sigma)$, v must have been made adjacent to all vertices of B i.e., $N(v,\sigma)=B$. Further, since $d_{s+1}(B,\sigma)=1$, there exists a vertex $x \epsilon V_{s+1}$ which is adjacent to all vertices of B. Therefore, B is not a maximal clique of $G_{s+1}(\sigma)$. Since $N(v,\sigma)=B$ and B is not a maximal clique of $G_{s+1}(\sigma)$, by definition, B is a base set of $G_s(\sigma)$. As $G_s(\sigma)$ is a subgraph of $G_{t+1}(\sigma)$, B is also a base set of $G_{t+1}(\sigma)$, a contradiction. Hence, $d_{t+1}(B,\sigma)=1$.

Now, we show that $d_i(B,\sigma) = d_{i+1}(B,\sigma)+1$, where $i \leq t$, if and only if $\sigma(i) \epsilon D(B,\sigma)$. Suppose $\sigma(i) \epsilon D(B,\sigma)$. In $G(V_i - B)$, $\sigma(i)$ is an isolated vertex and forms a dependent component of B. Further all the dependent components of B in G_{i+1} are also the dependent components of B in G_i as G_{i+1} is a subgraph of G_i. Therefore, $d_i(B,\sigma)= d_{i+1}(B,\sigma)+1$. Suppose $d_i(B,\sigma)= d_{i+1}(B,\sigma)+1$. It is straight forward to see that $\sigma(i)\epsilon D(B,\sigma)$.

Since there are $\mu(B,\sigma)$ dependent vertices of B in G, $d_1(B,\sigma)=d(B)=\mu(B,\sigma)+1$.□

Corollary 1. *If B is a base set of a chordal graph G wrt peo σ, then B is properly contained in at least $\mu(B,\sigma)+1$ maximal cliques of G.*

Corollary 2. *Let B be a base set of a chordal graph wrt σ. No two vertices of $D(B,\sigma)$ belong to the same dependent component of B.*

Theorem 2. *Let α and β be two peo's of a chordal graph G. (i) If B is a base set of G wrt α then it is also a base set of G wrt β, and (ii) $\mu(B,\alpha)=\mu(B,\beta)$.*

Proof. (i) Let t be such that B is properly contained in one maximal clique in $G_{t+1}(\beta)$, but is contained in two maximal cliques in $G_t(\beta)$. Such a t must exist because, being a base set of G wrt α, by Corollary 1, B is contained in at least two maximal cliques of G. If $v=\beta^{-1}(t)$ then $N(v,\beta)=B$ and B is not a maximal clique of $G_{t+1}(\beta)$. Thus B is a base set of G wrt β also. (ii) By Lemma 3, $\mu(B,\alpha)=\mu(B,\beta)=d(B)$-1. □

We will henceforth drop the phrase 'wrt a peo' while referring to base sets.

Lemma 4. *Let B be a base set of a chordal graph G. Then B is properly contained in exactly $\mu(B)+1$ maximal cliques of G if and only if B is a maximal base set of G.*

Proof. Let $D(B,\sigma)=\{x_1,x_2,\ldots,x_{\mu(B)}\}$ and let $t=\max\{\sigma^{-1}(x_i):x_i\epsilon D(B,\sigma)\}$, where σ is an arbitrary peo of G. Since $\sigma(t)$ is a dependent vertex of B wrt σ, B is properly contained in at least one maximal clique Q_0 in $G_{t+1}(\sigma)$. Let Q_i, $1\leq i\leq\mu(B)$, be a maximal clique of G that contains B and x_i. Since Q_0 does not contain any x_i, $1\leq i\leq\mu(B)$, $Q_0\neq Q_i$. By Corollary 2, x_i's belong to different dependent components of B. So, $Q_i\neq Q_j$ for $1\leq i,j\leq\mu(B)$. Now, $Q_0, Q_1, \ldots, Q_{\mu(B)}$ are $\mu(B)+1$ distinct maximal cliques of G, each containing B.

(If) We now claim that if B is a maximal base set of G then B is properly contained only in the maximal cliques $Q_0,Q_1,\ldots,Q_{\mu(B)}$. Suppose there is a maximal clique Q of G such that $Q\neq Q_i$, $0\leq i\leq$r and $B\subseteq Q$. Since B is a separator of G, either $Q\subseteq G_{t+1}(\sigma)$ or $Q\cap V_{t+1}(\sigma)=B$.

Case 1. $Q\subseteq G_{t+1}(\sigma)$.

Let s, $t+1 < s<n$, be the maximum integer such that in $G_s(\sigma)$, B is properly contained in exactly one maximal clique. Since B is contained in two maximal cliques Q and Q_0 in $G_{t+1}(\sigma)$, there must exist a vertex v, where $t+1\leq\sigma^{-1}(v)<s$, such that

the addition of v creates a new maximal clique $\{v\}\cup N(v,\sigma)$ which contains B. Now $B_1=N(v,\sigma)$ is a base set because the addition of v gives rise to a new maximal clique. We know that $B\subseteq B_1$. Suppose $B_1=B$. Then v is a dependent vertex of B because $N(v,\sigma)=B$. As $G_{t+1}(\sigma)$ does not contain any dependent vertex of B, B_1 properly contains B, contradicting the maximality of B. Thus B is properly contained in exactly $\mu(B)+1$ maximal cliques of G.

Case 2. $Q\cap V_{t+1}(\sigma)=B$.

Suppose $Q\cap Q_j=B$ for all j, $1\leq j\leq\mu(B)$. Since $Q\supseteq B$, there must be a dependent vertex of B in Q. This is not possible as there are only $\mu(B)$ dependent vertices of B. Therefore for some j, $Q\cap Q_j=B_1\supseteq B$. There exists a vertex y in Q-Q_j such that $N(y,\sigma)=B_1$ and similarly a vertex z in Q_j-Q such that $N(z,\sigma)=B_1$. Let $i=\sigma^{-1}(y)$ and $k=\sigma^{-1}(z)$ and wlg let $i>k$. Then, B_1 is not a maximal clique in $G_{k+1}(\sigma)$. So B_1 is a base set of G, contradicting the maximality of B. Thus B is contained in exactly $\mu(B)+1$ maximal cliques of G.

(Only if) Suppose B is properly contained in exactly $\mu(B)+1$ maximal cliques of G. Assume that there exists a base set B_1 which properly contains B. Let Q be a maximal clique which contains B_1 and a dependent vertex of B_1 wrt σ. Then B is proper ly contained in Q, in addition to Q_i, $1\leq i\leq\mu(B)$, a contradiction. Thus B is a maximal base set of G. □

3. BASE SETS AND PLANARITY OF CHORDAL GRAPHS

In this section, we present characterizations of planar k-trees and planar chordal graphs in terms of base sets. These results follow from an observation about the planarity of 3-trees.

In the following results, we prove planarity of graphs by showing that they have a planar embedding. A planar embedding of a graph partitions the plane into a number of simply connected regions, called *faces*, each bounded by the edges of the graph. A face F of a planar embedding P is denoted by a sequence of vertices $(u_1,u_2,\ldots,u_r)$ representing the boundary of F as we traverse it in counter clockwise direction. The *inside*(*outside*) of a face is the region to the left (right) as we traverse the boundary in counter clockwise direction.

Lemma 5. *A 3-tree is planar if and only if every base set of it is of multiplicity one.*
Proof. (If) Let G be a 3-tree such that every base set of G has multiplicity one. Let σ be a peo of G. Let P_i denote the planar embedding of G_i. We prove the following statement H by induction on t.

H:G_{n-t} has a planar embedding P_{n-t} such that the vertices of any 3-clique which is contained in a unique maximal clique of G_{n-t} *form* the boundary of a face in P_{n-t}.

For $0 \leq t \leq 3$, G_{n-t} is a $(t+1)$-clique and it is easy to verify that G_{n-t} has a planar embedding which satisfies the condition of the hypothesis. Suppose H is true for $t=j \geq 3$. We will show that we can obtain a planar embedding of $G_{n-(j+1)}$ from that of G_{n-j} such that it satisfies H. Let $V_{n-(j+1)}$- $V_{n-j}=v$. Let $B=N(v,\sigma)$. As G is a 3-tree, $|B|=3$. Since $|V_{n-j}| \geq 4$, B is not a maximal clique of G_{n-j}. Thus B is a base set of G. Note that every base set of a 3-tree is of size three and so is maximal. Since $\mu(B)=1$, by Lemma 4, B is properly contained in exactly two maximal cliques of G. As $B \cup \{v\}$ is one of them, B is contained in a unique maximal clique in G_{n-j}. By the induction hypothesis, there is a face F in P_{n-j} with the vertices of B forming its boundary. Now, to obtain $P_{n-(j+1)}$, place v inside the face F and add edges connecting it to all the vertices of B. Note that the newly created 3-cliques form boundaries of faces in $P_{n-(j+1)}$. Thus H is true for $t=(j+1)$. Hence, by induction, G has a planar embedding.
(Only if) Let G be a planar 3-tree. Suppose B is a base set of G such that $\mu(B) \geq 2$. By Corollary 1, B is contained in at least three maximal cliques of G. If Q_1,Q_2,Q_3 are three such maximal cliques, then clearly $K_{3,3}$ is a subgraph of the graph induced by $Q_1 \cup Q_2 \cup Q_3$, a contradiction.□

It is easy to verify that 2-trees are planar. Now, since K_5 is a subgraph of a k-tree with $k \geq 4$, the following is immediate.

Theorem 3. *A graph G is a planar k-tree if and only if G is either (1) a tree, or (2) a 2-tree, or (3) a 3-tree in which all base sets are of multiplicity one.*

Lemma 5 can be restated as follows: A 3-tree is planar if and only if it can be constructed as follows: Start with a 3-clique. Choose a 3-clique Q in the existing graph such that Q is contained in a unique maximal clique; add a new vertex and make it adjacent to all the vertices of Q. The above construction method can be extended to obtain a method of constructing planar chordal graphs by interleaving the construction methods of trees, 2-trees and planar 3-trees, as we show in the following theorem.

Theorem 4. *A chordal graph G is planar if and only if (i)* $\omega(G) \leq 4$ *and (ii) for any base set B of size three* $\mu(B)=1$.
Proof. (If) We prove the following statement H by induction on t.

H: G_{n-t} has a planar embedding P_{n-t} such that for any 3-clique K of G_{n-t} the following hold:
(i) If K is a maximal clique in G_{n-t} then there exist two faces in P_{n-t} such that each vertex of K lies on the boundary of both these faces.
(ii) If K is properly contained in a unique maximal clique of G_{n-t} then there exists a face in P_{n-t} such that the vertices of K lie on its boundary.

(Remark: The difference between the induction hypothesis of this proof and that of Lemma 5 is that the vertices of the 3-cliques of concern here need not *form* the boundary of a face but need only be *lying on* the boundary of a face.)

In the basis case where t=0, H is trivially true. Suppose H is true for t=j. We will show that we can obtain the required planar embedding of G_{n-j-1} from that of G_{n-j}. Let $\{v\}= V_{n-j-1}$-V_{n-j} and let B=$N(v,\sigma)$. $|B|\leq 3$ as $w(G)\leq 4$. Three cases arise depending on the cardinality of B.

Case 1. $|B|$=1. Let B=$\{u_1\}$. Let $F = (u_1, x_1, ..., x_r, u_1)$ be any face of P_{n-j} which has the vertex u_1 on its boundary. To obtain P_{n-j-1}, place vertex v inside the face F and connect it by an edge to u_1. P_{n-j-1} satisfies the induction hypothesis as there are no new 3-cliques in G_{n-j-1}.

Case 2. $|B|$=2. Let B=$\{u_1,u_2\}$. The edge (u_1,u_2) belongs to some face F=$(u_1,x_1,...,x_r,u_2,u_1)$ of P_{n-j}. To obtain P_{n-j-1}, place v inside F and add edges to connect it to u_1 and u_2. The face F now gets split into two faces F_1=(u_1, v, u_2, u_1) and $F_2 = (u_1, x_1, ..., x_r, u_2, v, u_1)$. The vertices $\{v, u_1, u_2\}$ of the newly created 3-clique are on the boundary of both F_1 and F_2. Further more if $\{x,y,z\}$ is any 3-clique such that x,y, and z are on the boundary of F, then they will now be on the boundary of F_2. Thus P_{n-j-1} is a planar embedding of G_{n-j-1} satisfying the required conditions.

Case 3. $|B|$=3. Let B=$\{u_1, u_2, u_3\}$. Two subcases arise.

Case 3.1. B is a maximal clique in G_{n-j}. By the induction hypothesis, we have two faces F_1,F_2 in P_{n-j}. To obtain P_{n-j-1}, place v inside F_1 and add edges to connect it to u_1,u_2 and u_3. B is now contained in a unique maximal clique and the existence of F_2 ensures that the condition (ii) of H is satisfied. Thus P_{n-j-1} satisfies the induction hypothesis.

Case 3.2. B is not a maximal clique of G_{n-j} and hence is a base set of G. Since $w(G)\leq 4$, B is a maximal base set of G. Since $\mu(B)$=1,by Lemma 4, B is properly contained in exactly two maximal cliques of G. As $B\cup$ $\{v\}$ is one of these, B is contained in a unique maximal clique in G_{n-j}. By the induction hypothesis, there exists a face F in P_{n-j} such that the u_i's are on the boundary of F. To obtain P_{n-j-1}, place v inside F and add edges to connect it to u_1, u_2 and u_3. P_{n-j-1} satisfies the induction hypothesis.

Hence G has a planar embedding.

(Only if) Let G be a planar chordal graph. Clearly, $\omega(G)\leq 4$. Suppose there exists a base set B of size 3 with $\mu(B)\geq 2$. By Corollary 1, there exist at least three maximal cliques say Q_1, Q_2 and Q_3 which properly contain B. Then, $K_{3,3}$ is a subgraph of the induced subgraph of $Q_1 \cup Q_2 \cup Q_3$, a contradiction.□

Figure 2 shows a planar chordal graph and its planar embedding.

4. PLANARITY TESTING FOR CHORDAL GRAPHS

In this section, we present a $O(|V|+|E|)$ time algorithm to test the planarity of a chordal graph by using the characterization developed in the previous section. We require to test if every base set of size three has multiplicity one. We do this efficiently by making use of a property of Lexicographic_Breath_First_Search (LBFS) peo of a chordal graph [G80].

Lemma 6. *Let σ be a LBFS peo of a chordal graph G and let B be a maximal base set of G. All vertices of $D(B,\sigma)$ occur consecutively in σ.*

Proof. Let $\mu(B)>1$, for otherwise we are through. Let $v_r, v_{r-1}, \ldots, v_1$ be the vertices of $D(B,\sigma)$ in the order they appear in σ. Let the label of v_1 be $x_1x_2\ldots x_s$ at the stage when v_1 is selected in the process of obtaining σ. Observe that the x_i's correspond to the peo numbers of the vertices of B and all other vertices of $D(B,\sigma)$ also have the same label at this stage. After v_1 is numbered, the only way any vertex can have a larger label compared to $x_1x_2\ldots x_s$ is that it be adjacent to all vertices of $B \cup \{v_1\}$. This is ruled out as B is a maximal base set with multiplicity at least two.□

Algorithm Chordal-Planar

1. { obtain a LBFS peo σ of G;
2. for all $v \in V(G)$ determine $N(v,\sigma)$; *planar*:=true;
3. for i:=1 to n do if $|N(\sigma(i),\sigma)| \geq 4$ then *planar*:=false;
4. for i:=1 to n do *base*[i]:=false; t:=n-1;
   /* *base*[i] is set true if $|N(\sigma(i),\sigma)|=3$ and $N(\sigma(i),\sigma)$ is a base set of $G_i(\sigma)$ */
5. while ($t \geq 1$) and *planar* do
6. { if $|N(\sigma(t),\sigma)|=3$ then
7. if $N(\sigma(t),\sigma) \neq N(\sigma(t+1),\sigma)$ then
   { /* $N(\sigma(t),\sigma)$ is encountered for the first time and so we need to test if it is a base set. */
8. r:= min{ $\sigma^{-1}(v)$:$v \in N(\sigma(t),\sigma)$};
9. if $N(\sigma(r),\sigma) \neq N(\sigma(t),\sigma)$-{$\sigma(r)$} then *base*[$t$]:=true;
10. }
11. else
12. { *base*[t]:=true;
13. if *base*[t+1]=true then *planar*:=false;
14. }
15. t:=t-1;
16. }
17. If *planar* then write("G is planar")
18. else write("G is nonplanar"); }

Lemma 7. *Algorithm Chordal-Planar correctly determines whether a given chordal graph G is planar.*

Proof. In Line 3, we check if for all vertices v of G, the size of $N(v,\sigma)\leq 3$. This will ensure that $\omega(G)\leq 4$. Since the peo being used is LBFS peo and since any base set of size three is maximal, by Lemma 6 , any two vertices v_1,v_2 such that $N(v_1,\sigma)=N(v_2,\sigma)$ and $|N(v_1,\sigma)|=3$, will appear consecutively in σ. If $N(\sigma(t),\sigma)=\{x,y,z\}$ for some t, we check in Line 7 if $N(\sigma(t+1),\sigma)=\{x,y,z\}$. If not then there is no $t_1>t$ such that $N(\sigma(t_1),\sigma)=\{x,y,z\}$. Thus to determine if $\{x,y,z\}$ is a maximal clique in $G_{t+1}(\sigma)$ (and hence not a base set of $G_t(\sigma)$), we need to check if the last added vertex among x,y and z is such that its neighbours with larger peo number are exactly the other two vertices. This is accomplished by Lines 8 and 9. If $N(\sigma(t),\sigma)=N(\sigma(t+1),\sigma)$ then $\{x,y,z\}$ is a base set of $G_t(\sigma)$ and hence of G. The multiplicity of this base set is ≥ 2 if $\{x,y,z\}$ is also a base set of $G_{t+1}(\sigma)$ which is indicated by *base*$[t+1]$. In Line 13 this is checked. Thus at the end of the while loop *planar* will be true only if every base set of size three has multiplicity one.□

Theorem 5. *Planar chordal graphs can be recognized in* $O(|V|+|E|)$ *time.*

Proof. Chordal graphs can be recognized in $O(|V|+|E|)$ time [G80]. It remains to show that the algorithm Chordal-Planar runs in the same time. Obtaining a LBFS peo σ can be done in $O(|V|+|E|)$ time [G80]. To compute $N(v,\sigma)$ for a vertex v, we traverse the adjacency list of v and delete from it all vertices which have lesser peo number compared to that of v. Thus finding $N(v,\sigma)$ for all vertices v can be done in $O(|V|+|E|)$ time. Each iteration of the while loop takes constant time as it deals with sets of constant size. □

Since the recognition of planar k-trees by using Theorem 3 also involves the testing of multiplicity of base sets of size three, the algorithm Chordal Planar can be modified to recognize planar k-trees. Thus we have,

Theorem 6. *Planar k-trees can be recognized in* $O(|V|+|E|)$ *time.*

5. BASE SETS AND MAXIMAL OUTERPLANAR GRAPHS

In this section, we show that a graph is a maximal outerplanar graph if and only if it is a hamiltonian 2-tree.

An *outerplanar* graph is a planar graph which can be embedded in the plane such that all its vertices lie on the same face. An outerplanar graph is *maximal outerplanar* (*mop*) if no edge can be added without losing outerplanarity. In the following lemma we give a characterization of maximal outerplanar graphs in terms of 2-trees.

Lemma 8. *Let G be a 2-tree. Then, G is a maximal outerplanar graph if and only if every base set of G has multiplicity one.*

Proof. (If) Let σ be an arbitrary peo of G. Let P_i denote the maximal outerplanar embedding of G_i. Wlg assume that all the vertices of G_i are on the outer face of P_i. The edges of P_i which form the outer face are called the external edges and the others are internal edges. We prove the following statement H by induction on t.

H: G_{n-t} has a maximal outerplanar embedding P_{n-t} in which an edge is an internal edge if and only if it is a base set of G_{n-t}.

For $0 \leq t \leq 2$, G_{n-t} is a $(t+1)$-clique and it can be easily verified that there exists a maximal outerplanar embedding of it which satisfies H. Assume that H is true for $t=j \geq 2$. Let $\{v\} = V_{n-(j+1)} - V_{n-j}$ and let $B=N(v,\sigma)$. Suppose B is base set of G_{n-j}. Then due to the addition of v, B will have multiplicity two. Therefore B is not a base set of G_{n-j}. By the induction hypothesis, B is an external edge in P_{n-j}. Now, to obtain $P_{n-(j+1)}$, place v in the outer face of P_{n-j} and add edges to connect it to the vertices of B. It is straightforward to show that $P_{n-(j+1)}$ satisfies H. Hence, by induction, G has a maximal outerplanar embedding.

(Only if) Let G be a mop with n vertices. G has $(2n\text{-}3)$ edges and every minimal vertex separator is a 2-clique [H69]. Thus G is a 2-tree [R72]. Suppose B is a base set of G with $\mu(B) \geq 2$. Then, by Corollary 1, B is contained in at least three maximal cliques of G, a contradiction since every edge in a mop is contained in at most two triangles. Thus $\mu(B)=1$ for every base set B of G. □

Theorem 7. *A 2-tree is hamiltonian if and only if it is a mop.*

Proof. (If) Obvious.

(Only if) Let G be a hamiltonian 2-tree. Let $B=\{u_1, u_2\}$ be any base set of G. Suppose $\mu(B) \geq 2$. By Lemma 3, B has at least three dependent components in G. As a hamiltonian circuit of G, starting at u_1, can go through only two of the dependent components of B before returning to u_1 , G does not have a hamiltonian circuit, a contradiction. Thus any base set of G has multiplicity one. By Lemma 8, G is a maximal outerplanar graph. □

CONCLUSIONS

In this paper, we have introduced the notion of base sets of a chordal graph. We have developed structural characterizations of planar k-trees and planar chordal graphs in terms of base sets. Using these characterizations we have given linear time algorithms for checking planarity of k-trees and chordal graphs. However, it needs to be investigated whether these algorithms can be extended to obtain planar embeddings also. We have also shown the equivalence of maximal outerplanar graphs and hamiltonian 2-trees. As one of the referees pointed out, it will be of interest to generalise this result to k-outerplanar graphs.

ACKNOWLEDGEMENTS

We thank our collegue Sudeb Pal for his critical comments on the manuscript which resulted in improved presentation. We also thank the referees for their helpful and detailed comments.

REFERENCES

[BFMY83] Beeri, C., Fagin, R., Maier, D., Yannakakis, M., *On the Desirability of Acyclic Database Schemes*, JACM 30(3), 479-513,1983.

[G80] Golumbic, M.C., *Algorithmic Graph Theory and Perfect Graphs*, Academic Press, New York, 1980.

[H69] Harary, F., *Graph Theory*, Addison Wesley, Reading, MA, 1969.

[HL89] Ho, C.,Lee, R.C.T., *counting Clique Trees and Computing Perfect Elimination Schemes in Parallel*, IPL, 31, 61-68, 1989.

[HT74] Hopcroft, J.,Tarjan, R.E., *Efficient Planarity Testing*, JACM, 21(4), 549-568, 1974.

[K88] Klein, P.N., *Efficient Parallel Algorithms for Chordal Graphs*, FOCS, 150-161, 1988.

[R72] Rose, D., *On Simple Characterizations of k-trees*, Disc., Math., 7, 317-322, 1972.

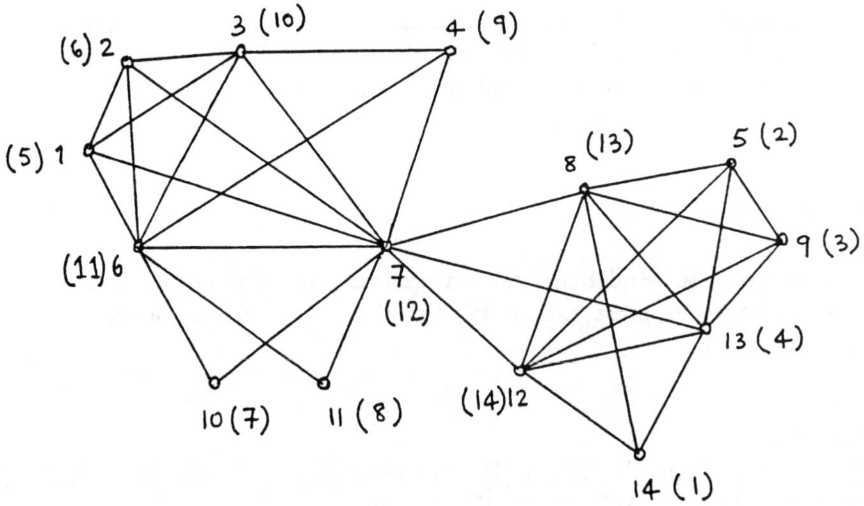

σ = (14, 5, 9, 13, 1, 2, 10, 11, 4, 3, 6, 7, 8, 12)

BASE SET	MULTIPLICITY
{ 7 }	1
{ 6, 7 }	2
{ 3, 6, 7 }	1
{ 8, 12, 13 }	2

(Numbers in parentheses indicate the position of the vertex in σ)

FIGURE 1

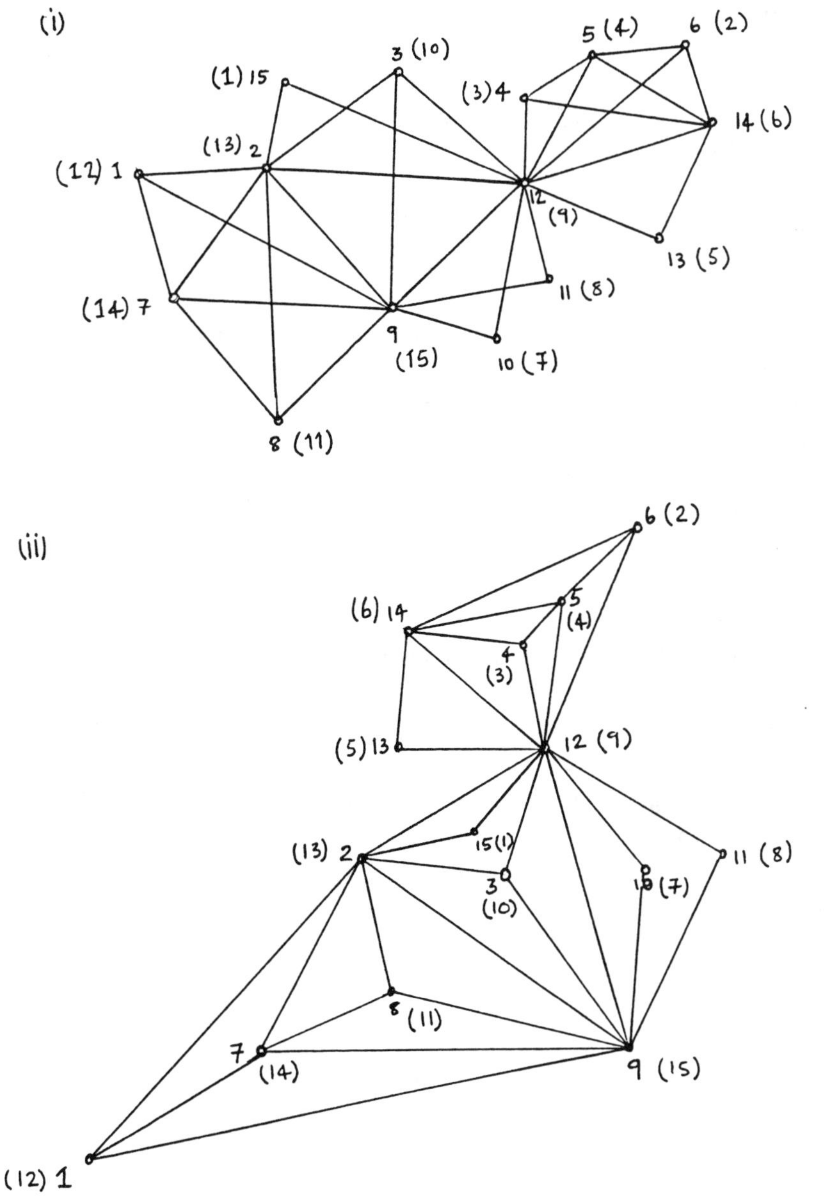

(i) A Planar Chordal Graph G

(ii) A Planar Embedding of G

σ = (15, 6, 4, 5, 13, 14, 10, 11, 12, 3, 8, 1, 2, 7, 9)

(Numbers in parentheses indicate the position of the vertex in σ)

FIGURE 2

OPTIMAL PARALLEL ALGORITHMS ON CIRCULAR-ARC GRAPHS

A.Srinivasa Rao and C.Pandu Rangan
Department of Computer Science & Engineering
I.I.T. Madras 600 036 India.

1. INTRODUCTION

Recently, a growing interest has been shown in designing parallel algorithms on restricted classes of graphs [10,11]. We present in this paper some optimal parallel algorithms on circular-arc graphs. Specifically, we present optimal parallel algorithms for finding (unweighted) maximum independent set, minimum clique cover and minimum dominating set in a unified way. Given the sorted array of end points of the arcs in the intersection model of the circular-arc graph, all the above mentioned problems can be solved sequen-tially in O(n) time where n is the number of arcs [9]. All our parallel algorithms run in O(log n) time on an O(n/log n)-processor EREW PRAM and hence they are optimal.

All the algorithms that we present will have the following form:

Stage 1: (*Pruning*) Delete a suitable subset of vertices of the given circular-arc graph G and obtain a graph G'.

Stage 2: (*Find Successor*) Define in a suitable manner a function on the vertex set of G' called NEXT.

Stage 3: (*Greedy Step*) Use NEXT function greedily ' and solve the problem on G'.

Stage 4: (*Extension Step*) Extend the solution of G' to G (if necessary).

2. PRELIMINARIES

All the graphs we consider in this paper are finite graphs with no multiple edges and self-loops.

Let G = (V,E) be a graph. A set of vertices $S \subseteq V$ forms a **clique** in G if every pair of vertices in S are adjacent. A **clique cover** of G is a partition of vertex set V into $V_1,\ldots,V_k$, such that each V_i, $1 \leq i \leq k$, forms a clique in G; k is the **size** of the clique cover. A clique cover with minimum size is called a **minimum clique cover** (MCC).

A set of vertices $S \subseteq V$ forms an **independent set** in G if no two vertices of S are adjacent. An independent set with maximum cardinality is called a **maximum independent set** (MIS).

A set $S \subseteq V$ of vertices **dominates** a set $S' \subseteq V$ if every vertex in $S'-S$ is adjacent to some vertex in S. If S dominates V, we say that S is a **dominating set** for the graph G. A dominating set with minimum cardinality is called a **minimum dominating set** (MDS).

The MCC, MIS, and MDS problems for an arbitrary graph are known to be NP-complete [7].

A graph G = (V,E) is a **circular-arc graph** if there exists a one-to-one correspondence of the vertex set V with a family AF of (closed circular) arcs on the unit circle such that two vertices are adjacent in the graph iff their corresponding arcs in the family intersect. The family AF is called an **intersection model** of the graph G. An example is given in Fig.1. The family AF is **proper** if no arc of AF is contained in some other arc of AF.

Circular-arc graphs arise in various applications such as traffic-control and information retrieval and they are well studied in literature [2,5,6,8,13,14,15]. From now on, let $AF = \{X_1, X_2, \ldots, X_n\}$ be a family of arcs on a unit circle and G = (V,E), $|V| = n$, be the circular-arc graph with AF as its intersection model. The arc X_i is represented by the ordered pair $(l(X_i), r(X_i))$, where $l(X_i)$ and $r(X_i)$ denote its **left** and **right** end points respectively. The arc X_i exists on the circle as a traversal in the clockwise direction from $l(X_i)$ to $r(X_i)$ along the circumference of the circle.

Instead of presenting the algorithms on the graph G, we will be working with the intersection model AF itself. For example, we will compute a maximum independent set of arcs (two arcs being independent if they do not intersect) to solve the MIS problem.

Let X_i and X_j be two arcs such that the arc X_j is totally contained in the arc X_i. Then X_i is called a **containing arc** and arc X_j is called a **contained arc**.

Let PL be the sorted array of 2n distinct end points of arcs in AF. These points appear in PL in the same order as they are encountered in the clockwise traversal of the circle beginning at $l(X_1)$. We note that if the end points are not sorted, then we can use the Parallel Merge Sort [3] to sort them in O(log n) time using O(n) processors.

Let L be a list of elements $a_1, a_2, \ldots, a_k$, $k > 0$, not necessarily in that order. Then, the **position** of an element a_i in the list L is the number of elements that precede it in L plus one.

For a nonempty set S of integers, let MAX(S) and MIN(S) denote a maximum element and a minimum element of S respectively.

3. MIS PROBLEM

3.1 Discussion

We first observe that the arcs in AF that properly contain some other arcs of AF do not contribute to the solution of this problem [6,13]. Hence all such arcs can be removed from AF. Let the new arc family be AF'. For sake of convenience, we still assume |AF'|=n.

Definition 3.1 : For each arc X_i in AF', define **NEXT(i)** to be the arc in AF' whose left end is the first encountered in a clockwise traversal from $r(X_i)$.

Definition 3.2 : For each arc X_i in AF', define **GD(i)** to be the (greedy) maximal independent set for AF' of the form $\{X_i, X_{i_1}, \ldots, X_{i_k}\}$, where X_{i_1} = NEXT(i) and X_{i_j} = NEXT(i_{j-1}), $2 \leq j \leq k$.

For example, in Fig.1 AF' = $\{X_1, X_3, X_4, X_5, X_6, X_8, X_{10}, X_{11}, X_{12}\}$; NEXT(1) = X_4, NEXT(3) = X_6, NEXT(11) = X_3; GD(1) = $\{X_1, X_4, X_8, X_{10}\}$, GD(10) = $\{X_{10}, X_{12}, X_3, X_6, X_8\}$.

The following Lemma shows the importance of greedy independent sets.

Lemma 3.1 [9] *: Let P be an independent set of AF' containing* X_i*. Then,* $|P| \leq |GD(i)|$.

Definition 3.3 : Define **RIGHT(1)** = { $X_i \in$ AF' | X_i contains $r(X_1)$, $i \neq 1$}, and **LEFT(1)** = {X_i AF'| X_i contains $l(X_1)$, $i \neq 1$}.

Let MAIN(1) = $\{X_1\}$ U LEFT(1) U RIGHT(1) throughout this section. The following Lemma gives a method to solve the MIS problem efficiently in parallel.

Lemma 3.2 *: A set of maximum size among { GD(i) |* $X_i \in$ *MAIN(1)} is an MIS of AF.*

Proof: Follows from the fact that any maximum independent set of AF contains either the arc X_1 or an arc of AF' that intersects with X_1.#

We now present the sequential form of our algorithm.

Stage 1 : Remove the containing arcs from AF to get AF'.

Stage 2 : Compute NEXT(i), for all $X_i \in$ AF'.

Stage 3 : Compute |GD(i)|, for all $X_i \in$ MAIN(1). Find an index a such that |GD(a)| = MAX{|GD(i)| : $X_i \in$ MAIN(1)}.

Stage 4 : Output GD(a). {GD(a) is an MIS of AF.}

3.2 Parallel Implementation

We now show that each stage can be implemented to run in O(log n) time and O(n) space using O(n/log n) processors in an EREW PRAM.

Stage 1 : To remove the containing arcs from AF, we modify the technique of removing contained arcs shown in [1]. First, we remove the arcs $X_i \in$ LEFT(1) for which there exists an arc X_j that is contained in the arc segment $(l(X_1),r(X_i))$. This can be done in a simple way using parallel prefix [12]. Then, we remove other containing arcs from AF as follows.

Recall that PL is the sorted array of 2n distinct end points of arcs in AF. Let PL_1 be obtained from PL by removing from it every $r(X_i)$ for which $X_i \in LEFT(1)$. Let PL_2 be obtained from PL by keeping in it only the $r(X_i)$'s for which $X_i \in LEFT(1)$. Finally, let $Pl_1.PL_2$ denote the concatenation of the lists PL_1 and PL_2.

Using parallel prefix [12], we compute for each element of $PL_1.PL_2$, its position in $PL_1.PL_2$. Next, we assign to every $r(X_i)$ of $PL_1.PL_2$, a weight equal to the position of $l(X_i)$ and to every $l(X_i)$, a weight zero. Finally, using parallel prefix on the weighted $PL_1.PL_2$, we find for every $r(X_i)$, the largest weight, say w(i), that occurs before it. If w(i) is greater than the weight of $r(X_i)$, then X_i is a containing arc and can be removed from AF. We also remove the end points of the arcs so removed from PL.

Lemma 3.3 : *The above procedure removes exactly those arcs in AF that contain some other arcs of AF.*

Proof: Let X_i be an arc such that w(i) is greater than the weight of $r(X_i)$. That means there exists an arc $X_{w(i)}$ such that $l(X_{w(i)})$ occurs after $l(X_i)$ in the list PL and $r(X_{w(i)})$ occurs before $r(X_i)$ in PL. Hence, X_i is a containing arc. The proof of the converse is simple. #

Stage 2 : In the array PL, we assign to each $l(X_i)$, a weight equal to its index i, and assign to each $r(X_i)$ a weight zero. Then using list ranking [4], we compute for each $r(X_i)$, the smallest weight, say, w'(i), that occurs to the right of $r(X_i)$ in PL. If w'(i)= 0, then NEXT(i) = $X_{w'(i)}$; otherwise NEXT(i) = X_1.

The correctness of this procedure follows from the definition of NEXT( ).

Lemma 3.4: *Let X_i and X_j be two arcs in AF' such that X_i contains $l(X_j)$ and NEXT(i) = NEXT(j). Also let X_k be an arc in AF' such that the segment$(l(X_i),l(X_j))$ contains $l(X_k)$. Then, NEXT(k) = NEXT(i).*

Proof : Observe that if the arcs in AF' are sorted on left end's in clockwise, then they will also be sorted on right end's in clockwise, because AF'is a proper family of arcs. Now it is clear that the segment $(r(X_i),r(X_j))$ contains $r(X_k)$ (See Fig.2). This, together with the fact that NEXT(i) = NEXT(j) implies that NEXT(k) = NEXT(i). #

Definition 3.4: For each $X_i \in$ AF', define $\mathbf{NEXT}^{-1}(\mathbf{i})=\{X_j \mid NEXT(j)=X_i\}$.

The above Lemma 3.4 shows that the arcs in $NEXT^{-1}(i)$ occur consecutively around the circle.

Computation of $NEXT^{-1}()$ is as follows [1]. For each X_i, we compute a pair (l_i, r_i) such that $NEXT^{-1}(i) = \{X_{l_i}, X_{l_{i+1}}, \ldots, X_{r_i}\}$, with the convention that $X_{n+j} = X_j$. For each X_i, we initialise $NEXT^{-1}(i) = \emptyset$. Then, for each X_i, if $NEXT(i) = X_j \neq NEXT(i+1) = X_k$, then we set $r_j = i$ and $l_k = i+1$.

Stage 3 : We will now outline the procedure to compute $|GD(i)|$, $X_i \in RIGHT(1)$, in parallel. To begin with, RIGHT(1) can be computed in O(log n) time using O(n/log n) processors. We create a new copy of each $X_i \in MAIN(1)$ and denote it by $X_{new(i)}$. We then modify the NEXT() function by replacing every $NEXT(j) = X_i$, $X_i \in MAIN(1)$, by $NEXT(j) = X_{new(i)}$. Also, we set NEXT(new(i)) equal to for every new(i).

Now, we form a directed graph H = (V',E'), where V' = {1,2,..., |AF'|}, and the directed edge(i,j) ∈ E iff $X_j = NEXT(i)$. It is easy to see that H is an in-forest. In this forest, the children list for each node except the leaves is available in the form of $NEXT^{-1}()$. This facilitates the use of the Euler Tour Technique [16] and Parallel Prefix on the trees of H. If X_i is an arc in AF', then the corresponding vertex in H is referred to as node i.

We define some terms on the forest H as follows.

Definition 3.5 : For every node i of H, define **ROOT(i)** to be the root of the tree in H to which i belongs.

Definition 3.6 : For every node i of H, define **DEPTH(i)** to be the number of nodes on the path from node i to ROOT(i) (both inclusive) in H.

We observe that the arrays ROOT(), and DEPTH() can be easily computed in O(log n) time with O(n/log n) processors using the Euler Tour Technique in conjunction with the Parallel Prefix by converting the forest H into a tree by adding an 'extra root'.

The following Lemma facilitates an easy computation of $|GD(i)|$, for all $X_i \in RIGHT(1)$.

Lemma 3.5: *For all $X_i \in RIGHT(1)$,*

$|GD(i)| = DEPTH(i)$, *if X_i and $X_{ROOT(i)}$ do not intersect;*

$= DEPTH(i)-1$, *otherwise.*

Proof: Follows from the definitions of GD(i), DEPTH(i), and ROOT(i). (See Fig.3) #

After computing $|GD(i)|$, for all $X_i \in RIGHT(1)$, we can compute $|GD(i)|$, for all $X_i \in LEFT(1)$ in a similar way. Computation of $|GD(1)|$ is straightforward.

Finally, we compute the maximum of $\{|GD(i)| : X_i \in MAIN(1)\}$, say $|GD(a)|$.

Stage 4 : Notice that the elements of GD(a), a maximum independent set of AF, are on the path from node a to ROOT(a) in H. Hence this stage consists of outputting the above path and this can be done in O(log n) time using O(n/log n) processors.

Finally, we note that the space complexity for each step is O(n). This completes the algorithm. Our parallel algorithm is optimal since the processor-time product is O(n).

From the above discussion, we have the following theorem.

Theorem 3.1 : *Given the sorted array of end points of arcs in an intersection model for a circular-arc graph, the maximum independent set problem can be solved in O(log n) time and O(n) space using O(n/log n) processors in an EREW PRAM.*

4. MCC PROBLEM

4.1 Discussion

Let AF' be a proper family of arcs as obtained in the MIS problem. Let CQ be an MCC for AF'. Then, it is easy to extend CQ to an MCC of AF as follows : We know that for each X_i in AF-AF', there exists an X_j such that X_j is properly contained in X_i. So, we can include X_i in the clique of CQ to which X_j belongs.

Definition 4.1: A clique is said to be **linear** if every arc in the clique contains a common point on the circle.

Definition 4.2: Define **LQ(i)**, for all $X_i \in$ AF', to be the linear clique that is formed by all the arcs in AF' that contain $r(X_i)$.

Definition 4.3: For each X_{i_1} in AF', let $GD(i_1)$, as defined by Definition 3.2, be $\{X_{i_1}, X_{i_2}, \ldots, X_{i_k}\}$.

1) Define $\mathbf{LAST}(i_1)$ to be $NEXT(i_k)$.

2) Define the (greedy) clique cover

$$\mathbf{GD_q(i)} = \{LQ(i_1), LQ(i_2), \ldots, LQ(i_k)\}, \text{ if } LAST(i_1)=X_k;$$
$$= \{LQ(i_1), LQ(i_2), \ldots, LQ(i_k), LQ'(i_{k+1})\}, \text{ otherwise,}$$
where $X_{i_{k+1}} = NEXT(i_k)$ and $LQ'(i_{k+1}) = LQ(i_{k+1}) - LQ(i_1)$.

For example, in Fig.1, $LQ(1) = \{X_1, X_3, X_2\}$, $LQ(12) = \{X_{12}, X_1, X_2\}$; $GD_q(1) = \{LQ(1), LQ(4), LQ(8), LQ(10), \{X_{12}\}\}$;
$GD_q(10) = \{LQ(10), LQ(12), LQ(3), LQ(6), LQ(8)\}$.

Lemma 4.1 [9] : *If AF' is not a clique, then there exists an MCC of AF' consisting of linear cliques.*

The following Lemma shows the importance of greedy clique covers.

Lemma 4.2 [9] : *Let* $LQ(S) = \{LQ(i_1), LQ(i_2), \ldots, LQ(i_k)\}$, *where* $S = \{X_i, \ldots, X_{i_k}\}$, *be a linear clique cover for a proper family AF', and* X_i *be any arc in S. Then,* $|GD_q(i)| \le |S|$.

Let LEFT' = $\{X_1\}$ U LEFT(1) throughout this section.

Lemma 4.3 : *A clique cover of minimum size among* $\{ GD_q(i) \mid$

$X_i \in$ *LEFT'} is an MCC of AF'.*

Proof : In view of Lemma 4.1, it is sufficient to consider clique covers consisting of only linear cliques. Let CQ be an MCC consisting of linear cliques, and C be the clique containing the arc X_1. Then, the clique C is either LQ(1) or LQ(i) for some $X_i \in$ LEFT(1). The result follows. #

We now present the sequential form of our algorithm.

Stage 1 : Remove the containing arcs from AF to get AF'.

Stage 2 : Compute NEXT(i), for all $X_i \in$ AF'.

Stage 3 : Compute $|GD_q(i)|$, for all $X_i \in$ LEFT'. Let $|GD_q(a)|$ = MIN{ $|GD_q(i)|$, $X_i \in$ LEFT'}. Construct $GD_q(a)$ from AF'.

Stage 4 : Extend $GD_q(a)$ by including the arcs in AF-AF' in the corresponding cliques of $GD_q(a)$ to get an MCC of AF.

4.2 Parallel Implementation

Stage 1 : This is similar to Stage 1 of MIS problem, except that we indicate for every removed arc X_i, an arc X_j in AF' such that X_i contains X_j.

Stage 2 : This is same as Stage 2 of MIS problem.

Stage 3 : The construction of a forest H is similar to that in MIS problem except that, here, new copies are created for the arcs in LEFT(1) instead of MAIN(1).

In view of Lemma 4.3, it is enough to compute $|GD_q(i)|$, for all $X_i \in$ LEFT'. Computation of $|GD_q(1)|$ is straightforward.

Lemma 4.4: *Let $GD_q(i_1)$, for all $X_i \in$ LEFT(1) be defined as in* Definition 4.3. *Then,*

$$|GD_q(i_1)| = \mathrm{DEPTH}(i_1)-1, \text{ if } ROOT(i_1)=new(i_1);$$
$$= \mathrm{DEPTH}(i_1), \text{ otherwise.}$$

Proof : Follows from the definitions of GD(i), DEPTH(i), and ROOT(i).#

Now, let $|GD_q(a)|$ = MIN{$|GD_q(i)|$: $X_i \in$ LEFT'}. That means $GD_q(a)$ is an MCC for AF'. The next step is to partition the arcs of AF' into the linear cliques of $GD_q(a)$. To do this, we set the vector LC to indicate LC(i) = j iff $X_i \in$ LQ(j). Let GD(a), as defined by Definition 3.2, be $\{X_{a_1},\ldots,X_{a_k}\}$. We discuss the case when $GD_q(a)$ = {LQ(a_1,...,LQ(a_k)}. The other case when $GD_q(a)$ = {LQ(a_1),...,LQ(a_k), LQ'(a_{k+1})} can be dealt with in a similar way. Initially, we assign weights LC(a_i) = a_i, $1 \leq i \leq k$, and LC(j) = 0, for others. Let SF be the sorted list of right ends of arcs in AF'. Note that SF can be easily obtained from the input list PL. Since AF' is a proper family, every arc X_m, $a_i \leq m < a_{i+1}$, $1 \leq i < k$, belongs to LQ(a_i). Also, every arc X_m, m >= a_k, belongs to LQ(a_k). Thus, we want for each r(X_m) in SF, the largest weight, say w, that occurs before it in LC.

Then, $X_m \in LQ(a_w)$. This can be done using parallel prefix.

Stage 4 : Recall that we have marked in Stage 1 some arc of AF' for every arc in AF-AF'. This marking can be used as mentioned at the beginning of this Section to distribute the arcs in AF-AF' among the linear cliques of $GD_q(a)$ in O(log n) time using n/log n processors.

Theorem 4.1: *Given the sorted list of end points of arcs in an intersection model for a circular-arc graph, the minimum clique cover problem can be solved in O(log n) time and O(n) space using O(n/log n) processors in an EREW PRAM.*

5. MDS PROBLEM

5.1 Discussion

Let AF" be the proper family of arcs obtained from AF by removing all the "contained arcs" from AF. Contrast AF" with AF' of previous problems. For each arc X_i which is properly contained in an arc X_j, a dominating set for AF containing X_i can be changed to another dominating set for AF by swapping X_i and X_j. Hence, to find an MDS for AF it suffices to consider the arcs in AF" only. However, we note that a dominating set for AF" is **not** necessarily a dominating set for AF. From now on, we assume that there is no single arc in AF that intersects all the arcs in AF. For sake of simplicity, we still assume |AF"| = n.

Definition 5.1: For each $X_i \in$ AF, define **N(i,AF)** to be the set of arcs in AF that intersect X_i. Similarly, for each X_i in AF", define **N(i,AF")** to be the set of arcs in AF" that intersect X_i.

Definition 5.2: For each $X_i \in$ AF", define the **first clockwise arc** denoted **FCA(i)**, to be the arc X_j in AF-N(i,AF) such that $r(X_j)$ is the first right end of an arc in AF-N(i,AF) encountered in a clockwise traversal of the circle starting from $r(X_i)$.

Definition 5.3: For each $X_i \in$ AF", define $\mathbf{NEXT_d(i)}$ to be the arc X_j in N(FCA(i), AF") such that $r(X_j)$ is the last right end of an arc in N(FCA(i),AF") encountered in a clockwise traversal of the circle starting from right end of FCA(i).

Definition 5.4: For each $X_i \in$ AF", define $\mathbf{NEXT_d^1(i)} = NEXT_d(i)$, and $\mathbf{NEXT_d^r(i)} = NEXT_d(j)$, where $X_j = NEXT_d^{r-1}(i)$, for $r \geq 2$.

Definition 5.5: For each $X_i \in$ AF", define the (greedy) dominating set $\mathbf{GD_d(i)}$ of the following form : $\{ X_i, NEXT_d^1(i),...,NEXT_d^r(i)\}$, where r is the smallest integer such that $GD_d(i)$ is a dominating set for AF.

For example, in Fig.1, AF" = $\{ X_1,X_2,X_4,X_5,X_6,X_7,X_9,X_{11},X_{12} \}$; $FCA(1) = X_4$, $FCA(6) = X_8$, $FCA(11) = X_3$; $NEXT_d(1) = X_6$, $NEXT_d(6) = X_7$, $NEXT_d(11) = X_5$; $GD_d(1) = \{X_1,X_6,X_7,X_{12}\}$; $GD_d(2) = \{X_2,X_7,X_{12}\}$.

Lemma 5.1 [9]: *Let D be a dominating set for AF such that $D \subseteq AF''$ and $X_i \notin D$. Then,* $|GD_d(i)| \leq |D|$.

Definition 5.6 : Define **RIGHT(1)** = $\{X_i \mid X_i \in AF''$ and X_i contains $r(X_1)$, $i \neq 1\}$, and **LEFT(1)** = $\{X_i \mid X_i \in AF''$ and X_i contains $l(X_1)$, $i \neq 1\}$.

Let MAIN(1) = $\{X_1\}$ U RIGHT(1) U LEFT(1) throughout this section.

Lemma 5.2: *A set of minimum size among* $\{GD_d(i) \mid X_i \in MAIN(1)\}$ *is an MDS for AF.*

Proof : Follows from the fact that any dominating set for AF contains either the arc X_1, or an arc in AF" that intersects with X_1. #

We now present the sequential form of our algorithm.

Stage 1 : Remove the contained arcs from AF to get AF".

Stage 2 : Compute $NEXT_d(i)$, for all $X_i \in AF''$.

Stage 3 : Compute $|GD_d(i)|$, for all $X_i \in$ MAIN(1).
Let $|GD_d(a)|$ be the minimum.

Stage 4 : $GD_d(a)$ is an MDS for AF.

5.2. Parallel Implementation

Stage 1 : This is similar to stage 1 of MIS problem except that, here, contained arcs are removed.

Stage 2 : First, we have to compute FCA(i), for all $X_i \in AF$. This is same as the computation of NEXT( ) in the MIS problem except for the following difference : here, list ranking is done on the input list PL that contains the end points of the arcs in AF (not of the arcs in AF") in sorted order.

We will now introduce an intermediate definition to help us to compute $NEXT_d()$.

Definition 5.7: For each $X_i \in AF$, define **NEXT'(i)** to be the arc X_j in AF such that X_j intersects X_i and $r(X_j)$ is the last right end that is encountered in a clockwise traversal of the circle starting from $r(X_i)$.

We proceed as follows to compute NEXT'(i). We obtain PL_1 from the input list PL by i) removing from it all the left end's, and ii) every $r(X_i)$ for which $X_i \in$ LEFT(1). Similarly, we obtain PL_2 from PL by keeping only the $r(X_i)$'s for which $X_i \in$ LEFT(1). Let $PL_1.PL_2$ be the concatenation of PL_1 and PL_2. We can easily obtain $PL_1.PL_2$ by applying parallel prefix. Next, using parallel prefix again, we compute for each element of $PL_1.PL_2$ its position in $PL_1.PL_2$. Now, we assign to every $l(X_i)$ of PL, a weight equal to the position of $r(X_i)$ in $PL_1.PL_2$, and to every $r(X_i)$ of PL, a weight equal to 0. Using parallel prefix again, we compute, for each $r(X_i)$ of $(PL-PL_2).PL_2$, the largest weight, say s(i), that occurs before it. Finally, using parallel prefix, we compute, for each $r(X_i)$ in PL, the largest weight, say y(i), that occurs before it.

If X_i does not contain $l(X_1)$, then $NEXT'(i) = X_{s(i)}$. If X_i contains $l(X_1)$, then

$$NEXT'(i) = X_{s(i)}, \text{ if } X_{s(i)} \text{ contains } r(X_{y(i)}),$$
$$= X_{y(i)}, \text{ otherwise.}$$

Let X_j = FCA(i). Then, it follows from the definitions of $NEXT_d()$, FCA(), and NEXT'() that $NEXT_d(i) = NEXT'(j)$, for all $X_i \in AF''$.

Definition 5.8: For each $X_i \in AF''$,

define $\mathbf{NEXT_d^{-1}(i)} = \{X_j \mid NEXT_d(j)=X_i\}$.

Similar to Lemma 3.4, we have

Lemma 5.3: *All the arcs in $NEXT_d^{-1}(i)$, $X_i \in AF''$, occur consecutively around the circle.*

The above Lemma implies that $NEXT_d^{-1}(i)$ can be computed in the same fashion as $NEXT^{-1}(i)$ was computed in the MIS problem.

Stage 3: Now, in view of Lemma 5.2, it suffices to compute $|GD_d(i)|$, for all $X_i \in MAIN(1)$.

We will now outline the procedure to compute $|GD_d(i)|$, for all $X_i \in RIGHT(1)$. We form a forest H from AF", like the one in MIS problem, using $NEXT_d^{-1}()$ function (instead of $NEXT^{-1}()$), and compute the arrays ROOT() and DEPTH().

Lemma 5.4: *Let $GD_d(i)$, for all $X_i \in$ RIGHT(1) be defined as in the* Definition 5.5. *Then,*

$$|GD_d(i)| = DEPTH(i)-1, \textit{ if } FCA(ROOT(i)) \textit{ and } X_i \textit{ intersect;}$$
$$= DEPTH(i), \textit{ otherwise.}$$

Proof : We note that every arc in AF which contains some point in the arc segment $(l(X_i),r(XROOT(i)))$ is dominated by some arc in $GD_d(i)$. Let $GD_d(i) = \{X_i, NEXT(i),\ldots,NEXT^r(i)\}$. If the arcs FCA(ROOT(i)) and X_i intersect, then r = DEPTH(i)-1 (since $NEXT_d^r(i)$ = ROOT(i)); otherwise r = DEPTH(i). (See Fig.4) #

The final step is to compute a minimum of $\{|GD_d(i)| : X_i \in MAIN(1)\}$, say $|GD_d(a)|$. It is obvious that $|GD_d(a)|$ can be obtained in O(log n) time using O(n/log n) processors.

Stage 4 : $GD_d(a)$, the elements of which are on the path from the node a to ROOT(a) in H, is an MDS for AF.

Theorem 5.1 : *Given the sorted list of end points of arcs in an intersection model for a circular-arc graph, the minimum dominating set problem can be solved in O(log n) time and O(n) space using O(n/log n) processors in an EREW PRAM.*

6. CONCLUSIONS

We have presented in a unified way optimal parallel algorithms for the unweighted versions of the MIS, MCC, and MDS problem on circular-arc graphs using greedy methods. It would be interesting to investigate whether our techniques can be extended to obtain efficient sequential and parallel algorithms for the weighted versions of these problems.

Acknowledgments

We thank an anonymous referee for his meticulous reading of the manuscript and for many helpful suggestions.

REFERENCES

[1] M.J.Atallah and D.Z.Chen, Optimal Parallel Algorithm For the Minimum Circle-cover Problem. Tech Rept. CSD-TR-813, Purdue University, Sep 1988.

[2] A.Apostolico and S.E. Hambrusch, Finding Maximum Cliques On Circular-arc Graphs, *Infom. Proc. Lett.*, **26** (1987), pp.209-215.

[3] Richard Cole , Parallel Merge Sort, *SIAM J. Comp.*, **17**(1988), pp.770-785.

[4] R.Cole and U.Vishkin, Approximate Parallel Scheduling. Part I: The Basic Technique With Applications To Optimal Parallel List Ranking in Logarithmic Time, *SIAM J. Comp.*, **17** (1988), pp. 128-142.

[5] M.C. Golumbic , Algorithmic Graph Theory And Perfect Graphs (Academic press, New York, 1980)

[6] M.C. Golumbic and Peter L. Hammer, Stability In Circular-Arc Graphs, *J. Algorithms*, **9** (1988), pp.314-320.

[7] M.R.Gary and D.S.Johnson, Computers and Intractability: A Guide To The Theory Of NP-Completeness (Freeman, San Francisco, CA, 1979).

[8] W.L.Hsu, Maximum Weight Clique Algorithms For Circular-Arc Graphs And Circle Graphs, *SIAM J. Comput.*, **14** (1985), pp.224-231.

[9] W.L.Hsu and K.H.Tsai, Linear Algorithms On Circular-arc Graphs, unpublished manuscript (1988).

[10] P.N. Klein, Efficient Parallel Algorithms For Chordal Graphs. *29th FOCS*, 1988, pp.150-161.

[11] P.N. Klein and J.H.Reif, An Efficient Parallel Algorithm For Planarity, *J. Comp. Sys. Sci.*, **37**(1988), pp.190-246.

[12] R.E.Ladner and M.J.Fischer, Parallel Prefix Computation, *J. of ACM*, **24**(1980), pp.831-838.

[13] S.Masuda and K.Nakajima, An Optimal Algorithm For Finding a Maximum Independent Set of a Circular-arc Graph,*SIAM J.Comput.*, **17** (1988), pp.41-52.

[14] W.K.Shih and W.L.Hsu, An O(n log n+ m log log n) Maximum Weight Clique Algorithm for Circular-Arc Graphs, *Inform.Process. Lett.* **31** (1989), pp. 129-134.

[15] A.Tucker, An Efficient Test For Circular-arc Graphs, *SIAM J. Comput.*, **9**(1980), pp.1-24.

[16] R.E.Tarjan and U.Vishkin, An Efficient Parallel Biconnectivity Algorithm, *SIAM J. Comput.*, **14**(1985), pp. 862-874.

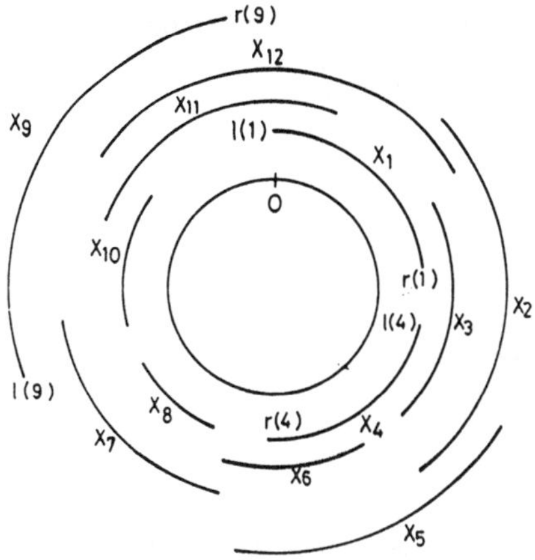

(a) An intersection model

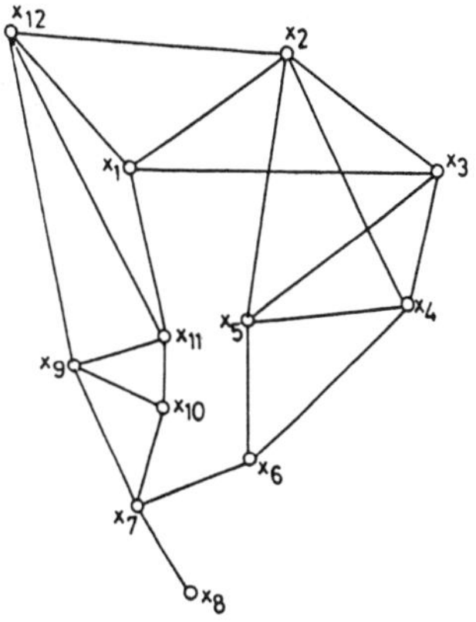

(b) Its circular-arc graph

Note: For simplicity, $l(X_i)$ is represented as $l(i)$

FIG. 1.

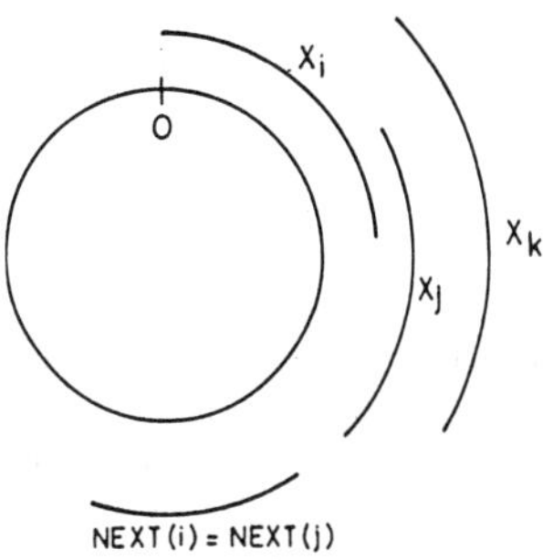

FIG.2.

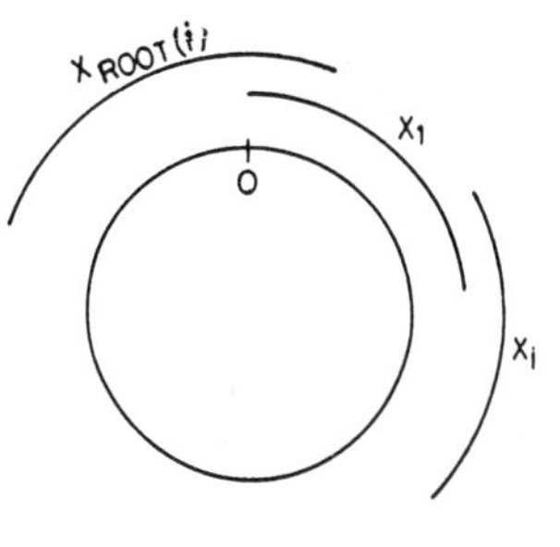

(a)

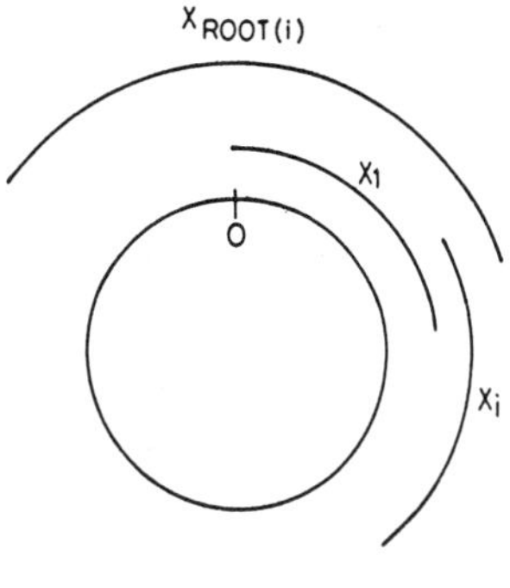

(b)

FIG.3.

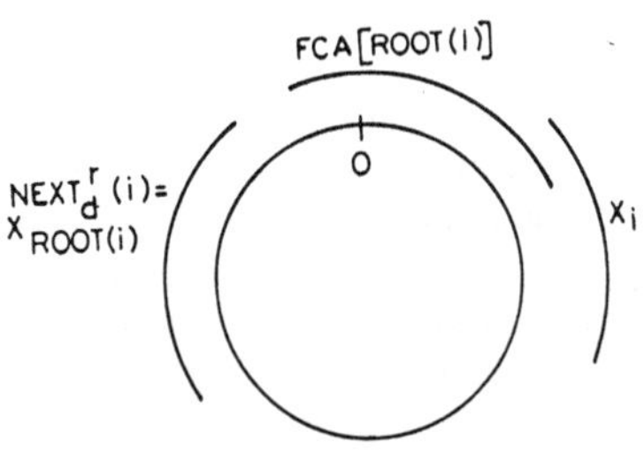

(a)

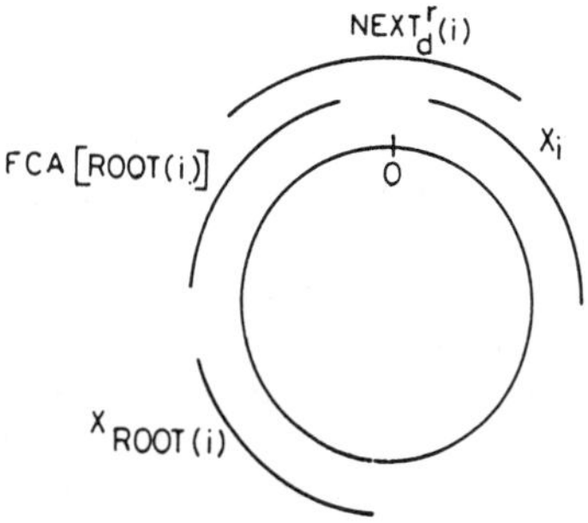

(b)

FIG.4.

Algebraic Properties of The Space of Multivalued and Paraconsistent Logic Programs

V.S. Subrahmanian

Department of Computer Science
University of Maryland
College Park, MD 20742.

Abstract

Paraconsistent logics are a class of logics proposed by Newton da Costa [7] that provide a framework for formal reasoning about inconsistent systems. In [4, 5, 6], Blair and Subrahmanian, and independently, Fitting [11], showed that paraconsistent logics may be successfully used for logic programming. In this paper, we study the algebraic properties of the space of paraconsistent logic programs over a complete lattice of truth values. We show that this set, under some natural operations generalizing those defined by Mancarella and Pedreschi [18], yields a distributive lattice that satisfies various important *non-extensibility* conditions. Intuitively, these non-extensibility conditions tell us that the algebraic characterization we provide cannot be (naturally) strengthened any further. As an interesting application, we generalize the notion of subsumption equivalence of classical logic programs to the case of multi-valued logic programs and derive necessary and sufficient conditions for multivalued logic programs to be subsumption-equivalent.

1 Introduction

Recently, there has been intense interest in utilizing paraconsistent logic as a programming language (cf. Blair and Subrahmanian[4, 5, 6], Fitting [10, 11]). The reason for this interest is that paraconsistent logics (cf. Da Costa [7]) provide a framework for automated reasoning in the presence of inconsistency. As very large databases and very large "knowledge bases" may often contain inconsistent and/or erroneous information, it is only natural that paraconsistent logics be used to reason about such knowledge bases. The computational formalism of logic programming provides a natural framework to express knowledge bases as programs. The basic foundations of paraconsistent logic as a programming language has been laid by the work of Blair and Subrahmanian [4, 5, 6] and Fitting [11, 12].

One of the main features a logic programming language should possess is *compositionality*, i.e. it must be possible to define the semantics of a program $P = P_1 \cup P_2$ by describing the semantics of its components P_1 and P_2. This point was realized recently by Mancarella and Pedreschi [18]. They realized that the correct approach to formalizing compositionality of logic programs is through algebraic methods. Mancarella and Pedreschi studied the algebraic properties of the space of *pure* (i.e. negation-free) two-valued logic programs. Earlier, [15], we studied the algebraic properties of the space of general logic programs (i.e. logic programs whose clauses may contain negated atoms in their body).

Our principal technical contributions in this paper are:

1. to carry out an in-depth study of the algebraic properties of multi-valued and paraconsistent logic programs. Thus, we generalize the results of Mancarella and Pedreschi[18] to the case of multi-valued logic programming over logics having a complete lattice of truth values.
2. to study the algebraic properties of the space of multivalued logic programs.
3. to derive necessary and sufficient conditions linking the cardinality of the Herbrand Base of the language in question with the possibility of *extending* this algebra to some other well-known formalisms like boolean algebras, rings, etc.
4. to study the equivalences of logic programs over these multivalued logics. In particular, we generalize the notion of subsumption equivalence (cf. Maher [17]) to the multi-valued case. (Maher's definitions, too, were restricted to pure classical logic programs). We derive necessary and sufficient conditions for two multi-valued logic programs to be subsumption equivalent.

Throughout the rest of this paper, we assume that the reader is familiar with work on paraconsistent logic programs (cf. [4, 5, 6]), and with elementary notions of lattice theory [13] and Boolean Algebras [14, 19, 22]. Due to space restrictions, proofs of the results presented here are omitted. They may be found in [24].

2 Algebraic Properties

We assume that $(\mathcal{T}, \leq)$ is a complete lattice of *truth values*. As usual, we use the notation $\sqcup$ and $\sqcap$ to denote l.u.b.'s and g.l.b.'s respectively, and use $\top$ and $\bot$ to denote the greatest element of $\mathcal{T}$ and the least element, respectively, of $\mathcal{T}$. We also assume that all programs are closed in the sense of [5]. We assume now that we have some fixed logical language L. We always assume that L satisfies the following two conditions:

(L1) L contains at least one predicate symbol and one constant symbol.

(L2) L contains finitely many constant, function and predicate symbols.

The Herbrand Base of L, denoted B_L, is the set of all variable free atoms that can be expressed in the language L. Conditions (L1) and (L2) above ensure that B_L is non-empty and that $card(B_L)$ is either finite or countably infinite. An annotated logic program (ALP, for short) is a finite set of clauses of the form:

$$A_0 : \mu_1 \Leftarrow A_1 : \mu_1 \ \& \ldots \& \ A_k : \mu_k.$$

Here, the A_i's are atoms, and the μ_i's are in $\mathcal{T}$. Interpretations are maps from B_L to $\mathcal{T}$. If A is a ground atom and $\mu \in \mathcal{T}$, then interpretation I satisfies $A : \mu$, denoted $I \models A : \mu$, iff $I(A) \geq \mu$. The definition of satisfaction is extended to complex formulas in the obvious way (cf. [4]). Let $\Upsilon(L)$ denote the set $\{T_P \mid P \text{ is a } \mathcal{T} \text{ valued ALP in language } L\}$. Now define two operations $\oplus$ and $\otimes$ on $\Upsilon(L)$ as follows:

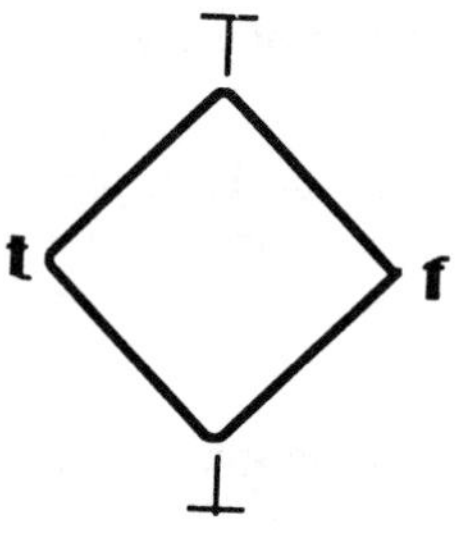

Figure 1: The Truth Value Lattice *FOUR*

$(T_P \oplus T_Q)(I) = \sqcup\{T_P(I), T_Q(I)\}$, and

$(T_P \otimes T_Q)(I) = \sqcap\{T_P(I), T_Q(I)\}$.

The first thing to verify is whether $(T_P \oplus T_Q)$ and $(T_P \otimes T_Q)$ are in $\Upsilon(L)$. The following two propositions confirm this.

Proposition 1 $(T_P \oplus T_Q) = T_{P \cup Q}$. □

Definition 1 Suppose $C1$ and C_2 are annotated clauses that are standarized apart (i.e. they share no common variables) of the form

$$A_1 : \mu_1 \Leftarrow B_1 : \rho_1 \& \cdots \& B_k : \rho_k$$

$$A_2 : \mu_2 \Leftarrow D_1 : \psi_1 \& \cdots \& D_m : \psi_m$$

such that A_1 and A_2 are unifiable via mgu θ. Then define the clause $C_1 @ C_2$ to be:

$$(A_1 : \mu \Leftarrow B_1 : \rho_1 \& \cdots \& B_k : \rho_k \& D_1 : \psi_1 \& \cdots \& D_m : \psi_m)\theta$$

where $\mu = \sqcap\{\mu_1, \mu_2\}$. Given ALPs P, Q over $\mathcal{T}$, define $P@Q$ to be the ALP $\{C_1 @ C_2 \mid C_1$ is an annotated clause in P, C_2 is a renamed version of a clause C in Q such that C_1 and C_2 share no common variable symbols $\}$.

For purposes of illustration, we show in Figure 1 a Hasse diagram of the four valued truth value lattice *FOUR*. Intuitively, in *FOUR*, $\perp$ stands for "unknown" or "undefined" while $\top$ stands for "inconsistently defined" or "over-defined". Due to lack of space, we are unable to go into the epistemological aspects of *FOUR*; the interested reader is referred to Fitting's [10] for an elegant epistemological discussion.

Proposition 2 Suppose P and Q are $\mathcal{T}$ valued ALPs in L. Then: $(T_P \otimes T_Q) = T_{P@Q}$. □

Example 1 Consider the *FOUR* valued logic programs P and Q below:

$P:$	$Q:$
$p(X,Y):\mathbf{t} \Leftarrow q(X):\mathbf{t}$	$p(a,Z):\mathbf{t} \Leftarrow w(Z):\mathbf{f}$
$q(a):\mathbf{t}$	$w(b):\mathbf{f}$

Then $P@Q$ is the program consisting of the single annotated clause:

$$p(a,Z):\mathbf{t} \Leftarrow q(a):\mathbf{t}\ \&\ w(Z):\mathbf{f}.$$

Proposition 3 Suppose $\mathcal{T}$ is any complete lattice of truth values. Then $\langle \Upsilon(L), \oplus, \otimes \rangle$ is a bounded distributive lattice. □

If X is a set of formulas in some language L', and L is a language that is a subset of L', then we use the notation $[X]_L$ to denote $X \cap L$, i.e. to denote that part of X that is in language L.

Proposition 4 (Blair, [3]) Suppose X is an r.e. subset of B_L. Then there is a pure logic program P (cf. Lloyd[16]) in language $L' \supseteq L$ such that $[T_P \uparrow \omega]_L = X$. □

Lemma 1 Suppose P is a $\mathcal{T}$ valued ALP. Then $\{\mu \mid (\exists A \in B_L) T_P \uparrow \omega(A) = \mu\}$ is finite. □

Theorem 1 Suppose $\mathcal{T}$ is a complete lattice of truth values and $\mathcal{T}'$ is a *finite* subset of $\mathcal{T} - \{\bot\}$. Let $(S_\mu)_{\mu \in \mathcal{T}'}$ be a collection of mutually disjoint, r.e. subsets of B_L. Then there is a $\mathcal{T}$ valued ALP P in language $L' \supseteq L$ such that:

1. for all $\mu \in \mathcal{T}'$, if $A \in S_\mu$, then $T_P \uparrow \omega(A) = \mu$ and
2. if $A \in \left(L - \bigcup_{\mu \in \mathcal{T}'} (S_\mu)\right)$, then $T_P \uparrow \omega(A) = \bot$. □

We assume that the reader is familiar with the notion of a Boolean algebra (cf. Sikorski [22], or Henkin, Monk and Tarski [14]).

Definition 2 A bounded distributive lattice $\langle D, +, \cdot \rangle$ is said to *have a Boolean extension* iff there is a unary operator $\neg : D \to D$ such that $\langle D, +, \cdot, \neg, \mathbf{0}, \mathbf{1} \rangle$ is a Boolean algebra (Here $\mathbf{0}$ is the least element of D and $\mathbf{1}$ is the greatest element of D.).

Throughout the rest of this paper, given a $\mathcal{T}$ valued interpretation I, and some $\mu \in \mathcal{T}$, we will use the notation $\Re(\mu, I)$ to denote the set $\Re(\mu, I) = \{A \in B_L \mid I(A) = \mu\}$. We also use the notation, $\wp(P, I)$ to denote $\wp(P, I) = \{\mu \in \mathcal{T} \mid (\exists A \in B_L)\, T_P(I)(A) = \mu\}$. Note that $\wp(P, I)$ is always finite. Also given any bounded distributive lattice, we use $\mathbf{0}$ and $\mathbf{1}$ to denote, respectively, the least and greatest element of D.

Lemma 2 Suppose P is a $\mathcal{T}$ valued logic program and I is a $\mathcal{T}$ valued Herbrand interpretation. Then: For all $\mu \in (\mathcal{T} - \{\bot\})$, if $\Re(\mu, I)$ is an r.e. subset of B_L, then $\Re(\mu, T_P(I))$ is an r.e. subset of B_L. □

Corollary 1 Let P be a $\mathcal{T}$ valued logic program. Then for all $\mu \in \mathcal{T} - \{\bot\}$, $\Re(\mu, T_P \uparrow \omega)$ is an r.e. subset of B_L. □

Theorem 2 (Weak Boolean Non-Extensibility Theorem.) Suppose B_L is infinite and $card(\mathcal{T}) \geq 2$. Then: the bounded distributive lattice $\langle \Upsilon(L), \oplus, \otimes \rangle$ has no Boolean extension. □

We now exhibit below a necessary and sufficient condition for a particular kind of Boolean extension, called strongly complemented Boolean extension, to exist.

Definition 3 A Boolean algebra $\langle D, +, \cdot, \neg, \mathbf{0}, \mathbf{1} \rangle$ is *strongly complemented* iff:

(SC1) $\neg$ is injective, i.e. for all $a, b \in D$, $a \neq b \Rightarrow \neg a \neq \neg b$.

Note that a Boolean algebra that satisfies (SC1) above as well as the condition that $\neg\neg a = a$ has been studied under the name *quasi Boolean algebras* due to Bialynicki-Birula and Rasiowa [2] and also Michael Dunn [9]. However, in this paper, we do not require the assumption that $\neg\neg a = a$. We also recall that in any Boolean algebra, $x \leq y \Rightarrow \neg(y) \leq \neg(x)$.

Definition 4 A bounded distributive lattice $\langle D, +, \cdot \rangle$ is said to *have a strongly complemented Boolean Extension* iff there is an operator $\neg : D \rightarrow D$ such that $\langle D, +, \cdot, \neg, \mathbf{0}, \mathbf{1} \rangle$ is a strongly complemented Boolean Algebra.

Suppose now that $\mathcal{T}$ is not only a complete lattice, but that under the operations of $\sqcup$ and $\sqcap$ and some (unspecified) operation $\sim: \mathcal{T} \rightarrow \mathcal{T}$, $\langle \mathcal{T}, \sqcup, \sqcap, \sim, \bot, \top \rangle$ is a strongly complemented Boolean algebra. When this is so, the set of $\mathcal{T}$ valued Herbrand interpretations of L forms a strongly complemented lattice with $(\neg I)(A) = \sim (I(A))$.

Theorem 3 (Strongly Complemented Boolean Non-Extensibility Theorem) Suppose $\langle \mathcal{T}, \sqcup, \sqcap, \sim, \bot, \top \rangle$ is a strongly complemented Boolean algebra. Then: $\langle \Upsilon(L), \oplus, \otimes \rangle$ has a strongly complemented Boolean extension iff $card(\mathcal{T}) = 1$. □

Definition 5 Suppose $\mathcal{T}$ is a complete lattice. An annotated clause:

$$A : \mu \Leftarrow Body$$

is *uninformative* iff $\mu = \bot$. A $\mathcal{T}$ valued ALP P is *uninformative* iff each clause in P is uninformative. P is *informative* iff P is not uninformative.

Note that the empty ALP is always (trivially) uninformative.

Lemma 3 Suppose $\mathcal{T}$ is a complete lattice. Then: $T_P(I) = \Delta$ for all interpretations I iff either $card(\mathcal{T}) = 1$ or P is uninformative. □

Definition 6 We say that the bounded distributive lattice $\langle \Upsilon(L), \oplus, \otimes \rangle$ has a *ring extension* iff there is a ring $\langle \Upsilon(L'), \oplus, \otimes \rangle$ such that: (1) $\Upsilon(L) \subseteq \Upsilon(L')$ and (2) $\oplus$ and $\otimes$ of $\langle \Upsilon(L'), \oplus, \otimes \rangle$, extend the corresponding operators on $\langle \Upsilon(L), \oplus, \otimes \rangle$, and (3) $\mathbf{0}$ of $\langle \Upsilon(L), \oplus, \otimes \rangle$ and $\langle \Upsilon(L'), \oplus, \otimes \rangle$ are identical.

Theorem 4 Suppose $\mathcal{T}$ is a complete lattice. Then: $\langle \Upsilon(L), \oplus, \otimes \rangle$ has a ring extension iff $card(\mathcal{T}) = 1$. □

Definition 7 An element $d \in D$ (where $\langle D, +, \cdot \rangle$ is a distributive lattice) is said to be *meet reducible* if there exist $x, y \in D$ such that $x \cdot y = d$ and x and y are distinct from d. If a distributive lattice has a least element **0** and the **0** is meet reducible (via some $x, y \in D$), then such x and y are called *zero divisors* of D and (x, y) is called a *zero divisor pair*. We denote the set of zero divisors of this distributive lattice by $\mathcal{Z}(D)$.

Theorem 5 (Weak Zero Divisor Theorem.) Suppose $\mathcal{T}$ is a complete lattice. Then:

1. if $card(B_L) \geq 2$ and $card(\mathcal{T}) \geq 2$ then $\langle \Upsilon(L), \oplus, \otimes \rangle$ has a zero divisor.
2. if $\langle \Upsilon(L), \oplus, \otimes \rangle$ has a zero divisor, then $card(\mathcal{T}) \geq 2$. □

The above theorem yields some conditions for the *existence* of zero divisors, but it does not tell us much about the syntactic structure of the ALPs whose associated T_P operators are zero divisors. We will now present a necessary and sufficient condition for identifying zero divisors.

Definition 8 Suppose P, Q are $\mathcal{T}$ valued ALPs. We say that P and Q are *contravening* iff whenever $C1$ is a clause in P having head $A_1 : \mu_1$, and $C2$ is a clause in Q having head $A_2 : \mu_2$, if A_1, A_2 are unifiable, then $\mu_1 \sqcap \mu_2 = \bot$.

Example 2 Consider the $FOUR$ valued programs P and Q, consisting respectively of the single clauses $\{p : \mathbf{t} \Leftarrow\}$ and $\{p : \mathbf{f} \Leftarrow\}$. Then P and Q are contravening.

The empty program is trivially contravening with any program P. Indeed, if Q is uninformative, then for all $\mathcal{T}$ valued programs P, P and Q are contravening. The following lemma is immediate.

Lemma 4 Suppose $\mathcal{T}$ is a complete lattice, and P and Q are $\mathcal{T}$ valued ALPs. Then: P and Q are contravening iff $P@Q$ is uninformative. □

Theorem 6 (Zero Divisor Identification Theorem.) Suppose $\mathcal{T}$ is a complete lattice and $card(\mathcal{T}) \geq 2$. Then: (T_P, T_Q) is a zero divisor pair iff P and Q are both informative and contravening. □

3 Generalized Subsumption Equivalence

Various notions of equivalences of logic programs have been proposed. These notions are of two types – semantical notions and syntactical notions (of course, there is often a close connection between these two).

For classical logic programs (pure and two valued), the syntactic notions have been carefully explored by Maher [17]. Of these notions, the most important is that of subsumption equivalence. In this section, we will show how to generalize the notion of subsumption equivalence to logic programming over complete lattices of truth values.

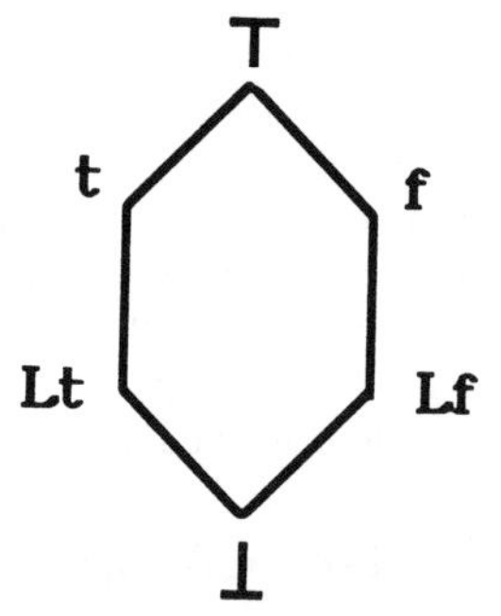

Figure 2: The Complete Lattice SIX of Truth Values

Definition 9 Suppose $\mathcal{T}$ is a complete lattice of truth values, and $C1$ and $C2$ are the following annotated clauses:

$$C1: \quad A_1 : \delta_1 \Leftarrow B_1 : \mu_1 \,\&\cdots\&\, B_k : \mu_k$$

$$C2: \quad A_2 : \delta_2 \Leftarrow D_1 : \phi_1 \,\&\cdots\&\, D_m : \phi_m$$

$C1$ *subsumes* $C2$ iff there is a (most general) substitution θ such that:

1. $A_1\theta = A_2$ and $\delta_2 \leq \delta_1$ and
2. for all $1 \leq j \leq k$, either:
   (a) $\mu_j = \bot$ or
   (b) there is some $\alpha(j)$, $1 \leq \alpha(j) \leq m$ such that $B_j\theta = D_{\alpha(j)}$ and $\mu_j \leq \phi_{\alpha(j)}$.

Example 3 Consider the complete lattice SIX shown in Figure 2.

Let C_1 and C_2 be:

$$C_1: \quad p(X, a) : \mathbf{t} \Leftarrow q(X) : \mathbf{Lf}$$

$$C_2: \quad p(b, a) : \mathbf{Lt} \Leftarrow q(b) : \mathbf{f}$$

Here, C_1 subsumes C_2.

Definition 10 Suppose $\mathcal{T}$ is a complete lattice of truth values and P and Q are $\mathcal{T}$ valued logic programs. P is said to *subsume* Q iff each annotated clause in Q is subsumed by some annotated clause in P. P and Q are *subsumption equivalent* iff P subsumes Q and Q subsumes P.

If C is an annotated clause, we use the notation T_C to denote $T_{\{C\}}$.

Lemma 5 Suppose $\mathcal{T}$ is a complete lattice of truth values and $C1, C2$ are annotated clauses. Then: If $C1$ subsumes $C2$, then $T_{C2} \leq T_{C1}$. □

The following result follows immediately from Lemma 5.

Theorem 7 Suppose $\mathcal{T}$ is a complete lattice and P, Q are $\mathcal{T}$ valued logic programs. Then:

1. If P subsumes Q, then $T_Q \leq T_P$.
2. If P and Q are subsumption equivalent, then $T_P = T_Q$. □

Definition 11 Suppose $\mathcal{T}$ is a complete lattice of truth values and suppose C is a variable free annotated clause. C is said to be *antecedent-sensible* iff for all distinct occurrences $A : \mu$ and $B : \mu'$ of annotated atoms in the body of C, it is the case that $A \neq B$. A (possibly infinite) set S of $\mathcal{T}$ valued clauses is *antecedent-sensible* iff every clause in S is antecedent-sensible.

Example 4 The $FOUR$ valued clause C_1 below is antecedent sensible.

$$p(X) : \mathbf{t} \Leftarrow p(X) : \mathbf{t} \,\&\, p(a) : \mathbf{f}$$

This is because $p(X) : \mathbf{t}$ and $p(a) : \mathbf{f}$ are not distinct annotated atoms. But the $FOUR$ valued clause C_2 below is not antecedent sensible:

$$p(X) : \mathbf{t} \Leftarrow q(X) : \mathbf{t} \,\&\, q(X) : \mathbf{f}.$$

This is because $q(X)$ occurs twice in the body of the above clause.

Intuitively, clauses that are not antecedent-sensible have redundant information in their bodies.

Theorem 8 Suppose $\mathcal{T}$ is a complete lattice of truth values and P, Q are $\mathcal{T}$ valued logic programs such that $grd(P)$ and $grd(Q)$ are antecedent-sensible. Then: $T_P = T_Q$ iff $grd(P)$ and $grd(Q)$ are subsumption equivalent. □

The restriction that the $\mathcal{T}$ valued programs P and Q be antecedent sensible in Theorem 8 is fairly reasonable because any collection of ground clauses (finite or infinite) can be converted into an equivalent set of antecedent-sensible clauses. Given a ground clause $C \equiv$

$$A : \mu \Leftarrow B_1 : \mu_1 \,\&\cdots\&\, B_k : \mu_k$$

which is not antecedent sensible (suppose $B_i = B_j$, where $i \neq j$ and $\mu_i \neq \mu_j$), the following clause is logically equivalent to C above and is also antecedent-sensible:

$$A : \mu \Leftarrow B_1 : \mu_1 \,\&\cdots\&\, B_{i-1} : \mu_{i-1} \,\&B_i : \rho \,\&\cdots\&B_{j-1} : \mu_{j-1} \,\&\, B_{j+1} : \mu_{j+1} \,\&\cdots\&\, B_k : \mu_k$$

where $\rho = \mu_i \sqcup \mu_j$.

4 Some Paraconsistent Logics

Before concluding the paper, a brief discussion of what kinds of logics fit into our framework is useful. Paraconsistent logics due to Newton da Costa [7] are a class of logics that allow us to reason *consistently* about systems that exhibit inconsistency (in the sense of classical logic).

Clearly, such an ability is of great interest because very large databases and knowledge bases may contain inconsistent information. Classical model theory would deem such a knowledge base to be meaningless even though a great deal of useful information may be contained in the knowledge base. Worse still, the very fact that the knowledge base is inconsistent may only be revealed after it has been used for a great deal of time. We now present below some examples of what $\mathcal{T}$ could look like and why such logics are useful.

Example 5 For instance, $\mathcal{T}$ could be the set $FOUR$ of truth values with $\sim$ defined as:

$$\sim(\mathbf{t}) = \mathbf{f}$$

$$\sim(\mathbf{f}) = \mathbf{t}$$

$$\sim(\bot) = \bot$$

$$\sim(\top) = \top$$

In that case, an ALP is intuitively like a classical logic program with negations allowed to occur both in the body of a clause as well as the head of clause. Such programs can clearly be inconsistent.

Example 6 The lattice SIX of truth values (Figure 2) represents *linguistic* truth values. Here, **Lt** and **Lf** stand, respectively, for *likely to be true* and *likely to be false*. We may take **Lt** and **Lf** to be *linguistic truth values* in the sense that the qualifier *likely to be ...* is often used by human beings in interacting with each other. This provides one way of reasoning about vague linguistic concepts. Negation is defined exactly as for $FOUR$ except that $\sim(\mathbf{Lt}) = \mathbf{Lf}$ and $\sim(\mathbf{Lf}) = \mathbf{Lt}$. Thus, using this set of truth values, we can express the linguistic sentence: *if it is snowing and John is driving, then John is likely to be late* by the annotated clause:

$$late(john) : \mathbf{Lt} \leftarrow snowing : \mathbf{t} \,\&\, driving(john) : \mathbf{t}$$

Sentences of this kind are frequently *spoken*, but their logical representation is not always clear. Using linguistic truth values, this is not very difficult.

Example 7 Alternately, take $\mathcal{T}$ to be the set $[0,1] \times [0,1]$ ordered as follows:

$$[\mu_1, \mu_2] \leq [\rho_1, \rho_2] \text{ iff } \mu_1 \leq_r \rho_1 \text{ and } \mu_2 \leq_r \rho_2$$

where $\leq_r$ is the usual "less than or equals" ordering on the reals. Here, the assignment of a truth value $[\mu_1, \mu_2]$ to an atom A by interpretation I may be taken as meaning that the degree of belief in A is μ_1 and the degree of disbelief in A is μ_2. There are no restrictions requiring that $(\mu_1 + \mu_2) \leq_r 1$. This allows us to incorporate both quantitative reasoning and paraconsistent reasoning in a single framework. The classical truth values **true** corresponds to $[1,0]$, **false** corresponds to $[0,1]$, $[0,0]$ corrsponds to complete lack of information while $[1,1]$ indicates *absolute* inconsistency. $\sim$ is defined as: $\sim([\mu_1, \mu_2] = [\mu_2, \mu_1]$.

Example 8 We could obtain a very weak form of temporal reasoning by taking $\mathcal{T}$ to be the power set of the natural numbers. $\mathcal{T}$ is ordered under inclusion and $\sim$ is set complementation. Then the assignment by interpretation I of a set X of natural numbers to an atom A intuitively means that:

A is true at time t w.r.t. I iff $t \in I(A)$.

Further discussions on how paraconsistent logics are useful in computational reasoning are contained in a forthcoming article by Newton da Costa and Subrahmanian [8].

5 Conclusions

The principal purpose of this paper was to study the algebraic properties of multivalued and paraconsistent logic programs which have recently proved to be of considerable interest to the logic programming community. For instance, the paraconsistent logic approach (based on $FOUR$) has provided a framework for mechanical reasoning in the presence of inconsistency. And different multivalued lattices (cf. Subrahmanian [23]) have proven useful in quantitative reasoning.

In addition, we have extended, to the case of multi-valued logic programs, the study of logic program equivalences. A current open problem is that of generalizing subsumption equivalence to multivalued logic programming. This paper provides such a generalization.

One future avenue for exploration is to study how the results in this paper change when we alter the definitions of $\oplus$ and $\otimes$ to reflect operators that conjoin programs together in different ways.

There are many alternative formulations of multivalued logics (Rasiowa's book [19] contains many details of logics based on Post algebras). In the framework considered here, many of the axioms of Post algebras are not required to hold (we only need a complete lattice with any unary complementation function). Future work may concentrate along studying the relationship between logic programming semantics and Post algebras. A start has been made in this direction by Rine [20].

Acknowledgements. I am grateful to Howard Blair, Newton da Costa, Melvin Fitting, Anil Hirani, Mike Kifer and Wiktor Marek for useful discussions. Thanks to an anonymous referee for pointing out a redundant condition in an earlier definition of strongly complemented boolean algebras. This work was partly supported by U.S. Air Force Contract F30602-85-C-0008.

References

[1] H. Andreka and I. Nemeti. (1978) *The Generalised Completeness of Horn Predicate Logic as a Programming Language*, Acta Cybernetica, 4, 1, pps 3-10.

[2] A. Bialynicki-Birula and H. Rasiowa. (1957) *On the Representation of Quasi-Boolean Algebras*, Bulletin of the Polish Academy of Sciences, Cl. III, 5, pps 259–261.

[3] H.A. Blair. (1986) *Decidability in the Herbrand Base*, in: Proc. of the Workshop on Foundations of Logic Programming and Deductive Databases, (ed. Jack Minker), College Park, MD.

[4] H. A. Blair and V.S. Subrahmanian. (1987) *Paraconsistent Logic Programming*, Proc. 7th Conference on Foundations of Software Technology and Theoretical Computer Science, Lecture Notes in Computer Science, Vol. 287, pps 340–360, Springer Verlag. Extended version to appear in: Theoretical Computer Science.

[5] H. A. Blair and V. S. Subrahmanian. (1988) *Strong Completeness Results for Paraconsistent Logic Programming*, submitted for publication.

[6] H. A. Blair and V. S. Subrahmanian. (1988) *Paraconsistent Foundations for Logic Programming*, to appear in: Journal of Non-Classical Logic.

[7] N.C.A. da Costa. (1974) *On the Theory of Inconsistent Formal Systems*, Notre Dame J. of Formal Logic, 15, pps 497-510.

[8] N.C.A. da Costa and V.S. Subrahmanian. (1989) *Paraconsistent Logics as a Formalism for Reasoning about Inconsistent Knowledge Bases*, to appear in: J. of Artificial Intelligence in Medicine.

[9] J. M. Dunn. (1982) *A Relational Representation of Quasi-Boolean Algebras*, Notre Dame Journal of Formal Logic 23, 4, pps 353–357.

[10] M. C. Fitting. (1987) *Bilattices and the Theory of Truth*, draft manuscript.

[11] M. C. Fitting. (1988) *Logic Programming on a Topological Bilattice*, Fundamenta Informatica, 11, pps 209–218.

[12] M. C. Fitting. (1988) *Bilattices and the Semantics of Logic Programming*, to appear.

[13] G. Grätzer. (1971) *Lattice Theory: First Concepts and Distributive Lattices*, W. H. Freeman and Company.

[14] L. Henkin, J. D. Monk and A. Tarski. (1971) *Cylindric Algebras, Part I*, North Holland.

[15] A. N. Hirani and V. S. Subrahmanian. (1988) *Algebraic Foundations of Logic Programming, I: The Distributive Lattice of Logic Programs*, to appear in: Fundamenta Informatica.

[16] J. W. Lloyd. (1984) *Foundations of Logic Programming*, Springer Verlag.

[17] M. J. Maher. (1988) *Equivalences of Logic Programs*, in: Foundations of Deductive Databases and Logic Programming, ed. Jack Minker, Morgan-Kauffman.

[18] P. Mancarella and D. Pedreschi. (1988) *An Algebra of Logic Programs*, in: Proc. 5th International Conference on Logic Programming (eds. R. Kowalski and K. Bowen), pps 1006-1023, MIT Press.

[19] H. Rasiowa. (1974) *An Algebraic Approach to Non-Classical Logics*, North Holland.

[20] D. C. Rine. *Some Relations between Logic Programming and Multiple Valued Logic*, manuscript.

[21] J. Sebelik and P. Stepanek. (1982) Horn Clause Programs for Recursive Functions, in: eds. K.L. Clark and S.-A. Tarnlund: Logic Programming, Academic Press, pps 325-340.

[22] R. Sikorski. (1964) *Boolean Algebras*, Springer Verlag.

[23] V. S. Subrahmanian. (1988) *Mechanical Proof Procedures for Many Valued Lattice Based Logic Programming*, to appear in J. of Non-Classical Logic.

[24] V. S. Subrahmanian. (1989) *Algebraic Foundations of Logic Programming, II: The Space of Multivalued and Paraconsistent Logic Programs*, manuscript.

An autoepistemic logical view of knowledge base

Y.J. Jiang
Computer Laboratory, Cambridge University,
Cambridge CB2, 3QG, UK

Abstract

Autoepistemic logic (AE) is a non-monotonic logic for modelling beliefs of agents who reflect on their own beliefs. In this paper, we will take such a logical view of knowledge base by treating its contents as its beliefs about a world and its integrity constraints as its beliefs about its contents. We will show how such a view can help us to represent and reason about incomplete knowledge, self-knowledge and negative information. We will also show that an AE logical closure of a knowledge base will neither suffer the inconsistency problem nor the logic-impurity problem that often persist in the standard nonmotonic closures of a kowledge base. In particular, we will show that an AE logic view of integrity constraints provides a finer way of defining integrity constraints than existing definitions. For the logic to be effective, we introduce a a *stratified AE proof theory* for evaluating queries and maintaining integrity constraints. It is shown that the AE logical view of a stratified knowledge base will yield a unique AE closure of the knowledge base.

Keywords: AI in Database, Deductive database, Incomplete knowledge, Non-monotonic logic, Autoepistemic logic, Closed World Assumption, Complete Database, Integrity Constraints. Nonstanard Logic, Possible worlds semantics, Modal logic.

1 Introduction

A knowledge base (KB) is generally an *incomplete* description of the world (or domain of application). An effective knowledge base management system therefore should make the proper plan on the basis of what currently the KB knows and does not know, rather than to wait for the state of complete world which could never be obtained. This suggests the need for a formalism to represent and reason about incomplete knowledge and self-knowledge.

The incompleteness problem is not new in database models. A number of solutions have been proposed. In Codd's relational model [Codd 82], the unknown number in "Mary's tele-no is not known" is indicated by a *null* value. This approach however is not sufficient enough to represent disjunctive incomplete knowledge such as "Mary's tele-no is 1 or 2". This problem is solved in Lipski's model by associating a set of elements for Mary's tele-no. If the set is empty, then it is not known; else if the set contains one element, then the value is known; otherwise , the value is only known to be a member of the set.

These solutions are nevertheless very restrictive. For example, they cannot represent accumulative objects, eg. "the person who likes Mary also likes Sue"; neither can they represent disjunctive information of the kind in which there is uncertainty regarding which object is being characterized, eg. "Mary's tele-no is 1 or John's teleno is 2".

Although many of these problems can be solved in a deductive logical view of database systems [Reiter 84, Galliare etal 84], they still cannot represent and reason about what a KB knows and does not know. Often, negative information cannot be represented. This is because positive information that is not present in the KB, is usually assumed *assymmetrically* to be negative in order to form a complete closure of a partial KB. As a result, negative connectives becomes non-logical, usually in the disguise of CLark's Negation as Failure [Clark 78].

These problems have been *partially* addressed by Levesque [84]. In his approach, a first order (FOL) knowledge base is characterized by an autoepistemic logic closure. In Levesque's view, a KB is simply a set of facts about the world; while queries and integrity constraints are treated as its beliefs about the contents of the KB. However Levesque's approach is limited to knowledge bases that contain only FOL formulae. Thus in Levesque's approach, we can make queries and integrity constraints about what a KB knows and does not know; but we cannot represent in the KB *itself* what it knows and does not know. For example, given Tele-no(Mary,100) in a KB, we can ask if the KB knows about Mary's tele-no; on the other hand, we cannot represent in a KB the knowledge "Mary's tele-no is known" (ie. ∃ x Know(Tele-no(Mary,x))) without giving the actual number.

Our position in this paper is to extend Levesque's approach by additionally viewing KB as a set of beliefs rather than facts about the world. In this way, a KB can express beliefs about its beliefs and non-beliefs of the world. For example, a KB can represent its belief "if it is not known that Mary works, then Mary is a housewife". We will formalize our position in an autoepistemic predicate logic. In particular in contrast with Levesque's approach which uses the full power of first order proof mechanization for his query evaluation, we will attempt to develop an effective epistemic proof procedure for query processing and integrity checking.

The paper is organized as follows. Section 2 introduces an AE predicate logic that allows quantifying-in variables. It also defines the semantics of such a logic view of KB. Section 3 and 4 compares and contrasts such a semantical view of KB with some existing semantics for queries and integrity constraints. Section 5 then develops an effective proof procedure for a stratified AE predicate logic which has the property of unique AE extension of a KB.

2 Autoepistemic predicate logic

Autoepistemic (AE) logic was defined by Moore [85] as a formal account of an agent reasoning about her own beliefs. In the autoepistemic view of a KB, the KB is identified as such an agent. It can thus express knowledge such as "It is not known that John has a telephone" and "It is known that John lives either in the city where he works or in the city where his wife lives". For convenience reason, we will use KB to denote the knowledge base both as an agent and as the initial set of AE formulae in the knowlege base.

AE logic was originally only defined for propositional case. Otherwise, the logic is restricted to *closed* epistemic formulae in the sense that no quantifying-in variables (ie. variables quantified outside the scope of their **B**-operators) are allowed. Although AE logic is often claimed for its ability to reason about incompleteness, however many types of incomplete knowledge in KB applications are quantifying-in types of AE formulae. For example, the beliefs "All the managers are known" and "There are definitely some girls who are not known" can be represented in a KB respectively as follows.

$\forall$ x (Manager(x) $\rightarrow$ **B**(Manager(x))).

$\exists$ x (Girl(x) $\wedge$ $\neg$**B**(Girl(x))).

In this section, we will therefore attempt to develop an AE logic that allows quantifying-in variables.

2.1 Semantics of AE logic of KB

The language of AE predicate logic is that of standard first order logic, augmented by the modal operator B. We will call a set of AE formulae an *AE theory.*

The standard semantics of an AE propositional logic is usually formulated in a recursive fashion (eg. [Konolige 87]). This makes it difficult to exhibit AE extensions. It also fails to establish a connection between the monotonic logic of belief [Halpern & Moses 85] and AE logic. To avoid these problems without changing AE logic, we reformulate the standard semantics of AE predicate logic (eg. [Konolige 89]) in a possible worlds semantics.

We define the following Kripke-style possible worlds model structure M=(W, D, S5, w_0) for AE predicate logic.

Definition 1 *1. W is a non-empty set of possible worlds;*

2. D is the constant domain of all possible worlds.

3. S5 denotes the equivalence *accessibility relation for all worlds in W; ie. W forms a* complete S5 structure.

4. w_0 is the actual world and every world in W is accessible from w_0.

5. A world is a function which assigns to each n-place function symbol a function from D^n to D, and which assigns to each n-place predicate symbol, a set of tuples of D^n; and which assigns to each non-domain constant an element in D.

Given the above semantic structure M, we can define the following standard satisfiability (or truth assignment) relation $\models_M$ recursively between a world and a belief as follows for AE predicate logic.

1. $w \models_M p(t_1,..,t_n)$ iff $<Val(t_1,w),..,Val(t_n,w)> \in w(p)$
   where $Val(t,w) = w(t)$ if t is a non-domain constant,
   $Val(t,w) = t$ if t is a domain element,
   $Val(f(t_1,..t_n),w) = w(f)(<Val(t_1,w),..,Val(t_n,w)>)$
2. $w \models_M B\phi$ iff for all $w' \in W$, $w' \models_M \phi$
3. $w \models_M \neg\phi$ iff $\neg(w \models_M \phi)$
4. $w \models_M \phi \vee \psi$ iff $w \models_M \phi$ or $w \models_M \psi$
5. $w \models_M \forall x\ \phi(x)$ iff for all $d \in D$ $w \models_M \phi(d/x)$ where $\phi(d/x)$ is obtained by replacing all x in the formula ϕ by d.

Definition 2 *An AE theory is satisfied/true in a world iff every formula in the theory is true in the world.*

Definition 3 *An AE theory is satisfied/true in a set of worlds W iff the theory is true in all the worlds of W.*

The semantical structure $M=(W,D,S5,w_0)$ defined so far thus corresponds to a weak S5 structure $M'=(W+w_0, D, K45)$ for a *monotonic* modal logic of belief. This is because W is a complete S5 structure, and all worlds in W are accessible from w_0, hence the union of W and w_0 forms a weak S5 structure. The question now is how the *nonmonotonic* part of AE logic comes into the possible worlds semantics. This is achieved by defining possible worlds interpretations of AE theory at a meta-level that would reflect the nonmonotonic part or reflective nature of the AE logic.

Definition 4 *A Kripke structure $M=(W,D,S5,w_0)$ is a possible worlds interpretation of an AE theory T iff T consists of all the formulae that are satisfied by W in M.*

Definition 5 *A possible world model of an AE theory T is a possible worlds interpretation of T such that T is true in w_0.*

Definition 6 *An AE theory is AE-satisfiable iff it has a possible world model.*

It can be shown that the possible world models of an AE predicate theory are the possible world interpretations of the theory where w_0 has the same satisfiability relation as one of the possible worlds in W in the Kripke structure $M=(W,D,S5,w_0)$.

Theorem 1 *If $M=(W,D,S5,w_0)$ is a possible world interpretation of an AE theory T, then M will be a possible world model of the theory iff $w_0 \in W$.*

Proof: The if-case is obvious. If $w_0 \in W$, naturally all formulae in T will be true in w_0. Hence M is a possible world model of T. To prove the only-if-case, we suppose that w_0 differs from all the worlds in W. Then we can construct a disjunction of atoms in such a way that each atom is selected from each world in W which differs from w_0. This disjunction is true in W but false in w_0. Since T contains this disjunction if M is its possible world interpretation, thus not all formulae in T will be true in w_0. Hence M cannot be a possible world model of T.

Our semantics can be compared with Levesque's (also reformulated in Reiter [88]) AE semantics of a FOL KB. In his formalization, an autoepistemic model of an autoepistemic theory of a FOL KB consists of a S5 world structure W which is formed of all the models of the sentences of the KB. The satsifiability relation between a possible world and an AE sentence is defined in the same way as our semantics. The following theorem establishes the relationship of Levesque's semantics and our semantics.

Theorem 2 *In the case of a FOL KB, Levesque's semantics $M=(W,D,S5)$ of FOL KB is equivalent to our semantics $M'=(W,D,S5,w_0)$ of the KB in which w_0 is an element of W.*

Proof: Since all the FOL consequence of KB is true in all the possible worlds of W(or models of FOL KB) in a Levesque's possible world model, for these consequences to be true in our corresponding possible world model, w_0 must be a model of FOL KB, ie. an element of W.

Now a traditional AE logical approach usually defines an AE extension T of a theory KB self-referentially in a non-constructive fixpoint as follows:

$$T = \{\phi \mid (KB + \{\mathbf{B}p \mid p \in T\} + \{\neg\mathbf{B}p \mid \neg(p \in T)\}) \models \phi\}.$$

We can avoid this self-referential problem by defining AE extension in a possible world semantics.

Definition 7 *T is an AE extension of a theory KB iff there exists a complete S5 structure (W,D,S5) such that, for every possible world interpretation M=(W,D,S5,w_0) of T that has KB true in W, KB is true in w_0 iff M is a possible world model of T (ie. $w_0 \in W$).*

This definition can be shown to be equivalent to the traditional definition [Jiang 89].

Theorem 3 *The possible world definition is equivalent to the self-referential definition.*

Correspondingly we can also define completeness and soundness in the possible worlds semantics that equivalent [Jiang 89] match their counterparts (ie. stableness and groundness) in the self-referential semantics.

Definition 8 *An AE theory T is semantically complete with respect to a set of premises KB iff there exists a possible world interpretation M=(W,D,S5,w_0) of T in which KB is true in W.*

Definition 9 *An AE theory T is semantically sound with respect to a set of premises KB iff there exists a complete S5 structure of worlds (W,D,S5) such that for all w_0 in all AE Kripke structures of the form M=(W,D,S5,w_0) such that KB and T are true in W, KB and T are true in w_0 iff $w_0 \in$ W of M.*

It can be easily seen that if T consists of all formulae that are true in all the worlds of W in the soundness definition, then T is also semantically complete. We thus have the following obvious theorem:

Theorem 4 *T is an AE extension of a set of premises KB iff T is semantically complete and sound with respect to KB.*

Another obvious theorem is:

Theorem 5 *An AE theory T that contains KB is AE-satisfiable if T is an AE extension of a KB; The converse however is not true (eg. let KB={**B**p}, then T={p,**B**p,..} is AE- satisfiable and contains KB, but it is not an AE extension of KB).*

3 AE closure, Closed World Assumption and Complete database

Given the above semantical characterization, queries to a knowledge base KB simply become formulae to be checked to be members of an AE extension of the KB and integrity constraints simply become members of such an AE extension. In this section, we will compare and contrast the approach of using an AE extension as a closure of KB with two notable closure functions in database semantic: Reiter's Closed World Assumption [Reiter 78] and Clark's Complete database [Clark 78]. Both functions are also intended to form a total closure on a partially complete database. The intuitive effect is that facts about the world that are not known to be positively true, are assumed to be false.

Theorem 6 *An AE extension of a KB is syntax independent.*

Our first observation is that unlike Completion of database which is syntax-dependent, an AE closure is not. For example, the completion of the database {p←q, p←p} is quite different from the completion of the database {p←q} although both databases are FOL semantically equivalent. In contrast, both sets of sentences would have the same AE extension.

The second observation is that unlike CWA or Comp, an AE closure will not affect the consistency property of a FOL KB. Formally, we have the following theorems.

Theorem 7 ***Assume KB is a FOL knowledge base, if CWA(KB) is FOL-satisfiable, then KB is FOL satisfiable; the converse however is not true.***

Theorem 8 ***Assume KB is a FOL knowledge base, if Comp(KB) is FOL-satisfiable, then KB is FOL satisfiable; the converse however is not true.***

Theorem 9 ***Assume KB is a FOL knowledge base, KB is FOL-satisfiable iff there exists an AE extension of KB (which implies that the extension is AE-satisfiable).***

Proof:

1. If KB is satisfiable, then construct a model structure M=(W,D,S5,w_0) of such that W is formed of all the models of KB and w_0 is a world in W. Let T be all the formulae that are true in W. T is an AE extension of KB.

2. If T is an AE extension of KB, then in any possible world model M=(W,D,S5,w_0) of T, KB will be satisfied in W (and w_0) as well. Now assuming KB is not FOL-satisfiable, then W must be empty. But according to the definition of an AE extension, W must not be empty, ie. a contradiction.

Although Lifschitz's [88] circumscriptive view of a KB also preserves the consistency property of a FOL KB, however it is not powerful enough to represent disjunctive incomplete knowledge and ignorance. For example, they can neither model $\mathbf{B}(p \vee q)$ nor $\neg\mathbf{B}(p \vee q)$.

Following Theorem 7, Theorem 8 and Theorem 9, we immediately have the following relationships between CWA, Comp and AE.

Lemma 1 ***Assume KB is a FOL knowledge base, then if CWA(KB) is FOL-satisfiable, then KB has an AE extension, hence AE-satisfiable; the converse however is not true.***

Lemma 2 ***Assume KB is a FOL knowledge base, then if Comp(KB) is FOL-satisfiable, then KB has an AE extension, hence AE-satisfiable; the converse however is not true.***

However it should be noted that an AE closure of a non-FOL KB may not be AE-satisfiable. Or more precisely, such a KB may not have an AE extension at all. For example, given $\mathbf{B}a \vee \mathbf{B}b$, the AE closure will become AE-unsatisfiable or empty. In addition, unlike FOL KB, there can be multiple AE extensions of a non-FOL KB in which a formula is true in one extension and false in another. These problems will addressed in Section 5 where we introduce a restricted AE logic to ensure that an AE closure of a KB is always unique and non-empty.

However for satisfiable FOL KB, we can have the uniqueness property. For this reason, we will use AE(KB) to indicate the unique closure of such a KB [Jiang 89].

Theorem 10 ***There exists a unique AE extension for the AE closure of a satisfiable FOL KB.***

Now it is well-known that CWA and Comp closures of a KB are both ***asymmetric*** assumptions about the incomplete information in the KB in the sense that only positive ground atoms are considered for candidates of negative conclusions. However often in KB applications, we also assume unspecified information to be true. For example, we generally regard that every one lives somewhere unless otherwise stated. The point is that we have a no-win situation for any asymmetric treatment. On the other hand, an AE closure would provide a ***symmetric*** treatment of assumption. If ϕ is not known in an AE extension of a KB, then $\neg\mathbf{B}\phi$ is known in the extension. Here ϕ can be either positive or negative atoms. In fact, it can be any formulae.

Another advantage of the AE treatment is that it can also represent negative information explicitly. This is not possible for the asymmetric treatment of assumption in CWA and Complete database. If negation is introduced, it usually appears in the form of "negation as failure" which makes the negation non-logical. In particular, it is not clear a "Yes" answer to a negative atomic query means "the query is proven to be negative" or " the query is not proven to be positive". In contrast, all the connectives are logical in our AE closure of KB.

It is well known that CWA is generally incompatible with Comp. This can be demonstrated by the following FOL database $\{p \leftarrow q, q \leftarrow \neg p, q \leftarrow q\}$. Although both CWA and Comp of the database is consistent, the union of the two closure is not. It appears that CWA and Comp closures may be compatible to AE closure since AE may bring out the possible incompatibility outside FOL into epistemic level. This however in fact is not possible as shown below.

Theorem 11 *Assume KB is a FOL database. Even if CWA(KB) is FOL satisfiable, CWA(KB)+AE(KB) may still not be AE-satisfiable.*

Proof: This is because AE closure is symmetric. So if both p and ¬p are not followed from a FOL database KB, CWA(KB) would have ¬ p true (when p is an atom); while AE(KB) would have ¬B¬p (and ¬Bp true) which is contradicting to the CWA closure.

Theorem 12 *Assume a FOL database KB. Even if Comp(KB) is FOL satisfiable, Comp(KB)+AE(KB) may still not be AE satisfiable.*

Proof: Similar to Theorem 11.

4 AE closure for integrity constraints

Introducing epistemic notions into knowledge base can also open a new era of research in Integrity Constraints (IC) [Reiter 88,Jiang 88]. Integrity constraints (IC) are meant to characterize the acceptable states of a Knowledge Base (KB) through incremental changes. In this section, we will argue, contrary to the prevailing view, that integrity constraints are ***autoepistemic*** in nature.

Traditionally, integrity constraints are usually formalized under the following two definitions.

Definition 10 Satisfiability *(eg. [Sadri & Kowalski 87])*

KB satisfies IC iff Closure(KB)+IC is satisfiable.

Entailment *(eg. [Lloyd & Topor 85])*

KB satisfies IC iff Closure(KB) $\models$ *IC*

The Closure concept is crucial here because it reflects the indexical nature of of integrity constraints satisfaction (This point is overlooked in Reiter's criticism of the two definitions). It generates a kind of complete extension of a KB based on the current context of KB.

Our formalization of integrity constraint is to identify the closure concept in the above definitions with an AE extension of a KB in our AE logic. In this case however, the standard concept of an integrity rule of the form p→q must be represented in AE logic as **B**p→**B**q (or equivalently **B**(p→q). If there is any NAF notions of the form not(p), then it will also be translated into ¬**B**p in AE logic. We denote these translations as IC^{AE}. The translations are necessary because the original formulae mention nothing explicitly about the current context although it is what it is intended. We may wonder why such a translation is not needed for CWA and Complete closures functions that are normally chosen for the two definitions. This is because these closures are based on FOL reflections of KB. As a result, the conclusions at epistemic level (eg. not provable(p)) are reduced to FOL level (eg. ¬p).

However it should be noted that the IC^{AE} is only defined for IC rules of standard concept in FOL formalization of a KB. In the context of an AE formalization of KB, we do not need such a translation function. IC simply denotes a set of AE formulae. Thus we are not only able to represent AE formulae of the form **B**p→**B**q (which replaces the standard FOL IC notion) where p,q are in FOL, but also of any form of AE predicate logic. In particular, we can represent quantifying-in IC rules that have no analogs in standard concept of FOL IC rules. For example, the standard notion of IC can say something like "for x to be a person, he must live somewhere"; while the AE notion of IC can additionally say something like "for x known to be a person, the KB must currently know where he lives".

We can now compare and contrast our AE formalization of integrity constraints with alternative formalizations. For this purpose, we first show that consistent CWA of a FOL database has the nice *catagorical* property of a unique model [Reiter 87].

Theorem 13 *FOL satisfiable CWA of a FOL KB is catagorical.*

Lemma 3 *FOL satisfiable CWA of a FOL KB entails either p or ¬p for any FOL formula p.*

Due to the complexity of AE logic, Reiter [88] introduces a way of combining AE closure with CWA in such a way that the satisfaction of AE integrity constraints become the satisfcation of FOL integrity constraints. This is shown by the following theorem:

Theorem 14 *Assume KB is FOL, AE(CWA(KB))* $\models IC^{AE}$ *iff CWA(KB)* $\models$ *IC where KB and IC are sets of FOL sentences.*

Proof: The reason for this to happen is that CWA(KB) is catagorical in the sense that it has at most one model. Thus in the case that there is no model, the theorem is trivally true. In the case that there is only one model, then this model must be the only possible world in an AE model of AE((CWA(KB)). Thus, we always have $\forall x p(x) \leftrightarrow \mathbf{B}p(x)$ for any FOL formula p with free variables x.

However Reiter's approach is too coarse-grain to distinguish the definite terms from indefinite terms. For example, given $p(a) \vee p(b)$, in our AE formalization of integrity constraints we would not have $\exists x \mathbf{B}p(x)$ true although $\exists x p(x)$ is true in FOL. However, they become indistinguishable when the closure of a knowledge base is CWA followed by an AE closure.

It is also interesting to note that under the AE closure for a consistent FOL KB, the two IC definitions mentioned earlier become equivalent for standard IC rules. This is however not true for other closures. The main reason for this is that AE closure preserves consistency and yields a unique AE extension for FOL KBs.

Theorem 15 *Let KB be a set of FOL formulae and IC a set of FOL formulae of standard notion, then the* entailment *definition of IC and the* satisfiability *definition of IC is equivalent iff CWA(KB) is consistent.*

Proof: : This is because consistent CWA(KB) is catagorical.

Theorem 16 *Let KB be a set of FOL formulae and IC a set of FOL formulae of standard notion, then the* entailment *definition of IC and the* satisfiability *definition of IC will not be equivalent even if Comp(KB) is consistent.*

Proof: : This is because Comp(KB) is not catagorical.

Theorem 17 *Let KB be a set of FOL formulae and IC a set of FOL formulae of standard notion, then the* entailment *definition of IC and the* satisfiability *definition of IC is equivalent under AE closure where IC becomes* IC^{AE} *iff KB is consistent.*

Proof: :

1. Assume the two definitions are equivalent. Then if the KB is inconsistent, then clearly the satisfiablity approach would invalid IC^{AE}; while the the entailment approach would entail or validify anything. Hence the two definitions become inequivalent; ie. contradicting the assumption.

2. Assume KB is consistent. If the two definitions are not equivalent, then there must exist an IC such that AE(KB) $\models IC^{AE}$ while AE(KB) + IC^{AE} is AE-unsatisfiable or $\neg$(AE(KB) $\models IC^{AE}$) while AE(KB) + IC^{AE} is AE-satisfiable. Since AE(KB) has a unique AE extension for consistent FOL KB according to Theorem 10, both cases would not be possible either.

Because of the lack of a unique AE extensions for a non-FOL KB, the two definitions will not be equivalent for the AE closure of a non-FOL KB. However as shown in the next section, a restricted kind of AE logic can ensure that there is a unique AE extension for a non-FOL KB. In this case, the two definitions would again become equivalent.

5 Stratified AE logic

Since the semantics of AE logic consists of a complete S5 structure together with an actual world, there appears to be a connection between a S5 modal logic and AE extensions. In this section, we thus attempt to establish such an connection proof theoretically.

We first note that the semantical structure of AE logic is a weak S5, thus the monotonic component of the proof theoretic connection is a proof theory for K45 epistemic logic.

Definition 11 *Epistemic K45 proof theory consists of the following set of axioms and rules of inference:*

the axioms are:

$$FOL--axioms$$
$$B(\phi \rightarrow \psi)\&B\phi \rightarrow B\psi$$
$$B\phi \rightarrow BB\phi$$
$$\neg B\phi \rightarrow B\neg B\phi$$

and the rules of inference are:

$$\phi,\phi\rightarrow\psi \Longrightarrow \psi$$
$$\phi \Longrightarrow B\phi$$

Because of the non-monotonic nature of the AE logic, the deployment of the above monotonic K45 mechanization to the AE logic need to be augmented by indexical introspections. This however presents several difficulties. To start with, the negative introspection is itself not even semi-decidable [Niemela 88]. Furthermore, these introspections are part of an AE extension itself, thus involving a circular way of making assumptions followed by checking on soundness. For example, from **B**p→p, an AE extension could assume *p* to be true and be justified through soundness.

We believe that the only way to solve the self-referential problem is to introduce some kind of stratification. This is essentially what Konolige's Hierarchical AE (HAE) Predicate Logic [Konolige 88] attempted to do although it does not appear to be so obvious. By allowing **B** formulae to introspect only formulae at a lower level theory in a hierarchical structure, HAE essentially removes the self-referential part of an AE proof theory. However to achieve this, HAE requires an unnaturally indexed set of B operators rather than a single **B** operator. Our solution is to introduce an explicitly stratified AE predicate logic. First, we introduce two rules characterizing introspections. Instead of having a general negation as failure type of introspection, we adopt an Epistemic Negation As Failure (ENAF) rule of inference:

Epistemic NAF:

If ¬ (A $\vdash_{AE}$ p), then A $\vdash_{AE}$ ¬**B**p

where p is ordinary and AE is an autoepistemic proof system that includes ENAF, K45 and PI(defined later).

The ENAF rule is in fact similar to Clark's NAF [Clark 78] except that it is made at an epistemic level and can be applied to non-grounded formulae as well. However like Clark's NAF, ENAF is not-semidecidable for general logic due to the semi-decidability of FOL. In addition, the ENAF can still result an inconsistent AE closure at epistemic level. For example, given **B**p, the ENAF would produce ¬**B**p. On the other hand, from an autoepistemic point of view, this kind of inconsistency would result an empty AE extension. Our solution is to restrict the AE logic to avoid an empty extension. This is a reasonable restriction for a rational agent such as KB. Since given some beliefs of an agent, the possibility of an empty AE extension appears to be intuitively contradictory. After all, the agent did have some beliefs before his reflection. We will show how to achieve the restriction later.

Next, to characterize the positive introspection, we introduce another rule of inference:

PI: If A $\vdash_{AE}$ p, then A $\vdash_{AE}$ **B**p

where p is ordinary and AE=K45+ENAF+PI.

This is in fact the kind of rule of inference used in McDermott's modal non-monotonic logics [82]. As pointed out by Moore [85], instead of treating the inference as part of a AE theory, ie. **B**p∈T if p∈T, the mere use of inference as a rule would result no AE extension of **B**p→p that contains p. To avoid this incompleteness problem, we will restrict the AE logic to one that does not define p recursively through **B**p as shown later.

The AE logic also suffers the problem of 'theoremhood' in the sense that there could be multiple AE extensions. Multiple extensions may be possible for human beings. They however do not seem to be reasonable in many practical Knowledge Base (KB) applications. We cannot afford to have p and ¬Bp at the same time from a KB due to its multiple extensions. Nor We can afford to find all AE extensions (which is possible for AE propositional logic) as indicated in [Gelfond 88] because this could be infinite for AE predicate logic.

To avoid (not solve) all these problems, we define a stratified AE predicate logic. We extend Gelfond's [87] definition for propositional logic to predicate logic. The intuition is that we want to avoid to define recursively a predicate through its introspection (positive or negative). We will also indicate how stratification would restrict certain kinds of formulae that cause problems in our AE proof system.

Definition 12 *An AE theory T is stratified if*

1. *T consists of clauses of the form S→V. V is a disjunction of FOL atoms and S is a conjunction of* **B** *literals and FOL atoms. Each* **B***-literal is not allowed to be nested. Hence the introspection rules only need to introspect ordinary FOL formulae.*
2. *There is a partition $T=T_0+..+T_n$ such that*
3. *T_0 is ordinary (possibly empty).*
4. *clauses with empty conclusions do not belong to T_k where $k>0$.*

   Thus the case **B***p; ie.* ¬**B***p → that would cause inconsistency of ENAF would not occur.*
5. *If a predicate p belongs to the conclusion of a clause in T_k, then (positive/negative) literals with predicate p do not belong to $T_0,..,T_{k-1}$ and where literals* **B***f and* ¬**B***f where f contains p, do not belong to $T_0,..,T_k$.*

   Thus the case **B***p→p and* ¬**B***p→p would not occur.*

Now Gelfond [87] has shown that every consistent stratified AE propositional theory has a unique AE extension. In [Jiang 89], we have shown that Herbrand theorem "a set of universal sentences is unsatisfiable iff a finite subset of its ground instances are" remains to be valid for epistemic logic with the introduction of level of intension. Thus with unification and Gelond's propositional result, we can have the following theorem:

Theorem 18 *Every consistent set of stratified AE predicate formulae has a unique AE extension.*

If we use K45+ENAF+PI to characterize the proof mechanization of our stratified AE predicate logic, we first can show the following soundness theorem.

Theorem 19 *If KB is a consistently stratified AE theory, then there exists a unique AE(KB) such that*

If KB $\vdash_{K45+ENAF+PI} \phi$, then AE(KB) $\models \phi$.

Since the stratified AE logic still allows ordinary FOL formulae in the AE logic, we thus cannot obtain full completeness result for our proof mechanization. Given the presence of function symbols in FOL, the ENAF and PI rules can only be semi-decidable. A consequence is that the stratified AE predicate logic itself is not even semi-decidable. Hence it is not complete either. However if we limit ourselves to function-free knowledge base which is generally the case for deductive database applications, we can obtain the following completeness result:

Theorem 20 *If KB is a consistently stratified and function-free AE theory, then there exists a unique AE(KB) such that*

If AE(KB) $\models \phi$, then KB $\vdash_{K45+ENAF+PI} \phi$,

We illustrate our proof theory on the following stratified AE KB (assuming the unique name assumption).

Query: Student(Tom)?.

Knowledge base :

1. teacher(John). "John is a teacher"
2. teacher(father(John)). "Father of John is a teacher"
3. $\neg$ B(teacher(x)) $\rightarrow$ student(x). "If x is not currently known to be a teacher, then x is a student"

From 3, we have:

4. $\neg$B(teacher(Tom)) $\rightarrow$ student(Tom)

Apply ENAF rule to the initial knowledge base, yield :

5. $\neg$B(teacher(Tom))

Apply modus poens between 4 and 5, yield student(Tom).

Note if we add $father(John) = Tom$, then 5 cannot be obtained.

Despite the catagorical property of stratified AE predicate logic which helps resolve the constructive proof theoretical problem of AE logic, it is still too restrictive for KB applications. For examples, the two quantifying-in formulae mentioned in Section 2 would fall outside the scope of our stratification. On-going research is to extend the boundary of AE logic and at the same time maintain the constructive nature of AE logic.

Acknowledgements

The author would like to thank Professor R. Reiter, Professor J. Lloyd for their helpful discussions. This research is supported by a British Telecolm Fellowship.

References

K. Clark (1978) *Negation as failure* in logic and database eds. H. Galliare and J. Minker, Plenum, New York, 293-322.
E.F. Codd (1982) *Relational database: A practical foundation for productivity* 25 CACM, 1982, pp.109-117.
H. Galliare etal (1984) *Logic and database: a deductive approach* ACM computing surveys, Vol.16, No.2, June 1984.
M. Gelfond (1987) *On stratified autoepistemic theories* AAAI 87, pp.207-211.
Y.J Jiang (1988c) *A self-referential data model of knowledge*, IFIP conference on the role of AI in database, 1988.
Y.J. Jiang (1989) *Stratified Autoepistemic Predicate Logic* Israel AI Conference, Dec., Jerusalem, 1989.
K. Konolige (1987) *On the relationship between default and autoepistemic logic* IJCAI 87.
K. Konolige (1988) *Hierarchical autoepistemic logic* SRI note, 1988.
H.J. Levesque (1984) *The logic of incomplete knowledge bases* On Conceptual Modelling, eds M.Brodie, J.Mylopouos & J.Schmidt, Springer-Verlag, 1984, pp.165-187.
V. Lifshitz (1988) *On the semantics of negation of logic programming* Fundations of deductive database and logic programming (J.Minker ed.) Morgan Kaufmann Publishers, L. Altos, CA, pp.19-85.
J. Llyod & W. Topor (1985) *A basis for deductive database systems*, J. of logic programming 2, pp.93-109.
D. McDermott (1982) *Non-monotonic logic II: non-motonic modal theories* in JACM 29 (1) 33-57.
R. C. Moore (1985) *Semantic considerations of non-monotonic logic* AI 25 (1).
I. Niemela *Autoepistemic Predicate logic* ECAI 88, pp.595-599.
R. Reiter (1978) *On closed world databases* Logic and Databases (H.Gallaire & J. Minker eds.), Plenum Press, pp.149-178.
R. Reiter (1984) *Towards a logical reconstruction of relational database theory.* in On Conceptual Modelling, eds M.Brodie, J.Mylopouos & J.Schmidt, Springer-Verlag, pp.49-83.
R. Reiter (1988) *On integrity constraints* Proc of Theoretical aspects of reasoning about knowledge, CA, 1988.
F. Sadri & R. Kowalski (1988) *An application of general purpose theorem proving to database integrity* Foundations of deductive database and logic programming (J.Minker ed.) Morgan Kaufmann Publishers, L. Altos, CA.

A NATURAL SEMANTICS FOR LOGIC PROGRAMS WITH NEGATION

Phan Minh Dung [1] **and Kanchana Kanchanasut** [2]

Division of Computer Science, Asian Institute of Technology,
P.O. Box 2754, Bangkok 10501, Thailand.

Abstract

Two natural ways to specify the declarative semantics of logic programs and deductive databases are the fixpoint theory of Van Emden and Kowalski [11] and Clark's predicate completion [2]. The fixpoint theory does not apply to general programs with negation; a generalization of the theory can be defined [1,12] only if the programs are stratified. Clark's predicate completion is defined for logic programs with negation. In general, it fails to capture their intended semantics [7,8,9].

In this paper, we introduce a new notion of quasi-interpretation as a set of ground clauses of the form $A \leftarrow \neg B_1, \ldots, \neg B_n$ and extend the classic fixed point theory in [11] to quasi-interpretations. The semantics of a logic program P is defined by Clark's predicate completion of the least fixpoint of a continuous operator T_P on quasi-interpretations. It is called the fixpoint completion of P, *fixcomp*(P). We then discuss the relations between *fixcomp*(P) and other approaches [5,7,8,9].

1 Introduction

A logic program can be viewed as a set of universally quantified first order clauses and its declarative semantics can be defined by specifying one or more models of this set. For definite Horn programs, the declarative semantics of a program is its least Herbrand model which is equivalent to the least fixed point of some operator associated with the program [11]. For programs with negation, there can be many minimal models for a given program and their corresponding opertor can have many minimal fixed point.

To handle logic programs with negation, Apt, Blair and Walker [1] and, independently, van Gelder [12] introduced the concept of *stratified programs*, where recursion through negation is forbidden. The declarative semantics of this class of programs is defined by an iterated fixed point construction. Przymunsinsky [7] introduced a concept of perfect model semantics and proved that for a class of *locally stratified* programs, a unique perfect model exists. Model-theoretic extensions to perfect model semantics to cover wider classes of logic programs include the weakly perfect model [8], the stable model [5], and the well-founded model [13].

In this paper, we propose a new method to specify the declarative semantics of logic programs by a simple and natural extension of the classic fixpoint approach of van Emden and Kowalski [11]. The basic idea is formalized by the introduction of quasi-interpretation as a set of ground clauses of the form $A \leftarrow \neg B_1, \ldots, \neg B_n$ where A, B_i are atoms. An operator on quasi-interpretations is defined which is monotonic and continuous. The declarative semantics is then defined as the Clark completion of the least fixed point of this operator. This is why we call our construction the *fixpoint completion* of P or *fixcomp*(P). Its naturalness will be demonstrated in the following examples.

Example 1.1 Let $P1$ be

[1]On leave from Institute of Computer Science and Cybernetics, National Center for Scientific Research of Vietnam, Lieugiai, Badinh, Hanoi, Vietnam

[2]Current Address: Department of Computer Science, University of Melbourne, Australia

$$p(x) \leftarrow q(x)$$
$$q(a) \leftarrow$$

Then the declarative semantics of $P1$ is the Herbrand model $\{p(a), q(a)\}$. This model can be determined uniquely by the following formula:

$$\forall x\ (p(x) \Leftrightarrow x = a) \wedge \forall x\ (q(x) \Leftrightarrow x = a).$$

■

Example 1.2 Let $P2$ be

$$p(a) \leftarrow \neg q(x)$$

The least fixpoint of our operator on quasi-interpretations is the set $p(a) \leftarrow \neg q(a)$. The declarative semantics is defined by Clark's completion of this set which has exactly one Herbrand model $\{p(a)\}$. Clearly, $\{p(a)\}$ is the intended meaning of $P2$. ■

We show the following results:

- The fixpoint completion is the basis for declarative semantics of logic programs.
- We introduce a new notion of *sufficient stratification*, which is more general than the local stratification. We show that for this class of programs our approach specifies their intended meaning naturally. Also there exists a constructive semantics based on the fixpoint completion, which allows us to construct their models bottom-up.
- In relation to other models, we will show that our approach is equivalent to the stable model approach. For locally stratified programs, our construction leads to the same semantics like the perfect model approach. If the program is weakly stratified, then its unique weakly perfect model is also the unique Herbrand model of our construction. The relationship to the well-founded model is demonstrated by defining a general notion of constructive semantics for logic programs.
- We show that constructive programs are those which have well-founded model, and that the sufficient stratification is a sufficient condition for the existence of the constructive semantics.

An earlier version of this paper [3], did not include the significant relationship of our approach to the well-founded semantics which should be the most general notion of constructive semantics for logic programs. See also [10].

2 The Fixpoint Completion

We assume the reader's familiarity with the notion in [6]. For safety, however, we recall some of them as follows.

A *program clause* is a clause of the form

$$A \leftarrow L_1, \ldots, L_n$$

where A is an atom and L_i are literals.

A *program* is a set of program clauses.

From now on, P denotes an arbitrary, but fixed program. The Herbrand universe (resp. the Herbrand base) of P is denoted by U_P (resp. B_P). The set of ground instances of P is denoted by G_P.

Definition. A *quasi-interpretation* is a set of ground program clauses of the form $A \leftarrow \neg B_1, \ldots, \neg B_n$, $n \geq 0$, where A, B_i are ground atoms. ■

A set of quasi-interpretations is denoted by QI. It is clear that QI is a complete lattice wrt the set inclusion.

Let C be ground clause $A \leftarrow \neg B_1, \ldots, \neg B_n, A_1, \ldots, A_m$ with $n \geq 0, m \geq 0$ and let C_i be ground clauses $A_i \leftarrow \neg B_{i_1}, \ldots, \neg B_{i_{n_i}}$ with $1 \leq i \leq m$ and $n_i \geq 0$. Then $T_C(C_1, \ldots, C_m)$ is the following clause

$$A \leftarrow \neg B_1, \ldots, \neg B_n, \neg B_{1_1}, \ldots, \neg B_{1_{n_1}}, \ldots, \neg B_{m_1}, \ldots, \neg B_{m_{n_m}}.$$

We now introduce the transformation T_P on quasi-interpretations

$$T_P : QI \rightarrow QI$$

$$T_P(I) = \{T_C(C_1, \ldots, C_m) \mid C \in G_P \text{ and } C_i \in I, 1 \leq i \leq m\}$$

Theorem 2.1 *T_P is continuous.*

Proof: The proof of this theorem is similar to the corresponding theorem in [6], page 37.

■

Let $LFP_n = T_P^n(\Phi)$, and

$$LFP = \bigcup\{LFP_n \mid n \geq 1\} \ (\textit{The least fixpoint of } T_P)$$

Let p be a predicate of P and $\{C_1, C_2, \ldots\}$ be the set of clauses in LFP whose heads are atoms with predicate p. C_i is a clause of the form $p(t) \leftarrow \neg B_1, \ldots, \neg B_n$. Then the *Clark completion of p* is

$$\forall(p(x) \Leftrightarrow E_1 \vee \ldots \vee E_m \vee \ldots)$$

where the right hand side is a (possibly infinite) disjunction. Every E_i is of the following form:

$$x = t \wedge \neg B_1 \wedge \ldots \wedge \neg B_n.$$

For the sake of simplicity, we assume that all predicates are unary predicates. An infinite disjunction is *true* wrt an interpretation if one of its elements is *true* wrt this interpretation. If there is no clause whose head are atoms with predicate p, then the completed definition of p is

$$\forall \neg p(x).$$

Clark's completion of LFP, which is called the *fixpoint completion* of P, *fixcomp*(P), is a collection of the completed definitions of predicates of P together with Clark's equality theory.

Let C be a clause. Then C^- (resp C^+) denotes the set of literals (resp. the atom) occuring in the body (resp. in the head) of C.

Theorem 2.2 (Basic theorem) a *Every Herbrand model of P is a model of LFP.*

b *Every Herbrand model of the fixpoint completion of P, fixcomp(P), is a model of the Clark's completion of P, comp(P).*

Proof: See [3] ■

Note: The following example show that, in general, the reverse of part b, theorem 2.2, does not hold.

Let P be

$$
\begin{array}{l}
a \leftarrow a \\
a \leftarrow \neg b \\
b \leftarrow b \\
b \leftarrow \neg c \\
c \leftarrow c \\
c \leftarrow \neg a
\end{array}
$$

Clark's completion of P is clearly consistent, but it is not meaningful because it does not provide any useful information about the declarative meaning of P. The fixpoint completion of P is inconsistent. However, this is not a weakness of the fixpoint completion, but a demonstration that, in general $comp(P)$ cannot properly specify the declarative semantics of P.

On the other hand, we believe that Clark's completion provides the most intuitive way of specifying the declarative semantics of logic programs. Our *fixcomp* approach, which is based on the Clark completion, will demonstrate how these drawbacks can be eliminated. The following examples are taken from [9]. Throughout this paper, we assume that Clark's equational theory axioms are satisfied.

Example 2.1 Let $P3$ be

$$
\begin{array}{l}
natural\!-\!number(0)\leftarrow \\
natural\!-\!number(succ(x)) \leftarrow natural\!-\!number(x)
\end{array}
$$

It is clear that Clark's completion of $P3$ specifies correctly the intended meaning of $P3$. So we cannot derive that IBM is a natural number from $comp(p)$. However, after adding to P a neutral (meaningless) clause:

$$natural\!-\!number(x) \leftarrow natural\!-\!number(x).$$

The new program has a different semantics, because its Clark's completion has many models and only one of them describes the intended semantics of the program.

Let us consider the fixpoint completion of the modified $P3$.

$$
\begin{array}{l}
LFP_1 = \{natural\!-\!number(o)\leftarrow\} \\
LFP_n = \{natural\!-\!number(succ^i(0)) \mid 0 \leq i < n\} \\
LFP = \{natural\!-\!number(succ^i(0)) \mid i \geq 0\}
\end{array}
$$

fixcomp(P) is the following formula:

$$\forall(natural\!-\!number(x) \Leftrightarrow x = o \vee x = succ(0) \vee \ldots \vee x = succ^i(0) \vee \ldots)$$

We see that *fixcomp*(P) describes uniquely the set of natural numbers. ∎

Example 2.2 Suppose now that $P4$ is given by the following clauses:

$$
\begin{array}{l}
edge(a, b)\leftarrow \\
edge(c, d)\leftarrow \\
reachable(a)\leftarrow \\
reachable(y) \leftarrow reachable(y), edge(y, x) \\
unreachable(x) \leftarrow \neg reachable(x)
\end{array}
$$

We obviously expect that vertices c, d to be unreachable and indeed, Clark's semantics implies *unreachable*(c) and *unreachable*(d). However, if we add a new clause edge (d, c) to $P4$, the new program no longer conclude that c and d are unreachable under Clark's semantics. *fixcomp* of the new program is demonstrated below:

$$\begin{aligned} LFP_1 = \{ \; & edge(a,b)\leftarrow \\ & edge(c,d)\leftarrow \\ & edge(d,c)\leftarrow \\ & reachable(a)\leftarrow\} \cup \{unreachable(x) \leftarrow \neg reachable(x) \mid x \in \{a,b,c,d\}\} \end{aligned}$$
$$LFP_2 = LFP_1 \cup reachable(b)$$
$$LFP_3 = LFP_2 = LFP$$

fixcomp(P) is the following formula:

$$\forall xy(edge(x,y) \Leftrightarrow (x = a \wedge y = b) \vee (x = c \wedge y = d) \vee (x = d \wedge y = c) \wedge$$

$$\forall x(reachable(x) \Leftrightarrow x = a \vee x = b) \wedge$$

$$\forall x(unreachable(x) \Leftrightarrow \begin{array}{l} (x = a \wedge \neg reachable(a)) \vee \\ (x = b \wedge \neg reachable(b)) \vee \\ (x = c \wedge \neg reachable(c)) \vee \\ (x = d \wedge \neg reachable(d))). \end{array}$$

It is clear that

$$fixcomp(P) \models \forall(unreachable(x) \Leftrightarrow x = c \vee x = d)$$

which means the fixpoint completion implies *unreachable*(c) and *unreachable*(d). The only Herbrand model of *fixcomp*(P) is clearly the intended model of the program. ∎

3 Relation to Other Approaches

We will briefly describe how our approach is related to the perfect model and the stable model semantics. See [3] for details. In [12], the well-founded model semantics is defined and it was shown that if a program has a well-founded model then this model also is the unique stable model. In section 3.3 we will also show that, in fact, the well-founded semantics is a "constructive" stable model semantics.

3.1 The Perfect Model Approach

The perfect model approach is based on the idea of assigning different *priorities* to predicate symbols [7]. Let M and N be two Herbrand models of P. We say that N is *preferable* to M, $N \ll M$, if for each $A \in (N - M)$ there is a $B \in (M - N)$ with $A < B$, where $<$ is the *priority relation* between atoms A, B in B_P. M is *perfect* if there is no other model preferable to M.

We introduce a class of *sufficiently stratified* programs which significantly extends the class of locally stratified programs and show that our fixcomp approach produces a unique Herbrand Model for such a class. This model coincides with the unique perfect model of a program P if P is locally stratified.

A relation $<$ is *noetherian* if there is no infinite sequence of $E_0 < E_1 < \ldots$.

Definition. A program P is *sufficiently stratified* if the priority relation of LFP is noetherian.

Theorem 3.1 *If P is sufficiently stratified, then fixcomp(P) has a unique Herbrand model.* ■

For locally stratified programs, the priority relation of P is noetherian. It is clear that the sufficiently stratified programs are more general than the locally stratified ones as illustrated in the following example.

Example 3.1 *Let P5 [5,8] be*

$$p(a,b)\leftarrow$$
$$q(x) \leftarrow p(x,y), \neg q(y)$$

$$LFP_1 = \{p(a,b)\leftarrow\}$$
$$LFP_2 = \{\ p(a,b)\leftarrow \quad q(a) \leftarrow \neg q(b)\}$$

$$LFP_3 = LFP_2 = LFP$$

$$\mathit{fixcomp}(P) : \forall x, y(p(x,y) \Leftrightarrow x = a \wedge y = b) \wedge \forall x(q(x) \Leftrightarrow x = a \wedge \neg q(b))$$

LFP is locally stratified but P is not. ■

The following theorem makes explicit the relations between the fixpoint completion and the perfect model semantics.

Theorem 3.2 *Assume that fixcomp(P) is consistent and P has one Herbrand perfect model. Then fixcomp(P) has exactly one Herbrand model which is also the unique Herbrand perfect model of P.* ■

Corollary 3.1 *If P is locally stratified then fixcomp(P) has exactly one Herbrand model which is the unique Herbrand perfect model of P.* ■

In example 3.1, *fixcomp*(P) has only one Herbrand model which is $\{p(a,b), q(a)\}$. But since P is not locally stratified, it has no perfect model.

3.2 Stable Model Semantics

Gelfond and Lifschitz [5] proposes an elegant definition of a stable model as one that is able to reproduce itself under certain kinds of transformation. A program may have zero, one, or many stable models, but a "well-behaved" program has a unique stable model.

Definition. Let M be a set of atoms of P. We define S_m as a program obtained from G_p be deleting

1. each clause that has a negative literal $\neg B$ in its body with $B \in M$
2. all negative literals in the bodies of the remaining clauses.

S_m is clearly a set of ground definite Horn clauses. If M coincides with the least Herbrand model of S_m, then M is a model of P and it is called a *stable model* of P.

Example 3.1 shows a program with a unique stable model which is the unique Herbrand model.

Theorem 3.3 *Every Herbrand model of fixcomp(P) is a stable model of P and vice versa.*

The two approaches are equivalent, but our fixpoint completion approach specifies the declarative semantics of logic programs from the syntactic definitions while the stable model describes a model or a set of models as the declarative semantics by a meta rule. This is similar to the relationship between circumscription and the closed world assumption in the theory of deductive database.

In [8], a class of *weakly stratified* programs is defined which is an extension of the locally stratified programs. For this class, the stable model semantics and the weakly perfect model semantics coincide.

3.3 The Well-Founded Semantics

Although the stable model semantics can describe declaratively the semantics of logic program, it is not constructive. The well-founded semantics was defined in [13] where it was shown that if a program has a well-founded model then this model is the unique stable model. A stepwise construction of the well-founded model was given, though the whole method is not constructive.

We will relate our fixcomp approach to the well-founded approach by introducing a notion of constructive semantics. We will show the relationship between the two approaches in three steps:

- We first introduce a rule-based semantics which constructs the unique Herbrand model for *fixcomp*(P) from *LFP*, for a restricted class of programs.
- Next we introduce a tree-based semantics which constructs a model directly from P and show its equivalence to the well-founded semantics.
- We then show that the equivalence of the two constructive semantics.

As a by product of this process, we can give an elegant proof that if a program has a well-founded model then it has a unique stable model.

The constructive semantics of P is defined by the rule-based construction [12] of the following sequence (SS_k, FS_k, RR_k).

a $SS_0 = \emptyset$, $FS_0 = \emptyset$, $RR_0 = LFP$

b Create SS_{k+1}, $FS_{k+1} from SS_k$, FS_k, RR_k as follows:

- Add to SS_k an atom A if the unit clause $A \leftarrow$ belongs to RR_k.
- Add to FS_k each atom which unifies with no heads of clauses from RR_k.
- Remove from RR_k each clause whose body contains one negative literal $\neg A$ with $A \in SS_{k+1}$.
- Delete from the body of the remaining clauses each negative literal $\neg A$ with $A \in FS_{k+1}$.

If k is a limit ordinal, we define

$$SS_k = \bigcup_{r<k} SS_r,\ FS_k = \bigcup_{r<k} FS_r,$$

$$RR_k = \{C \mid \exists r < k\ \forall r \leq s < k : C \in RR_s\}$$

Let τ be the least nonconstructive ordinal, and define

$$SS = \bigcup_{k<\tau} SS_k\ FS = \bigcup_{k<\tau} FS_k.$$

Example 3.2 *Let P6 be*

$a \leftarrow \neg b, \neg d$
$b \leftarrow \neg a, \neg c$
$c \leftarrow$

Then:

$SS_1 = \{c\}$	$FS_1 = \{d\}$	$RR_1 = \{\ c \leftarrow$ $a \leftarrow \neg b\}$
$SS_2 = \{c\}$	$FS_2 = \{d, b\}$	$RR_2 = \{\ c \leftarrow$ $a \leftarrow\}$
$SS_3 = \{c, a\}$	$SS_3 = \{d, b\}$	$RR_3 = RR_2$
$SS = \{c, a\}$	$FS = \{d, b\}$ ■	

Definition. A logic program P is said to be *constructive* if $FS \cup SS = B_P$

■

Theorem 3.4 *If P is constructive then SS is the unique Herbrand model of fixcomp(P).*

Proof: By induction on k, it is easy to see that:

$$\forall A \in SS_k : fixcomp(P) \models A$$

$$\forall A \in FS_k : fixcomp(P) \models \neg A.$$

The theorem follows directly from this proposition.

■

Note: The reverse is not valid as shown in the following example.

Example 3.3 *Let P7 be*

$d \leftarrow \neg a, \neg b, \neg c$
$a \leftarrow \neg b, \neg d$
$b \leftarrow \neg c, \neg d$
$c \leftarrow \neg a, \neg d$

It is clear that $\{d\}$ is the unique Herbrand model of fixcomp(P). But P is not constructive. ■

The next proposition shows the relation between the notion of constructive semantics and the notion of sufficient stratification. This is a very important result as it means that "sufficiently stratified", which is a syntactic condition of programs, ensures that a program is constructive.

Proposition 3.1 *If P is sufficiently stratified then P is constructive.*

Proof: Proof is similar to the proof of Theorem 3.1 in [3]. ■

The first example in this section shows that the reverse is not true.

We now give another constructive definition of (SS, FS) directly from P. We recall the definition of negation-as-failure derivation tree ($NF-tree$) in [12] with minor changes.

Definition. A *negation-as-failure derivation tree (NF-tree)* is a (possibly infinite) tree whose nodes are one of:

- a positive atom which is an internal node
- a negated atom which must be a leaf
- an empty node (denoted by a □) which must also be a leaf.

For each internal node there is a clause C from G_P such that the internal node is the head of C and the children of the internal node are the literals in the body of C. If C is a unit clause then the internal node has only one □ $-$ *child.*

A tree is called *positive* if it has no negative leaves.

It is easy to see that our $NF-tree$ correspond to the complete $NF-trees$ in [12].

We define now the tree-based negation-as-failure semantics of P by construction directly from P:

a $TSS_0 = \emptyset$, $TFS_0 = \emptyset$ RT_0 is the set of finite $NF-trees$.

b TSS_{k+1}, TFS_{k+1}, RT_{k+1} are created from TSS_k, TFS_k, RT_k as follows.

1. Add an atom which is the root os a positive tree in RT_k to TSS_k.
2. Add an atom which is not the root of any tree in RT_k to TFS_k.
3. Remove from RT_k each tree which has any negative leaf $\neg A$ with $A \in TSS_{k+1}$. On each remaining tree in RT_k, replace its negative leaf $\neg A$ where $A \in TSS_{k+1}$ by a □ $-$ *child.*

c If k is a limit ordinal then

$$TSS_k = \bigcup_{r<K} TSS_r, \; TFS_k = \bigcup_{r<k} TFS_r,$$

$$RT_k = \{tr \mid \exists r < k \; \forall r \leq s < k \; : \; tr \in RT_s\}$$

Let $TSS = \bigcup_k TSS_k$ and $TFS = \bigcup_k TFS_k$. The equivalence between the rule-based and the tree-based semantics is stated in the following proposition.

Proposition 3.2 *For every countable ordinal k, the following properties hold:*

a $TSS_k = SS_k$, $TFS_k = FS_k$

b *A clause C belongs to RR_k iff there is a tree in RT_k whose set of negative leaves is C^-.*

Proof: The proof is easily by induction on k, and is left to the reader. ■

The equivalence between constructive semantics and well-founded semantics [4] is stated in the next theorem.

Theorem 3.5 *(SS,FS) is the well-founded semantics of P.*

Proof: See [4]. ■

The following interesting relations follow:

Corollary 3.2 *P is constructive iff it has a well-founded model.*

Corollary 3.3 *If P has a well-founded model then this model also is the unique stable model of P.*

This is a strong indication that the well-founded semantics is a constructive stable model semantics. Constructiveness is a very nice semantic property which guarantees that a program have a unique stable model.

4 Conclusion

We have described a natural way to specify the declarative semantics of logic programs which is an extension of Clark's completion. For a class of constructive programs, their fixpoint completions have exactly one Herbrand model which is also their unique stable model. This model can be constructed step by step. A sufficient condition for the existence of constructive semantics, called the sufficient stratification, which is more general than the locally stratification is defined. Relations to other approaches in the literature are described. So far, we have considered only Herbrand-semantics which, as shown in [9], becomes incorrect wrt universal queries. An extension of our fixpoint completion along the line of [9] will be given in a forthcomming paper.

ACKNOWLEDGEMENTS: We thank Huynh Ngoc Phien and Tomonori Kimura for their assistance and support during the preparation of this paper. We also thank Harald Sondergaard for assisting us with the necessary literaturesand to the referees for their invaluable comments and suggestions.

References

[1] K. Apt, H. Blair and A. Walker. Towards a Theory of Declarative Knowledge, In J. Minker, editor, Foundation of Deductive Database and Logic Programming, *pages 89-148. Morgan Kaufmann, 1988.*

[2] K. Clark. Negation as failure. In H. Gallaire and J. Minker, editors, Logic and Databases, *pages 293–322. Plenum Press, 1978.*

[3] P. M. Dung and K. Kanchanasut. A Fixpoint Approach to Declarative Semantics of Logic Programs. In Proc of the North American Conference on Logic Programming, *Cleveland, Ohio, 1989.*

[4] P.M. Dung and K. Kanchanasut. Constructive Semantics for Logic Programs. Technical Report, AIT-CS, 6/89, April 1989.

[5] M. Gelford and V. Lifschitz. The stable model semantics for logic programs. In Proc of the Fifth International Conference on Logic Programming, *pages 1070-1079. Seatles, Washington, 1988.*

[6] J. W. Lloyd. Foundations of Logic Programming. *Springer-Verlag, second edition 1987.*

[7] T. C. Przymusinski. On the declarative semantics of deductive database and logic programming. In J. Minker, editor, Foundation of Deductive Database and Logic Programming, *pages 193-216. Morgan Kaufmann, 1988.*

[8] H. Przymusinska and T. C. Przymusinski. Weakly perfect model semantics for logic programs. In Proc of the Fifth International Conference in Logic Programming, *pages 1106-1120. Seatles, Washington, 1988.*

[9] T. C. Przymusinski. Perfect model semantics. In Proc of the Fifth International Conference in Logic Programming, *pages 1079-1096. Seatles, Washington, 1988.*

[10] T. C. Przymusinski. Non-Monotonic Formalisms and Logic Programming. In Proc of the Sixth International Conference in Logic Programming, *pages 655-674. Lisbon, 1989.*

[11] M. van Emden and R. Kowalski. The semantics of logic as a programming language. Journal of the ACM **23** *: 733–742, 1976.*

[12] *A. van Gelder. Negation as failure using tight derivations for general logic programs.* Journal of Logic Programming **6** *: 109-133, 1989.*

[13] *A. van Gelder, K. Ross and J.S. Schipf. Unfounded sets and well-founded semantics for general logic programs. In* Proc. of the Seventh ACM SIGACT-SIGMOD-SIGART Symposium on Principles of Database Systems, *page 221-230.*

A Transformation System for

Deductive Database Modules with Perfect Model Semantics

Michael J. Maher
IBM Thomas J. Watson Research Center,
P.O. Box 704, Yorktown Heights, NY 10598, U.S.A.

Abstract

We present a transformation system for deductive database (DDB) modules. We show that it preserves several data dependency properties of a DDB and is correct for the "perfect model" semantics of DDBs. Perfect models are not directly amenable to logical reasoning since logically equivalent DDBs may have different perfect models. We develop an approach which involves using a condition on data dependencies in DDBs (stratification compatibility) to pass from a logical equivalence to equivalence under perfect model semantics. This is readily applicable to the transformation system.

Introduction

The perfect model (or standard model) semantics of stratified deductive databases [11][2] has now become widely accepted. The semantics has a natural and intuitive interpretation in terms of finishing the definition of a predicate before the complement of the predicate is used. However the use of a semantics based upon a single model chosen by the syntactic structure of the deductive database (DDB) can create some problems. For example, logically equivalent DDBs may have different perfect models. This makes it difficult to straightforwardly exploit the considerable body of work on reasoning in first-order logic when optimizing or reasoning about queries using this semantics, despite the apparent close relation to logical notation.

The first result of this paper shows that, under the condition of *stratification compatibility*, two DDBs have the same perfect model if they are logically equivalent. More generally, it shows that for any semantics S which is coarser than perfect model semantics if two stratification compatible DDBs are equivalent under S then the DDBs have identical perfect models. (Here we take a semantics for a DDB to be the association of a set of models to the DDB, and we say that one semantics S_1 is *coarser* than another S_2 if $\forall Q \;\; S_1(Q) \supseteq S_2(Q)$.)

The second part of the paper exploits this result to show the correctness of a transformation system with respect to the perfect model semantics. Specifically, we independently show correctness with respect to the completion semantics [4], and the stratification compatibility of DDBs which differ by only a single transformation. The previous result allows us to conclude the correctness for perfect model semantics. We also demonstrate that the transformation system preserves several dependency properties [Kun87], even if the DDB acted upon does not have a perfect model semantics.

The transformation system contains Unfold, Fold and Replacement transformations, among others. It is essentially the transformation system discussed in [8] [9]. There are two complications to the transformation system: We allow constraints to be used in the DDB, and the transformation system operates on modules rather than entire DDBs.

The constraints are treated as in the CLP scheme [6], that is, our DDB language, transformation system and our results are all parameterized by the choice of a (generally many-sorted) data domain and the class of constraints which are allowed in DDBs. The extension of perfect model semantics to this scheme is relatively straightforward, but the formulation of the transformations is more difficult than for the usual Herbrand domain.

The parameterized treatment means that our results will hold for quite complex data domains and constraints, so that we are essentially treating programming languages as well as DDB languages. In most programming language cases the perfect model semantics is not computable, although for restrictions on the class of programs it can be (see, for example, [1]). Nevertheless the transformations are computable (provided certain basic operations on constraints are computable), and the results continue to hold irrespective of computability.

The next section provides some preliminary definitions. Following that we present definitions of program dependencies and introduce stratification compatibility. We show that, for any semantics coarser than perfect model semantics, if two programs are equivalent and stratification compatible then they have identical perfect model semantics. In section 4 we outline the kind of modules and module composition that we treat, define equivalence of modules, and extend the previous result from programs to modules. Section 5 presents the transformations. In section 6 we show that the transformation system preserves the perfect model semantics. We also show that many of the program dependency properties are preserved. We conclude by briefly discussing future work. Proofs, which are omitted, are given in [10].

Preliminaries

We use the symbols Σ and V to denote respectively the collection of function symbols and the infinite collection of variables. Terms are constructed from Σ and V in the usual way. The predicate symbols are partitioned into two sets: Π_D which are the pre-defined predicates and Π_U which are the predicates to be defined by the program. We assume that Π_D contains the predicate symbol $=$. The language of all first-order formulas built from these symbols is denoted by L. For any expression e, $var(e)$ denotes the set of free variables of e.

We assume throughout that there is an intended domain of computation $\mathcal{D}$. The structure $\mathcal{D}$ defines the set D of elements over which computation will be performed and defines the functions and relations associated to the symbols of Σ and Π_D. We will also use the extension $L_{\mathcal{D}}$ of L in which there is a new constant for each element of D. In an abuse of notation we will use D both for the set of elements of $\mathcal{D}$ and the set of constants denoting these elements. $L_{\mathcal{D}}$ is used in the meta-language, whereas programs and queries are formulas of L. $B_{\mathcal{D}} = \{p(d_1, \ldots, d_n) \mid p \text{ is } n\text{-ary}, p \in \Pi_U, d_1, \ldots, d_n \in D\}$.

An *atom* is of the form $p(t_1, \ldots, t_n)$ where p is an n-ary symbol in Π_U and the t_i are terms. A *literal* is either an atom or the negation of an atom. Where A is a literal, $pred(A)$ denotes its associated predicate symbol. A *constraint* is a first-order formula not involving symbols from Π_U.

A *$\mathcal{D}$-model* (which we will abbreviate to *model*) for a set of sentences S is a structure for $L_{\mathcal{D}}$ which extends $\mathcal{D}$ where the meaning of a constant d is the element d and is a model (in the usual sense) of S. By $S \models F$ we denote that F is valid in every $\mathcal{D}$-model of S. A conjunction of constraints C is said to be *consistent* (or *satisfiable*) if there are values (from $\mathcal{D}$) for the free variables y such that every constraint is true in $\mathcal{D}$, that is, $\models \exists y\, C$. A *valuation* v is a mapping from V to D which extends to map terms to D and $L_{\mathcal{D}}$ to $L_{\mathcal{D}}$ by replacing each free variable x in a formula of $L_{\mathcal{D}}$ with $v(x)$ and evaluating terms and constraints. We sometimes call the result of applying a valuation to a syntactic object a *ground instance* of that object. Thus the result of applying a valuation to a term, atom, etc is called a ground term, ground atom, etc.

A *deductive database* or *logic program* (or simply *program*) P is a collection of *rules* of the form

$$H \leftarrow C, A_1, \ldots, A_m, \neg B_1, \ldots, \neg B_n$$

where C is a constraint and $H, A_1, \ldots, A_m, B_1, \ldots, B_n$ are atoms ($m \geq 0, n \geq 0$). The positive literals and the negative literals are grouped separately purely for notational convenience. H is called the *head* of the rule and $A_1, \ldots, A_m, \neg B_1, \ldots, \neg B_n$ is called the *body*. If $m = n = 0$ then the rule is called a *unit rule*. A rule can be regarded logically as the sentence

$$\forall x\; H \vee \neg C \vee \neg A_1 \vee \ldots \vee \neg A_m \vee B_1 \vee \ldots \vee B_n$$

where x is the set of variables in the rule. A ground instance of a rule is the result of applying a valuation for x to the rule such that C evaluates to True under this valuation. The *Clark-completion* [4] of P, denoted by P^*, combines all the rules for each predicate into an if-and-only-if definition of the predicate.

To simplify the exposition we assume that the rules are in a standard form, where all arguments in atoms are variables and each variable occurs in at most one atom. This involves no loss of generality since a rule $p(t_1, t_2) \leftarrow C, q(s_1, s_2)$ can be replaced by the equivalent rule $p(x_1, x_2) \leftarrow x_1 = t_1, x_2 = t_2, y_1 = s_1, y_2 = s_2, C, q(y_1, y_2)$. We also assume that all rules defining the same predicate have the same head and that no two rules have any other variables in common (this is simply a matter of renaming variables).

Program Dependencies

In the following definitions we consider the set of rules formed by taking all ground instances of rules in a program P. We follow the notation of [7]. A and B range over ground atoms.

$A \sqsupseteq_{+1} B$ if A appears in the head of a ground rule and B is a positive literal in the body of that rule. $A \sqsupseteq_{-1} B$ if A appears in the head of a ground rule and $\neg B$ is a negative literal in the body of that rule. A dependency $A \sqsupseteq_i B$ *arises from* a program rule r if the ground rule used to demonstrate the dependency is an instance of r. $A \sqsupseteq B$ iff $A \sqsupseteq_{+1} B$ or $A \sqsupseteq_{-1} B$. $\geq$ is the transitive reflexive closure of $\sqsupseteq$. $A \approx B$ iff $A \geq B$ and $B \geq A$. $A > B$ iff $A \geq B$ and not $B \geq A$. $\geq_{+1}$ and $\geq_{-1}$ are the least relations such that $A \geq_{+1} A$ and, $A \sqsupseteq_i B$ and $B \geq_j C$ implies $A \geq_{i.j} C$, where $i.j$ denotes multiplication of i and j. Essentially $\geq_{+1}$ denotes a relation of dependence through an even number of negations and $\geq_{-1}$ denotes dependence through an odd number of negations. As is usual, we will write $A \leq B$ when $B \geq A$, and similarly for the other relations. $A \lessdot B$ iff $A \leq_{-1} B$ and not $A \approx B$. $\lessdot^*$ denotes the transitive closure of $\lessdot$.

The notion of stratified programs was developed in [3][2][5]. [7] expresses stratification and other properties in terms of dependencies on predicates. We expand this treatment by applying the definitions to elements of $B_{\mathcal{D}}$ in a manner somewhat similar to [11]. Any program which is stratified (strict, semi-strict) with regard to predicates will also be stratified (strict, semi-strict) in the following more general sense.

Let A, B range over elements of $B_{\mathcal{D}}$. A program P is

stratified if we never have $A \approx B$ and $A \geq_{-1} B$.

strict if we never have $A \geq_{+1} B$ and $A \geq_{-1} B$.

semi-strict (or *call-consistent* [12]) if we never have $A \geq_{-1} A$, or equivalently [7], if we never have $A \approx B$, $A \geq_{+1} B$ and $A \geq_{-1} B$.

well-founded if $<^*$ is well-founded.

Roughly, stratified programs have no recursion through negation, and the law of the excluded middle is inapplicable to strict programs. Every strict program is semi-strict, and every stratified program is semi-strict. The model-theoretic results of [7] for definitions with regard to predicate symbols extend, using the above definitions, to all well-founded programs. As one example, if a program P is semi-strict and well-founded then P^* is consistent.

Local stratification was defined in [11]. It is shown there that locally stratified programs over the Herbrand domain have a unique perfect Herbrand model. This result extends straightforwardly to other domains. We characterize local stratification in terms of dependency properties as follows.

Proposition.1 P has a local stratification iff P is stratified and well-founded.

Two programs, P_1 and P_2, are *stratification compatible* if $P_1 \cup P_2$ has a local stratification. The following theorem provides a powerful tool for determining whether a transformation preserves the perfect model semantics of a program. It shows that if a program P_1 is transformed to a stratification-compatible program P_2 and the transformation preserves a semantics defined by S, then the transformation preserves perfect model semantics.

Theorem.2 Suppose we have a method for associating with a program P a subset $S(P)$ of its models which includes the perfect model of P. Let P_1 and P_2 be stratification compatible. If $S(P_1) = S(P_2)$ then P_1 and P_2 have the same perfect model.

In particular the theorem applies to the program treated as a logic formula and the Clark-completion of the program:

Corollary.3 Let P_1 and P_2 be stratification compatible with perfect models M_1 and M_2.

(a) If $\models P_1 \leftrightarrow P_2$ then $M_1 = M_2$

(b) If $\models P_1^* \leftrightarrow P_2^*$ then $M_1 = M_2$

If we take $S(P)$ to be the set of minimal models of P then we obtain a formal proof of the fact that once the minimal models are fixed it is the form of the program, reflected in the stratification (or, more precisely, the dependency relations) which determines which minimal model is the perfect model. However it is slightly misleading to view the stratification as choosing a model from among the minimal models. As the theorem shows, *any* set of models which contains the perfect model could play the same role as the minimal models.

Modules

With the prospect of increasingly large and complex deductive database systems comes the problem of managing the many predicate definitions. A module system is a fundamental tool in handling this problem. A *module P* consists of predicate definitions and three disjoint sets of predicate symbols, which together include the predicate symbols occurring in the predicate definitions: the set *Exp*(*P*) of those predicate symbols defined in *P* which are accessible outside *P* (the *exported* predicates), the set *Imp*(*P*) of those predicate symbols used in *P* which are defined externally to *P* (the *imported* predicates), and the set of predicate symbols which are purely internal to *P* (the *local* predicates). Module composition associates exported predicates in some modules with imported predicates in another module. We do not discuss any particular syntax for expressing modules and their composition. However we do make some assumptions about the semantics and use of the module system:

> We assume that a module cannot in any way modify the sets of function symbols and constraints which may be used in the module. Although there may be great advantages in, for example, localizing the use of a function symbol to a single module this would introduce major complications to the semantics of modules and module composition.
>
> We assume that each predicate is defined within a single module. This assumption ensures locality properties: when a predicate definition is to be modified only one module is directly involved, and when a module is modified only those modules which depend on that module through module composition can be affected by the change.
>
> We assume a hierarchical calling pattern for modules. That is, a module may not import predicates through module composition which are defined in that module, nor may it import predicates from modules which depend on the module. This ensures that all recursion occurs within modules, and not between them.

These assumptions have several useful consequences for logic programs and deductive databases with negation. If every module of a program is well-founded then so is the program. Similarly, if every module is stratified then so is the entire program. Strictness may be violated by the program although every module is strict. For example if one module contains $p \leftarrow q, r.$ and is composed with another module containing $q \leftarrow s, t.$ and $r \leftarrow \neg s.$ then the resulting program is not strict. (Here we use identical predicate symbols to denote the association by module composition of predicate definition and predicate use.) However the weaker notion of semi-strictness is preserved under module composition. Essentially this is because semi-strictness only requires strictness between mutually dependent predicates and under the regime of a hierarchical calling pattern all mutual dependencies must occur within modules.

The perfect model semantics of a module *P* with a local stratification is defined as follows: The semantics of *P* is a mapping μ_P from relations for *Imp*(*P*) to relations for *Exp*(*P*), such that if *Q* is the set of ground atoms in the relations for *Imp*(*P*), then the relations for *Exp*(*P*) are given by the perfect model of $P \cup Q$, restricted to exported atoms. When there are no imported predicates and every predicate is exported this semantics is isomorphic to the perfect model semantics of a program. We write $P \sim P'$ iff $\mu_P = \mu_{P'}$.

We can also consider an equivalence of modules based on completions. Suppose that modules P_1 and P_2 have the same imported and exported predicates, but disjoint collections of local predicate symbols. Let D_1 and

D_2 be the definitions of the local predicates of the respective modules P_1 and P_2. Then define $P_1 \simeq P_2$ iff $\models P_1{}^* \wedge D_2{}^* \leftrightarrow P_2{}^* \wedge D_1{}^*$. If P_1 and P_2 are stratification compatible, then so also are P_1, D_2, Q and P_2, D_1, Q , for any relation Q for imported predicates. Using theorem 2 we obtain

Theorem.4 If P_1 and P_2 are stratification compatible and $P_1 \simeq P_2$ then $P_1 \sim P_2$.

The theorem generalizes to any semantics S coarser than perfect model semantics by taking $P_1 \simeq P_2$ to mean $\mu^S_{P1} = \mu^S_{P2}$, where $\mu^S_P(Q) = S(P \cup Q) \mid_P$, the semantics of $P \cup Q$ restricted to the exported predicates.

To avoid choosing a particular syntax, we represent a network N of composed modules as a directed acyclic graph (dag) with module names at the nodes and an edge from P_2 to P_1 labeled with α if P_1 calls P_2 and $\alpha : Imp(P_1) \twoheadrightarrow Exp(P_2)$ is the partial function associating exported predicates of P_2 with imported predicates of P_1 . This dag has the extra property that if P has incoming edges labeled with $\alpha_1, \ldots, \alpha_n$ then the domains of the α_i are disjoint. We also have $Imp(N)$, the set of imported predicate symbols not in the domain of any α, and $Exp(N)$, some subset of the set of all exported predicate symbols. Our previous assumptions are necessary for this representation to make sense. For simplicity we assume that each predicate symbol occurs in only one module.

The semantics of a module network $(N; P_1, \ldots, P_n)$ is a mapping from relations for $Imp(N)$ to relations for $Exp(N)$ defined inductively on the dag roughly as follows: Given relations Q for $Imp(N)$, the semantics of a minimal (in the dag ordering) module P_i determines relations for $Exp(P_i)$. Let Q' be obtained from Q by adding, as a relation for p, a duplicate of the relation for r, for each p and α such that $\alpha(p) = r$. Let N' be obtained from N by deleting the node for P_i and the edges from P_i. The process repeats for N' and Q'. Of the final set of relations, the subset corresponding to $Exp(N)$ is chosen.

Module composition corresponds to merging connected nodes in the dag. For definiteness we choose a particular semantics for module composition. Let P be a module with an incoming edge from Q labeled with α. We will write this as $P \leftarrow \alpha - Q$. Composition along $P \leftarrow \alpha - Q$ is allowed only if there is no module S such that $P \leftarrow \beta - S \leftarrow \gamma - Q$. (This ensures that a hierarchical calling pattern is maintained.) In this case the semantics is given by the module $R = P \otimes_\alpha Q$ with predicate definitions $P \cup \alpha(Q)$, $Exp(R) = Exp(P) \cup Exp(Q)$ and $Imp(R) = Imp(Q) \cup Imp(P) - domain(\alpha)$. $\alpha(Q)$ denotes the set of predicate definitions containing Q and a copy of the definition for q with the q predicate symbols renamed to p whenever $\alpha(p) = q$. For each module S in the network, if $P \leftarrow \beta - S$ and $Q \leftarrow \gamma - S$ then these edges are merged, and become $R \leftarrow (\beta + \gamma) - S$. Similarly, if $S \leftarrow \beta - P$ and $S \leftarrow \gamma - Q$ then these edges are merged. Note that the semantics of the resulting module is the same as the semantics of the network consisting only of $P \leftarrow \alpha - Q$.

Module composition satisfies some important properties. Compositionality justifies performing transformations on one module in isolation, ignoring the context in which it occurs. Independence justifies working with a localized part of a network of modules instead of the entire network.

Proposition.5 Compositionality: if $P_1 \sim P_2$ and $Q_1 \sim Q_2$ then $P_1 \otimes_\alpha Q_1 \sim P_2 \otimes_\alpha Q_2$.

Independence: if $P \leftarrow \alpha - Q$, $Q \leftarrow \beta - R$ and $P \leftarrow \alpha - R$ then
$(P \otimes_\alpha Q) \otimes_{\beta+\gamma} R \sim P \otimes_{\alpha+\gamma} (Q \otimes_\beta R)$, and
if $P \leftarrow \alpha - Q$, $P \leftarrow \beta - R$ and neither $Q \leftarrow \gamma - R$ nor $R \leftarrow \gamma - Q$ then
$(P \otimes_\alpha Q) \otimes_\beta R \sim (P \otimes_\beta R) \otimes_\alpha Q$.

Transformations for DDBs with Constraints

We need some further definitions to express the transformations. A *variable renaming* is an invertible substitution, that is, a substitution α such that for some substitution α^{-1}, $\alpha \circ \alpha^{-1} = \alpha^{-1} \circ \alpha = \varepsilon$ (ε is the identity substitution). A *variant* of a syntactic object is the result of applying a variable renaming to that object. By *new variant* we will refer to a variant which has no variables in common with the current context.

It is convenient for describing the transformations to extend the terminology introduced in [15]. A *molecule* is an existentially quantified (possibly empty) conjunction of constraints and literals $\exists x\ C \wedge A$. For simplicity we assume that atoms in A have only variables as arguments and no variable appears twice in A. No loss of generality is involved since every molecule is logically equivalent to such a molecule. Two molecules $\exists x_1\ C_1 \wedge A_1$ and $\exists x_2\ C_2 \wedge A_2$ are equal if there is a variable renaming α of the variables x_1 to the variables x_2 such that $A_1\alpha \equiv A_2$ and $C_1\alpha \leftrightarrow C_2$.

A molecule $\exists x_1\ C_1 \wedge A_1$ is a *submolecule* of the molecule $\exists x_2\ C_2 \wedge A_2$ if there is a variable renaming α of the variables x_1 to a subset of the variables x_2 such that $A_1\alpha \subseteq A_2$, $C_2 \rightarrow C_1\alpha$ and $var(A_2 - A_1\alpha) \cap x_1\alpha = \phi$. That is, $\exists x_1\ C_1 \wedge A_1$ is a submolecule of $\exists x_2\ C_2 \wedge A_2$ if $\exists x_2\ C_2 \wedge A_2 \leftrightarrow \exists z\ Z \wedge (\exists x_1\alpha\ C_1\alpha \wedge A_1\alpha)$ for some variables z and some conjunction of constraints and literals Z. In this case Z is said to be the result of subtracting $\exists x_1\ C_1 \wedge A_1$ from $\exists x_2\ C_2 \wedge A_2$. A rule body can be regarded as a molecule; the rule $A \leftarrow B$ is equivalent to $A \leftarrow \exists x\ B$ where x is the set of variables in the rule which appear in B but not in A.

For $p, q \in \Pi_U$, we say q *depends* on p, if $A_1 \leq A_2$ for ground atoms A_1, A_2 with $pred(A_1) = p$ and $pred(A_2) = q$.

In a series of module transformations we will denote the initial module by P_0, and the resultant series of modules is $P_0, P_1, P_2, \ldots, P_i, \ldots$. Let $L' \subseteq L$ be the largest language which only has predicate symbols from Π_U for imported and exported predicates. Every module P_i has a corresponding language L_i derived from the function symbols Σ and all predicate symbols in P_i or L', so that $L' \subseteq L_i$. To simplify the exposition we assume that if a predicate symbol p appears in L_i but not in L_{i+1} then p does not appear in any L_j for $j > i$.

The Transformations

We consider the following transformations on a module P. (Further transformations are dealt with in [10].)

Definition

The addition of a set of rules

$$A_j \leftarrow B_j \qquad j = 1, \ldots, k$$

to P where $\{pred(A_j): j = 1, \ldots, k\}$ is a set of new predicate symbols, that is, predicate symbols not appearing in P. In the context of a series of transformations $pred(A_j)$ must not have appeared in a previous module in the series.

Deletion

The deletion of all rules defining a set S of predicate symbols such that, for every $p \in S$, p does not occur in L' and every predicate symbol in P which depends on p appears in S.

Unfolding

The replacement of a rule (the *unfolded* rule)

$$A \leftarrow C, B$$

in P by the rules

$$A \leftarrow C \cup C_j \cup \{B' = H\}, B - \{B'\} \cup D_j \qquad j = 1, \ldots, m$$

where $B' \in B$ is a positive literal, and the rules

$$H \leftarrow C_j, D_j \qquad j = 1, \ldots, m$$

are new variants of the rules in P such that $C \cup C_j \cup \{B' = H\}$ is consistent. Note that if, for every rule in P, the constraint $C \cup C_j \cup \{B' = H\}$ is not consistent then the result of unfolding is to delete the unfolded rule.

We require (a) that the unfolded rule is never an unfolding rule, in other words, for no variable renaming ψ is $C \cup C\psi \cup \{B' = A\psi\}$ consistent, and (b) that the unfolded atom B' is not imported, that is, *pred*(B') is not an imported predicate symbol.

Folding

The replacement of a collection of rules (the *folded* rules)

$$A \leftarrow C_i, B_i \qquad i = 1, \ldots, k$$

in P by the single rule

$$A \leftarrow C, H\theta, D$$

provided (a) there are (new variants of) rules (the *folding* rules)

$$H \leftarrow C'_i, B'_i \qquad i = 1, \ldots, k$$

in P, (b) θ is a variable renaming which maps some variables of H to *var*(A, C, D), (c) there is a constraint C and conjunction of literals D such that $C'_i\theta$, $B'_i\theta$ is a submolecule of C_i, B_i for $i = 1, \ldots, k$ and $C \wedge D$ is the result of subtracting $C'_i\theta$, $B'_i\theta$ from C_i, B_i for $i = 1, \ldots, k$, and (d) for every rule

$$H \leftarrow C', B'$$

in P, if $C \wedge C'\theta$ is satisfiable then the rule is a folding rule. We require that no rule is simultaneously a folded rule and a folding rule. (This ensures that we do not destroy a rule by folding it with itself.)

Folding is said to be *reversible* when there is only one folding rule (and so also only one folded rule). This form of reversible folding differs from the reversible folding of [14] [15]. Here the folding rule is in P whereas in [15] the folding rule must come from P_0. One consequence is that reversible folding in this transformation system does not have the same power as reversible folding in [14] [15] (See [9]). However a comparison of the two entire systems is not so clear-cut.

Replacement

A *replacement rule* takes the form $J \Rightarrow K$ where J and K are molecules with the same free variables. Application of such a replacement rule to a rule

$$A \leftarrow B$$

consists of the replacement of a submolecule B' of B by $K\theta$ where $B' = J\theta$ and θ is a variable renaming which acts only on the free variables of J, to obtain

$$A \leftarrow (B - B') \cup K\theta$$

It is *legal* to apply a replacement rule to such a rule only when no predicate symbol appearing in the replacement rule depends on *pred*(A). We only allow replacement rules to be applied to P_i if $P_j^* \models J \leftrightarrow K$ for some $j \leq i$ and J and K are in L_i. (P_j is said to *validate* the replacement rule.) This condition allows the validity of replacement rules to be verified at whichever stage in the process of transformation is convenient, and not only at the first stage or at the current stage as some transformation systems implicitly require.

Preservation Theorems

A *basic transformation system* uses only the transformations defined above. Consequently a module undergoing transformation is totally isolated from other modules. In this section we discuss some properties which are preserved (i.e. held invariant) by the basic transformation system.

The correctness of the basic transformation system with respect to Clark-completion semantics can be viewed as simply another preservation theorem.

Theorem.6 Let P_i be obtained from P_0 by the basic transformation system. Then $P_i \simeq P_0$.

We now turn to dependency-related properties. It is clear that Deletions, and Unfolding both reduce the dependencies in a module and add none. Hence these transformations preserve semi-strictness, stratifiedness, well-foundedness, ... Definition transformations add dependencies. However such transformations will preserve each of the above properties except strictness, provided the new rules themselves satisfy the property. This is because the new rules in essence form a module which calls the module composed of the old rules. Preservation of strictness can require an examination of the entire program as pointed out in the section on modules.

For Folding and Replacement transformations preservation of these properties is not so obvious. The following theorem summarizes our results.

Theorem.7 Let P_i be obtained from P_0 by a series of transformations. Suppose that uses of the Definition transformation add subprograms which are stratified (semi-strict, well-founded).

If P_0 is stratified (semi-strict, well-founded) then P_i is stratified (semi-strict, well-founded)

Suppose the Definition transformations is not used, and Folding always uses at least one non-unit folding rule.

If P_0 is strict then P_i is strict

Folding with only unit rules can destroy strictness. An example is given in [10]. As a corollary to the proof of theorem 7 we have

Corollary.8 If P_0 has a local stratification and P_i, P_{i+1} are obtained from P_0 by a series of transformations then P_i and P_{i+1} are stratification compatible.

The correctness of the basic transformation system with respect to the perfect model semantics now follows by combining theorem 6 and corollary 8, using theorem 4.

Theorem.9 Let P_i be obtained from P_0 by a series of transformations. Suppose P_0 has a local stratification. Then P_i has a perfect model semantics and $P_i \sim P_0$.

A comparable result is shown in [13]. The two transformation systems are quite different since [13] discusses a transformation system based on Tamaki-Sato reversible folding.

The basic transformation system treats a module in isolation from any module network in which it appears. The applicability of theorem 9 in this setting follows from the property of compositionality (proposition 5). The transformation system can be extended with module composition and decomposition transformations, which provide the ability to exploit the specific context in which a module appears. In this case we can obtain a result similar to theorem 9 for module networks, using the independence property (proposition 5). However, as would be expected, the semantics of individual modules is not preserved.

References

[1] K. Apt & H. Blair, Arithmetic Classification of Perfect Models of Stratified Programs, *Proc. ICLP/SLP-5*, 765-779, 1988.

[2] K. Apt, H. Blair & A. Walker, Towards a Theory of Declarative Knowledge, in: *Foundations of Deductive Databases and Logic Programming*, J. Minker (Ed), Morgan Kaufmann, 89-148, 1988.

[3] A. Chandra & D. Harel, Horn Clause Queries and Generalizations, *Journal of Logic Programming* 1, 1-15, 1985.

[4] K. Clark, Negation as Failure, in *Logic and Databases*, H. Gallaire & J. Minker (Eds), Plenum Press, 293-322, 1978.

[5] A. van Gelder, Negation as Failure Using Tight Derivations for General Logic Programs, in: *Foundations of Deductive Databases and Logic Programming*, J. Minker (Ed), Morgan Kaufmann, 149-176, 1988.

[6] J. Jaffar & J-L. Lassez, Constraint Logic Programming, *Proc. POPL*, 111-119, 1987.

[7] K. Kunen, Signed Data Dependencies in Logic Programs, *Journal of Logic Programming*, to appear. Also CSTR 719, Computer Sciences Department, University of Wisconsin-Madison, 1987.

[8] M. Maher, Equivalences of Logic Programs, in: *Foundations of Deductive Databases and Logic Programming*, J. Minker (Ed), Morgan-Kaufmann, 627-658, 1988.

[9] M. Maher, Correctness of a Logic Program Transformation System, IBM Research Report, T. J. Watson Research Center, 1988.

[10] M. Maher, A Transformation System for Deductive Database Modules with Perfect Model Semantics, IBM Research Report, T. J. Watson Research Center, 1989.

[11] T. Przymusinski, On the Declarative Semantics of Deductive Databases and Logic Programs, in: *Foundations of Deductive Databases and Logic Programming*, J. Minker (Ed), Morgan Kaufmann, 193-216, 1988.

[12] T. Sato, On Consistency of First Order Logic Programs, TR-87-12, Electrotechnical Laboratory, 1987.

[13] H. Seki, Unfold/Fold Transformation of Stratified Programs, *Proc. ICLP-6*, 554-568, 1989.

[14] H. Tamaki & T. Sato, Unfold/Fold Transformation of Logic Programs, *Proc. ICLP-2*, 127-138, 1984.

[15] H. Tamaki & T. Sato, A Generalized Correctness Proof of the Unfold/Fold Logic Program Transformation, Information Science Technical Report 86-4, Ibaraki University, 1986.

An Efficient Distributed Algorithm for Finding Articulation Points, Bridges, and Biconnected Components in Asynchronous Networks

Mohan Ahuja and Yahui Zhu

Department of Computer and Information Science

The Ohio State University, Columbus, Ohio 43210

1 Introduction

The problems of finding articulation points, bridges and biconnected components are very important for fault tolerance in distributed systems. A node (an edge) in a connected network is called an *articulation point* (a *bridge*) iff the deletion of the node (the edge) disconnects the network into two or more nonempty components. A *biconnected component* is defined as a maximal subgraph which does not contain an articulation point. Failure of an articulation point or a bridge will cause a partition in a network, while a biconnected component can tolerant a node failure. Many researchers have studied the problems ([3, 6, 7, 8, 9, 11, 12]), and it is very desirable to have efficient distributed algorithms for them.

This paper presents an efficient distributed algorithm for these problems. Let a network be represented as G=(V,E), with $|V| = n$ and $|E| = m$. The algorithm uses the *distributed depth first search* (DDFS) algorithm proposed independently by Cidon [4] and Lakshmanan *et al* [10], both improved an earlier DDFS algorithm of Awerbuch [2] using the same idea. It can detect all the articulation points and bridges, and identify all the members of each biconnected component through one run of a DDFS. The algorithm is efficient in the sense that its time is only $2n - 2$ (which is optimal), number of messages is bounded by $4m - n$, each message size is bounded by $2\log n + 2$ bits and there is no complicated local computations. It can operate correctly in asynchronous networks, specially message passing does *not* need to be in *FIFO* order.

The first efficient solution for finding articulation points and biconnected components was obtained by Tarjan in [8], who gave a sequential algorithm based on *depth first search* (DFS). The algorithm has $O(m)$ time complexity. A sequential bridge algorithm based on postorder search was given by Tarjan in [9]. Later, Tsin and Chen extended the method to a general scheme, and showed that the scheme can be implemented by many different searching methods [11]. These algorithms for bridges also takes $O(m)$ time. More efficient parallel algorithms for these problems have also been pursued by researchers, $O(\log^2 n)$ time has been achieved on CREW PRAM model [6, 12] and $O(\log n)$ time on CRCW PRAM model [7].

A distributed algorithm for finding articulation points and biconnected components was gave by Chang in [3]. The time and message complexities of this algorithm are bounded by $2d$ and $4m - n$ respectively, where *d* is the diameter of a network. Although these two complexities are of the same order as ours, its message size bound is rather large. The algorithm needs to pass sets of node IDs, and in the worst case, message size can reach $O(n \log n)$ bits. For large networks, this bound is too high for efficient message passing. Also each node needs to do some complicated local computations, which makes the algorithm inefficient to implement. For the bridge problem, we will show that it can be naturally solved in our algorithm.

2 The Model and Some Definitions

The network model is the standard asynchronous model. All the processors have distinct identities (IDs). There is no common memory in the network and the processors communicate with each other by sending messages. All messages sent from one node to another node arrive correctly, within arbitrary but finite time, and *not* necessarily in *FIFO* order (non-FIFO). Each node is aware of its neighboring nodes and the incident edges. The *communication complexity* is the total number of messages sent during execution of an algorithm. The *time complexity* is the maximum time passed from the start to the end of an algorithm, assuming that the time of sending one message over each edge takes one unit of time. The algorithm operates correctly with any finite arbitrary message delivery time.

When a DFS is done on a graph, a directed *depth first spanning tree* (DFST) will be formed with the initial node as the *root*. Each node can be labeled with a *depth first number* (DFN), which corresponds to the order in which a DFS first visited that node. The edges of the DFST will be called *tree edges*, and all the others *back edges*. Each root node of the sub-DFST formed by a biconnected component will be called the *root* of that component. Also *father*, *son* etc. can be defined in the usual way [5].

3 The Algorithm

3.1 Preliminary Review

Our algorithm is based on the following lemmas, whose proofs are easy and omitted.

Lemma 3.1 *The root in a DFST of G is an articulation point iff it has at least two children; a node i ($\neq$ root) is an articulation point iff for every descendant v of i, if (v,w) is an back edge, then w is a descendant of i.*

Lemma 3.2 *If e is a bridge in G, then e is in every spanning tree of G.*

Lemma 3.3 *If (b,a) is an edge in any spanning tree of G, then (b,a) is a bridge iff for every descendant v of a or v = a, if (v,w) is a back edge, then w is a descendant of a.*

These observations lead us to define L(i) for each node i as:

$$L(i) = \min(\{DFN(i)\} \cup \{L(s) \mid s \text{ is a son of } i\} \cup \{DFN(j) \mid (i,j) \text{ is a back edge}\})$$

Intuitively, L(i) is the lowest DFN that can be reached from i using a path of descendants followed by at most one back edge. Then we can use DFN(i), L(i) and a DFST of G to detect articulation points and bridges as follows:

C1: if i $\neq$ root, i is an articulation point iff i has a son j such that L(j) $\geq$ DFN(i).

C2: if i = root, i is an articulation point iff it has at least two sons.

C3: if (j,i) is a tree edge with j being i's father, (j,i) is a bridge iff L(i) = DFN(i).

One can see that these three conditions are the same as those in lemma 3.1 and 3.3.

Our algorithm will label each node i with DFN(i) and compute L(i) as defined above through a DDFS. It will also set some pointers at each node for identifying the members of each biconnected component. Now we first introduce four kinds of messages employed by our algorithm and state their functions:

1. START: used just for starting the algorithm.

2. TOKEN: contains the *DFN counter* (DFNcnt), used so that all the nodes can be consistently labeled with DFN's.

3. VISITED: contains DFN, used for two purposes: 1) to notify its neighbors that it has been visited and 2) to pass its DFN to its descendants for computing their L's.

4. ECHO: contains L(i) and DFNcnt, used for two purposes: 1) to send L(i) to its father j for computing L(j) and 2) to send the current DFNcnt used by its subtree so that the father can continue the DFS with the correct DFNcnt.

Notice that ECHO's are the only kind of messages containing two labels: L and DFNcnt.

3.2 Informal Description of the Algorithm

The algorithm starts with a node *source* (or root) receiving a START message from the outside world. The root sets its DFN and L, and initializes the DFNcnt. Then it sends a TOKEN(DFNcnt) to one neighbor, and VISITED(DFN)'s to all the others.

Upon receiving the TOKEN(DFNcnt) for the first time, node i ($\neq$ root) changes to the *active* state, sets DFN(i) to the DFNcnt, and marks the sender as its father. Then it becomes the center of activity, calls Search procedure, and broadcasts VISITED(DFN(i))'s to all neighbors, excluding its father and the son.

Search at node i will try to find next unvisited neighbor to continue the DDFS. But if there is no such neighbor, then the DDFS by the current node is finished, so Search checks if (Father(i), i) is a bridge and shifts the center of activity back to Father(i) through ECHO. However, if the node happens to be the root, then the DDFS of the network is finished, so Search checks if the root is an articulation point and terminates the algorithm.

Upon receiving a TOKEN(DFNcnt) but not for the first time, node i just marks the sender's flag to indicate the sender is visited if necessary. But if the TOKEN is from its son j, which can happen when the center of activity comes back from a descendant j after j has sent a TOKEN to i and i now has sent a TOKEN to j also, then i knows that its last TOKEN has been sent to a visited descendant (i.e., j). So it tries to visit its next unmarked neighbor by calling Search. This is one place where we need the local DFNcnt(i), so that node i can recover the previous DFNcnt needed by Search.

Upon receiving an ECHO(L, DFNcnt) from a son, node i marks the son's flag if necessary, updates its local DFNcnt(i), checks if it is an articulation point using its DFN and the son's L in the ECHO, and sets the biconnected component pointer (Biptr) if necessary. Then it tries to visit its next unmarked neighbor by calling Search.

Upon receiving a VISITED(DFN), node i first marks the sender's flag if necessary. If the DFN is less than the minimum DFN (MinDFN) seen by i, i will record the DFN and its sender (in Minsdr): MinDFN is required here since it corresponds to the minimum DFN received from its ancestors over back edges needed for computing L(i), and Minsdr is required to distinguish between the MinDFN set by its father and its other ancestors. But if the VISITED is from its son, i knows that its last TOKEN has been sent to a visited node, so it tries to recover the mistake by calling Search. This is the other place where we need local DFNcnt(i).

If a VISITED message is from its father (due to the non-FIFO property), then since i already knows its father is visited, it just ignores this VISITED.

3.3 Formal Description of the Algorithm

The following local variables are used, with their initial values and meanings:

DFN(i):	0: DFN of node i,
L(i) :	0: L of node i,
DFNcnt(i):	0: the DFN counter at node i,
MinDFN(i):	∞: the minimum DFN received by i from its ancestors other than its father,
Minsdr(i):	i: the node ID who sends the DFN recorded in MinDFN(i),
State(i):	*inactive*: the state of node i,
Nghbors(i):	the set of nodes who are the neighbors of node i,
Father(i):	i: the father of node i,
Sons(i):	∅: the set of sons of node i,
Bridge(i):	*false*: set to *true* if (Father(i),i) is a bridge,
BiPtr(i):	∅: if nonempty, indicates i is an articulation point and contains the set of pointers to the biconnected components rooted at node i,
flag(i,j):	0: a flag for each neighbor j when i knows that j has been visited.

1. On receiving a START message by node i (*source*) from the outside world:

1.1 **if** State(i) = inactive **then**

1.2 State(i) := active; L(i) = DFN(i) = DFNcnt(i) :=1;

1.3 call Search;

1.4 send VISITED(DFN(i)) to all nodes in (Nghbors(i) – Sons(i));

2. On receiving a TOKEN(DFNcnt) message from a node j:

2.1 flag(i,j) := 1;

```
2.2  if   State(i) = inactive then
2.3       State(i) := active;   Father(i) := j;   L(i) = DFN(i) = DFNcnt(i) := DFNcnt;
2.4       call Search;
2.5       send VISITED(L(i)) to all nodes in (Nghbors(i) − Sons(i) − {Father(i)}) ;
2.6  else
2.7       if  j ∈ Sons(i) then       /* last TOKEN was sent to a visited descendant */
2.8            Sons(i) := Sons(i) − { j } ;
2.9            call Search;

3. On receiving an ECHO(L, DFNcnt) message from a node j:
3.1  if   j ∈ Sons(i) then
3.2       flag(i,j) := 1;
3.3       L(i) := Min ( L(i), L);      /* updates L(i) to reflect its son's smaller L */
3.4       DFNcnt(i) := Max (DFNcnt(i), DFNcnt);
3.5       if  (L ≥ DFN(i)) and (i ≠ source) then       /* checks for arti. point */
3.6            BiPtr(i) := BiPtr(i) ∪ { j } ;
3.7       call Search;

4. On receiving a VISITED(DFN) message from a node j:
4.1  flag(i,j) := 1;
4.2  if   DFN < MinDFN(i) then       /* records the min. DFN from ancestors */
4.3       MinDFN(i) := DFN;   Minsdr(i) := j;
4.4  if   j ∈ Sons(i) then      /* last TOKEN was sent over back edge (i,j) */
4.5       Sons(i) := Sons(i) − { j } ;
4.6       call Search;

5. Procedure Search:
5.1  if   ∃ k (flag(i,k) = 0) then       /* continues the DFS */
5.2       send TOKEN(DFNcnt(i) + 1) to k;
5.3       Sons(i) := Sons(i) ∪ { k } ;
5.4  else   if   i = source then      /* root checks for arti. point and terminates */
5.5       if   | Sons(i) | ≥ 2 then BiPtr(i) := Sons(i);
5.6       terminate;
5.7  else      /* a normal node has finished the visits to its subtree */
5.8       if   ( MinDFN(i) < L(i)) and (Minsdr(i) ≠ Father(i)) then
5.9            L(i) := MinDFN(i);      /* sets to the smaller min. DFN from ancestors */
5.10      if   (L(i) = DFN(i)) then    Bridge(i) := true;    /* checks for bridge */
5.11      send ECHO(L(i),DFNcnt(i)) to Father(i);
```

An example of how the algorithm works is given in Figure 1. The algorithm executes from a) to l). Several interesting cases should be noticed:

1. in a) the V's sent from a to d and f are not received until in g) and h);
2. in e) the T passes over the earlier V from a to d, and this V is ignored in g);
3. in g) the T from f is sent to an already visited node d, and f realizes the mistake when receives the V from a in h);
4. in j) L(e) is set to 6 despite that MinDFN(e) was set to 4 in g), because Minsdr(e) = Father(e) = d;
5. the two articulation points: a and d, and the bridge (d,e) are detected in l), k) and j) respectively.

Once the algorithm terminates, each articulation point in the network has its Biptr nonempty and each bridge has Bridge set to *true*. The members of each biconnected component can also be traced through Biptr's and Sons's at all the nodes. More precisely, each node i other than the root belongs to the biconnected component of its father's, together with the son not in BiPtr(i). And if BiPtr(i) is nonempty, then i is also the root of the biconnected components pointed to by each node in BiPtr(i). For the root node r, if its BiPtr(r) is nonempty, then it is the root of the biconnected components pointed to by each node in BiPtr(r). Otherwise, it is the root of the biconnected component pointed to by the son in Sons(r). For instance, in the last example, starting from the root a in m), we find the members of the three biconnected components: {a, b, c}, {a, d, f} and {d, e}.

4 Correctness and Complexities

Since it is trivial to show that the algorithm works correctly when the network has just one node, we assume that the network under consideration has at least two nodes. In the proof, we will refer to line numbers of the formal algorithm.

Lemma 4.1 *Each node ($\neq$ root) could send an ECHO only after it has received the first TOKEN message from its father, the VISITED's from all of its ancestors reachable through one back edges, and the ECHO's from all of its sons.*

Proof: First notice that an ECHO could only be sent by calling Search, and there are only four places where it can be called: lines 2.4, 2.9 3.7, and 4.6. Before a TOKEN is received by i ($\neq$ root), State(i) is *inactive* and Sons(i) empty, so 2.9, 3.7 and 4.6 can not be executed. Hence, line 2.4 is the only place left, and is invoked only after receiving the first TOKEN.

After receiving the first TOKEN, i becomes the center of activity and calls Search. Three cases arise now:

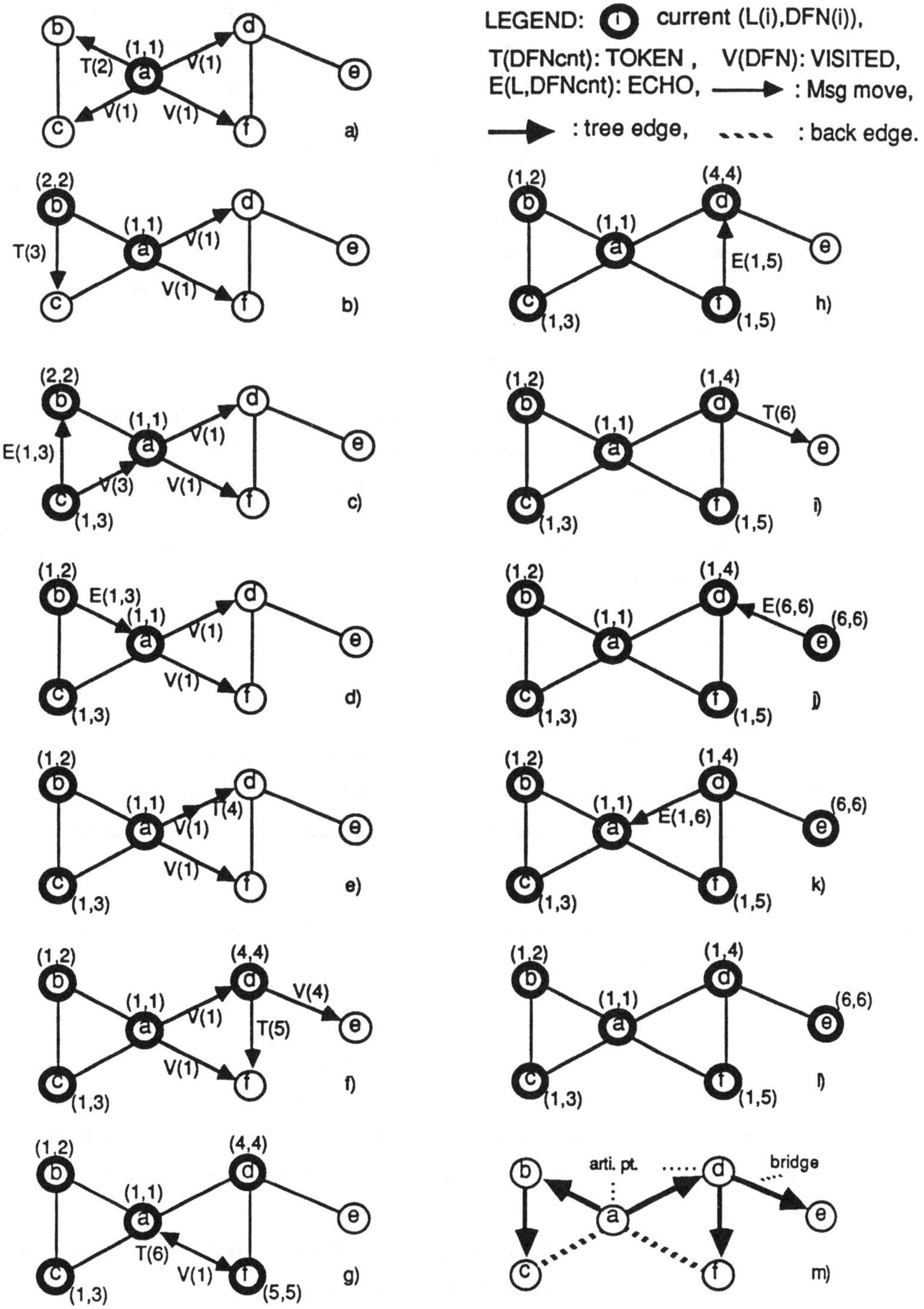

Figure 1: An example.

1. Search finds an unmarked neighbor which has actually been visited: then that node must be either an ancestor (but not a father) or a visited descendant (but not a son). So there must be a VISITED or TOKEN (sent in 2.5 or 5.2) on their way to i from the ancestor or the descendant respectively. After receiving the TOKEN or VISITED (in 2.7, 4.4), i realizes that the last TOKEN was sent to a wrong place, so it tries to visit the next unmarked neighbor by calling Search (2.9, 4.6).

2. Search finds an unmarked neighbor j which has not been visited yet: so j will become a son of i after receiving the TOKEN from i and the center of activity is also shifted to j. Since j has one less unvisited node to visit in its DFS than node i, j will eventually finish its DFS by induction argument and send an ECHO back to i (5.11). This ECHO will shift the center of activity back to i again, and i will try to visit the next unmarked neighbor by calling Search (3.7).

3. Search finds no unmarked neighbors: this means it has finished the DFS of its subtree. So it has received the VISITED's from all its ancestors connected to it by back edges and visited descendants, and all the ECHO's from its sons. Then it sends an ECHO back to its father along the tree edge (5.11).

So i will not send an ECHO to its father until it has received the VISITED's from all those ancestors connected to it by back edges and all the ECHO's from its sons. □

Corollary 4.2 *There are exactly $n - 1$ messages (ECHO's) with two DFN labels in them.*

Corollary 4.3 *The algorithm will terminate at the root node.*

Proof: Actually, lemma 4.1 also applies to the root node for its DFS, except that it receives the START instead of the first TOKEN. So it eventually will receive all ECHO's from its sons and all the VISITED's or TOKEN's from its other descendants. Then instead of sending an ECHO, it terminates the algorithm (5.6).

□

Lemma 4.4 *The root sets the correct DFN and L after receiving the START; each node ($\neq$ root) correctly sets its DFN after receiving the first TOKEN and computes its L before sending its ECHO.*

Proof: It is obvious that the root sets the correct DFN and L, both equal to 1, after receiving the START (1.2). And it also correctly sets the DFNcnt (= 2) in the TOKEN sent to the next node (5.2).

Before considering the other nodes, we first notice that the DFNcnt always contains the current DFN the next unvisited node should get. It always goes with the center of activity, either by TOKEN's to unvisited nodes (5.2) or by ECHO's back to fathers (5.11). And it is always recorded in local DFNcnt's in case recovering is needed (2.3,3.4).

Now let us consider the DFN(i) of node i ($\neq$ root). The algorithm will set its DFN(i) to the DFNcnt immediately after receiving the first TOKEN(DFNcnt) (2.3). And DFN(i) will not be changed anymore because State(i) is set to *active* also and line 2.3 is the only place to change DFN(i). By definition, this DFN(i) is the correct DFN for node i.

Next, suppose that node i is ready to send its ECHO to its father (i.e., just before 5.10 or 5.11). Notice that DFN(i) has been correctly set by the above argument. By **lemma 4.1**, i must have received the L's from all of its sons in their ECHO's, and L(i) is immediately updated upon receiving each of them (3.3); and also i must have received the DFN's of its ancestors connected by back edges in their VISITED's, and the minimum DFN of these DFN's and its sender are recorded in MinDFN(i) and Minsdr(i) (4.3). Before i sends its ECHO, L(i) is updated again with this MinDFN(i) (5.8-5.9). Since DFN(i), L's from its sons and DFN's from ancestors connected by back edges are the only data needed to compute L(i), so L(i) is fully computed now by its definition. □

Theorem 4.5 *The algorithm finds all the articulation points and bridges in a network.*

Proof: For a node i ($\neq$ root), after receiving the L from a son j, i checks if L $\geq$ DFN(i) (3.5-3.6). By **lemma 4.4**, this L is the correct L(j) of node j. So if L $\geq$ DFN(i), by condition **C1**, i is an articulation point. Then BiPtr(i) is updated by including j to indicate that it is an articulation point and also the root of the biconnected component pointed to by j.

For the root r, before the algorithm terminates, it checks $|$ Sons(r) $| \geq 2$ (5.5). By **corollary 4.3**, all of its sons have sent their ECHO's to r, and r has recorded them in Sons(i). So if $|$Sons(i)$| \geq 2$, by condition **C2**, r is an articulation point. It then sets BiPtr(i) to Sons(i) to indicate that it is an articulation point and also the roots of the biconnected components pointed to by each node in BiPtr(i).

And before i sends its ECHO, it checks if L(i) = DFN(i) (5.10). Since L(i) is fully computed by **lemma 4.4**, if L(i) = DFN(i) holds, then (Father(i), i) is a bridge by condition **C3** and Bridge(i) is set to *true*.

Therefore, when the algorithm terminates, all the articulation points will have their BiPtr's nonempty and each bridge (j,i) will have Bridge(i) be true. □

Since our algorithm is based on the DDFS algorithms from [4, 10], and for the completeness of the presentation, we include the result about the communication and time complexities from [10] in our next theorem (Although [4] proved that $3m$ is the upper bound of the number of messages needed, the proof seems to be incorrect as we showed in [1]). Also since all the messages in our algorithm contain at most two DFN labels (and only $n-1$ of them by **corollary 4.2**), plus 2 more bits to distinguish the four kinds of messages, we can conclude that the message size is bounded by $2\log n + 2$ bits.

Theorem 4.6 *The algorithm uses at most $4m - n$ messages and $2n - 2$ time, and has each message size bounded by $2\log n + 2$ bits.*

5 Discussion

It is known that $O(m)$ communication and $O(n)$ time complexities are needed, and $2m$ messages and $2n-2$ time are the lower bounds for the class of distributed algorithms which require network traversal and termination confirmation [10]. For the problem of biconnected component detection, our algorithm belongs to this class. It achieves the lower bound for time and comparable complexity for communication. Compared with the algorithm in [3] for biconnected component problem, our algorithm reduces the message size bound from $O(n \log n)$ bits to $O(\log n)$ bits and has only trivial local computations. But we do notice that Chang's algorithm may have some advantage when the diameter and size of a network are small.

For future research, we would study the fault tolerant aspect of the algorithm, and try to reduce the number of messages sent while preserving the optimal time complexity and the $O(\log n)$ message size bound. The messages can be reduced either by reducing messages in DDFS algorithms as asked in [4, 10] as well, or by finding more efficient solutions not based on DDFS.

References

[1] M. Ahuja and Y. Zhu, On the communication complexities in two distributed depth first search algorithms, OSU-CISRC-12/88-TR41, The Ohio State University.

[2] B. Awerbuch, A new distributed depth-first-search algorithm, Inform. Process. Lett. 20 (3) (1985) 147-150.

[3] E. J. H. Chang, Echo algorithms: depth parallel operations on general graphs, IEEE Trans. on Software Eng. SE-8 (4) (1982) 391-401.

[4] I. Cidon, Yet another distributed depth-first-search algorithm, Inform. Process. Lett. 26 (6) (1988) 301-305.

[5] E. Horowitz and S. Sahni, Fundamentals of Computer Algorithms, (Computer Science Press, Potomac, MD, 1978).

[6] C. Savage and J. Ja'Ja, Fast, efficient parallel algorithms for some graph problems, SIAM J. Comput. 10 (1981) 682-691.

[7] R. Tarjan and U. Vishkin, An efficient parallel biconnectivity algorithm, SIAM J. Comput. 14 (4) (1985) 862-874.

[8] R. Tarjan, Depth-first search and linear graph algorithms, SIAM J. Comput. 1 (2) (1972) 146-160.

[9] R. Tarjan, A note on finding the bridges of a graph, Inform. Process. Lett. 2 (1974) 160-161.

[10] K. Lakshmanan, N. Meenakshi and K. Thulasiraman, A time-optimal message-efficient distributed algorithm for depth first search, Inform. Process. Lett. 25 (2) (1987) 103-109.

[11] Y. Tsin and F. Chin, A general program scheme for finding bridges, Inform. Process. Lett. 17 (1983) 269-272.

[12] Y. Tsin and F. Chin, Efficient parallel algorithms for a class of graph theoretic problems, SIAM J. Comput. 13 (1984) 580-599.

Impossibility Results in the Presence of Multiple Faulty Processes

(Preliminary Version)

Gadi Taubenfeld* Shumel Katz† Shlomo Moran‡

Abstract. We investigate the impossibility of solving certain problems in an unreliable distributed system where multiple processes may fail. We assume undetectable crash failures which means that a process may become faulty at any time during an execution and that no event can happen on a process after it fails. A sufficient condition is provided for the unsolvability of problems in the presence of multiple faulty processes. Several problems are shown to be solvable in the presence of $t-1$ faulty processes but not in the presence of t faulty processes for any t. These problems are variants of problems which are unsolvable in the presence of a single faulty process (such as consensus, choosing a leader, ranking, matching). In order to prove the impossibility result a contradiction is shown among a set of axioms which characterize any fault-tolerant protocol solving the problems we treat. In the course of the proof, we present two results that appear to be of independent interest: first, we show that for any protocol there is a computation in which some process is a *splitter*. This process can split the possible outputs of the protocol to two disjoint sets. In case that the protocol is also fault-tolerant, then this splitter must be a *decider*, that can split its own output values into two different singletons. These results generalize and expand known results for asynchronous systems.

1 Introduction

In this paper we investigate the possibility and impossibility of solving certain problems in an unreliable distributed system where a number of processes may fail. We assume undetectable crash failures which means that no event can happen on a process after it fails and that failures are undetectable. For any $1 \leq t < n$, where n is the number of processes, we define a class of problems which cannot be solved in a completely asynchronous system where t processes may fail. This implies a (necessary) condition for solving a problem in such an unreliable system. These results generalize previously known impossibility results for completely asynchronous systems, and prove new results.

---

*Computer Science Department Yale University, New Haven, CT 06520. Supported in part by the National Science Foundation under grant DCR-8405478, by the Hebrew Technical Institute scholarship, and by the Guttwirth Fellowship.

†Computer Science Department, Technion, Haifa 32000, Israel.

‡Computer Science Department, Technion, Haifa 32000, Israel. Supported in part by Technion V.P.R. Funds - Wellner Research Fund, and by the Foundation for Research in Electronics, Computers and Communications, administrated by the Israel Academy of Sciences and Humanities.

Various authors have investigated the nature of systems where only a *single* process may fail (i.e., $t = 1$). It is proven in [FLP] that in asynchronous systems there cannot exist a nontrivial consensus protocol that tolerates even a single process (crash) failure. This fundamental result has been extended to other models of computation [DDS,DLS]. Various extensions [MW, Ta, BMZ], also for a single fault, prove the impossibility of other problems using several new techniques. Other recent works point out some specific problems that can be solved in asynchronous systems with numerous faulty processes, and prove impossibility results for other problems [ABDKPR,BW,DDS]. In [TKM2] a necessary and sufficient condition is provided for solving problems in an unreliable asynchronous message passing systems where undetectable *initial* failures may occur. Initial failures are a very weak type of failures where it is assumed that processes may fail only prior to the execution. Results for asynchronous shared memory systems which support only atomic read and write operations, similar to those presented here appear in [TM].

Define an input vector to be a vector $\vec{a} = (a_1, ..., a_n)$, where a_i is the input value of process p_i. A crucial assumption in all the above results (for a single process failure) is that the set of input vectors is "large enough". To demonstrate this fact, consider the consensus problem where only two input vectors are possible: either all processes read as input the value "zero" or all processes read as input the value "one". It is easy to see that under this restriction, the problem can be solved assuming any number of process failures. One of the consequences of our result is to identify a property (or a *promise* [ESY]) which a set of input vectors should satisfy so that a problem can be solved in the presence of $t-1$ faulty processes but not in the presence of t faulty processes.

We show variants of the problems which are known to be unsolvable in the presence of a single faulty process (such as consensus, choosing a leader, ranking, matching, and sorting) and prove that the variants can be solved in the presence of $t-1$ faulty processes but not in the presence of t faulty processes for any t. An example is the consensus problem where the promise is that for each input vector, $|\#1 - \#0| \geq t$. (i.e., the absolute difference between the number of ones and the number of zeroes is at least t.)

The proof of our result is constructed as follows. We first identify a class of *protocols* that cannot tolerate the failure of t processes, when operating in a completely asynchronous system. Then, we identify those *problems* which force every protocol which solves them to belong to the above class of protocols. Hence, these problems cannot be solved in a completely asynchronous system where t processes may fail.

As in [FLP], we differentiate between a process having *reached* a decision, and a stage at which the eventual decision to be reached by a process is *uniquely determined* (but usually not yet known at a process). The class of protocols for which we prove the impossibility result is characterized by two requirements on the possible input and decision (output) values of each member in the class. For the input, it is required that (for each protocol) there exists a group of at least $n-t$ processes and there exist input values such that after all the $n-t$ processes in the group read these input values, the eventual decision value of at least one of them is still not uniquely determined. As for the decision values, the decision of different processes should have the following mutual dependency: the eventual decision value of any (single) process is uniquely determined as soon as all other processes decide.

In order to prove the above result for protocols, we use an axiomatic approach for proving properties of protocols (and problems) due to Chandy and Misra [CM1,CM2]. The idea is to capture the main features of the model and the features of the class of protocols for which one wants to prove the result by a set of axioms, and to show that the result follows from the axioms. Unlike in [CM1], we define a model in which all messages are eventually delivered. We will present six axioms capturing the nature of asynchronous message passing systems, a single axiom expressing the fact that at most t processes may be faulty, and two axioms defining the class of protocols for which we want to prove the impossibility result. We then show that no protocol in the class can tolerate t faulty processes, by showing that the set of the nine axioms is inconsistent.

The rest of the paper is organized as follows. In Section 2 the notions of a problem and a protocol are defined. In Section 3 the properties of asynchronous message passing systems are stated. In Section 4 the notions of *decision* and *robustness* are introduced. In Section 5 we prove two results that appear to be of independent interest: first, we show that for any protocol there is a computation in which some process is a *splitter*. This process can split the possible outputs of the protocol to two disjoint sets. In case that the protocol is also fault-tolerant, then this splitter must be a *decider*, that can split its own output values into two different singletons. In Section 6, we use the result of the previous section along with a condition called dependency to show any protocol satisfying the conditions cannot tolerate t process failures. In Section 7, we finally identify the class of problems that cannot be solved in the presence of t process failures.

2 Definitions and Basic Notations

First, the type of problems we consider is described. Let I and D be sets of input values and decision (output) values, respectively. Let n be the number of processes, and let $\bar{I}$ and $\bar{D}$ be subsets of I^n and D^n, respectively. A problem T is a mapping $T : \bar{I} \rightarrow 2^{\bar{D}} - \{\emptyset\}$ which maps each n-tuple in $\bar{I}$ to subsets of n-tuples in $\bar{D}$. We call the vectors $\vec{a} = (a_1, ..., a_n)$ where $\vec{a} \in \bar{I}$, and $\vec{d} = (d_1, ..., d_n)$ where $\vec{d} \in \bar{D}$, the *input* vector and *decision* vector, respectively. In that case, we say that a_i is the input value of process p_i, and d_i is the decision value of process p_i.

Following are some examples of problems, referred to later in the paper (the input vectors for all problems are from I^n for an arbitrary set I): (1) The *permutation* problem, where each process $p_i (i = 1..n)$ decides on a value v_i from D, $D = 1, ..., n$, and $i \neq j$ implies $v_i \neq v_j$; (2) The *consensus* problem, where all processes are to decide on the same value from an arbitrary set D; (3) The (leader) *election* problem, where exactly one process is to decide on a distinguished value from an arbitrary set D; (4) The *sorting* problem, where all processes have input values and each process p_i decides on a value identical to the $i^t h$ smallest input value; and (5) The *rotation* problem, where each process p_i decides on a value identical to the input value of the process $p_{i(mod\ n)+1}$.

A *protocol* is a nonempty set C of *computations* and a set of process id's (abbv. processes), $N = \{p_1, ..., p_n\}$. A computation is a *finite* sequence of events. There are four types of events: *send*, *receive*, *input*, and *decide*. A *send* event, denoted $([send, m, p_k], p_i)$, represents sending a message m to process p_k by process p_i. A *receive* event, denoted $([receive, m], p_k)$, represents receiving a message m by process p_k. An *input* event, denoted $([input, a], p_i)$, represents reading a value a by process p_i. A *decide* event, denoted $([decide, d], p_i)$, represents deciding on a value d by process p_i. We use the notation (e, p_i) to denote an arbitrary event, which may be an instance of any of the above types of events. For an event (e, p_i) we say that it occurred *on* process p_i. An event is *in* a computation iff it is one of the events in the sequence which comprises the computation.

In the rest of this paper Q denotes a set of processes where $Q \subseteq N$. The symbols x, y, z denote computations. Also $\langle x; y \rangle$ is the sequence obtained by concatenating the two sequences x and y. An *extension* of a computation x is a computation of which x is a prefix. For an extension y of x, $(y - x)$ denotes the suffix of y obtained by removing x from y. For any x and p_i, let x_i be the subsequence of x containing all events in x which are on process p_i. Computation y *includes* x iff x_i is a prefix of y_i for all p_i.

We assume that all events are unique and all messages are distinguished. An event $([receive, m], p_k)$ is the *complement* of the event $([send, m, p_k], p_i)$ in a computation x iff both events are in x. An event $([send, m, p_k], p_i)$ is *fulfilled* in a computation x if it is in x and its complement event $([receive, m], p_i]$ is also in x. That is, the message m sent from process p_i to process p_k has already arrived. An event $([send, m, p_k], p_i)$ is *unfulfilled* in a computation x if it is in x, and it is not *fulfilled* in x.

Definition: x and y are *equivalent w.r.t.* p_i, denoted by $x \overset{i}{\sim} y$, iff $x_i = y_i$.
Note that the relation $\overset{i}{\sim}$ is an equivalence relation over system computations. For a computation x and p_i, we define the extensions of x which only have events on p_i.

Definition: $Extensions(x, i) \equiv \{y | y \text{ is an extension of } x \text{ and } x \overset{j}{\sim} y \text{ for all } j \neq i\}$.

Process p_i *reads* input a in x iff the input event $([input, a], p_i)$ is in x. Process p_i *decides* on d in x iff the decision event $([decide, d], p_i)$ is in x. A computation x is *i-input* iff for some value a, p_i reads input a in x. A computation x is *i-decided* iff for some value d, p_i decides on d in x. We assume that a process may read and decide only once.

A *protocol* $P = (C, N)$ *solves* a problem $T : \bar{I} \rightarrow 2^{\bar{D}} - \{\emptyset\}$ iff (1) For every input vector $\vec{a} \in \bar{I}$, and for every decision vector $\vec{d} \in T(\vec{a})$, there exists a computation $z \in C$ such that in z processes $p_1, \ldots, p_n$ read input values $a_1, \ldots, a_n$ and decide on $d_1, \ldots, d_n$; (2) For every computation $z \in C$ such that in z processes $p_1, \ldots, p_n$ read input values $a_1, \ldots, a_n$ and decide on $d_1, \ldots, d_n$, if $\vec{a} \in \bar{I}$ then $\vec{d} \in T(\vec{a})$; and (3) In any "sufficiently long" computation on input in $\bar{I}$ all processes decide (this last requirement is to be defined precisely later). It is also possible to define solvability so that (1) is replaced by the requirement that for each input vector $\vec{a} \in \bar{I}$, there exists a computation with $\vec{a}$ as input. In such a case we will say that a protocol P *minimally solves* a problem T.

We define when a set of input events is consistent. Intuitively, this is the case when all the input events in the set can happen in the same computation. Let P be a protocol that solves a problem $T : \bar{I} \rightarrow 2^{\bar{D}} - \{\emptyset\}$ For any input vector $\vec{a} \in \bar{I}$, the set $([input, a_1], p_1)$,..., $([input, a_n], p_n)$ is a consistent set of input events (w.r.t. T); and any subset of a consistent set of input events is also consistent. For simplicity of presentation, we assume that in any given computation the set of input events is consistent. An input event is said to be consistent with a *computation* y if it is consistent with the input events of y. Throughout the paper we consider a single protocol, $P = (C, N)$, that solves a problem $T : \bar{I} \rightarrow 2^{\bar{D}} - \{\emptyset\}$ and all references are made to that protocol.

3 Asynchronous Environment

In this section asynchronous message passing systems are characterized by stating six properties that any protocol which is operating in such an environment should satisfy.

The description considered here is similar to that of [Ta] and is based on [CM1,CM2]. We first introduce the notion of an *enabled* process. Process p_i is *enabled* at computation x iff there exists an event (e, p_i) such that $\langle x; (e, p_i)\rangle$ is a computation.

Definition: An *asynchronous protocol* is a protocol that satisfies the properties,

P1 Every prefix of a computation is a computation.

P2 Let x and y be computations such that y includes x and $x \overset{i}{\sim} y$. If $\langle x; (e, p_i)\rangle$ is a computation and (e, p_i) is not an input event which is inconsistent with y, then $\langle y; (e, p_i)\rangle$ is also a computation.

P3 For any computation x, process p_i and input value a, if the set of all input events in x together with $([input, a], p_i)$ is consistent, then there exists y in $Extensions(x, i)$, such that $([input, a], p_i)$ appears in y.

P4 For any computation $y = \langle x; (e, p_h)\rangle$ where (e, p_h) is an input event, any process $p_i \neq p_h$, and any computation $z \in Extensions(y, i)$, the sequence $\langle x; (z - y)\rangle$ is also a computation.

P5 For an *unfulfilled* event $([send, m, p_k], p_i)$ in a computation x, there exists an extension y of x such that $y \in Extensions(x, k)$, and $([send, m, p_k], p_i)$ is $fulfilled$ in y.

P6 For a computation x and an event $([receive, m], p_k)$, the sequence $\langle x; ([receive, m], p_k)\rangle$ is a computation only if $([receive, m], p_k)$ is the complement of some *unfulfilled* event in x.

Intuitively, property $P2$ means that if an event (e, p_i) can happen at a process p_i at some point in a computation, then the same event can happen at a later point, provided that p_i has taken no steps between the two points, and either it is not an input event or it is an input event consistent with the input events up to the later point. Property $P3$ means that a process which has not yet read an input value, may read any of the input values which do not conflict with the input values already read by other processes. Property $P4$ means that an input event on one process does not enable events of some other process. Property $P5$ means that it is always possible for a process to receive a message sent Property $P6$ means that a message is received only if it was sent previously and that it cannot be received twice.

Observation 1: In any asynchronous protocol, for computations x, y, z, if $y \in Extensions(x, i)$, z is an extension of x such that $x \overset{i}{\sim} z$ and y does not contain input events that are inconsistent with z, then $\langle z; (y - x)\rangle$ is a computation.

Observation 2: For any computations x and y, and for any process p_i; if y is an extension of x, p_i is *enabled* at x, and $x \overset{i}{\sim} y$ then p_i is *enabled* at y.

4 Decisions and Robustness

In this section we identify two classes of protocols, called *decision(t)* protocols, and *robust(t)* protocols, with t an integer, $0 \leq t < n$. In a decision(t) protocol every process tries to decide on a certain value, and additional conditions hold, to be defined below.

A decision is irreversible, that is, once a process decides on a value, the decision value cannot be changed. The important features of such protocols are the requirements on the possible input and decision (output) values. Here we require that there exists a group of at least $n-t$ processes and there exist input values such that after all the $n-t$ processes read these input values, the eventual decision value of at least one of them is still not uniquely determined. Compared with the usual requirement in other works where the above group should include all the processes, this requirement is very weak.

Typical examples of such protocols are those that solve any of the problems described in the Introduction and Section 2, where various assumptions, depending on the value of t, are made about the set of input vectors for each of these problems.

The following definition generalizes the notion of *valency* of a computation from [FLP]. Let d be a possible decision value and let U, W be sets of decision values.

Definition: A computation x is *(i, W)-valent* iff (1) for every $d \in W$, there is an extension z of x such that p_i decides on d in z, and (2) for every $d \notin W$, there is no extension z of x such that p_i decides on d in z.

A computation is *i-univalent* iff it is *(i,d)-valent* for some (single) value d. It is *i-multivalent* otherwise. It is *univalent* iff it is *i-univalent* for all $i = 1..n$. As we shall see later no computation in a protocol studied here is *$(i, \emptyset)$-valent*.

Lemma 1: In any asynchronous protocol, if x is *(i, W)-valent* computation, y is *(i, U)-valent* computation, and y *includes* x then $U \subseteq W$.

Proof: We prove that for an arbitrary value d, $d \in U$ implies $d \in W$. Assume $d \in U$. By the definition of *valency* there exists an extension z of y such that p_i decides on d in z. Clearly, the computation z includes x. It follows from properties $P1$, $P2$ and $P3$ that there exists an extension z' of x such that $z \overset{i}{\sim} z'$. (To see this, take z' as the concatenation of x with the subsequence of all events in z which are not in x.) Since, p_i decides on d in z and $z \overset{i}{\sim} z'$ it follows (from the definition of *decides*) that p_i decides on d in z'. Since z' is an extension of x, $d \in W$. □

Definition: Let y and y' be *(i, W)-valent* and *(i, W')-valent*, respectively. Then y and y' are *i-compatible* iff $W \cap W' \neq \emptyset$. They are *compatible* iff they are *i-compatible* for all $i = 1..n$.

Using the above notions we are now able to characterize decision(t) protocols formally.

Definition: A *decision(t) protocol* is a protocol that satisfies the requirement:

N(t): There exists a computation x, process p_j and set of processes Q, such that $|Q| \geq n-t$, for every $p_i \in Q$ x is *i-input*, $p_j \in Q$, and x is *j-multivalent*. (non-triviality.)

It is not difficult to see why any protocol that solves the variant of the consensus problem which is mentioned in the introduction (i.e., with the promise that for each input vector, $|\#1 - \#0| \geq t$) must satisfy $N(t)$. As will be shown later in Section 7, any problem that can be solved by a protocol that does not satisfy $N(t)$, can also be solved by a trivial protocol in which every process decides after having $n-t$ input values. Notice that $N(t)$ implies $N(t+1)$. This requirement generalizes a requirement from Lemma 2 of [FLP], that a nontrivial consensus protocol must have a bivalent initial configuration.

Next we identify the class of *robust(t)* protocols. A failure of a process means that no subsequent event can happen on this process. This is a very weak type of failure, called crash failure. Since we want to prove an impossibility result, it follows that if the result holds for crash failures it also holds for any stronger type of failure.

In order to define robust(t) protocols formally, we need the concept of a *Q-fair sequence*. Let Q be a set of processes, a *Q-fair sequence* w.r.t. a given protocol is a (possibly infinite) sequence of events, where: (1) Each finite prefix is a computation; (2) For an *enabled* process $p_i \in Q$ at some prefix x, there exists another prefix y which is an extension of x such that there is an event (e, p_i) in $(y-x)$; (3) For any event $([send, m, p_k], p_i)$ which is *unfulfilled* in some prefix, if process $p_k \in Q$, then $([send, m, p_k], p_i)$ is *fulfilled* in another prefix; (4) The sequence $\langle x; ([receive, m], p_k)\rangle$, is a prefix only if $([receive, m], p_k)$ is the complement of some *unfulfilled* event in x, and (5) Every process p_k not in Q appears only finitely often in the sequence.

A Q-fair sequence captures the intuition of an execution where all enabled processes which belong to Q can proceed, all messages sent to processes belonging to Q are eventually delivered and a message is received only if it was sent previously. By (5), a process not in Q eventually either is not enabled or simply stops taking actions. Notice that a Q-fair sequence may be *infinite* and in such a case it is not a computation. It follows from Observation 2, $P5$ and $P6$ that for every set of processes Q, any computation is a prefix of a Q-fair sequence. Requirement (4) follows from $P6$ and requirement (1).

Definition: A *robust(t) protocol* is a protocol that satisfies the requirement:

R(t): For every set Q of processes where $|Q| \geq n-t$, every Q *-fair sequence* has a finite prefix that is i *-decided* for every $p_i \in Q$.

Note that the class of robust($t+1$) protocols is included in the class of robust(t) protocols. Furthermore, from examples of protocols which are robust(t) but not robust($t+1$), we can see that the inclusion is strict. Requirement $R(0)$ formally expresses requirement (3) from the definition of *solves* given in Section 2. It follows from $R(0)$ and from the fact that every computation is a prefix of some N-fair sequence that (in asynchronous robust(0) protocols) no computation is $(i, \emptyset)$*-valent*.

Lemma 2: In any asynchronous robust(0) protocol, for any *i-input* computation x, for any computation $y \in Extensions(x, i)$ and for any extension z of x, if $x \overset{i}{\sim} z$ then y and z are *compatible*.

Proof: Assume $x \overset{i}{\sim} z$. From Observation 1, $\langle z; (y-x)\rangle$ is a computation. The computation $\langle z; (y-x)\rangle$ includes both y and z. Thus, from Lemma 1 and the fact that no computation is $(i, \emptyset)$*-valent* (for all $i = 1..n$), y and z are *compatible*. □

5 Splitters and Deciders

In this section we prove that for any asynchronous, non-trivial protocol there is a computation in which some process is a *splitter*. This process can split the possible outputs of the protocol to two disjoint sets. This result holds both for fault-free and for fault-tolerant protocols. In fault-tolerant protocols, this splitter must be a *decider*, that can split its own output values into two different singletons. Our Decider Theorem generalizes a previous result by Chandy and Misra [CM1, Theorem 1], in which they proved a similar condition for commit protocols in the presence of a single faulty process. A result resembling our Decider Theorem was presented independently in [BW].

Let us consider the eight requirements mentioned so far. All of them capture very natural concepts: $P1 - P6$ and $R(t)$ express the well known notions of asynchronous and robust protocols respectively, while $N(t)$ requires that a given solution is not trivial. This motivates the question of what can be said about protocols that satisfy all the above requirements. For later reference we call these protocols Decision(t) Asynchronous Robust(t) Protocols (abbv. DEAR(t) P's).

In order to state our result, we first define the notions of a *j-splitter* and a *decider*. Informally, a process p_i is a *j-splitter* at a computation x, if it is possible to extend x with two sequences of events on process p_i only, in such a way that the (single) value some process p_j can (still) decide on in each of the resulting two computations, differ. In particular when process p_i is an *i-splitter*, we say that p_i is a *decider* at x.

Definition: A process p_i is a *j-splitter* at a computation x iff there exist two *j-univalent* computations y and y', both belonging to *Extensions*(x, i), such that y and y' are not *j-compatible*. A process p_i is a *decider* at a computation x iff p_i is an *i-splitter* at a computation x.

Lemma 3 (The Splitter Lemma): In any asynchronous robust(0) protocol, if x is a *j-multivalent* computation then there is an extension v of x and a process p_i such that p_i is a *j-splitter* at v.

Proof: Let x be a *j-multivalent* computation. We must show an extension v of x and a process p_i such that *Extensions*(v, i) contains *j-univalent* computations y and y' which are not *j-compatible*. We use the following definition. Computation x is *j-open w.r.t. process* p_i iff any $y \in$ *Extensions*(x, i) is *j-multivalent*. We consider two cases.

Case 1: Assume that there exists a *j-multivalent* extension x' of x and a process p_i such that any extension v of x' is not *j-open w.r.t. process* p_i.

Let v be an extension of x' as above. We denoted by $\Phi(v)$, one (arbitrary) *j-univalent* extension of v, with events only on p_i (such an extension must exist because v is not *j-open w.r.t.* p_i). If v is not *i-input*, we choose an extension $\Phi(v)$ that includes an input event on p_i (this is possible due to $P3$). Since x' is *j-multivalent*, there is an extension z of x' ($z \neq x'$) such that z and $\Phi(x')$ are not *j-compatible*. Consider the extensions of x' which are also prefixes of z. Since z and $\Phi(x')$ are not *j-compatible*, there exist two extensions y and y' of x' such that $\Phi(y)$ and $\Phi(y')$ are not *j-compatible*, and where y is a one event extension of y'. Therefore $y = \langle y'; (e, p_h)\rangle$ for some event (e, p_h).

If $p_i = p_h$, then $\Phi(y)$ and $\Phi(y')$ both belong to *Extensions*(y', i), and the lemma is proven. If $p_i \neq p_h$, and either y' is *i-input* or (e, p_h) is not an input event, then by Observation 1, $w = \langle y; (\Phi(y') - y')\rangle$ is a computation. From the construction, $w \in$ *Extensions*(y, i). Since w includes $\Phi(y')$ (which is *j-univalent*), by Lemma 1 w is also *j-univalent*, with the same value. Moreover, since $\Phi(y)$ and $\Phi(y')$ are not *j-compatible*, it follows that $\Phi(y)$ and w are also not *j-compatible*, and the Lemma again holds.

If $p_i \neq p_h$, and both (e, p_h) is an input event on p_h, and y' is not *i-input*, then the w above may not be a computation, because the input event (e, p_h) could be inconsistent with an input event on p_i. However, by $P4$, $w' = \langle y'; (\Phi(y) - y)\rangle$ (i.e., not including the input event on p_h) is a computation. By $P2$ and the definition of Φ, $\langle \Phi(w'); (e, p_h)\rangle$ (i.e., adding the input event on p_h) is a *j-univalent* computation (here we use the fact that $(\Phi(y) - y)$ has an input event on p_i which *is* consistent with (e, p_h)). By Lemma 1, $\langle \Phi(w'), (e, p_h)\rangle$ is *j-compatible* with $\Phi(w')$. Since $\langle \Phi(w'); (e, p_h)\rangle$ includes $\Phi(y)$, also $\Phi(w')$

and $\Phi(y)$ are *j-compatible*. This, and the fact that $\Phi(y)$ and $\Phi(y')$ are not *j-compatible*, imply that $\Phi(w')$ and $\Phi(y')$, which both belong to $Extension(y', i)$, are both *j-univalent* and are not *j-compatible*. This implies the lemma.

Case 2: The negation of Case 1. That is, assume that for every *j-multivalent* extension x' of x and for every p_i, there exists an extension v of x' which is *j-open w.r.t.* p_i.

Using this assumption, we derive a contradiction similar to that in [FLP] by constructing an N-fair sequence $\mathcal{F}$ such that all its finite prefixes are *j-multivalent*.

The construction of $\mathcal{F}$ is done in steps. At each step m we extend the *j-multivalent* sequence $\mathcal{F}_{m-1}$ constructed at step $m-1$ to a *j-multivalent* sequence $\mathcal{F}_m$. $\mathcal{F}_0$ is the given *j-multivalent* computation. At each step $m \geq 1$, we set $i = m \ (mod\ n)$. If p_i is not enabled at $\mathcal{F}_m$ then we let $\mathcal{F}_m = \mathcal{F}_{m-1}$. If p_i is enabled, we first extend $\mathcal{F}_{m-1}$ to a computation v which is *j-open w.r.t.* p_i. Since we can extend the computation v by an arbitrary (possible) event on p_i and still get a *j-multivalent* computation, we choose one such extension so that p_i eventually reads its input and receives each message sent to it. The resulting sequence is $\mathcal{F}_m$. Thus we can construct an N-fair sequence which is everywhere *j-multivalent*, contradicting $R(0)$. This case is therefore impossible. □

Lemma 4: In any asynchronous robust(1) protocol, for any *i-input* computation x and any process p_j where $i \neq j$, process p_i is not a *j-splitter* at x.

Proof: Let y and y' both belong to $Extensions(x, i)$. Apply $P1 - P6$ and $R(1)$ to conclude that there is a *j-univalent* extension z of x such that $x \overset{i}{\sim} z$. From Lemma 2, both y, z and y', z are compatible. Since z is *j-univalent*, y and y' are *j-compatible*. □

THEOREM 1 (The Decider Theorem): In any DEAR(t) P, there exists a *j-input* computation v and a process p_j, such that p_j is a *decider* at v.

Proof: Let x be a *j-multivalent* computation satisfying $N(t)$, and let Q be the corresponding set of processes, where $p_j \in Q$. By Lemma 3, there is an extension v of x and a process p_i such that p_i is a *j-splitter* at v. We must show that $i = j$. Assume, for contradiction, that $i \neq j$, and let y and y' be any two computations in $Extension(v, i)$. We will show that y and y' must be *j-compatible* if $j \neq i$, which will contradict the assumption that p_i is a *j-splitter* at v.

If the computation v above is *i-input*, then we are done by Lemma 4. Otherwise, v is not *i-input*, and by $N(t)$ $p_i \notin Q$, by $N(t)$. By $R(t)$, there is a *j-univalent* extension z of v such that only processes from Q are activated in $(z - v)$; in particular, $(z - v) \overset{i}{\sim} v$ and $(z - v)$ contains no input events (since those from Q were already in v).

Let $w = \langle y; (z - v) \rangle$ and $w' = \langle y'; (z - v) \rangle$. By Observation 1, both w and w' are computations. Also, since both w and w' include z, and since z is *j-univalent*, w and w' are *j-compatible*. Since w includes y and w' includes y', y and y' are also *j-compatible*. This is the desired contradiction, and the Theorem is proven. □

6 Robust(t) Asynchronous Dependent(t) Protocols

In the previous sections we have defined several classes of protocols. In this section we investigate the class of robust(t) asynchronous dependent(t) protocols (abbv. ROAD(t) P's). The class of ROAD(t) P's is defined by the previous eight axioms, plus the following requirement, which we call *dependency*.

Definition: A *dependent(t) protocol* is a protocol that satisfies the requirement:

D: For any computation x, if every process has read an input value in x and x is a *j-decided* computation for all $j = 1..i-1, i+1..n$ then x is *i-univalent.* (dependency.)

Requirement D means that as soon as all processes except one have made their decisions, and all processes have read their input, the eventual decision value of the remaining process is uniquely determined. All protocols which solve the problems mentioned in the Introduction and in Section 2 satisfy D. Notice that, for two *univalent* computations x and y which are *j-compatible* for all $j = 1..i-1, i+1..n$, it does not follow from requirement D that x and y are also *i-compatible.*

We prove in this section that for any $1 \leq t \leq n$, the class of ROAD(t) P's is an *empty* class. Put another way, we show that there does not exist any ROAD(t) P.

Lemma 5: In any ROAD(t) P, for any *i-input* computation x, there exists a *univalent* extension z of x such that $x \overset{i}{\sim} z$.

Proof: It follows from Observation 2, $P5$ and $P6$, that for any process p_i, any computation x is a prefix of some $(N-\{p_i\})$-fair sequence. Apply requirement $R(1)$ to the above sequence to conclude that, for any computation x and any process p_i, there exists an extension z' of x such that $x \overset{i}{\sim} z'$ and z' is *j-decided* for any $j \neq i$. By $P3$ there is an extension z of z' in which all processes read their input and $x \overset{i}{\sim} z$. From D the computation z is *univalent.* □

Lemma 6: In any ROAD(t) P, for any *i-input* computation x, any two computations y and y' which belong to *Extensions*(x, i) are *compatible.*

Proof: Let y and y' both belong to *Extensions*(x, i). Apply Lemma 5 to conclude that there is a *univalent* extension z of x such that $x \overset{i}{\sim} z$. From Lemma 2, both y, z and y', z are compatible. Since z is *univalent*, y and y' are *compatible.* □

Now the main theorem can be stated and proven.

THEOREM 2: There is no ROAD(t) P.

Proof: By Theorem 1 there exists a computation x and process p_i for which p_i is a decider at x. However, this means precisely that there are two computations in *Extensions*(x, i) which are not compatible, contradicting Lemma 6. □

7 Dependent(t) Problems

In this section we identify the problems that cannot be solved in an unreliable asynchronous message passing system. We do this by identifying those problems which are solved only by ROAD(t) protocols. Hence, the impossibility of solving these problems will follow from Theorem 2.

We say that a problem can be solved in an environment where t processes may fail, if there exists a robust(t) protocol that solves it. Since we assume that up to t processes may fail, any protocol that solves a problem should satisfy properties $P1 - P6$, and the requirement $R(t)$. Thus, we are now left with the obligation of identifying those problems which force any protocol that solves them also to satisfy requirements $N(t)$ and D. Let Q

denote a set of processes, and $\vec{v}$ and $\vec{v'}$ be vectors. We say that $\vec{v}$ and $\vec{v'}$ are *Q-equivalent*, if they agree on all the values which correspond to the indices (of the processes) in Q. A set of vectors H is *Q-equivalent* if any two vectors which belong to H are *Q-equivalent*. Also, we define: $T(H) \equiv \bigcup_{\vec{a} \in H} T(\vec{a})$.

Definition: A problem $T : \bar{I} \rightarrow 2^{\bar{D}} - \{\emptyset\}$ is a *dependent(t) problem* iff it satisfies:

T1(t): There exists a set of processes Q where $|Q| \geq n-t$, and there exists a *Q-equivalent* set $H \subseteq \bar{I}$ such that $T(H)$ is not a *Q-equivalent* set.

T2: For every $\vec{a} \in \bar{I}$, every set of processes Q where $|Q| = n-1$, and every two different decision vectors $\vec{d}$ and $\vec{d'}$, if both $\vec{d}$ and $\vec{d'}$ belong to $T(\vec{a})$ then they are not *Q-equivalent*.

Requirement $T1(t)$ means that $n-t$ input values (in an input vector) do not determine the corresponding $n-t$ decision values (in the decision vectors). Any problem that does not satisfy requirement $T1(t)$ can easily be solved in a completely asynchronous environment where t processes may fail. (Each process sends its input value to all other processes, then it waits until it receives $n-t$ values; assuming it does not satisfies $T1(t)$, it has now enough information to decide.) Note that $T1(t)$ implies $T1(t+1)$. Requirement $T2$ means that a single input vector cannot be mapped into two decision vectors that differ only by a single value.

THEOREM 3: A dependent(t) problem cannot be solved in an asynchronous message passing system where up to t failures may occur.

A problem $T : \bar{I} \rightarrow 2^{\bar{D}} - \{\emptyset\}$ *includes* a problem $T : \bar{I'} \rightarrow 2^{\bar{D}'} - \{\emptyset\}$ iff $\bar{I'} = \bar{I}$, and for every $\vec{a'} \in \bar{I'}$: $T'(\vec{a'}) \subseteq T(\vec{a'})$. It is easy to see that a protocol P *minimally solves* a problem T iff there exists a problem T' which is included in T such that P *solves* T'. A problem $T' : \bar{I} \rightarrow 2^{\bar{D}'} - \{\emptyset\}$ is a *sub-problem* of a problem $T : \bar{I} \rightarrow 2^{\bar{D}} - \{\emptyset\}$ iff $\bar{I'} \subseteq \bar{I}$, and for every $\vec{a'} \in \bar{I'}$: $T(\vec{a'}) = T'(\vec{a'})$. It is easy to see that if a protocol P *solves* (*minimally solves*) a problem T then P *solves* (*minimally solves*) any sub-problem T' of T.

8 Discussion

We showed that for the message passing model there exists a resiliency hierarchy. That is, for each $0 \leq t < n-1$ there are problems that can be solved in the presence of $t-1$ failures but can not be solved in the presence of t failures.

The identities of processes have been used by us for the purposes of the metadiscussion in the proofs. However, no assumption has been made about whether or not process ids are known (available) to the processes themselves. Thus the impossibility result we have proven holds even for the strongest possible assumption about identifiers, namely that all processes have distinct identifiers which are universally known.

It is simple to modify the presentation to allow an atomic *broadcast* instead of the usual *send* event. Also, by simply modifying property $P6$, we can show that the result holds even under the assumption that messages sent from one process to another are received in the order they were sent (i.e., FIFO). Few more generalizations of the results mentioned so far are included in [TKM1, Section 8].

Acknowledgements: We are most grateful to Nissim Francez, Oded Goldreich, Joe Halpern, and Yaron Wolfstahl for many helpful discussions concerning this work.

References

[ABDKPR] Attiya, H., Bar-Noy, A., Dolev, D., Koller, D., Peleg, D., and Reischuk, R. Achievable cases in an asynchronous environment, *ACM-FOCS* 1987, 337-346.

[BMZ] Biran, O., Moran S., and Zaks, S. A Combinatorial characterization of the distributed tasks which are solvable in the presence of one faulty processor, *ACM-PODC* 1988, 263-275.

[BW] Bridgland, M., and Watro, R. Fault-tolerant decision making in totally asynchronous distributed systems, *ACM-PODC* 1987, 52-63.

[CM1] Chandy, M., and Misra, J. On the nonexistence of robust commit protocols, Unpublished manuscript, November 1985.

[CM2] Chandy, M., and Misra, J. How processes learn, *Distributed Computing* 1986, 40-52.

[DDS] Dolev, D., Dwork, C., Stockmeyer, L. On the minimal synchronism needed for distributed consensus, *JACM 34*, 1, 1987, 77-97.

[DLS] Dwork, C., Lynch, N., Stockmeyer, L. Consensus in the presence of partial synchrony, *JACM 35*, 2, 1988, 288-323.

[ESY] Even, S., Selman A., and Yacobi, Y. The complexity of promise problems with applications to public-key cryptography, *Information and Control* 1984, 159-173.

[FLP] Fischer, M., Lynch, N., Paterson, M. Impossibility of distributed consensus with one faulty process, *JACM 32*, 2, 1985, 374-382.

[MW] Moran, S., and Wolfstahl, Y. An extended impossibility result for asynchronous complete networks, *IPL 26*, November 1987, 145-151.

[Ta] Taubenfeld, G. Impossibility Results for Decision Protocols, Technion Technical Report #445, January 1987. Revised version, Technion TR #506, April 1988.

[TKM1] Taubenfeld, G., Katz, S., and Moran, S. Impossibility results in the presence of multiple faulty processes, Technion Technical Report #492, January 1988.

[TKM2] Taubenfeld, G., Katz, S., and Moran, S. Initial failures in distributed computations, Technion Technical Report #517, August 1988.

[TM] Taubenfeld, G., and Moran, S. Possibility and impossibility results in a shared memory environment, To appear in *3rd International workshop on distributed algorithms*, Nice, France, September 1989. Also, *Yale technical report YALEU/DCS/TR-708* (May 1989).

AN ADAPTIVE REGULATOR APPROACH
FOR THE DESIGN OF LOAD SHARING ALGORITHMS

By
F. Bonomi,
AT&T Bell Laboratories, Holmdel, New Jersey, USA,
and
P.J. Fleming and P. Steinberg,
AT&T Bell Laboratories, Naperville, Illinois, USA

1. *INTRODUCTION*

In this paper we present a description and an application of a general approach to the design of load sharing algorithms for a class of multiprocessor systems, which is somewhat inspired by the so called ***adaptive regulators*** of control system theory. Regulators are controlled systems which tend to maintain a given operating condition.

The most important performance indices for a load sharing algorithm on a multiprocessor computer are the user-perceived performance measures usually described in terms of response time and throughput. Often, these indices are too high-level to be of immediate use to an automatic load sharing algorithm.

The underlying philosophy of our approach is that there is some internal state (or states) of the system that need to be maintained in order to provide optimal (or near optimal) user-perceived performance. Maintaining the system in such "desirable" internal states involves maintaining balance in some easily quantified load measure such as the average queue length at a processor, or the average fraction of time a processor is idle (known commonly as "idle time"). More specifically, we can formulate our design approach in the following steps:

- Identify suitable load indices characterizing the state of the system.
- Identify a desirable operating condition for the system, defined in terms of the adopted load indices.
- Determine a measure of deviation from such desired condition which can be estimated by measuring the load indices on the system.
- Define a load assignment algorithm which drives the system to achieve and maintain the desired operating condition.

This sequence of steps can be recognized in the definition of the load sharing algorithm for a UNIX® multiprocessor sytem discussed in this paper. The algorithm has been successfully implemented on the AT&T 3B4000 computer system.

In the UNIX® systems we consider, load sharing is performed by assigning each newly created process (created, for example, via the `exec(2)` system call in the UNIX® System V Operating System) to a particular processing element, where it will remain until termination. Thus we do not consider the option of process migration. We utilize a combination of the available instantaneous information about the number of processes active on each processing element and periodically collected average CPU run-queue-length information in an algorithm that is an adaptive version of the Join-the-Biased-Queue policy [13]. The bias components are recalculated periodically by using a simple stochastic approximation procedure. The algorithm tries to maintain a balance in the normalized average CPU run queue lengths at the various processors. In practice, it behaves as an adaptive regulator where the criterion of performance is the deviation of the observed normalized run queue lengths from a condition of balance. The algorithm is simple to implement and the processing overhead is very small. We refer to this algorithm as AJBQ, which stands for "Adaptive Join the Biased Queue." Implementation experience, simulation studies and laboratory measurements, confirm that AJBQ is characterized by superior response time and throughput performance, stability, and robustness with respect to workload, file system and hardware configurations.

Our approach has wide applicability in multiserver architectures with a distinguished processor that assigns new work to processors. We provide a concrete reference for the study of the behavior and performance of AJBQ, compared to other practical load sharing algorithms, by discussing its implementation on the AT&T 3B4000 multiprocessor computer system. For references in the vast literature on load sharing problems see [3,4,7,12] for more theoretical studies, and [5,6,8,10] for works emphasizing implementations.

The presentation is organized as follows. In Section 2 we discuss the types of loosely-coupled computer systems where AJBQ can be successfully applied and, as a particular case, we briefly describe the AT&T 3B4000 computer system. In Section 3 we define AJBQ. In Section 4 we present the results of a comparative study of load sharing algorithms with simulation experiments and laboratory measurements. Section 5 contains our conclusions.

2. ARCHITECTURAL FRAMEWORK

The approach to load sharing described in this paper applies generally to distributed computing systems possessing a distinguished processor (called a master processor) which assigns dispatchable entities to the various processing elements of the system. The dispatchable entities may be processes, as in the UNIX® System V Operating System, or threads as in the MACH operating system [1] or a database management system, or data network packets or circuits as in a data communication network. We call these dispatchable entities "processes" for the sake of discussion, since our implementation study was done on a UNIX® system. This category is general enough to include systems with different speed processors and distributed file systems, as described in [2], where a significant fraction of the processing and disk resources used by a process are remote from the processor where the process resides. For example, a process may be assigned to a processor that has no mass storage device directly attached to it. Thus, when the process requires data (or text) from a storage device attached to another processor in the distributed system, it expends CPU cycles on that remote processor. The master processor usually won't know about the remote resource requirements of a new or currently running process.

To compound the problem, processes have large variance in the amount of system resources required during their lifetime. Some processes sleep waiting for a stimulus for hours, while other processes are CPU- or disk-intensive. These attributes of a process cannot be known at the time the process is assigned except in rare cases.

A concrete reference architecture where the approach to the design of load sharing argorithm presented here has been successfully applied is provided by the AT&T 3B4000 computer system. The AT&T 3B4000 computer system is a multiprocessor system that runs a distributed version of the AT&T UNIX® System V operating system. It contains a Master Processor (MP) and up to 16 Adjunct Processing Elements (APEs), connected together via a very high bandwidth system bus. The MP can run stand-alone, and the APEs are added as processing and I/O capabilities are needed. The APEs can be of two different types according to their function as Adjunct Communication Processor (ACP) or as a regular Adjunct Processing Element (EADP). While the MP and the ACPs are AT&T minicomputers (AT&T 3B15 and AT&T 3B2/600, respectively), the EADPs are single board computers. The relative CPU speeds of MP, ACPs, and EADPs are approximately 1, 1.6, and 2, respectively. The architecture has many of the features of a highly-coupled network of supermini-computers. The main difference is that from the user/programmer point of view the system looks like a single UNIX® machine. See reference [14] for a detailed description of the hardware components of the system. For a more comprehensive treatment of the software architecture, see reference [15]. Each adjunct runs a separate kernel in which accesses to main memory are local. The basic mechanism used in the operating system to implement the distributed operating system is the remote procedure call. Embedded within each system call is a filter function that determines whether the resource being requested is local to the APE on which the system call occurs or remote. Here "resource" refers to file descriptors, message queues, pipes, etc. If the resource is local, the local kernel continues by way of the standard UNIX® operating system implementation. If it is remote, the request is packaged and sent, by way of the kernel-to-kernel protocol, to the appropriate APE. The request may be sent directly to the agent of the requesting process on another APE, termed a ***stub process***, or simply, a stub. A stub process is a sleepable, dispatchable portion of an extended process that resides on an APE or the MP remote from the main user portion of the process.

There are two observations about the AT&T 3B4000 computer operating system that are key to understanding the design of its automatic load-balancing algorithm. First, the fact that every user process **must** have a stub on the MP means that the MP knows where the user process image is at all times and also knows when it terminates (i.e., exits). However, the MP is not aware of the existence of stubs on other processors. This information will be used in the load sharing algorithm proposed in this paper. Second, the MP receives a packet of data, called a "sanity packet", at regular intervals from each APE to make the MP aware of the ability of an APE to execute a process. Data related to the load of each individual APE can be "piggy-backed" with these sanity packets with negligible additional overhead.

3. THE ADAPTIVE JOIN THE BIASED QUEUE ALGORITHM

The adaptive algorithm described in this paper attempts to balance, over the various processors, the queue lengths of processes ready to receive CPU processing (i.e., the CPU run-queue lengths), normalized by processor speed. However, the use of average CPU idle time is an alternative, and has been proposed in a similar context [4]. Our choice of the average CPU run-queue length as a load index is based on the fact that CPU is the scarce resource for the system we consider. For systems where this is not true, various generalizations of the average queue length index are possible (see, for example [8]).

In the next section we define and discuss the algorithm we designed in order to maintain the desired balance in the average CPU run-queue lengths among the various processing elements.

3.1 Description of the AJBQ Algorithm

We first formally define the AJBQ algorithm. As mentioned above, the key rationale behind the design of AJBQ is that a condition of balance in the normalized average CPU run queue lengths for the various processors provides a desirable operating point for the system, in terms of throughput and average response time.

With this observation in mind, let M be the number of processing elements in the multiprocessor system (including the master processor), and let μ_i, i=1,...,M be the service rate of processor i. Let $N_i(t)$, i=1,...,M, be the number of active processes, that is, the number of processes, both user and system initiated, assigned to processor i at time t. Each such process could be in any state (runnable, sleeping, etc.). Remote work is not included in the number of active processes $N_i(t)$. Let us consider the time axis as divided into intervals of length τ as shown in Figure 1.

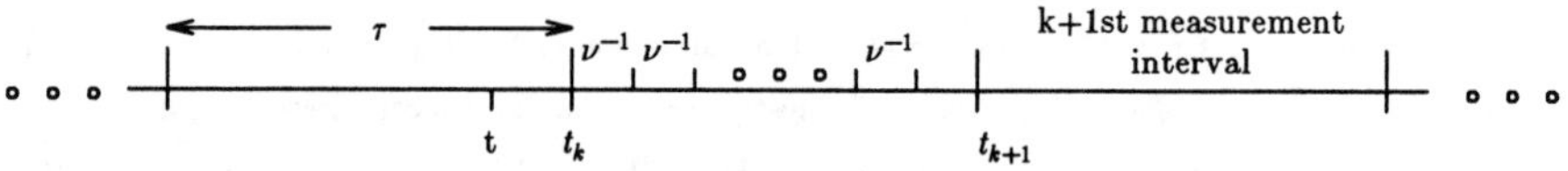

Figure 1. The Measurement Interval

During each measurement interval a simple information collection mechanism allows the estimation of the average CPU run queue length for each processor, averaged over the last measurement interval. We can thus assume that at the end of each interval such estimates are known at the master processor. In particular, the measurement involves the independent sampling, with frequency ν, of the various CPU run queues. In this way, at the end of the k−th measurement interval, (t_k, t_{k+1}), the process assignment algorithm at the Master Processor is able to compute the estimate $\hat{n}_{i,k}$ for the asymptotic average CPU run queue length at processor i, denoted by $n_{i,k}$. If we use the notation $q_{i,k}^{(j)}$ for the number of processes found in the CPU run queue of the i−th processor in the j−th sample of the k−th interval, then, $\nu\tau$ being the total number of samples in the measurement interval, $\hat{n}_{i,k}$ is simply obtained as

$$\hat{n}_{i,k} = \sum_{j=1}^{\nu\tau} \frac{q_{i,k}^{(j)}}{\nu\tau} \quad . \tag{1}$$

At a time t in a measurement interval, the load of the processors is characterized by the ***biased-queue-lengths*** [13]

$$c_i(t) = N_i(t) + \Delta_{i,k}, \qquad t \epsilon (t_k, t_{k+1}), \quad i = 1, 2,\dots M, \quad k \geq 0, \tag{2}$$

where the queue-length bias terms $\Delta_{i,k}$ are bounded as $-\overline{\Delta} \leq \Delta_{i,k} \leq \overline{\Delta}$, for i = 1,..., M, $k \geq 0$. Here $\overline{\Delta} \geq 0$ is an adjustable parameter to be suitably chosen. When at time t a new process is created via, for example, an `exec(2)` system call, it is assigned for execution to the processor with minimum biased queue length, i.e., to processor j with

$$c_j(t) \leq c_i(t) \qquad \text{for all } i \neq j \quad i,j{=}1,\dots,M \quad , \quad t \,\epsilon\, (t_k, t_{k+1}) \quad . \tag{3}$$

This kind of an assignment policy is inspired by the so-called *Join-the-Biased-Queue* policy proposed by Yum [13]. However, in our case, the value of the bias terms is not a constant, but is periodically updated, based on the information on the average queue lengths at the various CPUs. In order to describe the updating mechanism for the bias terms, we let the vector of bias terms on interval k be denoted by $\Delta_k = [\Delta_{1,k}, \dots \Delta_{M,k}]^T$. Let us also define the feasible region S for the vectors of bias terms as

$$S = \left\{ \text{all vectors } \Delta = [\Delta_1, \ldots, \Delta_M]^T \text{ such that } \sum_{i=1}^{M} \Delta_i = S_o, \quad -\bar{\Delta} \leq \Delta_i \leq \bar{\Delta} \text{ for all } i \right\} . \tag{4}$$

As from the definition of S, we require the sum of the bias terms to maintain a constant value S_o (usually $S_o = \sum_{i=1}^{M} \Delta_{i,0}$) at all times, while each component remains within its bounds. This requirement is motivated by the need to prevent any of the bias terms from becoming unbounded, which would reduce the algorithm's ability to adapt to sudden changes in the workload/configuration combination.

Let π_S be the orthogonal projection operator into the feasible region S. The orthogonal projection of Δ into S is the point $\Delta^* = \pi_S[\Delta] \in S$ which is the closest to Δ in the sense of the Euclidean distance $\sum_{i=1}^{M} (\Delta_i - \Delta_i^*)^2$. A simple implementation for π_S is presented in [5]. Also, let the vector $\underline{\epsilon}_k = [\epsilon_{1,k}, \ldots, \epsilon_{M,k}]^T$ be defined as

$$\epsilon_{i,k} = \frac{\hat{n}_{i,k}}{\mu_i} - \frac{1}{M} \sum_{j=1}^{M} \frac{\hat{n}_{j,k}}{\mu_j} . \tag{5}$$

We can interpret the meaning of the vector $\underline{\epsilon}_k$ by observing that each component $\epsilon_{i,k}$ expresses the deviation of the normalized average run queue length estimated for processor i, with respect to the average over all the processors of the estimated normalized average queue lengths. The sequence of bias terms is now generated by the following scheme

$$\Delta_{k+1} = \pi_S\left[\Delta_k + \alpha\, \underline{\epsilon}_k\right], \quad k \geq 0 , \tag{6}$$

with the initial vector of bias terms Δ_o given, and $\alpha > 0$ an appropriate scalar gain factor. The updating mechanism of Eq. (6), which is of the Stochastic Approximation type [9], is thus driven by the vector of deviations of the normalized average queue lengths from the desired balance expressed by

$$\frac{n_{i,k}}{\mu_i} = \frac{n_{j,k}}{\mu_j} \quad i \neq j \quad i, j = 1, \ldots, M . \tag{7}$$

Consequently, when the condition expressed by Eq. (7) is achieved, the updating of the bias vector will cease. Also, we can reasonably expect that AJBQ will converge to a neighborhood of the operating condition characterized by Eq. (7). Although the convergence of Stochastic Approximation schemes in this class has been treated to some extent, the rigorous convergence proof for our case requires more work. However, an extensive series of simulation experiments suggests the satisfactory convergence properties of our procedure.

In [5] we studied a detailed model of the measurement process which provides a characterization of the measurement noise and a basis for the choice of some important parameters (e.g., the measurement interval τ and the sampling frequency ν). An obvious observation is that the larger τ is, the more accurate is the measurement, and hence, the more accurate is any control algorithm derived from it, but the less frequently we are able to update the control. Our study and experience support the conclusion that a measurement interval of 400-800 times the mean service time requirement is sufficient, when ν is chosen such that the number of samples in the measurement interval is ~50 to 100. Note that the mean service time requirement can be estimated by evaluating the average execution requirement per CPU visit for the particular workload considered. However, even with smaller values of τ, the control algorithm seems to perform very well. By using the values of mean service time requirements for the type of workloads we commonly encounter in a wide variety of computing environments, we decided that appropriate ranges for τ and ν are 10 sec $\leq \tau \leq$ 60 secs, ν = 50 to 100 per second.

Note that another trade-off exists with respect to the choice of $\bar{\Delta}$. In fact, a large value of $\bar{\Delta}$ would guarantee a more effective discrimination between processors due to the wider range achievable by the bias terms, while it would reduce the responsiveness of the algorithm in the face of dramatic changes in workload. The choice of $\bar{\Delta}$ should depends on the maximum number of processes that can be assigned to a particular processing element, and should not be affected by the system configuration considered. Our simulation and laboratory experience suggests that a value for $\bar{\Delta}$ in the range 80-100 is appropriate. Finally, based on the same experience, it seems appropriate to choose α = 1~2 for a wide range of computing environments. The choice of the algorithm parameters appears however to be rather robust with respect to changes in the workload or in the system configuration.

4. ALGORITHM BEHAVIOR AND PERFORMANCE: THE AT&T 3B4000 COMPUTER SYSTEM CASE STUDY

In this section we present a brief performance evaluation for the load sharing algorithm introduced in this paper. A more extensive treatment is offered in [5]. Our study uses the AT&T 3B4000 computer as the reference system. Both simulation results and prototype measurements are discussed. The workload used in the laboratory measurements, and modeled in the simulation model, is based on a benchmark meant to represent a system-level view of the computer system and the aim is to reproduce a UNIX® computation center workload. The actual code executed during a benchmark run is determined by a shell script containing about 115 instances of commonly-used UNIX® commands. For purposes of summarizing benchmark results, the commands in the script are divided into four categories, *simple, complex, editor,* and *ignored.* The simple commands are those commands that the user can reasonably expect to wait one second or less for a response from the system, but do not include commands executed during a editing session. The complex commands are those commands for which response time is not as critical. The editor commands are those commands that are submitted while the user is in an editing session, while the ignored commands are those commands that do not return any characters to the users terminal after execution. The simulation model described below only has two classes, *simple* and *other.* The *other* class includes all commands other than the simple commands.

In order to investigate the behavior of the proposed algorithm and to compare its performance with other similar procedures, we developed a SIMSCRIPT [11] simulation model of the AT&T 3B4000 computer whose basic structure is described by a queueing network. The processing nodes (MP, EADPs, and ACPs) are modeled as processor sharing nodes with possibly different service speeds, while the disk nodes are modeled by FCFS nodes with unlimited buffers. The nodes describing user terminal screen painting and think-type times are modeled as pure exponential delays. The model describes file access and other remote work by probabilistic routing of "read/write jobs." Disk caches are also accounted for by assuming appropriate cache hit ratios. We assumed all service time distributions to be exponential. The model parameters were identified by using the measurements obtained under the UNIX® workload described above.

We begin by presenting a set of simulation results which focus on the algorithm behavior. The system configuration includes the Master Processor , 4 EADPs and 3 ACPs. The number of UNIX® users is 100. The bounds for the bias terms are set by choosing $\overline{\Delta} = 50$. We assume that the load due to file accesses and interprocessor communication over the ABUS (remote work or stub load), is distributed so that the MP has about 40% of such load, with the rest assigned asymmetrically to the 4 EADPs. Twice, at time 800 seconds and again at time 1600 seconds the load on two of the EADPs (EADP1 and EADP2) is interchanged, in the sense that their respective percentage of stub load is interchanged. This tests the algorithm's ability to adapt to sudden changes in load conditions. In Figures 2a we present the evolution of the bias terms characterizing the MP, EADP1 and EADP2, when the measurement interval is $\tau = 30$, with the gain $\alpha = 1$. We set $\Delta_o = (0,0,0,0,0,0,0,0)^T$. Figures 2b shows the evolution of the objective function $\sum_{i=1}^{M} \epsilon_{i,k}^2$ (see Eq. (5)) for the same of experiment. These results show the convergence of the bias terms and the adaptivity of the algorithm in the face of sudden load changes.

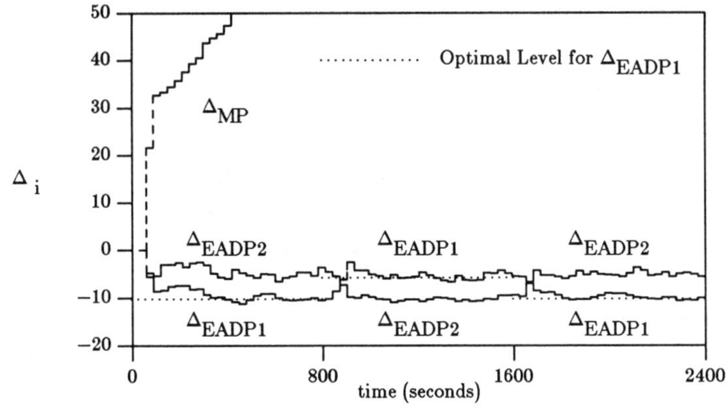

Figure 2a. Bias Terms versus Time

Stoch. Approx. Algorithm with Constant Gain ($\alpha = 1$). Measurement Interval = 30 secs.

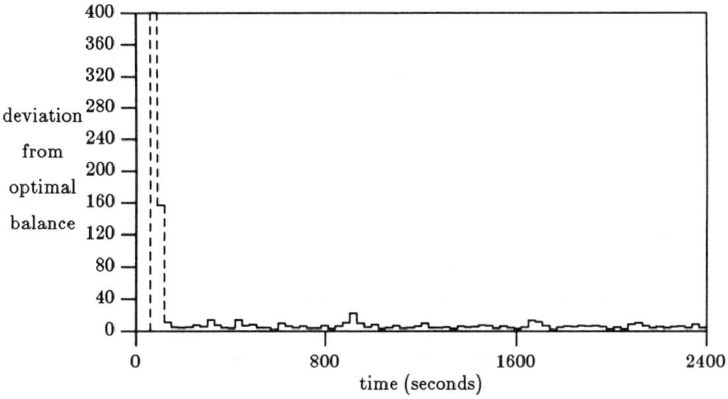

Figure 2b. Unbalance versus Time (The vertical axis is truncated).

Next, we will discuss a sample of a large performance study of load sharing algorithms, based on lab experiments on the AT&T 3B4000 multiprocessor system. The performance measures of interest will be both (average) response times and throughput. We will compare the performance of AJBQ with $\alpha = 1$ and $\alpha = 0$, to that of a simple round robin assignment procedure, a static procedure where processors are selected in cyclic order. We note that when $\alpha = 0$ the adaptive algorithm simply does not update the bias terms. Thus, if we initially set all the bias terms to 0, the algorithm selects for assignment the server with the smallest number of active processes.

With this understanding we will refer to the three load sharing algorithms as Adaptive-Join-the-Biased-Queue (AJBQ) and Join-the-Shortest-Active-Queue (JSAQ), for the adaptive algorithm with $\alpha = 1$ and $\alpha = 0$, respectively, and Round-Robin (RR).

We first consider a response time test on a machine including the MP, 4 EADPs and 4 ACPs. In Tables 1, 2, and 3 we show the 90-th percentile (Note the 90-th percentile of response time is the number t such that 90% of all commands of the given class, executed during the measurement interval, have a response time less than t), and the mean response time for two classes of commands in the benchmark, simple and complex, for each algorithm, when the number of users is 120, 160, and 190, respectively. All the estimates, except where otherwise noted, are obtained as the average over 6 samples of each measurement experiment. The numbers in parenthesis are the standard deviations in the samples.

The new adaptive procedure provides a remarkable improvement in response time performance, in terms of 90-th percentile, mean and of standard deviations. In particular, AJBQ reduces the standard deviation in measured run-to-run response time by a factor of ten in many cases. This reduction in variance is reflected in the vastly improved 90-th percentiles in Table 3 where the total system load is heaviest. The evident improvement in the standard deviations presented is important when fairness of service is considered a relevant performance measure. In Table 3 we do not present results for the RR algorithms, since it was not able to handle the load imposed by 190 users (i.e., response time became very long and erratic causing scripts to time-out and fail to continue). This phenomenon confirms our simulation results showing the degradation in the performance of this algorithm under large loads.

Algorithm	Simple 90-th Perc.	Simple Mean	Complex 90-th Perc.	Complex Mean
RR	0.66 (0.36)	0.35 (0.09)	12.36 (2.80)	5.90 (1.22)
JSAQ	0.83 (0.69)	0.43 (0.18)	20.10 (5.76)	9.91 (2.28)
AJBQ	0.70 (0.032)	0.35 (0.012)	12.45 (1.31)	5.78 (0.37)

TABLE 1. Average Response Time Comparison of Algorithms on 3B4000 System with MP, 4 EADPs, and 4 ACPs, and with 120 Users. Standard Deviations are in Parenthesis.

Algorithm	Simple 90-th Perc.	Simple Mean	Complex 90-th Perc.	Complex Mean
RR	1.32 (0.36)	0.66 (0.09)	26.67 (2.80)	13.89 (1.22)
JSAQ	1.64 (0.69)	0.76 (0.18)	48.18 (5.76)	23.38 (2.28)
AJBQ	0.91 (0.032)	0.47 (0.012)	19.70 (1.31)	9.17 (0.37)

TABLE 2. Average Response Time Comparison of Algorithms on 3B4000 System with MP, 4 EADPs, and 4 ACPs, and with 160 Users. Standard Deviations are in Parenthesis.

Algorithm	Simple 90-th Perc.	Simple Mean	Complex 90-th Perc.	Complex Mean
RR	-	-	-	-
JSAQ	2.20 (0.351)	0.90 (0.110)	60.1 (6.86)	30.19 (5.76)
AJBQ	1.28 (0.035)	0.79 (0.036)	42.1 (1.88)	20.34 (0.905)

TABLE 3. Average Response Time Comparison of Algorithms on 3B4000 System with MP, 4 EADPs, and 4 ACPs, and with 190 Users. Standard Deviations are in Parenthesis.

A comparison of throughput performance under the same benchmark and configuration is presented in Figure 3, where each point is obtained as the average over three repetitions of each experiment. We observe that, for the configuration considered, the RR algorithm provides a throughput which is noticeably lower than that of the other two algorithms. However, the throughput of the JSAQ algorithm is here close to that of the AJBQ algorithm, since in this test a large number of long sleeping processes (login shells, gettys, etc.), typical of real computing environments and of the response time testing environment, is not present. Therefore, it is clear that the gains that were measured in the response time characterization were not at the cost of throughput.

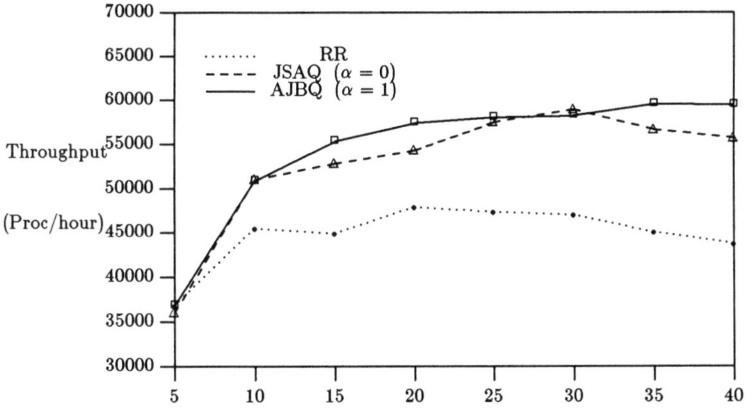

Figure 3. Throughput Comparison. The Configuration includes MP and 4 EADPs.

5. CONCLUSIONS

In this work we presented a novel approach to the design of load sharing algorithms for a class of multiprocessor systems. This approach was used in the definition of an adaptive load balancing algorithm, which we call AJBQ, which is successfully implemented on the AT&T 3B4000 UNIX® multiprocessor. The algorithm led to a significant improvement in system performance with a very small overhead, and has been designed to take advantage of software and hardware mechanisms available on the system. The adaptive (i.e., learning) properties of the proposed procedure offer advantages in terms of ability to react to sudden changes in the system configuration and workload, reduced hand-tuning requirements, and robustness with respect to workload/configuration combinations.

A brief performance study of the AJBQ algorithm, including simulation results on a simulation model, and laboratory measurements on a prototype, has been presented. The algorithm performance justified the adoption of a process assignment procedure which requires the collection of information on the state of the system. In fact, we show that the performance improvement with respect to a simple static procedure, such as the Round Robin algorithm, as well as with respect to dynamic procedures, such as JSAQ, is significant. We expect that the adaptive load sharing approach described here will be applicable to a wide range of distributed systems with a centralized resource manager.

REFERENCES

[1] Accetta, M., et al, "Mach: A New Kernel Foundation for UNIX Development," Computer Science Department, Carnegie-Mellon University, Pittsburg, DRAFT, May 1, 1986.

[2] Bach, M.J., "The Design of the UNIX Operating System", Prentice-Hall, New Jersey, 1986.

[3] Bonomi, F.,and Kumar, A.,"Adaptive Optimal Load Balancing in a Heterogeneous Multiserver System with a Central Job Scheduler", to appear on IEEE Transactions on Computers.

[4] Bonomi, F.,and Kumar, A.,"Adaptive Optimal Load Balancing in a Heterogeneous Multiserver System with a Central Job Scheduler", Proc. of 8th ICDCS, San Jose', CA, June 1988, pp. 500-509.

[5] Bonomi, F., Fleming, P.J., and Steinberg, P., "An Adaptive Load Balancing Algorithm for a Class of UNIX® Multiprocessor Systems", submitted to the IEEE Transactions on Computers.

[6] Bonomi, F., "Performance Analysis of Some Process-to-Processor Assignment Algorithms for a UNIX® Multiprocessor System", Proc. of 1987 IFIP Conf. on Distributed Processing, Amsterdam, Oct. 1987, pp. 491-504.

[7] Eager, D., Lazowska, E. and Zahorjan, J.," Adaptive Load Sharing in Homogeneous Distributed Systems", *IEEE Trans. on Software Engg.*, Vol. SE-12, No. 5, pp. 662-675, May 1986.

[8] Ferrari, D., and Zhou, S., "A load Index for Dynamic Load Balancing", Proc. 1986 Fall Joint Computer Conference, Dallas, TX, pp. 1138-1149, November 1986.

[9] Kushner, H.J., and Clark, D.S., *Stochastic Approximation Methods for Constrained and Unconstrained Systems*, Springer-Verlag, New York, 1978.

[10] Leland, W. E., and Ott, T.J., "UNIX® Process Behavior and Load Balancing Among Loosely Coupled Computers", Teletraffic Analysis and Computer Performance Evaluation, 1986, pp. 191-208.

[11] Russell, E. C., "*Building Simulation Models with SIMSCRIPT II.5* ", C.A.C.I., Los Angeles, 1983.

[12] Wang, Y.T., and Morris, R.T.J., "Load Sharing in Distributed Systems", IEEE Trans on Computers, vol. C-34, March 1985, pp. 204-217.

[13] Yum, T. P., "The Join-Biased-Queue Rule and its Applications to Routing in Computer Communication Networks", *IEEE Trans. on Communications*, vol. Com-29, no. 4, pp. 505-511, April 1981.

[14] AT&T 3B4000 Computer Hardware Description, Doc. No. 303-303, 1988.

[15] AT&T 3B4000 Computer Software Architecture, Doc. No. 303-310, Issue 1, 1988.

An Algebraic Compositional Semantics of an Object Oriented Notation with Concurrency

Ruth Breu
Fakultät für Mathematik und Informatik
Universität Passau
Postfach 2540, D-8390 Passau - West Germany
EMail: rbreu@unipas.uucp

Elena Zucca
Dipartimento di Matematica
Università di Genova
Via L. B. Alberti 4, 16132 Genova - Italy
EMail: astes@igecuniv.bitnet

Introduction

This paper presents an algebraic compositional semantics for a schema of an object-oriented syntax which models many existing features as class hierarchies, polymorphism and concurrency, using a pattern which could be applied to different concrete languages (in what follows O-O stands for "object-oriented"). The semantics is defined in a classical denotational style, ie giving an abstract syntax, the semantic domains and the interpretation of the syntactic operators. From this point of view the paper yields a formalization of the model which underlies an O-O notation as done for example in [Wo] for Smalltalk-80. However our approach is different from the traditional one for at least two reasons. First, the given semantics is algebraic in the sense that the value denoted by a *class* (the basic language unit in an O-O notation) is in general a class of algebras described by an algebraic specification. In particular, we use the algebraic specification language ASL ([Wi]). This approach allows to model in a natural way some typical O-O features related to combining classes. A class combinator (eg inheritance) is semantically interpreted in this framework as a function which handles classes of algebras or, in an equivalent way, since we use an algebraic specification language, as a specification combinator (see [Wi] for foundations). Moreover, our schema of semantic definition allows to model also concurrent features of the O-O language if any, by underlying an approach to concurrency based on *algebraic transition systems* (see for example [AR] for foundations and [AGRZ] for a recent survey with already some hints on the treatment of objects). In this respect our aim is not to present a particular language but to give a general framework in which different concurrent features, like synchronization primitives between active objects or mutual exclusion, can easily be inserted. A formal semantics for a particular parallel O-O language in a classical denotational style may be found for example in [ABKR].

In this paper we consider a schema of programming languages. This means that the description of a class includes an implementation part containing method bodies where *method* is the O-O notion which corresponds to the function/procedure notion in Pascal-like languages. Its semantic counter-part is a set of axioms in the specification associated with the class, each one corresponding to a method body. However the overall approach presented here also works in a framework in which properties of methods are specified by more general axioms. In this sense the O-O syntax presented in the paper, if we do not consider method bodies, can be viewed as a starting point for an O-O specification language, following an idea of [GM]. A paper in this direction is in preparation ([BZ2]).

Due to the lack of space, this paper is mainly devoted to illustrate the main ideas of our semantics, trying to avoid as much as possible technicalities and details. It is organized in a top-down way. Sect. 1 presents the syntax and semantics of class combinators, showing how they are modelled by compositionality; this section is concerned with structuring classes and is independent from the kind of dynamics of the system (sequential or concurrent). Sect. 2 shows how the treatment of concurrency is inserted into the framework. Sect. 3 is concerned with method implementations; this part is illustrated by an example. For the formalization of this part the reader may refer to a more detailed version in [BZ1]; a revised full version of this paper with also other examples of applications is in preparation.

This paper has been written largely as a result of the experience gained by the authors during the work in the Esprit project DRAGON, in which one of the tasks is the development of an object-oriented notation particularly suitable for reuse and distribution ([DRAGON]).

1 Composing classes

We consider throughout this paper a schema of O-O languages which includes the features listed below.

Each object belongs to a *class*; each class specifies which are the *attributes*, the *methods* and (possibly) the *thread* of the object. Classes in the sequel are called *active* if they have a thread, *passive* otherwis.e New classes can be defined using a set of *class combinators*; the most important relations between classes we consider are the *inherit* and *use* relations. A class C_1 which *inherits* from a class C_2, called an *heir* of C_2 (which is called a *parent* of C_1), has all the attributes and methods of C_2 to which it may add its own. A class can have several parent classes, ie we consider *multiple inheritance.* A class C_1 which *uses* a class C_2, called a *client* of C_2, can have attributes and method parameters of class C_2. These two class relations are modelled by a unique syntactic combinator in our language schema. Moreover we consider two other class combinators, an *export* operator (which allows to hide methods to the outside) and a *rename* operator (which allows to rename methods). Visible methods (ie methods which are not hidden by using the *export* operation) represent the interface of an object of the class when used in a context.

Attributes are *typed* where in this paper *type* always means either a basic type (as integer, boolean and so on), or a class. A restricted form of *polymorphism* is allowed for attributes, since to an attribute of class C can be assigned an object of any heir class of C (so notice that the type of the object which the attribute refers to can change *dynamically*, ie during execution). This feature is of particular interest since it allows us to consider a more significant class hierarchy (with full polymorphism of variables as in Smalltalk-80 the *use* relation would make no sense), but at the same time modelling this feature in the typically typed framework of algebraic specifications poses in the essence the same problems as modelling full polymorphism. The restricted form of polymorphism considered in the paper, as other language features, are essentially the same as in [M].

Before giving our abstract syntax, we present a small example in order to give an idea of the kind of language we are considering.

```
class RECTANGLE is r where r =
   LENGTH,WIDTH: INTEGER;
   procedure  SET-L (L: INTEGER);
   procedure  SET-W (W: INTEGER);
   function   AREA return INTEGER;
class body RECTANGLE is
   procedure SET-L (L: INTEGER) is
       begin LENGTH:= L end;
   procedure SET-W (W: INTEGER) is
       begin WIDTH:= L end;
   function AREA return INTEGER is
       begin return LENGTH*WIDTH end;
end class RECTANGLE;
```

```
class USER is u where u =
   uses RECTANGLE;
   A:RECTANGLE;
   V:INTEGER;
class body USER is
   thread
      begin
         A.CREATE;
         A.SET-L(3);
         A.SET-W(5);
         V:= A.AREA
      end;
end class USER;
```

```
class CUBOID is c where c =
   inherits RECTANGLE;
   HEIGHT:INTEGER;
   procedure  SET-H (H: INTEGER);
   function   VOLUME return INTEGER;
class body CUBOID is
   procedure SET-H (H: INTEGER) is
       begin HEIGTH:= H end;
   function VOLUME return INTEGER is
       begin return AREA*HEIGTH end;
end class CUBOID;
```

The example contains three classes: two passive classes describing rectangles and cuboids, where the cuboid class is an heir of the rectangle class; moreover, an active class USER uses the rectangle class and executes a simple sequence of commands in its thread. Method bodies and thread are provided for showing a complete example, but we do not fix any syntax for them in the sequel. The expressions r, c and u are class expressions defined in the abstract syntax below (enriched with some syntactic sugar). In the declaration part of a class the attributes and methods are declared. In the example, the rectangle class has two attributes (LENGTH and WIDTH) which are of a basic type (integer) and three methods (SET-L, SET-W, AREA), the first ones being procedures and the last one being a function. The cuboid class has all the preceding attributes and methods (inherited from the rectangle class), a further attribute (HEIGHT) of a basic type (integer) and two further methods (SET-H, VOLUME), the first one being a procedure and the last one being a function. Finally, the user class has two attributes (A, V), the first one of the rectangle class and the last one of a basic type (integer), no methods and a thread (ie USER is an active class).

We give now formally the syntax:

Class::=	Flat | Export | Rename | Inherits-Uses	Type-Id::=	Basic-Type | Class-Id
Inherits-Uses::=	Set(Class) Set(Class) Flat	Method::=	Method-Id List(Param) [Type-Id]
Flat::=	Set(Attr) Set(Method) Body	Param::=	Id Type-Id
Export::=	Set(Method) Class	Body::=	Set(Method) Method-Body) [Thread]
Rename::=	Renaming Class	Thread::=	Method-Body
Attr::=	Id Type-Id	Method-Body::=	Command

A hierarchical class is constructed starting from two sets of classes which are the inherited and the used classes respectively . Notice that a flat class can be viewed as a hierarchical class in which these two sets are empty; nevertheless we treat generally the flat case separately as a help to the reader. A method whose body is defined in the class body must be declared in the method set part of the class. Notice that as a particular effect of inheritance a method which was *deferred* in a parent class (ie without a corresponding method body) can be *concreted* in an heir class. Moreover a method can also be *redefined* in an heir class. We assume that the types of the attributes and of the method parameters of a class are either basic types or used classes or the class itself (ie we assume that the *use* relation is reflexive). In the last case, we call the class *recursive.*

In the following we will use c, d to range over classes, C, D, E to range over class identifiers, X, Y, Z to range over attribute identifiers, T to range over type identifiers, r to range over renamings. Moreover we assume for simplicity that in a class term a unique class identifier, denoted by Name(c), is associated with each class subterm c.

We now give some general ideas on the semantic model presented in this paper. The semantics of a class c with name C consists of a specification *Spec*(C, c), modelling the objects of the class together with their methods, called the *class specification*, and of a signature *Interface*(C, c) describing the interface of the class to the client classes, called the *interface signature.*

The class specification can be informally thought as consisting of two parts, as follows: it is based on a specification modelling the internal structure of objects of the class (*Obj*(C, c)), ie *what objects of the class are* (depending only on the attributes of C and those of the used classes), together with a part modelling the methods of C and those of the used classes, ie *how objects of the class behave.* In particular we have in the signature of the class specification a sort corresponding to the class (it will in the sequel be denoted itself by C in the sequel for simplicity) and an operation for each method. Operations related to the internal structure of objects are hidden (using the ASL *export* operator) in *Spec*(C, c), modelling that an object is something which is only visible from outside through its behaviour (its methods). The interface signature *Interface*(C, c) is a subset of the full signature of *Spec*(C, c) and represents the interface to users (containing only visible methods). This section is mainly devoted to the formal definition of the visibility relationships between classes. Moreover the axioms of the the class specification define properties of these methods based on their implementation in the body of the class, if any; the translation of bodies into axioms is exemplified in Sect. 3.

The specification of the internal structure of objects *Obj*(C, c) can be in turn thought as consisting of two parts; it is based on a specification *Obj-Env*(C, c) which gives a semantic view of objects which is independent from the fact that we deal with concurrency, together with a part modelling these objects as components of a concurrent environment. The first specification is only informally described since the formalization is quite straightforward (it can be found in the Appendix), while the second part is given in Sect. 2.

We need some preliminary notations and assumptions.

In the following, BASE denotes a specification of the basic data types with signature Σ_{BASE}, including a subspecification NAME of an infinite set of object names (of sort *name*), each one with an associated class (of sort *class-id*), individuated by an operation Class: name $\rightarrow$ class-id.
We assume to have in our specifications built-in *functional sorts* (for each couple of sorts s_1, s_2 we have in the signature also the sort $(s_1 \rightarrow s_2)$) and *cartesian product sorts* (for each n-tuple of sorts $s_1, \ldots, s_n$ we have in the signature also the sort $(s_1 \times \ldots \times s_n)$; we assume that for $n = 0$ $(s_1 \times \ldots \times s_n) = \text{null}$ (the sort whose carrier has only one element (denoted by Null), assumed to be in the specification BASE).

Set $\text{RES} = \{(s_1 \times \ldots \times s_n) \mid s_1, \ldots s_n \in \text{sorts}(\Sigma_{BASE})\}$, intuitively the set of all the values which may be sent as message parameters: they are indeed either basic values or *references* to objects .

For each type T we denote by $\underline{T}$ a sort which is the corresponding basic sort in Σ_{BASE} if T is a basic type, *name* otherwise (ie if T is a class identifier).

We assume in this section that for each class C there is a signature $\Sigma\text{-PR}_C$, called in the sequel a *process signature*, intuitively the signature of processes which act on objects of class C, which will be defined in Sect. 2 when dealing with concurrency. For understanding this section it is sufficient to know that $\Sigma\text{-PR}_C$ contains, for each $r_1, r_2 \in$ RES, a sort $(r_1 \to r_2\text{-process}_C)$, called in the sequel a *process sort*, intuitively the sort of the processes acting on an object of class C which are parameterized on a value of sort r_1 and return as final result a value of sort r_2. A help for the reader can be to see processes as a generalization of functions: indeed in the sequential case everything in this section holds by replacing each sort $(r_1 \to r_2\text{-process}_C)$ by just $((r_1 \times C) \to (r_2 \times C))$. As a particular case of process sorts we have constant process sorts (of the form $r\text{-process}_C$) and sorts of processes which do not return any final value (ie of the form $r_1 \to \text{null-process}_C$, which we write just $r_1 \to \text{process}_C$).

In writing specifications we adopt the ASL notation ([Wi]); in particular our semantic domains, eg Sig, Spec, Axioms, are sets of ASL expressions of a certain type (*mode*), eg the set of the ASL signatures, specifications, axiom sets.

We give now the clauses defining the visible signature of a class.

Interface: Class-Id × Class → Sig
Interface(C, Flat(attrs, methods, body)) $=_{def}$
  enrich $\Sigma_{BASE} + \Sigma\text{-PR}_C$ **by sorts** {C} **opns** *Method-Opns*(C, methods)
Interface(C, Export(methods, d)) $=_{def}$
  enrich $\Sigma_{BASE} + \Sigma\text{-PR}_C$ **by sorts** {C} **opns** opns(*Interface*(C, d)) ∩ *Method-Opns*(C, methods)
Interface(C, Rename(r, d)) $=_{def}$ **rename** *Interface*(C, d) **by** *Sigmorph*(r)
(*Sigmorph*: Renaming → Sigmorph translates a renaming into the corresponding signature morphism)
Let c = Inherits-Uses($\{c_1, ..., c_n\}$, $\{c_1', ..., c_m'\}$, attrs, methods, body), then
 Interface(C, c) $=_{def}$
  enrich $\Sigma_{BASE} + \Sigma\text{-PR}_C$ + *Interface*(C, c_1) + ... + *Interface*(C, c_n) **by sorts** {C} **opns** *Method-Opns*(C, methods)

The visible signature of a hierarchical class is obtained by combining the new methods and the *inherited* visible signatures of the parent classes (*Interface*(C, c_1), ... , *Interface*(C, c_n) above); their are equal to the visible signatures of the parent classes up to renaming of the main sort. This follows from the following fact:

Interface(C, c) = **rename** *Interface*(D, c) **by** [C → D]

(Here it is assumed that the given signature morphism also renames indices.)

Note moreover that the interface of a class used by C is not visible to clients of C, ie clientship is not a transitive relation.

The auxiliary semantic function *Method-Opns* defines the operations of the class specification based on the method declarations (second parameter) and on standard methods (in the sequel we assume only the creation of objects to be a standard method).

Method-Opns: Class-Id × Set(Method) → Opns
Method-Opns(C, methods) $=_{def} \bigcup_{m \in methods}$ {*Method-Opn*(C, m) } ∪ *Standard-Opns*(C)

Standard-Opns: Class-Id → Opns
Standard-Opns(C) $=_{def}$ {Create: → process_C}

Method-Opn : Class-Id × Method → Opn
Method-Opn(C, m-id (x_1: T_1, ..., x_n: T_n)) $=_{def}$ m-id: ($\underline{T}_1$, ..., $\underline{T}_n$) → process_C
Method-Opn(C, m-id (x_1: T_1, ..., x_n: T_n) **return** T) $=_{def}$ m-id: ($\underline{T}_1$,..., $\underline{T}_n$) → $\underline{T}\text{-process}_C$

We also define an auxiliary semantic function *Full-Sig* (which will be used in the definition of *Spec*) which defines the *full* signature of a class. It is the sum of a signature containing all the methods of the class (*Sig*(C, c)) and of the *used* visible signatures of the used classes. The set of used classes contains the used classes of parent classes too. Using a signature means that every operation in the used class is replaced by an operation with an additional parameter of sort *name*. Moreover a used procedure returns the name of the called object (that is in order to allow in the syntax chains of procedure calls to the same object). The last component models the fact that classes are clients of their own, ie the clientship relation is reflexive.

Full-Sig: Class-Id × Class → Sig
Full-Sig(C, c) $=_{def}$ *Sig*(C, c) + +*Use-Sigs*(C, c) + Use-Sig(C, *Sig*(C, c))

Sig: Class-Id × Class → Sig defined in an analogous way to the *Interface* function with the only difference that:
 Sig(C, Export(methods, c)) $=_{def}$ *Sig*(C, c).

Use-Sigs: Class-Id × Class → Sigs
Use-Sigs(C, Flat(attrs, methods, body)) $=_{def}$ ∅
Use-Sigs(C, Inherits-Uses($\{c_1, ..., c_n\}$, $\{c_1', ..., c_m'\}$, attrs, methods, body)) $=_{def}$
 $\bigcup_{i=1..n}$ *Use-Sigs*(C, c_i) ∪ { Use-Sig(C, *Interface*(C_i', c_i')) | i=1, ..., m, Name(c_i') = C_i' }
Use-Sigs(C, Export(methods, d)) $=_{def}$ *Use-Sigs*(C, Rename(r, d)) $=_{def}$ *Use-Sigs*(C, d)

sigfunct Use-Sig $=_{def}$ (λ **sort** C, **signature** Σ).
    enrich Σ-PR_C **by**
        sorts sorts(Σ) $\cup$ {C}
        opns { _.opn: (name, $s_1, \ldots, s_n$) $\rightarrow$ s'-$process_C$
            | opn: ($s_1, \ldots, s_n$)$\rightarrow$ s-$process_D$ $\in$ opns(Σ), s' = s if s $\neq$ null, s' = name otherwise }

Note that an heir class has visibility of all the features of a parent class. This follows from the fact that *Full-Sig*(C, c) $\supseteq$ *Full-Sig*(C, d), where c = Inherits-Uses(inh-classes, used-classes, attrs, methods, body) and d $\in$ inh-classes. Thus the full signature defines the interface of a class to heir classes. This implies the transitivity of the inheritance relation. Notice moreover that from the definitions above follows that:

Interface(C, c) $\subseteq$ *Full-Sig*(C, c) for every class identifier C and class expression c.

Fig. 1 summarizes the visibility relations between classes. Arrows indicate dependencies. Here Σ, $H\Sigma$ denote visible and full (hidden) signatures respectively.

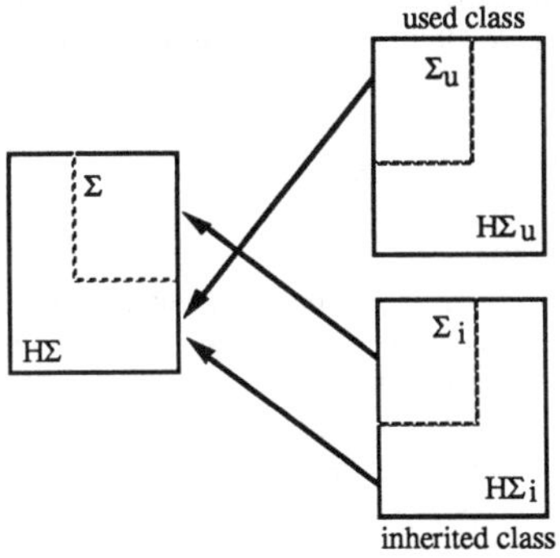

Fig. 1

We now define the structured specification of a class. The specification of a compound class relies on the specification of the internal structure of the objects (given formally in the Appendix and informally in next section) and on the *used* specifications of the used classes. As for the full signature, the second part of the definition models the reflexivity of the clientship relation.

Spec: Class-Id $\times$ Class $\rightarrow$ Spec
Spec(C, c) $=_{def}$ *Non-Refl-Spec*(C, c) + Use-Spec(C, *Sig*(C, c), *Non-Refl-Spec*(C, c), C)
Non-Refl-Spec: Class-Id $\times$ Class $\rightarrow$ Spec
Non-Refl-Spec(C, c) $=_{def}$
    export *Full-Sig*(C, c) **from**
        enrich *Obj*(C, c) + $+$*Use-Specs*(C, c) **by**
            sorts { C } **opns** opns(*Sig*(C, c)) $\cup$ opns(Use-Sig(C, *Sig*(C, c)))
            axioms *Method-Axioms*(c, $\varnothing$) $\cup$ {*Create-Axiom*(C , c) }
If the class expression c is constructed by the *rename* or *export* operation we can directly define
Spec(C, Export(methods, d)) $=_{def}$ *Spec*(C, d)
Spec(C, Rename(r, d)) $=_{def}$ **rename** *Spec*(C, d) **by** *Sigmorph*(r)

The functions *Method-Axioms*, giving the axioms of the specification based on the method implementations and *Create-Axiom*, giving an axiom for the standard create method, are defined in Sect. 3.

Using a specification means that operations _.opn of a class C being client of a class D are defined by "propagating" the semantics of opn in D to the client class C using the operation Use_D, defined in the next section, which maps a process acting on an object of class D onto a process acting on an object of class C.

Use-Specs: Class-Id $\times$ Class $\rightarrow$ Specs
Use-Specs(C, Flat(attrs, methods, body)) $=_{def}$ $\varnothing$
Use-Specs(C, Inherits-Uses({$c_1, \ldots, c_n$}, {$c_1', \ldots, c_m'$}, attrs, methods, body)) $=_{def}$
    $\bigcup_{i=1..n}$ *Use-Specs*(C, c_i) $\cup$ { Use-Spec(C_i', *Interface*(C_i', c_i'), *Spec*(C_i', c_i'), C) | i = 1, ..., m, Name(c_i') = C_i' }
Use-Specs(C, Export(methods, d)) $=_{def}$ *Use-Specs*(C, Rename(r, d)) $=_{def}$ *Use-Specs*(C, d)

specfunct Use-Spec $=_{def}$ (λ **term** D, **sig** Σ, **spec** USED-SP, **sort** C).
  export Use-Sig(C, Σ) **from**
    enrich USED-SP **by**
      sorts sorts(Use-Sig(C, Σ)) **opns** opns(Use-Sig(C, Σ))
      axioms
        $\{ \ \text{Class}(n) = D \Rightarrow n.opn(x_1, ..., x_k) = \text{Use}_D(n, opn(x_1, ..., x_k))$
          $\mid \_.opn \in \text{opns}(\text{Use-Sig}(C, \Sigma)), opn: (s_1, \dots, s_n) \rightarrow \text{s-process}_D, s \neq \text{null} \}$
        $\cup \{ \text{Class}(n) = D \Rightarrow n.opn(x_1, ..., x_k) = \text{Use}_D(n, opn(x_1, ..., x_k));$ **return** n
          $\mid \_.opn \in \text{opns}(\text{Use-Sig}(C, \Sigma)), opn: (s_1, \dots, s_n) \rightarrow \text{process}_D \}$

Inheritance enhances the top-down design of programs. Starting with abstract descriptions of classes by using deferred methods, heirs may concrete methods and add new features. Thus, heirs can be seen as implementations or specializations of the parent class. This point of view is reflected in the semantics as follows.

Fact Let c = Inherits-Uses(inh-classes, used-classes, attrs, methods, body) and let $d \in$ inh-classes, ie c inherits d. Then the following properties hold (here Mod(S) denotes the set of the models of a specification S):

(1) $\text{Mod}(Obj(C, c))|_{sig(Obj(C, d))} \subseteq \text{Mod}(Obj(C, d))$

(2) If no method visible in d is redefined in c and c,d are either both passive or active classes then
$$\text{Mod}(Spec(C, c))|_{sig(Spec(C,d))} \subseteq \text{Mod}(Spec(C, d)),$$
Note that methods of d may be concreted in c.

Proof omitted (it can be found in [BZ1]).

Property (2) says that every model of the specification of an heir class restricted to the signature of the parent class is a model of the parent class (if the name of the parent class is replaced by the name of the heir class). Hence inheritance corresponds to an implementation relation on the specification level (see [Wi]). If a class (in an extended approach) also may contain abstract properties of deferred methods, it restricts the set of possible heirs to those fulfilling fact (2). As there are no restrictions for redefining a method and we do not consider any semantic equivalence of processes, the second property does not hold if methods are redefined in the heir class.

2 An algebraic semantics of objects in a concurrent environment

In this section we deal with the process specification related to a class. Considering a concurrent environment, an object in a (possibly) concurrent context can be thought of as a system consisting of (the passive part of) the object and of many processes which can all act in parallel on the object executing either some methods or the thread. As mentioned in the introduction, our approach to concurrency is based on algebraic transition systems. That means that processes are modelled by *labelled transition systems* ie specifying a set of *process states*, a set of *actions* (*labels*) and a set of *transitions* (ie triples of the form <pr, a, pr'> where pr, pr' are states and a is an action, usually written $pr \xrightarrow{a} pr'$). Moreover labelled transition systems are specified algebraically, in particular we have in the labelled transition system modelling processes:

- Each state of a process is modelled by an element of a constant process sort r-process_C.
- Each action is modelled by an element of a sort act_C; actions which processes can perform on the object are basically creation of new objects and reading/updating attributes (which we model in detail), together with actions related to the particular concurrent features of the language (left unspecified in this paper).
- The transition relation is modelled by a family of boolean operations (one for each $r \in \text{RES}$):
  $\_ \xrightarrow{r} \_ : (\text{r-process}_C, \text{act}_C, \text{r-process}_C) \rightarrow \text{bool}.$
- The whole system is modelled in turn as a labelled transition system in which a state is a couple consisting of the passive part of the object and the concurrent user (a parallel composition of processes). The corresponding transition relation will be indicated in the sequel by $\Longrightarrow$. Notice that since the object can be in general an *open* object (in the sense that its attributes can refer also to external objects) the evolution of the system can involve interaction with the outside.
- The *thread* is modelled as a process acting on the passive part of the object as a component of a concurrent user.

The formal definition of the process signature associated with a class is as follows:

$\Sigma\text{-PR}_C =_{def}$
  enrich Σ_{BASE} **by**
  sorts $\{ \ \text{act}_C \} \cup \{\text{r-process}_C \mid r \in \text{RES} \}$
  opns $\{\_ \xrightarrow{r} \_ : (\text{r-process}_C, \text{act}_C, \text{r-process}_C) \rightarrow \text{bool} \mid r \in \text{RES} \}$

In order to understand how actions which processes can perform on objects are modelled, we give an informal description of the internal structure of an object (formalized by the auxiliary function *Obj-Env* given in the Appendix). As mentioned before, a class defines which are the attributes of each object of the class ($X_1, \ldots, X_n$ in Fig.2). Attributes refer in general to other objects; the reference can be either to a *subobject*, ie an object which is created during the life of the object we are considering (as X_n in the picture) or to an *external* object, ie an object which is already existing when the object we are considering is created (as X_1 in the picture). Both these subobjects and external objects must be of used classes. Attributes of subobjects in turn can refer to other objects (as Y_m in the picture), which again may be either subobjects or external objects. We say that a class C *transitively uses* a class D if either C uses D or C uses E and E transitively uses D for some class E. Thus all subobjects and external objects must be of transitively used classes. Moreover attributes can assume values of basic types (as Y_1 and Z_1 in the picture). Following this intuition, (the passive part of) an object of the class is modelled as an *object environment* (a value of sort C), ie an association from names (values of the sort *name*,

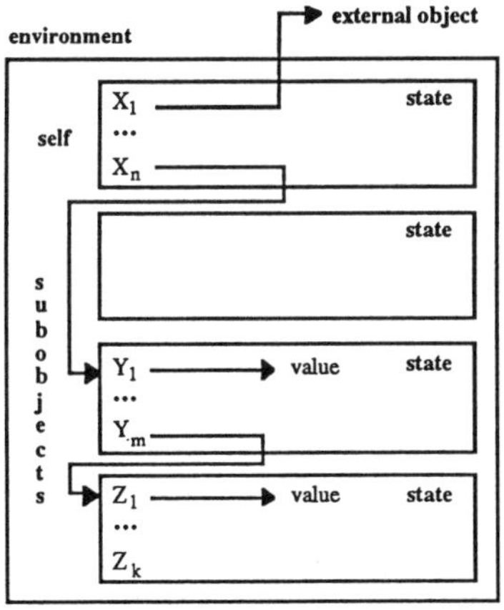

Fig. 2

which model references to objects represented by arrows in the picture) into *object states*, where an object state is a tuple with one component for each attribute. Each component is either a basic value (if the corresponding attribute is of a basic type) or a name (if the attribute refers to an object). In the object environment a special name (Self, assumed to be a constant in NAME) is associated with the state of the object itself. Notice that the splitting in two steps of the association between an attribute and the denoted object allows to model a typical feature of O-O languages which is object sharing (two attributes can refer to the same object).

We now give the formal specification of the interactions between an object and the concurrent environment. We assume a specification $PROCESS_C$ of the processes acting on objects of class C, whose signature contains $\Sigma\text{-}PR_C$. We do not need to fix this specification as long as we are not considering the implementation part of classes; in Sect. 3, in order to give an example of the semantic counterpart of method bodies, we use an example definition of $PROCESS_C$ which is formally given in the Appendix. Moreover, $MSET(PROCESS_C)$ denotes the specification of the multisets of processes, omitted here: the multiset of the processes $pr_1, \ldots, pr_n$ is denoted by $pr_1 \mid \ldots \mid pr_n$ (the vertical bar "|" is used to suggest parallel composition).

Obj: Class-Id × Class → Spec
Obj(C, c) $=_{def}$ *Attrs-Actions*(C, c, C, c) + *Create-Action*(C, c, C, c)

The specification of the actions of reading/updating attributes and of the actions related to objects of transitively used classes (which both depend on the attributes of the class) is returned by the function *Attr-Actions*, while the specification of the action of creation of an object of the given class is returned by the function *Create-Action*.

Attrs-Actions: Class-Id × Class × Class-Id × Class → Spec
Let d = Flat(attrs, methods, body), then
Attrs-Actions(C, c, D, d) = + {*Attr-Actions*(C, c, X: T) | X: T ∈ attrs })
Let d = Inherits-Uses($\{c_1, \ldots, c_n\}$, $\{c_1', \ldots, c_m'\}$, attrs, methods, body), Name(c_i') = C_i' for i = 1, ..., m, then
Attr-Actions(C, c, D, d) $=_{def}$
  + {*Attrs-Actions*(C, c, C, c_i) | i = 1, ..., n} ++ {*Attrs-Actions*(C, c, C_i', c_i') | i = 1, ..., m}
  ++ { *Create-Action*(C, c, C_i', c_i') | i = 1, ..., m }
  ++ {*Attr-Actions*(C, c, X: T) | X: T ∈ attrs } + *Create-Action*(C, c, D, d)

For each attribute X: T of a transitively used class we have two actions. One (_.ASSIGN-X_T) corresponds to assigning a new value to the attribute, one (_.GET-X_T) corresponds to reading the present value of the attribute. For each one of these actions we have two axioms: the first is related to the case in which the action is performed on a subobject (including the object itself) and the corresponding transition of the system is an internal action (denoted by TAU); the second is related to the case in which the action is performed on an external object and the corresponding transition of the system is the "propagation to the outside" of the action. Here o_C ranges over object environments of class C and σ ranges over object states; $o_C[n]$ denotes the object state associated with the name n in o_C, $o_C[n \to \sigma]$ denotes the new object environment which is equal to o_C except that it gives σ on n, IsUnused(o_C, n) is true iff n is not in the domain of o_C, $X_T(\sigma)$ denotes the X_T-labelled component of the tuple σ, $\sigma[x/X_T]$ denotes the tuple which is equal to σ except for the X_T-labelled component which is x.

Attr-Actions: Class-Id $\times$ Class $\times$ Attr $\to$ Spec
Attr-Actions(C, c, X: T) $=_{def}$
  enrich *Obj-Env*(C, c) + MSET(PROCESS$_C$) **by**
  sorts { syst-act$_C$}
  opns
    { _.ASSIGN-X_T, _.GET-X_T: name , $\underline{T} \to$ act$_C$, _.ASSIGN-X_T, _.GET-X_T: name , $\underline{T} \to$ syst-act$_C$,
    TAU: $\to$ syst-act$_C$,
    $\langle\_,\_\rangle \overset{-}{\Longrightarrow} \langle\_,\_\rangle$: (mset(process$_C$), C, syst-act$_C$, mset(process$_C$), C) $\to$ bool }
  axioms
    { $pr \xrightarrow{n.ASSIGN\text{-}X_T(x)} pr' \wedge \sigma' = o_C[n][x/X_T] \Rightarrow \langle pr \mid prset, o_C\rangle \xRightarrow{TAU} \langle pr' \mid prset, o_C[n \to \sigma']\rangle$,
    $pr \xrightarrow{n.GET\text{-}X_T(x)} pr' \wedge X_T(o_C[n]) = x \Rightarrow \langle pr \mid prset, o_C\rangle \xRightarrow{TAU} \langle pr' \mid prset, o_C\rangle$,
    $pr \xrightarrow{n.ASSIGN\text{-}X_T(x)} pr' \wedge \text{Is-Unused}(o_C, n) \Rightarrow \langle pr \mid prset, o_C\rangle \xRightarrow{n.ASSIGN\text{-}X_T(x)} \langle pr' \mid prset, o_C\rangle$,
    $pr \xrightarrow{n.GET\text{-}X_T(x)} pr' \wedge \text{Is-Unused}(o_C, n) \Rightarrow \langle pr \mid prset, o_C\rangle \xRightarrow{n.GET\text{-}X_T(x)} \langle pr' \mid prset, o_C\rangle$ }

For each transitively used class D we have one action (_.CREATE$_D$) corresponding to the creation an object of the class D. For each one of these actions we have one axiom, modelling that a new object with an unused name is added to the object environment. The function Use$_D$ maps a process pr_D acting on an object of class D onto a process acting on an object o_C of class C which performs the same actions of pr_D on a subobject of o_C.

Create-Actions: Class-Id $\times$ Class $\times$ Class-Id $\times$ Class $\to$ Spec
Create-Action(C, c, D, d) =
  enrich *Obj-Env*(C, c) + MSET(PROCESS$_C$)+ *State*(D, d) + PROCESS$_D$ **by**
    sorts {syst-act$_C$ }
    opns
      { _.CREATE$_D$: (name , state$_D$, process$_D$) $\to$ act$_C$, TAU: $\to$ syst-act$_C$,
      $\langle\_,\_\rangle \overset{-}{\Longrightarrow} \langle\_,\_\rangle$: (mset(process$_C$), C, syst-act$_C$, mset(process$_C$), C) $\to$ bool }
    $\cup${ Use$_D$: (name, r-process$_D$) $\to$ r-process$_C$ | r $\in$ RES}
    axioms
      { $pr \xrightarrow{n.CREATE_D(\langle\sigma_D, thread_D\rangle)} pr' \wedge \text{Is-Unused}(o_C, n) \wedge (\text{Class}(n) = D \vee n = \text{Self})$
        $\Rightarrow \langle pr \mid prset, o_C\rangle \xRightarrow{TAU} \langle pr \mid prset \mid Use_D(n, thread_D), o_C[n \to \sigma_D]\rangle$ }
    $\cup${ $pr_D \xrightarrow{Self.ACT} pr'_D \Rightarrow Use_D(n, pr_D) \xrightarrow{n.ACT} Use_D(n, pr'_D)$ | for every action _.ACT }

Notation In the following we denote every action Self.ACT by just ACT for every action _.ACT.

In the example given in Sect. 1, the actions of the class USER are two creation actions (creation of a user and creation of a rectangle) and the reading/updating actions related with the attributes V and A of the class USER and the attributes LENGTH and WIDTH of the class RECTANGLE.

3 Method implementations

The axioms of a class specification describe properties of the methods; they are obtained by translating each method implementation contained in the body of the class into a process term. Deferred methods, ie methods without an implementation, have no related axiom. Thus the interpretation of a deferred method in a model of the class specification is an arbitrary process. With the expressive power of the specification language also abstract properties of the deferred methods could be defined.

Method-Axioms: Class × Set(Method) → Axioms
Method-Axioms(Flat(attrs, methods, body), ms) $=_{def}$
$\bigcup_{m \in \text{methods}}$ {*Method-Axiom*(m, com) | m ∉ ms, (m, com) is in body }
Method-Axioms(Inherits-Uses({c_1, ..., c_n}, {c_1', ..., c_m'}, attrs, methods, c-body), ms) $=_{def}$
$\bigcup_{i=1..n}$ *Method-Axioms*(c_i, ms ∪ methods)
∪ $\bigcup_{m \in \text{methods}}$ {*Method-Axiom*(m, com) | m ∉ ms, (m, com) is in body }

Create-Axiom(C, Inherits_Uses({c_1, ..., c_n}, {c_1', ..., c_m'}, attrs, methods, body)) $=_{def}$
Create-Axiom(C, c_i) if c_i is active for some i, otherwise:
Create-Axiom(C, c) $=_{def}$ CREATE(Init_State$_C$, **skip**) Δ **skip**, if the body of c contains no thread
Create-Axiom(C, c) $=_{def}$ CREATE(Init_State$_C$, *Eval*(th) ω) Δ **skip**, if the body of c contains a thread th
Here ω denotes the totally undefined local environment.

Method-Axiom: Method × Command → Axiom
Let method = m-id (X_1: T_1, ..., X_n: T_n) **return** T and assume for simplicity $T_1, \ldots, T_k$ to be classes, $T_{k+1}, \ldots, T_n$ to be basic types, for some k, $0 \le k \le n$, then
Method-Axiom(method, com) $=_{def}$
$\wedge_{i=1..k}\, n_i \in \text{Names}(T_i) \Rightarrow$
$m(n_1, \ldots, n_k, x_{k+1}, \ldots, x_n) = Eval(\text{com})[X_1 \to n_1, \ldots, X_k \to n_k, X_{k+1} \to x_{k+1}, \ldots, X_n \to x_n]$

Eval: Command → Local-Env → Term

Local-Env $=_{def}$ [Param → Variable]

The axioms of a hierarchical class are obtained by both translating the implementations of the methods contained in the body of the class and by inheriting the axioms of the parent classes. Thereby the axioms related with the methods being redefined in the heir class have to be forgotten. The second argument of *Method-Axioms* indicates this set of methods. Notice that in case of multiple inheritance name clashes between methods may lead to an inconsistency of the heir class specification. In order to avoid this, it is left to the programmer to avoid name clashes by renaming the methods of parent classes. The axiom related with a method is obtained by evaluating its implementation yielding a process term. The precondition states that a variable corresponding to a parameter whose type is a class refers to an object either of this class or of an heir class (described by the Names function contained in the specification NAME). The definition of the axioms is based on an evaluation function which translates a command into a process term. The local environment is a mapping from formal parameters (occurring in the method headers) to variables. We now exemplify the definition of *Eval* in a concrete case on the example introduced in Sect. 1. Here we assume to fix a process specification (given formally in the Appendix) in which the following process combinators are available:

- action prefixing: the process a Δ pr can perform the action a and then become the process pr; this is the basic combinator for expressing the activity of a process in terms of a sequence of actions;
- non-deterministic choice: the process **choose** x: r **in** pr(x) can (nondeterministically) behave as each pr(t) for every defined term t of sort r.
- sequential composition: the activity of **def**$_r$ x = pr **in** pr'(x) consists in the activity of pr until it terminates; if pr terminates returning a value t of sort r, then pr'(t) follows, otherwise the process returns the value to an outer frame. The process **return**$_r$ t represents a terminated activity returning the value t of sort r.

Sort indexes in process combinators are omitted in the example. We assume here that the sort symbols corresponding to the class identifiers RECTANGLE, CUBOID, USER are respectively R, C, U. Modelling reflexivity of clientship is omitted, as the classes are not recursive. We assume the internal structure of the objects to be given.

Interface(RECTANGLE, r) $=_{def}$ Σ_R $=_{def}$
enrich Σ_{BASE} + Σ-PR$_R$ **by**
sorts {R} **opns** {Set-L, Set-W: int → process$_R$, Area: → int-process$_R$, Create$_R$: → process$_R$}

Spec(RECTANGLE, r) $=_{def}$ SP$_R$ $=_{def}$
export Σ_R **from**
enrich *Obj*(RECTANGLE, r) **by**
sorts {R} **opns** opns(Σ_R)
axioms
{ Set-L(l) = ASSIGN-LENGTH$_{int}$(l) Δ **skip**, Set-W(w) = ASSIGN-WIDTH$_{int}$(w) Δ **skip**,
Area = **choose** l **in** GET-LENGTH$_{int}$(l) Δ **choose** w **in** GET-WIDTH$_{int}$(w) Δ **return** l∗w,
Create$_R$ = CREATE(Init-State$_R$, **skip**) Δ **skip** }

Interface(CUBOID, c) $=_{def}$ Σ_C $=_{def}$
enrich Σ_{BASE} + Σ-PR$_C$ **by**
sorts {C} **opns** { Set-L, Set-W, Set-H: int → process$_C$, Volume, Area: → int-process$_C$, Create$_C$: → process$_C$ }

Spec(CUBOID, c) =
  export Σ_C **from enrich** *Obj*(CUBOID, c) **by**
    sorts {C} **opns** opns(Σ_C)
    axioms
      { Set-H(h) = ASSIGN-HEIGHT$_{int}$(h) Δ **skip**,
        Volume = **def** a = Area **in choose** h **in** GET-HEIGHT$_{int}$(h) Δ **return** a∗h,
        Create$_C$ = CREATE(Init-State$_C$, **skip**) Δ **skip**, ... }

Interface(USER, u) =$_{def}$ Σ_U =$_{def}$ **enrich** Σ_{BASE} + Σ-PR$_U$ **by sorts** {U} **opns** {Create: → process$_U$}
Full-Sig(USER, u) =Σ_U + Σ_{use} where Σ_{use} =$_{def}$
  enrich Σ-PR$_U$ **by**
    <sorts(Σ_{BASE}) ∪ {R, U},
      { _.Set-L, _.Set-W: (name, int) → name-process$_U$, _.Area: name → int-process$_U$,
        _.Create: name → name-process$_U$ }
Spec(USER, u) =
  export *Full-Sig*(USER, u) **from**
    enrich *Obj*(USER, u) + SP$_{use}$ **by**
      sorts { U } **opns** { Create: → process$_U$ }
      axioms
        { pr = **choose** n **in** n.Create Δ ASSIGN-A$_R$(n) Δ **skip**;
          choose n **in** GET-A$_R$(n) Δ n.Set-L(3);
          choose n **in** GET-A$_R$(n) Δ n.Set-W(5);
          def a = **choose** n **in** GET-A$_R$(n) Δ n.Area **in** ASSIGN-V$_{int}$(a) Δ **skip**
        ⇒ Create = CREATE$_U$(Init-State$_U$, pr) Δ **skip** }
SP$_{use}$ =$_{def}$
  export Σ_{use} **from**
    enrich SP$_R$ **by**
      sorts sorts(Σ_{use}) **opns** opns(Σ_{use})
      axioms
      { Class(n) = RECTANGLE ⇒ n.Set-L(l) = Use$_R$(n, Set-L(l)),
        (note that here Use$_R$(n, Set-L(l)) is equivalent to n.ASSIGN-LENGTH$_{int}$(l) Δ **return** n) ... }

Concluding Remarks

In the preceding sections an algebraic semantics of an object-oriented programming language has been presented. Each class corresponds to an algebraic specification which describes in a loose approach the objects of the class together with the related methods. In particular, we give a framework for objects in a concurrent environment modelling the methods of a class by processes acting on the object passive parts which are determined by the attributes of the class.

Future work has to be done in at least two directions. One is to introduce an *observational semantics* of objects and processes, ie to define a semantics of a class by abstracting away from the internal structure of objects, only considering their properties when used in a context. In particular for processes this is related to the well-known techniques of expressing quotient structures as for example bisimulation (see [AGRZ]). With them it can be specified what we want to observe of a process which is acting on an object of a class.

The second topic is the extension of our framework to an object-oriented specification language. As mentioned above, the expressive power of the algebraic specification language allows not only to translate method implementations into axioms, but also to describe properties of methods in an abstract way. This is particularly relevant in the case in which the object oriented language is used in the design phase of a program as for example pursued in [M]. As shown in Sect.1, inheritance corresponds to an implementation relation on the algebraic specification level. Thus, this approach can be combined with notions developed in the area of reusability of algebraic specifications (for example in [WHB] a language for defining a structured system of algebraic specifications related by an implementation relation has been presented). Classes defining abstract properties of methods can be concreted step by step in the heir classes by adding either further properties or concrete implementations. At the end of this chain (or tree structure if various design decisions are taken on one level of abstraction) the concrete machine executable target programs can be found.

Acknowledgment. The authors are grateful to their colleagues in the DRAGON project, especially to Martin Wirsing, Rolf Hennicker (for the Passau side), Egidio Astesiano and Gianna Reggio (for the Genova side) for many helpful discussions and comments.

References

[ABKR] America, P.; de Bakker, J.; Kok, J.; Rutten, J. "Denotational semantics of a parallel object-oriented language", Report CS-R8626, Centre for Mathematics and Computer Science, Amsterdam, the Netherlands, August 1986.

[AGRZ] Astesiano, E.; Giovini, A.; Reggio, G.; Zucca, E. "An integrated algebraic approach to the specification of data types, processes and objects", to appear in (Wirsing, M. ed.) *Proc. Meteor 1987 Workshop*, Berlin, Springer Verlag, 1988 (Lecture Notes in Computer Science n. ...).

[AR] Astesiano, E.; Reggio, G. "SMoLCS-Driven Concurrent Calculi", *Proc. TAPSOFT'87*, vol.1, Berlin, Springer Verlag, 1987 (Lecture Notes in Computer Science n. 249), pp. 169–201.

[BW] Broy, M.; Wirsing, M. "Partial abstract data types", Acta Informatica 18, pp. 47-64, 1982.

[BZ1] Breu, R.; Zucca, E. "An algebraic compositional semantics of an object-oriented notation with concurrency", in : Breu, R.; Hennicker, R.; Wirsing, M.; Astesiano, E.; Giovini, A.; Reggio, G.; Zucca, E. "Towards an Algebraic Compositional Semantics for DRAGOON, Deliverable of the DRAGON project (Esprit 1550), March 1989 (revised version in preparation).

[BZ2] Breu, R.; Zucca, E. "An object-oriented specification language", in preparation.

[DRAGON] Bayan, R.; Kaag, F.; Spasojevic, A.; Di Maio, A.; Cardigno, C.; Gatti, S.; Crespi Reghizzi, S.; Astesiano, E.; Giovini, A.; Gautier, B.; Atkinson, C.; Wirsing, M.; Hennicker, R. "An object oriented approach to DRAGON", Deliverable of the project "DRAGON" (Esprit 1550), February 1988.

[GM] Goguen, J.A.; Meseguer, J. "Unifying functional, object-oriented and relational programming with logical semantics, *Research Directions in Object-Oriented Programming* (Shriver, B.; Wegner, P. editors), Computer Systems Series, MIT Press, 1987.

[M] Meyer, B. "Object Oriented Software Construction", Prentice Hall, New York , 1988.

[Wi] Wirsing, M. "Structured algebraic specifications", in Theoretical Computer Science 43, 1986, pp. 123-250.

[WHB] Wirsing, M.; Hennicker, R.; Breu, R. "Reusable specification components", *Proc. MFCS 1988*, Berlin, Springer Verlag, 1988 (Lecture Notes in Computer Science n. 324), pp 121-137.

[Wo] Wolczko, M. "Semantics of Smalltalk-80", in ECOOP '87, Lecture Notes in Computer Science n. 276, Springer Verlag, 1987.

Appendix

A. The Specification of the Object Environment

The internal structure of an object is in essence a map from names into object states. Object states are tuples with a component for each attribute. Compare the formal definition given here with Fig. 2.

Obj-Env: Class-Id × Class → Spec

Let FIN-MAP_C = FIN-MAP(NAME, name, *States*(C, c), { $\text{state}_D \mid \text{state}_D \in \text{sorts}(\text{sig}(\text{STATE}_D))$, $\text{STATE}_D \in$ *States*(C, c) }, C) } be the specification of the finite maps from names into states of the transitively used classes, omitted here, then

Obj-Env(C, c) $=_{def}$
  enrich FIN-MAP_C **by**
    opns { $\text{Obj}_C: \text{state}_C \to C$ }
    axioms
      { $\text{Obj}_C(\sigma_C) = \text{Empty}[\text{Self} \to \sigma_C]$, $D(o_C[\text{Self} \to \sigma]) \mid \_[\_ \to \_]: C, \text{name}, \text{state}_C \to C$ }
      $\cup$ { $o_C \neq \text{Empty} \Rightarrow D(o_C[\text{Self}]) \mid \_[\_]: C, \text{name} \to \text{state}_C$ }
      $\cup$ { $n \neq \text{Self} \Rightarrow (D(o_C[n \to \sigma]) \Leftrightarrow \text{Class}(n) = E) \mid \_[\_ \to \_]: C, \text{name}, \text{state}_E \to C$ }

An auxiliary semantic function defines all the object states in the internal structure of the objects of the given class, ie one for each transitively used class.

States: Class-Id × Class → Specs
States(C, Flat(attrs, methods, body)) $=_{def}$ *State*(C, Flat(attrs, methods, body))
States(C, Export(methods, d)) =*States*(C, Rename(r, d)) $=_{def}$ *States*(C, d)
Let c = Inherits-Uses($\{c_1, ..., c_n\}$, $\{c_1', ..., c_m'\}$, attrs, methods, body), $C_i' = \text{Name}(c_i')$, then
States(C, c) $=_{def}$ *State*(C, c) $\cup \bigcup_{i=1..n}$ (*States*(C, c_i) - *State*(C, c_i)) $\cup \bigcup_{i=1..m}$ (*States*(C_i', c_i'))

Note in the last clause that *State*(C, c_i), i = 1, ..., n, ie the state specifications of the inherited classes, are eliminated since they are all replaced by the new state specification *State*(C, c). A constant Init-State_C defines the initial state related to a class: attributes of basic types are initialized by predefined values, while the others refer to a constant Nil (the null name).

Here we assume a predefined specification SUM(A,B) defining the disjoint union of data types A and B and a specification NIL containing a sort nil and a constant Nil.
State: Class-Id × Class → Spec
State(C, Inherits-Uses($\{c_1, ..., c_n\}$, $\{c_1', ..., c_m'\}$, attrs, methods, body)) $=_{def}$
    enrich BASE + SUM(NAME, NIL) + *State*(C, c_1) + ... + *State*(C, c_n) **by**
        sorts { $state_C$ }
        opns
            { Init-$State_C$: → $state_C$ }
            ∪{ X_B: $state_C$ → B, _[_/X_B]: ($state_C$, B) → $state_C$ | X: B ∈ attrs, B basic type }
            ∪{ X_E: $state_C$ → sum(name, nil), _[_/X_E]: ($state_C$, sum(name, nil)) → $state_C$ | X: E ∈ attrs, E class}
        axioms
            { C inherits C_i | i =1, ..., n, C_i = Name(c_i) } (inherits is a boolean operation in NAME)
            ∪{ D(σ[x / X_B]) | _[_/X_B]: ($state_C$, B) → $state_C$, B basic type }
            ∪{ D(σ[n / X_E]) ⇔ n ∈ Names(E) | _[_/X_E]: ($state_C$, name) → $state_C$), E class }
            ∪{ X_T(σ[x / X_T]) = x | X_T: $state_C$ → T, _ [_ / X_T]: ($state_C$, T) → $state_C$ }
            ∪{ $Y_{T'}$(σ[x / X_T]) = $Y_{T'}$(σ) | $Y_{T'}$: $state_C$ → T', _ [_ / X_T]: ($state_C$, T) → $state_C$, X: T ≠ Y: T'}
            ∪{ X_B(Init-$State_C$) = v_B | X_B: $state_C$ → B, B basic type, v_B a default value of type B }
            ∪{ X_E(Init-$State_C$) = Nil | X_E: $state_C$ → name, E class }
State(C, Export(methods,d)) = *State*(C, Rename(r,d)) $=_{def}$ *State*(C,d)

B An example of process specification

$PROCESS_C =_{def}$
    enrich Σ-PR_C **by**
        opns
            { _Δ_: (act_C , r-$process_C$) → r-$process_C$,
              $\textbf{choose}_r\textbf{in}$_: (r → r'-$process_C$) → r'-$process_C$,
              $\textbf{def}_r$_**in**_: r-$process_C$ → (r → r'-$process_C$) → r'-$process_C$,
              $\textbf{return}_r$ _: r → r-$process_C$,
        axioms
            { a Δ pr $\xrightarrow{a}$ pr }
            ∪ {prf(t) $\xrightarrow{a}$ pr' ⇒ $\textbf{choose}_r\textbf{in}$ prf $\xrightarrow{a}$ pr' | r ∈ RES}
            ∪ {$\textbf{def}_r$ ($\textbf{choose}_{r'}$ **in** prf) **in** prf' = $\textbf{choose}_{r'}\textbf{in}$ λt. ($\textbf{def}_r$ prf(t) **in** prf')
                | r ∈ RES, t not free in prf, prf' }
            ∪ {$\textbf{def}_r$ a Δ pr **in** prf = a Δ $\textbf{def}_r$ pr **in** prf,
              $\textbf{def}_r$($\textbf{return}_r$ t) **in** prf = prf(t),
              pr $\xrightarrow{a}$ pr' ⇒ $\textbf{def}_r$ pr **in** prf $\xrightarrow{a}$ $\textbf{def}_r$ pr' **in** prf | r ∈ RES}
            ∪ {$\textbf{def}_r$ ($\textbf{return}_{r'}$ t) **in** prf = $\textbf{return}_{r'}$ t | r, r' ∈ RES, r ≠ r'}

<u>Notations</u>
- sort indexes are omitted in process combinators when there is no ambiguity;
- $\textbf{choose}_r\textbf{in}$ λx.pr(x) is written **choose** x: r **in** pr(x);
- **def** pr **in** λx.pr'(x) is written **def** x = pr **in** pr'(x);
- **return** Null is written **skip**, $\textbf{def}_{null}$ pr **in** pr' is written pr; pr'.

AN AXIOMATIZATION OF EVENT STRUCTURES

Madhavan Mukund and P. S. Thiagarajan
The Institute of Mathematical Sciences, Madras 600 113, INDIA

0. Introduction

We present here a sound and complete axiomatization of event structures. Event structures are a poset-based model of distributed systems. In an event structure, the three fundamental phenomena of causality, choice and concurrency are clearly separated from each other.

Event structures are pleasant mathematical objects possessing a rich theory [NPW]. They have a very natural connection to the theory of Petri nets [NPW]. Event structures can be used to provide the non-interleaved denotational semantics of a large family of CCS-like languages [W1]. Hence there is a good deal of motivation for developing a logic to reason about the behaviour of a distributed system represented in terms of an event structure. The logic we present here is a temporal logic with two additional unary modalities which directly express choice and concurrency.

In the next section we introduce event structures. In Section 2 we define the logical language and specify a Kripke-style semantics using event structures as frames. We then illustrate with the help of some simple examples how this language can be used to express interesting properties of distributed computations. The axiomatization is presented in Section 3. In Section 4, we sketch the proof of completeness of the axiomatization, which is the main contribution of this paper. The concluding section discusses related work and directions for future research.

1. Event Structures

An event structure essentially consists of a partially ordered set of event occurrences augmented with a binary conflict relation.

Definition 1.1:

An **event structure** is a triple $ES = (E, <, \#)$ where

(i) E is a set of **events**.

(ii) $< \subseteq E \times E$ is an irreflexive and transitive **causality relation**.

(iii) $\# \subseteq E \times E$ is an irreflexive and symmetric **conflict relation**.

(iv) $\#$ is inherited via $<$ in the sense that $e_1 \# e_2 < e_3$ implies that $e_1 \# e_3$ for every e_1, e_2, e_3 in E.

□

To be precise, the objects we have defined above are usually referred to as prime event structures in the literature [W2]. Here, for the sake of convenience, we always refer to them simply as event structures. Usually the causality relation is required to be a partial ordering relation. We have made it a strict partial ordering relation because it fits in better with the completeness argument presented in Section 4.

Let $ES = (E, <, \#)$ be an event structure. Then

$$id \triangleq \{(e,e) \mid e \in E\}$$

$$> \triangleq \{(e,e') \mid (e',e) \in <\}$$

$$\leq \triangleq < \cup\, id$$

$$\geq \triangleq > \cup\, id \text{ and}$$

$$co \triangleq E \times E - (\leq \cup \geq \cup \#).$$

The relation co captures concurrency. Observe that $\{<, >, \#, co, id\}$ is a partitioning of $E \times E$.

Before we consider an example it will be convenient to define one more auxiliary relation. Let $ES = (E, <, \#)$ be an event structure and $e, e' \in E$. Then

$$e \#_\mu e' \triangleq e \# e' \text{ and } \forall e_1, e_1' \in E.[\, e_1 \leq e \text{ and } e_1' \leq e' \text{ and } e_1 \# e_1' \text{ implies } e_1 = e \text{ and } e_1' = e' \,].$$

$\#_\mu$ in some sense identifies the "minimal elements" (under $<$) of the $\#$ relation. As a result, we can specify an event structure by displaying its $<$ and $\#_\mu$ relations. The $\#$ relation is then uniquely determined by part (iv) of Definition 1.1.

Figure 1.1 is an example of an event structure. The squiggly lines represent the $\#_\mu$ relation. The causality relation is shown in the form of the associated Hasse diagram.

In this event structure, $e_1 \# e_6$ because $e_1 \#_\mu e_2 < e_6$. It is also easy to see that $e_6\ co\ e_7$.

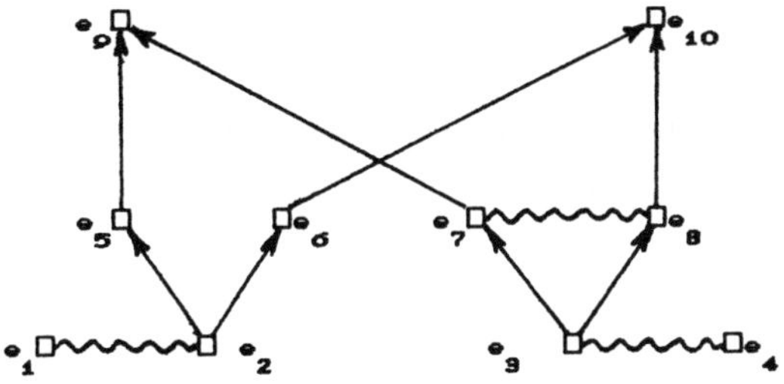

FIGURE 1.1

The states of an event structure are called configurations. A configuration identifies a set of events that have occurred "so far". An event can occur only if all the events in its "past" have occurred. Two events that are in conflict can never both occur in the same stretch of behaviour. Before formalizing these notions it will be convenient to adopt the following notation.

Let ES = (E,<,#) be an event structure and $X \subseteq E$. Then

$$\downarrow X = \{e' \mid \exists e \in X.\ e' \leq e\}$$

For the singleton {e}, we shall write $\downarrow e$ instead of $\downarrow\{e\}$.

Definition 1.2:
Let ES = (E,<,#) be an event structure and $c \subseteq E$. Then c is a **configuration** iff

(i) $c = \downarrow c$ (left-closed)

(ii) $(c \times c) \cap \# = \emptyset$ (conflict-free)

□

For the event structure shown in Figure 1.1, $\{e_2,e_5,e_6\}$ is a configuration. $\{e_2,e_5,e_{10}\}$ is not a configuration because it is not left-closed and $\{e_3,e_7,e_8\}$ is not a configuration because it is not conflict-free.

In this paper, we will be concerned with only the **local configurations** of an event structure. The notion of a local configuration is based on a simple but crucial observation which lies at the heart of the theory of event structures [NPW].

Proposition 1.3:
Let ES = (E,<,#) be an event structure and $e \in E$. Then $\downarrow e$ is a configuration.

Proof: Follows easily from the definitions.

□

We now define $LC_{ES} = \{\downarrow e | e \in E\}$ to be the set of **local configurations** of the event structure $ES = (E,<,\#)$. We shall interpret the formulas of our logical language only at the local configurations of an event structure. We view "global" configurations as states whose holdings can be neither verified (without a global clock, which we do not wish to assume) nor provably denied. We do not pursue this important issue here due to lack of space. The interested reader is referred to [LT1,KP,PW] for a sample of discussions on this topic.

2. The Language and its Models

We fix $P = \{p_1,p_2,\ldots\}$, a countably infinite set of **atomic propositions**. We let p,q with or without subscripts range over P. The formulas of our language are then defined inductively as follows:

(i) Every member of P is a formula.

(ii) If α and β are formulas then so are $\sim\alpha$, $\alpha \vee \beta$, $\Box\alpha$, $\boxminus\alpha$, $\triangledown\alpha$ and $\blacktriangle\alpha$.

$\Box$ and $\boxminus$ will denote the future and past modalities of tense logic [B1] respectively. $\triangledown$ will capture conflict and $\blacktriangle$ will capture concurrency. The operator $\triangledown$ was used first by Penczek [P] in a slightly different context, which we explain in the concluding section.

For the rest of the paper, Φ will denote the set of formulas of our language. We let α,β and γ with or without subscripts range over Φ.

A **frame** is an ordered pair $Fr = (ES,LC_{ES})$ where $ES = (E,<,\#)$ is an event structure and LC_{ES} is the set of local configurations of ES. The members of LC_{ES} will play the role of possible worlds in the Kripke-style semantics we are about to define.

A **model** is an ordered pair $M = (Fr,V)$ where $Fr = (ES,LC_{ES})$ is a frame and $V:P \longrightarrow 2^{LC_{ES}}$ is a **valuation function**.

Let $M = (Fr,V)$ be a model with $Fr = (ES,LC_{ES})$, where $ES = (E,<,\#)$ and $\downarrow e \in LC_{ES}$. Then the notion of a formula α being satisfied at the local state $\downarrow e$ in the model M is denoted as $M,\downarrow e \models \alpha$ and is defined inductively as follows:

$M,\downarrow e \models p$ iff $\downarrow e \in V(p)$

$M,\downarrow e \models \sim\alpha$ iff $M,\downarrow e \not\models \alpha$

$M,\downarrow e \models \alpha \vee \beta$ iff $M,\downarrow e \models \alpha$ or $M,\downarrow e \models \beta$

$M,\downarrow e \models \Box\alpha$ iff $\forall e' \in E.[\ e < e'$ implies $M,\downarrow e' \models \alpha\ ]$

$M,\downarrow e \models \boxminus\alpha$ iff $\forall e' \in E.[\ e' < e$ implies $M,\downarrow e' \models \alpha\ ]$

$M, \downarrow e \models \nabla\alpha$ iff $\forall e' \in E.[\ e \# e'$ implies $M, \downarrow e' \models \alpha\ ]$

$M, \downarrow e \models \Delta\alpha$ iff $\forall e' \in E.[\ e\ co\ e'$ implies $M, \downarrow e' \models \alpha\ ]$

The formula α is **satisfiable** if there exists a model $M = (Fr, V)$ with $Fr = (ES, LC_{ES})$ and a local state $\downarrow e$ of ES such that $M, \downarrow e \models \alpha$. α is **M-valid** iff $M, \downarrow e \models \alpha$ for every $\downarrow e \in LC_{ES}$. α is **valid** — and this is denoted by $\models \alpha$ — if α is M-valid for every model M.

One remark is in order before we begin to study this language with the chosen semantics. Let us call the language defined above L1. There is a closely related language L2 which is more useful and more expressive. L2 differs from L1 only in that the operator ∇ is replaced by the operator ∇_μ. The semantics of L2 is the same as that of L1 except that the clause corresponding to $\nabla\alpha$ is replaced by:

$$M, \downarrow e \models \nabla_\mu\alpha \text{ iff } \forall e' \in E.[\ e \#_\mu e' \text{ implies } M, \downarrow e' \models \alpha\ ]$$

∇ becomes a *derived* modality in L2 and is given by:

$$\nabla\alpha \triangleq \nabla_\mu\alpha \wedge \nabla_\mu\Box\alpha \wedge \boxminus\nabla_\mu\alpha \wedge \boxminus\nabla_\mu\Box\alpha$$

We have, in fact, an axiomatization of event structures in terms of L2 [MT3]. Here however we have chosen to present an axiomatization in terms of L1 because it exhibits all the basic aspects of the theory based on L2 in a much cleaner way. Technically, both the axiomatization and the completeness proof for L2 is merely a "messier" version of the material presented here.

Returning to L1, we define the derived connectives of the Propositional Calculus (PC) such as $\wedge, \supset$ and $\equiv$ in terms of $\sim$ and $\vee$ in the usual way. In addition, we define

$$\Diamond\alpha \triangleq \sim\Box\sim\alpha$$

$$\diamondminus\alpha \triangleq \sim\boxminus\sim\alpha$$

$$\triangledown\alpha \triangleq \sim\nabla\sim\alpha$$

$$\vartriangle\alpha \triangleq \sim\Delta\sim\alpha$$

A number of interesting properties of distributed computations can be expressed in our language.

To illustrate, consider a finite set of sequential agents $A_1, A_2, \ldots A_n$. Assume that $\{Q_1, Q_2, \ldots Q_n\}$ is a collection of pair-wise disjoint finite non-empty sets. Q_i is the set of local states that the agent A_i can assume. The agents communicate with each other asynchronously. The means for associating an event structure with such a system of communicating sequential agents will be assumed to be available (see for example [MT1]).

Suppose that for each i and each $q \in Q_i$ we have an atomic proposition, also called q for convenience, which denotes that the current local state is q. Then $at_i = \bigvee_{q \in Q_i} q$ will denote the fact that the current local state belongs to A_i. The formula $\bigwedge_i (at_i \supset \blacktriangle(\sim at_i))$ captures the fact that the individual agents are *sequential* — i.e. they exhibit no concurrency in their local behaviours. The fact that for every local state q_i of agent A_i, there exists at least one local state q_j of agent A_j $(j \neq i)$ that can co-exist with q_i (i.e. q_i and q_j are *both* part of a reachable global state) can be expressed as $at_i \supset \bigwedge_{j \neq i} \Delta(at_j)$.

We can also use propositions to *uniquely* name local states of an event structure. Let $p \in P$ and let $\hat{p}$ denote the formula $p \wedge \Box{\sim}p \wedge \boxminus{\sim}p \wedge \blacktriangledown{\sim}p \wedge \blacktriangle{\sim}p$. Clearly, $\hat{p}$ can be satisfied at at most one local stated in any model. Hence, p uniquely identifies the local state where $\hat{p}$ is true.

Now suppose that the agents are running a common protocol to achieve a *stable property* expressed by the formula α. By a stable property, we mean that the formula $\bigwedge_j at_j \supset (\alpha \supset \Box_j \alpha)$ is valid over the model. Here, and through the rest of this section we shall use $\odot_j \beta$ to abbreviate $\odot(at_j \supset \beta)$ for $\odot \in \{\Box, \boxminus, \blacktriangle, \blacktriangledown\}$.

In other words, if A_i achieves a local state satisfying α as a result of running the protocol then starting from any global state containing such a local state every other agent must also eventually achieve a local state satisfying α. For instance each A_i could be a local data base manager controlling the ith copy of a distributed data base. α could denote that an agent has decided, as a result of running the protocol, to go through with an update on the local copy (see [PW] for a concrete example of this situation).

Let p be the proposition naming the local state of agent i where α has been achieved. Then

$$at_i \wedge \alpha \wedge \hat{p} \supset \bigwedge_{j \neq i} \blacktriangle_j[\alpha \vee (\Diamond(at_j \wedge \alpha \wedge (\Delta\hat{p} \vee \blacklozenge\hat{p})) \wedge \Box_j(\alpha \vee \Diamond(at_j \wedge \alpha \wedge (\hat{\Delta} p \vee \hat{\blacklozenge} p))))]$$

expresses the correctness of the protocol.

For most "reasonable" protocols, including the one described in [PW], the simpler formula

$$at_i \wedge \alpha \supset \bigwedge_{j \neq i} \blacktriangle_j[\alpha \vee (\Diamond(at_j \wedge \alpha) \wedge \Box_j(\alpha \vee \Diamond(at_j \wedge \alpha)))]$$

is sufficient for expressing correctness.

Finally we note that in L2 we can also assert $at_i \supset \blacktriangledown_\mu at_i$, which would express the important fact that (non-deterministic) choices in the behaviour are made locally by the individual agents. L1 does not seem capable of expressing this fact.

3. The Axiom System

Our axioms are a combination of standard axioms of modal logic and tense logic [HC,B1], along with a few new axioms which reflect the restrictions imposed on the relations $<$, # and *co* in the definition of an event structure. We first present the axiom scheme in full, and then provide some explanatory remarks.

AXIOMS

(A1) All the substitution instances of the tautologies of propositional logic.

(A2) (i) $\Box(\alpha \supset \beta) \supset (\Box\alpha \supset \Box\beta)$ (Deductive Closure)
(ii) $\boxminus(\alpha \supset \beta) \supset (\boxminus\alpha \supset \boxminus\beta)$
(iii) $\blacktriangledown(\alpha \supset \beta) \supset (\blacktriangledown\alpha \supset \blacktriangledown\beta)$
(iv) $\blacktriangle(\alpha \supset \beta) \supset (\blacktriangle\alpha \supset \blacktriangle\beta)$

(A3) (i) $\Box\alpha \supset \Box\Box\alpha$ (Transitivity of $<$)
(ii) $\boxminus\alpha \supset \boxminus\boxminus\alpha$

(A4) (i) $\alpha \supset \blacktriangledown\nabla\alpha$ (Symmetry of # and *co*)
(ii) $\alpha \supset \blacktriangle\Delta\alpha$

(A5) (i) $\alpha \supset \Box\blacklozenge\alpha$ (Relating past and future)
(ii) $\alpha \supset \boxminus\Diamond\alpha$

(A6) $\nabla\alpha \supset \Box\nabla\alpha$ (Conflict inheritance)

(A7) $\Delta\alpha \supset \boxminus(\Delta\alpha \vee \Diamond\alpha)$ (Conflict-free past)

(A8) (i) $\Diamond\alpha \supset \Box(\alpha \vee \Diamond\alpha \vee \blacklozenge\alpha \vee \nabla\alpha \vee \Delta\alpha)$ (Relating weak and strong modalities)
(ii) $\nabla\alpha \supset \blacktriangledown(\alpha \vee \Diamond\alpha \vee \blacklozenge\alpha \vee \nabla\alpha \vee \Delta\alpha)$
(iii) $\Delta\alpha \supset \blacktriangle(\alpha \vee \Diamond\alpha \vee \blacklozenge\alpha \vee \nabla\alpha \vee \Delta\alpha)$
(iv) $\blacklozenge\alpha \supset \boxminus(\alpha \vee \Diamond\alpha \vee \blacklozenge\alpha \vee \Delta\alpha)$

(A9) $\nabla\alpha \supset \blacktriangle(\Diamond\alpha \vee \nabla\alpha \vee \Delta\alpha)$ (Relating $\blacktriangle$ and $\blacktriangledown$)

(A10) $\nabla\alpha \supset \boxminus(\Diamond\alpha \vee \nabla\alpha \vee \Delta\alpha)$ (Relating $\blacktriangledown$ and $\boxminus$)

(A11) $\Delta\alpha \supset \Box(\blacklozenge\alpha \vee \nabla\alpha \vee \Delta\alpha)$ (Relating $\blacktriangle$ and $\Box$)

INFERENCE RULES

(MP) $\dfrac{\alpha,\ \alpha \supset \beta}{\beta}$

(TG) (i) $\dfrac{\alpha}{\Box\alpha}$ (ii) $\dfrac{\alpha}{\boxminus\alpha}$ (iii) $\dfrac{\alpha}{\blacktriangledown\alpha}$ (iv) $\dfrac{\alpha}{\blacktriangle\alpha}$

(UNIQ) $\dfrac{\hat{p} \supset \alpha}{\alpha}$ where p is an atomic proposition not appearing in α and $\hat{p} \triangleq p \wedge \Box{\sim}p \wedge \boxminus{\sim}p \wedge \blacktriangle{\sim}p \wedge \triangledown{\sim}p$

Axioms A1 and A2 and inference rules MP and TG are standard. A3 and A4 are versions of the modal logical axioms T and B respectively which express the transitivity of < and the symmetry of # and *co*. A5 is the standard tense logical axiom relating the past and future modalities. A6 expresses the fact that conflict is inherited through <. A7 ensures that any two events related by *co* have consistent (i.e. conflict-free) pasts. The remaining axioms are necessary to ensure that the relations $<, <^{-1}$, # and *co* "cover" the event structure — i.e., any two events are related by one of these relations. The rule UNIQ is adapted from [B2]. Notice that given an atomic proposition p, the formula $\hat{p}$ can be true at at most one local state, by the definition of $\hat{p}$. Hence, we can label events with distinct formulas $\hat{p}_i$. The rule UNIQ will allow us to construct this labelling, which will be crucial in the completeness proof.

A formula α is a **thesis** if it is derivable in our axiom system. We denote that α is a thesis by $\vdash\alpha$.

Theorem: (Soundness) If $\vdash\alpha$ then $\models\alpha$.

Proof:

It is routine to verify that the axioms A1 to A11 are valid and that the inference rules MP and TG preserve validity. To show that UNIQ preserves validity is not so straightforward. A proof can be found in [MT2].

□

4. Completeness of the Axiom System

We now wish to show that the axiom system presented in the previous section is complete. We merely sketch the proof idea here. A detailed account can be found in [MT2].

As usual, by a **consistent** formula, we shall mean a formula whose negation is not a thesis of our axiom system. Our proof of completeness will establish that every consistent formula is satisfiable.

By a Maximal Consistent Set (MCS) we mean a consistent set of formulas which is not properly included in any other consistent set.

We can define three binary relations over MCSs as follows.

Definition 4.1:

Let A,B be maximal consistent sets.

(i) $A \hat{<} B \triangleq \{\alpha \mid \Box\alpha \in A\} \subseteq B$

(ii) $A \hat{\#} B \triangleq \{\alpha \mid \triangledown\alpha \in A\} \subseteq B$

(iii) $A \hat{co} B \triangleq \{\alpha \mid \blacktriangle\alpha \in A\} \subseteq B$

□

We can give equivalent definitions for $\hat{<}$, $\hat{\#}$ and $\hat{co}$ by exploiting the fact that □ and ⊟ are "inverses" of each other and that ▲ and ▽ are symmetric operators. It follows at once from axioms A3 and A4 that $\hat{<}$ is transitive and $\hat{\#}$ and $\hat{co}$ are symmetric. Henceforth we let $\hat{>}$ denote $(\hat{<})^{-1}$.

The semantic relations defined on MCSs are designed to behave like their counterparts in an event structure. Let ES = (E,<,#) be an event structure with $e_1,e_2,e_3 \in E$ and let $R_1,R_2 \in \{<,>,\#,co\}$ such that $e_1\ R_1\ e_2$ and $e_1\ R_2\ e_3$. We are guaranteed that for any choice of R_1 and R_2, we can always complete the "triangle" with $e_2\ R_3\ e_3$, where $R_3 \in \{<,>,\#,co\}$ such that the definition of an event structure is not violated. The next lemma establishes an analogous result for MCSs.

Lemma 4.2:

Let A,B and C be *distinct* MCSs such that $A\ \hat{R}_1\ B$ and $A\ \hat{R}_2\ C$ for $\hat{R}_1,\hat{R}_2 \in \{\hat{<},\hat{>},\hat{\#},\hat{co}\}$ as specified in Table 4.1. Then it must be the case

$\hat{R}_1$	$\hat{R}_2$	$\hat{R}_3$
$\hat{<}$	$\hat{<}$	$\hat{<}$, $\hat{>}$, $\hat{\#}$, $\hat{co}$
$\hat{<}$	$\hat{>}$	$\hat{>}$
$\hat{<}$	$\hat{\#}$	$\hat{\#}$
$\hat{<}$	$\hat{co}$	$\hat{>}$, $\hat{\#}$, $\hat{co}$
$\hat{>}$	$\hat{>}$	$\hat{<}$, $\hat{>}$, $\hat{co}$
$\hat{>}$	$\hat{\#}$	$\hat{<}$, $\hat{\#}$, $\hat{co}$
$\hat{>}$	$\hat{co}$	$\hat{<}$, $\hat{co}$
$\hat{\#}$	$\hat{\#}$	$\hat{<}$, $\hat{>}$, $\hat{\#}$, $\hat{co}$
$\hat{\#}$	$\hat{co}$	$\hat{>}$, $\hat{\#}$, $\hat{co}$
$\hat{co}$	$\hat{co}$	$\hat{<}$, $\hat{>}$, $\hat{\#}$, $\hat{co}$

TABLE 4.1

that B $\hat{R}_3$ C, $\hat{R}_3 \in \{\hat{<},\hat{>},\hat{\#},\hat{co}\}$, for at least one of the options specified for $\hat{R}_3$ in the corresponding row of Table 4.1.

Proof:
The result follows by appealing to the definition of $\hat{<}$, $\hat{\#}$ and $\hat{co}$ and axioms A3 and A6 to A11.

□

Next, we need to define the notion of a chronicle on an event structure.

Definition 4.3:
Let ES = (E,<,#) be an event structure.

(i) A **chronicle** on ES is a function T which assigns an MCS to each $e \in E$.

(ii) T is a **coherent chronicle** iff it satisfies the following requirements.

(a) $\forall e,e' \in E.\ e < e'$ implies $T(e)\ \hat{<}\ T(e')$

(b) $\forall e,e' \in E.\ e \# e'$ implies $T(e)\ \hat{\#}\ T(e')$.

(c) $\forall e,e' \in E.\ e\ co\ e'$ implies $T(e)\ \hat{co}\ T(e')$.

(iii) A **chronicle structure** is a pair (ES,T) where T is a coherent chronicle on ES.

□

A chronicle structure may contain "unfulfilled" formulas, in the following sense.

Definition 4.4:
Let (ES,T) be a chronicle structure, where ES = (E,<,#).

(i) A **live prophetic requirement** is a pair $(e,\Diamond\alpha)$ such that $e \in E$ and $\Diamond\alpha \in T(e)$ and for all $e' \in E$, $e < e'$ implies that $\alpha \notin T(e')$.

(ii) A **live historic requirement** is a pair $(e,\Diamond\!\!\!\!-\,\alpha)$ such that $e \in E$ and $\Diamond\!\!\!\!-\,\alpha \in T(e)$ and for all $e' \in E$, $e' < e$ implies that $\alpha \notin T(e')$.

(iii) A **live choice requirement** is a pair $(e,\nabla\alpha)$ such that $e \in E$ and $\nabla\alpha \in T(e)$ and for all $e' \in E$, $e \# e'$ implies that $\alpha \notin T(e')$.

(iv) A **live concurrent requirement** is a pair $(e,\Delta\alpha)$ such that $e \in E$ and $\Delta\alpha \in T(e)$ and for all $e' \in E$, $e\ co\ e'$ implies that $\alpha \notin T(e')$.

(v) A **live requirement** is a pair (e,β) such that (e,β) is a live prophetic requirement or a live historic requirement or a live choice requirement or a live concurrent requirement.

□

We are interested in chronicle structures which do not have certain classes of live requirements. First we need to define the closure of a formula α.

Definition 4.5:
Let α be a formula. CL(α), the **closure** of α is defined as follows:

$$CL(\alpha) = CL'(\alpha) \cup \{\sim\beta \mid \beta \in CL'(\alpha)\}$$

where $CL'(\alpha)$ is the least set of formulas containing α such that:

$\sim\beta \in CL'(\alpha)$ implies $\beta \in CL'(\alpha)$

$\beta_1 \vee \beta_2 \in CL'(\alpha)$ implies $\beta_1, \beta_2 \in CL'(\alpha)$

$\odot\beta \in CL'(\alpha)$ implies $\beta \in CL'(\alpha)$ where $\odot \in \{\Box, \boxminus, \nabla, \blacktriangle\}$

□

Definition 4.6:
Let (ES,T) be a chronicle structure, with ES = (E,<,#) and let α be a formula. (ES,T) is an **α-perfect chronicle structure** iff it has no live requirement (e,β) with $e \in E$ and $\beta \in CL(\alpha)$.

□

Given an α-perfect chronicle structure, we can specify a valuation function on the frame defined by the underlying event structure.

Definition 4.7:
Let (ES,T) be an α-perfect chronicle structure, where ES = (E,<,#). The **α-valuation induced by T** on the frame Fr = (ES, LC_{ES}) is denoted by V_T^{α} and is given by

$$\forall p \in P.\ V_T^{\alpha}(p) = \begin{cases} \{\downarrow e \in LC_{ES} \mid p \in T(e)\}, & \text{if } p \in CL(\alpha) \\ \emptyset, & \text{otherwise} \end{cases}$$

□

We can now use this induced valuation to extract a model for formulas in CL(α).

Lemma 4.8:
Let (ES,T) be an α-perfect chronicle structure, with ES = (E,<,#). Let $M_T^{\alpha} = (Fr, V_T^{\alpha})$, where Fr = (ES, LC_{ES}). Then

$$\forall\beta \in CL(\alpha).\ M_T^{\alpha}, \downarrow e \models \beta \text{ iff } \beta \in T(e)$$

Proof:
This is straightforward to establish by induction on the structure of β.

□

Hence, by Lemma 4.8, to construct a model for a consistent formula α, it is sufficient to construct an α-perfect chronicle structure (ES,T) with ES = (E,<,#) such that for some $e \in E$, $\alpha \in T(e)$.

For the rest of the section, we fix a consistent formula α_0 and a countably infinite set of events $E = \{e_0, e_1, e_2, \ldots\}$. Now, let

$\{q_0,q_1,\dots,q_n\}$ be the set of atomic propositions that appear in α_0. We fix an enumeration of P in the form $q_0,q_1,\dots,q_n,p_0,p_1,\dots$ We also fix an enumeration of $E \times CL(\alpha_0)$.

We shall inductively build up a chronicle structure $CH = (ES,T)$ which will have $\alpha_0 \in T(e_0)$, with e_0 an event in ES, and will eventually be α_0-perfect. At stage i, we shall assume that we have built up a structure CH_i where:

(i) $CH_i = (ES_i, T_i)$.
(ii) $ES_i = (E_i, <_i, \#_i)$ is an event structure.
(iii) $E_i = \{e_0, e_1, \dots, e_i\}$.
(iv) T_i is a coherent chronicle on ES_i.
(v) For $0 \le j \le i$, $\hat{p}_j \in T_i(e_j)$.

The last condition ensures that each event e_j that is present in E_i has a unique "name" $\hat{p}_j$ present in $T_i(e_j)$. This "name" is crucial for consistently extending CH_i to CH_{i+1}.

First, we define CH_0 to conform to our inductive definition. We have to ensure that $\alpha_0 \in T_0(e_0)$ and that $\hat{p}_0 \in T_0(e_0)$ as well.

We begin by defining the function $g:P \longrightarrow P$ as follows:

$$\forall x \in P.\ g(x) = \begin{cases} x, & \text{if } x \in \{q_0,q_1,\dots,q_n\} \\ p_{i+1}, & \text{if } x = p_i \text{ for } i \in \{0,1,2,\dots\} \end{cases}$$

In other words, replace p_0 by p_1, p_1 by p_2 . . . but leave the atomic propositions $q_0,q_1,\dots q_n$ *untouched*. g extends in an obvious way to $\hat{g}:\Phi \longrightarrow \Phi$. We abbreviate $\hat{g}(\alpha)$ by α'.

Extend $\{\alpha_0\}$ to a maximal consistent set A. Let $A' = \{\alpha' \mid \alpha \in A\}$. It is straightforward to show that A' is consistent and $\alpha_0 \in A'$. Furthermore, we can use UNIQ to establish that $A' \cup \{\hat{p}_0\}$ is also consistent. Let A_0 be a maximal consistent extension of $A' \cup \{\hat{p}_0\}$.

Let $CH_0 = ((\{e_0\},\emptyset,\emptyset), T_0)$, where $T_0(e_0) = A_0$. Clearly CH_0 satisfies all the properties assumed inductively for CH_i.

We now proceed to construct CH_{i+1} from CH_i. Let $e \in E_i$ and $\beta \in CL(\alpha_0)$ such that (e,β) is a live requirement which, among all live requirements in CH_i, has the least index in the enumeration of $E \times CL(\alpha_0)$. If no such live requirement is present set $CH_{i+1} = CH_i$. Otherwise, let $e = e_j$, where $j \in \{0,1,\dots,i\}$.

We shall outline the main steps for the case where β is of the form $\Diamond\beta_o$. The other cases can be dealt with in a similar fashion.

We have to add an event e_{i+1} and extend T_i to T_{i+1} such that $(e_j, \Diamond\beta_o)$ is not a live requirement in (ES_{i+1}, T_{i+1}).

To begin with, we "reserve" p_{i+1} for naming e_{i+1}. Define a function $h: P \longrightarrow P$ as follows.

$$\forall x \in P.\ h(x) = \begin{cases} x, & \text{if } x \in \{q_o, q_1, \ldots, q_n, p_o, p_1, \ldots, p_i\} \\ p_{k+1}, & \text{if } x = p_k \text{ for } k \in \{i+1, i+2, \ldots\} \end{cases}$$

In other words, replace p_{i+1} by p_{i+2}, p_{i+2} by p_{i+3} . . . but leave $q_o, q_1, \ldots q_n, p_o, p_1, \ldots, p_i$ *untouched.* Let $\hat{h}: \Phi \longrightarrow \Phi$ be the obvious extension of h to formulas. We abbreviate $\hat{h}(\alpha)$ by α''.

For $e_k \in E_i$, let A_k denote the MCS $T_i(e_k)$. A_k'' denotes the set $\{\alpha'' \mid \alpha \in A_k\}$. It is easy to show that A_k'' is consistent, though of course not maximal.

Consider A_j'' (recall that our live requirement is $(e_j, \Diamond\beta_o)$). Define $A_{i+1}'' = \{\alpha'' \mid \Box\alpha'' \in A_j''\} \cup \{\hat{p}_{i+1}\} \cup \{\beta_o\}$. Using UNIQ we can establish that A_{i+1}'' is consistent. Let $\hat{A}_{i+1}$ be a maximal consistent extension of A_{i+1}''. Clearly $\beta_o \in \hat{A}_{i+1}$.

Now, let $A_j^* = \{\nu \mid \boxminus\nu \in \hat{A}_{i+1}\}$. We can show that $A_j'' \cup A_j^*$ is consistent. Let $\hat{A}_j$ be a maximal consistent extension of $A_j'' \cup A_j^*$. Clearly $\hat{A}_j \hat{<} \hat{A}_{i+1}$. Thus if we ensure that $T_{i+1}(e_j) = \hat{A}_j$ and $T_{i+1}(e_{i+1}) = \hat{A}_{i+1}$, we know that $(e_j, \Diamond\beta_o)$ will not be a live requirement in CH_{i+1}.

For the other types of live requirements ($\beta \equiv \Diamond\beta_o, \nabla\beta_o$ and $\Delta\beta_o$) the procedure followed is similar. The definition of A_{i+1}'' would change depending on the requirement to be satisfied.

We now have to extend A_k'' for each $e_k \in E_i - \{e_j\}$ to an MCS. While doing this, we preserve the relationship of each A_k'' with respect to A_j''. For example, let $e_k \in E_i = \{e_j\}$ such that $e_k \#_i e_j$. Since T_i was assumed to be coherent, we know that $A_k \hat{\#} A_j$. Let $A_k^* = \{\beta \mid \nabla\beta \in \hat{A}_j\}$. It turns out that $A_k'' \cup A_k^*$ is consistent. Let $\hat{A}_k$ be a maximal consistent extension of $A_k'' \cup A_k^*$. Clearly $\hat{A}_k \hat{\#} \hat{A}_j$ as well. Similarly we extend each A_l'', using analogous arguments for $e_l <_i e_j$, $e_l >_i e_j$ and $e_l\ co_i\ e_j$.

At this stage, we have the following situation. We have managed to find MCSs $\hat{A}_0, \hat{A}_1, \ldots, \hat{A}_i, \hat{A}_{i+1}$ such that:

(i) For $0 \le k \le i$, $A''_k \subseteq \hat{A}_k$ where $A''_k = \{\alpha'' \mid \alpha \in T_i(e_k)\}$,

(ii) $\hat{p}_k \in \hat{A}_k$ for $0 \le k \le i+1$.

(iii) $\beta_0 \in \hat{A}_{i+1}$ and $\hat{A}_j \mathrel{\hat{<}} \hat{A}_{i+1}$.

(iv) For $0 \le k \le i$,
if $k \ne j$ and $(e_k, e_j) \in <_i$ (resp. $>_i, \#_i, co_i$) then
$(\hat{A}_k, \hat{A}_j) \in \hat{<}$ (resp. $\hat{>}, \hat{\#}, \hat{co}$)

We now have to verify that we have extended the MCSs in a consistent manner, so that live requirements "killed" at earlier stages remain "dead". We first need the following key result. Recall that for $p \in P$, $\hat{p} \triangleq p \wedge \Box{\sim}p \wedge \boxminus{\sim}p \wedge \triangledown{\sim}p \wedge \blacktriangle{\sim}p$.

Lemma 4.9:

Let A and B be MCSs such that $\hat{p} \in A$, where $p \in P$. Then A and B can be related by at most one semantic relation.

□

We can then show that for all $e_k, e_l \in E_i - \{e_j\}$, $\hat{A}_k$ and $\hat{A}_l$ are in the same semantic relation as A_k and A_l. This follows from the fact that $\hat{A}_k$ and $\hat{A}_l$ are both related to $\hat{A}_j$ and must thus be in *at least* one semantic relation, by Lemma 4.2. But, since $\hat{p}_k \in \hat{A}_k$, we appeal to Lemma 4.9 to deduce that they must be in *exactly* one semantic relation. The way we have preserved the relationship between A_k and A_j and A_l and A_j when extending A''_k to $\hat{A}_k$ and A''_l to $\hat{A}_l$ ensures that the unique relation between $\hat{A}_k$ and $\hat{A}_l$ is the same as that between A_k and A_l.

Finally, using a similar argument, we can show that for $0 \le l \le i$, $\hat{A}_{i+1}$ is in exactly one semantic relation with $\hat{A}_l$.

We can now "extend" CH_i to CH_{i+1} as follows.

(i) $E_{i+1} = E_i \cup \{e_{i+1}\}$

(ii) $<_{i+1} = <_i \cup \{(e_k, e_{i+1}) \mid 0 \le k \le i \text{ and } \hat{A}_k \mathrel{\hat{<}} \hat{A}_{i+1}\}$
$\cup \{(e_{i+1}, e_k) \mid 0 \le k \le i \text{ and } \hat{A}_{i+1} \mathrel{\hat{<}} \hat{A}_k\}$.

(iii) $>_{i+1} = (<_{i+1})^{-1}$.

(iv) $\#_{i+1} = \#_i \cup \{(e_k, e_{i+1}), (e_{i+1}, e_k) \mid 0 \le k \le i \text{ and } \hat{A}_k \mathrel{\hat{\#}} \hat{A}_{i+1}\}$.

(v) $co_{i+1} = co_i \cup \{(e_k, e_{i+1}), (e_{i+1}, e_k) \mid 0 \le k \le i \text{ and } \hat{A}_k \mathrel{\hat{co}} \hat{A}_{i+1}\}$.

(vi) $\forall k \in \{0,1,\ldots,i+1\}.\ T_{i+1}(e_k) = \hat{A}_k$.

Clearly $E_{i+1} = \{e_0, e_1, \ldots e_{i+1}\}$ and $\forall e_k \in E_{i+1}$, $\hat{p}_k \in T_{i+1}(e_k)$. Since we assumed that T_i is a coherent chronicle on ES_i, by the definition of CH_{i+1} it is clear that T_{i+1} is a coherent chronicle on ES_{i+1}, provided ES_{i+1} is an event structure.

Lemma 4.10: ES_{i+1} is an event structure.

Proof:

Note that $E_i \subseteq E_{i+1}$ and $R_i = R_{i+1} \upharpoonright (E_i \times E_i)$ for $R \in \{<,>,\#,co\}$, where $ES_i = (E_i, <_i, \#_i)$ is an event structure by the induction hypothesis. Lemma 4.2 guarantees that the relationships between MCSs in T_{i+1} respect the definition of an event structure. By Lemma 4.9, only one semantic relation can exist between any two MCSs in our chronicle structure. Since T_{i+1} is coherent on ES_{i+1}, it then follows from our construction that ES_{i+1} must be an event structure.

□

In this way, we can construct an infinite sequence of coherent chronicle structures.

To extract a model, first note that in passing from $CH_i = (ES_i, T_i)$ to $CH_{i+1} = (ES_{i+1}, T_{i+1})$, ES_{i+1} is a *proper extension* of ES_i. In other words $E_i \subseteq E_{i+1}$ and $R_i = R_{i+1} \upharpoonright (E_i \times E_i)$ for $R \in \{<,>,\#,co\}$. Hence we can construct the event structure $ES = (E,<,\#) = \bigcup_{i=0}^{\infty} ES_i$ where

$$E = \bigcup_{i=0}^{\infty} E_i, \quad < = \bigcup_{i=0}^{\infty} <_i, \quad \text{and } \# = \bigcup_{i=0}^{\infty} \#_i$$

To construct an α_0-perfect chronicle on ES, we first define a series of languages $L_0, L_1, \ldots$, where L_i is the set of formulas built from the set of propositions $P_i = \{q_0, q_1, \ldots q_n, p_0, p_1, \ldots p_i\}$ using the connectives $\sim$ and $\vee$ and the operators $\Box, \boxminus, \triangledown$ and $\blacktriangle$. We then define a function T as follows:

$$\forall e_i \in E.\ T(e_i) = \bigcup_{j \geq i} (T_j(e_i) \cap L_j).$$

Notice that for all $k \geq j \geq i$, $T_k(e_i) \cap L_j = T_j(e_i) \cap L_j$. Thus, $T(e_i) \cap L_j$ is fixed once and for all at stage j. From this, it is easy to verify that for each $e_i \in E$, $T(e_i)$ is an MCS. Our construction then ensures that (ES,T) is an α_0-perfect chronicle structure.

Let $V_T^{\alpha_0}$ be the α_0-valuation induced by T. By Lemma 4.8, we know that $M_T^{\alpha_0}, \downarrow e_0 \models \alpha_0$, so α_0 is satisfiable. Thus we have established

Theorem 4.11: (Completeness) If $\models \alpha$ then $\vdash \alpha$.

□

5. Discussion

In this paper we have obtained, for the first time, a sound and complete axiomatization of event structures. The logic we have designed explicitly deals with the three fundamental phenomena present in distributed computations — causality, choice and concurrency. $\Box$ and $\boxminus$ capture causality, $\triangledown$ captures choice and $\vartriangle$ captures concurrency. Our language seems to be a fairly expressive one — and the language L2, defined in Section 2, obtained by replacing $\triangledown$ with $\triangledown_\mu$ even more so — for dealing with distributed computations.

Aspects of branching time logic [EH] are captured in our language by "looking sideways" along a "cut" rather than by looking along a path as done in branching time logics. It will be interesting to determine the expressive power of our logic relative to the various branching time logics that have been studied in the literature.

Our completeness proof is a novel one in that it uses in a crucial way the inference rule UNIQ. This surprising and powerful inference rule — as already pointed out — is essentially due to Burgess [B2]. It is not clear at present whether completeness can be obtained *without* this inference rule.

The results presented here may be viewed as a generalization of the results presented in [LT1]. In [LT1], only $\Box$ and $\boxminus$ are used and, using special atomic propositions, a sound and complete axiomatization of a subclass of event structures is obtained. These restricted event structures are meant to model the behaviour of a finite set of sequential agents that communicate with each other asynchronously. (Incidentally [LT1] contains a flaw in the completeness proof which has since been repaired [LT2]).

Our work is also related, though in a less direct way, to the work of Penczek [P]. His use of the $\triangledown$ operator inspired us to invent, in addition, the $\vartriangle$ operator. He however is interested — inspite of the title of his paper — in the partially ordered computations generated by an event structure rather than in the event structure itself. A similar remark applies to the work reported in [PW] and [KP].

A number of extensions of the logic considered here are in order. The first, and the most important one, is to axiomatize *finitary* event structures. A finitary event structure ES = (E,<,#) has the property that $\downarrow e$ is a finite set for every $e \in E$. The motivation underlying this restriction should be clear. We conjecture that the logical system presented here augmented with the two axiom schemes

(i) $\ominus\alpha \supset \ominus(\alpha \wedge \boxminus\sim\alpha)$ (Well Foundedness)

(ii) $\alpha \wedge \Box\alpha \wedge \triangledown\alpha \wedge \blacktriangle\alpha \supset \ominus\Box\alpha \vee \boxminus\bot$ (Backward Discreteness)

is sound and complete for the class of finitary event structures. One can also consider adding axiom schemes to our system to characterize interesting subclasses of event structures such as sequential, determinate and the so-called confusion-free event structures. It seems that the property called confusion-freeness [W2] can be captured only in the language L2. We shall address these issues in our future work.

At present we do not know whether satisfiability in our logic is decidable. Clearly our logic does not have the finite model property. Hence it is not clear how one should go about attacking this decidability problem. Nevertheless, we wish to conclude by conjecturing that the satisfiability problem in our logic is decidable.

References:

[LNCS stands for Springer Lecture Notes in Computer Science]

[B1] Burgess, J. P.: "Basic Tense Logic", in *Handbook of Philosophical Logic*, Vol. II, Gabbay and Guenthner (eds.), D. Reidel Publishing Co., Dordrecht (1984), 89-133.

[B2] Burgess, J. P.: Decidability for Branching Time", *Studia Logica* **XXXIX**, 2/3 (1980) 203-218.

[EH] Emerson, E. A. and Halpern, J. Y.: " Decision Procedures and Expressiveness in the Temporal Logic of Branching Time", *J Comput. Syst. Sci.*, **30**, 1 (1985), 1-24.

[HC] Hughes, G. E. and Cresswell, M. J.: *An Introduction to Modal Logic*, Methuen and Co., London (Reprinted in 1982).

[KP] Katz, S. and Peled, D.: "Interleaving Set Temporal Logic", *Proc. 6th ACM-PODC Symposium*, Vancouver, Canada (1987) 178-190.

[LT1] Lodaya, K. and Thiagarajan, P. S.: "A Modal Logic for a Subclass of Event Structures", LNCS **267** (1987) 290-303.

[LT2] Lodaya, K. and Thiagarajan, P. S.: "A Correction to 'A Modal Logic for a Subclass of Event Structures'", *Report* DAIMI-PB-275, Computer Science Department, Aarhus University, Aarhus, Denmark (1989).

[MT1] Mukund, M. and Thiagarajan, P. S.: "A Petri Net Model of Asynchronously Communicating Sequential Processes", in *A Perspective in Theoretical Computer Science — Commemorative Volume for Gift Siromoney*, R. Narasimhan (ed.), World Scientific, Singapore (1989) 165-198.

[MT2] Mukund, M. and Thiagarajan, P. S.: "An Axiomatization of Event Structures", *Report* IMSc/89/7, The Institute of Mathematical Sciences, Madras, India (1989).

[MT3] Mukund, M. and Thiagarajan, P. S.: "A More Powerful Axiomatization of Event Structures", *Internal Report*, The Institute of Mathematical Sciences, Madras, India.

[NPW] Nielsen, M., Plotkin, G. and Winskel, G. : "Petri Nets, Event Structures and Domains, Part I", *Theor. Comput. Sci.* **13**, 1 (1980) 86-108.

[P] Penczek, W.: "A Temporal Logic for Event Structures", *Fundamenta Informaticae*, **XI** (1988) 297-326.

[PW] Pinter, S. and Wolper, P.: "A Temporal Logic for Reasoning about Partially Ordered Computations", *Proc. 3rd ACM-PODC Symposium*, Vancouver, Canada (1984) 28-37.

[W1] Winskel, G.: "Event Structure Semantics of CCS and Related Languages", LNCS **140** (1982) 561-576.

[W2] Winskel, G.: "Event Structures", LNCS **255** (1987) 325-392.

DEDUCING CAUSAL RELATIONSHIPS IN CCS

Jeremy Gunawardena,
Hewlett-Packard Laboratories, Information Systems Centre,
Filton Road, Stoke Gifford, Bristol BS12 6QZ.

Abstract

We introduce ***purely parallel processes***, a class of finite CCS processes defined by a restricted syntax which allows synchronization but forbids choice. Such processes are deterministic in the sense of Milner, [7]. We define a function which associates to each purely parallel process a labelled partially ordered set which is also deterministic but in the sense of Vaandrager, [10]. Our main result is that this induces a ***bijection*** from equivalence classes of purely parallel processes, under weak bisimulation, to finite deterministic pomsets. The motivation for this work comes from practical problems in verification and we give two applications of our results.

1 Introduction

In this paper we are concerned with studying the causal relationships between events in a CCS process. We concentrate on the subset of *purely parallel processes*, which is defined by a syntax which allows synchronization - of a restricted form - but forbids explicit use of the choice operator. The restrictions force all purely parallel processes to be deterministic in the sense of Milner, [7, Chapter 11]. In particular, the behaviour of such a process (ie: its equivalence class under weak bisimulation) is entirely determined by its traces.

We construct a function γ which associates to each purely parallel process, P, a labelled partially ordered set (poset), $\gamma(P)$, which encodes the causal relationships between the occurrences of observable actions. This gives, in effect, a causal denotational semantics for purely parallel processes. A key property is that the traces of P coincide with the sequences (linearizations) of $\gamma(P)$.

The poset $\gamma(P)$ is also deterministic, but now in the sense of Vaandrager, [10]. Vaandrager has shown that two deterministic event structures are isomorphic if, and only if, they have the same set of step sequences. We observe that when the event structures are conflict-free (ie: they correspond to posets) a stronger result holds: two deterministic posets are isomorphic if, and only if, they have the same set of sequences. It follows that the isomorphism class of $\gamma(P)$ is also determined by trace level information.

Our main result is that γ induces a bijection from equivalence classes of purely parallel processes, under weak bisimulation, to isomorphism classes of finite, deterministic posets. In one direction this follows from the properties mentioned above of determinism for processes and posets. We relate the weak bisimulation class of the process to the isomorphism class of the poset by "bouncing" off the trace level. The other direction requires a careful explicit construction. We sketch the proofs; full details may be found in [1].

In the second part we discuss two applications of the above results. The first is the verification of a proprietary key-distribution protocol. This provided the original motivation for the work described here. The second is a rigorous justification of a test, due to Kung, [4], for deadlock-freedom of systolic programs.

It is a pleasure to thank Robin Milner for his remarks on an early version of this paper; they provided an essential stimulus at a critical stage of the work. We are also grateful to two anonymous referees whose comments led to a considerable improvement in presentation. This work was undertaken as part of project VESPA at Hewlett-Packard's Information Systems Centre in Bristol, England.

2 Purely Parallel Processes

We shall assume familiarity with CCS, as expounded in either [6] or, more recently, [7], and also with a few of the elementary concepts of the theory of event structures, [11]. For the purposes of this paper a more appropriate reference for the latter is [10].

A few comments on notation and terminology may be appropriate. CCS processes engage in *actions*. The observable actions are assumed to be elements of some universe, $\Im$, which does not include the hidden action τ. The notation $P \xrightarrow{\alpha} Q$, where $\alpha \in \Im \cup \{\tau\}$, indicates that the process P engages in the action α and evolves into the process Q. This indexed relation can be extended, in a well-known way, to a relation,

$\overset{s}{\Longrightarrow}$, indexed over strings $s \in \Im^*$ of observable actions, where hidden events are now ignored. A string s is a *trace* of P if $P \overset{s}{\Longrightarrow} Q$ for some Q. The empty string ε is always a trace: by definition $P \overset{\varepsilon}{\Longrightarrow} P$.

We shall always use the weak semantics for CCS: processes P and Q are deemed to have the same behaviour if there is a weak bisimulation between them, denoted $P \approx Q$. Since all our processes are finite we shall feel free to use the phrase "observational equivalence" as a synonym for this.

In describing causal relationships it appears essential to employ a different mathematical setting to the algebra of expressions used in CCS or other process calculi. Causality exists not at the level of actions but at the level of action occurrences. In the event structure view, action occurrences, or *events*, are the primitive notion. The action is recovered from the event by a labelling function which provides the necessary extra layer of abstraction: different events may have the same action label and hence represent (different occurrences of) the same action.

Semantics based on causality are frequently assumed to adopt the true concurrency view: the interleaving equation $a|b = a.b + b.a$ is assumed not to hold. We should stress that this is not the case in the present paper.

2.1 Pure parallelism, confluence and determinism

A *purely parallel process* is an expression constructed from the following syntax.

$$P ::= (\, NIL \mid \alpha \mid P;P \mid P\backslash M \mid P||P\,)$$

The set of all such expressions will be denoted $\wp^3$. With the exception of the operator ";", which corresponds to sequentiality, all the operators in the syntax are derived from the standard CCS operators. Instead of describing them in this way, it may be more illuminating to write down the derived rewrite rules which they obey. This defines $\wp^3$ as a mini concurrency language in its own right but we shall prefer to think of it as a subset of CCS. The introduction of sequentiality in place of prefixing - which may be recovered as a special case via $\alpha.P = \alpha;P$ - is very convenient in applications but is essentially unnecessary. It turns out, as a Corollary to the proof of Theorem 3 below, that any $P \in \wp^3$ is observationally equivalent to a process written in the syntax

$$P ::= (\, NIL \mid \alpha.P \mid P||P\,).$$

The rewrite rules have the following form.

- NIL does nothing and has no rules.
- α introduces an action which may be the hidden action τ.

$$\alpha \overset{\alpha}{\longrightarrow} NIL$$

- $Q;R$ is sequential composition. Recall from [6, §5.6] that P is directly equivalent to NIL, written $P \equiv NIL$, if and only if P offers no actions, hidden or otherwise.

$$\frac{Q \overset{\alpha}{\longrightarrow} Q_1}{Q;R \overset{\alpha}{\longrightarrow} Q_1;R} \qquad\qquad \frac{R \overset{\beta}{\longrightarrow} R_1 \;\; (Q \equiv NIL)}{Q;R \overset{\beta}{\longrightarrow} Q;R_1}$$

- $Q\backslash M$ is restriction over a set M of actions.

$$\frac{Q \overset{\alpha}{\longrightarrow} Q_1 \;\; (\alpha \notin M)}{Q\backslash M \overset{\alpha}{\longrightarrow} Q_1\backslash M}$$

- $Q||R$ is parallel composition of a restricted form. In order to form $Q||R$ it is necessary that $L(Q) \cap L(R) = \emptyset$. Here, $L(Q)$ denotes the *strict sort* of P which is defined by structural induction as in [6, §5.5]. Let $L(Q,R)$ denote the set of actions on which Q and R can synchronize: $L(Q,R) = (L(Q) \cap \overline{L(R)}) \cup (L(R) \cap \overline{L(Q)})$,

$$\frac{Q \xrightarrow{\alpha} Q_1 \ (\alpha \notin L(Q,R))}{Q||R \xrightarrow{\alpha} Q_1||R} \qquad \frac{R \xrightarrow{\beta} R_1 \ (\beta \notin L(Q,R))}{Q||R \xrightarrow{\beta} Q||R_1}$$

$$\frac{Q \xrightarrow{a} Q_1 \quad R \xrightarrow{\overline{a}} R_1}{Q||R \xrightarrow{\tau} (Q_1||R_1)\backslash\{a,\overline{a}\}}$$

This parallel operator is not associative in general.

Milner has considered essentially these same operations but for rather different reasons: they arise in his work on determinism in CCS, [7, Chapter 11]. Informally, a process is deterministic if its present behaviour is only dependent on what it did in the past; a precise definition may be found in [7, §11.1, Definition 3]. Deterministic processes have the following crucial properties. Firstly, determinism is a behavioural property: if P is deterministic and $P \approx Q$ then Q is also deterministic. Secondly, behaviour is determined by traces: if P and Q are both deterministic then $P \approx Q$ if, and only if, $traces(P) = traces(Q)$.

Determinism is important because deterministic processes abound in nature and reasoning about their behaviour is particularly easy. The fly in the ointment, however, is that determinism is not a compositional property. If P and Q are both deterministic there is no reason why $P|Q$ or $P+Q$ should also be so. Milner's answer to this is to introduce the stronger notion of *confluence*, [7, §11.3, Definition 5]. Confluent processes are necessarily deterministic and confluence does have limited compositionality. Indeed, it is preserved by all of the operations in the syntax of $\wp^3$, [7, §11.4, Proposition 19]. (In actual fact, Milner does not deal with sequentiality, but it seems easy to do so.) This allows us to deduce the following essential fact.

Proposition 1 *Any purely parallel process is confluent and (hence) deterministic.*

This result can also be proved directly without relying on Milner's work and this is the method adopted in [1]. It can be shown, [1, §7], that there are (finite) confluent processes which are not purely parallel, even up to weak bisimulation. In other words, there are confluent behaviours which cannot be built compositionally. The causal structure of confluence can still be explicated but requires a more sophisticated approach to that taken here. The interested reader should refer to [2] for more details.

2.2 Posets, event structures and determinism

The partially ordered sets which we shall work with may be regarded as conflict-free event structures of the "prime with binary conflict" variety, [10, Definition 2.1]. We shall give precise definitions at the level of posets but refer the reader to [10] for notation and terminology relating to event structures.

Definition 1 *A labelled partially ordered set - poset for short - is a triple $(A, \preceq, \ell)$ where A is a set, $\preceq \subseteq A \times A$ is a partial order on A, and $\ell : A \to \Im$ is a labelling function. We assume the principle of finite causes: for all $a \in A$, the set $\{x \preceq a\}$ is finite.*

If $(A, \preceq_A, \ell_A)$ and $(B, \preceq_B, \ell_B)$ are two posets, a *morphism* between them is a function $f : A \to B$ such that $(u \preceq_A v) \Rightarrow (f(u) \preceq_B f(v))$ and $\ell_A(u) = \ell_B(f(u))$ for all $u, v \in A$. This yields a category of posets and morphisms. An isomorphism of posets is defined in the usual categorical manner. A *pomset* is an isomorphism class of posets. If A is a poset then $[A]$ will denote the corresponding pomset.

A poset B is a *linearization* of a poset A if the ordering on B is a total order and there is a morphism of posets $f : A \to B$ which is a bijection on the underlying sets. Note that if B is a poset with a total order then the pomset $[B]$ corresponds to a (possibly infinite) string over $\Im$. If A is a poset, the *sequences* of A are those strings $s \in \Im^*$ which, for some linearization B of A, are (finite) prefixes of $[B]$. The set of sequences of A will be denoted $seq(A)$.

Vaandrager has given a definition of determinism for event structures, [10, §3.6], and has shown that on this class both the interleaving equivalences and the lattice of non-interleaving equivalences collapse. More precisely he proves the following result.

Theorem 1 (F.W. Vaandrager, [10, §3.9,§5.1]) *If E and F are deterministic event structures then*

1. *bisimulation coincides with sequence equivalence: $E \leftrightarrows F$ if, and only if, $E \equiv_{seq} F$;*

2. isomorphism coincides with step sequence equivalence: $E \cong F$ *if, and only if,* $E \equiv_{step} F$.

When there is no conflict, Vaandrager's definition of determinism reduces to the following condition which corresponds to property T of [1, Definition 3.5].

Definition 2 (F.W. Vaandrager, [10, §3.8]) *A poset* $(A, \preceq, \ell)$ *is deterministic if for any* $a, b \in A$ *with* $\ell(a) = \ell(b)$ *either* $a \preceq b$ *or* $b \preceq a$.

Note that, in the absence of conflict, isomorphism of event structures is equivalent to isomorphism of posets, as defined above, and $E \equiv_{seq} F$ is equivalent to $seq(E) = seq(F)$. The following observation extends Vaandrager's theorem.

Proposition 2 *If A and B are deterministic posets (ie: conflict-free deterministic event structures) then isomorphism coincides with sequence equivalence:* $[A] = [B]$ *if, and only if,* $seq(A) = seq(B)$.

The proof is in two parts. When the posets are finite one uses induction on the number of elements in the poset, [1, Theorem 3.1]. Infinite posets are then approximated as a colimit of finite ones. Because of the principle of finite causes, a deterministic poset has no non-identity automorphism which is needed to show compatibility of the isomorphisms constructed over the finite approximations.

(Since writing this paper, it has come to our attention that Proposition 2 was essentially anticipated by Pratt, [9]. He points out, [9, Theorem 1], that an unlabelled poset can be recovered from its set of linearizations and, [9, §2.6], that this remains true - by "an easy exercise" - for pomsets "when all vertices with the same label are linearly ordered".)

2.3 Constructing the poset representation

We now move on to discuss the function γ from $\wp^3$ to (finite) deterministic posets. It is defined in a syntax-directed fashion and an appropriate rule is given for each production in the syntax of $\wp^3$.

If $P = NIL$ then $\gamma(P)$ is the empty poset. If $P = \alpha$, where $\alpha \neq \tau$ is an observable action, then $\gamma(P)$ consists of a single element with the label α:

$$\gamma(P) = (\{e\}, \{(e,e)\}, \ell(e) = \alpha).$$

If $P = \tau$ then once again $\gamma(P)$ is the empty poset. If $P = Q;R$ then $\gamma(P)$ is formed from the disjoint union of $\gamma(Q)$ and $\gamma(R)$ by insisting that every element of $\gamma(Q)$ precedes every element of $\gamma(R)$. These constructions are all very obvious.

The parallel operator, $||$, is much more interesting and requires more work. (Restriction will fall out during the course of this.) It will be convenient, for reasons which will become obvious, to work with graphs rather than partial orders, as in [1].

Definition 3 *The Hasse diagram of the poset* $(A, \preceq, \ell)$ *is the labelled acyclic directed graph* $(A, \rightarrow, \ell)$ *where the edge relation* $\rightarrow \subseteq A \times A$ *is given by the rule* $u \rightarrow v$ *if, and only if, u immediately precedes v. That is,*

- $u \preceq v$*; and*
- *if* $u \preceq w \preceq v$ *then either* $w = u$ *or* $w = v$.

The poset can be recovered from the Hasse diagram by taking the transitive closure of the edge relation. When dealing with graphs we allow nodes to be labelled with the hidden action τ.

Suppose that $\gamma(P)$ and $\gamma(Q)$ have already been constructed as acyclic directed graphs and we want to construct $\gamma(P||Q)$. Suppose that $a \in L(P)$ is an event which can synchronize with $\overline{a} \in L(Q)$. The first point to note is that, by Definition 2, all the nodes in $\gamma(P)$ which have label a are totally ordered in (the transitive closure of) the edge relation. Hence it makes perfect sense to refer to "the first node with label a", "the second node with label a" and so on.

We now take the disjoint union of the two graphs $\gamma(P)$ and $\gamma(Q)$ and identify the corresponding nodes with labels a and $\overline{a}$. That is, the first node with label a in $\gamma(P)$ is identified with the first node with label $\overline{a}$ in $\gamma(Q)$ and so on. The new nodes are given the temporary label τ, for obvious reasons. This *merging* procedure must be done for all possible synchronizations: for all pairs of events $\{\beta, \overline{\beta}\} \subseteq L(P,Q)$.

The merging has two effects. Most importantly it may have introduced cycles into the graph. These correspond to deadlocks and must be removed. This is where we have to move outside the framework of partial orders and where graphs are a more convenient formalism. To explain how the cycles are removed we need a few definitions. An *initial* node of a graph is one which has no edges leading into it; a *dead* graph is one which has no initial nodes. Define the *core* of a graph to be its maximal dead subgraph. It is easy to check that this is well-defined. Removing the core corresponds to restoring acyclicity to a graph; what remains is referred to as the *acyclic part* of the graph. This is the crucial construction.

The other effect of merging is to introduce nodes with the label τ. These may still remain after forming the acyclic part and have to be removed by a procedure called *condensation*, [1, §3.4]. This introduces extra edges in the graph to record any causal relationships which may have been propagated via the τ nodes.

Finally there may still remain nodes with labels in the synchronization set. These are removed by a procedure called *restriction*, [1, §3.4] which also cuts out any nodes which are causally dependent on those with labels in $L(P,Q)$. (The same procedure is used for the restriction operator $P\backslash M$.)

It is rather important that these procedures are carried out in the right order, since they mostly do not commute with each other. What emerges at the end is another acyclic, directed graph without any τ labelled nodes. Taking the transitive closure of the edge relation gives the poset $\gamma(P||Q)$.

The other operators in the syntax of $\wp^3$ are much easier to deal with. When the effect of each operator has been specified, γ is effectively defined on all purely parallel processes by structural induction.

At one level, γ provides a semantic denotation for a purely parallel process. But it does rather more than this: by concentrating on observable actions only, it also squeezes out all the flab resulting from synchronizations, deadlocks and hidden actions. The following example should bring this point home.

$$P = ((\bar{a};(b||x))||((\bar{c};a)||z))||(\bar{b};(y;c)).$$

P is evidently purely parallel. The actions a, b and c all synchronize in P while x, y and z do not. However, there is a deadlock which prevents x and y from being offered; indeed, $traces(P) = \{\varepsilon, z\}$. The poset $\gamma(P)$ has just the one element labelled with z:

$$\boxed{z}\,.$$

2.4 Properties of γ

The definition of γ given above may well have seemed rather *ad hoc*. However, by Proposition 2, the following property characterizes it up to isomorphism of posets.

Theorem 2 *If* $P \in \wp^3$ *then* $traces(P) = seq(\gamma(P))$.

The proof is by structural induction and is fairly tedious, [1, Theorems 4.1, 4.2]. If γ_1 is any other function from $\wp^3$ to deterministic posets with the same property then $[\gamma_1(P)] = [\gamma(P)]$ for all $P \in \wp^3$.

The sequences of a finite poset which are of maximal length have the following obvious property. They are all permutations of each other. Theorem 2 suggests that a similar property should hold for traces of a purely parallel process. Let us say that a string $s \in \Im^*$ is a *maximal trace* of a process P if $P \stackrel{s}{\Longrightarrow} Q$ and $Q \approx NIL$. In other words, Q does not offer any further observable actions although it may engage in hidden actions. A finite CCS process is *permutable* if all its maximal traces are permutations of each other.

It is important to realize that this is a property of P rather than of $traces(P)$. The expression $\tau.NIL + a.NIL$ has both ε and a as maximal traces while $a.NIL$ has only a. However, both expressions have the same trace set $\{\varepsilon, a\}$. One cannot infer that maximal traces are permutations directly from Theorem 2. However, the missing ingredient is evidently determinism and we can appeal to Proposition 2 to deduce the following result.

Proposition 3 *All purely parallel processes are permutable.*

Permutability is a very useful property. If the action a appears on some trace of a permutable process P then it must eventually appear on any trace of P. It is sufficient to run through a *single* execution sequence to determine whether P offers any particular action; it is not necessary to examine the entire state space. This provides a simple and inexpensive method of checking deadlock-freedom which has useful applications, as we show in §3.2.

Proposition 3 is not really new. Permutability holds more generally for finite confluent processes and can be deduced easily from Milner's results. However, its utility in practice seems, to the best of our knowledge, not to have been noted before.

We can now state the main result on purely parallel processes.

Theorem 3 *The mapping γ induces a bijection from equivalence classes of purely parallel processes under weak bisimulation to finite deterministic pomsets.*

In one direction the result follows immediately from what we have done above. Suppose $P, Q \in \wp^3$. Proposition 1 tells us that P and Q are both deterministic so, by the properties of determinism, $P \approx Q$ if, and only if, $traces(P) = traces(Q)$. We know from Theorem 2 that $traces(P) = seq(\gamma(P))$ and similarly for Q. Since $\gamma(P)$ and $\gamma(Q)$ are deterministic posets by construction, it follows from Proposition 2 that $seq(\gamma(P)) = seq(\gamma(Q))$ if, and only if, $[\gamma(P)] = [\gamma(Q)]$. Hence γ induces a injective function on equivalence classes of purely parallel processes.

It remains to show that this is a surjection onto finite deterministic posets. This is harder to prove and requires some care. We content ourselves with a sketch of the argument.

Suppose given a finite deterministic poset A. We need to show that there is a purely parallel process P such that $[\gamma(P)] = [A]$. It is easier to work with the Hasse diagram of A, as above. The proof proceeds by induction on the number of nodes in this graph. The idea behind the inductive step is to choose some initial node of the graph - say one with label a - and then, roughly speaking, to "cut out" all the nodes with that label from the graph. The subgraph which remains has fewer elements and the inductive hypothesis yields a purely parallel process R with an isomorphic graph. Because A is deterministic, the nodes labelled a are totally ordered in (the transitive closure of) the edge relation. This makes it easy to build another purely parallel process Q which carries these nodes in the same relative order that they had in A. One may then take $P = Q||R$. Because all of the nodes with label a have been placed in Q, one can avoid falling foul of the restriction $L(Q) \cap L(R) = \emptyset$ when forming the parallel composition.

It is not quite as easy as we have made out; R must be suitably modified, ensuring that it remains purely parallel, so that the correct synchronizations take place to knit the nodes labelled a back into the graph. Finally, it must be checked that, as posets, $[\gamma(P)] = [A]$; see [1, Theorem 6.1] for the fine print.

The proof gives a (not very efficient) algorithm for constructing a purely parallel process from a finite deterministic pomset. There is little need to fine-tune the algorithm: it is usually enough to know that a suitable process exists; it is unnecessary to know exactly what it looks like. One useful feature of the proof is that it makes do with prefixing rather than sequentiality and avoids restriction altogether. This explains the remark made in §2.1 about a simplified syntax for processes in $\wp^3$.

The final result rounds off our understanding of purely parallel processes. It follows easily from Theorem 3 and the properties of determinism.

Theorem 4 *A CCS process P is observationally equivalent to a purely parallel process if, and only if, P is deterministic and there exists a finite deterministic poset A such that $traces(P) = seq(A)$.*

Unfortunately, this criterion is difficult to use in practice because of the difficulty of knowing when a CCS process is deterministic. As Milner shows us, the most painless way to prove determinism is to construct the process as a purely parallel one in the first place!

3 Applications

3.1 Verifying a key-distribution protocol

The original motivation for purely parallel processes came from a practical problem in protocol verification. We were concerned with the key-distribution phase of the Secure Messaging System, [5]. SMS is a proprietary system for providing security services (authentication, integrity and confidentiality) for a store-and-forward electronic mail system. Cryptographic techniques are essential to implement these services and the main problem is to manage distribution and replacement of the hierarchy of cryptographic keys. SMS uses a central trusted Key Distribution Centre, K, to distribute the keys via the underlying mail system.

The most complex part of key distribution occurs when one user, A, requests K to set up a secure link to another user B. The protocol is specified as a set of CCS equations in Figure 1. The equations describe the

$$
\begin{aligned}
K0 &= \overline{ak\_reqlmk}; kb\_q\_link; \overline{bk\_accept}; (kb\_ack1 \,||\, K1 \,||\, K2)\\
K1 &= kb\_rxlmk; \overline{bk\_lmkrx}; (kb\_ack2 \,||\, K3)\\
K2 &= ka\_rxlmk; \overline{ak\_lmkrx}; (ka\_ack2 \,||\, K4)\\
K3 &= ka\_txlmk; \overline{ak\_lmktx}; ka\_ack1; k1; NIL\\
K4 &= kb\_txlmk; \overline{bk\_lmktx}; kb\_ack3; k2; NIL
\end{aligned}
$$

$$
\begin{aligned}
A0 &= ak\_reqlmk; (A1 \,||\, A2)\\
A1 &= \overline{ka\_txlmk}; ak\_lmktx; (\overline{ka\_ack1} \,||\, A3)\\
A2 &= \overline{ka\_rxlmk}; ak\_lmkrx; (\overline{ka\_ack2} \,||\, A4)\\
A3 &= ab\_ldk; \overline{ba\_ldkack}; ab\_ack; a1; NIL\\
A4 &= \overline{ba\_ldk}; ab\_ldkack; \overline{ba\_ack}; a2; NIL
\end{aligned}
$$

$$
\begin{aligned}
B0 &= \overline{kb\_q\_link}; bk\_accept; (\overline{kb\_ack1} \,||\, B1 \,||\, B2)\\
B1 &= \overline{kb\_rxlmk}; bk\_lmkrx; (\overline{kb\_ack2} \,||\, B3)\\
B2 &= \overline{kb\_txlmk}; bk\_lmktx; (\overline{kb\_ack3} \,||\, B4)\\
B3 &= \overline{ab\_ldk}; ba\_ldkack; \overline{ab\_ack}; b1; NIL\\
B4 &= ba\_ldk; \overline{ab\_ldkack}; ba\_ack; b2; NIL
\end{aligned}
$$

Figure 1: The SMS key-distribution protocol

behaviour of three processes $K0$, $A0$ and $B0$ corresponding to the three entities K, A and B. Only a single run of the protocol is modelled. Message exchange is represented by synchronization. SMS assumes that the underlying mail system is basically unreliable and provides appropriate mechanisms to ensure delivery. This feature is below the level of abstraction of the CCS specification. However, the possibility that messages might be delayed with respect to each other was incorporated into the equations and accounts for their high level of parallelism.

These remarks are intended merely as background information. For the purposes of this paper, we may take the equations as given.

The behaviour of the whole system comprising K, A and B can be modelled by the expression $P = K0||(A0||B0)$ which is purely parallel. In order to verify the correctness of the protocol, it is necessary to find a CCS description of the behaviour expected from P. Note that if every event in the equations is part of a message exchange, P will offer no observable events to its environment and the only thing that could be said is that $P \approx NIL$. Hence, special "signal" events have been included in the descriptions of K, A and B. These events $k1$, $k2$, $a1$, $a2$ and $b1$, $b2$ are offered to the environment when, and only when, K, A and B respectively have successfully completed their parts of the protocol. It would be possible, and indeed sensible, to checkpoint K, A and B elsewhere in the protocol: our choice is merely the simplest for purposes of illustration.

It takes some guesswork to arrive at a description of P's expected behaviour. This is one of the drawbacks of this style of verification. A good guess would seem to be that each of the signal events should appear in every possible order. The non-appearance of any one event would correspond to some deadlock in the protocol and, if there is no deadlock, there seems to be no obstruction to the events appearing in all possible orders. This suggests that the correct behaviour of P is captured by the purely parallel process C shown below.

$$C = (k1||k2||a1||a2||b1||b2).$$

(There is no synchronization so we need not worry about associativity of the parallel operator.) To verify the key-distribution protocol amounts to proving that $P \approx C$.

The first attempt at this used a prototype version of the Edinburgh Concurrency Workbench, [8], and was a complete failure. The Workbench expired after some 27 hours of effort with its heap space exhausted.

By using the theory of purely parallel processes the verification can be done by hand in a matter of minutes. It is only necessary to calculate $\gamma(P)$ following the prescriptions sketched in §2.3 above. The poset consists of six elements carrying the labels $k1$, $k2$, $a1$, $a2$, $b1$, $b2$ with no edges between them. This is clearly isomorphic to $\gamma(C)$ and it follows immediately from Theorem 3 that $P \approx C$. This completes the verification.

3.2 Deadlock checking for systolic programs

Kung has studied the problem of deadlock-avoidance for systolic programs, [4]. We first summarise the systolic architecture which he considers and then describe the algorithm which is used to check deadlock-freedom. We then comment on the mathematics which underlies this.

Kung's systolic system consists of several *cells*[1] arranged in some interconnection topology. Communication between cells takes place via *queues* positioned between "adjacent" cells. There may be several queues between a given pair of cells.

Each cell carries its own *program* which is a finite sequence of instructions consisting either of operations on data values or of communications between cells. A communication between two cells, which need not be adjacent, takes the form of a *message* with specified *sender* and *receiver*. Each message consists of several individual *words*. Given a message A, with sender $C1$ and receiver $C2$, the program in cell $C1$ can transmit a word of the message with a write instruction $W(A)$. Similarly, the program in cell $C2$ can read a word of the message with a read instruction $R(A)$.

For the purposes of deadlock avoidance it is only necessary to concentrate on the communication behaviour as expressed by the read/write instructions. An important feature of systolic systems is that the communication behaviour is independent of the data. Kung further assumes that each cell program is straight line and consists of a linear sequence of read/write instructions.

Depending on the interconnection topology, a message may have to use several queues between different cells in order to get from sender to receiver. However, a cell has only to respond to messages which are sent to it or sent by it: a word which is in transit along a link between two cells is not under the control of the cell programs at either end but is handled by a separate I/O subsystem.

Systolic systems employ a circuit-switched communication paradigm. Each message is assigned a fixed route between cells and a fixed choice of queue on each leg of the route. Queues are not shared between messages and a particular queue can only be re-assigned to a new message if all the words of the old message have passed through it. This paradigm requires more computation at compile time, for routing and queue assignment, but minimizes computation at run time.

An important problem in executing systolic programs is to ensure that queues are assigned to messages in a sensible and efficient manner. Different messages which are routed across the same link in the system may compete for the same queue. Which message should be given priority? If the wrong choice is made, the system could suffer a *queue-induced deadlock*. The central problem which Kung addresses is how to avoid this and he presents an elegant algorithm for queue-assignment which is based on a labelling of messages, [4, §5].

Kung addresses only the problem of queue-assignment and not that of routing. In effect, he assumes that a route has been chosen and then considers how best to assign queues to the message.

The main requirement for Kung's procedure to work, [4, Theorem 1], is that the systolic system be *deadlock-free* in the first place. This is the notion which we want to discuss here. It is a property only of the communication behaviour of the system and is independent of queue-assignment. A deadlock-free program may still encounter queue-induced deadlock if there are not enough queues or if the queue-assignment is poor. Conversely, a program which is not deadlock-free will be unable to reach completion no matter how clever the queue-assignment. To define a deadlock-free systolic system, Kung uses a procedure called *crossing-off*. He discusses first the situation in which the queues have no buffering capability (ie: queue size 0), [4, §3.1], and then allows for queues with positive capacity by adding *lookahead* to the crossing-off procedure, [4, §8.1].

In the simpler case, crossing-off amounts to simulating a particular execution history of the systolic system by finding *executable pairs* of the form $(W(A), R(A))$ and successively removing them from the list of instructions in each program. At any step there may, of course, be a choice of executable pair; they can be crossed off in any order. If this procedure terminates with all instructions crossed off, then Kung defines the program to be deadlock-free, [4, §3.1].

[1] Italic type indicates a word whose exact meaning is defined in Kung's paper, [4].

In the case when the queues have capacity greater than zero, the search for an executable pair is aided by the lookahead procedure. This allows skipping of write operations to a given message, up to a number determined by the total buffering capacity along the entire route of that message. Skipping read operations is forbidden (since writes must precede reads). It is easy to see that this procedure also amounts to simulating a particular execution history of the system where now the words of each message are carried by a single corresponding queue having the total buffering capacity for the whole route. The skipping amounts to loading the queue with words of the message. Once again, if this procedure terminates with each instruction crossed off then Kung defines the systolic system to be deadlock-free, [4, §8.1]

The first remark to be made about this algorithm is that it runs through only one possible execution sequence of the systolic system. It is clear that this particular sequence is free of deadlock, but it is not clear, *a priori*, that all other execution sequences must hence also be deadlock-free. Kung presents no argument to explain why this should be so. Perhaps it is worth pointing out that a small alteration to the communication mechanism would invalidate the procedure.

Consider the case of two cells, $C1$ and $C2$, which communicate through a pair of registers. Like queues, the registers can be read or written by either cell. However, unlike queues, we assume that the reads are destructive and that after reading a register a cell must write back the contents before the register can be read by the other cell. Initially, both registers are considered written and may be read by either cell. Suppose that $C1$ and $C2$ run the programs shown below where RA and WA are instructions having the obvious meaning of "read register A" and "write register A" respectively.

C1	**C2**
RB	RA
RA	RB
WB	WA
WA	WB

One possible execution sequence is for $C1$ to first run through its four instructions and then for $C2$ to run through its four. Clearly, there is no deadlock on this sequence. However, another possible sequence is when $C1$ reads register B and then $C2$ reads register A. This does result in a deadlock: $C1$ cannot now read A because $C2$ has not written to it and $C2$ cannot read B because $C1$ has not written to it; no further progress is possible. This is, of course, a disguised version of the famous Dining Philosophers, [3, §2.5].

To provide a rigorous foundation for Kung's procedure, we model the behaviour of the systolic system as a purely parallel process. Provided this can be done, the correctness of the procedure follows immediately from Proposition 3.

The cell programs present no problem since they are straight line. If message A has 5 words in it, the writes to it can be modelled by the actions $wa1$, $wa2$, $wa3$, $wa4$, $wa5$ and the reads similarly by $ra1, \cdots, ra5$. Each cell program can then be written in the form $wa1; rb1; \ \cdots \ ; wxn$ which is purely parallel. The difficulty arises with the queues.

Consider the queue for the message A above. It will need to use the actions $\overline{wa1}, \cdots, \overline{wa5}$, where synchronization (with $wa1, \cdots, wa5$) represents writing to the queue, and $\overline{ra1}, \cdots, \overline{ra5}$, where synchronization (with $ra1, \cdots, ra5$) represents reading. If the total buffering capacity of the route assigned to A is, say 2, then the behaviour of the queue must also respect this restriction.

One has a clear intuitive understanding of how the queue ought to behave. The basis of this is the causal relationship between action occurrences: $\overline{wa1}$ must precede both $\overline{ra1}$ and $\overline{wa2}$, $\overline{wa3}$ must be preceded by $\overline{ra1}$ and so on. This causal understanding makes it easy to write down a graph which captures the implied causal relationships. It is shown in Figure 2. This graph is acyclic and the poset which results from taking the transitive closure of the edge relation - call it A - is evidently deterministic. But now Theorem 3 immediately tells us that there is some purely parallel process P with $[\gamma(P)] = [A]$. This works for a graph of any capacity and messages of any length.

It is now clear that the behaviour of any systolic system, of the form considered by Kung, can be modelled by a purely parallel process. Hence, by Proposition 3, all maximal execution sequences (traces) are permutations of each other and it is only necessary to check one of them to determine whether the system is deadlock-free. This justifies Kung's procedure.

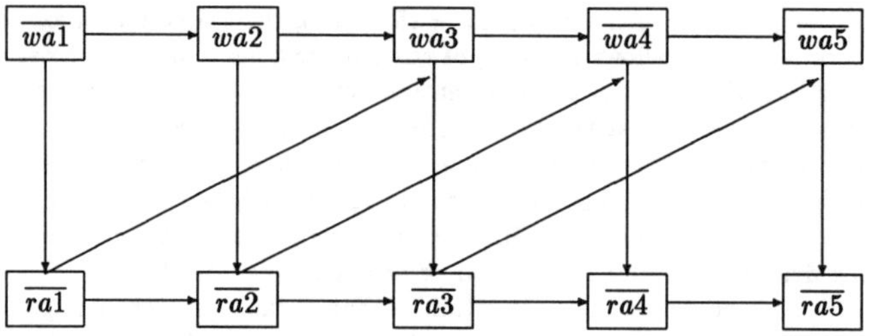

Figure 2: Hasse diagram for a queue of size 2 which accepts 5 words

4 Conclusion

In this paper we have discussed several restricted classes of concurrent processes: deterministic, permutable, confluent and purely parallel. We have provided a very complete theory of the last of these, which, notwithstanding its simplicity, has useful practical applications. We believe that the study of such specialized classes, and the identification of new ones, is an important and interesting problem: an essential step in developing a genuine *applied mathematics* of concurrency.

References

[1] J. Gunawardena, *"Purely Parallel Processes"*, Technical Memo, Hewlett-Packard Laboratories, Information Systems Centre, HPL-ISC-TM-89-002, March 1989; submitted to *Information and Computation.*

[2] J. Gunawardena, *"Causal Automata I: Confluence* $\equiv$ {AND, OR} *Causality"*, Technical Memo, Hewlett-Packard Laboratories, Information Systems Centre, HPL-ISC-TM-89-078, July 1989.

[3] C.A.R. Hoare, *"Communicating Sequential Processes"*, International Series in Computer Science, Prentice-Hall, 1985.

[4] H.T. Kung, *"Deadlock Avoidance for Systolic Communication"*, Journal of Complexity, 4, pp 87-105, 1988.

[5] A. Marshall, G. Proudler, *"Cryptographic key management for a store-and-forward messaging system"*, Proceedings of SECURICOM '87, 5th Worldwide Congress on Computer and Communications Security and Protection, Paris, France, 4-6th March 1987.

[6] R. Milner, *"A Calculus of Communicating Systems"*, Springer Lecture Notes in Computer Science No 92, Springer-Verlag 1980.

[7] R. Milner, *"Communication and Concurrency"*, International Series in Computer Science, Prentice-Hall, 1989.

[8] J. Parrow, *"Verifying a CSMA/CD-Protocol with CCS"*, LFCS Report ECS-LFCS-87-18, University of Edinburgh, January 1987.

[9] V. Pratt, *"Modelling Concurrency with Partial Orders"*, International Journal of Parallel Programming, 15(1), pp 33 - 71, 1986.

[10] F. W. Vaandrager, *"Determinism* $\rightarrow$ *(Event structure isomorphism = Step sequence equivalence)"*, Report CS-R8839, CWI Amsterdam, October 1988.

[11] G. Winskel, *"Event Structures"*, in W. Brauer, W. Reisig, G. Rozenberg (eds), "Advances in Petri Nets", SLNCS 255, Springer-Verlag.

ANNOTATED PROGRAM TRANSFORMATIONS

Viktor N.Kasyanov
Computing Center Siberian Branch of USSR Ac. Sci.
Novosibirsk 630090,USSR

Transformation of annotated programs is a method of program processing which takes into account program application information a priori known and conveyed in annotations. A scheme and languages of annotated programming are described within whose framework many kinds of practical work with programs (e.g. execution, partial evaluation, optimization) can be performed. The problem of global dataflow analysis of annotated programs that covers conventional forward and backward dataflow problems is formulated and solved. A transformation machine concept as an integrated environment for transformations of annotated programs is presented.

Introducton

Transformation techniques are gaining in importance for both theoretical and technological programming. Systems of equivalent transformations have been conventionally used in the optimizing compilers and are currently widely applied to the so called transformation programming systems where the program development from a specification is a formal, mechanically supported process [1, 2].

Investigations of transformation systems and their applications to various kinds of program manipulations show that when performing transformations it is important to take into account information known about program applications, as well as to employ generalizing and specializing transformations which are nonequivalent. A well-known example of specializing transformation is the so-called partial evaluation (or mixed computation) of programs on partially given inputs [3].Partial evaluation can be applied to compiling, program generation, including compiler generation and generation of a compiler generator, and metaprogramming without order-of-magnitude loss of efficiency [4].

The main idea of the paper is to consider program processing aimed at improving the program given by a qualitative criterion (memory, time, reliability, etc.) not interfering with the program meaning within the scope of a subfield restricted by formalized comments (annotations) of the program transformed. The class of correct transformations of annotated programs covers various kinds of work with basic programs. It contains both all equivalent transformations and a number of such nonequivalent transformations which specialize or generalise a program to be transformed, in particular partial evaluation. The approach also permits specializing and generalizing transformations of basic programs and to employ for their investigation equivalent transformation techniques developed in terms of program schemata theory [6]. Within the approach, transformations can change not only basic programs but their annotations as well. It allows systems of annotated program transformations to be used for solving problems of dataflow analysis and verification. Another advantage of the approach outlined here is the possibility to perform global transformations of basic programs by iterative application of elementary transformations of annotated programs, to construct a system which consists of a relatively small number of elementary transformations of annotated programs and covers a sufficiently broad class of program manipulations including program execution, partial evaluation and optimization.

1. Model for annotated programming

A program model described below is based on large-scale program schemata that covers a broad class of programs and their transformations [5, 6].

Let $S = \{s\}$ be a set of memory states such that for any state $s \in S$ a partition of the set of all variables $V = \{v\}$ into two sets $A(s)$ and $I(s)$ of *accessible* and *inaccessible* variables, respectively, is given and for every accessible $v \in A(s)$ its value $s(v)$ is defined. Let s^1 and s^2 be two memory states. s^1 and s^2 are *equal on a set* of the variables $W \subseteq V$ if for any $v \in W$ either $s^1(v) = s^2(v)$ or $v \in I(s^1) \cap I(s^2)$. s^1 *expands* s^2 (denoted by $s^2 \leqslant s^1$) if s^1 and s^2 are equal on the set $A(s^2)$.

A *program* π is a tuple (g,f,p,r,a,d) which consists of

(1) a *flowgraph* $g = (X,U,x_0,y_0)$, where $x_0 \in X$ is the *entry* statement having no ingoing arcs (i.e. $IN(x_0) = \emptyset$) and only one outgoing arc denoted by u_0 (i.e. $OUT(x_0) = \{u_0\}$) and $y_0 \in X$ is the *exit* statement having no outgoing arcs (i.e. $OUT(y_0) = \emptyset$), and for every arc $u = (x^1,x^2) \in U$ the functions **source**$(u) = x^1$ and **target**$(u) = x^2$ are defined;

(2) a function of *memory transformation* $f : X \Rightarrow (S \Rightarrow S)$;

(3) a function of *control transfer* $p : X \Rightarrow (S \Rightarrow U)$;

(4) *argument* and *result* functions $a,r: X \Rightarrow (S \Rightarrow 2^V)$;

(5) *applicability* predicate $d : X \Rightarrow (S \Rightarrow \{\textbf{true},\textbf{false}\})$,

such that for any $v \in V$, $x \in X$ and $s,s^1,s^2 \in S$ the following properties hold:

(1) the memory states s and $f(x)(s)$ are equal on the set $V \setminus r(x)(s)$;

(2) if s^1 and s^2 are equal on $a(x)(s^1)$ then $d(x)(s^1) = d(x)(s^2)$, $p(x)(s^1) = p(x)(s^2)$, $a(x)(s^1) = a(x)(s^2)$, $r(x)(s^1) = r(x)(s^2)$ and the memory states $f(x)(s^1)$ and $f(x)(s^2)$ are equal on the set $r(x)(s^1)$;

(3) if $I(s) \cap a(x)(s) \neq \emptyset$, then $d(x)(s)$ is **false**;

(4) $a(x_0)(s) = A(f(x_0)(s))$, $a(y_0)(s) = \emptyset$ and for every $x \in \{x_0,y_0\}$ the memory states s and $f(x)(s)$ are equal on the set $A(f(x)(s))$;

(5) $p(x)(s)$ is an arc u outgoing from x, i.e. **source**$(u) = x$.

The program π computes function $\pi : S \Rightarrow S$ defined by the following rules. The value of the function for a given memory state s_1 is *defined*(π is *applicable* to s_1) and equal to s_2 if there is a finite sequence **seq**$(\pi, s_1) = (x_0 = x^0, s^0, u^0, x^1, s^1, u^1, \ldots, x^n, s^n, u^n, x^{n+1} = y_0)$ called an *execution sequence* of π on s_1 such that $s^0 = f(x_0)(s_1)$, $s_2 = f(y_0)(s^n)$ and for any i the following properties hold: $d(x^i)(s^{i-1})$ is **true**, $s^i = f(x^i)(s^{i-1})$, $u^i = p(x^i)(s^{i-1})$ and $x^i =$ **target**(u^{i-1}). If there is no finite execution sequence **seq**(π, s_1) then π is *inapplicable* to s_1 and the value $\pi(s_1)$ is *undefined*. If the value $\pi(s_1)$ is defined then the variables $v \in a(x_0)(s_1)$ are called the *arguments* of $\pi(s_1)$.

Let π^1 and π^2 be two programs. π^1 *generalizes* π^2 if for any memory state s^2 which π^2 is applicable to, there is such a memory state s^1 that s^2 is equal to s^1 on the set of arguments of $\pi^2(s^2)$, π^1 is applicable to s^1 and $\pi^1(s^1) \leqslant \pi^2(s^2)$. π^1 and π^2 are *eguivalent* programs if they compute the same function.

Let a nonempty set of objects called *annotations* be given. It is assumed that the set is divided into two disjoint subsets: *assertions* $E = \{e\}$ and *directives* $Q = \{q\}$. Every assertion $e \in E$ is a predicate on S. A memory state s is said to be *admissible* with respect to e, denoted $s \dashv e$, if $e(s)$ is **true**. It is assumed that E contains minimum and maximum elements $\perp$ and $\top$ such that any memory state is admissible with respect to $\top$ and inadmissible with respect to $\perp$. Every directive $q \in Q$ is a statement on S. In other words, the functions f, a and r and the predicate d of any program are extended on the set Q. It is assumed that Q contains *identity* directive q_0 such that $a(q_0)(s) = r(q_0)(s) = \emptyset$ for any $s \in S$, and for any memory state $s \in S$ and set $W \subseteq V$ there is such a directive $q_{s,W} \in Q$ that for all $s^1 \in S$ the following properties hold: $a(q_{s,W})(s^1) = \emptyset$, $r(q_{s,W})(s^1) = W$ and s and $f(q_{s,W})(s^1)$ are equal on W.

Annotated program π^1 is a triple (π, m, t) where π is a program on which π^1 is *based*, m and t are annotating functions which attach to every arc u of π some assertion $m(u) \in E$ and directive $q(u) \in Q$. Like basic program any annotated program π^1 computes a function $\pi^1 : S \Rightarrow S$. The function is defined by the following rules. For a diven $s_1 \in S$ the value $\pi^1(s_1)$ is *defined* (π^1 is *applicable* to s_1) and equal to s_2 if there is a finite execution sequence **seg**$(\pi^1, s_1) = (x^0 = x_0, \bar{s}^0, u^0, \tilde{s}^0, x^1, \bar{s}^1, u^1, \tilde{s}^1, \ldots, x^n, \bar{s}^n, u^n, \tilde{s}^n, x^{n+1} = y_0)$ such that $\bar{s}^0 = f(x_0)(s_1)$, $s_2 = f(y_0)(\tilde{s}^n)$ and for any i the following properties hold: $d(x^i)(\tilde{s}^{i-1})$ and $d(t(u^i))(\bar{s}^i)$ are true, $\bar{s}^i = f(x^i)(\tilde{s}^{i-1})$, $u^i = p(x^i)(\tilde{s}^{i-1})$, $x^i =$ **target**(u^{i-1}), $\bar{s}^i \dashv m(u^i)$and $\tilde{s}^i = t(u^i)(\bar{s}^i)$. Thus, the equivalence and generalization relations are defined on the set Π of all annotated and basic programs. π^1 is *semibasic* if $m(u) = \top$ and $t(u) = q_0$ for any $u \in U$. π^1

is *well-defined* if π=**base**(π^1) generalizes π^1.

Proposition 1. Any semibasic program π is equivalent to **base**(π), by this for any memory state s which π is applicable to, **seq**(**base**(π),s) can be obtained from **seq**(π,s) by removing all $\tilde{s}^i$ and consists of memory states s^i such that $s^i = \tilde{s}^i = \bar{s}^i$ for any i.

Proposition 2. A program π is well-defined if there is such a subset $W \subseteq V$ that for any statement x, memory state s and arc u the following properties hold: (1) $a(x)(s) \subseteq W$; (2) $A(f(x_0)(s)) \subseteq W$; (3) $r(t(u))(s) \cap W = \emptyset$; (4) $r(x)(s) \subseteq W$ if $x \neq y_0$; (5) $A(f(y_0)(s)) \subseteq W$.

2. Classes of transformations

Any function $h : \Pi \Rightarrow \Pi$ is called a (program) *transformation*. It is said h to be *correct* (or *generalizing*) if $h(\pi)$ generalizes π for any $\pi \in \Pi$ and *equivalent* if π and $h(\pi)$ are equivalent for any $\pi \in \Pi$.

Let us consider how equivalent transformations can be possibly applied for the definition of the program equivalence relation without using the concept of the execution sequence. $\pi \in \Pi$ is called *simple* if $t(u)=q_0$ for any $u \in U$ and $m(u) = \top$ for any $u \in U$, distinct from u_0. A given memory state s is *valid* at a point y (arc or node) of π if there is $s^1 \in S$ such that s immediately follows y in **seq**(π,s^1). An annotation e is a *complete* invariant at the point y if for any $s \in S$, s is valid at the point y iff $s \dashv e$. π is called a *single execution* program if $m(u_0)$ is a complete invariant at the arc u_0 and only one memory state is admissible with respect to $m(u_0)$.

Let R be the following system of equivalent transformations:

1. Reduction of ingoing arcs. If $u_0 \in IN(x)$ and $x \neq y_0$, then the node x can be replaced by two copies x^1 and x^2 in such a way that $IN(x^1)=\{u_0\}$ and $IN(x^2) = IN(x^1) \setminus \{u_0\}$

2. Reduction of outgoing arcs. An arc $u \in OUT(x)$ can be removed if $IN(\mathbf{source}(u)) = \{u_0\}$, $|OUT(\mathbf{source}(u))|>1$ and $u \neq p(\mathbf{source}(u))(t(u_0)(s))$ for any $s \dashv m(u_0)$.

3. Reduction of useless nodes. Any node distinct from x_0 and y_0 together with all outgoing arcs can be removed if $\mathbf{target}(u_0) = y_0$.

4. Reduction of directives. A directive $t(u_0)$ can be replaced by a directive $q_{s,Y(s)}$ if $\mathbf{target}(u_0) = y_0$ and for any $s^1 \dashv m(u_0)$ both $s \leqslant t(u_0)(s^1)$ and s is equal to $t(u_0)(s^1)$ on $A(f(y_0)(s^1))$.

5. Reduction of constant statements. A node x and arcs u_0 and u^1 can be replaced by an arc u if $IN(x) = \{u_0\}$, $OUT(x) = \{u^1\}$, $m(u) = m(u_0)$ and there is such $W \subseteq V$ and $s \in S$ that $t(u)=t(u^1) \circ q_{s,Y(s)} \circ t(u_0)$ and for any $s^2=t(u_0)(s^1)$ where $s^1 \dashv m(u_0)$ the following properties hold: $d(x)(s^2)$ is **true**, $W = r(x)(s^2)$, $f(x)(s^2) \dashv m(u^1)$, the memory states s and $f(x)(s^2)$ are equal on W.

Proposition 3. The system R reduces any simple single-execution program π to an equivalent program π_1 such that the folowing properties hold: the flowgraph of π_1 consists of two nodes and a single arc, and for any simple single-execution program π_2 equivalent to π, π_1 is the only normal form of π_2 with respect to R.

Thus the reduction system R is a foundation on which various kinds of program interpreters can be constructed. It should be noted that the process of annotated program transformation involving basic program evaluation can be accompanied by gathering additional information (e.g. evaluation trace, dynamic errors) on the evaluation in annotations.

Partial evaluation [3, 4] is another well-known way to handle programs resulting in a correct transformation only for some inputs. It can be formulated as follows in terms of the above computational model. A function $\mathbf{mix}:\Pi\times S\Rightarrow S$ is *partial evaluation* if for any program $\pi\in\Pi$ and memory states $s^1,s^2\in S$ the following property holds: if $s^1\leqslant s^2$ and π is applicable to s^2, then there is $s^3\in S$ such that $s^3\leqslant s^2$, $A(s^3)=$ $=A(s^2)\setminus A(s^1)$, $\pi^1=\mathbf{mix}(\pi,s^1)$ is applicable to s^3 and $\pi(s^2)=\pi^1(s^3)$.

For any $\pi\in\Pi$ and $s\in S$ let us denote by $\mathbf{annot}(\pi,s)$ an annotated program π^1 such that the following properties hold: (1) $\mathbf{base}(\pi^1)$ is obtained from the $\mathbf{base}(\pi)$ by replacing x_0 by such a node x_0^1 that $A(f^1(x_0)(s^1))=$ $A(f(x_0)(s^1))\setminus A(s)$ for all $s^1\in S$; (2) $m(u)=_T$ for any $u\in U^1$; (3) $t(u_0^1)=$ $q_{s,Y(s)}$; (4) $t(u)=q_0$ for any $u\in U$ distinct from u .

For any correct transformation h, program π and memory state s the program $\mathbf{base}(h(\mathbf{annot}(\pi,s)))$ will be denoted by $\mathbf{mix}_h(\pi,s)$.

Proposition 4.A function $\mathbf{mix}_h$ is a partial evaluation, if for any $\pi\in\Pi$ and $s\in S$ the program $h(\mathbf{annot}(\pi,s))$ is a simple one.

So, to construct a partial evaluation we may use an equivalent transformation h which converts the directive $t(u_0)$ of the source annotated program into a sequence of assignment statements of result basic program . In many cases however, it is necessary to employ another concretizing transformation by way of h which in a sense makes the most use of the information contained in the annotations of source programs.

Let some partial order relation « that is caled a quality relation be defined on Π. A program π^1 is called a *concretization* of a program π^2 with respect to « (denoted by $\pi^1\in K(\pi^2,«)$), if $\pi^1«\pi^2$ and π^1 generalizes π^2. A concretization π^1 of a given program π^2 with respect to « is *complete* if $\pi^1«\pi^3$ for any $\pi^3\in K(\pi^2,«)$. A transformation h is *concretizing* (or *specializing*) with respect to « if $h(\pi)\in K(\pi,«)$ for any $\pi\in\Pi$.

An important subclass of the concretizing transformations consists of the so-called *property* transformations h altering neither base program nor their directives, i.e. for any $\pi^1,\pi^2\in\Pi$, if $\pi^2=h(\pi^1)$, then $\mathbf{base}(\pi^1)$ $=\mathbf{base}(\pi^2)$ and $t^1=t^2$. Here belong transformations aimed at solving verification and dataflow analisys problems [7,8]. For any property transformation h it is naturally assumed that $\pi^2=h(\pi^1)\ll\pi^1$ if for all arcs u∈U and memory states s∈S, $s\dashv m^2(u)$ implies $s\dashv m^1(u)$.

According to the main criteria of program quality the set of other concretizing transformations further falls into the four subsets:

(1) optimizing transformations aimed to improve efficiency of programs (Though they do it in conventional for the optimizing compiler way, they are source-to-source transformations and take into account the parameters of both compilation and execution environment.);

(2) transformations resulting in a more self-descriptive and clear annotated program; they can annotate the source basic program by assertions on its properties, improve the program structure by renaming objects, inserting descriptions, etc.;

(3) transformations providing a debugging version of a source program by adding the statements which test program properties described in the annotations;

(4) transformations aimed at a statical check of a source annotated program for correctness and supplementing it with annotations presenting discrepancies discovered in the program; e.g, the transformations can elicit the so-called *implausibility* properties due to certain discrepancies between the program text and the executions which it represents; test for implausibility permits statical detection of some dynamic errors and formal detection of some informal erros [9].

3. Dataflow analysis of annotated program

The goal of dataflow analysis of a program represented by a flowgraph is to produce a property assignment, i.e. to assign to each node in the flowgraph a program fact, the information that will be valid every time the node is reached during every possible execution. A dataflow analysis problem conveniently considered is either a forward problem or a backward problem [7,8]. Given a point in a program, forward problem determine what could happen before program execution reaches that point; backward problems determine what could happen during or after execution at that point. For a forward problem, the complete invariant at the initial node and all dependencies between properties of any state and its previous states are known. Backward problem assumes that the complete invariant at the exit node and all dependencies between properties of any state and its following states are known.

If annotations conveying additional information on program applications are available in a program, its dataflow analysis problem falls outside the limits of conventional formulation for the following reasons: annotated program can contain an annotation not deduced from the basic program; none of annotations of a source program can be complete invariant at the corresponding point; a priori known information on internal points of a source program requires taking into account opposite dependencies between the analysed properties of program states

The problem of dataflow analysis of annotated program can be formulated as follows.

Let $L \sqsubseteq E$ and $\sqsubseteq$ be a set of all properties being analysed and a partial order relation on L called an *approximation* relation, respectively, such that the following properties hold: (1) for any e^1, $e^2 \in L$ if $e^1 \sqsubseteq e^2$, then $s \dashv e^2$ for any $s \dashv e^1$; (2) $\bot \in L$; (3) $\top \in L$; (4) the pair $(L, \sqsubseteq)$ is a bounded (contains no infinite descending chains) lattice. Let us denote by $\sqcap$ and $\sqcup$ meet and join operations on the lattice $(L, \sqsubseteq)$, i.e. for any $e^1, e^2 \in L$, $e^1 \sqsubseteq e^2$ iff $e^1 \sqcap e^2 = e^1$ and $e^1 \sqcup e^2 = e^2$.

A *monotone dataflow scheme* $\sigma = (\mu, \phi, \psi, \iota, \tau, \nu)$ for a program π incorporates: (1) a control flow graph $\mu = (Z, W)$; (2) such a one-to-one function $\phi : Z \Rightarrow X \cup \{x_0, y_0\} \cup \{(u, t(u)) : u \in U\}$ that $\phi^{-1}(x_0)$ and $\phi^{-1}(y_0)$ are the initial and exit nodes of the graph ; (3) such a function $\psi : W \Rightarrow U$ that for any $z^1, z^2 \in Z$ and $w \in W$, $w \in OUT(z^1) \cap IN(z^2)$ iff one of the three following properties holds: $\psi(w) \in OUT(\phi(z^1)) \cap IN(\phi(z^2))$, $\psi(w) \in OUT(\phi(z^1))$ and $\phi(z^2) = (\psi(w), t(\psi(w)))$, $\psi(w) \in IN(\phi(z^2))$ and $\phi(z^1) = (\psi(w), t(\psi(w)))$; (4) a function $\iota : Z \Rightarrow L$ of the known properties; (5) two functions $\tau, \nu : W \Rightarrow (L \Rightarrow L)$ of property transformations, such that for any $w \in W$ and $e^1, e^2 \in L$, $e^1 \sqsubseteq e^2$ implies $\tau(w)(e^1) \sqsubseteq \tau(w)(e^2)$ and $\nu(w)(e^1) \sqsubseteq \nu(w)(e^2)$.

Given a scheme σ of a dataflow problem, the ideal result of dataflow analysis is to produce the *meet-over-all-paths-assignment*, the map *MOP*: $Z \Rightarrow L$ such that for all nodes z, $MOP(z) = \sqcap\{r(\alpha)(z) : \alpha \in PATHS(\mu, z)\}$.

Here $PATHS(\mu, z)$ is the set of all paths from the initial node of μ to its exit node passing through the node z and $r(\alpha)(z) = \sqcap\{h(\beta)(\iota(\mathbf{source}(\beta))) : \beta \in SEMIPATHS(\alpha, z)\}$ where $SEMIPATHS(\alpha, z)$ is the set of all semipaths in α terminated by z, $\mathbf{source}(\beta)$ is the first node of the semipath β, and $h(\beta) : L \Rightarrow L$ is the function associated with semipaths β as follows: (1) if β is the empty semipath, then $h(\beta)(e) = e$ for any $e \in L$; (2) if $\beta = (z_1, u_1, z_2, u_2, \ldots, z_k)$ for some $k > 1$, then $h(\beta) = h_k \circ \ldots \circ h_2 \circ h_1$ where $h_i = \tau(u_i)$ if $\mathbf{source}(u_i) = z_i$ and $h_i = \nu(u_i)$ if $\mathbf{source}(u_i) = z_{i-1}$.

Let b^1 and b^2 be two assignments of the scheme σ. b^1 is a *correct* assignment if for all nodes z and memory states s, $s \dashv b^1(z)$ if one of the following priperties holds: $\phi(z) = (u, t(u))$ and s is valid at the arc u; $\phi(z) \in X \cup \{x_0, y_0\}$ and s is valid at the node $\phi(z)$. b^1 is a *more precise* assignment than b^2 (denoted by $b^1 \sqsubseteq b^2$) if $b^1(z) \sqsubseteq b^2(z)$ for all $z \in Z$.

The scheme σ is *well-defined* if for any node z, arc u, property e, memory state s the following properties hold: (1) if either $\phi(z) \in X$, $u \in IN(\phi(z))$ and $s = t(u)(s^1)$ for a memory state $s^1 \dashv m(u)$ or $\phi(z) = (u, t(u))$

and $s \dashv m(u)$, then $s \dashv \iota(z)$; (2) if $\phi(z)=(u,t(u))$ and $w \in OUT(z)$, then $t(\psi(w))(s) \dashv \tau(w)(e)$ when $s \dashv e$ and $s \dashv \nu(w)(e)$ when $t(\psi(w))(e) \dashv e$; (3) if $\phi(z) \in X$ and $w \in OUT(z)$, then $f(\phi(z))(s) \dashv \tau(w)(e)$ when $s \dashv e$ and $s \dashv \nu(w)(e)$ when $f(\phi(z))(s) \dashv e$.

Proposition 5. If a given monotone dataflow scheme is well-defined, then its *MOP* is a correct assignment.

Proposition 6. A monotone dataflow scheme σ describes a forward problem if $\iota(z)=\top$ for any $z \in Z$ distinct from $\phi^{-1}(x_0)$ and $\nu(w)(e)=\top$ for any $w \in W$ and $e \in L$; σ describes a backward problem if $\iota(z)=\top$ for any $z \in Z$ distinct from $\phi^{-1}(y_0)$ and $\tau(w)(e)=\top$ for any $w \in W$ and $e \in L$.

Proposition 7.The problem of finding *MOP* assignment in the class of monotone dataflow schemes is unsolvable. There exists an algorithm to construct for any monotone dataflow scheme such a correct assignment b that $b(z)=(\sqcap\{\tau(w)(b(\mathbf{source}(w))):w \in IN(z)\}) \sqcup \iota(z) \sqcup (\sqcap\{\nu(w)(b(\mathbf{target}(w))) :w \in OUT(z)\})$ for any $z \in Z$.

Proposition 8.Let b be a correct assignment of a well-defined scheme of an annotated program $\pi^1=(\pi,m,t)$. Then $\pi^2=(\pi,b,t)$ generalizes π^1.

4.Transformation machine

To construct annotated program transformation tools, we may make use of the concept of *transformation machine*,i.e.an abstract device which has elementary transformations as its instruction set [3].

Various processes of correct transformations of annotated programs seem to have a relatively small number of underlying elementary transformations being correct in the class of all annotated programs. Thus, it possible to develop a transformation matine (*TM*), whose data and instructions are the annotated programs and their transformations, respectively [10]. Transformation rules used as *TM* instructions are of the three types: (1) instructions for moving active points about the programs processed; they make one or few points of the program accessible for transformations; (2) control instructions to express higher level transformation rules in terms of lower ones; (3) elementary transformations which are rules of correct transformations of annotated programs which alone are able to modify the program processed.

Thus unlike the transformation machine described in [3], *TM* employs no instructions of whose application correctness depends not only on the fragment but on program as a whole. So, every program in the *TM* instruction language defines a correct transformation.

The set of all elementary transformations of *TM* is subdivided into four subsets: property and schematic transformations to be outlined below, elementary transformations which reflect the semantics of language constructions (e.g. CASE *const* OF *const:statement*; *seguence*

END ⇒ *statement*) and elementary transformations that originate from object domain laws(e.g., 1+2⇒3 ; *exp**1 ⇒ *exp* ; *exp*/0 ⇒ **error-division-by-zero**). The subset of the schematic transformations includes removing and inserting inaccessible fragments; removing and inserting useless computations; replacing the terms according to their properties; replacing the variables; deadlock standartization; copying the fragments and pasting copies together; folding and unfolding for the defined functions and procedures; removing and inserting unessential branches. Property transformations are intended to generate new annotations by extracting information from a basic program constructions, to propagate information, taking into account the property modification which originates from a relevant language construction and to update annotations through the new information logically inferred from current annotations.

The transformation implemented by *TM* can be considered as some programmer-guided manipulation of annotated programs. This process may involve significant system-programmer interactions.

TM instruction language also allows writing procedures to define more complex rules in terms of elementary ones and contains a set of built-in procedures. For example, there are built-in procedures for dataflow analysis for the extraction of such properties as equality of terms, ranges of variables and a number of properties which can be described by finite sets of predicates. Different strategies of program transformation can be expressed in the instruction language as procedure with transformations being formal parameters. For example, there are built-in procedures to realize algorithms of dataflow analysis, to convert various constructions of annotated program into canonical forms, for logical inference and so on.

Conclusion

The transformational approach described above enables us to construct program transformation tools of various types. An example is a program transformer performing a collection of connected concretizations: optimizer, debugger, analyser, etc. It is also possible to implement concretization system as integrated device for constructing program concretizators [6,10]. Concretization systems are based on the transformation machine concept and support operational environments ensuring safe and rapid programming of a variety of program processors, as well as their application in combinations previously impossible (for example, to optimize the debugging version of a source program). Reliability of tools implemented by means of the concretization system is provided by applying only such transformation rules that preserve the meaning of the program processed. The language level for writing transformation tools is getting higher, which contributes to a greater automation of program development. It should be noted that tools can be extended and implement self-descriptive processes of program transformation (the history of development is presented by a sequence of applied transformations). In the environment supported by a concretization system it seems practical to create experimental tools for program transformation as well as tools for "single" and "individual" applications, i.e. tools constructed to transform a specific program or designed for one programmer.

Of great interest is an implementation of the transformation machine to program concretization in a language which is an extension of the inplementation language. If *TM* basic language and its implementation language were the same, mutual applications of program processors would be possible which would provide us with the opportunity to make a compiler from an interpretater, a compiler generator from a partial evaluator and other applications usually considered as motivations for partial evaluation [3, 4].

References

1. H.Partsh, R.Steinbruggen. Program transformation systems. - ACM Comput.Surveys 15,3(1983), 199-236.

2. M.S.Feather. A survey and classification of some program transformation approaches and techniques. - In: Program specification and transformation, North-Holland, Amsterdam,1987, 165-195.

3. A.P.Ershov. Mixed computation: potential applications and problems for study. - Theoretical Computer Science, Vol. 18, 1982, 41-67.

4. New Generation Computing. Vol 6, Nos. 2, 3, 1988.

5. V.N.Kasyanov. Basis for program optimization.-In:Information processing 83, North-Holland, Amsterdam,1983,315-320.

6. V.N.Kasyanov. Optimizing program transformations.- Moscow:Nauka, 1988. - 336 p.(in russian).

7. J.B.Kam, J.D.Ullman. Monotone data flow analysis framework.- Acta Informatica, Vol. 7, No. 3, 1977, 305-318.

8. Program Flow Analysis: Theory and Applications / Ed. S.S.Muchnick and N.D.Jones, Englewood Cliffs, NJ: Prentice Hall, 1981.- 418 p.

9. V.N.Kasyanov, I.V.Pottosin. Application of optimizations techniques to correctness problems. - In: Constructing Quality Software, North Holland, Amsterdam, 1978, 237-248.

10. V.N.Kasyanov, V.K.Sabelfeld. Tools for program transformation. - In:Ihformatika 88: Actes du seminaire Franco-Sovietique, Rocquencourt, INRIA, 1988, 89-100.

Algebraic Software Development Concepts for Module and Configuration Families [1]

Hartmut Ehrig, Werner Fey, Horst Hansen, Michael Löwe
Institut für Software und Theoretische Informatik, Technische Universität Berlin
Franklinstraße 28/29, D-1000 Berlin 10

Dean Jacobs
Computer Science Department, University of Southern California
Los Angeles, CA 90089-0782

Abstract

Configuration families are the means of keeping track of structural and historical relationships between the components of a system as they evolve over time. Thus they form a kernel of a configuration management system. In this paper, we study configuration families within a formal semantic framework for modules and their interconnection operations. Our goal is to formulate and prove formally fundamental ideas in this area to serve as a guide to the design of methodologies and tools for software engineering.

The module concept we use is based on abstract data types and algebraic specifications and includes a set of fundamental operations on interface and module specifications for horizontal structuring, vertical development steps, which refine abstract specifications into more concrete ones, and realization of interface specifications by module specifications.
In the paper we study the construction and evolution of module families, i.e., collections of conceptually related modules, usually revisions and variants, which have developed over time. We show how horizontal structuring operations can be applied to entire module families to produce configuration families, and explain how vertical refinement steps of underlying modules induce refinements of configurations. The construction of modules, module families, and configuration families is illustrated by a simple desk calculator.

CR classification: D.2.1 Specification, D.2.2 Modules and interfaces, D.2.7 Version control, D.2.9 Software configuration management, D.2.10 Design methodologies, D.3.3 Abstract data types, modules, F.3.1 Specification techniques

Keywords: modules, module families, configuration families, algebraic specifications, formal specification development, software engineering

Introduction

The importance of decomposing large software systems into modules to improve their clarity, facilitate proofs of correctness, and support reusability has been widely recognized within the software engineering community. As practical experience using modules has accumulated, considerable interest has developed in configuration management, i.e., in techniques such as configuration families for keeping track of structural and historical relationships between modules as a system evolves over time. In this paper, we study configuration families within a formal semantic framework for modules based on algebraic specifications. This framework allows us to identify and exploit semantic relationships between modules. Our goal is to formulate and prove formally fundamental ideas in this area to serve as a guide to the design of methodologies and tools for software engineering.

We use an algebraic module concept that has evolved over the last ten years into its present form. Its origin is in the early work on abstract data types and algebraic specifications, [LZ 74], [ADJ 76], and [TWW 78], and the work of Parnas [Par 72] on module specifications. Practical experience lead to an informal version of our concepts of interface and module specifications ([WE 86]), which were given a formal algebraic definition in [BEP 87] and [EFHLP 89]. Other proposals for an algebraic formulation of the notion of modules can be found e.g. in [GM 82], [Rei 85], and [ST 85]. But none of these papers studies module and configuration families.

Our interface and module specifications can be interconnected by a set of fundamental operations which go well beyond the capabilities of Module Interconnection Languages (MILs) (see [PN82] and [NS87]). These include

[1] This work was carried out as part of a research exchange program between TUB and USC.

- horizontal structuring operations for building up specifications,
- vertical development steps which refine abstract specifications into more concrete forms, and
- realization of interface specifications by module specifications.

This provides three dimensions for specification development as shown in figure 1. We use the following notations in this figure: H(I) and V(I) mean horizontal and vertical development steps on interface specifications, H(M) and V(M) mean corresponding steps on module specifications, and R means realization.

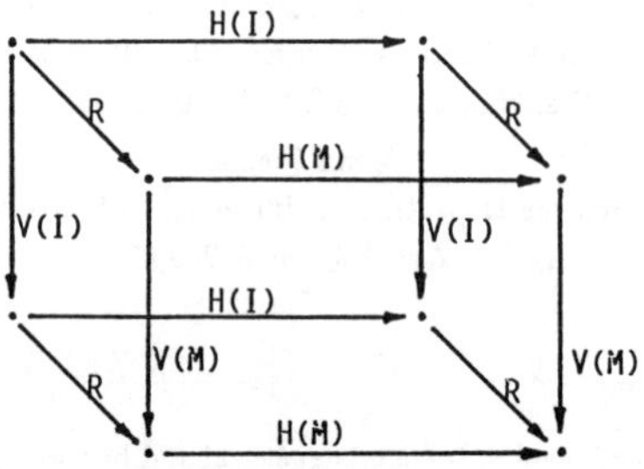

Figure 1.1: Dimensions of Program Development

A variety of different specification development methodologies can be formulated within this framework. For example, a top-down methodology might start with high-level requirements expressed as interface specifications. Then, vertical development steps could be taken to elaborate the design, perhaps introducing some horizontal structure. Eventually, the interface specifications would be realized by module specifications to produce a high-level description of the implementation. Finally, additional vertical development steps could be taken until an acceptable implementation is produced

The algebraic framework allows us to study semantic interactions between horizontal and vertical development. In particular, compatibilities between the different kinds of operations correspond to different faces of the cube in figure 1. The front and back faces correspond to compatibility of horizontal structuring with vertical development. The key issue here is whether a compound module (or interface) is refined when its submodules (or interfaces) are refined. Similarly, the left and right faces correspond to compatibility of realization with vertical development and the top and bottom faces correspond to compatibility of horizontal structuring with realization. These operations and results concerning their compatibilities are discussed in detail in [EFHLP 89].

Our most recent work, introduced here and in more detail in our technical report [EFHJLLP 88], has been to study the construction and evolution of module families. A module family is a collection of conceptually related modules, usually revisions and variants, which have developed over time. Module families provide structure to a module library, facilitating the storage, access, and reuse of its members. In addition, module families allow the members of a group of conceptually related systems to be manipulated all at once rather than individually. In our framework, a module family is defined to be a set of module specifications, each of which realizes a common interface specification. Each module family has a set of relations, such as *refinement_of*, *revision_of*, and *variant_of*, defined on its members. We show how the horizontal operations on interface and module specifications can be applied to entire module families to produce configuration families and explain how vertical refinement steps of the underlying modules induce refinements of configurations.

This paper is an extension of [EFHJL 89]. It is organized as follows: Section 1 presents an overview of the basic concepts of modules, horizontal and vertical development steps, and module and configuration families. Section 2 develops a specification for a simple desk calculator as an example. Section 3 provides an outline of the algebraic theory underlying our work. Finally, section 4 summarizes this work and discusses our future research plans.

1. Overview of Basic Concepts

Our module concept was designed to be the main structuring mechanism for a software system. The organizational structure provided by our modules is suitable for all stages of the software development process. It may be used as the basis for a high-level specification language with pure algebraic semantics.

We view a module as being a completely self-contained software unit which is independently developed for later incorporation in a system. Each module contains import and export interfaces which describe all assumptions made about the environment in which it will be used. Flexible operations for combining modules are provided to facilitate reusability. This aim is also furthered by a parameterization mechanism which allows modules to play the role of generic software units.

1.1 Interface and Module Specifications

An interface specification consists of three parts called the import, export, and parameter parts. A module specification consists of an interface specification and a fourth part called the body. Each of these parts is in the basic case an algebraic data type specification, see [EM 85], containing sorts, declarations of operations on those sorts, and equations describing those operations.

Import Part: The import part identifies the sorts and operations which are to be imported into the module. In general, the equations in the import part describe properties of these operations rather than defining them completely. This feature is particularly useful in the stepwise development of software systems. It allows a module specification to demand special properties that are essential to its functioning, leaving inessential details up to the imported module.

Export Part: The export part identifies the sorts, operations, and equations that are visable outside the module. Again, the equations may describe properties of the operations without defining them completely. The export part supports three different aspects of information hiding which are essential to the module concept.

1. It prevents the construction of modules which depend on the internal structure of other modules, i.e. it hides the representation of data and operations.
2. It prevents auxiliary operations and sorts from being used outside the module, i.e., it supports hidden sorts and functions.
3. It may be used to define an application-specific view of a generic body. As such, it may give access to only a subspace of the total value space in order to enforce application-dependent integrity constraints.

Parameter Part: The parameter part contains sorts, operations, and equations which are common to the import and export parts. These elements are conceptually copied from the parameter part to the import and export parts and need not be repeated. These elements are intended to be essential parameters of the entire modular system. Generic software units are constructed by combining module specifications through their import and export parts, leaving the parameter part open. Note that the parameter part and the import part are similar except that components of the former appear automatically in the export part while components of the later must be explicitly included, if this is desired.

Body: The equations in the body of a module specification define the export part operations in terms of the import part operations. The sorts, operations, and equations of the import and export parts are conceptually copied to the body and need not be repeated. The body may contain auxiliary sorts and operations which do not belong to any other part of the module specification.

1.2 Horizontal Structuring Operations

Horizontal structuring operations are used to build up interface and module specifications. We have defined a wide variety of these operations, including composition, actualization, union, extension [BEP 87], recursion, product and iteration. The first three of these are the ones most commonly used.

Composition: The import part of module MOD_1 is connected to the export part of module MOD_2 by taking their composition, denoted $MOD_1 \bullet MOD_2$. The connection is established by a specification morphism h which maps sorts and operations in the import part to sorts and operations in the export part. We require that the translated version of every equation in the import part be satisfied in the export part and that h maps the parameter part of MOD_1 onto the parameter part of MOD_2. $MOD_1 \bullet MOD_2$ has the same import part as MOD_2, the same export and parameter parts as MOD_1, and a body given by the union of the bodies of MOD_1 and MOD_2 w.r.t. the common import part of MOD_1.

Two interface specifications can be combined using composition by restricting it to the import, export, and parameter parts.

Actualization: The parameter part of a module specification MOD can be actualized by a data type specification $SPEC$ or a parameterized data type specification $PSPEC$. The actualized module $act(PSPEC, MOD)$ has the same parameter part as PSPEC while its import part, export part, and body are given by the union of the body of $PSPEC$ with the corrresponding parts of MOD w.r.t. the common parameter part of MOD. Note that actualization adds new components to the import and export parts, while composition provides exactly the import part of MOD_2 and the export part of MOD_1.

1.3 Vertical Development Steps and Realization

Vertical development steps transform abstract module specifications into more concrete forms. There are several different kinds of vertical steps on interface and module specifications, including refinement and simulation. In addition, an interface specification may be realized by a module specification.

Refinement: Intuitively, a refined specification more completely describes the resources that will be produced and the resources that are required to produce them. Refinement can be used to elaborate requirements during the initial phase of software development or to incorporate changes during the maintainence phase. Technically, a refined interface or module specification has additional sorts, operations, and equations in its import, export, and parameter parts. More specifically, a module specification is connected with its refined version by three specification morphisms on the import, export, and parameter parts; these morphisms are inclusions in most cases. A weak refinement satisfies only these basic syntactic requirements; more generally, a module and its refinement must be semantically compatibility with respect to their common parts.

Simulation: Intuitively, specification A is simulated by specification B if they are upwardly compatible, i.e., B can appear in any context where A can appear. Simulation can be used during the maintainence phase of software development to enhance a system without otherwise changing its behavior. Technically, specification A is simulated by specification B if the import part of B has fewer sorts and operations then the import part of A and the export part of B has more sorts and operations then the export part of A. A weak simulation satisfies only these basic syntactic requirements; more generally, a module and its simulation must be semantically equivalent.

Realization: Intuitively, a realization of an interface specification is a module specification which implements it. Realization is used to make the transition from requirement specification to design specification. Technically, a realization is simply a refinement between an interface specification and the interface of a module specification. If all three morphisms which establish the realization are identities, it is said to be exact; this means that only the body has been added. If all three morphisms are inclusions, the realization is said to be faithful.

1.4 Module and Configuration Families

Our approach to configuration management is based on collecting conceptually related modules into groups, called module families, to facilitate their storage, access, and reuse. We define a module family to be a set of module specifications, each of which realizes a common interface specification called the abstract interface of the module family. Recall that a realization need not be exact; in general, the abstract interface may be mapped to members of the module family using specification morphisms. This provides great flexibility for inserting new modules into a module family. Each module family has a set of relations, such as *refinement_of*, *revision_of*, and *variant_of*, defined on its members. These relations are updated as the module family is updated.

A configuration family is a set of compound modules which have been constructed in a uniform way from an n-tuple of module families. Members of a configuration family are constructed using an n-ary operation OP built up from the horizontal operations introduced in1.2. Version functions are used to select appropriate combinations of modules from the module families. Relations on members of a configuration family, such as *refinement_of*, *revision_of*, and *variant_of*, are induced by relations on the module families. Under suitable conditions, each configuration family defines a new module family.

1.5 Correctness and Compatibility Issues

The algebraic framework allows us to identify certain kinds of incorrect or incomplete module specifications. First, if the body of a module specification is overdetermined, in the sense that it gives several different results for some function w.r.t. the given import, then certain elements of the import algebras become identified. Second, if the body is underdetermined, in the sense that it does not define some function completely w.r.t. the given import, then new elements are added to the import algebras.

A module specification is said to be correct if it leaves in its semantics every possible import algebra unchanged. Algebraic theory provides support for checking the correctness of modules. A horizontal operation is said to be correctness preserving if it always produces correct results from correct arguments. We have shown that composition, actualization, and union are all correctness preserving. Thus, to show the correctness of a compound module constructed from these operations, it suffices to show the correctness of its atomic modules, which can be accomplished using existing algebraic techniques and tools.

A horizontal operation is said to be compositional if the semantics of its result can be constructed from the semantics of its arguments, and clean if it is both correctness preserving and compositional. We have shown that if composition, actualization, and union are used with correct modules, then they are compositional and therefore clean. Clean operations have a number of useful properties. First, they satisfy algebraic laws, such as associativity and distributivity, which can be used to restructure compound modules. Second, they are compatible with certain vertical development steps, such as refinement and realization, in the following sense. Suppose we have a compound module M_1 constructed from a set of modules A using clean operations and a compound module M_2 constructed from refinements of modules in A using the same operations, then M_2 is a refinement of M_1. This allows modular vertical development and consistent updates of module and configuration families; see 3.9.

2. The Evolution of a Simple Desk Calculator

In this section, we develop the specification of a simple desk calculator to illustrate the construction of modules, module families, and configuration families. We emphazise the overall structural aspects rather than the definition of the user operations.

The primary module of our example system, calculator, exports a function **eval:string → rational** which evaluates arithmetic expressions over the rational numbers. A calculator is a compound module composed of a scanner module and a driver module. The scanner exports a function **scan:string → scanresult** which breaks the input string up into tokens. The driver implements **eval** by repeatedly calling **scan** and interpreting the sequence of tokens it produces. The driver assumes this sequence of tokens is in postfix form and implements **eval** using a stack of rationals. If an error occurs while the input string is being scanned or parsed, **eval** returns the error rational **errorrat**.

All modules in the system have a common parameter part, called **system_parameter**, which provides the sorts boolean, alphabet, string, rational, and stack(rational) with their standard operations and interpretation.

In the following examples we assume there are explicitly specified boolean operations for equality and inequality on all sorts, which we use in the premisses of conditional equations. To enhance readability we denote them by '=' and '≠'.

2.1 The Scanner Module Family

As a first step, we define the scanner module family with its abstract interface. No elements are imported other than those provided already by the parameter part.

```
module family scanner
   parameter system_parameter
   import
   export
      sorts tokentype, scanresult
      opns
         scan:     string       → scanresult
         gettype: scanresult   → tokentype
         getvalue:scanresult   → rational
         getrest: scanresult   → string
         plus, minus, number, endinput, errortoken:→ tokentype
      eqns
         gettype(scan(emptystring))=endinput
         getvalue(x)=errorrat ← gettype(x) ≠ number
         getrest(x)=errorstring ← gettype(x) = errortoken
         ...Definition of the normal cases for scan ...
   end export
end scanner
```

Intuitively, the function **scan** identifies the next token on the input string and produces a scanresult to describe it. A scanresult includes the token's type, either **plus**, **minus**, **number**, **endinput**, or **errortoken** and, if the tokentype is **number**, its value. In addition, a scanresult includes the remainder of the input string. The functions **gettype**, **getvalue**, and **getrest** produce these values from a scanresult. The explicitly given equations only partially specify the operation **scan**; for brevity we omit the equations for the normal cases.

We now construct a scanner module called **small_scanner**. The parameter, import, and export parts of this module are taken from the abstract interface of the scanner module family.

```
module small_scanner
   parameter scanner.parameter
   import scanner.import
   export scanner.export
   body
      opns
         tup:        tokentype, rational, string → scanresult
         isnum:      string → boolean
         convertnum: string → rational
         skipnum:    string → string
      eqns
         gettype(tup(t,r,s)) = t
         getvalue(tup(t,r,s)) = r
         getrest(tup(t,r,s)) = s
         scan(s) = tup(endinput,errorrat,errorstring) ← isempty(s) = true
         scan(s) = tup(plus,errorrat,rest(s)) ← first(s) = '+'
         scan(s) = tup(minus,errorrat,rest(s)) ← first(s) = '-'
         scan(s) = tup(number,convertnum(s),skipnum(s)) ← isnum(s) = true
         scan(s) = tup(errortoken,errorrat,errorstring)
                   ← ...all conditions of the equations above are false ...
         ...definition of isnum, convertnum, skipnum ...
   end body
end small_scanner
```

The functions **isnum**, **convertnum**, and **skipnum** are used to process a rational constant: **isnum** determines whether a prefix of the input string is a rational constant, **convertnum** converts the largest such prefix to a rational, and **skipnum** returns the input string with this prefix removed. For brevity, we omit the specifications of these functions.

In the previous section, we stated that a module is correct if it leaves the semantics of every possible import algebra unchanged. We can show that this module is correct given that the allowable algebras for the system parameter are restricted to those which have the standard interpretation.

We now update the scanner module family to include **small_scanner** using an exact realization.

```
update scanner with small_scanner using identities
```

2.2 The Driver Module Family

We now define the driver module family and its abstract interface.

```
module family driver
   parameter system_parameter
   import scanner.export
   export
      opns
         eval:  string → rational
      eqns ...properties of eval ...
   end export
end driver
```

We now construct a driver module called **small_driver**. The parameter, import, and export parts of this module are taken from the abstract interface of the driver module family.

```
module small_driver
   parameter driver.parameter
   import driver.import
   export driver.export
   body
```

```
    opns
        evalrec:  string, stack(rational) → rational
    eqns
        eval(s) = evalrec(s,emptystack)
        evalrec(s,t) = top(t) ← gettype(scan(s)) = endiput and
                       t ≠ emptystack and pop(t) = emptystack
        evalrec(s,t) = errorrat ← gettype(scan(s)) = errortoken
        evalrec(s,t) = evalrec(getrest(scan(s)),push(top(t)+top(pop(t)),pop(pop(t))
                       ← gettype(scan(s)) = plus and t ≠ emptystack and
                                      pop(t) ≠ emptystack
        ...analog equation for minus ...
        evalrec(s,t) = evalrec(getrest(scan(s)), push(getvalue(scan(s)),t))
                       ← gettype(scan(s)) = number
        evalrec(s,t) = errorrat
                       ← ...all conditions above are false ...
  end body
end small_driver
```

Again, we can show that this module is correct given that the allowable algebras for system parameter are restricted to those which have the standard interpretation, and the imported tokens are all different.

We now update the driver module family to include **small_driver** using an exact realization.

```
update driver with small_driver using identities
```

2.3 The Calculator Configuration Family

We now define the calculator configuration family with respect to the scanner and driver module families. The operation used to combine scanners and drivers is simply composition. No elements are imported other than those provided by the parameter part.

```
configuration family calculator
  with s:scanner, d:driver operation d • s
  parameter system_parameter
  import
  export
    opns
      eval:  string → rational
    eqns ...properties of eval ...
  end export
end calculator
```

The abstract interface consistency condition, which requires that the abstract interface for the calculator configuration family be equal to composition applied to the abstract interfaces of the scanner and driver module families, clearly hold in this case.

We now update the calculator configuration family to include **small_calculator**, a compound module composed from **small_scanner** and **small_driver** using identity morphisms.

```
update calculator with small_calculator(small_scanner, small_driver) using identities
```

The calculator configuration family induces a module family which can be used in the construction of subsequent configuration families. Since composition is a clean operator, and the scanner and driver modules are correct, we are guaranteed that the calculator module is correct.

2.4 Enlarging the Module and Configuration Families

We now construct a new calculator module which supports multiplication and division. As a first step, we refine **small_scanner** into a new module, **big_scanner**, which recognizes these tokentypes. The parameter and import parts of this module are the same as in **small_scanner**. The export part is the same as in **small_scanner** with the addition of two new functions `times: → tokentype` and `division: → tokentype`. The body is constructed by inserting two more equations.

```
scan(s) = tup(times,errorrat,rest(s)) ← first(s) = '*'
scan(s) = tup(division,errorrat,rest(s)) ← first(s)= '/'
```

We now add **big_scanner** to the scanner module family using a faithful realization; the realization morphisms must be inclusions, rather than identities, because the export part of **big_scanner** has more operations. **big_scanner** is only a weak refinement of **small_scanner** since they do not have the same behavior on errortokens.

```
update scanner with big_scanner using inclusions
        weakly refining small_scanner using inclusions
```

Similarly, we refine **small_driver** into a new module, **big_driver**, which interprets the additional tokentypes **times** and **division**. The parameter and export parts of this module are the same as in **small_driver**. The import part is the same as in **small_driver** with the addition of the new functions `times: → tokentype` and `division: → tokentype`. The body is constructed by inserting two equations.

```
evalrec(s,t) = evalrec(getrest(scan(s)),push(top(t)*top(pop(t)),pop(pop(t)))
        ← gettype(scan(s)) = times and t ≠ emptystack and pop(t) ≠ emptystack
... analog equation for division ...
```

We now add **big_driver** to the driver module family using a faithful realization. **big_driver** is a refinement of **small_driver** since they have the same behavior on their common elements.

```
update driver with big_driver using inclusions
        refining small_driver using inclusions
```

New members of the calculator module family can now be generated. The modules **big_scanner** and **big_driver** can be combined using identity morphisms to produce **big_calculator** which supports multiplication and division.

```
update calculator with big_calculator(big_scanner,big_driver) using identities
```

Since **big_scanner** and **big_driver** weakly refine **small_scanner** and **small_driver**, we get an induced weak refinement between **small_calculator** and **big_calculator**. In addition, **big_scanner** and **small_driver** can be combined to produce **mixed_calculator_1** using inclusions. **mixed_calculator_1** is semantically equivalent to **small_calculator** since **small_driver** treats all unknown tokentypes as errors.

```
update calculator with mixed_calculator_1(big_scanner,small_driver) using identities
```

Since every module is a refinement of itself, this update induces two more weak refinements; one between **small_calculator** and **mixed_calculator_1** and one between **mixed_calculator_1** and **big_calculator**.

We can combine **small_scanner** and **big_driver** to create **mixed_calculator_2** by mapping all extra tokens required by **big_driver** to the errortoken provided by **small_scanner**. This demonstrates the power of using morphisms to connect modules.

```
update calculator with mixed_calculator_2(small_scanner,big_driver)
        using identities on sorts
              times → errortoken
              division → errortoken
              identities otherwise on operations
```

The refinements among the four calculators are shown in figure 2.1.

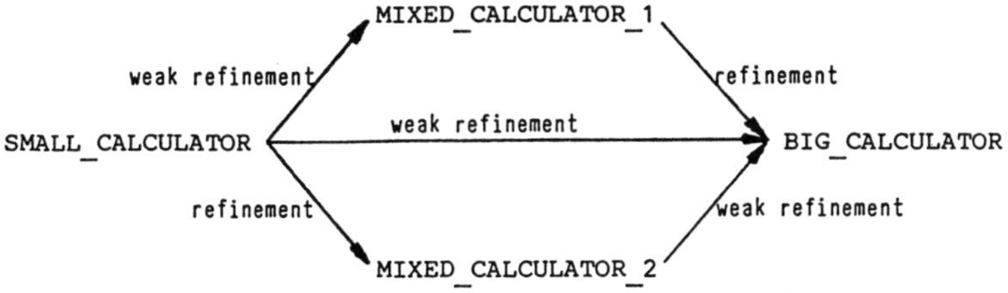

Figure 2.1: Refinements Among the Calculators

3. Outline of Algebraic Theory

In this section, we give an overview of the algebraic theory underlying our concepts of module specifications, horizontal and vertical development steps, and module and configuration families. A more detailed discussion can be found in our technical report [EFHJLLP88].

Our concept of module specifications is based on algebraic data type specifications $SPEC = (S, OP, E)$ where S, OP, and E are sets of sort symbols, operation symbols, and equations respectively. A specification morphism $f : SPEC_1 \rightarrow SPEC_2$ between specifications $SPEC_i = (S_i, OP_i, E_i)$ for $i = 1,2$ is a pair $f = (f_S : S_1 \rightarrow S_2, f_{OP} : OP_1 \rightarrow OP_2)$ of functions such that for each $N : s_1, \ldots, s_n \rightarrow s$ in OP_1 we have $f_{OP}(N) : f_S(s_1) \ldots f_S(s_n) \rightarrow f_S(s)$ in OP_2, and for each e in E_1 the translated equation $f^{\#}(e)$ is provable from E_2.

A $SPEC$-algebra $\mathcal{A}$ consists of a base set A_s for each $s \in S$ and an operation $N_A : A_{s_1} \times \ldots \times A_{s_n} \rightarrow A_s$ for each operation symbol $N : s_1, \ldots, s_n \rightarrow s$ in OP. The operations are required to satisfy all equations in E. $SPEC$-algebras and homomorphisms between them define a domain $Alg(SPEC)$ used to define the semantic of modules. For each specification morphism $f : SPEC_1 \rightarrow SPEC_2$ there is a forgetful construction $FORGET_f : Alg(SPEC_2) \rightarrow Alg(SPEC_1)$, which forgets all base sets and operations not in $f(SPEC_1)$, and a free construction $FREE_f : Alg(SPEC_1) \rightarrow Alg(SPEC_2)$ which transforms each $SPEC_1$-algebra $\mathcal{A}_1$ into a freely generated $SPEC_2$-algebra. For more details we refer to [EM 85].

3.1 Definition and Remarks: Module Specifications

1. A module specification $MOD = (PAR, IMP, EXP, BOD, i, e, s, v)$ consists of four algebraic specifications: the parameter part PAR, the import part IMP, the export part EXP, and the body BOD; and four specification morphisms: $i : PAR \rightarrow IMP$, $e : PAR \rightarrow EXP$, $s : IMP \rightarrow BOD$, and $v : EXP \rightarrow BOD$ such that the diagram in figure 3.1 commutes.

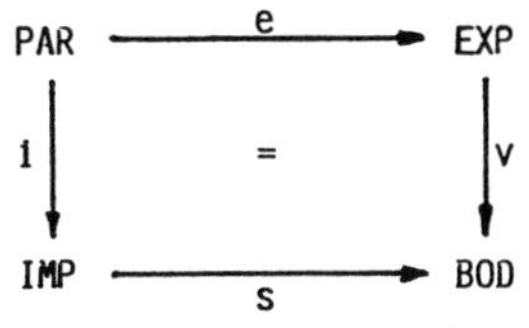

Figure 3.1 : Module specifications

The morphisms may be arbitrary specification morphisms, however they are always inclusions in the previous sections of this paper.

2. The semantics SEM of MOD is the construction $SEM = FORGET_v \circ FREE_s : Alg(IMP) \rightarrow Alg(EXP)$. SEM is a transformation from import into export algebras, i.e. export algebras are constructed from import algebras by applying the free construction $FREE_s$ and then the forgetful construction $FORGET_v$.
3. A module specification MOD is said to be correct, as discussed in 1.5, if the free construction $FREE_s$: $Alg(IMP) \rightarrow Alg(BOD)$ is strongly persistent. Strong persistence of $FREE_s$ means that every import algebra $\mathcal{A} \in Alg(IMP)$ remains unchanged after the free construction $FREE_s$.

As a typical example of a horizontal operation on module specifications, we give the formal definition of composition.

3.2 Definition: Composition of Module Specifications

The composition of two module specifications MOD_1 and MOD_2 via a pair $h = (h_1, h_2)$ of specification morphisms $h_1 : IMP_1 \rightarrow EXP_2$ and $h_2 : PAR_1 \rightarrow PAR_2$ is the module specification $MOD_3 = MOD_1 \bullet_h MOD_2$ given by the diagram in figure 3.2.

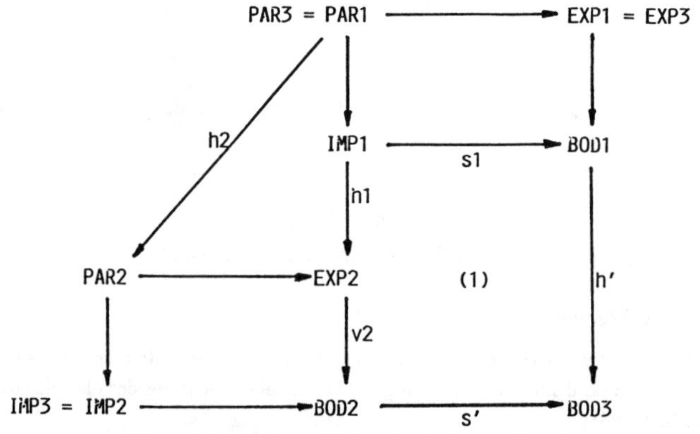

Figure 3.2 : Composition of module specifications

The subdiagrams (1), (2), and (3) are assumed to commute and in (4) BOD_3 is built from BOD_1 by textual replacement of $s_1(IMP_1)$ by BOD_2. This induces the specification morphisms $h\prime$ and $s\prime$ (see [EM85]).

3.3 Fact: Correctness and Compositionality of Composition

Given correct module specifications MOD_1 and MOD_2, the composition MOD_3 as above is correct and its semantics $SEM_3 = SEM_1 \circ FORGET_{h_1} \circ SEM_2$. (For a proof see [BEP 87].)

Thus, composition is correctness preserving and compositional and therefore clean as discussed in 1.5.

As a typical example of a vertical development step, we give the formal definition of refinement.

3.4 Definition: Refinement of Module Specifications

1. A weak refinement $r : MOD_1 \rightarrow MOD_2$ from MOD_1 to MOD_2 is given by a triple $r = (r_P, r_E, r_I)$ of specification morphisms $r_P : PAR_1 \rightarrow PAR_2$, $r_E : EXP_1 \rightarrow EXP_2$, and $r_I : IMP_1 \rightarrow IMP_2$ such that all subdiagrams in figure 3.3 commute.

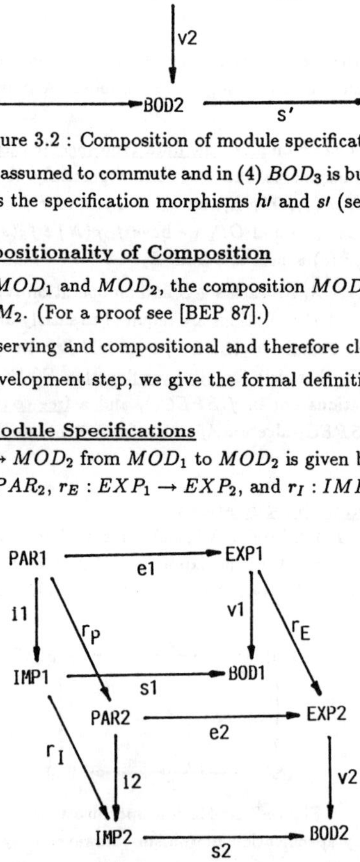

Figure 3.3: Refinement of module specifications

2. A weak refinement $r : MOD_1 \rightarrow MOD_2$ is called a refinement if $SEM_1 \circ FORGET_{r_I} = FORGET_{r_E} \circ SEM_2$ holds, i.e., if the semantics SEM_1 and SEM_2 of MOD_1 and MOD_2 are compatible up to forgetful functors.

3.5 Fact: Compatibility of Refinement with Composition

Given (weak) refinements $r_i : MOD_i \rightarrow MOD'_i$ for $i = 1, 2$, and well-defined compositions $MOD_3 = MOD_1 \bullet_h MOD_2$, and $MOD'_3 = MOD'_1 \bullet_{h'} MOD'_2$ satisfying $h'_1 \circ r_{1I} = r_{2E} \circ h_1$ and $h'_2 \circ r_{1P} = r_{2P} \circ h_2$ there is an induced (weak) refinement $r_3 : MOD_3 \rightarrow MOD'_3$ with $r_3 = (r_{1P}, r_{1E}, r_{2I})$. (For a proof see [EFHLP 89].)

3.6 Remarks: Interface Specifications and Realization

1. The notion of an interface specification $INT = (PAR, IMP, EXP, i, e)$ can be obtained from that of a module specification by dropping the body BOD and the morphisms s and v.

2. The notions of composition and refinement can be restricted to interface specifications.
3. A realization $r : INT \rightarrow MOD$ of an interface specification INT by a module specification MOD is given by a triple $r = (r_P, r_E, r_I)$ of specification morphisms satisfying the same conditions as a weak refinement.

We now outline the formal definitions of module and configuration families.

3.7 Definition: Module family

A module family $MODFAM = (INT, (MOD_j, r_j)_{j \in J}, REL)$ consists of an interface specification INT, called the abstract interface of $MODFAM$, a family of module specifications MOD_j and realizations $r_j : INT \rightarrow MOD_j$ for each $j \in J$, and a set of relations REL on J. REL is intended to include different relations between the versions of $MODFAM$, like $refinement\_of$, $revision\_of$, and $variant\_of$.

3.8 Definition and Remarks: Configuration family

Given an n-tuple of module families $MODFAM_i = (INT_i, (MOD_{i_j}, r_{i_j})_{j \in J_i}, REL_i)$ for $i = 1, \ldots, n$

a configuration family $CONFAM = (INT, OP, J, f, REL)$ w.r.t. $MODFAM_i$ $(i = 1, \ldots, n)$ consists of an interface specification INT, called the abstract interface of $CONFAM$, an n-ary horizontal operation OP, a version index set J, an n-tuple of version functions $f = (f_i : J \rightarrow J_i)_{i=1,\ldots,n}$, to select compatible n-tuples of module specifications from each module family, and a set of relations REL on J. Four basic consistency conditions (see [EFHJLLP 88]), such as abstract interface consistency as mentioned in 2.3, and version consistency are required to hold.

The version functions select n-tuples of module family members to be combined, using OP, to produce members of the configuration family. Each such n-tuple defines one configuration given by some $j \in J$. The corresponding n-tuple is $(MOD^*_{1j}, \ldots, MOD^*_{nj})$ with $MOD^*_{ij} = MOD_{i,f_i(j)}$ for $i = 1, \ldots, n$. Version consistency makes sure that these tuples of modules can be combined to a configuration $CONF_j$ using the operation OP.

3.9 Main Facts: Compatibility Results for Module and Configuration Families

Given a configuration family $CONFAM$ w.r.t. module families $MODFAM_i$ as above, we have the following results (see [EFHJLLP 88]):

1. Induced Module Family: There is an induced module family corresponding to the result of applying OP to those members of $MODFAM_i$ given by the version functions.
2. Induced Refinement: Refinements between members of the module families induce refinements between corresponding configurations in $CONFAM$, provided that certain basic compatibility conditions hold.
3. Induced Updates: Given an update $MODFAM_i'$ of $MODFAM_i$ by additional realizations, there is an induced update $CONFAM'$ of $CONFAM$ by additional realizations, provided that certain basic compatibility conditions hold.

4. Summary and Future Research

In this paper we introduced a new approach to modular software development and configuration management that is based on the theory of algebraic module specification development [EFHLP 89]. The formal nature of this approach permits reasoning about the horizontal and vertical structure of a software systems in a precise manner. At the same time, it introduces very flexible concepts that are well-suited for practical use. This flexibility arises from the fact that all module interconnections, on the horizontal and vertical levels, are established by specification morphisms that incorporate features like renaming, identification and restriction. Thus it is possible to adjust and reuse modules in quite different contexts.

One direction for future research is to develop a notion of refinement for module families and configuration families to model evolution on the system architecture level. A possible approach could use the following terminology: A refinement of one module family by another is given by a refinement of their interfaces. With this notion every module that can be put into the refining module family can also be used to update the original module family. Thus, an update of a refining family results in updates of all families that are refined by it.

This refinement notion of module families generalizes to a notion of configuration family refinement. Given two n-tuples of module families, such that $MODFAM_i$ is refined by $MODFAM'_i$, then a configuration family $CONFAM$ w.r.t. $MODFAM_i$ $(i = 1, \ldots, n)$ is refined by a configuration family $CONFAM'$ w.r.t. $MODFAM_i'$ $(i = 1, \ldots, n)$, if there is a refinement of the interfaces of the configuration families and the horizontal operation of both configuration families are identical.

As with module families any update of a configuration family $CONFAM$ induces updates of every configuration family which $CONFAM$ refines. Thus we get downward compatibility of system architectures in the case of configuration family refinements.

A number of questions arise in this setting concerning upward compatibility of system architectures. Suppose we are given a configuration family refinement $CONFAM$ w.r.t. $MODFAM_i$ $(i = 1, \ldots, n)$ by $CONFAM'$ w.r.t. $MODFAM'_i$ $(i = 1, \ldots, n)$, module refinements MOD_i by MOD'_i and an update of $CONFAM$ with $MOD_1, \ldots, MOD_n$. Is there (under some additional assumptions) an induced update of $CONFAM'$ with $MOD'_1, \ldots, MOD'_n$ and how are they semantically related? We will address these issues in our future research.

5. References

[ADJ 76] Goguen, J.A., Thatcher, J.W., Wagner, E.G. : "An Initial Algebra Approach to the Specification, Correctness and Implementation of Abstract Data Types ", IBM Research Report RC 6487, 1976. Also : Current Trends in Programming Methodology IV : Data Structuring (R. Yeh, ed.), Prentice Hall, 1978, pp. 80-144

[BEP 87] Blum, E.K., Ehrig, H., Parisi-Presicce, F.:"Algebraic Specification of Modules and Their Basic Interconnections", JCSS Vol. 34, 1987, pp. 293-339

[BHK 86] Bergstra, J.A., Heering, J., Klint, P.: "Module Algebra", Centre for Mathematics and Computer Science, Amsterdam, Report CS-R 8617, 1986

[EFHJL 89] Ehrig, H., Fey, W., Hansen, H., Jacobs, D., Löwe, M.: Algebraic Concepts for the Evolution of Module Families, in Proc. AMAST (International Conference on Algebraic Methodology and Software Technology), Iowa City (USA), May 22-24, 1989, pp. 85-88

[EFHJLLP 88] Ehrig, H., Fey, W., Hansen, H., Jacobs, D., Langen, A., Löwe, M., Parisi-Presicce, F.: "Algebraic Specification of Modules and Configuration Families", Research Report No. 88-17, Department of Computer Science, TU Berlin, 1988

[EFHLP89] Ehrig, H., Fey, W., Hansen, H., Löwe, M., Parisi-Presicce, F. : "Categories for the Development of Algebraic Module Specifications", in Ehrig, H., Herrlich, M., Kreowski, H.-J., Preuß, G. (eds.) : "Categorical Methods in Computer Science with Aspects from Topology", LNCS 393, 1989, Springer Verlag

[EM85] Ehrig, H., Mahr, B. : "Fundamentals of Algebraic Specification 1 ", Springer Verlag, Berlin, 1985

[EW86] Ehrig, H., Weber, H. : "Programming in the Large with Algebraic Module Specifications", Proc. IFIP Congress '86, Dublin, September 1986, pp. 675-684

[GM 82] Goguen, J.A., Messeguer : "Universal Realization, persistent Interconnection and Implementation of Abstract Modules", Proc. 9th ICALP, LNCS 140, 1982, pp. 265-281, Springer Verlag

[HJ 87] Hull, R., Jacobs, D. : "Towards a Formalism for Module Interconnection and System Evolution", Proceedings of 'First Workshop on Database Programming Languages', Roscoff, 1987

[LZ 74] Liskov, B., Zilles, S. : "Programming with Abstract Data Types", SIGPLAN Notices 9, 1974, pp. 55-59

[NS 87] Narayanaswamy, K., Scacchi, W. : "Maintaining Configurations of Evolving Software Systems", IEEE Transactions on Software Engineering, Vol. SE-13, March 1987, pp. 324-334

[Par 72] Parnas, D. L. : "A Technique for Software Module Specification with Examples", Communications of the ACM, Vol. 15, No. 5, 1972, pp. 330-336

[Par 76] Parnas, D. L. : "On the Design and Development of Program Families", IEEE Transactions on Software Engineering, Vol. SE-2, 1976, pp. 1-9

[PN 82] Prieto-Diaz, R., Neighbors, J. : "Module Interconnection Languages: A Survey", ICS Technical Report 189, University of California, Irvine, 1982; also in: The Journal of Systems and Software, Vol. 6, 1986, pp. 307-334

[Rei 85] Reichel, H. : "Behavioural Program Specification", Proc. Category Theory and Computer Programming, Guildford, September 1985, LNCS 240, pp. 390-411, Springer Verlag

[ST 85] Sannella, D., Tarlecki, A. : "Extended ML: an institution-independent framework for formal program development" Proc. Category Theory and Computer Programming, Guildford, September 1985, LNCS 240, pp. 364-389, Springer Verlag

[TWW 78] Thatcher, J.W., Wagner, E.G., Wright, J.B. : "Data Type Specification: Parameterization and the Power of Specification Techniques ", 10th Symp. Theory of Computing, 1978, pp. 119-132 Trans. Prog. Languages and Systems 4, 1982, pp. 711-732

[WE 86] Weber, H., Ehrig, H. : "Specification of Modular Systems", IEEE Transaction on Software Engineering, Vol. SE-12, 1986, pp. 786-798

On the Limitations of Locally Robust Positive Reductions

Lane A. Hemachandra* and Sanjay Jain†
Department of Computer Science
University of Rochester
Rochester, New York 14627, USA

Abstract

Polynomial-time positive reductions, as introduced by Selman, are by definition globally robust — they are positive with respect to all oracles. This paper studies the extent to which the theory of positive reductions remains intact when their global robustness assumption is removed.

We note that two-sided locally robust positive reductions — reductions that are positive with respect to the oracle to which the reduction is made — are sufficient to retain all crucial properties of globally robust positive reductions. In contrast, we prove absolute and relativized results showing that one-sided local robustness fails to preserve fundamental properties of positive reductions, such as the downward closure of *NP*.

1 Introduction

In this paper we study the relative powers of different positive reducibilities. Informally, a reduction is positive if converting some "no" answers to "yes" does not cause a previously accepted string to be rejected.

Selman, in his seminal paper [Sel82b], defines and considers the properties of polynomial-time positive reductions. His positive reductions are by definition globally robust in the positivity.

*Supported in part by the National Science Foundation under grants CCR-8809174, CCR-8996198 and Presidential Young Investigator Award CCR-8957604.

†Supported by National Science Foundation grant CER 5-285-25 to the University of Rochester.

An oracle machine, or a set of oracle machines, is said to robustly have a property P if it has property P for all oracles. Recent work on the power of robustness [Sch85, BI87, HH87, Ko87, Tar87] suggests that global robustness is a strong restriction. For example, it is known that if two nondeterministic machines N_1 and N_2 are robustly complementary — that is, complementary for every oracle — then for all oracles A, $L(N_1^A) \in P^{A \oplus NP}$ [HH87]. This, and the desire to broaden the domain of application of Selman's techniques, motivate us to relax the global robustness restriction.

Accordingly, we introduce three notions of locally robust polynomial-time positive reductions. We show that the Turing versions of these reducibilities differ. However, our ability to distinguish among the truth-table versions of these reducibilities depends on the structure of *NP*. In particular, we show that if *P*=*NP* then these polynomial-time locally robust truth-table reducibilities are the same. However, if there exist uniformly log*-sparse tally sets in *NP*−*P*, then the reducibilities differ.

We study the extent to which the theory of positive reductions, as studied by Selman, remains intact for locally robust reductions. We prove results identifying the crucial properties of positive reductions required to obtain the results of [Sel82b]. One reason for introducing new reducibilities is that it is more likely that a set A reduces to B by locally positive reductions than by globally positive reductions. Our results thus enrich the domain in which Selman's techniques can be applied.

2 Notations

Let $\mathcal{N}$ denote the set of natural numbers. Σ is an alphabet set, usually $\{0, 1\}$. A language is a subset of Σ^*. $\emptyset$ denotes the empty set. $M_0, M_1, \ldots$ denotes some standard enumeration of polynomial-time deterministic Turing machines. $N_1, N_2, \ldots$ denotes some standard enumeration of polynomial-time nondeterministic Turing machines. We assume that the running times of machine M_i (N_i) is bounded by deterministic (nondeterministic) time $n^i + i$. P denotes the class of all languages accepted by some polynomial-time deterministic Turing machine [HU79]. *NP* denotes the class of languages accepted by some polynomial-time nondeterministic Turing machine and *coNP* denotes the class of languages whose complement is in *NP* [HU79]. $L(M)$ denotes the language accepted by the machine M. E and NE denote respectively the class of languages accepted by exponential time deterministic and nondeterministic Turing machines; that is, $E = \bigcup_{c>0} DTIME[2^{cn}]$ and $NE = \bigcup_{c>0} NTIME[2^{cn}]$. $L(M^A)$ denotes the language accepted by the oracle machine M with the oracle A [HU79].

$A \leq_T B$ means there exists a machine M such that $A = L(M^B)$. $\leq_T^P$ denotes polynomial-time Turing reduction. $\leq_{tt}$ and $\leq_m$ similarly denote truth-table and many-one reductions. $P_r(A)$ denotes the class of languages r-reducible to A in polynomial time (see [BK88]). A tally language is a subset of 1^*. $\overline{A}$ denotes the complement of A, i.e., $\Sigma^* - A$. χ_A denotes the characteristic function of A. We sometimes denote a string x of length n by $x_1 x_2 \ldots x_n$, where x_i is the ith character of x. $|x|$ denotes the length of x. $A^{\leq n}$ denotes the set of strings in A with length at most n.

3 Polynomial-time positive reducibilities

In this section, we review Selman's notion of positive reducibility, which by definition is globally robust, and we introduce new notions of locally robust positive reducibility.

Positive reducibility was first studied for polynomial-time truth-table reductions in [LLS75]. Selman, in [Sel82b], extended the definition to Turing reductions. We first give the definition of globally positive reducibility due to Selman.[1]

Definition 3.1 *[Sel82b, Sel82a] A query machine M is globally positive if $(\forall x)(\forall A, B)[x \in L(M^B) \Rightarrow x \in L(M^{A \cup B})]$.*

Intuitively, a machine M is positive if converting some "no" answers to "yes" answers does not make the machine reject a previously accepted string. Moreover, this property holds for all oracles given to the machine (hence the term *globally* positive). Positive reducibility can now be defined using these globally positive machines.

Definition 3.2 *[Sel82b, Sel82a] $A \leq_{pos}^P C$ if $A \leq_T C$ by some polynomial-time, globally positive Turing machine M.*

The conditions placed here on positive Turing reductions are analogous to those in the definition of positive truth-table reductions in [LLS75], which defined globally positive truth-table reductions.

Definition 3.3 *[LLS75] $A \leq_{ptt}^P C$ if $A \leq_T C$ by some polynomial-time, globally positive machine M, and there is a polynomial-time computable function $f : \{0,1\}^* \to \{c, 0, 1, \}^*$ such that M on input x makes queries only from the list $f(x)$ (here c acts as a separator of elements of the list). M above can be equivalently represented by a polynomial time evaluator e such that for all oracles C, $e(x, \chi_C(y_1), \chi_C(y_2) \ldots) = M^C(x)$, where $y_1, y_2, \ldots$ are the elements in the list $f(x)$.*[2]

Definition 3.4 *[LLS75] $A \leq_{pbtt}^P C$ if $A \leq_T C$ by some polynomial-time, globally positive machine*

[1] This reducibility is simply referred to as "positive" in [Sel82b]. However, we'll refer to it throughout this paper as "globally positive" in order to distinguish it from the locally positive reducibilities we define.

[2] In [LLS75] the first argument of e is $\alpha(x)$, however without loss of generality we can take this to be x and let e do the (polynomial time) computations required to obtain α.

M, and a polynomial-time computable function $f : \{0,1\}^* \rightarrow \{c,0,1,\}^*$ such that M on input x makes queries only from the list $f(x)$. Moreover the number of elements in the list $f(x)$ is bounded by some constant independent of x. M above can be equivalently represented by a polynomial time evaluator e such that for all oracles C, $e(x, \chi_C(y_1), \chi_C(y_2), \ldots) = M^C(x)$, where $y_1, y_2, \ldots$ are the elements in the list $f(x)$.

The above definitions require global robustness; given *any* oracle A, $L(M^A)$ must never decrease when A is increased in *any* way. Note that all $\leq_m^P$ reductions are globally positive. However, global robustness is a strong restriction on Turing transducers. Machines exhibiting global robustness are known, in other contexts, to be weak [BI87, HH87, Tar87].

A more moderate definition of "positive" might require a reduction to be robust *only with respect to the particular set to which the reduction is being made.* We introduce three notions of locally robust positive reductions. In these definitions we require the machine to be robust only with respect to the oracle to which the reduction is made.

Definition 3.5 *A query machine M is locally right positive with respect to B if $(\forall x)(\forall A)[x \in L(M^B) \Rightarrow x \in L(M^{A \cup B})]$.*

Intuitively, M is locally right robust with respect to B if converting some "no" answers from the oracle B to "yes" answers does not make the machine reject a previously accepted string. Left robustness is just the other side of the above definition.

Definition 3.6 *A query machine M is locally left positive with respect to B if $(\forall x)(\forall A)[x \in L(M^{B-A}) \Rightarrow x \in L(M^B)]$ (or equivalently $(\forall x)(\forall A)[x \notin L(M^B) \Rightarrow x \notin L(M^{B-A})]$).*

Definition 3.7 *A query machine M is locally right-left positive with respect to B if M is both right and left positive with respect to B.*

Locally robust reductions can now be defined with respect to reductions involving locally robust machines.

Definition 3.8 *$A \leq_{rpos}^P B$ if $A \leq_T B$ by some polynomial-time machine that is locally right positive with respect to B.*

Definition 3.9 *$A \leq_{lpos}^P B$ if $A \leq_T B$ by some polynomial-time machine that is locally left positive with respect to B.*

Definition 3.10 *$A \leq_{rlpos}^P B$ if $A \leq_T B$ by some polynomial-time machine that is locally right-left positive with respect to B.*

$\leq_{rlptt}^P, \leq_{rptt}^P, \leq_{lptt}^P, \leq_{rlpbtt}^P, \leq_{rpbtt}^P$ and $\leq_{lpbtt}^P$ reductions can be defined similarly.

4 Relationships between different polynomial-time positive reducibilities

In this section, we compare the relative power of different polynomial-time positive reducibilities. Clearly:

Proposition 4.1 *$A \leq_s^P B \Rightarrow A \leq_{rls}^P B \Rightarrow [A \leq_{rs}^P B \wedge A \leq_{ls}^P B]$, where s is in $\{pos, ptt, pbtt\}$.*

We first consider the elementary properties of the reductions. The following proposition is easy to prove.

Proposition 4.2

1. *$A \leq_{pos}^P B$ and $B \leq_{pos}^P C \Rightarrow A \leq_{pos}^P C$.*
2. *$A \leq_{rpos}^P B$ and $B \leq_{rpos}^P C \Rightarrow A \leq_{rpos}^P C$.*
3. *$A \leq_{lpos}^P B$ and $B \leq_{lpos}^P C \Rightarrow A \leq_{lpos}^P C$.*
4. *$A \leq_{rlpos}^P B$ and $B \leq_{rlpos}^P C \Rightarrow A \leq_{rlpos}^P C$.*

Results similar to those of Proposition 4.2 can also be proved for bounded truth-table and truth-table reductions.

Proposition 4.3 *$A \leq_{lpos}^P B \Rightarrow \overline{A} \leq_{rpos}^P \overline{B}$.*

Proof: Let $A \leq_{lpos}^P B$ via M. Let M_1 be such that $M_1^C(x) = 1$ iff $M^{\overline{C}}(x) = 0$. Clearly $x \in L(M_1^{\overline{B}}) \Leftrightarrow x \notin L(M^B)$. Thus M_1 reduces $\overline{A}$ to $\overline{B}$. If $C \supseteq \overline{B}$ and $x \in \overline{A}$ (and thus $\overline{C} \subseteq B$ and

$x \notin A$) then $x \notin L(M^{\overline{C}})$, since M is locally left positive, and thus $x \in L(M_1^C)$. So M_1 is locally right positive. ▮

A similar proof can be used for $\leq_{pos}^P, \leq_{rpos}^P$, $\leq_{rlpos}^P, \leq_{ptt}^P, \leq_{lptt}^P, \leq_{rptt}^P, \leq_{rlptt}^P$, yielding the following result.

Proposition 4.4

1) $A \leq_{rpos}^P B \Rightarrow \overline{A} \leq_{lpos}^P \overline{B}$.

2) $A \leq_{rlpos}^P B \Rightarrow \overline{A} \leq_{rlpos}^P \overline{B}$.

3) (implicit in [Sel82b]) $A \leq_{pos}^P B \Rightarrow \overline{A} \leq_{pos}^P \overline{B}$.

4) $A \leq_{lptt}^P B \Rightarrow \overline{A} \leq_{rptt}^P \overline{B}$.

5) $A \leq_{rptt}^P B \Rightarrow \overline{A} \leq_{lptt}^P \overline{B}$.

6) $A \leq_{rlptt}^P B \Rightarrow \overline{A} \leq_{rlptt}^P \overline{B}$.

7) ([LLS75], Proposition 3.1(v)) $A \leq_{ptt}^P B \Rightarrow \overline{A} \leq_{ptt}^P \overline{B}$.

We now consider the relative power of different locally robust positive reductions. Selman showed that globally robust positive Turing reductions are more powerful than truth-table reductions.

Theorem 4.5 *[Sel82b] There exist recursive sets A and B such that* $A \leq_{pos}^P B$ *but* $A \not\leq_{tt}^P B$.

Also, it is easy to see as a corollary of previous work on disjunctive reductions that (i) there exist recursive sets A and B such that $A \leq_{ptt}^P B$ but $A \not\leq_{btt}^P B$, and (ii) there exist recursive sets A and B such that $A \leq_{pbtt}^P B$ but $A \not\leq_m^P B$ [LLS75].

Though locally robust positive reductions are in general more flexible than globally robust positive reductions, the following theorem shows that local robustness does not add extra power for the special case of positive *bounded* truth-table reductions.

Theorem 4.6 *For all* $A, P_{pbtt}(A) = P_{rpbtt}(A) = P_{lpbtt}(A)$.

Proof: Let $B \leq_{rpbtt}^P A$ via M. Let $f(x)$ be the polynomial time computable list such that M, on input x, makes queries only from the list $f(x)$. Let e be the evaluator equivalent to M (as in the definition of $\leq_{pbtt}^P$ reduction). Recall that this means that the size of list $f(x)$ is bounded by some constant c and e is positive with respect to A. Thus if $f(x) = x_1, x_2, \ldots x_c$, $\chi_A(x_i) = b_i$ and $e(x, b_1, \ldots b_c) = 1$, then converting some of b_i from 0 to 1 does not make e evaluate to 0. To make a globally robust reduction from B to A we need to convert this e to e' that is positive with respect to all oracles. We do this by converting some evaluation of e from 1 to 0.

Let $e'(x, b_1, \ldots, b_c) = 1$ iff $(\forall d_1, \ldots, d_c,\ b_j = 1 \Rightarrow d_j = 1)\ [e(x, d_1, \ldots, d_c) = 1]$ (Example: if $c = 2, e(x,0,0) = 1,\ e(x,0,1) = 1,\ e(x,1,0) = 0$ and $e(x,1,1) = 1$ then we replace e by e', where $e'(x,0,0) = 0,\ e'(0,1) = 1,\ e'(x,1,0) = 0$ and $e'(x,1,1) = 1$). This makes e' globally positive, and does not effect the reduction from B to A (since e was right positive with respect to A). Thus, f and e' form a positive bounded truth-table reduction from B to A. A similar proof can be used to show that $P_{lpbtt}(A) = P_{pbtt}(A)$. ▮

For *unbounded* truth-table reductions, the distinction between different positive reducibilities depends on the structure of *NP*, as shown by the following two theorems.

Theorem 4.7 *If* P=NP, *then for all* $A, P_{ptt}(A) = P_{rlptt}(A) = P_{rptt}(A) = P_{lptt}(A)$.

Theorem 4.8 *Let* $g(0) = 1,\ g(n+1) = 2^{g(n)},\ n > 0$. *If there exist tally sets in* $\bigcup_{c>0} NTIME[g^c(n)] - \bigcup_{c>0} DTIME[g^c(n)]$ *then there is a recursive set A such that* $P_{rptt}(A) - P_{lptt}(A) \neq \emptyset$ *and* $P_{lptt}(A) - P_{rptt}(A) \neq \emptyset$.

Proof (of Theorem 4.7): We prove that $P_{rptt}(A) = P_{ptt}(A)$. Proof for $P_{lptt}(A) = P_{ptt}(A)$ is similar. $P_{rlptt}(A) = P_{ptt}(A)$ follows from Proposition 4.1.

Let $B \leq_{rptt}^P A$ via M. Let $f(x)$ be the polynomial time computable list such that M, on input x, makes queries only from the list $f(x)$. Let e be the evaluator equivalent to M (as in the definition of $\leq_{ptt}^P$ reduction). We now proceed as in Theorem 4.6. Let $e'(x, b_1, b_2, \ldots, b_{p(n)}) = 1$ iff $[(\forall d_1, \ldots, d_{p(n)}, b_j = 1 \Rightarrow d_j = 1)\ [e(x, d_1, \ldots, d_{p(n)}) = 1]]$. Note that e' can be calculated in polynomial time if *NP=P*. Clearly, f and e' witness that $B \leq_{ptt}^P A$. ▮

Proof (of Theorem 4.8): We only prove that $(\exists A)[P_{rptt}(A) - P_{lptt}(A) \neq \emptyset]$. The proof can be easily modified to show that $[(\exists A)[P_{rptt}(A) - P_{lptt}(A) \neq \emptyset \wedge P_{lptt}(A) - P_{rptt}(A) \neq \emptyset]]$.

Let N be a polynomial-time nondeterministic machine accepting a tally language $L \subseteq \{1^{g(k)} : k \in \mathcal{N}\}$ which is not in P (the existence of such a machine follows from the assumption that there exist tally sets in $\bigcup_{c>0} NTIME[g^c(n)] - \bigcup_{c>0} DTIME[g^c(n)]$, by the techniques of [HIS85][3]).

W.l.o.g., let all certificates of $x \in L$ be of length $|x|^j + j$ and w.l.o.g., $0^{|x|^j+j}$ is never such a certificate. Let r be the polynomial-time predicate associated with N and L, i.e., $r(x,y) = 1$ iff y is a certificate for x. Let $e(x, y_1, \ldots y_{n^j+j}) = 1 - r(x,y)$, where $y = y_1 \ldots y_{n^j+j}$. Let $plus(a,j)$ be the string j greater than a in standard lexicographical order; e.g., $plus(1010, 3) = 1101$. Let c be the separation character from the definition of f (see Definitions 3.3 and 3.4). Let $f(x) = plus(x,1)\, c\, plus(x,2)\, c \ldots c\, plus(x, |x|^j + j)$. Clearly, functions f and e are computable in polynomial time.

A will be defined so that e is locally right positive. Also all strings not of the form $x, plus(x, 1), plus(x, 2), \ldots, plus(x, |x|^j + j)$, where $x \in \{1^{g(k)} : k \in \mathcal{N}\}$, are not in A. $\chi_A(plus(x, 1)) \ldots \chi_A(plus(x, |x|^j + j))$ will be $0^{|x|^j+j}$ if $x \notin L$, and otherwise will be a certificate of the fact that $x \in L$. Let R_i be the requirement that $M_i : \overline{L} \not\leq^P_{lptt} A$, that is, M_i does not $\leq^P_{lptt}$ reduce $\overline{L}$ to A. Below A_s denotes the strings of A determined before stage s. Go to stage 0.

<u>Stage s</u>

1. Let x be the least element in $\{1^{g(k)} : k \in \mathcal{N}\}$ not considered until this stage.

2. Let i be the least requirement not satisfied until now.

3. Let e_i, f_i be the evaluator and set calculator (as in the definition of positive truth-table reducibility) for the truth-table reducer M_i.

4. If $x \notin L$ then let $A_{s+1} = A_s$.

5. Else If $(\exists z)[z$ is a certificate for x and $e_i(x, \chi_{D(z)}(q_1), \chi_{D(z)}(q_2), \ldots) = 1]$, where $f_i(x) = q_1 c q_2 \ldots$ and $D(z) = A_s \bigcup \{plus(x, i) : z_i = 1\}$, then let y be least such certificate z. Set $A_{s+1} = A_s \bigcup \{plus(x, i) : y_i = 1\}$. (Note that here R_i is satisfied.)

6. Else Let $A_{s+1} = A_s \bigcup \{plus(x, i) : y_i = 1\}$, where y us the least certificate for x.

<u>end stage s.</u>

It is clear that $\overline{L} \leq^P_{rptt} A$ via the functions f and e. This is because when $x \in \overline{L}$, then $e(x, y) = 1$ for *any* length $|x|^i + i$ string y; so even if A has some strings added—and the "address" $\chi_A(plus(x, 1)) \cdots \chi_A(plus(x, |x|^i + i) = 0^{|x|^i+i}$ thus has some zeros corrupted to ones—$e(x$, corrupted address) will nonetheless accept.

Now consider the following cases:

case 1: All requirements are satisfied.

Clearly, $\overline{L} \not\leq^P_{lptt} A$.

case 2: R_i is the least requirement not satisfied.

In this case we show that $L \in P$. Let n be so large that $2^{n/10} > n^i + i$, and all the smaller requirements have been satisfied before stage s, $n > g(s)$. Clearly, when $m \in \{g(k) : k \in \mathcal{N}\}$, then $A^{\leq m-1}$ can be determined in time polynomial in m (by just going through all possible certificates). Now for $x \in \{1^{g(k)} : k \in \mathcal{N}\}, |x| > n$, we have $x \notin L \Rightarrow e_i(x, \chi_{A^{\leq |x|-1}}(q_1), \chi_{A^{\leq |x|-1}}(q_2), \ldots) = 1$ (since $A^{\leq |x|-1} = A^{\leq |x|^j+j}$ due to step 4 of the construction, and M_i reduces $\overline{L}$ to A). And similarly, we have $x \in L \Rightarrow e_i(x, \chi_{A^{\leq |x|-1}}(q_1), \chi_{A^{\leq |x|-1}}(q_2), \ldots) = 0$ (since $A^{\leq |x|-1} \subseteq A$ and $\overline{L} \leq^P_{lptt} A$ via M_i). This gives us a polynomial-time decision procedure for L contrary to the assumption.

Thus all requirements are satisfied. ∎

Note that the above proof can also be used to distinguish between $\leq^P_{rptt}$ and $\leq^P_{lpos}$ reductions, under the same assumption.

We now consider the relationship between various positive Turing reducibilities.

[3]Though recent work by Allender [All] has corrected parts of [HIS85], the techniques of [HIS85] as used here are correct.

Theorem 4.9 $(\exists A)[P_{rpos}(A) - P_{lpos}(A) \neq \emptyset \wedge P_{lpos}(A) - P_{rpos}(A) \neq \emptyset]$.

Corollary 4.10 $(\exists A)[P_{rpos}(A) - P_{rlpos} \neq \emptyset \wedge P_{lpos}(A) - P_{rlpos}(A) \neq \emptyset]$.

Proof: Let $g(0) = 1, g(n+1) = 2^{g(n)}$. Consider the following languages:

$L_A = \{1^n : n = g(k)$ for some even $k \wedge 1^n b_0 b_1 b_2 \ldots b_{n-1} \in A$ where $b_j = \chi_A(0^{n+j})\}$.

$L'_A = \{1^n : n = g(k)$ for some odd $k \wedge 1^n b_0 b_1 b_2 \ldots b_{n-1} \in A$ where $b_j = \chi_A(0^{n+j})\}$.

To ensure that $L_A \leq^P_{rpos} A$ it suffices to construct A so that for all n of form $g(2k)$, for $b_j = \chi_A(0^{n+j})$, we have $[[1^n b_0 b_1 \ldots b_{n-1} \in A] \wedge [b_j = 1 \Rightarrow d_j = 1]] \Rightarrow [1^n d_0 d_1 \ldots d_{n-1} \in A]$. Thus an oracle machine M^B which accepts 1^n iff $n = g(k)$ for some even k and $1^n a_0 a_1 \ldots a_{n-1} \in B$, where $a_i = \chi_B(0^{n+i})$ witnesses that $L_A \leq^P_{rpos} A$.

Similarly, $L'_A \leq^P_{lpos} A$ is ensured if for all n of form $g(2k+1)$, for $b_j = \chi_A(0^{n+j})$, $[[1^n b_0 b_1 \ldots b_{n-1} \notin A] \wedge [b_j = 0 \Rightarrow d_j = 0]] \Rightarrow [1^n d_0 d_1 \ldots d_{n-1} \notin A]$.

We now construct A in stages. A will satisfy the conditions above so that $L_A \leq^P_{rpos} A$ and $L'_A \leq^P_{lpos} A$.

At stage s we decide the membership in A of strings of length $g(s), \ldots, g(s+1)-1$. We always assume that strings not of the form $0^{g(k)+i}, i < g(k)$ or $1^{g(k)}\{0,1\}^{g(k)}$, are not in A (without explicitly mentioning it below).

Let R_{2i} be the requirement that $M_i : L_A \not\leq^P_{lpos} A$, that is, M_i does not $\leq^P_{lpos}$ reduce L_A to A. Let R_{2i+1} be the requirement that $M_i : L'_A \not\leq^P_{rpos} A$, that is, M_i does not $\leq^P_{rpos}$ reduce L'_A to A. Note that if all the requirements are satisfied then $L_A \not\leq^P_{lpos} A$ and $L'_A \not\leq^P_{rpos} A$. Below A_s denotes the strings of A determined before stage s. Go to stage 0.

<u>Stage $2s$</u>

1. Let R_{2i} be the least unsatisfied even requirement.

2. Let $n = g(2s)$.

3. If $2^{n/10} \leq n^i + i$ then exclude from A all strings of length l, $g(2s) \leq l < g(2s+1)$.

4. Else If $M_i^A(1^n)$ rejects when all new questions x (i.e., those not decided in A_{2s}) are answered by the rule *"If x is of form $1^n\{0,1\}^n$ then YES; If x is of form 0^{n+i} then NO,"* then let A_{2s+1} be such that all strings of form $1^n\{0,1\}^n \in A_{2s+1}$ and all other strings of length $l, g(2s) \leq l < g(2s+1)$ not in A_{2s+1}. (Note that in this case R_{2i} is satisfied.)

5. Else

   - Let S be the set of questions of form $1^n\{0,1\}^n$ asked in the computation by M_i in step 4 above.
   - For all $x \in S$, let $x \in A$.
   - If x is of form $1^n\{0,1\}^n$ and $x \notin S$ then let $x \notin A$.
   - Let y be a question of form $1^n\{0,1\}^n$ not asked by M_i (there exists such a y).
   - Let $0^{n+i} \in A \Leftrightarrow y_{n+i+1} = 1$ for $i < n$.
   - (Note that on this A, M_i either accepts incorrectly or rejects. In the latter case, since $A \supseteq A_{2s} \bigcup S$ on which M_i accepts, M_i is not a $\leq^P_{lpos}$ reduction. Either way, R_{2i} is satisfied.)

<u>end stage $2s$</u>

Stage $2s+1$ is similar:

<u>Stage $2s+1$</u>

1. Let R_{2i+1} be the least unsatisfied odd requirement.

2. Let $n = g(2s+1)$.

3. If $2^{n/10} \leq n^i + i$ then exclude from A all strings of length l, $g(2s+1) \leq l < g(2s+2)$.

4. Else If $M_i^A(1^n)$ accepts when all new questions x (i.e., those not decided in A_{2s}) are answered by the rule *"If x is of form $1^n\{0,1\}^n$ then NO; If x is of form 0^{n+i} then YES,"* then let A_{2s+1} be such that all strings of form $1^n\{0,1\}^n \notin A_{2s+2}$ and all strings of form 0^{n+i}, $i < n$ in A_{2s+2}. (Note that in this case R_{2i+1} is satisfied.)

5. Else

- Let S be the set of questions of form $1^n\{0,1\}^n$ asked in the above computation by M_i.
- For all $x \in S$, let $x \notin A$.
- If x is of form $1^n\{0,1\}^n$ and $x \notin S$ then let $x \in A$.
- Let y be a question of form $1^n\{0,1\}^n$ not asked by M_i (there exists such a y).
- Let $0^{n+i} \in A \Leftrightarrow y_{n+i+1} = 1$ for $i < n$.
- (Note that on this A, either M_i rejects incorrectly, or M_i accepts. In the latter case, since $A \subseteq A_{2s} \bigcup \{0^{n+i} : i < n\} \bigcup \{1^n z : |z| = n, z \notin S\}$ on which M_i rejects , M_i is not a $\leq^P_{rpos}$ reduction. In either case, R_{2i+1} is satisfied.)

end stage $2s+1$

Let $M^B(1^n) = 1$ iff $n = g(2k)$ for some k and $1^n b_0 b_1 \ldots b_{n-1} \in B$, where $b_j = 1$ iff $0^{n+j} \in B$. Clearly, $L_A \leq^P_{rpos} A$ via M (since 1^n is placed in L_A only in step 4 in which case all strings of form $1^n z, |z| = n$ are also placed in A). Similarly $L'_A \leq^P_{lpos} A$. We claim that $L_A \not\leq^P_{lpos} A$. Suppose by way of contradiction that $L_A \leq^P_{lpos} A$ via M_i. Also let M_i be the least such machine. Then for sufficiently large s in stage $2s$, $2^{n/10} > n^i + i$ and all smaller even requirements have been satisfied. Thus at this stage by construction M_i will be fooled. Thus no such machine can exist. It can be similarly shown that $L'_A \not\leq^P_{rpos} A$. This proves the theorem. ∎

Whether $\leq^P_{pos}$ and $\leq^P_{rlpos}$ are different is at present an open problem.

5 Basic properties of reductions

In this section we consider some of the basic properties of positive reduction in *NP*. Selman, in [Sel82b], showed that *NP* is closed downward under globally robust positive Turing reductions. We note that, though Selman's techniques suffice to prove that *NP* is closed downwards under two of the locally robust reductions, the remaining locally robust reduction fails to leave *NP* closed downwards in some relativized worlds. As a corollary, we note that rpos and lpos reductions do not share the complementation property of globally robust positive reductions (Proposition 4.4, part 3). A proof of Theorem 5.1 can be found in the full version of this paper [HJ89].

Theorem 5.1 NP *is closed downward under* $\leq^P_{lpos}$ *reductions.*

Corollary 5.2

1. coNP *is closed downward under* $\leq^P_{rpos}$ *reductions.*

2. NP *and* coNP *are closed downward under* $\leq^P_{rlpos}$ *reductions.*

3. [Sel82b] NP *and* coNP *are closed downward under* $\leq^P_{pos}$ *reductions.*

However the proof does not work for right positive reductions. We give a relativized world in which *NP* is not closed downward under locally right robust positive reductions.

Theorem 5.3 *There is a recursive oracle B such that* NP^B *is not closed downward under* $\leq^P_{rpos}$ *reductions. That is, there are recursive sets A, B and C such that $C \leq^P_{rpos} A$, $A \in \mathrm{NP}^B$, and $C \notin \mathrm{NP}^B$.*

Proof: This proof is similar to the proof of Theorem 4.9 . Let $g(0) = 1, g(n+1) = 2^{g(n)}$. We will define sets A and B. Let $A = \{x : (\exists y)|y| = |x|, xy \in B\}$. Clearly $A \in NP^B$. Let $L_A = \{1^n : n = g(k)$ for some k and $1^n b_0 b_1 \ldots b_{n-1} \in A$ where $b_j = 1 \Leftrightarrow 0^{n+j} \in A\}$. If $[1^n b_0 b_1 \ldots b_{n-1} \in A \bigwedge b_j = 1 \Rightarrow d_j = 1] \Rightarrow [1^n d_0 d_1 \ldots d_{n-1} \in A]$, where $b_j = 1 \Leftrightarrow 0^{n+j} \in A$, then $L_A \leq^P_{rpos} A$ (via machine M which with oracle B accepts 1^n iff $n = g(k)$ for some k and $1^n a_0 a_1 \ldots a_{n-1} \in B$, where $a_i = \chi_B(0^{n+i})$). We will construct B so that A satisfies the above property. In addition we will ensure that $L_A \notin NP^B$. Taking $C = L_A$ proves the theorem.

Let R_i be the requirement that $L(N_i^B) \neq L_A$. A will contain strings of form $1^n z, |z| = n$ and $0^{n+i}, i < n$ where $n = g(k)$ for some k (this thus restricts some elements to be out of B. We assume that such elements are not in B without explicitly mentioning so). At stage s we decide the membership of strings of length l, $g(s) \leq l < g(s+1)$ in A (and strings of length l, $2g(s) \leq l < 2g(s+1)$ in B). Below B_s denotes the strings of B determined before stage s. Go to stage 0.

Stage s

1. Let R_i be the least unsatisfied requirement.
2. Let $n = g(s)$.
3. If $2^{n/10} \leq n^i + i$ then exclude from A all strings of length l, $n \leq l < 2^n$.
4. Else If $N_i^{B_s \bigcup \{0^{2(n+i)} : i \geq n/2\} \bigcup \{1^n z 0^{2n} : |z| = n, z \geq 0^{n/2} 1^{n/2}\}}(1^n)$ rejects then let $B_{s+1} = B_s \bigcup \{0^{2(n+i)} : i \geq n/2\} \bigcup \{1^n z 0^{2n} : |z| = n, z \geq 0^{n/2} 1^{n/2}\}$. (Note that in this case we have already fooled N_i, since $1^n \in L_A - L(N_i^B)$).
5. Else
   - Fix an accepting path of $N_i^{B_s \bigcup \{0^{2(n+i)} : i \geq n/2\} \bigcup \{1^n z 0^{2n} : |z| = n, z \geq 0^{n/2} 1^{n/2}\}}$ running on input 1^n.
   - Let S be the set of questions asked by N_i which are in $\{0^{(n+i)} w : |w| = n + i\} \bigcup \{1^n z 0^{2n} : |z| = n, z \geq 0^{n/2} 1^{n/2}\}$.
   - Let $y, |y| = n, y \in \{0,1\}^{n/2} 1^{n/2}$ be such that $1^n y 0^{2n} \notin S$ (clearly, such a y exists).
   - Let s_{n+i} be a string of length $n+i$ such that $0^{(n+i)} s_{n+i} \notin S$.
   - Let $B_{s+1} = B_s \bigcup \{w : w \in \{0^{2(n+i)} | i \geq n/2\} \bigcup \{1^n z 0^{2n} : |z| = n, z \geq 0^{n/2} 1^{n/2}$ and $1^n z 0^{2n} \in S\}\} \bigcup \{0^{(n+i)} s_{n+i} : y_i = 1\}$.
   - (Note that in this case $1^n \in L(N_i^B) - L_A$).

end stage s.

Clearly, $L_A \leq_{rpos}^P A$. If all requirements are satisfied then clearly $L_A \notin NP^B$. So assume that R_i is the least requirement not satisfied. But then let s be so large that $2^{n/10} > n^i + i$, and all requirements less that i are satisfied by stage s. Then by construction R_i will be satisfied at stage s. Thus all the requirements are satisfied. ∎

Though $A \leq_{pos}^P B \Rightarrow \overline{A} \leq_{pos}^P \overline{B}$ (Proposition 4.4), the analog of this result fails for rpos and lpos reductions, as an immediate corollary of Theorems 5.1 and 5.3 and Corollary 5.2.

Corollary 5.4

1. *There exist recursive oracles A and B such that $A \leq_{rpos}^P B$ but $\overline{A} \not\leq_{rpos}^P \overline{B}$.*
2. *There exist recursive oracles A and B such that $A \leq_{lpos}^P B$ but $\overline{A} \not\leq_{lpos}^P \overline{B}$.*

6 P-selectivity and positive reductions

Selman, in [Sel79], introduced the notion of P-selectivity. Intuitively, A is P-selective if given two strings x and y, a polynomial-time function can determine which of x or y is more "likely" to be an element of A.

Definition 6.1 *[Sel79] A is P-selective if there exists a polynomial-time computable function f such that:*

1. *$(\forall x, y) f(x,y) \in \{x, y\}$, and*
2. *$x \in A \vee y \in A \Rightarrow f(x,y) \in A$.*

Selman [Sel82b] showed that if $A \leq_{pos}^P \overline{A}$ and A is P-selective then A is in P. Selman's proof can be easily seen to generalize to the following:

Theorem 6.2 *$A \in P$ if and only if $A \leq_{rlpos}^P \overline{A}$, and A is P-selective.*

We leave it as an open problem whether $\leq_{rpos}^P$ or $\leq_{lpos}^P$ reducibility suffice to obtain the above theorem. Below, we show that weak P-selectivity does not suffice.

Ko [Ko83] generalized Selman's notion of P-selectivity.

Definition 6.3 *[Ko83]*

A preorder R on Σ^* is partially polynomial-time computable if there is a polynomial-time computable function f such that

1. $f(x,y) = f(y,x) = x$ *if* xRy *but not* yRx,

2. $f(x,y) = f(y,x) \in \{x,y\}$ *if* xRy *and* yRx, *and*

3. $f(x,y) = \#$ *otherwise.*

Let xSy if and only if xRy and yRx. Let R' be an induced ordering on Σ^*/S, i.e., $\overline{x}R'\overline{y}$ iff xRy, where $\overline{x}$ denotes the equivalence class of x under the relation S.

Definition 6.4 *[Ko83] A partial ordering* R *is p-linear if for all* n, *the set* $\Sigma_n = \{x : |x| \leq n\}$ *can be decomposed into at most* $p(n)$ *many pairwise disjoint sets* $B_1, \ldots B_m, m \leq p(n)$, *for some polynomial* p *such that:*

1. If x *and* y *are in the same set* B_i *then* $xRy \vee yRx$, *and*

2. if x *and* y *are in two different sets then neither* xRy *nor* yRx.

Definition 6.5 *[Ko83] A is weakly P-selective if and only if there is a partially polynomial-time computable preorder* R *with the induced equivalence relation* S *and partial ordering* R' *such that*

1. R' *is p-linear, and*

2. for all n, $A_n = \{x \in A : |x| \leq n\}$ *is the union of initial segments of* R' *chains in* Σ_n.

In contrast to Theorem 6.2 we show that:

Theorem 6.6 *There exists recursive oracle* Q *and a recursive set* A *such that* A *is weakly* P^Q-*selective,* $A \leq^P_{pos} \overline{A}$ *but* $A \notin P^Q$.

Proof: We will define A and Q in the following. Q will act as a weak P-selector for A. Thus A will be trivially weakly P^Q-selective.

Let $g(0) = 1$, $g(n+1) = 8^{g(n)}$. A and Q will be such that

1) $A \subseteq S$ where $S = [\{1^{g(n)} : n \in \mathcal{N}\} \cup \{1^{g(n)}0^k : n \in \mathcal{N} \wedge 0 < k \leq 2g(n)\} \cup \{1^{4g(n)}y : n \in \mathcal{N} \wedge |y| = 1 + g(n)\}]$.

2) $1^{g(n)}0^{2k+1} \in A \Leftrightarrow 1^{g(n)}0^{2k+2} \notin A$, for $k < g(n)$.

3) for $|y| = g(n)$, $1^{4g(n)}y1 \in A \Leftrightarrow 1^{4g(n)}y0 \notin A$.

4) $1^{g(n)} \in A \Leftrightarrow 1^{4g(n)}y1 \in A$ where $y = \chi_A(1^{g(n)}0^2)\chi_A(1^{g(n)}0^4)\ldots\chi_A(1^{g(n)}0^{2g(n)})$.

For partial ordering R we have

5) $B_n = \{x : |x| = n\}$ (for B_i in the definition of p-linear partial ordering).

6) $\langle x, y\rangle \in Q$ if and only if $|x| = |y|$ and xRy.

Clearly, $A \leq^P_{pos} \overline{A}$ and A is weakly P^Q-selective.

Following construction diagonalizes to ensure that every P^Q machine fails to accept A. Assume without loss of generality that M_i^Q queries only strings of form $\langle x, y\rangle$ such that $|x| = |y|, x \in S$ and $y \in S$. At stage s we determine the membership in A for all strings of length l, $g(s) \leq l < g(s+1)$. We also define Q on all pairs of strings of length between $g(s)$ and $g(s+1)$. We explicitly give the membership in A only for strings in S. Also we define the relation R only for strings in S which are of same length. A and R on other values can be predetermined using (1) and (5) above.

Let R_i be the requirement that $L(M_i^Q) \neq A$. Go to stage 0.

<u>Stage s</u>

1. Let $x = 1^{g(s)}$.

2. Let i be the least requirement not satisfied until now. Let $n = g(s)$.

3. . If $n^i + i \geq 8^{n/10}$ then let $1^n \notin A$, $1^n0^{2k} \in A, k \leq n$, and $1^{4n}y1 \notin A$ for all $y, |y| = n$. Define Q in some way consistent with A.

4. Else run M^i on 1^n, answering all questions $\langle z, y\rangle$ in the following way: *"If* $5g(s) + 1 = |z| = |y|$, *then let* $z = uc, y = wr; r, c \in \{0,1\}$; *Put* $u0, w0 \in A$ *and* $u1, w1 \notin A$; *Answer the question in a way consistent with the previous answers and A as determined so far."*

5. Let y be such that neither $1^{4n}y0$ nor $1^{4n}y1$ has appeared in any query until now. Let $\chi_A(1^n0^2)\chi_A(1^n0^4)\ldots\chi_A(1^n0^{2n}) = y$.

6. Let $1^{4n}y1 \in A$ if and only if M rejected in the above simulation.

7. (Note that M_i has been fooled in this stage)

end stage s

Clearly, $A \le_{pos}^{P} \overline{A}$. Also A is weak P^{Q}-selective. Suppose by way of contradiction that $M_i^Q = A$. Also let M_i be the least such machine. Then for sufficiently large s in stage s, $8^{n/10} > n^i + i$ and all smaller requirements are satisfied. Thus at this stage by construction M_i will be fooled. Thus no such machine can exist. ∎

Selman [Sel82b] showed that if $A \le_{pos}^{P} B$ ($B \neq \emptyset, B \neq \Sigma^*$) and B is P-selective, then there exists an algorithm that runs in time polynomial in the number of queries in the computation tree of the reducer and outputs a set I such that $x \in A \Leftrightarrow I \subseteq B$. We observe that Selman's proof holds even for $\le_{rlpos}^{P}$ reductions. Detailed proofs of Proposition 6.7 and Corollary 6.8 appear in the the full version of this paper [HJ89].

Proposition 6.7 *[implicit from the techniques of [Sel82b]] Let $A \le_{rlpos}^{P} B$ via machine M, $B \neq \emptyset, B \neq \Sigma^*$. Let B be P-selective. Then there exists an algorithm that runs in time polynomial in the length of the input x and the number of queries in the computation tree of M on x, that outputs a set I such that $x \in A \Leftrightarrow I \subseteq B$.*

Corollary 6.8 *If $A \le_{rlpos}^{P} B$, $B \neq \emptyset, B \neq \Sigma^*$ and B is P-selective then for some polynomial p, $A \le_m B$ by a function g computable in time $2^{p(|x|)}$.*

It is easy to convert a $\le_{rpos}^{P}$ computation tree to a $\le_{rlpos}^{P}$ computation tree in exponential time. Thus we also have:

Corollary 6.9 *If $A \le_{lpos}^{P} B$, $B \neq \emptyset, B \neq \Sigma^*$ and B is P-selective then for some polynomial p, $A \le_m B$ by a function g computable in time $2^{p(|x|)}$*

Corollary 6.10 *If $A \le_{rpos}^{P} B$, $B \neq \emptyset, B \neq \Sigma^*$ and B is P-selective then for some polynomial p, $A \le_m B$ by a function g computable in time $2^{p(|x|)}$*

For *rlptt* reductions the number of queries in the computation tree is polynomial in the length of the input; thus we have:

Corollary 6.11 *If $A \le_{rlptt}^{P} B$, $B \neq \emptyset, B \neq \Sigma^*$ and B is P-selective then $A \le_m^P B$.*

Corollary 6.12 *If A is $\le_{rlptt}^{P}$ self reducible and A is P-selective then A is in P.*

Theorem 6.13 *[Sel82b] For every tally language A there exist sets A and B such that:*

1) $B \le_{ptt}^{P} A \le_{T}^{P} B$.

2) $C \le_{tt}^{P} A \le_{T}^{P} C$.

3) $B \le_{ptt}^{P} C \le_{tt}^{P} B$.

4) B is P-selective, and

5) C P-selective $\Rightarrow C \in P$.

As a corollary we obtain:

Corollary 6.14 *Let A be a tally language not in P. Then there exist $\le_{T}^{P}$ equivalent sets B, C such that $C \le_{tt}^{P} B$ but $C \not\le_{rlptt}^{P} B$. Also $\overline{B} \not\le_{rlpos}^{P} B$.*

Corollary 6.15 *If $E \neq NE$ then there exists sets B and C such that:*

1. $B \in \mathrm{NP} - P$,

2. $B \le_{ptt}^{P} C$,

3. $C \le_{tt}^{P} B$,

4. $C \not\le_{rlptt}^{P} B$, and

5. $\overline{B} \not\le_{rlpos}^{P} B$.

Corollary 6.16 *If $NE \neq E$ then there exists a $\le_{tt}^{P}$ degree in NP that does not consist of single $\le_{rlpos}^{P}$ degree.*

Corollary 6.17 *If $NE \neq E$ then there exists a $\le_{rlptt}^{P}$ degree in NP which consists of a single $\le_{m}^{P}$ degree.*

Corollary 6.18 *If $NE \bigcap coNE \neq E$ then there exists sets B and C in NP such that $B \le_{ptt}^{P} C$ and $C \le_{tt}^{P} B$ but $C \not\le_{rlptt}^{P} B$.*

7 Conclusions and Open Problems

In this paper we defined locally positive reductions as more moderate versions of Selman's (globally) positive reductions. We compared the different locally positive polynomial-time Turing reductions and identified the properties required by positive reductions to obtain the results of Selman—thus enriching the domain in which his results are applicable and delimiting the boundaries of their application.

Some open problems arise out of our work. It is open at present whether there exist relativized worlds in which $\leq_{rlpos}^{P}$ and $\leq_{pos}^{P}$ are different. The construction of such worlds would show that rlpos reductions are indeed more flexible than pos reductions; in this paper, we proved that rpos and lpos reductions are mutually incomparable, and that each is more flexible than rlpos and pos reductions. Another open problem is whether Theorem 6.2 fails for $\leq_{rpos}^{P}$ or $\leq_{lpos}^{P}$ in some relativized world.

8 Acknowledgements

We thank William Gasarch for helpful comments on the paper.

References

[All] E. Allender. Limitations of the upward separation technique. In *Automata, Languages, and Programming (ICALP 1989)*. Springer-Verlag *Lecture Notes in Computer Science* . To appear.

[BI87] M. Blum and R. Impagliazzo. Generic oracles and oracle classes. In *28th Annual IEEE Symposium on Foundations of Computer Science*, October 1987.

[BK88] R. Book and K. Ko. On sets truth-table reducible to sparse sets. *SIAM Journal on Computing*, 17(5):903–919, 1988. own.

[Boo74] R. Book. Tally languages and complexity classes. *Information and Control*, 26:186–193, 1974.

[BWSD78] R. Book, C. Wrathall, A. Selman, and D. Dobkin. Inclusion languages and the Berman-Hartmanis conjecture. *Mathematical Systems Theory*, 11:1–8, 1978.

[HH87] J. Hartmanis and L. Hemachandra. One-way functions, robustness, and the non-isomorphism of NP-complete sets. In *Proceedings 2nd Structure in Complexity Theory Conference*, pages 160–174. IEEE Computer Society Press, June 1987.

[HIS85] J. Hartmanis, N. Immerman, and V. Sewelson. Sparse sets in NP-P: EXPTIME versus NEXPTIME. *Information and Control*, 65(2/3):159–181, May/June 1985.

[HJ89] L. Hemachandra and S. Jain. On the limitations of locally robust positive reductions. Technical Report TR-300, University of Rochester, Department of Computer Science, Rochester, NY, 14627, July 1989.

[HU79] J. Hopcroft and J. Ullman. *Introduction to Automata Theory, Languages, and Computation.* Addison-Wesley, 1979.

[Ko83] K. Ko. On self-reducibility and weak P-selectivity. *Journal of Computer and System Sciences*, 26:209–221, 1983.

[Ko87] K. Ko. On helping by robust oracle machines. *Theoretical Computer Science*, 52:15–36, 1987.

[LLS75] R. Ladner, N. Lynch, and A. Selman. A comparison of polynomial time reducibilities. *Theoretical Computer Science*, 1(2):103–124, 1975.

[Sch85] U. Schöning. Robust algorithms: A different approach to oracles. *Theoretical Computer Science*, 40:57–66, 1985.

[Sel79] A. Selman. P-selective sets, tally languages, and the behavior of polynomial time reducibilities on NP. *Mathematical Systems Theory*, 13:55–65, 1979.

[Sel82a] A. Selman. Analogues of semirecursive sets. *Information and Control*, 52:36–51, 1982.

[Sel82b] A. Selman. Reductions on NP and P-selective sets. *Theoretical Computer Science*, 19:287–304, 1982.

[Tar87] G. Tardos. Query complexity, or why is it difficult to separate $NP^A \cap coNP^A$ from P^A by random oracles A. Manuscript, July 1987.

QUERY EVALUATION WITH NULL VALUES: HOW COMPLEX IS COMPLETENESS?

V.S. Lakshmanan[1]
Department of Computer Science
University of Toronto
Toronto, Canada M5S 1A4

Abstract

The problem of evaluating queries on a relational database which is allowed to contain null values has been extensively studied. In general, most of the approaches to query evaluation in the literature seem to fall into two categories. Those in the first guarantee that answers to queries can be efficiently computed (*i.e.* in time polynomial in the database size), while being "incomplete" in the sense that they do not compute all "valid" answers to certain queries. The second kind guarantee "completeness" but unfortunately suffer from intractability. In this paper, we reexamine the proof-theoretic approach proposed by Reiter [Re 86] (which as proposed is incomplete) and present a "natural" interpretation of null values based on various possible null assignments. We show that this approach leads to completeness of query evaluation. We bring out the drawback of such an extension by showing that evaluation of even "simple" queries using this approach is co-NP-complete. We then propose an approach based on intuitionistic logic for the problem. The advantages are that query evaluation is now guaranteed to be complete (w.r.t. the new approach) *and* computable in time polynomial in the database size.

1. INTRODUCTION

The importance of allowing relations in a database to contain null values to model incomplete information has been well recognized. Indeed, various types of nulls have been studied in the literature. Of the vast literature in this area we only refer to [Co 79, Vas 79, Li 81, Bi 81, Za 82, IL 84, Va 85, Re 86, Va 86, AGK 86, YC 88] in this paper. The interested reader is referred to [IL 84, Za 82] for a survey. Of particular importance among the various types of nulls studied, are nulls representing "existing but unknown" values which we study in this paper. Traditionally, relational databases have been viewed as first order structures [Co 70], with the interpretation of queries based on the Tarskian notion of validity. However, with the introduction of null values, this viewpoint breaks down. *Null values* in databases were introduced as a device to model incomplete information. Thus, for instance, we might know that Smith's salary must be in the range \$35,000 - \$40,000 but might not have the exact value with us at the moment. One of the ways of incorporating this partial knowledge into the database is to store a "null value" (denote it δ) in the appropriate tuple in the database and somehow record its possible range. However, at our present state of knowledge we do not have an exact value for δ. This has the consequence that a database containing one or more nulls may no longer be viewed

[1]Currently at Concordia University, Montreal, Canada

as a first order structure. The reason is that in a first order structure all individuals (i.e. elements of the universe) are *explicitly known* to be distinct. This is not the case when the database contains nulls. To overcome this problem (among a host of others) the viewpoint that databases are logical theories was first advocated in [NG 78]. Here, a database is viewed as a set of first order sentences (in the language associated with the vocabulary of the database) asserting facts *known to be true* about the reality being modeled. As an example, the knowledge above about Smith's salary could be represented as a sentence $(\exists x)NaSal(Smith, x) \wedge (\forall x)(NaSal(Smith, x) \rightarrow 35,000 \leq x \leq 40,000)$. Thus, whereas physical databases (this term is due to Vardi [Va 85]) try to model the reality itself, logical databases model what is known about the reality. (See [GM 78, NG 78] for an interesting discussion of the *theory vs. interpretation* viewpoints of databases). It is by now well known that the *theory* viewpoint of databases is most suitable for handling null values [FUV 83, GMN 84, Re 84, Va 85, Re 86, Va 86]. In [Re 86] Reiter laid a logical foundation for studying null values and developed an algorithm for evaluating queries in their presence. Specifically, he generalized relational algebra to accommodate nulls and developed a query evaluation algorithm based on this algebra. Although complete for the classes of *positive* and *universal conjunctive* queries, his algorithm is in general incomplete.

A database possibly containing null values really represents a *set of possible first order structures* arising from the various values that the null values might assume. The source of incompleteness lies in the "traditional" interpretation of databases with nulls. We develop a formal theory of databases with nulls based on "possibility structures" and generalize relational algebra to this extended setting. Our generalized relational algebra reduces to the traditional one when restricted to databases without nulls. We show how evaluation of queries against our interpretation can always be made complete. The philosophy of using some form of "possibility structures" has appeared *e.g.,* in the works of [Li 81, Bi 83, Ma 83]. However, we are not aware of any previous works using it in the framework of classical logic. Thus, although our possibility structures have the flavor of Kripke structures associated with modal logics (see e.g., [RS 63, Fi 69]), the underlying semantics used here is still that of classical logic. Finally, we analyze the complexity of evaluating certain "simple" classes of queries and conclude that the requirement for completeness considerably increases the complexity of query evaluation. (See Vardi [Va 85] for a similar complexity result.) Abiteboul *et al* [ABK 86] study the complexity of query evaluation when the null values in relations are constrained by various types of conditions. Recently, Yuan and Chiang [YC 88] have proposed an extension to Reiter's approach in order to make the evaluation complete. It is a simple matter to see that their approach readily leads to intractability of query evaluation owing to its exhaustive nature.

While completeness of query evaluation may well be important for many applications, a high complexity price for that is clearly unreasonable. Indeed, for typical database applications computations requiring more than polynomial time in the database size are just not feasible. A natural question to ask then is whether there is any approach, possibly based on different foundations, that guarantees *feasible* (in the sense of polynomial time computability) *completeness.* Some works in this direction are [Li 81, Bi 83, IL 84]. Lipski [Li 81] proposes an approach based on a kind of modal logic to deal with the several possibilities represented by null values. Although attractive from a theoretical point of view, the computational complexity of query evaluation algorithms based on this is quite high. Also, [Li 81] does not study all the relational algebraic operators in detail. In [Bi 83], a very practical (and hence feasible!) approach is proposed based on Codd's [Co 79] notion of *sure* and *maybe* tuples. The approach is essentially algebraic and is still incomplete in the sense of classical logic on which it is based, although tight approximations (to the set all of "correct" answers) based on precise notions of "adequacy" and "restrictedness" are provided. Furthermore, the approach assumes that the null values in the database are not constrained by any equality or inequality axioms. In addition, the approach is based on a single null value appearing in several places in the database and hence does not achieve the tight approximation above for complex algebraic expressions. As the author himself points out, several marked nulls are necessary for this purpose. [IL 84] presents several systems for query evaluation with nulls. The most important among these supports evaluation of positive conjunctive queries. Although very practical, this does not cover all possible queries of interest. The complete approach that is proposed there is only of theoretical interest owing to its high complexity. Minker [Mi 82], in an attempt to extend Reiter's closed world assumption (CWA) to handle arbitrary clauses of literals in a database developed a generalized CWA (GCWA). Among other results, he proposed to use GCWA to handle null values. However, his approach does not handle the case where a null value need not be one of the nonnull values already known to exist in the database. Another important work is described in [Va 85], where in addition to many complexity results, the author describes a method for "approximate simulation" of a complete system and shows that the method only takes polynomial time in the database size.

We answer the above question about feasible completeness in the affirmative by describing one such approach based on first order intuitionistic logic and showing that it possesses the desirable features of completeness and practicability. The important differences from Biskup's approach are that we allow constraints on null values and deal with several marked nulls. It should be stressed that constraints on nulls is of more than mere academic interest. Thus, the setting where nulls are allowed to take on arbitrary values is a very special case of the more realistic situation where we have some partial knowledge about the nulls in the form of equality/inequality constraints. Besides, while [Bi 83] does not describe a nonprocedural language (although developing one corresponding to it is not too hard), we desribe both procedural (*i.e.* algebraic) and nonprocedural (*i.e.* logical) approaches and show their equivalence. It can also be shown that when applied to complete information databases (*i.e.* ones without nulls) our approach coincides with the traditional relational algebra. This is a nice feature since it offers the possibility of implementing our approach on top of existing data management systems. Due to space limitations, we suppress all proofs and discussions. These will appear in the full paper [La 89].

2. PRELIMINARIES

Most of the notions in relational database theory and null values can be found in the texts [Ul 80, Ma 83] or earlier literature [Va 85, Va 86, Re 86]. (See Section 1 for other literature.) We present the most essential ones here. A *relational database* over a database scheme **R** (**R** is just a finite set of relation symbols) is a finite first order structure for the vocabulary **R**. The structure interprets each relation symbol in the vocabulary against a *universe of values* assigning finite relations to the relation symbols. Each relation symbol R may be viewed as a set of attributes with the cardinality of the set equal to the arity of R. For simplicity we ignore the type information of attribute values in this paper, and regard the universe of the structure (*viz.* the database) as the domain of all attributes. Members of the relations of a database are called *tuples* and are essentially mappings of attributes to the universe. Notice that this definition of a database assumes that the database does not contain any nulls.

In the following, we shall briefly (and informally) outline Reiter's notion of "extended relational theories". (For complete details see Reiter [Re 86].) A *relational language* L is a first order language built up from a vocabulary consisting of finitely many constant symbols, finitely many relation symbols including the standard equality predicate, and individual variables. A *logical database* is a couple (L, Γ), where L is a relational language and Γ is a finite theory (i.e. a finite consistent set of sentences) in L. A logical database has in general several possible relational databases as *models* which satisfy the sentences in its theory. To deal with null values Reiter [Re 86] specially proposed *extended relational theories* defined as follows. A finite set of sentences Γ in L is called an *extended relational theory* if it exactly contains the following: (i) for each relation symbol R in L, an extension axiom saying what the legal tuples in R are; (ii) a (possibly empty) set of *unique name axioms* of the form $\neg c = c'$, for distinct constant symbols c, c' of L; (iii) the domain closure axiom $(\forall x)(x = c_1 \vee ... \vee x = c_n)$ saying that the only elements in the universe are those that we know about. (The *closed world assumption* saying that the only tuples in a relation R are those that the theory Γ says are in R is embodied in (i).) Thus, Reiter's model for null values does not distinguish between null and nonnull values in a database. Reiter argues that for representing null values, the only important feature of their unknown character is the absence of some of their unique name axioms. However, in this setting, technically one cannot identify null values, for even the "nonnull" constants do not in general have all unique name axioms involving them in the theory Γ (for instance, the ones involving them and some nulls). Thus any explicit reference to null values in the database would lead to some technical difficulties. To overcome this, we assume that L has disjoint sets (call them NONNULL and NULL) of constant symbols to denote the nonnull and null values of a database. There is nothing artificial about this assumption, since the null values in a real database can always be told apart from the nonnull values. Thus, while any structure has to map two distinct (nonnull) constant symbols of L to distinct elements of its universe, it can assign arbitrary values to the null symbols.

Queries in L are expressions of the form $Q \equiv \{\mathbf{x}|\Psi(\mathbf{x})\}$, where Ψ is a formula in L and $\mathbf{x}$ is a sequence of all distinct free variables of Ψ. The answer to such a query Q against an extended relational theory (L,Γ) is an $|\ \mathbf{x}\ |$-ary relation defined as $\|\ Q\ \|_\Gamma = \{\mathbf{t} \in D^{|\mathbf{x}|}|\Gamma \models \Psi(\mathbf{x})\}$. where D denotes the (finite) universe of the database. In this paper, $\models$ ($\models_i$) will denote classical (intuitionistic) entailment. We note that by the closed world assumption and the domain closure axiom, finite implication can be replaced by unrestricted implication, which explains our definition above. (See also [Va 85].) By completeness of first order logic, this definition is equivalent to Reiter's definition based on proof theory [Re 84, Re 86].

It is now well known that the complexity of query evaluation can be studied either as a function of the size of the database (which is viewed as the input) while treating the size of the query expression as a fixed parameter - this is called the *data complexity* - or as a function of the size of the query expression (which is viewed as the input now) while treating the database size as a fixed parameter - this is called the *expression complexity.* For formal definitions, see [Va 85]. In this paper, we shall be concerned only with the data complexity.

3. THE PROBLEM WITH THE TRADITIONAL APPROACH

In this section, we study the incompleteness problem of query evaluation methods based on "traditional" interpretations of databases containing null values. We also identify the source of such problems. First, we consider the following example from Reiter [Re 86]. The theory Γ contains two constant symbols a, b, no unique name axioms, and a single unary relation symbol P with the extension axiom $(\forall x)(P(x) \equiv x = a)$. The query to be evaluated is $Q \equiv \{x|P(x) \vee \neg P(x)\}$. The answer is of course the set $\{a,b\}$. However, when the query is decomposed into $\{x|P(x)\} \cup \{x|\neg P(x)\}$, the answer that results is just $\{a\}$. This is because $\Gamma \not\vdash P(b)$ and $\Gamma \not\vdash \neg P(b)$. Notice that it is important for efficient query processing to be able to recursively decompose complex queries into simpler subqueries. This example shows that decomposing on disjunction may lose us some answer tuples in general. This is one of the reasons for incompleteness (see [Re 86]).

A similar problem arises with queries containing certain types of existentially quantified expressions. The following example from [Re 86] illustrates that. Γ contains a binary relation symbol P, the constant symbols a, b, c, d, the unique name axiom $\neg a = b$, and the extension axiom $(\forall x,y)(P(x,y) \equiv x = d \wedge (y = a \vee y = b))$. The query is $Q \equiv \{x|(\exists y)(P(x,y) \wedge \neg y = c)\}$. It is not hard to see that the answer is $\{d\}$. On the other hand, decomposition gives $\pi_1(\{xy|\Gamma \vdash P(x,y)\} \cap \{xy|\Gamma \vdash \neg y = c\}) = \Phi$. The reason is that $\Gamma \not\vdash \neg a = c$ and $\Gamma \not\vdash \neg b = c$. Once again, a natural way of processing query by decomposition gives us an incomplete answer to a query. We would ideally like to obtain the complete set of answers in both the above cases.

A careful examination of these problems leads to the following observations. Firstly, Reiter's model does not make explicit the fact that a relation containing one or more nulls really represents a *set of possible relations* not containing nulls. Thus, a database with nulls similarly represents a set of possible databases (without nulls). Secondly, in decomposing disjunctions and evaluating individual disjuncts separately, the semantics used is the one associated with *intuitionistic*, rather than classical, logic. Thus, in the first example above, suppose without loss of generality that a represents a null while b is a nonnull. The other case is symmetric. Now, to say that $\Gamma \not\vdash P(b)$, and $\Gamma \not\vdash \neg P(b)$ means that we are taking all possibilities for a at once. That is, we use the semantics that $A \vee B$ is true in a given state if and only if either A is true in all states possible from the given state, or B is true in all such states, where A, B are any sentences. This is precisely the semantics of disjunction in intuitionistic logic (see [RS 63, Fi 69], e.g.). On the other hand, for classical logic, $A \vee B$ is true in a given state if and only if in each state possible from the given one either A is true or B is true. This is the interpretation we use when we evaluate the query directly without splitting into disjuncts. Thus it should not be surprising that the two answers do not coincide!

Similarly, for the second example, the semantics used is that $(\exists x)A(x)$ is true in a given state if and only if there is a fixed value a such that $A(a)$ is true in all states possible from the given one. This is again quite different from the classical semantics for existential quantification which would define the formula above to be true in a given state if and only if for each possible state from the given one, there is a value a making $A(a)$ true in that state. As with the previous example, we are using the classical semantics for the original formulation of the query but intuitionistic semantics for the transformed one. This explains the reason the two formulations evaluate unequally.

In order to ensure that the same type of semantics is associated with all (formulations of) queries, we need to clarify the model theory somewhat to deal with the infamous null values. This we do by explicitly representing the fact that databases with nulls correspond to a collection of possible databases without nulls, in *one single* structure. This will be accomplished by treating nulls as functions as in the next section. It should be noted that the notion of possible structures is by no means new (it appears *e.g.,* in [Li 81, Bi 83, Ma 83]), while our way of handling them is.

4. A MODEL THEORY FOR DATABASES WITH NULLS

We begin with a series of definitions. We occasionally blur the distinction between tuples of constant symbols in a logical database and the corresponding tuple in a structure for the database. By a *generalized tuple* of a database (L, Γ) (with nulls), we mean a tuple possibly containing one or more nulls. Recall that by our assumption L has a distinguished set of constant symbols to denote nulls and thus the above notion is well defined. This notion can be extended to relations and databases in the obvious manner. Since the constant symbols (null as well as nonnull) are a finite set, we may associate a particular ordering with them. By Herbrand's Theorem (see [Sh 67]) we need only consider structures over the fixed universe consisting of the constants of L (- there are no function symbols -) in order to determine the validity of sentences, and hence to evaluate queries. Since some symbols correspond to nulls, we need to consider several structures corresponding to different assignments of values to the null symbols of L. More precisely, each structure for (L, Γ) interprets each nonnull constant symbol of L as itself and interprets each null symbol of Γ either as a nonnull constant or as a new value in its universe. In the former case, the null value is interpreted as one of the existing values and in the latter as a new value ("not present in the physical database"). Thus, a structure for (L, Γ) exactly contains an element corresponding to each nonnull constant symbol of L and an element corresponding to each null symbol of L. The interpretation of nulls is arbitrary, while that of any nonnull constant is fixed.

A *null assignment function* (or *naf* for short) associated with a structure $\Im$ is a function $f : \text{NULL} \rightarrow \mid \Im \mid$ that assigns each null constant of L an element of the universe $\mid \Im \mid$. For ease of exposition, we assume in the sequel that in the logical database (L, Γ), Γ does not contain any unique name axioms involving any null constants. It should be noted that this assumption is *not* essential to the model theory presented here, as it can be readily adapted to the case without this assumption. The assumption also does not affect the complexity results for both the approaches presented in this paper. We further assume that Γ does not contain any integrity constraints for the database. Let $\delta_1, ..., \delta_n$ be the fixed ordering of the null constants of L. For two nafs f, g associated with a structure $\Im$, define $f \leq g$ exactly when either f and g are identical, or $f(\delta_1) < g(\delta_1)$, or $f(\delta_j) = g(\delta_j), 1 \leq j \leq i$, for some $i, 1 \leq i \leq n-1$, and $f(\delta_{i+1}) < g(\delta_{i+1})$, where $\leq$ denotes the ordering associated with the constants of L. Each naf may be regarded as a "possible structure" (equivalently, state of knowledge) with particular values assigned to all null constant symbols. Thus, using nafs we are able to deal with *several* structures collectively. It is convenient to extend the nafs to include nonnull constant symbols. Thus we may view a naf as a function $f : \text{CONST} \rightarrow \mid \Im \mid$, with the restriction that $f(c) = c, \forall c \in \text{NONNULL}$. With this machinery, the semantics for a generalized tuple may now be formalized. The interpretation of a generalized tuple t under a given (Herbrand) structure $\Im$ is $t^{\Im} = \langle f_1(t), f_2(t), ..., f_N(t) \rangle$, where $f_1, ..., f_N$ is the ordering of the nafs, and we are assuming that nafs have been extended to tuples. (Notice that since there are only a finite number of constant symbols in L, and hence the Herbrand structure is finite, the number of nafs is finite as well.) A tuple t is *ordinary* (i.e. it contains no nulls) exactly when $f_i(t) = f_j(t), 1 \leq i, j \leq N$. It is clear that $t^{\Im}$ can be regarded as a function from a finite subset of natural numbers to tuples of constants over $\mid \Im \mid$ where the value for i is the (ordinary) tuple that the generalized tuple t would take on as a value if the naf corresponding to the appropriate values for the nulls were to apply. This interpretation easily generalizes to generalized relations and databases. For a generalized relation r, the interpretation $r^{\Im}$ is defined as $\{t^{\Im}|t \in r\}$. This can again be viewed as a function on a finite subset of natural numbers as before. The value of this function for any number gives a possible value for the generalized relation. The same remarks carry over to interpretations of generalized databases. We note that frequently we refer to a generalized tuple t by its *extension*, i.e. the set of possible values $\{f_1(t), ..., f_N(t)\}$, for t.

We next present our extension of relational algebra for generalized relations.

Extended Relational Algebra for Generalized Relations. In the following, we extend the definitions of the relational operators to generalized relations. We remark that our definitions of operators correspond to the case where we are interested in the result vaild in *all* possible structures. It is easy to define operations corresponding to results valid in *some* possible structure along similar lines. In the following, r, s denote generalized relations, and we assume that the nafs are totally ordered as $f_1, f_2, ..., f_N$.

Union: $r \cup s = \{t|t \in r, \text{ or } t \in s\}$. (Here, t is a generalized tuple.)

Difference: $r \setminus s = \{t \in r|f_i(t) \notin f_i(s), 1 \leq i \leq N\}$.

Cartesian Product: $r \times s = \{u|u[R] \in r, u[S] \in s\}$, where $u[R]$ denotes the restriction of u to the attributes R of relation r, and is defined in the same way as for usual relations.

Selection: For a generalized relation r and a selection formula F (as in [Ul 80]), the selction operation is defined as $\sigma_F(r) = \{t \in r|\Im \models F(f_i(t)), 1 \leq i \leq N\}$.

Projection: For a generalized relation r, and a subset X of its attributes R, the projection is defined as $\pi_X(r) = \{t[X]|t \in r\}$.

Intersection: For generalized relations r, s, the intersection is given by $r \cap s = \{t|f_i(t) \in f_i(r), f_i(t) \in f_i(s), 1 \leq i \leq N\}$.

Division: For a generalized relation r and a unary relation s', the division is given by $\Delta_{s'}(r) = \{t|t.x \in r, \forall x \in s'\}$, where "." denotes concatenation.

The definitions above are in terms of the intensional representations of generalized tuples. We need to relate them to their extensions. Given the extension of a generalized tuple $\{t_1, ..., t_k\}$, let $t_1, ..., t_k$ be the lexicographical ordering of the t_i's induced by the ordering on the constants of L (see the beginning of this section). Then the intension of this generalized tuple is the tuple t (involving possibly the null and nonnull constant symbols of L), such that for $1 \leq j \leq k, \exists i_j, 1 \leq i_j \leq N$, such that $f_{i_j}(t) = t_j$, for

$1 \leq i \leq N, \exists j_i, 1 \leq j_i \leq k$, such that $f_i(t) = t_{j_i}$, and for $1 \leq j < j' \leq k, i_j < i_{j'}$. The intuition behind a generalized tuple t with extension $\{t_1, ..., t_k\}$ is easily seen by considering the semantics of the statement $\Gamma \vdash R(t)$, which is equivalent to $\Gamma \models R(t)$, and with the interpretation that this should be true for all nafs, the semantics of the original statement becomes that of $\Gamma \vdash R(t_1) \vee ... \vee R(t_k)$.

Notice that only the definitions of difference, selection, and intersection differ from their counterparts for ordinary relations (not containing nulls). We now have

Lemma 1. *The extended relational algebra defined satisfies the following. For any generalized relations r, s, and a binary operation ∇, $t \in r \nabla s$ iff $f_i(t) \in (f_i(r) \nabla f_i(s)), 1 \leq i \leq N$. Moreover, for a selection formula F, $t \in \sigma_F(r)$, iff $f_i(t) \in \sigma_F(f_i(r)), 1 \leq i \leq N$; for projection, $t \in \pi_X(r)$ iff $f_i(t) \in \pi_X(f_i(r)), 1 \leq i \leq N$.*

□

We next need to define the interpretation of queries with respect to our model theory. For any formula $\Psi(\mathbf{x})$, the query $\{\mathbf{x} | \Psi(\mathbf{x}\}$ is interpreted as $\| Q \|_\Gamma = \{\mathbf{c} | \Gamma \models \Psi(f_i(\mathbf{c})), 1 \leq i \leq N\}$. We call a generalized relation r *redundant* if there are two tuples t, t' in r such that the extension of t is a subset of the extension of t'. Now, in order to obtain a nonredundant set of tuples as answers to queries, we define $\| Q \|_\Gamma = \{\mathbf{c} | \Gamma \vdash \Psi(\mathbf{c}), \mathbf{c}$ minimal$\}$. (Notice that $\mathbf{c}$ above can contain nulls and is thus a generalized tuple and that the minimality is w.r.t. $\subseteq$.) We argue that since databases containing nulls stand for several possible structures, this is the correct interpretation, if we want to operate in the framework of classical logic. We now have

Theorem 2. *Let (L, Γ) be an extended relational theory. Let Q_1 and Q_2 be the queries $\{\mathbf{x} | \Psi_1(\mathbf{x})\}$ and $\{\mathbf{x} | \Psi_2(\mathbf{x})\}$. Also, let Q' be the query $\{\mathbf{x}y | \Psi(\mathbf{x}y)\}$. Then for a query Q on this database, we have the following:*

(i) if Q is of the form $\{\mathbf{x} | \Psi_1(\mathbf{x}) \wedge \Psi_2(\mathbf{x})\}$, then $\| Q \|_\Gamma = \| Q_1 \|_\Gamma \cap \| Q_2 \|_\Gamma$;

(ii) If Q is of the form $\{\mathbf{x} | \Psi_1(\mathbf{x}) \vee \Psi_2(\mathbf{x})\}$, then $\| Q \|_\Gamma = \| Q_1 \|_\Gamma \cup \| Q_2 \|_\Gamma$;

(iii) If Q is of the form $\{\mathbf{x} | \neg \Psi_1(\mathbf{x})\}$, then $\| Q \|_\Gamma = 2^{D^{|\mathbf{x}|}} \setminus \{\mathbf{x} | \Psi_1(\mathbf{x})\}$, upto minimality;

(iv) If Q is of the form $\{\mathbf{x} | (\forall y) \Psi(\mathbf{x}y)\}$, then $\| Q \|_\Gamma = \Delta_D(\| Q' \|_\Gamma)$, where D is the universe of the structure $\Im$ and is to be viewed as a unary relation.

(v) If Q is of the form $\{\mathbf{x} | (\exists y) \Psi(\mathbf{x}y)\}$, then $\| Q \|_\Gamma = \pi_X(\| Q' \|_\Gamma)$, where X names the attributes corresponding to $\mathbf{x}$.

(All operations mentioned above ($\cup, \cap, \setminus$, etc.) are extended relational operations. These reduce to their their usual meaning when restricted to relations without nulls such as $f_i(r)$. The set differene in (iii) is from $2^{D^{|\mathbf{x}|}}$ rather than $D^{|\mathbf{x}|}$ since extensionally, generalized tuples are sets of ordinary tuples, and the equality there is upto minimality.)

□

We note that the reason exact equality holds in (ii) and (v) above as opposed to the strict inclusion in Reiter's model [Re 86] is because of the way tuples containing nulls are explicitly handled here and our definitions of the extended relational operators. We illustrate this point by revisiting one of the examples of Section 3. The other example is similar and is left to the reader. We first reformulate the example suitably to reflect our convention of using distinguished symbols for nulls.

Example 1. Γ consists of the constant symbols a, b, c, δ, where δ is the only null, a binary relation symbol R with the extension $(\forall xy)(R(x,y) \equiv (x = a \wedge (y = b \vee y = c)))$, the only unique name axiom $\neg b = c$, and the usual domain closure axiom. The query is $Q \equiv \{x|(\exists y)(R(x,y) \wedge \neg y = \delta)\}$. Let $\Im$ be a structure for L with universe $D = \{a, b, c, d\}$, which interprets the nonnull constant symbols as themselves and the null δ as any one of the elements of D. The crucial thing to note is that $\{y|\neg y = \delta\}$ evaluates to $\{\{a,b\},\{a,c\},\{a,d\},\{b,c\},\{b,d\},\{c,d\}\}$ using our interpretation. Note that the member $\{a,b\}$ of the above set captures the fact that $\Gamma \vdash \neg\delta = a \vee \neg\delta = b$. (Technically, the member $\{a,b\}$ corresponds to the function $g : \{1,...,4\} \rightarrow D$ defined as $g(1) = a, g(i) = b, 2 \leq i \leq 4$.) Note that each member of the above set is a minimal generalized tuple y such that $\Gamma \vdash \neg y = \delta$. Hence, $\{xy|R(x,y) \wedge \neg y = \delta\} = \{xy|R(x,y)\} \cap \{xy|\neg y = \delta\} = \{ab, ac\} \cap \{\{aa, ab\}, ..., \{ab, ac\}, ..., \{ac, ad\}, ..., \{dc, dd\}\}$, and extended relational intersection gives us the set $\{ab, ac\}$. Hence, Q interpreted as $\pi_1(\{xy|R(x,y) \wedge \neg y = \delta\})$ evaluates to $\{a\}$, as required.

□

5. COMPLEXITY

In this section, we analyze the complexity of queries over generalized databases (i.e. ones containing nulls). As we shall see, evaluating queries over such databases is in general intractable. Specifically, we shall show that testing if a generalized tuple is a valid answer to certain types of queries is NP-Complete. This is analogous to the result of Vardi [Va 85]. The queries we shall consider involve testing if a generalized tuple, specified by its extension, is not a member of a given generalized relation R, where (L, Γ) is a logical database with L containing the relation symbol R. We show that evaluation of this simple query is co-NP-complete by reduction from k-COLORABILITY for graphs (see [GJ 79]). Given an instance of k-COLORABILITY, a graph $G = (V = \{u_1, ..., u_n\}, E)$ and the colors $\{1, ..., k\}$, construct an instance of the above problem as follows. L consists of the constant symbols $\{1, ..., k\} \cup V$. Γ contains the unique name axioms $\{\neg i = j|$ for distinct $i, j, 1 \leq i, j \leq k\} \cup \{\neg u = v|(u,v) \in E\}$. (We assume without loss of generality that the graph G is simple.) We are not concerned with distinguishing the null and the nonnull constants for the purposes of analyzing the complexity. Γ contains the unary predicate R and an extension axiom saying that the members of R are exactly $1, ..., k$. Finally, the generalized tuple is $t = \{u_1, ..., u_n\}$. The query is the simple one - whether t is not a member of R. Notice that such a query naturally arises while evaluating, e.g., the difference of two generalized relations. We can prove that

Theorem 3. *For the construction above, $\Gamma \not\vdash \neg R(t)$ if and only if G is k-colorable.*

□

Clearly, the transformation above can be done in polynomial time. We have the trivial NP algorithm for finding if $\Gamma \not\vdash \neg R(t)$, namely testing if $\Gamma \cup \{R(f_i(t))\}, 1 \leq i \leq N$, has a model. Thus, the problem of deciding if t is provably not a member of R is co-NP-complete. This is analogous to the complexity result in Vardi [Va 85].

6. AN INTUITIONISTIC APPROACH - THE LOGIC

We have observed that most of the approaches to query evaluation with nulls in the literature do not guarantee feasible completeness. Our above attempt at completeness based on Reiter's [Re 86] original proposal unfortunately led to a high complexity price. As pointed out in the introduction, there is a natural need to seek out a system guaranteeing feasible completeness that is possibly based on different foundations. We propose one such approach based on intuitionistic logic in this section. Before we go any further, it must be noted that any notion of feasible completeness must, of necessity, be weaker than the classical notion of completeness. This is obvious from complexity arguments. While we are at it, we simply cannot designate the set of answers coming from a "good" feasible approximation system (such as that of Reiter [Re 86] or that of Vardi [Va 85]) as complete for a new system and develop a notion of completeness based on that. We need a logical foundation based on which we will be able to justify the absence of certain tuples (as also the presence of certain others) in the answer generated by our system. Intuitively, we would like our system to respond to queries by providing not just those tuples which are provably in the answer, but tuples whose presence or absence in the answer is indefinite as well, and we want our system to tell the user about the status of tuples in the answer provided by it. In this section, we argue that intuitionistic logic provides the "right" foundation for this situation. Fitting [Fi 69] is an excellent text for the subject.

As we shall see shortly, treatment of the tuples in a relation possibly having nulls can be made "natural" by supposing that the relation contains zero or more tuples which are "indefinite". A similar approach was taken by Codd [Co 79] and later formalized by Biskup [Bi 83]. The meaning of an indefinite tuple is that using the knowledge about the possible values that the tuple might take on, it is impossible to conclude whether the tuple is in (or is not in) the relation. Since unlike in [Bi 83] we allow constraints on nulls (in the form of inequalities), a straightforward way of checking if a tuple is indefinite could be very inefficient. We shall show later on that it is possible to circumvent this difficulty using an efficient method for checking if a tuple is indefinite.

We would like an "ideal" system to answer queries giving as much information related to the query as possible from the database. Let us formalize this notion. Since we are dealing with incomplete information, our definitions have to provide for *certain* and *indefinite* conclusions. Formally, we call a query evaluation system *sound* if for any query $\Psi(\mathbf{x})$ and for any database (L, Γ), (i) if $\mathbf{a}$ is a certain tuple returned by the system, then $\Gamma \models_i \Psi(\mathbf{a})$, and (ii) if $\mathbf{a}$ is an indefinite tuple returned by the system, then $\Gamma \not\models_i \Psi(\mathbf{a})$ and $\Gamma \not\models_i \neg\Psi(\mathbf{a})$. We call the system *complete* when the reverse implications in (i) and (ii) above hold.

For the inference system, instead of giving an axiom system along the traditional lines, we prefer to work with "model sets" introduced by Hintikka, which are sets of statements having certain properties. We argue that in some sense, such sets closely correspond to the way information is stored in real databases and are therefore a "natural" device to work with. In addition, the resultant "axioms and inference rules" of the formal system become extremely simple. Since we are dealing with intuitionistic logic, we can conveniently work with Smullyan's *signed* formulas [Sm 68]. However, we depart from the traditional use of model sets in an important way. We do not represent negative information explicitly in model sets. Rather, we let absence of any adorned form of a fact stand for the negation of that fact. Truth will be indicated by the presence of the fact with the prefix T in the model set, and indefiniteness with the prefix I. The reason for this choice is that in real databases it is just not feasible to explicitly list down negations of all facts which are known not to hold in the world modeled by the database. However, this departure calls for a different definition of notions such as "saturation" which we provide below. Statements of our logic are built up as usual, from the vocabulary of the database, the equality predicate and the various connectives.

Definitions. A signed statement is a statement of the form TX or IX, where X is a statement of the logic. A set S of signed statements is *upward saturated* if the following conditions are satisfied (we abbreviate ($TX \notin S$ *and* $IX \notin S$) by $X \notin S$):

1. $TX \in S$ and $TY \in S \Rightarrow TX \wedge Y \in S$,
2. $X \notin S$ or $Y \notin S \Rightarrow X \wedge Y \notin S$,
3. ($TX \in S$ and $IY \in S$), or ($IX \in S$ and $TY \in S$), or ($IX \in S$ and $IY \in S$) $\Rightarrow$ $IX \wedge Y \in S$,
4. $TX \in S$ or $TY \in S \Rightarrow TX \vee Y \in S$,
5. ($TX \notin S$ and $IY \in S$) or ($IX \in S$ and $TY \notin S$) $\Rightarrow IX \vee Y \in S$,

1. $(X \notin S \text{ and } Y \notin S) \Rightarrow X \vee Y \notin S$,
2. $X \notin S \Rightarrow T\neg X \in S$,
3. $TX \in S \Rightarrow (T\neg X \notin S \text{ and } IX \notin S)$,
4. $IX \in S \Rightarrow I\neg X \in S$,
5. $TR(a)$ for all constants a in the database $\Rightarrow T(\forall x)R(x) \in S$,
6. $R(a) \notin S$ for some constant $a \Rightarrow (\forall x)R(x) \notin S$,
7. $IR(a) \in S$ for some constant a and for all other constants b, either $TR(b) \in S$ or $IR(b) \in S \Rightarrow I(\forall x)R(x) \in S$,
8. $TR(a) \in S$ for some constant $a \Rightarrow T(\exists x)R(x) \in S$,
9. $IR(a) \in S$ for some constant a and $TR(b) \notin S$ for all other constants $b \Rightarrow I(\exists x)R(x) \in S$,
10. $R(a) \notin S$ for all constants $a \Rightarrow (\exists x)R(x) \notin S$.

S is said to be *downward saturated* if all the reverse implications of the above hold. Finally, S is *saturated* if it is both upward saturated and downward saturated. S is *consistent* if for every statement X, not more than one of $TX, IX, T\neg X$ is in S. S is a *model set* in the intuitionistic sense if it is saturated and consistent. The valuation on statements induced by a model set S is that $v_S =$ **true** if $TX \in S$, **false** if $X \notin S$, and **indefinite** if $IX \in S$.

A remark about the definition of model sets above is that rules such as (7) pertaining to negative information are not intended to be explicitly represented in a database. We only use them in the inference of some facts. It is fairly straightforward to see that any set S can be extended to a *smallest* saturated set. Specifically, we have

Proposition 4. *If S is consistent and downward saturated, then S can be extended to a model set.*

□

Given a relational database with null values and with relations possibly containing indefinite tuples, the strategy to process queries is to first convert the database into a set of signed statements S and then extend S into a model set, say M. Then for a query $\Psi(\mathbf{x})$, the membership of a tuple $\mathbf{a}$ in the answer set is determined as follows. $\mathbf{a}$ is in the *certain* answer set iff $T\Psi(\mathbf{a}) \in M$; $\mathbf{a}$ is in the *indefinite* answer set iff $I\Psi(\mathbf{a}) \in M$. We have

Theorem 5. *Let* Γ *be an extended relational theory and let* M *be the intuitionistic model set derived from it. For a fact* X, $TX \in M$ *if and only if* $\Gamma \models_i X$; $IX \in M$ *if and only if* $\Gamma \not\models_i X \& \Gamma \not\models_i \neg X$, *Furthermore, because of saturation, query decomposition always leads to complete set of answers.*

□

Note that membership in M essentially corresponds to a proof from Γ, or lack of it depending on the sign of the statement and the above theorem thus proves the completeness of this approach. The "axiom system" of our approach is much simpler than the one in [Li 81]. Also, the approach has the advantage of allowing recursive definition of answers while still maintaining completeness (w.r.t. this logic). While such an approach may work in principle, a proof of its feasibility (see Section 1) is needed before it can be adopted for practical systems. Although it is possible to provide such a proof based on the logic alone, we prefer to do it by providing a corresponding relational algebra (in the next section). We then prove the equivalence of the two languages and show that operations of this algebra are polynomial time computable even while working with nulls. The formulation of query processing on algebraic footing has the advantage of enabling easy implementation and offering the scope for optimization of queries. Before closing this section, let us illustrate some of the ideas above with some examples.

Example 2. Let us return to the database of Example 1. The model set M corresponding to the theory Γ there can be readily computed. In particular, the reader can check that (i) $\{xy|TR(x,y) \wedge \neg y = \delta \in M\} = \{xy|TR(x,y) \in M\} \cap \{xy|T\neg y = \delta \in M\} = \Phi$; (ii) $\{xy|IR(x,y) \wedge \neg y = \delta \in M\} = (\{xy|TR(xy)\} \cap \{xy|I\neg y = \delta\}) \cup (\{xy|IR(x,y)\} \cap \{xy|T\neg y = \delta\}) \cup (\{xy|IR(x,y)\} \cap \{xy|I\neg y = \delta\}) = \{ab, ac\} \cap \{aa, ab, ac, ba, ..., cc, \delta c\} \cup \{a\delta\} \cap \Phi \cup \{a\delta\} \cap \{aa, ab, ..., \delta c\} = \{ab, ac\}$. Thus, we intend that our system respond to the query $\{xy|\Gamma \vdash (\exists y)(R(x,y) \wedge \neg y = \delta)\}$ with the answer sets $certain = \Phi$, $indefinite = \{a\}$. Similarly, for the other example in Section 3, it is easy to check that our system would provide the answer sets $certain = \{a\}$, $indefinite = \{b\}$.

□

Example 3. We now consider a more concrete example. Γ contains a single relation EMP with attributes *name, age, salary, sex* and the extension axiom $(\forall xyzw)EMP(xyzw) \equiv ((x = \text{'}Kirk\text{'} \wedge y = \delta_1 \wedge z = \delta_2 \wedge w = \text{'}M\text{'}) \vee (x = \text{'}Spock\text{'} \wedge y = 40 \wedge z = 90000 \wedge w = \text{'}M\text{'}) \vee (x = \text{'}Ilia\text{'} \wedge y = \delta_3 \wedge z = \delta_4 \wedge w = \delta_5) \vee (x = \text{'}Seizhenka\text{'} \wedge y = \delta_6 \wedge z = 60000 \wedge w = \delta_7))$. Suppose the unique name axioms say that values in any two distinct "columns" of EMP are disjoint. (*E.g.*, they could say $\neg\delta_1 = \text{'}Kirk\text{'}$, *etc.*) In addition, let Γ contain the constraints $\delta_1 \geq 0, \delta_2 \geq 0, \delta_3 \geq 35, \delta_4 \geq 80000, \delta_4 \leq 100000, \delta_6 \geq 45, \delta_6 \leq 55$. Let the query be $\{x|(\exists yzw)\ EMP(xyzw) \wedge \neg y < 50 \wedge ((z > 50000 \wedge z \leq 60000) \vee (w = \text{'}M\text{'}))\}$. Intuitively, the query asks for the names of all employees with age 50 or over and who are either earning between 50000 and 60000 or are males. The answer to the query may be verified to be $certain = \Phi$ and $indefinite = \{\text{'}Kirk\text{'}, \text{'}Seizhenka\text{'}\}$. Of course, the answer is invariant under any decomposition of the query. This example also illustrates the usefulness of constraints on null values used to model partial knowledge.

□

7. AN INTUITIONISTIC APPROACH - THE ALGEBRA

In this section, we describe the procedural counterpart of the logical approach of the previous section. For want of space, we directly provide the definitions of the operators. Discussions can be found in the full paper.

We first adapt some notions from [Re 86] to our setting. Two tuples s, t (possibly containing nulls) are said to *disagree* w.r.t. a theory Γ if $\Gamma \vdash_i s \neq t$, where $\vdash_i$ denotes intuitionistic provability. Since we work with signed facts, we incorporate different strengths of disagreement by defining s, t *certainly disagree* if $Ts \neq t \in M$ and s, t *indefinitely disagree* if $Is \neq t \in M$, where M is the model set corresponding to Γ. In order to decide if two given tuples certainly disagree w.r.t. Γ we can use the following algorithm of [Re 86]. We essentially test if $\Gamma \cup \{s = t\}$ is unsatisfiable. Since a contradiction can only arise from the inequality axioms in Γ it is sufficient to do the following. Collect the equivalence classes induced by the equalities $s = t$ (these may well be nontrivial because of possible repetitions of constants or nulls in the tuples). s, t certainly disagree iff there are two elements u, v in the same equivalence class and Γ has the inequality axiom $u \neq v$. Now, to test if two tuples s, t indefinitely disagree, we first see if they certainly disagree. If they do not, then indefinitely disagree iff they are not (syntactically) identical. It is clear that finding if two tuples disagree with a certain strength (if at all) can be done quite efficiently (*i.e.* trivially in polynomial time). (A remark about the validity of "proof by contradiction" in an intuitionistic setting is that contradictions here involve conjunctions of the form $Tu = v \wedge T\neg u = v$ which cannot hold simulataneously, even in an intuitionistic logic.) The notion of tuple disagreement is central to any reasonable definition of the difference operator.

Example 5. Let Γ contain, among other things, the inequalities $\neg\delta_1 = a, \neg\delta_2 = b$ and the extension axiom $(\forall xy)(R(xy) \equiv (x = \delta_2 \wedge y = c) \vee (x = \delta_1 \wedge y = c))$. We want to determine if R contains the tuple (ca) or not. First check if ca disagrees with the tuples of R. *E.g.*, the equality $ca = \delta_2 c$ generates the single equivalence class $\{a, c, \delta_2\}$. Since there is no inequality axiom contradicting this, we conclude that ca indefinitely disagrees with $\delta_2 c$. The equality $ca = \delta_1 c$ creates the equivalence class $\{a, c, \delta_1\}$, which violates the axiom $\neg\delta_1 = a$, implying that ca certainly disagrees with $\delta_1 c$. Finally, we infer that ca is indefinitely (not) in R.

□

(Intuitionistic) Definition of Extended Relational Operators.

Below, p, q, r are relations possibly containing nulls. Their arities and attributes are assumed to be appropriate for the operator in question to be well defined.

Union: $p \cup q = r$, where $certain(r) = certain(p) \cup certain(q)$, $indefinite(r) = indefinite(p) \cup indefinite(q)$. Here, $certain(p)$ ($indefinite(p)$) refers to the certain (indefinite) tuples of p.

Selection: $\sigma_{A=a}(p) = r$, where $certain(r) = \{t \in certain(p) | t[A] = a\}$ (equality here means identity); $indefinite(r) = \{t \in indefinite(p) | t[A] = a\} \cup \{t | \exists s \in p$, s.t. t and s agree on all attributes except A, and $s[A] = \delta_i, t[A] = a$, and Γ does not contain the axiom $\delta_i \neq a\}$. $\sigma_{A=B}(p) = r$, where $certain(r) = \{t \in certain(p) | t[A] = t[B]\}$, $indefinite(r) = \{t \in indefinite(p) | t[A] = t[B]\} \cup \{t | \exists s \in p$, s.t. at least one of $s[A], s[B]$ is a null and Γ does not contain the axiom $\neg s[A] = s[B]$, and t is s with the higher of $s[A]$ and $s[B]$ replacing the lower value$\}$. The priority is that a nonnull constant is higher than a null and between two distinct marked nulls the lower marked one is the higher one.

Cartesian Product: $p \times q = r$, where $certain(r) = certain(p) \times certain(q)$; all other combinations of course lead to tuples in $indefinite(r)$.

Difference: $p - q = r$, where $certain(r) = \{t \in certain(p) |$ t certainly disagrees with *every* tuple of $q\}$, and $indefinite(r) = \{t \in r |$ t indefinitely disagrees with one tuple of q, and either certainly or indefinitely disagrees with all other tuples of $q\}$.

Projection: Suppose that X is a subset of the attributes of p. Then $\pi_X(p) = r$, where $certain(r) = \{t[X] | t \in certain(p)\}$ (as usual, since this is a set duplicates are eliminated), and $indefinite(r) = \{t[X] | t \in indefinite(p)$, and $t[X] \notin certain(r)\}$.

It can be easily verified that the algebra above coincides with the standard one on databases without nulls. As with the traditional relational algebra, operators such as join, division, intersection, etc may be defined in terms of these operators and we omit the details here. We freely use some of these additional operators below, the notation being the standard one. Our next theorem proves the equivalence between the algebraic and logical query languages. We use the following abbreviations. For a query Q, let $| Q |$ denote the answer computed using (extended) relational algebra. Let Γ be a theory and M its associated model set. Then for a query $Q \equiv \{\mathbf{x} | \Psi(\mathbf{x})\}$, we mean by the equality $\| Q \|^i_\Gamma = | Q |$ the conjunction of the equalities $\{\mathbf{x} | T\Psi(\mathbf{x}) \in M\} = certain(| Q |)$ and $\{\mathbf{x} | I\Psi(\mathbf{x}) \in M\} = indefinite(| Q |)$. In the above, the superscript i means that the interpretation is intuitionistic. When the RHS $| Q |$ is replaced by a more complicated algebraic expression, this abbreviation generalizes in a natural way. Finally, we have

Theorem 6. *Let (L, Γ) be an extended relational theory. Let Q_i be the query $\{\mathbf{x} | \Psi_i(\mathbf{x})\}$, $i = 1, 2$, and let Q' be the query $\{\mathbf{xy} | \Psi(\mathbf{xy})\}$. Let D be the universe of the structure $\Im$.*

Then for a query Q on this database, we have the following:

(i) if Q is of the form $\{\mathbf{x}|\Psi_1(\mathbf{x}) \wedge \Psi_2(\mathbf{x})\}$, then $\| Q \|_\Gamma^i = | Q_1 | \cap | Q_2 |$;

(ii) If Q is of the form $\{\mathbf{x}|\Psi_1(\mathbf{x}) \vee \Psi_2(\mathbf{x})\}$, then $\| Q \|_\Gamma^i = | Q_1 | \cup | Q_2 |$;

(iii) If Q is of the form $\{\mathbf{x}|\neg\Psi_1(\mathbf{x})\}$, then $\| Q \|_\Gamma^i = D^{|\mathbf{x}|} \setminus | Q_1 |$;

(iv) If Q is of the form $\{\mathbf{x}|(\forall y)\Psi(\mathbf{x}y)\}$, then $\| Q \|_\Gamma^i = \Delta_D(| Q' |)$, where D is to be viewed as a unary relation.

(v) If Q is of the form $\{\mathbf{x}|(\exists y)\Psi(\mathbf{x}y)\}$, then $\| Q \|_\Gamma^i = \pi_X(| Q' |)$, where X names the attributes corresponding to $\mathbf{x}$.

□

In addition to showing the equivalence between the logic and the algebra, Theorem 6 also tells us that in our setting, recursive query decompostion can be performed without the risk of losing any answer tuples. Also, in view of Theorem 4, the algebraic approach also gives us complete answers to queries. Finally, as discussed earlier, the algebraic approach also throws open possibilities of query optimization. Now, let us quickly show that the completeness achieved using our approach is feasible. This is done by checking that each operator above can be computed in polynomial time in the size of the operands just as for the traditional algebra. The only nontrivial cases are selection and difference. These operators can be clearly evaluated in polynomial time using the efficient method of testing if two tuples certainly (indefinitely) disagree or not, outlined earlier.

8. SUMMARY AND FUTURE RESEARCH

Of the many approaches proposed for query evaluation with nulls, most suffer from incompleteness or intractability. This motivated us to propose and study the notion of feasible completeness. We first examined an approach that is a straightforward extension of Reiter's principles. We showed that this approach, while complete, still leads to intractability of query evaluation. We proposed an alternate approach based on intuitionistic footing. For this, we proposed a nonprocedural language based on the logic as well as its procedural counterpart based on an extended relational algebra. We showed the completeness of this approach. Among the advantages of this system are the following. The approach allows recursive decompostion of queries and the algebra offers possibilities of query optimization. Finally, since the algebra coincides with the traditional one when applied to a database without nulls, and because of its feasible completeness, it can be directly implemented on top of existing relational systems.

More research is needed to extend the results developed here to the case where more complex conditions on nulls are allowed. Another question is the effect of data dependencies on the theory developed here. We would also like to investigate our approach here in the context of non-Horn databases and logic programs featuring incompleteness of information in the form of indefinite conclusions. Finally, since the (feasible) approach is intuitionistic, it would be interesting to investigate the relationship between the extended relational algebra given here and *pseudo boolean algebras* which are an algebraization of intuitionistic logic.

REFERENCES

[AGK 86] S. Abiteboul, G. Grahne, and P. Kanellakis, "The Data Complexity of Null Values," SIGMOD 86, 1986.

[Bi 81] J. Biskup, "Null Values in Database Relations," In *Advances in Database Theory*, vol.1, H. Gallaire, J. Minker, and J.M. Nicolas, Eds., Plenum Press, NY, 1981.

[Bi 83] J. Biskup, "A Foundation of Codd's Relational Maybe Operations," *ACM TODS* 8, 4 (Dec. 1983), 608-636.

[Co 70] E.F. Codd, "Further Normalization of the Database Relational Model," In *Database Systems*, R. Rustin, Ed., Prentice Hall, NJ, 1972.

[Co 79] E.F. Codd, "Extending the Database Relational Model to Capture more Meaning," *ACM TODS*, 4, 4(Dec. 1979), 397-434.

[FUV 83] R. Fagin, J.D. Ullman, and M.Y. Vardi, "On the Semantics of Updates in Databases," *Proc. 2nd ACM Symp. PODS*, 1983, pp. 352-365.

[Fi 69] M. Fitting, *Intuitionistic Logic - Model Theory and Forcing*, North Holland, Amsterdam, 1969.

[GJ 79] M.R. Garey and D.S. Johnson, *Computers and Intractability*, Freeman, San Fransisco, 1979.

[GM 78] H. Gallaire and J. Minker, *Logic and Databases*, Plenum Press, NY, 1978.

[GMN 84] H. Gallaire, J. Minker, and J.M. Nicolas, " Logic and Databases: A Deductive Approach," *Computing Surveys*, 16, 2(June 1984), 151-185.

[IL 84] T. Imielinski and W. Lipski, "Incomplete Information in Relational Databases," *JACM*, 31, 4(Oct. 1984), 761-791.

[La 89] V.S. Lakshmanan, "Query Evaluation with Null Values: Different Notions of Completeness and Their Complexity," in preparation.

[Li 81] W. Lipski, "On Databases with Incomplete Information," *JACM*, 28, 1(Jan. 1981), 41-70.

[NG 78] J.M. Nicolas and J. Minker, "Database Theory vs. Interpretation," In *Logic and Databases*, Plenum Press, NY, 1978, pp. 33-54.

[Ma 83] D. Maier, *The Theory of Relational Databases*, Computer Science Press, Maryland, 1983.

[Mi 82] J. Minker, "On Indefinite Databases and the Closed World Assumption," *Proc. 6th Conf. Automated Deduction*, LNCS, vol. 138, Springer Verlag, 1982, pp. 292-308.

[Re 84] R. Reiter, "Towards a Logical Reconstruction of Relational Database Theory," In *On Conceptual Modeling* (M.L. Brodie et al Eds.), Springer, NY, 1984, pp. 191-233.

[Re 86] R. Reiter, "A Sound and Sometimes Complete Query Evaluation Algorithm for Relational Databases with Null Values," *JACM*, 33, 2(Apr. 1986), 349-370.

[RS 63] H. Raisowa and R. Sikorski, *The Mathematics of Metamathematics*, Pnastwowe Wydawnictwo Naukowe, Warszawa, 1963.

[Sm 68] R.T. Smullyan, "First Order Logic," *Springer*, Berlin, 1968.

[Sh 67] J.R. Shoenfield,*Mathematical Logic*, Addison-Wesley, Mass., 1969.

[Ul 80] J.D. Ullman, *Principles of Database Systems*, Computer Science Press, Maryland, 1980.

[Va 85] M.Y. Vardi, "Querying Logical Databases," *Proc. 4th ACM Symp. PODS*, 1985, pp. 57-65 (also see *JCSS* 33, 2 (Oct 1986), 142-160).

[Va 86] M.Y. Vardi, "On the Integrity of Databases with Incomplete Information," *Proc. 5th ACM Symp. PODS*, 1986, pp. 252-266.

[Vas 79] Y. Vasiliou, "Null Values in Database Management: A Denotational Semantics Approach," *Proc. ACM SIGMOD Conf. ICMOD*, 1979, pp. 162-169.

[YC 88] L.C. Yuan and D.-A. Chiang, "A Sound and Complete Query Evaluation Algorithm for Relational Databases with Null Values," *ACM SIGMOD*, 1988.

[Za 82] C. Zaniolo, "Database Relations with Null Values," *Proc. 1st ACM Symp. PODS*, 1982, pp. 27-33 (also see *JCSS* 28 (1984), 142-166).

Average case complexity analysis of RETE pattern-match algorithm and average size of join in Databases

Luc ALBERT *

Abstract. *The* RETE *algorithm [Forg 82] is a very efficient method for comparing a large collection of patterns with a large collection of objects. It is widely used in rule-based expert systems. We studied ([AF 88] or [Alb 88]) the average case complexity of the* RETE *algorithm on collections of patterns and objects with a random tree structure. Objects and patterns are often made up of a head-symbol and a list of variable or constant arguments (OPSV [Forg 81], Xrete [LCR 88] ...). In this paper, we analyse the theoretical performance of* RETE *algorithm on this widely used type of pattern and object with the theory of generating functions. We extend this work to the study of the performance of composed queries in relational Databases and we generalize Rosenthal's theorem on the average size of an equijoin [Rosen 81]. We give some numerical examples based on our results.*

CR classification : F.2 (Analysis of algorithms), I.2 (Artificial Intelligence), H.2 (Database).

I. Introduction

The RETE pattern match algorithm [Forg 79] [Forg 82] has been introduced by C. Forgy in the line of his work on production systems [Forg 81].

Production systems, or more generally rule-based systems, are widely used in Artificial Intelligence for modelling intelligent behaviour [LNR 87] and building expert systems. They are quite easy to use and have many advantages : modularity, relative independence of each rule and the same expressivity as a Turing machine. However the inference engine is algorithmically inefficient. The most time consuming process in a rule-based system is the *pattern match* phase that consists of maintaining the set of satisfied rules among changes in the data base. This computation can represent more than 90 % of the overall computation time in an application [DNM 78].

RETE algorithm is an efficient method for computing the set of satisfied rules incrementally after each rule execution. The incremental computation is justified in expert systems applications by the fact that the execution of a rule affects a relatively small number of objects (or facts or terms) in comparison to the total number of objects. Therefore most of the previous pattern match work remains valid. RETE algorithm realizes a total indexing of the data base according to rule conditions. Conditions common to several rules are shared in such a way that several rules can be found to be satisfied by testing some patterns only once.

Forgy [Forg 79] proved, thanks to simplifying hypotheses, that with RETE algorithm the worst case time complexity for computing the set of satisfied rules is linear in the number of rules, and polynomial in the number of objects (with degree being the maximum number of conditions in a rule). In the best case the complexity is a constant. Between these extremes the sensitivity of pattern match time to the size of the data base is highly dependent on rule characteristics. We already studied the theoretical average case complexity of RETE algorithm when it compares objects and patterns having any tree structure. ([AF 88], [Alb 88]). In real applications, objects and patterns are often made up of a function symbol and a list of variable or constant arguments. The height of their usual tree structure is therefore one and we analyse in this article the average performance of the algorithm in the case of these *"flat terms"*.

* Institut National de Recherche en Informatique et Automatique, Domaine de Voluceau, Rocquencourt, BP 105, 78150 Le Chesnay Cedex France. mail : albert@inria.inria.fr

Laboratoire Central de Recherches, Thomson-CSF, Domaine de Corbeville, BP 10, 91401 Orsay Cedex France.

There are many motivations in searching for a more accurate model of computation and an average case complexity analysis of **RETE** algorithm. First, **RETE** algorithm admits many variants and optimizations, concerning the representation of local memories [Forg 79], the sharing of conditions (the **ARBRE D'UNIFICATION** : [Gha 87], [Alb 88]), the computation of joins [Mir 87], the total compilation principle [Fag 86] [fag 88], the parallelization of the algorithm [Gupt 84] etc ... An average case complexity analysis can be used to evaluate these optimizations and propose new ones. Second, run-time performance prediction is a necessity for the development of *real-time* expert systems [WGF 86], [SF 88]. A mathematical model of run-time requirements can be used to extrapolate from the run-time performance of a prototype the performances of the expert system in real size. It define the range of its applicability in terms of number of objects that can be treated at a given time. Third, a mathematical model can be used also to work out significant benchmarks in order to compare several implementations according to the relevant characteristic parameters of a knowledge base [GF 83]. Lastly, we shall show that all this analysis applies not only to the study of the performance of pattern-match in expert systems but also to the estimation of the average size of composed queries in Relational Databases. In this paper we present an average case complexity analysis of **RETE** algorithm and of the average size of composed queries in Relational Databases using the generating function theory ([Fla 85], [FS 86], [FV 87]) (that introduces mathematical methods of independent interest). One can find a more detailed version of this study in [Alb 89].

Only equality tests are considered first. In Part **2**, we briefly present **RETE** algorithm, and develop an Example. We define also the cost of this algorithm and precise the fundamental quantities for its computation. In Part **3**, we introduce the generating function theory that is used to analyse the average case complexity of algorithms **(3.2)** and the asymptotic analysis necessary to simplify the expressions we previously obtained **(3.3)**. Thus we obtain a result under a first model in which the Database is represented as an ordered list of terms **(3.4)**. In Part **4**, we determine the complexity under a second model that considers the Database as a multiset of terms. In Part **5**, we extend the previous results by considering several separate ranges of variation for constants **(5.1)**. Then we generalize our results for taking into account different frequency coefficients for symbols **(5.2)** (by the way we shall consider inequality tests). In Part **6**, we consider the negation between arguments and between patterns.

Lastly in Part **7**, we apply all these results to the study of composed join in Relational Database. We illustrate the results we obtain throughout the article with some examples. The example of figure 1 is numerically developed in the appendix.

II. RETE algorithm

2.1. Presentation

The production systems we shall consider are composed of a fixed set, denoted by RB (for *Rule Base*), of *if-then rules* called *productions*, and a changing set of *facts*, called the *Working Memory* and denoted by WM. Facts are formed on a finite alphabet F of function symbols given with their arity. Arguments are taken in a finite set C of symbols of arity 0, the constants. For instance, given symbols h of arity 3, f of arity 2 and constants $a1$ and $a2$ one can form the following terms : $(f\ \ a1\ a1)$, $(f\ \ a2\ a1)$, $(h\ \ a1\ a2\ a1)$, $(h\ \ a1\ a2\ a2)$ etc ... The set of flat terms is denoted by $FT(F)$. The Working Memory is formalized as an ordered or unordered set of such terms.

The if-part of a rule (its *left-hand side*) is a conjonction of *patterns*, represented as a tuple $(P_1, \ldots, P_n)$. A pattern is a term some of whose arguments can be variable. Variables are denoted by $X, Y, \ldots$, they are taken from an enumerable set of variables V. Patterns are partial descriptions of facts. A pattern P *matches* a fact t if one can find a *substitution* of pattern's variables, $\sigma : V \rightarrow C$, such that $\sigma P = t$. For example the substitution of X by $a1$ and of Y by $a2$ in pattern $(h\ \ X\ Y\ X)$ matches the term $(h\ \ a1\ a2\ a1)$.

We say that the left-hand side of a rule $(P_1, \ldots, P_n)$ is *instanciated* (or that the rule is *satisfied*) when there exists a tuple of facts $(t_1, \ldots, t_n)$ with $t_i \in WM$, called the instance, and a substitution σ such that $\sigma P_i = t_i$. We remark that since a pattern in a rule can match several facts in the Working Memory, a rule can be instanciated in multiple ways. The then-part of a rule (its *right-hand side*) is a sequence of *actions* that can add (resp. remove) a fact in (resp. from) the Working Memory.

Example : Let h be a function symbol of arity 3, f and g of arity 2 and constants $a0$, $a1$, $a2$, $a3$, $a4$, $a5$. We can consider the three following rules, in which we omitted the right-hand side :

$$\begin{array}{ll} (R1: & (g \quad X\ Y)\ \neg(f \quad a0\ X)\ (h \quad a1\ X\ Y) \longrightarrow \ \ldots) \\ (R2: & (h \quad a0\ X\ a1)\ (g \quad X\ Y)\ (f \quad a0\ a1) \longrightarrow \ \ldots) \\ (R3: & (f \quad X\ a1)\ (f \quad Y\ a2)\ (h \quad a2\ X\ Y) \longrightarrow \ \ldots) \end{array}$$

(The negation "¬" is studied in Part **6**.)

The cycle of inference consists in three steps:

- *match* the patterns with the facts in the Working Memory in order to determine the set of satisfied rules (called the *conflict set*) : this is the *pattern match* phase;
- *select* one rule 's instance in the conflict set;
- *execute* the actions of the rule.

In **RETE** algorithm the pattern match step is not separated from the execution step. In fact, it occurs at each modification in the Working Memory, that is at initialisation time when facts are entered, and then at each assertion or retraction during execution steps. Since the **RETE** multi-pattern match algorithm is solely concerned with the left-hand sides of rules, from now on we shall identify rules with their left-hand sides (we shall consider right-hand sides in **5.2** when we distinguish apparition frequencies of symbols). Rules are compiled in a discrimination network. At run-time when a fact is asserted or retracted, it is processed in the network from the root. If the fact matches a pattern it is memorized in (or removed from) the network. If other memorized facts can jointly satisfy a rule, the instance is added to (or suppressed from) the conflict set. In this way both rules and facts are represented in the network.

Two types of tests are distinguished in rule left-hand sides:

- *one-pattern tests* are tests concerning solely the fact to be characterized. They test the equality of the function symbol and of constants between the fact and the pattern. When a variable has several occurrences in the pattern, they test the equality of the corresponding constants of the fact.
- *multi-pattern tests* are the tests of several patterns belonging to the same left-hand side of a rule. When the same variable appears in several patterns, they check the equality of the corresponding constants of facts. They perform a *join* in the sense of Databases (*i.e.* they produce as output the cartesian product of input data discriminated with tests).

In **RETE** pattern-match algorithm, one-pattern tests are executed first, then multi-pattern tests are executed at each join with memorized facts to verify consistent binding of variables across multiple patterns in a rule's left-hand side. Consequently the network is formed of two parts.

Figure 1 represents the **RETE** network corresponding to the three previous rules.

The first part is a tree composed of one-pattern tests, called the *discrimination tree*. In this tree each node is labelled with a single one-pattern test. The discrimination tree has as many leaves as the number of different patterns in the left-hand sides of the rules; that is 8 leaves in our example. (two patterns being equal up to variable renaming). We define the *i-pattern* of a node i as the pattern corresponding to the tests cumulated on the path from the root to node i (*i.e.* the pattern needed to reach node i). The root-pattern is a variable, *i.e.* a non-selective pattern (it matches any fact). The i-pattern of the leaves of the discrimination tree are all the patterns which appear in the rule left-hand sides. Several successors to a node correspond to several branches to follow. At run-time one fact typically reaches several leaves which correspond to different matching patterns. Thus in our example, the pattern $(h \ \ a0\ X\ Y)$ corresponds to node **8** and term $(f \ \ a0\ a1)$ reaches nodes **4**, **5** and **10**.

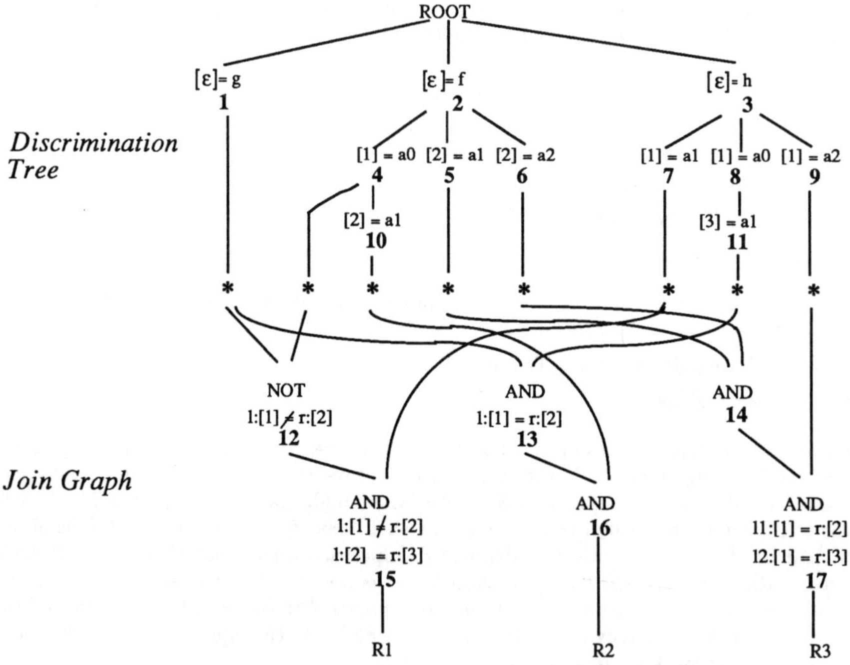

Figure 1 † : Rete Graph

The second part is a graph formed with binary joins between the leaves of the initial part. In these nodes, i-patterns are tuples of patterns $(P_1, \ldots, P_l)$, in which the sharing of variables between patterns is determined by the multi-pattern tests. Outputs are in a one-to-one correspondence with the rules. i-pattern of output nodes are the left-hand sides of the rules up to variable renaming. They are reached at run-time with the instances of the rules.

At run-time when a tuple reaches a join node, it is memorized in a *local memory* or *memory node*, and the memory of the opposite input of the join node is searched in order to find a compatible tuple according to the multi-pattern tests. Thus at node **17** of figure 1, are memorized in left input, pairs of the type $(f \;\; X \; a1)(f \;\; Y \; a2)$, and in right input $(h \;\; a2 \; U \; V)$ and we select as output triplets with the following multi-pattern tests $X = U$ and $Y = V$. In many implementations the right input of a join node is restricted to be a leaf of the initial tree (not the output of a join node) as in figure 1, so that the structure of the join network is a set of *combs*. This eliminates a possibility of optimization consisting of grouping together the most selective patterns together (we shall study the general case to perform calculations).

Hashing techniques can be used to reduce the complexity of the search in local memories, by exploiting all equality tests in a join in order to hash the input memories. In the same way, if inequality predicates are to be considered, the local memories can be organized in search trees.

Negation of patterns has not been considered yet. A negated pattern expresses the non-existence of a fact matching the pattern. Negated patterns are treated in RETE algorithm by adding a second type of join nodes (see node **12**). In these nodes the local memory on the left input stores the number of elements in the right memory (the negated elements) which are compatible with each "left-tuple" according to the

---

† We denote by [j] the jth leftmost son of the root ([ϵ]) of the i-pattern ; r (resp. l) denotes the pattern of the right (resp. left) input of a join node (lj precise the jth pattern of the left input list).

multi-pattern tests. When a counter gets to zero (resp. one) the left tuple is propagated in the network in assert (resp. retract) mode. In our example, as long as there is no fact of the type $(f \;\; a0 \; X)$ in the Working Memory, the fact reaching the left input of the node **12** reaches the node **15**. The existential quantifier can be treated in a symmetrical way. In fact it is possible to generalize RETE algorithm in order to accept in the left-hand sides of rules any first order logic formula with an arbitrary degree of imbrication of quantifiers ([Fag 88]).

2.2. Cost of the algorithm

The RETE algorithm spends most of its time performing the pattern match step. We are going to determine the average cost of the algorithm by considering an arbitrary Working Memory and a given RETE network. We shall do an average calculation over all the possible input-Working Memory. More precisely we shall determine the average time needed by the algorithm to compute the conflict set from an arbitrary input-Working Memory. For the facts, the time devoted to move through the discrimination tree is negligible when compared to the time devoted to joins. We shall therefore determine the average time devoted to perform the multi-pattern tests at the join nodes. Thus our complexity measure will be the time of performing one multi-pattern test. At a join node, the global average time is proportional to the average number of tuples of facts to be tested at this node. When there is no hashing at the join nodes, this quantity is the product of the average number of tuples stored at the memory nodes in left and right input of the join node (the product of the average *size* of the memory nodes). When local memories are hashed according to equality tests performed at the join node, the average number of tuples of facts to be tested coincide with the average number of tuples that output this node with success; that is the average size of the output local memory.

The average size of memory nodes thus appears to be a fundamental quantity to calculate. We shall thus be able to determine the average cost of the algorithm and the precise average size of each local memory.

We can model the input-Working Memory as an ordered list of facts. This is a good representation of the succession of the inputs of the RETE network at each cycle of the inference engine. This yields the results for the *list-model.* Since the final state of the local memories is independent of the order of adding of facts of the input-Working Memory, we can also model the Working Memory with a multiset of facts (we always enable repetitions of facts in order to take into account the possibility for the same fact to be added and suppressed several times during the cycle of the inference engine). This yields the results for the *multiset model.*

III. List model

3.1. Combinatorial study

Let c_0 be the number of constants. Let c_j denotes the number of function symbols of arity j in F. The arity of the function symbols lies between m (the minimal arity) $(m > 0)$ and M (the maximal one). We define the size $|t|$ of a term t as the number of the arguments of the function symbol minus m (the arity of its function symbol minus m). We associate with $FT(F)$ the characteristic generating function:

$$A(z) = \sum_{t \in FT(F)} z^{|t|} = \sum_{i=0}^{M-m} a_i z^i$$

with a_n the number of terms of size n in $FT(F)$. It is easy to see that $a_i = c_{i+m} c_0^{i+m}$. Since the number of function symbols and the number of constants are finite, the number of terms in $FT(F)$ is finite too and $A(z)$ is a polynomial with degree $M - m$. Remark that $a_0 \neq 0$. We can introduce the average size of terms in $FT(F)$, that is

$$\frac{1}{\lambda} = \frac{A'(1)}{A(1)}$$

Remark : In the case where $m = M$, we have $\frac{1}{\lambda} = 0$!! It is easy to study directly this specific case and the result we obtain is only a particular case of the formula described later. From now on, we have $0 < \frac{1}{\lambda} < M - m$.

Example : In our previous example, we have $c_0 = 6$, $c_1 = 0$, $c_2 = 2$ and $c_3 = 1$. Thus $m = 2$, $M = 3$ and $A(z) = 72 + 216z$ and $\frac{1}{\lambda} = 3/4$.

We consider that the **RETE** network takes as input an arbitrary Working Memory with k facts and of total size n (*i.e.* n is the sum of the sizes of terms composing the Working Memory). The generating function of a list of k terms determined by $A(z)$ is given by $A(z)^k$. Thus the nth coefficient in $A(z)^k$, $[z^n]A(z)^k$, represents the number of lists of k terms with total size n.

For a node i of the discrimination tree, we introduce the generating function of the terms that match at i : $B_i(z) = \sum_{n\geq 0} b_{i,n}z^n$, with $b_{i,n}$ the number of terms of size n that match the i-pattern. We introduce some notations for a node i of the discrimination tree :

- ω_i denotes the arity of the function symbol of the i-pattern;
- x_i is the number of different variable argument of the i-pattern.

Example : for node **8** of the network of figure 1, we have $\omega_8 = 3$ and $x_8 = 2$. For the pattern $(Head\ \ X\ X\ Y\ a)$, we have $\omega_i = 4$ and $x_i = 2$.

It is now easy to prove that :

THEOREM 1 : *The generating function of the terms that match at a node i of the discrimination tree is :*

$$B_i(z) = c_0{}^{x_i} z^{\omega_i - m}$$

Example : We have at node **11** of figure 1 : $B_{11}(z) = 6z$. And we see that $B_{root}(z) = A(z)$.

Let us consider now a node i of the join network. That node outputs l-tuples of facts that partially instanciate the left-hand side of a rule. $B_i(z) = \sum_{n\geq 0} b_{i,n}z^n$ is the associated generating function. $b_{i,n}$ is the number of l-tuples of total size n that match the i-pattern. We know the l leaves j_i of the discrimination tree which match each of the components of the output-l-tuples of the node i. L_i stands for this set of the l associated patterns. Let us denote :

- $\omega_i = \sum_{j_i \in L_i} \omega_{j_i}$
- $x_i = \left(\sum_{j_i \in L_i} x_{j_i}\right) + y_i \qquad y_i \leq 0$

with y_i a correcting term due to the multi-pattern tests between variables of the l different patterns. *If we consider the global set of all the variables of the different l-patterns, x_i still represents the number of distinct variables in this set.* Thus we determine easily y_i in function of the similar variables tested at node i and we have: $y_i \leq 0$ because the join increase *a priori* the number of identical variables.

From this, we prove in the same way as previously:

THEOREM 2 : *Considering as input an arbitrary Working Memory with k facts and of total size n ,the generating function of the l-tuples of terms which match at node i in the join network is:*

$$B_i(z) = c_0{}^{x_i} z^{\omega_i - lm}$$

From this, we deduce

THEOREM 3 : *The average number of terms that match at a node i of the discrimination tree is :*

$$\overline{b_{i,n,k}} = \frac{k c_0{}^{x_i} [z^{n-\omega_i+m}] A(z)^{k-1}}{[z^n] A(z)^k}$$

PROOF : The basic idea is to split the generating function $A(z)$ in: $A(z) = B_i(z) + R_i(z)$ with $R_i(z)$ the "rest function" *i.e.* the generating function of all the terms which don't match with the i-pattern. Then we shall mark the matching at i elements with the variable u and note:

$$A_i(z, u) = uB_i(z) + R_i(z) = A(z) + (u-1)B_i(z)$$

Thus $f_{i,n,p,k} = [u^p z^n](A_i(z,u)^k)$ represents the number of lists of size n with k terms among which there is exactly p terms matching at node i.
Therefore $\overline{b_{i,n,k}}$ is the quotient of $\sum_{p=0}^{+\infty} pf_{i,n,p,k} \left(= \sum_{p=0}^{k} pf_{i,n,p,k}\right)$ by the total number of lists of k terms and of total size n, that is

$$\overline{b_{i,n,k}} = \frac{\sum_p pf_{i,n,p,k}}{[z^n]A(z)^k}$$

We have $(A_i(z,u)^k) = \sum_{p,n} f_{i,n,p,k} u^p z^n$ thus :

$$\frac{\partial}{\partial u}\left(A_i(z,u)^k\right) = \sum_{p,n} f_{i,n,p,k} p u^{p-1} z^n$$

whence

$$\frac{\partial}{\partial u}\left(A_i(z,u)^k\right)\bigg|_{u=1} = \sum_n \left(\sum_p pf_{i,n,p,k}\right) z^n$$

Therefore

$$\overline{b_{i,n,k}} = \frac{[z^n]\frac{\partial}{\partial u}\left(A_i(z,u)^k\right)|_{u=1}}{[z^n]A(z)^k}$$

And since

$$\begin{aligned}\frac{\partial}{\partial u}\left(A_i(z,u)^k\right)\bigg|_{u=1} &= kA(z,u)^{k-1}\frac{\partial}{\partial u}\left(A_i(z,u)\right)\bigg|_{u=1} \\ &= kA(z)^{k-1}B_i(z)\end{aligned}$$

the theorem is established. ■

We shall now determine the average number of l-tuples of terms that match at a node i of the join network. Our demonstration will express the two antagonist sides of a join. We actually know the l nodes j_i of the discrimination tree "associated" to i, and thanks to theorem 3, we know the $\overline{b_{j_i,n,k}}$. The *expansion* side of a join can be expressed by the quantity $\overline{L} = \prod_{j_i=1}^{l} \overline{b_{j_i,n,k}}$, which represents (under the hypothesis of independent distribution laws at the j_i) the average number of l-tuples which would reach the node i if there were no multi-pattern tests. On the other hand a reasoning close to that of theorem 3 expresses the "selection" side of a join :

THEOREM 4 : *The average number of l-tuples of terms that match at a join node i from a list of total size n of L l-tuples of terms of which each component matches at an associated node j_i is :*

$$\overline{\gamma_{i,L,n}} = L\frac{[z^n]B_i(z)\left(\prod_{j_i=1}^{l} B_{j_i}(z)\right)^{L-1}}{[z^n]\left(\prod_{j_i=1}^{l} B_{j_i}(z)\right)^{L}}$$

(see [Alb 89]). Note that we shall use $\overline{b_{i,n,k}}$ both for discrimination and join nodes to denote *average number* of (tuples of) terms. From theorem 4 it follows :

THEOREM 5 : *For a node i of the join network, the average number of l-tuples of terms that match the i-pattern is :*

$$\overline{b_{i,n,k}} = c_0{}^{y_i}\left(\prod_{j_i=1}^{l} \overline{b_{j_i,n,k}}\right) \quad (y_i \le 0)$$

Those exact results could be studied using the Lagrange inversion theorem but they lead to expressions that are hard to use (multinomial coefficients ...). In order to express them simply we shall derive an asymptotic expansion with respect to k and n.

3.2. Asymptotic evaluation

To derive simple expressions, we use singularity analysis methods. We estimate the value of integrals with complex analysis methods (saddle-point method). We consider a Working Memory of size n with k terms as a given data of the algorithm. Thus we consider that k and n are both increasing.

According to the previous Section, we have to evaluate coefficients such as: $a_{n,k} = [z^n]A^k(z)$, from which we shall deduce the expression of $\overline{b_{i,n,k}}$. By Cauchy's theorem this quantity can be expressed as the following integral

$$a_{n,k} = \frac{1}{2i\pi}\int_{\Gamma}\left(A(z)^k\right)\frac{dz}{z^{n+1}}$$

where the contour Γ lies inside the domain of analycity of A and simply encircles the origin. In order to get an equivalent of this integral when k and n tend both to infinity, we shall use the saddle point method (See [dB 58] and [Henr 74]). In order to simplify this asymptotic analysis, we use the fact that, in real applications, the size of the terms is approximatively constant (say 4, 5, 6 ...). Thus, we can consider that $k = \lambda n$. The quite long calculations needed to obtain the following formula are detailed in [Alb 89] (similar ones are made in [Alb 88] and [AF 88]). We have :

$$a_{n,k} = \frac{A(1)^{\lambda n}}{2\sqrt{\pi}}\left(\frac{1}{2}(1-\frac{1}{\lambda}) + \frac{\lambda A''(1)}{2A(1)}\right)^{-\frac{1}{2}} n^{-\frac{1}{2}}\left(1+O\left(\frac{1}{n}\right)\right)$$

and this quantity has to be multiplied by δ when $A(z) = N(z^\delta)$ (HCF condition). From this we deduce (the constant δ disappears by cancelling the the $\overline{b_{i,n,k}}$ fraction) :

THEOREM 6 : *The average number of l-tuples of facts that match at a join node i is :*

$$\overline{b_{i,n,k}} = c_0{}^{x_i}\frac{1}{A(1)^l}k^l\left(1+O\left(\frac{1}{n}\right)\right) = c_0{}^{x_i}\frac{\lambda^l}{A(1)^l}n^l\left(1+O\left(\frac{1}{n}\right)\right) = \Pi_i n^l\left(1+O\left(\frac{1}{n}\right)\right)$$

with $l = 1$ when i is a node of the discrimination tree.

We can define now a matching-rate $\overline{\alpha_i}$ at a node i of the RETE network which expresses the probability for a term or a l-tuple of terms to match at a node i in the RETE network.

THEOREM 7 : *For a node i in the* RETE *network, the matching-rate is*

$$\overline{\alpha_i} = \frac{\overline{b_{i,n,k}}}{k^l} \simeq \frac{c_0{}^{x_i}}{A(1)^l}$$

Remark : Of course $\overline{\alpha_i} \leq 1$ and we can verify that at the first level of the discrimination tree (nodes **1**, **2** and **3** of figure 1 of our example), if we made the summation over all the function symbols of $FT(F)$, we find

$$\sum_i \overline{\alpha_i} = \sum_i \frac{c_i c_0{}^i}{A(1)} = 1 \ !$$

(a term of $FT(F)$ has always its function symbol in F).

3.3. Average cost of the algorithm with the list model

We can now evaluate the average cost of the RETE algorithm, given an arbitrary Working Memory and a fixed RETE network. We shall estimate the average time needed by the RETE algorithm to produce the conflict set from a given input-Working Memory. We determine the average number of multi-patterns tests realized at join nodes (this is as we previously said the main part of the total time cost). Let us recall that our complexity measure is the time of realization of one multi-pattern test. Since we know the average size of local memories in the RETE network, it is easy to determine the average number of those tests performed at the join nodes. Let us denote by l_i the number of components of the output-tuples at a join node i and β_i the number of multi-patterns tests performed at i considering only one l_i-input-tuple (in our example, $\beta_{17} = 2$, $\beta_{14} = 0$, $\beta_{13} = 1$ ...). The average number of tests performed at i is the average number of l_i-tuples tested at i multiplied by β_i. To obtain the average number of l_i-tuples that reaches i we just have to consider that at i no test is performed (*i.e.* $y_i = 0$) and evaluate the so modified $\overline{b'_{i,n,k}}$. Let us denote by $\Pi'_i n^{l_i}$ this quantity (notice that this quantity is precisely equal to $\overline{b_{i1,n,k}} \times \overline{b_{i2,n,k}}$ where $i1$ and $i2$ design the two nodes inputs of i).

Then, we can propose

$$\overline{cost_n} \simeq K \sum_{i\ join-node} \beta_i \Pi'_i n^{l_i} = K \sum_{i\ join-node} \beta_i (\Pi_{i1}\Pi_{i2}) n^{l_i} \tag{1}$$

with K an implementation constant.

Of course asymptotically with respect to n, we get the main part of this expression keeping only the nodes with the larger l_i. But the interest of an average case complexity analysis is the precise determination of all the proportionality constants, which can be, as we shall see in appendix, very small for large l_i, and therefore very important.

Remark : By hashing local memories according to equality tests at the join nodes, the average number of semi-unifications performed at a join node i is only the number of output-tuples *i.e.* $\overline{b_{i,n,k}}$. Thus in the above formula we just have to replace Π'_i by Π_i.

From this result, *that can be made fully precise on any case*, we can *a posteriori* assume Forgy's hypotheses (See [Forg 79]). Thus if we assume that the number of condition-patterns per left-hand side is constant equal to c in the Rule Base, the previous result becomes :

$$\overline{cost_{|WM|}} \simeq K\lambda^c |WM|^c \left(\sum_{j=1}^{|RB|} \beta_j \Pi'_j \right) = K\lambda^c |WM|^c \left(\sum_{j=1}^{|RB|} \beta_j \Pi_{j1}\Pi_{j2} \right)$$

with $j1$ and $j2$ denoting the two inputs of the last join node j of the Rj rule.
And we find the same type of relation proposed by Forgy: a linear cost as a function of the number of rules and a polynomial cost as a function of the size of the Working Memory $|WM|^c$ (we have determined the time needed by the RETE algorithm with an input of $|WM|$ modification terms, Forgy found a cost of $|WM|^{c-1}$ because he considered only one modification term as input).

IV. Multiset model

4.1. Combinatorial formulae

As we previously explained at the end of Section **(2.2)**, we shall now model the Working Memory as a multiset of facts. We shall use the "usual" definition of the size of a term : the number of its arguments plus 1 *i.e.* the number of nodes in its usual tree representation. Thus we have a new characteristic generating function :

$$P(z) = \sum_{t \in FT(F)} z^{|t|} = \sum_{n \geq 0} p_n z^n = \sum_{l=m+1}^{M+1} (c_{l-1} c_0^{l-1}) z^l$$

We can introduce the usual average size of a term

$$\frac{1}{\lambda_u} = \frac{P'(1)}{P(1)} \quad and \quad \frac{1}{\lambda_u} = \frac{1}{\lambda} + m + 1$$

Note that $A(1) = P(1)$ is the number of terms in $FT(F)$.

We consider as input of the RETE network, any Working Memory of total size n (without even considering the number of its terms). The generating function of multisets of terms of $FT(F)$ is :

$$M(z) = \prod_{t \in TP(F)} \left(\frac{1}{1 - z^{|t|}} \right) = \prod_{i=m}^{i=M} \left(\frac{1}{1 - z^{i+1}} \right)^{p_i}$$

Thus $[z^n]M(z)$ is the number of multisets of terms of total size n.

Example : In our example, we have

$$M(z) = \left(\frac{1}{1-z^3}\right)^{72}\left(\frac{1}{1-z^4}\right)^{216}$$

We keep on using the same notations $B_i(z)$, ω_i, x_i and y_i for a node i in the **RETE** network. We thus obtain :

THEOREM 8 : *The generating function of terms or l-tuples of terms that match at a node i is :*

$$B_i(z) = c_0{}^{x_i} z^{\omega_i+1}$$

with $l = 1$ in the case of a node of the discrimination tree.

With a reasoning close to that of theorem 3, we obtain

THEOREM 9 : *The average number of terms that match at a node i of the discrimination tree is :*

$$\overline{b_{i,n}} = \frac{c_0{}^{x_i}[z^{n-\omega_i-1}]\{M(z)/(1-z^{\omega_i+1})\}}{[z^n]M(z)}$$

For a join node i, the order of instanciation of the l local memories j_i is fundamental because it expresses the instanciation of different patterns. The reasoning of theorem 5 is valid and the average number of l-tuples of terms that match the i-pattern is still :

$$\overline{b_{i,n}} = c_0{}^{y_i}\left(\prod_{j_i=1}^{l}\overline{b_{j_i,n}}\right)$$

4.2. Asymptotic analysis

In order to simplify the expressions we have just obtained, we shall analyse specific fractions of the type $m_n = [z^n]\prod_j (1/(1-z^j)^{p_j})$. The modulus of all the singularities of this kind of rational fraction is always 1. Let us denote δ the highest common factor of the *arity* $+1$ of the function symbols of $FT(F)$. We know that

$$[z^n]\frac{1}{(1-z)^\alpha} = \frac{n^{\alpha-1}}{\Gamma(\alpha)}\left(1+O\left(\frac{1}{n}\right)\right)$$

In the case of $\delta = 1$, 1 is the singularity with the greatest multiplicity $(\sum_j p_j)$ and, as before, δ disappears in the average expression of $\overline{b_{i,n}}$. We obtain ([Alb 89]) :

$$m_n = \delta\prod_j \frac{1}{j^{p_j}}\frac{n^{\sum_j p_l - 1}}{\Gamma(\sum_j p_j)}$$

4.3. Results with the multiset model

Thanks to previous formulae, we obtain for the multiset model :

THEOREM 10 : *For an arbitrary input-Working Memory of total size n, at a node i*

- *of the discrimination tree, the average number of matching terms is*

$$\overline{b_{i,n}} = c_0{}^{x_i}\frac{1}{P(1)}\frac{1}{\omega_i+1}n\left(1+O\left(\frac{1}{n}\right)\right) = \Phi_i n\left(1+O\left(\frac{1}{n}\right)\right)$$

- *of the join network, the average number of matching l-tuples of terms is*

$$\overline{b_{i,n}} = c_0{}^{x_i}\frac{1}{P(1)^l}\frac{1}{\prod_{j_i=1}^{l}(\omega_{j_i}+1)}n^l\left(1+O\left(\frac{1}{n}\right)\right) = \Phi_i n^l\left(1+O\left(\frac{1}{n}\right)\right)$$

with j_i the l associated nodes of the discrimination tree.

We still can consider that $k \simeq \lambda_u n$, and define :

THEOREM 11 : *The matching rate at a node i of the discrimination tree is*

$$\overline{\mu_i} \simeq {c_0}^{x_i} \frac{1}{P(1)} \frac{1}{\omega_i + 1} \frac{1}{\lambda_u}$$

and for a join node i

$$\overline{\mu_i} \simeq {c_0}^{x_i} \frac{1}{P(1)^l} \frac{1}{\prod_{j_i=1}^{l} (\omega_{j_i} + 1)} \frac{1}{\lambda_u^l}$$

We can see that the multiset model yields to the *same type of expression for the cost of the algorithm*; we just have to substitute Φ_i for Π_i in Eq. (1).

Let us compare the results of the two models (let us recall that $A(1) = P(1)$). In the multiset model, there appears the ratio of the average size $\frac{1}{\lambda_u}$ to the size of the terms at the j_i. If we denote by $\sigma = \frac{1}{\lambda_u}$ the average size of terms, then

$$\overline{\mu_i} = \overline{\alpha_i} \prod_{j_i=1}^{l} \left(\frac{\sigma}{\omega_{j_i} + 1} \right)$$

and $\omega_{j_i} + 1$ is the size of the terms at the node j_i.

V. Multiple ranges of variation and probability

5.1. Multiple ranges of variation for the constants

Up to now, we have considered that there was only one set of c_0 constants in $FT(F)$. It meant that any constant could instanciate any argument of any function symbol, without any semantic consideration. We shall now distinguish p separate ranges of variation for the constants $D_1, \ldots, D_p$ of cardinality $d_1, \ldots, d_p$. We consider that an equality test can only happen between two variables of the same set. We have to precise the range of variation of each argument of each function symbol. Let i be a node of the discrimination tree. The arity of the function symbol of the i-pattern is ω_i and let us denote by $f_{i,r}$ the number of arguments of f_i that vary in D_r (we have $\sum_{i=1}^{p} f_{i,r} = \omega_i$ and of course the value of some of the $f_{i,r}$ can be zero).

This precision will lead to a slight modification of the previous results; indeed we have

$$P(z) = \sum_{f_i \in F} \left(\prod_{r=1}^{p} {d_r}^{f_{i,r}} \right) z^{\omega_i + 1} = z^{m+1} A(z)$$

Remark : Of course if $p = 1$ *i.e.* there is only one set of c_0 constants, we find again $[z^n]P(z) = c_{n-1}{c_0}^{n-1}$.

We always have $\frac{1}{\lambda_u} = \frac{P'(1)}{P(1)}$ but instead of x_i we have to define a p-tuple $x_{i,1}, \ldots, x_{i,p}$ with $x_{i,r}$ the number of *distinct* arguments of the i-pattern belonging to D_r (and the previous x_i is equal to $\sum_{r=1}^{p} x_{i,r}$). Hence

THEOREM 12 : *The generating function of the terms that match at a node i of the discrimination tree is, for the list model :*

$$B_i(z) = \left(\prod_{r=1}^{p} {d_r}^{x_{i,r}} \right) z^{\omega_i - m}$$

(for the multiset model, one just has to change the power of z).

Example : Let us consider the pattern :

$$(f \;\; a \; b \; a \; X \; Y \; X' \; X \; Z \; X)$$

with $X,\ X' \in D_1$, $Y \in D_2$ and $Z \in D_3$ and a, b some constants. Thus we have $x_{i,1} = 2$, $x_{i,2} = 1$ and $x_{i,3} = 1$ whence $B_i(z) = ({d_1}^2 d_2 d_3) z^{9-m}$.

For a node i of the join network, we denote $x_{i,r} = \sum_{j_i=1}^{l} x_{j_i,r} + y_{i,r}$ with $y_{i,r}$ (≤ 0) the corrective term due to joins in D_r at i. *With those notations we see that nothing is modified in the calculations of the previous Parts and in the final results one just has to substitute* $(\prod_{r=1}^{p} d_r^{x_{i,r}})$ *for* $c_0^{x_i}$.

This notion of multiple ranges of variation for the constants will enable us to consider a test of inequality : if at a node i, we have to test $X > a$ with a a constant of the set D and X a variable. D is therefore assumed to be ordered and we are then able to determine the set $D_a = \{ Y \in D \mid Y > a \}$ of cardinality d_a. This inequality test will therefore match d_a times as many terms as the equality test $X = b$ with b any constant in D and its cost has to be multiplied by the same constant d_a too.

5.2. Probability

The models studied up to now consider a uniform distribution over all the terms of the same size n in $FT(F)$. In order to get an even more likely modelling, we shall consider a model taking into account the fact that certain symbols are more frequent than others (see [Alb 88], [AF 88] and [FSS]). Thus we present here a *weighted model.* Let w be a *weight function* that assigns to each function symbol $f \in F$ (resp. to each constant c) a non negative real number $w[f]$ (resp. $w[c]$). Then this weight is extended multiplicatively to terms. If t is a term, its weight is defined as

$$w[t] = \prod_{symbol \in t} w[symbol]$$

In order to use a probabilistic weighted model for symbols we choose :

$$\sum_{f \in F} w[f] = |F| \quad and \quad \sum_{c \in D_r} w[c] = d_r \quad \forall r$$

(with $|F|$ the cardinality of F). We have chosen to use a weight function rather than a probabilistic model (in which all the above summations would have been equal to 1) to maintain the compatibility with the multiple ranges of variation and to keep similar results. We have indeed :

THEOREM 13 : *The generating function associated to our set of weighted terms is :*

$$W(z) = \sum_{t \in TP(F,w)} w(t) z^{|t|} = \sum_{f_i \in F} w(f_i) \left(\prod_{r=1}^{p} d_r^{f_{i,r}} \right) z^{\omega_i + 1}$$

(for the usual size for example).

For a node i of the discrimination tree, we define the weight of the i-pattern W_i as the product of the weight of its already instanciated symbols (variables having by convention a weight equal to 1). For a node i of the join network, we define the weight of the i-pattern as $W_i = \prod_{j_i=1}^{l} W_{j_i}$. With these conventions, once more, *all the previous results are only modified by the multiplicative constant* W_i, *the weight of the i-pattern.*

One can determine ***statically*** the weights of the symbol by considering the initial Working Memory, or ***dynamically*** by considering the right handside of the rules and the adding or suppression of certain patterns.

VI. The negation

We have explained at the end of **(2.1)** the functioning of a NOT join node (note that the length of output tuples is the length of the left input tuples). We can easily extend the previous calculations to a model taking into account the *negation.* More precisely, we can also consider non-equality tests between variables and the negation of condition-patterns in the left-hand side of the rules.

In the former case one considers negation inside patterns. Let us consider the following example : $(Head\ \ X\ \neg X)$. The average number of terms matching with this pattern is equal to the average number of terms matching with $(Head\ \ X\ Y)$ minus the average number of terms matching with $(Head\ \ X\ X)$. That can be easily extended to the negation of several variables in a pattern.

Let us consider now the negation of a condition-pattern or of a tuple of condition-patterns.

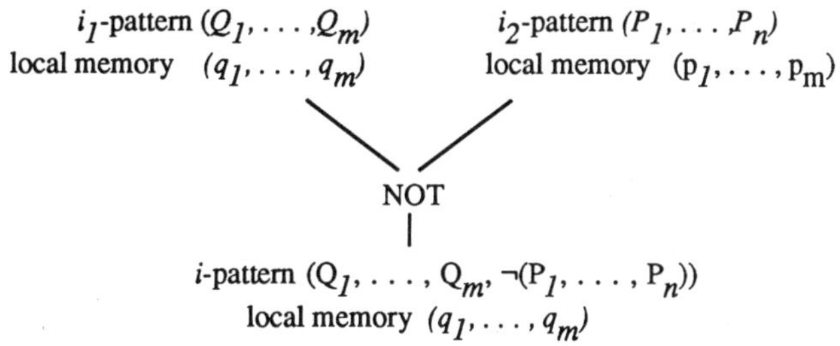

Figure 2 : NOT Join

Let us consider a NOT-join node i (see figure 2). We know the matching-rate of the node i_2 : $\overline{rate_{i_2}}$ and the matching-rate of the node i_1 : $\overline{rate_{i_1}}$. The matching rate of the pattern $\neg(P_1, \ldots, P_n)$ is $1 - \overline{rate_{i_2}}$ and thus the matching rate of the node i corresponding to the i-pattern $(Q_1, \ldots, Q_m, \neg(P_1, \ldots, P_n))$ is $\overline{rate_i} = \overline{rate_{i_1}}(1 - \overline{rate_{i_2}})$ (if the variables of all the P_i are distinct from the variables of all the Q_j, otherwise we modify in this formula $rate_{i_2}$ with the previous reasoning as for node **12** in our example, see appendix). The matching rates of the join nodes that are under this node i (*i.e.* that can be reached from i) are modified in the same way: we determine their usual matching rate forgetting the existence of the tuple of patterns $\neg(P_1, \ldots, P_n)$ and we multiply this result to obtain the real matching rate by the coefficient $(1 - \overline{rate_{i_2}})$ (that implies that the computation of the matching rates is easier top-down in the network).

VII. Composed queries in Relational Databases

In this Part, we shall show that our previous calculations can be easily extended to estimate the average size of a composed query (with possible selections) in a Relational Database.

7.1. Model for the equijoin

From now on, according to Database's vocabulary, we will represent the *relation* $R[X, Y]$ instead of the previous pattern $(R \;\; X \;\; Y)$. To determine a *query* in a Relational Database means to find the number of *tuples* (previously terms) that instanciate a relation. *Selection* operations correspond to the tests of the discrimination tree. The *size of a relation* is from now on the average number of tuples that instanciate this relation (we have to forget the previous notion of size of a term).

The type of join we have studied is called *equijoin* in Relational Database; we shall keep on using the word join in what follows. We represent the join between a relation A and a relation B on the attribute (or argument) X by $A[X, Y] \bowtie B[X, Z]$. We are going to determine the average number of tuples (l-tuples) that instanciate a composed query (after possible selections) (see [Alb 89], [Rosen 81], [GP 84] and [GP 88]). For example we want to find the average size of

$$R[a_0, X, Y] \bowtie S[a_1, X, Z] \bowtie T[Y, Z, U, b, Z'] \bowtie \ldots$$

which can be seen as the instanciation of the left-hand side of a rewriting rule.

7.2. Combinatorial study with a Database of k tuples

The tuples are always formed as in $FT(F)$ and we denote their set by $T(F)$. We still denote by $D_1, \ldots, D_p$ the ranges of variation for the constants and by $f_{i,1}, \ldots, f_{i,p}$ the p-tuple that describes the variation of the arguments of a relation symbol f_i. Since we are not interested in the size of a tuple, we can propose for all of them a size 1. Thus the generating function associated with $T(F)$ is :

$$Q(z) = \sum_{f \in F} \left(\prod_{r=1}^{p} d_r^{\,f_{i,r}} \right) z$$

We have to adapt the modelling for the Relational Database. There are indeed no repetitions in Databases and we shall represent a Relational Database with a *set* of tuples. The generating function that counts the sets of tuples of $T(F)$ is :

$$E(z) = \prod_{t \in T(F)} (1+z) = (1+z)^{\sum_{f \in F} (\prod_{r=1}^{p} d_r^{f_{i,r}})} = (1+z)^{Q(1)}$$

For a relation i, $x_{i,r}$ still denotes the number of distinct variables of i belonging to D_r; we have

THEOREM 14 : *The generating function of the tuples that instanciate relation i is*

$$B_i(z) = \left(\prod_{r=1}^{p} d_r^{x_{i,r}} \right) z$$

We can now prove (see [Alb 89]) :

THEOREM 15 : *Considering any Relational Database with k tuples, the average number of tuples that instanciate a relation i is :*

$$\overline{b_{i,k}} = \left(\prod_{r=1}^{p} d_r^{x_{i,r}} \right) \frac{k}{Q(1)}$$

When we consider a composed join i, we define the same corrective factor $y_{i,r}$ due to the join in D_r. The reasoning of theorem 5 is still valid and we have :

THEOREM 16 : *The average number of l-tuples that instanciate a composed relation i (from l initial relations) is :*

$$\overline{b_{i,n}} = \left(\prod_{r=1}^{p} d_r^{x_{i,r}} \right) \frac{k^l}{Q(1)^l}$$

and the matching rate of this composed join is :

$$\overline{\varrho_i} = \frac{(\prod_{r=1}^{p} d_r^{x_{i,r}})}{Q(1)^l}$$

Let us note that the results we have obtained are exact (and they correspond to the estimation found with the multiset model).

Often we have some more precise information on a Relational Database, and this will enable us to precise the previous study.

7.3. Databases with known sizes of relation

In real applications, one often has an idea of the initial sizes of relation in the initial Relational Database (empirically or with a distribution law). Therefore, we shall not perform average calculations over an arbitrary Database of k tuples any longer but over an arbitrary Database that follows these characteristics. Let us denote k_i the supposed size of relation i; we can propose a more precise generating function for $T(F)$:

$$Q(u_1, \ldots, u_{|F|}) = \sum_{j=1}^{|F|} \left(\prod_{r=1}^{p} d_r^{f_{j,r}} \right) u_j$$

with u_j marking the maximal size of relation j. Thus, the generating function of sets formed with tuples of $T(F)$ is :

$$E(u_1, \ldots, u_{|F|}) = \prod_{j=1}^{|F|} (1+u_j)^{\prod_{r=1}^{p} d_r^{f_{j,r}}}$$

$[u_1^{q_1} \ldots u_{|F|}^{q_{|F|}}] E(u_1, \ldots, u_{|F|})$ is the number of Relational Databases with exactly q_j tuples that instanciate relation j. We obtain :

THEOREM 17 : *The generating function of the tuples that instanciate relation i is :*

$$B_i(u_1, \ldots, u_{|F|}) = \left(\prod_{r=1}^{p} d_r{}^{x_{i,r}} \right) u_i$$

and we find ([alb 89]) :

THEOREM 18 : *The average number of tuples that instanciate a relation i is :*

$$\overline{b_{i,k_1,\ldots,k_{|F|}}} = \left(\prod_{r=1}^{p} d_r{}^{x_{i,r} - f_{i,r}} \right) k_i \qquad (x_{i,r} - f_{i,r} \leq 0)$$

for an arbitrary input Relational Database with q_j tuples that instanciate relation j.

Example : Let us consider the relation $A[a_0, Y]$. If there is k_a tuples that have A as relation symbol in any input Relational Database; if the range of variation for the first variable (resp. the second) of A has d_1 elements (resp. d_2); we have

$$\overline{b_{k_a}} = \frac{k_a}{d_1}$$

since $f_1 = 1$, $f_2 = 1$, $x_1 = 0$ and $x_2 = 1$.

Remark : As we see, the average size of relation i only depends on its initial size. *From now on, we shall not need the initial sizes of other relations.*

The average size for a composed join i, can always be obtained with the reasoning of theorem 5. Thus

THEOREM 19 : *Let us consider any input Relational Database with q_j tuples that instanciate relation j and a multiple equijoin from l initial relations j_i. The average number of l-tuples that instanciate relation i is :*

$$\overline{b_{i,k_1,\ldots,k_{|F|}}} = \left(\prod_{r=1}^{p} d_r{}^{x_{i,r}} \right) \frac{\prod_{j_i=1}^{l} k_{j_i}}{\prod_{j_i=1}^{l} \prod_{r=1}^{p} d_r{}^{f_{j_i,r}}}$$

and the matching rate of i is :

$$\overline{\chi_i} = \frac{(\prod_{r=1}^{p} d_r{}^{x_{i,r}})}{\prod_{j_i=1}^{l} (\prod_{r=1}^{p} d_r{}^{f_{j_i,r}})}$$

with $x_{i,r}$ the number of distinct variables of relation i in D_r.

Example : Let us consider the average size of the standard join i :

$$R[X, Y] \bowtie S[X, Z]$$

Let us assume that we know the size of the initial relations $R[X, Y]$ and $S[X, Z]$, *i.e.* respectively r and s. Let us denote by d_X, d_Y and d_Z the sizes of the ranges of variation of variables X, Y and Z. We have $x_{i,X} = 1$, $x_{i,Y} = 1$, $x_{i,Z} = 1$, $f_{R,X} = 1$, $f_{R,Y} = 1$, $f_{R,Z} = 0$, $f_{S,X} = 1$, $f_{S,Y} = 0$ and $f_{S,Z} = 1$ whence

$$\overline{b_{i,r,s}} = d_X d_Y d_Z \frac{rs}{d_X d_Y d_X d_Z} = \frac{rs}{d_X}$$

and we find again the well-known result of Rosenthal ([Rosen 81]).

Lastly we shall detail the example of Section **7.1** :

$$R[a_0, X, Y] \bowtie S[a_1, X, Z] \bowtie T[Y, Z, U, b, Z']$$

Let us denote the sizes of the ranges of variation of the variables by d_X, d_Y, d_Z (Z and Z' are two different variables that vary in the same range), d_U, d_a and d_b (the sizes of the range of variation of constants a_0, a_1 and b respectively). We know the number of tuples with function symbol R, S or T, *i.e.* r, s and t respectively. We have $f_{R,X} = 1$, $f_{R,Y} = 1$, $f_{R,Z} = 0$, $f_{R,U} = 0$, $f_{R,a} = 1$, $f_{R,b} = 0$, $f_{S,X} = 1$, $f_{S,Y} = 0$,

$f_{S,Z} = 1$, $f_{S,U} = 0$, $f_{S,a} = 1$, $f_{S,b} = 0$, $f_{T,X} = 0$, $f_{T,Y} = 1$, $f_{T,Z} = 2$, $f_{T,U} = 1$, $f_{T,a} = 0$, $f_{T,b} = 1$. and for relation i $x_{i,X} = 1$, $x_{i,Y} = 1$, $x_{i,Z} = 2$, $x_{i,U} = 1$, $x_{i,a} = 0$, $x_{i,b} = 0$. Therefore we have with theorem 19 :

$$\overline{b_{i,r,s,t}} = d_X d_Y {d_Z}^2 d_U \frac{rst}{d_a d_X d_Y d_a d_X d_Z d_Y {d_Z}^2 d_U d_b} = \frac{rst}{d_X d_Y d_Z {d_a}^2 d_b}$$

VIII. Conclusion

We have precised in Section **(2.2)** the notion of average cost for RETE algorithm. This average time complexity is given by formula (1) in Section **3.3**. Formula (1) gives the average cost to compute the set of satisfied rules from the set of initial facts and a fixed set of rules with RETE algorithm. This result is given in function of the average sizes of local memories in the RETE network. These quantities are formulated according to the different models in theorem : 6 for the list model, 10 for the multiset model, at the end of **5.1** when you consider multiple ranges of variation for constants, at the end of **5.2** when you consider different probabilities on symbols. All these expressions can be computed from the parameters of any particular Rule Base and Working Memory.

These theoretical results are experimented on the inference engine Xrete [LCR 88] and we develop for this system an automatic performance analyser from the results of this paper (Clark developed "similar" experimentations on LISP language [Clark 79]). Besides, these theoretical results enable us to propose, as an optimization of the algorithm, a reordoring of the nodes of the network in order to decrease the sizes of local memories.

We saw in Section **5.1** and in Part **6** that we can take into account a test of inequality and negation. As it has been mentioned in the case of the hashing of local memories, the formulae we have obtained can be adapted to many variants of RETE algorithm (see [Alb 88] for the ARBRE D'UNIFICATION).

We can use the same reasoning in Relational Databases. Indeed, in Part 7 theorem 16, we have presented the average size of a composed equijoin (with possible selections) considering any Relational Database with k tuples. We even have precised these results when the initial sizes of relations to be joined are known (**7.3** theorem 19). These results are also used to improve queries in Relational Databases. (system COSMA [RS 89]).

The work presented in this article, proves once more the power and the easy use of the generating function theory for the precise analysis of algorithms.

IX. Bibliography

[Alb 87] L. Albert, "Présentation et évaluation de la complexité de l'algorithme RETE de multi-pattern matching dans les systèmes de règles de production", rapport de DEA, Université de PARIS XI, ENS, rapport de recherche 87-8 LCR Thomson-CSF, 1987.

[Alb 88] L. Albert, "Présentation et évaluation de la complexité en moyenne d'algorithms de filtrage dans les moteurs d'inférences (Rete et arbre d'unification)", *Revue d' intelligence artificielle*, volume 2, Hermes, 1988, pp. 7-40.

[Alb 89] L. Albert, "Complexité en moyenne de l'algorithme de multi-pattern matching RETE sur des ensembles de patterns et d'objets de profondeur 1", INRIA Research Report 1009, 1989.

[AF 88] L. Albert, F. Fages, "Average case complexity analysis of the RETE pattern match algorithm", proceedings of the 15th International Colloquium on Automata, Languages and Programming, Lecture Notes in Computer Science, 317, Springer-Verlag, Tampere, Finland, July 1988.

[dB 58] NG de Bruijn, *Asymptotic Methods in Analysis*, Dover 1958.

[CKS 86] C.Choppy, S.Kaplan, M.Soria, "Algorithmic complexity of term rewriting systems", Proceedings of the First Conference on Rewriting Techniques and Applications, Dijon, France, 1986.

[Clark 79] D.W. Clark, "Measurements of Dynamic List Structures Use in Lisp", IEEE Transactions on Software Engineering SE-5(1), pp. 51-59. (Jan. 1979).

[Dieu 68] J. Dieudonné, *Calcul infinitésimal*, Hermann, 1968.

[Dufr 84] P. Dufresne, "Contribution algorithmique à l'inférence par règles de production", Thèse Université Paul Sabatier, Toulouse, 1984.

[DNM 78] J. McDermott, A. Newell, J. Moore , "The efficiency of certain production system implementations", in *Pattern-Directed Inference Systems* (Waterman et Hayes-Roth ed.) Academic Press, New York, 1978, pp. 155-176.

[Fag 86] F. Fages, "On the proceduralization of rules in expert systems", First France-Japan Symposium on Artificial Intelligence, Programming of Future Generation Computers, Addison-Wesley, Eds. M. Nivat and K. Fuchi, Tokyo, Nov., 1986.

[Fag 88] F. Fages, "Rulebased extension of programming langages", Proceedings of Les systèmes experts et leurs applications, Avignon, 1988.

[Fla 85] P. Flajolet, "Mathematical methods in the analysis of algorithms and data structures", INRIA, Research Report 400, 1985. To appear in A Graduate Course in Computer Science,Computer Science Press, 1987.

[Fla 87] P. Flajolet, "The symbolic operator method", *Mathematical methods in the analysis of algorithms and data structure*, L.N.C.S., Springer Verlag, to appear, 1987.

[Forg 79] C. Forgy, "On the efficient implementation of production systems", PhD Thesis, Carnegie Mellon University, 1979.

[Forg 81] C. Forgy, "OPS-V user's manual", Computer Science Department, Carnegie Mellon University, Pittsburgh, MA, 1981.

[Forg 82] C. Forgy, "RETE, a fast algorithm for the many patterns many objects Match problem", *Artificial Intelligence* 19, 1982, pp. 17-37.

[FS 86] P. Flajolet, R. Sedgewick, "Mathematical analysis of algorithms", Computer Science 504, Lecture Notes for Princeton University, 1986.

[FSS] P. Flajolet, P. Sipala et J.M. Steyaert, "The analysis of tree compaction in symbolic manipulations", preprint.

[FV 87] P. Flajolet, J. Vitter,"Average Case Analysis of Algorithms and Data Structures", in *A Handbook of Theoretical Computer Science*, North-Holland, 1987.

[GD 84] M. Ghallab, P. Dufresne, "Moteurs d'inférences pour systèmes de règles de production : techniques de compilation et d'interprétation", Colloque d'Intelligence Artificielle, Marseille, Oct. 1984, pp. 89-103.

[GF 83] A. Gupta et C.L. Forgy, "Measurements on production systems", Carnegie Mellon University, Technical Report CMU-CS-83-167, 1983.

[Gha 80] M. Ghallab, "New optimal decision tree for matching patterns in inference and planning system", 2nd Int. Meeting on Artificial Intelligence, Leningrad, Oct. 1980.

[GP 84] D. Gardy, C.Puech, "On the size of projection: a generating function approach", Information Systems, Vol. 9, No 3/4, pp. 231-235, 1984.

[GP 88] D. Gardy, C.Puech, "On the effect of join operations on relation sizes", to appear in ACM Transactions On Database Systems.

[Gupt 84] A. Gupta, "Parallelism in production Systems : the sources and the expected Speed-up", Carnegie Mellon University Technical Report CMU-CS-84-169, 1984.

[Henr 74] P. Henrici, *Applied and Computational complex Analysis*, Volumes 1-3, Wiley, New-York.

[LCR 88] Laboratoire central de Recherches, *Xrete : manuel de référence*, Thomson-CSF, domaine de Corbeville 91401 Orsay Cedex France, 1988.

[Mir 87] D.P. Miranker, "TREAT: A Better Match Algorithm for AI Production Systems", Proceedings of the 1987 National Conference on Artificial Intelligence, Seattle, Washington, 1987.

[MM 78] A. Meier, J.W. Moon, "On the altitude of nodes in random trees", *Canadian Journal of Math* 30, 1978, pp. 997-1015.

[Rosen 81] A.S. Rosenthal, "Note on the expected size of a join", SIGMOD Record 11(4), pp. 19-25, july 1981.

[RS 89] M. Regnier, E. Simon, "Efficient evaluation of production rules in a DBMS", Proceedings of V^{ièmes} Journées Bases de Données Avancées, Genève, 1989.

[SF 83] J.M. Steyaert, P. Flajolet, "Patterns and pattern match in trees : an analysis", *Information and Control* 58, 1983, pp. 19-58.

[SF 88] Schang T. and Fages F. "A Real-Time Expert System for On-Board Radar Identification" 55th Symposium AVP-AGARD on Software Engineering and its Applications to Avionics, 1988.

[Stey 84] J.M. Steyaert, "Complexité et structures des algorithmes", Thèse d'Etat, Université de Paris 7, 1984.

[Vien 86] G. Viennot, "La combinatoire bijective par l'exemple", Université de Bordeaux 1, 1986.

[WGF 86] M.L. Wright, M.W. Green, G.Fiegl, P.F. Cross, "An Expert System for Real-Time Control", SRI International, in IEEE Software, March 1986.

Appendix

We develop numerically the example of the three rules of Section **2.1**, the RETE network of which is represented in figure 1. In **3.1**, we precised the characteristics of this example (generating function, average size, ...). We present on the drawing of the network the matching rate of each node for the list and the multiset models with only one range of variation for constants and a uniform distribution. Matching rates are in *italic* for the list model and **bold-faced** for the multiset model.

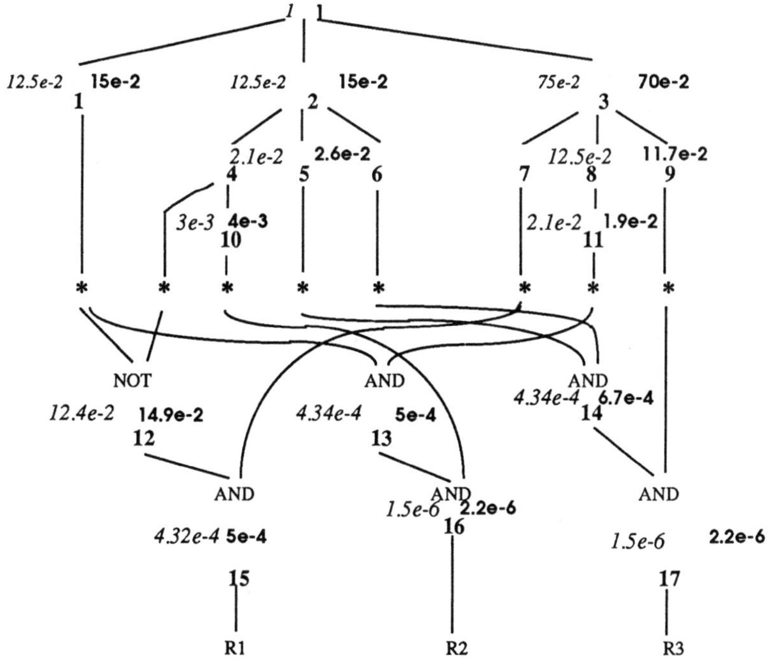

(for writing conveniences, we wrote but once the matching rates at nodes **4**, **5**, **6** and **7**, **8**, **9**. Because we have $\overline{rate_4} = \overline{rate_5} = \overline{rate_6}$ and $\overline{rate_7} = \overline{rate_8} = \overline{rate_9}$ in both models).

We obtained the matching rate at node **12** with :

$$\overline{rate}((g\ \ X\ Y), \neg(f\ \ a0\ X)) = \overline{rate}(g\ \ X\ Y) - \overline{rate}((g\ \ X\ Y), (f\ \ a0\ X))$$

Remark : Note that the average number of terms or of l-tuples of terms that match at a node i is obtained by multiplying the matching rate by k^l with k the number of terms of the input Working Memory and l the length of the output tuples of terms at i.

THE FROBENIUS PROBLEM

Ravi Kannan[1]
Department of Computer Science, Carnegie-Mellon University
Pittsburgh, PA, USA 15213

Abstract This paper considers the "Frobenius problem" : Given n natural numbers $a_1, a_2, \dots a_n$ such that the greatest common divisor of $a_1, a_2, \dots a_n$ equal to 1, find the largest natural number that is not expressible as a nonnegative integer combination of them. This problem is NP-hard; but for the cases $n = 2, 3$ polynomial time algorithms are known to solve it. Here a polynomial time algorithm is given for every fixed n. This is done by first proving an exact relation between the Frobenius problem and a geometric concept called the "covering radius". Then a polynomial time algorithm is developed for finding the covering radius of any polytope in a fixed number of dimensions. The last algorithm relies on a structural theorem proved here that describes for any polytope K, the set $K + \mathbf{Z}^n = \{x : x \in \mathbf{R}^n ; x = y + z ; y \in K ; z \in \mathbf{Z}^n\}$. The proof of the structural theorem relies on some recent developments in the Geometry of Numbers. In particular, it draws on the notion of "width" and covering radius introduced in Kannan and Lovàsz [7], a theorem of Hastad [5] bounding the width of lattice-point-free convex bodies and the techniques of Kannan, Lovász and Scarf [8] to study the shapes of a polyhedron obtained by translating each facet parallel to itself. The concepts involved are defined from first principles.

Notation

$\mathbf{R}^n$ is Euclidean n space. The lattice of all integer vectors in $\mathbf{R}^n$ is denoted $\mathbf{Z}^n$. For any two sets $S, T \subseteq \mathbf{R}^n$, we denote by $S + T$ the set $\{s + t : s \in S; t \in T\}$. For any positive real, λ, we denote by λS, the set $\{\lambda s : s \in S\}$. For any set W in $\mathbf{R}^{n+l}$ and any set V in $\mathbf{R}^l$, we denote by W/V the set

$$\{x : x \in \mathbf{R}^n \text{ such that there exists a } y \in V \text{ with } (x, y) \in W\}.$$

W/V is the set obtained by "projecting out" V from W.

A **copolyhedron** is the intersection of a finite number of half spaces - some of them closed and the others open. ("co" for closed / open.) If a copolyhedron is bounded, I will call it a copolytope.

Some statements in the paper will assert "the algorithm *finds* copolytope P_i.......". The precise meaning of this statement is as follows : suppose P_i is in $\mathbf{R}^n$. The algorithm will find a rational $m \times (n + l)$ matrix A and a rational $m \times 1$ vector b where l is at most some polynomial function of n and for each row of A, either the $\leq$ or the $<$ sign such that P_i equals

$$\{x : x \in \mathbf{R}^n \text{ such that there exists a } y \in \mathbf{R}^l \text{ with } A\binom{x}{y}\binom{\leq}{<}b\}.$$

By a "rational polyhedron", we mean a polyhedron that can be described by a system of inequalities that have rational coefficients; the inequalities may have irrational right hand sides.

In much of the paper A will be a fixed $m \times n$ matrix. If the meaning of A is clear from the context, for any b in $\mathbf{R}^m$, the polyhedron $\{x \in \mathbf{R}^n : Ax \leq b\}$ will be denoted by K_b.

A basis B of the lattice $\mathbf{Z}^n$ is a set of n linearly independent vectors $\{b_1, b_2, \dots b_n\}$ in $\mathbf{Z}^n$, such that each member of $\mathbf{Z}^n$ can be expressed as an integer linear combination of $\{b_1, b_2, \dots b_n\}$. The "fundamental parallelopied" corresponding to B is the set $\{x : x = \sum_{i=1}^{n} \lambda_i b_i$ where $\lambda_i \in \mathbf{R}$ satisfy $0 \leq \lambda_i < 1\}$. It is denoted $F(B)$. For each point y in $\mathbf{R}^n$, there is a unique lattice point z such that $z + F(B)$ contains y. The parallelopied $z + F(B)$ is denoted $F(B; y)$.

In most of the paper, the only lattices that occur are $\mathbf{Z}^r$ for some natural number r. In section 2, we use more general lattices. A lattice in general is the set of all integer linear combinations of a set of linearly independent vectors in Euclidean space.

[1]Supported by NSF-Grant CCR 8805199

1 Introduction

The Frobenius problem can be rephrased as follows : "Given n coins of denominations $a_1, a_2, \ldots a_n$, with $\text{GCD}(a_1, a_2, \ldots a_n)$ equal to 1, what is the largest integer amount of money for which change cannot be made with these coins ? " Note that the GCD condition implies that we can in fact make change for any large enough integer amount of money. The simple statement of the Frobenius problem makes it attractive. It is possible to show that the problem is NP-hard in general; the proof is not given here. For the special case of $n = 2$, the answer is explicitly known - it is $a_1a_2 - a_1 - a_2$. The proof of this is elementary. (See for example [16]) A polynomial time algorithm to solve the Frobenius problem in the case $n = 3$ was developed in 1977 by Rödseth [12] based on the results of Selmer and Beyer[17]. There is some literature on the general problem - see for example [3] and [16]. No polynomial time is known for fixed n greater than 3. This paper develops one for any fixed n. It might seem that this result would follow from the result of Lenstra [10] that Integer Programming in a fixed number of variables can be solved in polynomial time ; but note that a näive solution to the Frobenius problem involves solving (in the worst case) an exponential number of Integer Programs - one each to determine for each natural number b whether b can be expressed as a nonnegative integer combination of $a_1, a_2, \ldots a_n$. Some pruning is possible, but no such direct method is known to work.

The Frobenius problem is related to the study of maximal lattice point free convex bodies, a topic of long-standing interest in the Geometry of Numbers. This relation is described by Lovász in [11]. He also formulates a conjecture which he proves would imply a polynomial time algorithm for the Frobenius problem for a fixed number of integers. The structural result of this paper does not prove this conjecture, but does imply a closely related one as shown in section 6 . Scarf and Shallcross [14] have recently observed a somewhat direct relation between maximal lattice free convex bodies and the Frobenius problem. There have been some applications of the Frobenius problem to a sorting method called Shell-Sort - see for example Incerpi and Sedgwick [6] and Sedgwick [15].

In section 2, the Frobenius problem for n coins is exactly related to the "covering radius" of a certain simplex in $\mathbf{R}^{n-1}$. The notion of covering radius for the so-called centrally symmetric convex sets is a classical notion in the Geometry of Numbers ; in [7], it was introduced and studied for general convex sets. It is defined as follows :

For a closed convex set P of nonzero volume in $\mathbf{R}^n$, and a lattice L of dimension n also in $\mathbf{R}^n$, the least positive real t so that $tP + L$ equals $\mathbf{R}^n$ is called the "covering radius" of P with respect to L. It will be denoted by $\mu(P, L)$.

In words, the covering radius is the least amount t by which we must "blow up" P and one copy of P placed at each lattice point so that all of space is covered.

Suppose K is a closed bounded convex set in $\mathbf{R}^n$ and v is an element of $\mathbf{R}^n$. The **width of K along** v is $\max\{v \cdot x : x \in K\} - \min\{v \cdot x : x \in K\}$. The **width of K** (with respect to the lattice $\mathbf{Z}^n$) is defined to be the minimum width of K along any nonzero integer vector. Note that this differs from the usual definition of the geometric width of K, where the minimum is over all unit vectors v rather than all nonzero integer vectors. The width as defined here is greater than or equal to the geometric width since nonzero integer vectors have length at least one.

The following so-called "flatness theorem" is proved by Hastad [5] using the results of Lagarias, Lenstra and Schnorr [9].

Flatness Theorem If the width of a closed bounded convex set K in $\mathbf{R}^n$ of nonzero volume is at least $n^{5/2}/2$, then K contains a point of $\mathbf{Z}^n$.

Remark : The condition of nonzero volume is necessary as seen by the following example : $K = \{x \in \mathbf{R}^2 : x_1 \geq 1; x_1 = \sqrt{2}x_2\}$. However, in the case that K is a rational polyhedron, i.e., K is described by a system of linear inequalities with rational coefficients, the assumption of nonzero volume can be dispensed with in the above theorem. (This follows from the simple observation that if such a polyhedron has zero volume, than its width must be zero along some nonzero integer direction, namely along one of its facet directions.) I will, in fact, use this version of the theorem for rational polyhedra.

Kannan, Lovász and Scarf [8] show that for any fixed $m \times n$ matrix A satisfying some nondegeneracy condition, there is a small finite set V of nonzero integer vectors such that for any "right hand side" b, there is some $v(b)$ belonging to V such that the polytope $K_b = \{x : Ax \leq b\}$ has approximately the smallest width along $v(b)$; more precisely, the width of K_b along $v(b)$ is at most twice the width of K_b along any nonzero integer vector. Section 3 of this paper states a result in the same spirit; its proof is deferred to the final paper. There are two differences - here, I do not assume any nondegeneracy condition. Secondly in the result here, b is allowed to vary over some subset of $\mathbf{R}^m$ and the upper bound on the cardinality of V is in terms of the dimension of the affine hull of this subset. Letting the subset be the whole of $\mathbf{R}^m$, we can recover a result similar to [8].

The result of section 3 will be used in the structural theorem proved in section 4 which describes the set $K + \mathbf{Z}^n$ where K is a polyhedron. The proof of this theorem is by induction ; the inductive proof will need a "uniform" description of $K + \mathbf{Z}^n$ as each facet of K is moved parallel to itself in some restricted fashion. In this context, the theorem of section 3 comes in useful.

Section 5 gives an algorithm for finding the covering radius in a fixed number of dimensions using the theorem of section 4.

2 Frobenius problem to Covering Radius

For $a_1, a_2 \ldots, a_n$ positive integers with $gcd(a_1 \ldots, a_n) = 1$, let $Frob(a_1 \ldots, a_n) =$ largest natural number t such that t is not a nonnegative integer combination of $a_1 \ldots, a_n$. The aim of this section is to relate $Frob(a_1, a_2, \ldots a_n)$ to the covering radius of a certain $n-1$ dimensional simplex. This is done in Theorem (2.2).

(2.1) Theorem [2]

$$Frob(a_1 \ldots, a_n) = \max_{l \in \{1,2\ldots,a_n-1\}} \min t_l - a_n \tag{2.1}$$

where $t_l =$ the smallest positive integer congruent to l modulo a_n, that is expressible as nonnegative integer combination of $a_1 \ldots, a_{n-1}$.

Proof: The proof is rather simple. Let N be any positive integer. If $N \equiv 0 (mod\ a_n)$, then N is a nonnegative integer combination of a_n alone. Otherwise, if $N \equiv l(mod\ a_n)$, then N is a nonnegative integer combination of $a_1 \ldots, a_n$ iff $N \geq t_l$.

$$\text{Let} \quad L = \{(x_1 \ldots, x_{n-1}) : x_i \text{ integers and } \sum_{i=1}^{n-1} a_i x_i \equiv 0(mod\ a_n)\} \tag{2.2}$$

$$\text{and let} \quad S = \{(x_1, x_2 \ldots, x_{n-1}) : x_i \geq 0 \text{ reals and } \sum_{i=1}^{n-1} a_i x_i \leq 1\} \tag{2.3}$$

(2.2) Theorem $\mu(S, L) = Frob(a_1, a_2 \ldots, a_n) + a_1 + a_2 + \ldots + a_n$ where $\mu(S, L)$ is the covering radius of S with respect to L.

Proof: Abbreviate $Frob(a_1, a_2, \ldots, a_n)$ by F and $\mu(S, L)$ by μ. First, I show $\mu \leq F + a_1 + a_2 \ldots + a_n$. Suppose $y \in \mathbf{Z}^{n-1}$, and $\sum_1^{n-1} a_i y_i \equiv l(mod\ a_n)$. By definition of t_l, $\exists x_1, \ldots, x_{n-1}, x_n \geq 0$ integers such that

$\sum_{i=1}^{n-1} a_i x_i = t_l = l + a_n x_n$; thus with $x' = (x_1 \ldots, x_{n-1})$, we have $(y - x') \in L$ and $(y - x') + t_l S$ contains $y - x' + x' = y$. Since this is true of any $y \in \mathbf{Z}^n$, and $t_l \leq F + a_n$, we have:

$$\mathbf{Z}^{n-1} \subseteq (F + a_n)S + L \tag{2.4}$$

Further it is clear that $\mathbf{R}^{n-1} \subseteq \mathbf{Z}^{n-1} + (a_1 + \ldots + a_{n-1})S$. To see this, note that for $z \in \mathbf{R}^{n-1}$, we have $\lfloor z \rfloor = (\lfloor z_1 \rfloor, \ldots \lfloor z_{n-1} \rfloor) \in \mathbf{Z}^{n-1}$ and $(z - \lfloor z \rfloor) \in (a_1 + a_2 \ldots + a_{n-1})S$. Hence I have shown

$$\mathbf{R}^{n-1} \subseteq \mathbf{Z}^{n-1} + (a_1 + \ldots + a_{n-1})S \subseteq (F + a_1 + \ldots + a_n)S + L \tag{2.5}$$

Now for the converse: Consider $(F + a_n)S + L$. I claim that $F + a_n$ is the smallest positive real t such that $tS + L$ contains $\mathbf{Z}^{n-1}$. First suppose, for some $t' < F + a_n$, $t'S + L$ contains $\mathbf{Z}^{n-1}$. Then for any $l \in \{1, \ldots, a_n - 1\}$, pick a $y \in \mathbf{Z}^{n-1}$, such that $\sum_1^{n-1} a_i y_i \equiv l(mod\ a_n)$. y is in $t'S + x$ for some x in L, so $(y - x)$ is in $t'S$. But $\sum_1^{n-1} a_i(y_i - x_i) \equiv l(mod\ a_n)$ and $y_i - x_i \geq 0 \forall_i$, implies that $t_l \leq t'$. Since this is true of any l, we have $F \leq t' - a_n < F$ a contradiction (using Theorem (2.1)).

Conversely, for any $y \in \mathbf{Z}^{n-1}$, if $\sum_1^{n-1} a_i y_i \equiv l(mod\ a_n)$, since $t_l \leq F + a_n$, $\exists x_1, \ldots,, x_{n-1} \geq 0$ integers so that $\sum_1^{n-1} a_i x_i \equiv l \equiv \sum_1^{n-1} a_i y_i (mod a_n)$ and $\sum_1^{n-1} a_i x_i = t_l$. Then $(y - x) \in L$ and $(y - x) + t_l S$ contains $(y - x) + x = y$, so $L + (F + a_n)S$ contains y. Thus I have shown:

$$F + a_n = \min\{t : t > 0, \text{ real and } tS + L \supseteq \mathbf{Z}^{n-1}\} \tag{2.6}$$

By (2.6), we see that $\exists y \in \mathbf{Z}^{n-1}$, such that for any $x \in L$, with $y_i - x_i \geq 0 \forall_i$, we have $\sum_{i=1}^{n-1} a_i(y_i - x_i) \geq F + a_n$. Now let ϵ be any real number with $o < \epsilon < 1$ and consider the point $p = (p_1, p_2, \ldots p_{n-1})$ defined by $p_i = y_i + (1 - \epsilon) \forall i$. Suppose q is any point of L such that $p_i \geq q_i \forall i$. Then q_i are all integers, so we must have $q_i \leq y_i \forall_i$.

$$\text{So, } \sum_1^{n-1} a_i(p_i - q_i) = (\sum_1^{n-1} a_i)(1 - \epsilon) + \sum_1^{n-1} a_i(y_i - q_i) \geq (1 - \epsilon) \sum_1^{n-1} a_i + (F + a_n)$$

by the above.

Since this argument holds for any $\epsilon \in (0\ \ 1)$, we have $\mu \geq F + \sum_1^n a_i$.

Together with (2.5) now, Theorem (2.2) is proved.

∎

Remark : By applying a suitable linear transformation, we can "send" L to $\mathbf{Z}^{n-1}$. This sends the simplex S to some simplex whose constraint matrix is still rational. I assume this has been done ; in the coming sections, I will deal only with covering radii of sets with respect to the standard lattice of integer points.

3 Vectors along which K_b have small width

(3.1) Lemma : Suppose A is an $m \times n$ matrix of integers. For each $b \in \mathbf{R}^m$, we denote by K_b the polyhedron $\{x : Ax \leq b\}$. Let P be a copolytope in $\mathbf{R}^m$ of affine dimension j_o such that for all $b \in P$, K_b is nonempty and bounded . Let M be $\max\{|b| : b \in P\}$. There is an algorithm that finds a partition of P into copolytopes $P_1, P_2, \ldots P_r$ and for each copolytope P_i, it finds a nonzero integer vector v_i and $n \times m$ matrices T_i, T_i' such that

for all i, $1 \leq i \leq r$ and all $b \in P_i$, we have

- The point $T_i b$ maximizes the linear function $v_i \cdot x$ over x in K_b.
- The point $T_i' b$ minimizes the linear function $v_i \cdot x$ over x in K_b and

•

$$\text{either} \quad \text{Width}_{v_i}(K_b) \leq 1$$
$$\text{or } \forall u \neq 0, u \in \mathbf{Z}^n, \ \text{Width}_{v_i}(K_b) \leq 2\text{Width}_u(K_b).$$

Further, the algorithm works in time polynomial in data and $\log M$ if n, j_o are fixed.

Proof A complete proof is rather long and so is deferred to the final paper. Here, I try to give a very brief idea of the proof, in fact only of what the nonzero integer vectors $v_1, v_2, \ldots$ are. The first few of them will be the rows of A. This leaves us to worry only about the K_b of nonzero volume that have width at least one along each of the facet directions. After translating any such K_b so that its center of gravity is now 0, it will be of the form $\{x : Ax \leq c\}$ where $1/(n+1) \leq c_i \leq M2^\alpha$ for all i where α is bounded by a polynomial in the length of the input . This plus the fact that for any $b, b' \geq 0$ with $b' \leq b \leq 2b'$, we have $K_{b'} \subseteq K_b \subseteq 2K_{b'}$ are used in the proof.

(3.2) Lemma : Suppose K is a rational polyhedron in $\mathbf{R}^n$ and $v \in \mathbf{Z}^n \setminus \{0\}$ satisfies

$$\text{either} \ \ \text{Width}_v(K) \leq 1$$
$$\text{or } \forall u \neq 0, u \in \mathbf{Z}^n, \ \text{Width}_v(K) \leq 2\text{Width}_u(K).$$

Suppose also that y is in K and $v \cdot y = \alpha$. For $\beta \in \mathbf{R}$, denote by $H(\beta)$ the set $\{x \in \mathbf{R}^n : v \cdot x = \beta\}$. Let $s = n^{5/2} + 1$. Then for all $\gamma \in (\alpha \ \ \alpha + 1]$, we have

$$(K + \mathbf{Z}^n) \cap H(\gamma) = \left[K + \left(\bigcup_{k=-s}^{s} (\mathbf{Z}^n \cap H(k))\right)\right] \quad \cap \quad H(\gamma).$$

Proof : Follows from the Flatness theorem. Left to the final paper.

4 The Main Theorem

In this section, the main theorem is stated and proved. The idea of the theorem is to describe the set $K + \mathbf{Z}^n$ where K is a polyhedron . We assume K is described by m linear inequalities $Ax \leq b$ where A is an $m \times n$ matrix and b an $m \times 1$ vector. If it happens that K is contained in the fundamental parallelopiped $F(B)$ corresponding to some basis B of $L = \mathbf{Z}^n$, then clearly, $K + L = (K \cap F(B)) + L$. This of course is not true in general.

In spirit, the theorem below states that in general, it is enough to look at the portion of $K + L$ (where $L = \mathbf{Z}^n$), contained in some parallelopipeds which are lattice translates of the fundamental parallelopiped corresponding to some bases (note the plural) of L. Further, we need to consider only a "small" number of lattice translates. The number of bases of L as well as the number of lattice translates is bounded above by a function of n alone. The proof of the theorem will be by induction; in the body of the inductive proof, we will look at sets of the form $K' + L'$ where K' is the intersection of K with some lattice hyperplane and L' the intersection of L with the subspace parallel to the hyperplane. We will need to derive a "uniform" description of these sets as the hyperplane is translated parallel to itself. The sections then can be all described as $\{y : A'y \leq b'\}$ where the b' varies as an affine function of b and the position of the hyperplane. To facilitate such an inductive proof, we will consider a more general setting than $K + L$, namely $K_b + L$ where $K_b = \{x : Ax \leq b\}$ and now, we let b vary over a copolytope P in $\mathbf{R}^m$. The theorem will say that for fixed n and the affine dimension of P, we can partition P into a polynomial number of copolytopes such that in each part, there is an uniform description of $K_b + L$.

(4.1) Theorem Let A be an $m \times n$ matrix of integers. Let P be a copolytope in $\mathbf{R}^m$ of affine dimension j_o such that for all $b \in P$, the set $K_b = \{x : Ax \leq b\}$ is nonempty and bounded . There is an algorithm which for any fixed n, j_o runs in time polynomial in the size of A and $\log(\max_{b \in P}(|b|+1))$ and finds subsets $S_1, S_2, \ldots$ of $P \times \mathbf{R}^n$ such that :

1. Each S_i is of the form $S_i'/\mathbf{Z}^l$ where S_i' is a copolyhedron in $\mathbf{R}^{m+n+l}$ and $l \leq n^{3n}$.
2. Letting $S_i(b) = \{x \in \mathbf{R}^n : (b, x) \in S_i\}$, we have for all $b \in P$, $S_i(b) \cap S_j(b) = \emptyset \quad \forall i \neq j$.
3. For all $b \in P$, $\bigcup_i S_i(b) = \mathbf{R}^n$.(i.e., the S_i form a partition of $P \times \mathbf{R}^n$.)
4. For all i and all $b \in P$, $S_i(b) + \mathbf{Z}^n = S_i(b)$.

The algorithm also finds corresponding to each S_i, a collection $\mathcal{B}_i$ of at most n^{3n} bases of $\mathbf{Z}^n$. Corresponding to each basis B in each $\mathcal{B}_i$, it finds an affine transformation $T(B) : \mathbf{R}^m \to \mathbf{R}^n$ and a set $Z(B)$ of at most 2^{n^2} points of $\mathbf{Z}^n$ such that for all i and all $b \in P$, we have

$$(K_b + \mathbf{Z}^n) \cap S_i(b) =$$

$$\left[\left\{\bigcup_{B \in \mathcal{B}_i} ((K_b + Z(B)) \cap F(B; T(B)b))\right\} + \mathbf{Z}^n\right] \cap S_i(b).$$

/*END OF STATEMENT OF THE THEOREM*/

Remark Reminder on some notation : $F(B; y)$ is the lattice translate of the fundamental parallelopiped $F(B)$ corresponding to the basis B, that contains the point y.

Proof : The proof is by induction on n. First, I do the case $n = 1$. Here each row of A can be assumed to be ± 1 ; say the first k rows are $+1$ and the rest -1. We will have $S_1, S_2, \ldots S_k \subseteq P \times \mathbf{R}^1$ defined by

$$S_i = \{(b, x) : b_i \leq b_1, b_i \leq b_2, b_i \leq b_3, \ldots b_i \leq b_k\}.$$

For $(b, x) \in S_i$, we have $b_i \in K_b$. Let $\mathcal{B}_i = \{\{1\}\}$ for all i and let $T(B)$ be the affine transformation defined by $T(B)b = b_i$ for the single basis B in $\mathcal{B}_i$. Finally, let $Z(B) = \{0, -1\}$ for all B. It is easy to check that the theorem is valid with these quantities; this completes the proof for $n = 1$.

It is useful to remark that the role of $T(B)$ is to "get a hold of a point" $T(B)b$ that is guaranteed to be in K_b. We then know that we have all the information needed regarding $K_b + \mathbf{Z}$ by just looking at the intersection of K_b with the parallelopiped containing that point and a neighbouring parallelopiped.

Now we go to general n. First, we may restrict attention to each of the copolytopes that lemma (3.1) partitions P into in turn. So without loss of generality, assume that we know a linear transformations T, T' and a nonzero integer vector v such that for all $b \in P$, we have K_b has "small" width (i.e., width of at most 1 or a width at most twice the minimum width along a nonzero integer direction) along v and Tb minimizes $v \cdot x$ over x in K_b and $T'b$ maximizes $v \cdot x$ over x in K_b.

After a suitable unimodular transformation, we may assume that v is the first unit vector e_1.

Let now $e_1 \cdot Tb = \alpha$. For any real number γ, let $H(\gamma) = \{x \in \mathbf{R}^n : e_1 \cdot x = \gamma\}$. Let $L = \mathbf{Z}^n$.

The idea now will be to obtain an expression for $(K_b + L) \cap H(\gamma)$ as γ varies over $(\alpha \quad \alpha + 1]$. The inductive assumption will enable us to get an expression for each such section and then we will put the sections together.

For any $\beta \in \mathbf{R}$, let $Q(b, \beta) = K_b \cap H(\beta)$. We can find an integer $m \times (n-1)$ matrix C, an $m \times m$ affine transformation D and an $m-$ vector d such that

$$\forall b, \beta \quad Q(b, \beta) = \{(\beta, \hat{x}) : \hat{x} \in \mathbf{R}^{n-1} \text{ satisfies } C\hat{x} \leq Db + \beta d\}.$$

Let $\hat{Q}(b,\beta) = \{\hat{x} \in \mathbf{R}^{n-1} : C\hat{x} \le Db + \beta d\}$.

For $\gamma \in (\alpha \quad \alpha+1]$, we have by lemma (3.2), (with $s = n^{5/2}+1$)

$$(K_b + L) \cap H(\gamma) =$$
$$\left(K_b + \cup_{k=-s}^{s}(L \cap H(k))\right) \cap H(\gamma) =$$
$$\cup_{k=-s}^{s}\{(K_b \cap H(\gamma - k)) + (L \cap H(k))\} =$$
$$\cup_{k=-s}^{s}((Q(b,\gamma-k) + L') + ke_1) \tag{4.2}$$

where $L' = L \cap H(0) = 0 \times \mathbf{Z}^{n-1}$. As stated earlier, γ will vary over the range $(\alpha \quad \alpha+1]$, so $\beta = \gamma - k$ will vary over the range $(\alpha - s \quad \alpha + s + 1]$. Let $I(b) = \{\beta \in (\alpha - s \quad \alpha+s+1] : Q(b,\beta) \ne \emptyset\}$ which is equal to $(\alpha - s \quad \alpha+s+1] \cap [Tb \quad T'b]$. Let $b' = Db + \beta d$. As b varies over P, and β varies over $I(b)$, b' varies over some copolytope P' of affine dimension at most $j_o + 1$. Further, clearly, we can obtain a natural number ν' so that it is bounded in size by a polynomial in the size of A and $\log(\max_{b \in P}(|b|+1))$ and P' is contained in a ball of radius ν' about the origin in $\mathbf{R}^m$. Also, for all $b' \in P'$, we have $\hat{Q}(b') = \{\hat{x} : C\hat{x} \le b'\}$ is nonempty and bounded.

Applying the inductive assumption on $\hat{Q}(b') + \mathbf{Z}^{n-1}$ will give us a partition of $P' \times \mathbf{R}^{n-1}$; clearly, we may substitute $b' = Db + \beta d$ to make this a partition of $P_0 \times \mathbf{R}^{n-1}$ where $P_0 = \{(b,\beta) : b \in P; \beta \in I(b)\}$. So by induction, we get

(4.3) subsets $R_1, R_2, \ldots R_t$ of $P_0 \times \mathbf{R}^{n-1}$ such that

1. R_i is of the form $R_i'/\mathbf{Z}^l$ where R_i' is a copolyhedron in $\mathbf{R}^{m+n+l}$ and $l \le n^{3(n-1)}$ and for all $(b,\beta) \in P_0$

2. $$R_i(b,\beta) \cap R_j(b,\beta) = \emptyset \forall i \ne j$$ [2]

3. $$\bigcup_i R_i(b,\beta) = \mathbf{R}^{n-1}$$

4. $$R_i(b,\beta) + \mathbf{Z}^{n-1} = R_i(b,\beta).$$

For technical convenience, we let $R_0 = \{(b,\beta,x) : T'b < \beta \le \alpha + s + 1; b \in P\}$ and $R_{t+1} = \{(b,\beta,x) : \alpha - s < \beta < Tb; b \in P\}$. Now conditions 1 through 4 above are valid for all (b,β) in $P \times (\alpha - s \quad \alpha+s+1]$.

We also get corresponding to each subset R_i, for $1 \le i \le t$ a collection $\mathcal{B}_i$ of bases of $\mathbf{Z}^{n-1}$ containing at most $n^{3(n-1)}$ bases, and corresponding to each basis B, an affine transformation $T(B)$ and a set $Z(B)$ of points in $\mathbf{Z}^{n-1}$ so that for all $i = 1, 2, \ldots t$ and all $(b,\beta) \in P_0$, we have

$$\left(\hat{Q}(b,\beta) + \mathbf{Z}^{n-1}\right) \cap (R_i(b,\beta)) =$$
$$\left\{\bigcup_{B \in \mathcal{B}_i}\left[(\hat{Q}(b,\beta) + Z(B)) \cap F(B; T(B)\begin{pmatrix} b \\ \beta \end{pmatrix})\right] + \mathbf{Z}^{n-1}\right\} \cap R_i(b,\beta) \tag{4.4}$$

We let $\mathcal{B}_0 = \mathcal{B}_{t+1} = \emptyset$. Since, $\hat{Q}(b,\beta) = \emptyset$ for $\beta \notin [Tb \quad T'b]$, (4.4) is now valid for all (b,β) in $P \times (\alpha - s \quad \alpha + s + 1]$. The subsets of $P \times \mathbf{R}^n$ with which I prove the theorem are obtained as follows : Let $J = \langle i_{-s}, i_{-s+1}, \ldots i_0, \ldots i_s\rangle$ be any $(2s+1)$ - tuple of integers each in the range $[0 \quad t+1]$. There will

[2] Reminder on notation : $R_i(b,\beta) = \{x \in \mathbf{R}^{n-1} : (b,\beta,x) \in R_i\}$.

be one subset S_J in the partition of $P \times \mathbf{R}^n$ for each such J. It is defined as the set of $(b, \beta, x) : b \in P, \beta \in \mathbf{R}, x \in \mathbf{R}^{n-1}$ such that

$$\exists z \in \mathbf{Z} : \beta + z \in (\alpha \quad \alpha + 1] \text{ and } (b, \beta + z - k, x) \in R_{i_k} \text{ for } k = -s, -s+1, \ldots s$$

Note here that b "comes from" P and (β, x) "come from" $\mathbf{R}^n$. It is obvious that the sets S_J are of the form $S'_J/\mathbf{Z}^l$ where the S'_J is a copolyhedron and l is not too high. (In fact, $l \leq 1 + (2s+1)n^{3(n-1)} \leq n^{3n}$.) To show for any b, the intersection of $S_J(b)$ and $S_{J'}(b)$ is empty for $J \neq J'$, we proceed as follows : J and J' must differ in one of their "coordinates", say, in the k th coordinate J has j and J' has j' with $j \neq j'$. For any $b \in P$, and $\beta \in (\alpha - s \quad \alpha + s + 1]$, we have that $R_j(b, \beta)$ and $R_{j'}(b, \beta)$ do not intersect, from this it follows that $S_J(b)$ and $S_{J'}(b)$ do not intersect.

The other two properties required of the collection $\{S_J\}$ - that their union is $\mathbf{R}^n$ for any fixed b and they are invariant under $\mathbf{Z}^n$ also follow easily.

We must now associate a certain set of bases of $\mathbf{Z}^n$ with each S_J. I do this after giving an idea of what the set must be. For each J, say $J = \langle i_{-s}, i_{-s+1}, \ldots i_0, \ldots i_s \rangle$, and for $\gamma \in (\alpha \quad \alpha + 1]$, we get using (4.2),

$$((K_b + L) \cap H(\gamma)) \cap S_J(b) =$$

$$\gamma \times \left[\bigcup_{k=-s}^{s} \left(\hat{Q}(b, \gamma - k) + \mathbf{Z}^{n-1} \right) \right] \quad \cap \quad S_J(b) \tag{4.5}$$

$$\subseteq \bigcup_{k=-s}^{s} \gamma \times \left\{ \left(\hat{Q}(b, \gamma - k) + \mathbf{Z}^{n-1} \right) \cap R_{i_k}(b, \gamma - k) \right\}$$

where the last containment comes from the fact that for γ in the range $(\alpha \quad \alpha + 1]$, if $(b, \gamma, \hat{x})$ belongs to S_J, then $(b, \gamma - k, \hat{x})$ belongs to R_{i_k}. Now, by (4.4), we get,

$$\left(\hat{Q}(b, \gamma - k) + \mathbf{Z}^{n-1} \right) \quad \cap \quad R_{i_k}(b, \gamma - k) = \tag{4.6}$$

$$\left\{ \mathbf{Z}^{n-1} + \left\{ \bigcup_{B \in \mathcal{B}_{i_k}} \left[\left(\hat{Q}(b, \gamma - k) + Z(B) \right) \cap F\left(B; T(B) \begin{pmatrix} b \\ \gamma - k \end{pmatrix} \right) \right] \right\} \right\} \quad \cap \quad R_{i_k}(b, \gamma - k).$$

We can write $T(B)\binom{b}{\beta}$ as $T'_0 b + w'\beta$ where T'_0 is an affine transformation and w' is an $(n-1) \times 1$ vector. Let T_0 be the $n \times m$ matrix with 0 's in the first row and T'_0 in the other rows ; let w be the n vector $\binom{0}{w'}$. Let $z \in \mathbf{Z}^{n-1}$ be such that

$$w' \in F(B) + z.$$

We "complete " B to a basis B' of L as follows : if $B = \{b_1, b_2, \ldots b_{n-1}\}$, then we let B' be the set $\{(0, b_1), (0, b_2), \ldots (0, b_{n-1}), (1, z)\}$.

To define $T(B')$, we proceed as follows : let $B \in \mathcal{B}_{i_k}$. Let $y = T(B)\binom{b}{\gamma - k} = T'_0 b + w'(\gamma - k)$. Let $y' = (0, y)$ and let $y_o = (\gamma - k)e_1 + y'$. Then as γ varies over $(\alpha \quad \alpha + 1]$, y_o varies on the straight line segment p from $T_0 b + (\alpha - k)(e_1 + w) = z_o$, say, to $z_o + e_1 + w$. We can express z_o as Ub where U is an affine transformation. Then it is easy to see that $p \subseteq F(B'; Ub) + C$, where C is the set of 2^n corners of $F(B')$. So we get,

$$\left[0 \times F\left(B; T(B) \begin{pmatrix} b \\ \gamma - k \end{pmatrix} \right) \right] + (\gamma - k)e_1 \subseteq C + F(B'; Ub) \tag{4.7}$$

We will let $U = T(B')$ be the affine transformation corresponding to B'. We let $Z(B') = (0 \times Z(B)) - C$ where again C is the set of corners of $F(B')$. So, we have $|Z(B')| \leq 2^n |Z(B)| \leq 2^{n^2}$ using the inductive assumption. The collection $\mathcal{B}_J$ of bases of L corresponding to S_J is defined as the set of B' defined as above - one for each B in each R_{i_k} for $k = -s, -s+1, \ldots 0, \ldots s$.

Now, for γ belonging to $(\alpha \quad \alpha+1]$, we have

$$(\gamma-k)\times\left[\left(\hat{Q}(b,\gamma-k)+Z(B)\right)\cap F\left(B;T(B)\begin{pmatrix}b\\ \gamma-k\end{pmatrix}\right)\right]$$

$$\subseteq [(K_b+Z(B'))\cap F(B';Ub)]+C \tag{4.8}$$

By substituting this into (4.6), and then into (4.5), we get the theorem. The details are left to the final paper.

5 Algorithm to find the covering radius

(5.1) Proposition : There is a polynomial $p(\cdot)$ such that for any rational polytope P and rational lattice L, with total size N, $\mu=\mu(P,L)$ is a rational number of size at most $p(N)$.

Proof : Left to the final paper.

Given a rational polyhedron $K_b=\{x: Ax\leq b\}$ in $\mathbf{R}^n$, we wish to compute its covering radius. Since this is a fraction with numerator and denominator polynomially bounded in size, we can do this by binary search provided for any rational t, we can check whether $tK_b+\mathbf{Z}^n$ equals $\mathbf{R}^n$. Without loss of generality, we may assume that $t=1$. We appeal to the theorem of the last section to find the $S_i, \mathcal{B}_i$ etc. where P is assumed to be the singleton $\{b\}$. Then we check in turn for each S_i whether there exists an $x\in S_i$ so that $x\notin K+\mathbf{Z}^n$. We will formulate the last as several mixed integer programs each with polynomially many constraints and a fixed number of integer variables (for fixed n). For each B in $\mathcal{B}_i$, and for each $z\in Z(B)$, we wish to assert that the unique lattice translate $x(B)$ of x that falls in the parallelopiped $F(B;T(B)b)$ is not in K_b+z. To express this by linear constraints, we consider all mappings f of the following sort : f takes two arguments - a B in $\mathcal{B}_i$ and a z in $Z(B)$. The range of f is $\{1,2,\ldots m\}$. We will consider each possible such mapping f and for each solve a mixed integer program that asserts that there exists an x in S_i such that for each $B\in\mathcal{B}_i$ and for each $z\in Z(B)$, there is a $y(B)$ in $\mathbf{Z}^n$ such that $x+y(B)$ belongs to $F(B;T(B)b)$ and $x+y(B)-z$ violates the $f(B,z)$ th constraint among the m constraints $Ax\leq b$. If any of the MIP's is feasible , then we know that $K_b+L\neq\mathbf{R}^n$, otherwise $K_b+L=\mathbf{R}^n$. We use Lenstra's [10] algorithm to solve each MIP in polynomial time.

This concludes the description of the algorithm to find the covering radius of a polytope in a fixed number of dimensions.

Acknowledgments I thank Imre Bárány, Bill Cook, Mark Hartmann, Laci Lovász, Herb Scarf and David Shallcross for many helpful discussions.

References

1. D.E.Bell, *A theorem concerning the integer lattice*, Studies in Applied Mathematics, 56, (1977) pp187-188

2. A.Brauer and J.E.Shockley, *On a problem of Frobenius*, Journal für reine und angewnadte Mathematik, 211 (1962) pp 215-220

3. P.Erdös and R.Graham, *On a linear diophantine problem of Frobenius*, Acta Arithmetica, 21 (1972).

4. M.Grötschel, L.Lovász and A.Schrijver, *Geometric algorithms and combinatorial optimization*, Springe Verlag (1988)

5. J.Hastad, Private Communication.

6. J. Incerpi and R.Sedgwick, *Improved upper bounds on ShellSort*, 24 th FOCS, (1983) .

7. R.Kannan and L.Lovász, *Covering minima and lattice point free convex bodies*, in Lecture Notes in Computer Science 241, ed. K.V.Nori, Springer-Verlag (1986) pp 193-213. Final version in Annals of Mathematics, November (1988).

8. R.Kannan, L.Lovász and H.E.Scarf, *The shapes of polyhedra*, Cowles Foundation Discussion paper No. 883, September (1988). To appear in Mathematics of Operations Research.

9. J.Lagarias, H.W.Lenstra and C.P.Schnorr, *Korkine-Zolotarev bases and successive minima of a lattice and its reciprocal lattice*, To appear in Combinatorica (1989)

10. H.W.Lenstra, *Integer programming with a fixed number of variables*, Mathematics of Operations research, Volume 8, Number 4 Nov (1983) pp 538-548

11. L.Lovász, *Geometry of Numbers and Integer Programming*, Proceedings of the 13 th International Symposium on Mathematical Programming, (1988)

12. O.J.Rödseth, *On a linear diophantine problem of Frobenius*, Journal für Mathematik, Band 301, (1977).

13. H.E.Scarf, *An observation on the structure of production sets with indivisibilities*, Proceedings of the National Academy of Sciences, USA, 74, pp 3637-3641 (1977).

14. H.E.Scarf and D.Shallcross, Private Communication.

15. R.Sedgwick, *A new upper bound for ShellSort*, Journal of Algorithms, 7 (1986).

16. E.S.Selmer, *On the linear diophantine problem of Frobenius*, Journal für Mathematik, Band 293/294 (1977).

17. E.S.Selmer and O.Beyer, *On the linear diophantine problem of Frobenius in three variables* Journal für Mathematik, Band 301, (1977).

18. A.Schrijver, , *Theory of Linear and Integer Programming*, Wiley (1986).

An efficient implicit data structure for path testing and searching in rooted trees and forests

(draft paper)

Giorgio Gambosi
Istituto di analisi dei sistemi ed informatica del CNR
Viale Manzoni 30, 00185 Roma, Italy

Marco Protasi
Dipartimento di Matematica
II Università di Roma "Tor Vergata"
Via Orazio Raimondo, 00173 Roma, Italy

Maurizio Talamo
Dipartimento di Matematica
Università dell'Aquila
Via Roma, 67100 L'Aquila, Italy
and
Istituto di analisi dei sistemi ed informatica del CNR
Viale Manzoni 30, 00185 Roma, Italy

CR Classification: E1 (Data structures), F2 (Analysis of algorithms and problem complexity)

Abstract
In this paper, an implicit data structure is presented which makes it possible to represent a tree-structured partial order in such a way to efficiently perform operations of path testing and searching among elements of the ground set of the poset. The data structure makes it possible to represent the order relation by referring only to internal nodes of the tree and by associating to each element of the ground set a pair of integer values derived from specific linear extensions of the partial order.

Introduction

The study of efficient (with respect to time and space) implicit data structures, that is data structures in which pointers are not allowed and contiguous representation of data is used, has been extensively afforded in last years for many problems; for example in ([AMM84], [F83], [M86]) the dictionary problem has been considered while in ([ASSS86], [SS85], [GNT89]) the problem of managing priority queues has been studied with respect to several operations. In general, however, the above mentioned problems regard set inputs on which totally ordered relations are defined. So, for istance, in the dictionary problem, the operations of search, insert and delete are performed on a totally ordered set.

In this paper, instead, we consider a problem whose input is given by a set S on which a relation of partial order R is defined. We are interested to represent R in such a way to efficiently query about its structure.

Moreover, we restrict our study to consider only partial orders which are tree-structured, that is, whose Hasse diagram is a forest.

As a consequence, instead of presenting the problem using a poset and describing the operations that we want to perform in a set-like formulation, we will directly introduce the problem in a tree-like formulation. Given a rooted forest, we are interested in performing two operations: 1) given two nodes, decide if the two nodes are on the same path (in terms of a partial order on a set this means that we want to decide if two elements of the sets are incomparable).2) given a node, find the father.

According to the implicit approach, the input, that is the nodes of the forest and the relation among them, will be represented in a contiguous and pointer free way. A trivial solution to solve this problem in an implicit way consists in using an array of size n-1 (if n is the number of the nodes of the forest); every element of the array is divided in two fields and in every element is stored an edge, that is a couple of nodes. It is then easy to show that it is possible to find the father in constant time and decide if two nodes are on the same path in linear time.

In this paper we show how to solve the problem more efficiently with respect to time and space.

More precisely, in Section 3, we consider the case of binary trees. Given a tree of n nodes, we build an implicit data structure with space occupation 2m (m is the number of the internal nodes of the tree), on which it is possible to decide if two nodes are in the same path in constant time and it is possible to find the father of a given node in O(logn) steps. Note that, in order to avoid the trivial O(n) bound on the space complexity, we have to introduce some specific assumption: in particular, we assume that queries do not refer directly to element identifiers. Instead, we assume that queries refer to labels which are associated to elements and which are introduced in order to code the structure of relation R.

In Section 4 we extend these results to the case of rooted trees with unbounded degree and to the case of forests. For these more complicated structures, the path operation is still performed in costant time while to find a father requires $O(\log^2 n)$ time complexity.

Finally we note that the problem afforded in this paper has applications in the study of taxonomies, and more generally, in systems for representing knowledge.In this framework, forest-like structures are widely used and hierarchy properties can be investigated by operations of path testing and father search.

The figures used in the text are given in the Appendix at the end of the paper.

1. Basic definitions

Let $\mathbb{T}=(\mathbb{N},\mathbb{A})$ be a rooted binary tree: given a node $v \in \mathbb{N}$ let us define as father(v), the (unique) node $v' \in \mathbb{N}$ such that there exists an arc $(v',v) \in \mathbb{A}$: it is intended that father(v) is not defined if v is the root (*root(* $\mathbb{T}$*)*) of $\mathbb{T}$.

Given a node $v \in \mathbb{N}$, the heigth $h(v)$ of v is the length of the longest path from v to a leaf, that is $h(v)=0$ if v is a leaf and $h(v)=\max\{h(v_1), h(v_2)\}+1$, where v_1 and v_2 are the sons of v.

A *labeling* L: $\mathbb{N} \rightarrow \{1,..,n\}$, (where $n=|\mathbb{N}|$) of a tree $\mathbb{T}$ is an assignment of values belonging to the set $\{1,..,n\}$ to nodes of $\mathbb{T}$ such that for any couple of nodes v_i, v_j, $i \neq j$, $L(v_i) \neq L(v_j)$.

In this paper, an implicit representation of rooted trees is given such that it is possible to efficiently perform the following operations:

- *father(v)*, where $v \in \mathbb{N}$, which returns the node v'=father(v) if v is not the root;
- *path(* v_i, v_j*)*, where v_i, $v_j \in \mathbb{N}$, which returns *true* iff there exists a path from v_i to v_j.

2. Labeling algorithms

In the following sections, we will show how to efficiently perform the introduced operations by referring to a pair of labels associated to each node of the tree. Each label is assigned according to a specific labeling algorithm, which produces a linear extension of the given poset. Let us note that, by the theory of partial orders, two different linear extensions are necessary to represent any tree-structured poset.

Let us now introduce the two different labelings L1, L2 which make it possible to answer efficiently to *father(v)* and *path(* v_i, v_j*)* queries. Such labelings are derived from two specific algorithms Visit1, Visit2 for the visit of the tree.

Essentially, both Visit1 and Visit2 perform a postorder visit of $\mathbb{T}$ with the additional condition that, in order to visit a tree with root v:

- Visit1 visits first the subtree having as root the son of v of maximal height, ties are broken according to increasing lexicographic order;
- Visit2 visits first the subtree having as root the son of v of minimal height, ties are broken according to decreasing lexicographic order.

Thus, Visit2 visits the sons of a node v in the opposite order with respect to Visit1.

More formally, the algorithm for Visit1 is given below in a Pascal-like notation; the algorithm for Visit2 can be derived immediately.

```
Procedure Visit1(T: tree);

Procedure V1(v: node of T; var label: integer);
begin
    if "v is a leaf"
    then
    begin
            L1(v):=label;
            label:=label+1
    end
    else
            if "there exists only one son v1 of v"
                    then
                    begin
                            V1(v1, label);
                            L1(v):=label;
                            label:=label+1
                    end
                    else
                    begin
                            "choose the son of v of largest height,
                            in case of ties choose the greatest son
                            according to lexicographic order: let v1
                            be the chosen son and v2 be the other one";
                            V1(v1, label);
                            V1(v2, label);
                            L1(v):=label;
                            label:=label+1
                    end
end;

begin
    label:=1;
    V1(root(T), label)
end;
```

An example of the pairs resulting from both visits is given in figure 1.

Proposition 1:
The labeling of a binary tree of n nodes by means of the algorithms Visit1 and Visit2 requires an O(n) time complexity.

Proof:
Since we are considering binary trees, algorithms Visit1 and Visit2 require O(n) steps and, since it is possible to assign to each node v its height *h(v)* in O(n) time, the overall tree labeling has O(n) time complexity.

•

3. Implicit data structure and search algorithms

In order to present the data structure, let us first introduce some properties of the above labelings.

Lemma 1:

Given two nodes $v,v' \in \mathbb{N}$, let us denote as (x,y) the labels of v derived from algorithms Visit1, Visit2. Analogously let (x',y') be the labels of v'. If v'=father(v) then $x'>x$, $y'>y$ and $x'=x+1$ or $y'=y+1$.

Proof:

Trivial. It is sufficient to note that both Visit1 and Visit2 are postorder visits.

•

Note that if v is the only son of v', then both $x'=x+1$ and $y'=y+1$.

Lemma 2:

Given three nodes $u,v,v' \in \mathbb{N}$, let (x,y), (x',y') be the labels of v,v' and v'=father(v)=father(u). If $x'=x+2$ (and $y'=y+1$ by Lemma 1), then u is a leaf.

Proof:

Derives from Lemma 1 and from the characteristics of Visit1 algorithm, where it is required that the last son to be visited is the one of smallest height.

•

Lemma 3:

Given three nodes $u,v,v' \in \mathbb{N}$: let (x,y), (x',y') be the labels of v,v' and v'=father(v)=father(u). If $x'=x+1$ and $y'>y+1$, then h(v) is less than h(u).

Proof:

The proof derives from the same considerations in the proof of Lemma 2.

•

The data structure is defined on a set of m pairs of values (where $m<n$ is the number of internal nodes of $\mathbb{T}$) such that to a given internal node v with labels (x,y) a pair (a,b) is associated where a=x and b is derived according to the following rules.

Let (x',y') be the labels of v'=father(v):

R1. if $x'=x+1$, $y'=y+1$ (that is, v has no brother) then $b=x'$;

R2. if $x'=x+1$, $y'\neq y+1$ then $b=y'$;

R3. if $x'=x+2$, $y'=y+1$ (that is, the brother of v is a leaf) then $b=y'$;

R4. if $x'>x+2$, $y'=y+1$ then $b=x'$.

Note that, if v is the root of $\mathbb{T}$, $a=x=n$ and we may leave b undefined (in the following, b is left =0). Moreover, if n=1, that is the tree is only one node, such a node is considered as an internal node.

Note that, in cases 2,4, b has the value of the label of v' whose value is "farthest" from the value of the corresponding label of v. In general, b has the same value of one of the two labels of v'=father(v) and the value of the other label of v' is derivable.

In figure 2, the same tree of figure 1 is given with the a and b values corresponding to each node. For completeness, the pairs (a,b) have been also considered for the the leaves of the tree, even if not needed for the following.

Let us moreover introduce a partition of the set of internal nodes into two sets X,Y such that, for each internal node v with father v' having labels (x',y') and associated pair (a,b):

$v \in X$ iff b=x' (rules R1,R4 above);

$v \in Y$ iff b=y' (rules R2,R3 above);

Let us assume that, in general, root($\mathbb{T}$)$\in$X.

The (implicit) data structure for the representation of tree $\mathbb{T}$ is an array $\mathcal{T}$[0..m], where m<n is the number of internal nodes of $\mathbb{T}$: the i-th element of the array is a pair of integers (a_i, b_i), corresponding to the pair of values introduced above.

$\mathcal{T}$[1..m] is decomposed into two subarrays $\mathcal{T}$[1..|X|], $\mathcal{T}$[|X|+1..m]: pairs corresponding to nodes in X are stored in $\mathcal{T}$[1..|X|] in order of increasing a_i values, while pairs corresponding to nodes in Y are stored in $\mathcal{T}$[|X|+1..m] in order of increasing a_i values too. Note that the value |X| may be held in the first location of $\mathcal{T}$[0].

In figure 3, the array corresponding to the tree considered in figures 1, 2 is given.

In the following, we will assume that query formulation refers to pairs of labels instead of identifiers of nodes; that is, we assume that a pair of labels is always used as an element identifier.

A first theorem can now be stated for what regards the *path* operation.

Theorem 1:

Given the two labelings L1, L2, for each two nodes v_i, v_j, the *path* operation can be performed in constant time.

Proof:

Let (x_i, y_i), (x_j, y_j) be the pairs of labels of nodes v_i, v_j, respectively.

By the characteristics of the visit algorithms, it is easy to note that there is a path from v_i to v_j iff $x_i < x_j$ and $y_i < y_j$.

•

Let us now consider how to perform the *father (v)* operation.

Let (x,y) be a pair of labels of some node v and let (x',y') be the desired labels of v'=father(v). Let us moreover denote as a-values (b-values) the values of the first (second) component of items in $\mathcal{T}$. The search of x' and y' is performed by the following algorithm.

```
Algorithm Father -Search -1
begin
"let f be the first value in T[0]";
"perform a binary search  of x on the a-values in T[1..f]";
if "x has been found"
     then begin
            "let (a,b) be the pair determined";
            if b=0 then "the root has been found"
                    else begin
                            x':=b;                        (case 1)
                            y':=y+1
                            end
            end
     else "perform a binary search of x on the a-values in T[f+1,m]";
     if "x has been found"
                  then begin
                          "let (a,b) be the pair determined";
                          if b=y+1
                                then begin
                                        x':=x+2;       (case 2)
                                        y':=y+1
                                        end
                                else  begin
                                        x':=x+1;       (case 3)
                                        y':=b
                                        end
                          end
                  else "failure"
end;
```

If v is an internal node, the labels of the father of v are thus obtained; otherwise, if a failure has been obtained, the (x,y) pair is associated to some leaf which, by definition, is not represented in the array.

In order to find the father of a leaf v let us now introduce a second algorithm.

```
Algorithm Father-Search-2
begin
"perform binary searches of x+1 on the a-values in T[1..f] and in T[f+1..m]";
if "x+1 has  not been found"
     then begin
            x':=x+2;                              (case 4)
            y':=y+1
```

```
        end
else
        if x = 1 then
                begin
                        x':=x+1;        (case 5)
                        y':=y+1
                end
        else "perform a binary search of x-1 on the a-values in T[1..f]";
                if "x-1 has been found"
                then begin
                        x':=x+1;        (case 6)
                        y':=y+1
                        end
                else  begin
                        "perform a binary search of x-1 on the a-
                        values in T[f+1..m]";
                        if "x-1 has been found"
                        then begin
                                "let (a,b) be the pair determined";
                                x':=x+1;        (case 7)
                                y':=b
                                end
                        else begin
                                x':=x+1;        (case 8)
                                y':=y+2
                                end
                        end
end;
```

Let us now state the following theorems.

Theorem 2:
Given an internal node v, algorithm Father-Search-1 returns the pair of labels of node v'=father(v) in O(lgn) time.

Proof:
In order to prove the correctness of the algorithm, let us consider the different configurations which may occur among node v and node v'=father(v). It is easy to note that only the four configurations in figure 4 may occur.

Configuration 1
From Lemma 1 and since also u is an internal node, one of the two conditions i) ii) below holds:

i) x'=x+1, y'>y+2 (rule R2)

in such a situation, there is a pair (x,y') in $\mathcal{T}$[f+1..m]: such a pair is found according to case 3 of the algorithm;

ii) y'=y+1, x'>x+2 (rule R4)

in such a situation, there is a pair (x,x') in $\mathcal{T}$[1..f]: such a pair is found according to case 1 of the algorithm.

Configuration 2

In such a configuration, since v has no brothers, the only possible condition is:

x'=x+1, y'=y+1 (rule R1)

in such a situation, there is a pair (x,x') in $\mathcal{T}$[1..f]: such a pair is found according to case 1 of the algorithm.

Configuration 3

In such a configuration, since v has a brother node which is a leaf, from Lemma 3 it derives that:

x'=x+2, y'=y+1 (rule R3)

in such a situation, there is a pair (x,y') in $\mathcal{T}$[f+1..m]: such a pair is found according to case 2 of the algorithm.

Configuration 4

In such a configuration, v is the root of the tree: a value b=0 is found by the algorithm in $\mathcal{T}$[1..f].

This completes the proof of the correctness of the algorithm.

The complexity of the algorithm is trivially O(lgn), since a constant number of binary searches are performed on an array of size m=O(n).

•

Theorem 3:

Given a leaf node v, algorithm Father-Search-2 returns the pair of labels of node v'=father(v) in O(lgn) time.

Proof:

In order to prove the correctness of the algorithm, let us consider the different configurations (figure 5) which may occur among node v, node v'=father(v) and the brother u of v: let us denote as (x,y) the labels of v, (x',y') the labels of v', (x", y") the labels of u.. Note that in figure 5 $x=x_v$ and $x''=x_u$.

Configuration 1

In such a configuration, since u is not a leaf, from Lemma 3 it derives that:

x'=x+1, x"=x-1 (rule R2)

in such a situation, there is a pair (x",y') in $\mathcal{T}$[f+1..m]: such a pair is found according to case 7 of the algorithm.

Configuration 2

In such a configuration, from Lemma 1 and by hypothesis on the order of labeling of u and v,

x'=x+2, y'=y+1 (rule R3)

x"=x+1, y"=y-1

in such a situation, there is no pair with a=x+1 in the array: the correct values are found according to case 4.

Configuration 3

In such a configuration, from Lemma 1 and by hypothesis on the order of labeling of u and v,

x'=x+1, y'=y+2 (rule R2)

x"=x-1, y"=y+1

in such a situation, there is a pair with a=x+1 and there is no pair with a=x-1 in the array: the correct values are found according to case 8.

Configuration 4

In such a configuration, from Lemma 1 it derives that

x'=x+1 (rule R1)

y'=y+1

in such a situation, let us first consider the particular case in which x=1; the correct values are found according to case 5.

Otherwise let us denote as w the node such that x_W=x-1. Assume w is a leaf: this would imply that either i) w is the brother of v or ii) the father of w is an ancestor of v (figure 6). Case i) is in contradiction with the hypothesis about configuration 4, while case ii) would imply, by Lemma 3, that $x<x_W$. Hence, w is not a leaf and, by the characteristics of the postorder visit, it must be the son of an ancestor z of v (figure 7).

By construction, since w is not a leaf and $y_Z = y_W+1$, there must exist an element (a,b) in $\mathcal{T}$[1..f] with a=x_W and b=x_Z.

Since both x+1 and x-1 are found in $\mathcal{T}$, case 6 holds and the correct values x',y' are returned.

This completes the proof of the correctness of the algorithm.

The complexity of the algorithm is trivially O(lgn), since a constant number of binary searches are performed on an array of size m=O(n).

•

Theorem 4:

The space needed by the above algorithms is 2m, where m is the number of internal nodes in $\mathbb{T}$.

Proof:

A space occupation 2m+2 can be easily derived by observing that array $\mathcal{T}$ holds a pair of integers for each internal node in $\mathbb{T}$. Moreover, the first location in $\mathcal{T}$[0] holds the value |X|.

However, the space occupation can slightly be reduced to 2m by observing that value |X| can be held in the second location of $\mathcal{T}$[m], which can always be associated to the root of $\mathbb{T}$. Algorithms above can be easily modified to correctly manage such a situation.

In the following section, some extensions of the introduced approach are given.

4. Extensions to rooted trees and forests with unbounded degree

In order to extend the introduced representation to general rooted trees and forests, let us note that rooted trees with unbounded degree can be managed by reducing them to binary trees by means of the introduction of k-2 new nodes for every node with k sons. This implies that, in the worst case, the number of nodes is increased from n to 2n-3.

The data structure and the search algorithms above can then be modified to obtain the following performances.

Theorem 5:

It is possible to introduce an implicit data structure for the representation of rooted trees of n nodes with unbounded degree with space occupation <2n, such that the search algorithms perform a *path* operation in O(1) time and a *father* operation in $O(lg^2n)$ time.

Proof:

The proof will be given in the full paper.

•

For what concerns the representation of forests of rooted trees, the following theorems holds.

Theorem 6:

It is possible to introduce an implicit data structure for the representation of binary rooted forests of n nodes with space occupation 2m (where m is the number of internal nodes), such that the search algorithms perform a *path* operation in O(1) time and a *father* operation in O(lgn) time.

Proof:

The proof will be given in the full paper.

•

Theorem 7:

It is possible to introduce an implicit data structure for the representation of rooted forests of n nodes with space occupation <2n, such that the search algorithms perform a *path* operation in O(1) time and a *father* operation in $O(lg^2n)$ time.

Proof:

The proof will be given in the full paper.

•

5. References

[AMM84] H.Alt,K.Melhorn,J.I.Munro "Partial match retrieval in implicit data structures" Inf. Proc; Lett., 19, 2, (1984).

[ASSS86] M.D.Atkinson,J.R.Sack,N.Santoro,T.Strohotte "Min-Max heaps and generalized priority queues" Comm.A.C.M., 29,10, (1986).

[BFMUW86] A.Borodin,F.E.Fich,F.Meyer auf der Heide,E.Upfal, A.Widgerson "A tradeoff between search and update time for the implicit dictionary problem" Proc. 13th ICALP Conf., Lect. Not. in Comp. Sci., 226, Springer Verlag, (1986).

[F83] G.N.Frederickson "Implicit data structures for the dictionary problem" J. Ass. Comp. Mach., 30,1, (1983).

[GNT89] G.Gambosi,E.Nardelli,M.Talamo "A pointer-free data structure for merging heaps and min-max heaps" Proc.16th ICALP Conf., Lect. Not. in Comp. Sci., 372, Springer Verlag, (1989).

[M86] J.I.Munro "An implicit data structure supporting insertion,deletion and search in $O(\log^2 n)$ time" J. Comp. Syst. Sci., 33, 1, (1986).

[MS80] J.I.Munro, H.Suwanda "Implicit data structures for fast search and update" J. Comp. Syst. Sci., 21, 2, (1980).

[SS85] J.R.Sack,T.Strothotte "An algorithm for merging heaps" Act. Inf., 22, (1985).

APPENDIX

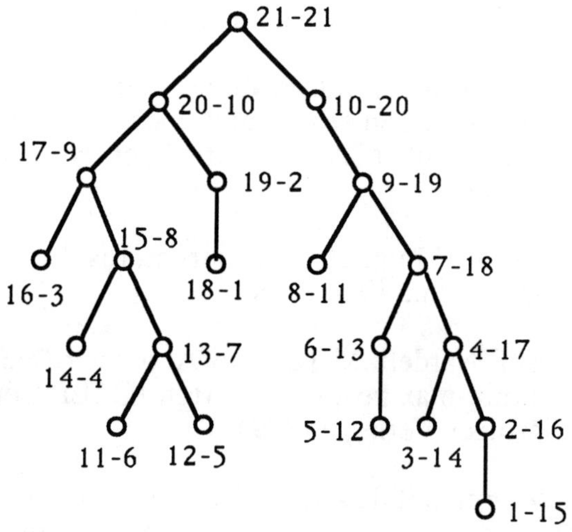

Figure 1

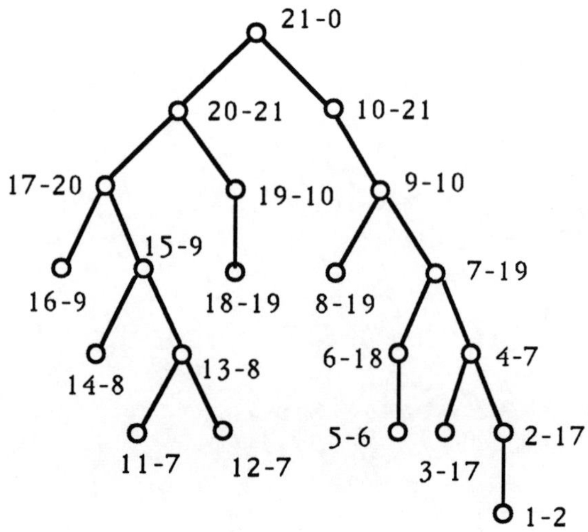

Figure 2

5	4	9	10	17	21	2	6	7	13	15	19	20
-	7	10	21	20	0	17	18	19	8	9	10	21
0	1	2	3	4	5	6	7	8	9	10	11	12

Figure 3

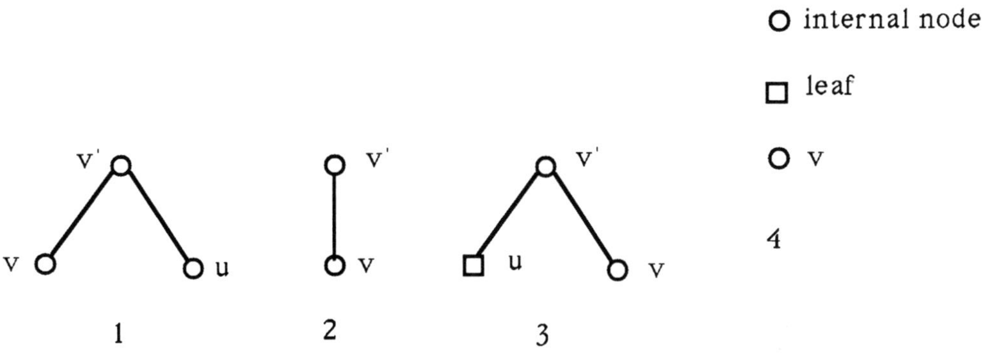

Figure 4

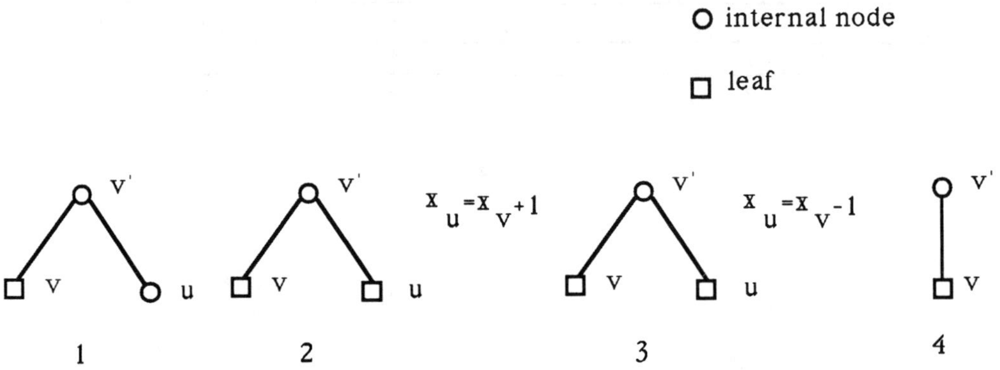

Figure 5

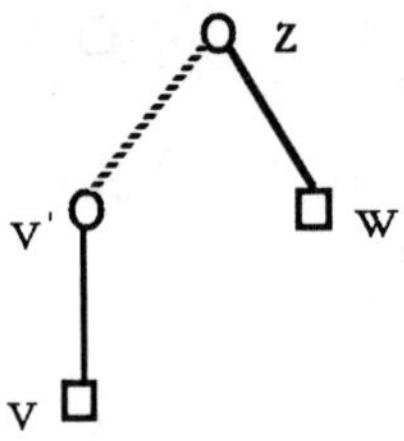

Figure 6

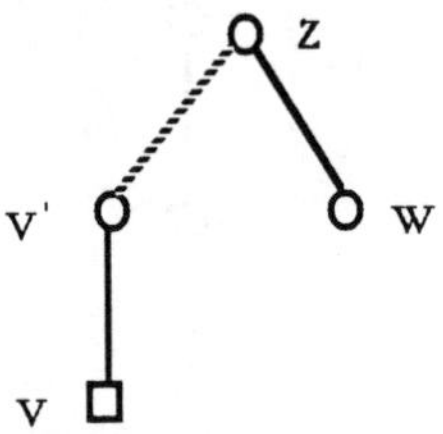

Figure 7

Robust Decompositions of Polyhedra *

Chanderjit L. Bajaj *Tamal K. Dey*

Department of Computer Science
Purdue University
West Lafayette, IN 47907

Abstract

We present a simple and robust algorithm to compute a convex decomposition of a non-convex polyhedron of arbitrary genus. The algorithm takes a topologically correct representation of a non-convex polyhedron S and produces a worst-case optimal $O(N^2)$ number of topologically correct representations of convex polyhedra S_i, with $\bigcup_i S_i = S$, in $O(nN^2 + N^4)$ time and $O(n\,N + N^3)$ space, where n is the number of edges of S, N is the total number of *notches* or reflex edges. Our algorithm can be made to run in $O((nN + N^3)\,logN\,)$ time if robustness is not desired. The robustness of the algorithm stems from its ability to handle all degenerate configurations as well as to maintain topological consistency, while doing floating-point numerical computations. The convex decomposition algorithm is independent of the precision used in the numerical calculations. With slight modifications it also yields a triangulation of the polyhedra into a set of tetrahedra.

1 Introduction

Motivation: The main purpose behind decomposition operations is to simplify a problem for complex objects into a number of subproblems dealing with simple objects. In most cases a decomposition, in terms of a finite union of disjoint convex pieces is useful and this is always possible for polyhedral models [5, 9]. Convex decompositions lead to efficient algorithms, for example, in geometric point location and intersection detection, see [9]. Our motivation stems from the use of geometric models in a physical simulation system being developed at Purdue [2]. Specifically, a disjoint convex decomposition of simple polyhedra allows for more efficient algorithms in motion planning, in the computation of volumetric properties, and in the finite element solution of partial differential equations.

Robust Computations: When programming geometric operations on polyhedra and arbitrary solid models, stemming from practical applications, one cannot ignore the degenerate geometric configurations that often arise, as well as the need to make specific topological decisions based on imprecise floating-point numerical computations, [15, 17, 25]. When making decisions about polyhedral features (vertices, edges, faces) which are very close together, so that computed numerical values are not reliable, one considers the topological constraints of the geometric configurations to arrive at a correct choice. An apriori threshold ε is set for all numerical computations such that one relies on the *sign* of computations, only if the computed value is greater than ε. A computed value, less than or equal to ε signals a region of local topological uncertainity[1]. For the decomposition operation we adopt the paradigm of reasoning with uncertainity. In particular, in regions of uncertainity, the choices are all equally likely that the computed quantity, is negative, zero or positive. Such decision points of uncertainity, where several choices exist, are either "independent" or "dependent". At independent decision points, any choice may be made from the finite set of local topological possibilities, while the choice at dependent decision points ensures the invariant state of global topological consistency.

*Supported in part by ARO Contract DAAG29-85-C0018 under Cornell MSI, NSF grant DMS 88-16286 and ONR contract N00014-88-K-0402.

[1] Usually, ε is chosen to depend on machine precision and the minimum feature separation of the input polyhedra, however as shall be exhibited, the correctness of the decomposition algorithm is independent of the value of ε, allowing it to be arbitrarily chosen by the user.

Problem Statement: Given a topologically correct representation of a non-convex polyhedron S, possibly with holes, in three dimensions, generate topologically correct representations for pairwise disjoint, convex polyhedra, whose union is S.

Related Work: The problem of partitioning a non-convex polyhedron into a *minimum* number of convex parts is known to be NP-hard [18, 20]. Rupert and Seidel [22] also show that the problem of partitioning a non-convex polyhedron into tetrahedra, without introduction of Steiner points, is NP-hard. For the decomposition problem, allowing Steiner vertices, Chazelle [5, 6] established a worst-case, $O(n^2)$ lower bound on the complexity of the problem and gave an algorithm that produces a worst-case, optimal number, $O(N^2)$ of convex polyhedra in $O(nN^3)$ time and $O(nN^2)$ space, where n is the number of edges of the polyhedron S and N is the number of *notches* or reflex edges of S. Recently, Chazelle and Palios [7], improved the above time bound to $O(nN + N^2 \ logN)$. All these results are based on exact RAM models of computation, assuming generic geometric configurations. Hence, issues of degeneracy and topological consistency due to finite precision numerical calculations are not considered.

The latter considerations have recently taken added importance because of the increasing use of geometric manipulations in computer-aided design, and solid modeling [1]. Edelsbrunner and Mucke [10], and Yap [26], suggest using expensive symbolic perturbation techniques for handling geometric degeneracies. Sugihara and Iri [25], and Dobkin and Silver [8], describe an approach to achieving consistent computations in solid modeling, by ensuring that computations are carried out with sufficiently higher precision than used for representing the numerical data. There are drawbacks however, as high precision routines are needed for all primitive numerical computations, making algorithms highly machine dependent. Furthermore, the required precision for calculations is difficult to apriori estimate for complex problems. Similarly, Segal and Sequin [23] require estimating various numerical tolerances, tuned to each computation, to maintain consistency. Milenkovic [19] presents techniques for modifying planar geometry to remove uncertainity, however such techniques are still not general to handle geometric configurations in three dimensions. Hoffmann, Hopcroft and Karasick [15], and Karasick [17], propose using geometric reasoning and apply it to the problem of polyhedral intersections. Sugihara [24] uses geometric reasoning to avoid redundant decisions, which lead to topological inconsistency, in the construction of planar Voronoi diagrams. Guibas, Salesin and Stolfi [14] propose a framework of computations called ε-geometry , in which they compute an exact solution for a perturbed version of the input. So does Fortune [12] who applies it to the problem of triangulating planar polygons. The methods of topological reasoning in this paper are related to these latter works, however presents new techniques for achieving robustness for the specific task of decomposing a polyhedron.

Results: We present a simple and robust algorithm to compute a disjoint convex decomposition of a polyhedron of arbitrary genus[2]. The algorithm takes a topologically correct representation of a polyhedron S and produces a worst case optimal $O(N^2)$ number of topologically correct representations of convex polyhedra S_i, with $\bigcup_i S_i = S$, in worst-case $O(nN^2 + N^4)$ time and $O(n\ N + N^3)$ space, where n is the number of edges of S, N is the total number of *notches* or reflex edges. The convex decomposition algorithm is also independent of the precision used in the numerical calculations and with additional $O(nN + N^3)$ operations on the decomposed pieces yields a triangulation of the polyhedron into tetrahedra. If robustness is not desired our algorithm can be modified to run in $O((nN + N^3) log\ N)$ time.

2 Preliminaries

Notation and Data Structure

The intersection of a polyhedron S with a plane P is, in general, a set of simple polygons, possibly with holes. We call this set of polygons as the *cross-sectional graph* of P and denote it by GP. If G is a simple polygon with vertices $v_1, v_2, ..., v_n$ in clockwise order, a vertex v_i is a notch of G if the inner angle between the edge (v_{i-1}, v_i) and (v_i, v_{i+1}) is $> 180°$. Between any two consecutive notches v_i, v_j in the clockwise order, the sequence of vertices $(v_i, v_{i+1}, ..., v_j)$ is called a *convex polygonal-line*. Each polygonal-line can be partitioned into *convex-chains*, which are maximal pieces of a polygonal-line, with the property that its vertices form a convex polygon. Each convex-chain can be further partitioned into at most three x-monotone maximal pieces called *subchains*, i.e., vertices of a subchain have x-coordinates in either strictly increasing or decreasing order.

[2]The genus of a polyhedron is equal to the number of holes it possesses

Data Structure: A polyhedron S with arbitrary number of holes, is represented by a collection of vertices, edges, and faces.
Vertices: Each vertex is represented with following fields.

1. *vertex.coordinates*: contains the coordinates of the vertex.
2. *vertex.adjacencies*: contains the edges incident on that vertex.

Edges: Each edge is represented with the following fields.

1. *edge.vertices*: contains two vertices which are its endpoints.
2. *edge.faces*: contains orientations of an edge with respect to each of its incident faces. An edge orientation with respect to a face f is such that a traversal of the edge has face f to its right.

Faces: Each face is represented with following fields.

1. *face.equation*: contains the equation of the plane on which the face lies.
2. *face.edges*: contains a collection of directed edge-cycles on a plane, and bounding the face, with edges oriented such that a clockwise traversal of edge-cycles always has the face to the right. Each subchain in the edge-cycles is stored in a balanced binary search tree (e.g. 2-3 tree).

Algorithm Synopsis Let S be a simple polyhedron, possibly with holes, and having n vertices : $\{v_1, v_2, ..., v_n\}$ t edges : $\{e_1, e_2, ..., e_t\}$ and q faces : $\{f_1, f_2, ..., f_q\}$. An edge g of S is a *notch* if the inner-angle γ between two incident faces of g, is greater than 180°. Nonconvexity in S, is a result of the presence of these notches in the polyhedron. Our algorithm proceeds in removing all notches of S, by repeatedly cutting and splitting S with planes containing the notches, finally producing convex polyhedra S_i, with $\bigcup_i S_i = S$. If edge g is a notch, with f_g^-, f_g^+ as its incident faces, then a plane P which contains the notch g and subtends an inner-angle greater than $\gamma - 180°$ with both f_g^- and f_g^+, is a valid notch plane for g. The chosen plane P is also called the *notch plane* of g. Clearly for each notch g, there exist an ∞^1 choices for P. Note that P may intersect other notches, thereby producing subnotches.

Essential properties need to be satisfied in the choice of a notch plane and in the splitting of a polyhedron by notch planes, to guarantee a worst-case, optimal number of convex pieces.

1. all subnotches of a notch need to be eliminated by the same notch plane.
2. if the elimination of a notch reduces the genus of a polyhedron then, the intersection of the notch plane should not increase the number of polyhedra. See Figure 5.2.

If minimality of the number of convex pieces is not desired, one may simply choose as a notch plane, one of the many planes incident on the notch.
Combinatorial Lemmas For time analysis in next sections we also need the following Lemmas, from Chazelle's thesis [5].
Lemma 2.1: Let G be a simple polygon with N_G notches, then number of convex-chains C_G in G is bounded as $C_G \leq 2(1 + N_G)$.
Proof: See ([5], page 22, Theorem 3). ♣
Lemma 2.2: Let G be a simple polygon with N_G notches, then number of subchains C_{SG} in G is bounded as $C_{SG} \leq 6(1 + N_G)$.
Proof: It is easy to see that there are at most 3 subchains per convex-chain. This fact together with Lemma 2.1 yields the bound. ♣
Lemma 2.3: Let G be a simple polygon with N_G notches. No line can intersect G in more than $2N_G$ segments.
Proof: See ([5], page 121, Lemma 18). ♣

When N_G is zero, one line can intersect G in at most one segment. We therefore modify the above Lemma to be
Lemma 2.4: Let G be a simple polygon with N_G notches. No line can intersect G in more than $max(1, 2N_G)$ segments or $max(2, 2N_G + 1)$ points.

3 Robust Intersection & Incidence Tests

All intersections and incidences between vertices, edges and faces are carried out by vertex-plane, edge-plane, face-plane classifications as described below.

Vertex-Plane Classification: To classify the incidence of a vertex $v_i = (x_i, y_i, z_i)$ w.r.t the plane $P: ax+by+cz+d = 0$, we compute the normalized algebraic distance of v_i from P by computing $ax_i+by_i+cz_i+d$ divided by a norm of the coefficients. The *sign* of this computation, viz., zero, negative, or positive, classifies v_i as "on" P (zero), "below" P (negative) or "above" P (positive), where "above" is the halfspace containing the plane normal (a, b, c). We rely on the sign of the computation if the above distance of v_i from P is larger than ε. Otherwise, we apply geometric reasoning rules, as we now detail, to classify vertex v_i w.r.t. the plane P.

Consider the edges incident at v_i. Let e be any such edge with m incident planes $P_1, P_2, ..., P_m$, where $P_i: a_ix+b_iy+c_iz+d_i = 0$. We compute the intersection point $\mathbf{r}$ of e and the plane P by computing the least squares solution of the over-determined linear system, viz., $A^TA\mathbf{r} = A^T\mathbf{d}$ where $A = \begin{bmatrix} a & b & c \\ a_1 & b_1 & c_1 \\ a_2 & b_2 & c_2 \\ \cdots & \cdots & \cdots \\ a_m & b_m & c_m \end{bmatrix}$ $\mathbf{d} = [-d, -d_1, -d_2, \ldots, -d_m]^T$. The linear system is solved using Gaussian elimination with scaled partial pivoting and iterative refinement.

If the distance between the computed point $\mathbf{r}$ and v_i is greater than ε we classify v_i as follows. To classify v_i "above" or "below" consistently, we simultaneously classify w, the other incident vertex of e. The classifications of v_i and w are made consistent with the computed point $\mathbf{r}$ by observing the following rules. (i) The classification of v_i is made to be of opposite sign to that of w if $\mathbf{r}$ lies in the interior of edge e. (ii) Similarly, the classification of v_i is set to the same sign as that of w if $\mathbf{r}$ lies in the exterior of edge e. On examining all edges e's incident to v_i in this manner to obtain a consistent classification of v_i with all w's , it may transpire (due to numerical computation error) that two computed edge-plane intersections $\mathbf{r}$'s (both greater than ε from v_i), yield a contradiction in the desired "above" or "below" classification of v_i, based on the above rules (i) and (ii). Further it may happen that for all edges e's incident on v_i, the computed intersection points $\mathbf{r}$'s are within ε of v_i. In both cases we mark v_i as "maybeon". All such "maybeon" vertices are consistently classified later when the faces containing them are classified w.r.t. the plane P.

Edge-Plane Classification: An edge can get any of the three classifications which are "not-intersected", "intersected", and "on". The classifications of the edge vertices are used to classify an edge e. If both vertices of an edge e are of the same classification, e is classified as "not-intersected". If the two vertices are of different classifications, e is classfied as "intersected". If the intersection point $\mathbf{r}$ for e and P was not already computed (during vertex classification), it is computed now, via the aforementioned least squares computation. If $\mathbf{r}$ does not lie in the interior of e, we force it to be so by considering the intersection point to be a point on e which is at a distance of ε from the vertex nearest to the computed point. If both the vertices are classified as "on" the plane, e is classified as "on". If one of the vertices is classified as "on", the edge is classified as "intersected" and the "on" vertex is taken as the point of intersection.

Face-Plane Classification: If a face f is intersected by a plane P the points of intersection of edges of f and P, should necessarily be (i) collinear with the line of intersection of the plane of f and P, and (ii) all the vertices of f on one side of the intersection line, should all be of the same classification w.r.t. the plane P. We classify vertices which have been temporarily classified as "maybeon", in a consistent way, i.e., they satisfy the above two properties (i) and (ii), with perturbations of atmost ε.

The different classifications of the vertices of a face f w.r.t. P yield the following cases.

1. All the vertices of f have been classified as "maybeon". We classify f as "on" the plane and change the classification of all these vertices to "on".

2. At least one vertex v_u of f has been classifed "above", or "below" the plane P, but no edge of f has its two vertices classified with opposite signs("below" and "above"). If there is only one "maybeon" vertex, we can choose that vertex as the point of intersection between f and P. Otherwise, we arbitrarily choose any two of the vertices which have been classified as "maybeon" and take the line

of intersection of f and P as the line L joining these two vertices. All other "maybeon" vertices which are more than ε away from this line are classified by using the classification of v_u. Any vertex which is more than ε away from L and which lies on the same (opposite) side of L as v_u does, gets the classification (opposite classification) of v_u. All other "maybeon" vertices which could not be classified by this method are classified as *on*. Note that these vertices are within the distance of ε from L. Hence, they will be collinear with perturbations of atmost ε. See Figure 3.1.

3. At least one edge e is known to intersect P, as its two vertices have opposite sign classification w.r.t. P. If there is no other edge which has been decided to be intersected by P, take the line joining the intersection point of e and any "maybeon" vertex as the line of intersection of f and P and then apply the method as described in case (ii) to classify other "maybeon" vertices. If more than two edges have been decided to be intersected by P, take the line which fits in a least square sense all the points of intersection and apply the method of classification as described in (ii).

The following lemma related to consistent vertex classification is used in later sections.

Lemma 3.1: If we know the classification of a vertex defined by any two planes P_i, P_j and a third plane P w.r.t. another plane P_k and if $\frac{\varepsilon}{sin\alpha} \leq \frac{M}{2}$ holds then we can classify the vertex defined by P_i, P_j, P_k w.r.t. P consistently. Here ε is the tolerance in computation. α is the angle between P_i and P on plane P_j. M is the largest (or smallest) possible value representable in the machine floating point arithmetic.

Proof: Consider the vertex v which is defined by the intersection of three planes P_i, P_j, P as shown in Figure 3.2. We denote this by $v = V(P_i, P_j, P)$. Let P_j denote the plane of the paper. The intersection lines between P_j and other planes are shown in Figure 3.1. Suppose we know the classification of v w.r.t. P_k. If the distance between P and $\hat{v} = V(P_i, P_j, P_k)$ is $> \varepsilon$ then we can determine the classification of $\hat{v}$ unambiguously. Otherwise, we translate the plane $P_k : ax + by + cz + d = 0$ to $P_{\hat{k}} : ax + by + cz - M = 0$ if $d > 0$, or to $P_{\hat{k}} : ax + by + cz + M = 0$ if $d \leq 0$. Note that $P_{\hat{k}}$ is the plane P_k translated by the amount $M + |d|$. In the first case P_k is translated to the positive side and in the latter P_k is translated to the negative side. Henceforth, we will call such transformation given to any plane P_k as max-translation and the transformed plane $P_{\hat{k}}$ as $(P_k)_{maxtranslate}$. If P_k is translated to the same side in which v lies then the classification of $\hat{v} = V(P_k, P_i, P_j)$ w.r.t. P is opposite to that of $\tilde{v} = V(P_{\hat{k}}, P_i, P_j)$ if P_k is translated by more than ℓ where ℓ is the distance between P_k and $v = V(P_j, P_i, P)$. Conversely, if P_k is translated to the side which does not contain v , then classification of $\hat{v} = V(P_i, P_j, P_k)$ w.r.t. P is same as that of $\tilde{v} = (P_{\hat{k}}, P_i, P_j)$. Hence, classification of $\hat{v}$ can be determined consistently if classification of $\tilde{v}$ can be asserted unambiguously.

Suppose the distance between $\tilde{v} = V(P_{\hat{k}}, P_i, P_j)$ and the plane P is d and the distance between $v = V(P_i, P_j, P)$ and the plane $P_{\hat{k}}$ is $\hat{\ell}$. From simple geometry, $\hat{\ell} < \frac{d}{sin\alpha}$. For $\tilde{v}$ to be classified unambiguously, we require $d \geq \varepsilon$. Since $d > \hat{\ell}sin\alpha$, we note that $\hat{\ell}sin\alpha \geq \varepsilon$ or $\hat{\ell} \geq \frac{\varepsilon}{sin\alpha}$ is a sufficient condition for unambiguous classification of $\tilde{v}$. The total amount of translation given to the plane P_k is $\hat{\ell} \pm \ell$. Further, since $\hat{v}$ could not be classified unambiguously, $\ell < \frac{\varepsilon}{sin\alpha}$. Hence in the worst case $\ell + \hat{\ell} \geq \frac{\varepsilon}{sin\alpha} + \frac{\varepsilon}{sin\alpha} = \frac{2\varepsilon}{sin\alpha}$ is a sufficient condition for unambiguous classification of $\tilde{v}$. Since maximum translation we can give to P_k is $M + |d|$, $M + |d| \geq \frac{2\varepsilon}{sin\alpha}$ is a sufficient condition for $\tilde{v}$ to be classified reliably. Now $min|d| = 0$, hence $M \geq \frac{2\varepsilon}{sin\alpha}$ or $\frac{\varepsilon}{sin\alpha} \leq \frac{M}{2}$ is a sufficient condition for $\tilde{v}$ to be classified unambiguously.♣

4 Nesting of Polygons

The following problem arises as a subproblem in our polyhedral decomposition.

Problem: Given a set of m simple polygons $P_i, i = 1..., m$, for each polygon P_i determine (i) the polygon P_k s.t. P_k contains P_i and any other polygon P_j which contains P_i also contains P_k. We call P_k as parent of P_i. Note, there may not exist any such P_k in which case we say parent of P_i is *Null*. (ii) The polygons $P_{i1}, P_{i2}, ...P_{it}$ whose parent is P_i. We call $P_{i1}, P_{i2}, ...P_{it}$ as children of P_i. Note, there may not exist any such child in which case we say children of P_i is *Null*.

Theorem 4.1: The problem of polygon nesting for m polygons can be robustly solved in $O(n + (m + N)\log(m + N))$ time where n is the total number of vertices and N is the total number of notches of all polygons.

Proof: See [4]. ♣

5 Convex Decomposition

Since decomposing a polyhedron S with N notches consists of a sequence of intersections with notch planes, we first describe the method of cutting a polyhedron S by the *notch plane* P of a notch g.

Cross-Sectional Graph (GP): The cutting plane P: $ax + by + cz + d = 0$ divides the 3-dimensional space into two open half spaces $P^+ : ax + by + cz + d > 0$ and $P^- : ax + by + cz + d < 0$. The closure of P^+ is $P^u = P^+ \cup P_\ell$, where $P_\ell : ax + by + cz + d = 0$ is the oriented plane P with normal (a, b, c) pointing into the exterior of P^+. Similarly, the closure of P^- is $P^b = P^- \cup P_r$ where $P_r : -ax - by - cz - d = 0$ is the oriented plane P, with normal $(-a, -b, -c)$ pointing into the exterior of P^-.

Cutting a solid S with plane P is equivalent to computing

$$S \cap P^u = (S \cap P^+) \cup (S \cap P_\ell)$$
$$S \cap P^b = (S \cap P^-) \cup (S \cap P_r).$$

$S \cap P_\ell$ and $S \cap P_r$ are planar graphs embedded in $\Re^3$. We denote the planar graphs $S \cap P_\ell$ and $S \cap P_r$ as GP_ℓ and GP_r respectively. We also frequently refer to GP_ℓ and GP_r as cross-sectional graphs. Note that for a solid S, and a plane P, the cross-sectional graphs GP_ℓ and GP_r may be different. See for e.g., Figure 5.1.

The constructions of both GP_ℓ and GP_r are the crucial part in splitting a solid S into new solids S^+ and S^- about a plane P. We determine the unique polygons Q_l,Q_r from GP_l and GP_r called the *polygon-cuts*, supporting the notch g. After determining the polygon-cuts , we need to split S along these cuts . Actually splitting S along the cuts instead of cross-sectional graphs, is sufficient to remove the notch g of S. Note that because of this, S may not get separated into two different pieces after the split. See also Figure 5.2.

- **Step I**: Determine Q_l,(Q_r). This calls for the following steps
  - *Step I(a)*: Determine the outer boundary of $Q_l(Q_r)$.
  - *Step I(b)*: Determine the inner boundary(s) of $Q_l(Q_r)$ (if any).
- **Step II**: Separate S. While describing the algorithm we assume S is separated into two pieces by cuts $Q_l(Q_r)$. We refer to [3] for the case where S is merely spliced by $Q_l(Q_r)$ instead of getting separated into two pieces.

Details of Step I with Geometric Reasoning for Robustness:

Constructing GP_ℓ and GP_r: The edges of GP_ℓ and GP_r are either the edges transferred from solid S (old edges), or edges newly generated from $S \cap P$ (new edges). Note, all new edges will be present in both cross-sectional graphs while only some of the old edges may be present in either GP_ℓ or in GP_r. As with the edges, some of the vertices of the cross-sectional graphs will be old vertices while some of them will be new vertices. To generate old and new edges on these cross-sectional graphs, we compute the intersection points of each face f with the cutting plane using the vertex-plane, edge-plane, face-plane classification as described before.After computing all intersection vertices (new and old) lying on face f, we sort these vertices along the line of intersection $f \cap P$.

Robust Sorting of intersection vertices along line $f \cap P$: Consider the face f as shown in Figure 5.3. Let edges e_1 and e_2 intersect plane P at points v_1 and v_2, both necessarily lying on line $L = f \cap P$. Further let v_1 and v_2 be new vertices. If v_1 and v_2 happen to be very close together, it may not be possible to determine their local ordering on L reliably. However, the classification of v on $f \cap P$ can be used to decide this ordering consistently. The plane P is translated to $P_{maxtranslate}$ and the points $e_1 \cap P_{maxtranslate}$ and $e_2 \cap P_{maxtranslate}$ are computed. Let these intersection points be $\hat{v_1}$ and $\hat{v_2}$ respectively. As the angle between edges e_1 and e_2 cannot be arbitrarily small (minimum feature criteria) there exists a certain translation such that the distance between $\hat{v_1}$ and $\hat{v_2}$ will be $> \varepsilon$. We set the minimum angle α_{min} between two edges to be such that $\frac{\varepsilon}{sin\alpha_{min}} \leq \frac{M}{2}$. By Lemma 3.1 the distance between $\hat{v_1}$ and $\hat{v_2}$ will be $> \varepsilon$ and thus $\hat{v_1}$ and $\hat{v_2}$ can be ordered on L unambiguously. The ambiguity in ordering of old vertices along $f \cap P$ does not arise because of our assumption of minimum feature separation for elements of our original solid S.

Generating new edges: Suppose we have $(v_1, v_2, ..., v_k)$ as sorted sequence of intersection vertices of a face on the line of intersection L. We need to decide consistently whether there should be an edge between two consecutive vertices v_i and v_{i+1} of this sorted sequence. It is easy to see that if v_i is a new vertex then there would be an edge between v_i and v_{i+1} if there were no edge between v_{i-1} and v_i and vice versa. But if v_i is an old vertex there can be edge between v_i and v_{i+1} disregard of presence of edge between v_{i-1}, v_i. Hence, if v_i is an old vertex we need to decide whether there should be an edge between v_i, v_{i+1} in a consistent manner.

Consider two vertices v_i, v_{i+1} as shown in Figure 5.4. Let v_i be the old intersection vertex. We check if there is an old edge between v_i and v_{i+1} decided to be on the plane P. This edge may be transferred to GP_ℓ or GP_r or both. Transferring of old edges which are decided to be on plane P is discussed later. Now we consider the case where there is no old edge between v_i and v_{i+1}. Let e_1, e_2, ..., e_k be the edges connected to v_i. Let e_1, e_2, ..., e_m be the edges whose other vertex has been classified to be on same side of P. We transform P to $P_{maxtranslate}$ and compute the intersections points of $P_{maxtranslate}$ with the edges e_1, e_2, ..., e_m. Due to minimum feature criteria and Lemma 3.1, the ordering of these intersection points on the intersection line can be decided unambiguously and hence we can determine the edge corresponding to the highest intersection point (in the sense of same ordering with which v_i, v_{i+1} were ordered). In Figure 5.4 e_m will be that particular edge. There should be an edge between v_i and v_{i+1} if and only if e_m is oriented on face f in such a way that if we traverse e_m from v_i to the other vertex of e_m the face f is to the right side. From the orientation of e_m on f it can be determined easily.

Repeating the above described procedure for all the intersected faces of S we can generate all the new edges of GP_ℓ while recognising all the old edges of them. Now for each such old edge we need to decide whether that edge should be transferred to GP_ℓ or GP_r or to both.

Transfer of old edges: The old edge e_o should be transferred to GP_ℓ (resp. GP_r) if any face (or a part of it) containing e_o which has not been decided to be on the cutting plane, gets transferred to GP_ℓ (resp. GP_r). For e.g. the edge e_p in Figure 5.1 should be transferred to GP_ℓ but not to GP_r. For each old edge e_o decided to be on the plane P we check all of its oriented edges on different faces which have not been decided to be on the cutting plane. Suppose f_o is such a face. Classify any vertex v_o of f_o w.r.t e_o which can be done by classifying v_o w.r.t any plane containing the edge e_o. Now if it is on the same side of e_o to which f_o lies then e_o(oriented edge) should be transferred to GP_ℓ (resp. GP_r) if v_o has been classified to lie in P^+ (resp. P^-). It is trivial to decide the side of e_o to which f_o lies from the oriented edge of e_o on f_o.

Consistent vertex-plane, edge-plane and face-plane classification takes overall $O(t)$ time where t is the total number edges of the solid S. The above bound follows from the fact that we visit each edge of S $O(1)$ time while determining the intersection points of S with the cutting plane P. The sorting of intersection points adds $O(N \log N + r)$ where r is the total number of faces decided to be cut by the intersecting plane. The above bound follows from the fact that any line segment intersects a face with N_i notches in no more than $max(2, 2N_i + 1)$ points (Lemma 2.4). **Step I(a)**: Once we construct the graphs GP_ℓ and GP_r, it is trivial to recognise the boundary contaning notch g. **Step I(b)**: If there are m polygons and p' points in the cross-sectional graphs $GP_\ell(GP_r)$ we can determine children and parent of all the polygons in $O(p' + (m+N) \log (m+N))$ time (Theorem 4.1).The inner boundaries of $Q_\ell(Q_r)$ are the children of the outer boundary of $Q_\ell(Q_r)$. Since $m = O(N)$, detection of inner boundaries takes $O(p' + N \log N)$ time. Combining the complexity of determining the edges of GP_ℓ (resp. GP_r) and Step I(a), I(b), we conclude that the outer and inner boundary(s) of $Q_\ell(Q_r)$ can be determined in $O(t + p' + N \log N) = O(t + N \log N)$ time.

Details of Step I without robustness: Since we do not need techniques for robust computations, we can avoid checking all the vertices of the solid being cut and thus improving the time complexity. We describe the method of determining any boundary of the set of polygons of the cross-sectional graphs. Suppose we have an initial point a_1 on the boundary B. We can determine other points on B in the following way. Let a_1 be on the edge u_1 of the face f_i. Let $a_2, ..., a_k$ be other intersection points of f_i with P on the edges $u_2, u_2, ..., u_k$. We need to determine $a_2, ..., a_k$ which will be on B. Since intersection of f_i and P is a line L, in general, determining $a_2, ..., a_k$ requires nothing more than determining the intersection points of L with the simple polygon representing f_i.

Since we store the subchains of faces in a 2-3 tree, the intersection point in each subchain c_i can be determined in $O(log\ p_i)$ time by binary search where p_i is the number of vertices in the subchain c_i. By Lemma 2.4, $k \leq max(2, 2N_i + 1)$ where N_i is the number of notches in f_i. By Lemma 2.2, the number of subchains h_i in f_i is bounded by $6(1 + N_i)$. So, determination of $a_2, ..., a_k$ takes at most $\sum_{j=1}^{h_i} log\ p_j$. We sort a_i's on the line of intersection L. This takes $O(max(1, N_i\ log\ N_i)) = O((1 + N_i\ log\ N_i))$ time since $k \leq max(2, 2N_i + 1)$.

In the following, for convenience, we assume that a_i's are new vertices. To remove this restriction, requires only a slight modification of the argument below. We join a_1 and a_2 and keep $a_3, a_4, ..., a_k$ in a list associated with f_i for future use as described below. We examine u_2 and get the face f_{i+1} associated with u_2 other than f_i. Now, in face f_{i+1}, all the intersection points might have been determined earlier. We check the list of boundary points (intersection points) associated with f_{i+1}. If the list is empty, we follow the above procedure to determine it, otherwise we join a_2 with a'_3 in the list $a'_2, a'_3, ..., a'_k$ associated with f_{i+1}. We delete a'_2, a'_3 from this list. Note a'_2 and a_2 are the same point. Now we proceed from a'_3 and go on following the above procedure, until we reach the initial point a_1, on the boundary B. Obviously, the time taken to determine all the points on B is $O(\sum_{i=1}^{h}(\ log\ p_i) + \sum_{i=1}^{r}(N_i\ log\ N_i + 1))$, where h is the total number of subchains in all the faces intersected by P and r is the number of such faces. Note p_i is the number of vertices in the ith such subchain.

Now, we describe how to determine the outer and inner boundary(s) of $Q_\ell(Q_r)$. **Step I(a):** The notch g will be on the outer boundary of Q_ℓ and Q_r. So, we can take any vertex of g as the initial point to start with determining the outer boundary of Q_ℓ and Q_r by the above method. **Step I(b):** Let I_i be any inner boundary of $Q_\ell(Q_r)$. I_i itself constitutes a simple polygon. Polygon I_i will have at least one (actually at least three) vertex, which is not a notch. Since I_i is the inner boundary of $Q_\ell(Q_r)$, the vertices which are not notches of polygon I_i are notches of $Q_\ell(Q_r)$. Definitely,notches of $Q_\ell(Q_r)$ lies on notches of S. This guarantees us that all inner boundaries of $Q_\ell(Q_r)$ will have a point which is the intersection point of P with a notch of S. So, we determine the set W of intersection points of all notches of S with P. We take one such point as the initial point and determine the corresponding boundary and mark all the intersection points in W, which appear on the boundary. We determine all such boundaries until all vertices in W are marked. Note $|W| = O(N)$. If there are p' points on the boundaries of cross-sectional graphs we can determine the inner boundaries of $Q_\ell(Q_r)$ from $GP_\ell(GP_r)$ in $O(p' + N log N)$ time using Theorem 4.1. Combining the complexity of Step I(a) and I(b), we conclude that without regarding robustness the outer and inner boundary(s) of $Q_\ell(Q_r)$ can be determined in $O(\sum_{i=1}^{h}(\ log\ p_i) + N\ log\ N + p')$ time, since $\sum_{i=1}^{r}(N_i\ log\ N_i + 1) = O(N\ log\ N + p')$, where r is the number of faces intersected by P. Obviously, r is $O(p')$ since each such face contributes at least one point on the boundary.

Details of Step II

Separation of S corresponding to the polygon-cut $Q_\ell(Q_r)$ is carried out by splitting the faces which are cut by the plane P. Suppose f_i is such a face which is to be split at $a_1, a_2, ..., a_k$ which are on the edges $u_1, u_2, ..., u_k$. The splitting of f_i consists of splitting the trees corresponding to the subchains in which $(a_1, a_2, ..., a_k)$ lies and inserting $a_1, a_2, ..., a_k$ in proper trees. For each such intersection points (which can be an old or new vertex) we do the following

New Vertex: Let the edge on which new vertex v_n lies be $e_s = (v_1, v_2)$. We generate edges between v_1, v_n and between v_2, v_n. Since we know the half spaces in which v_1 and v_2 lies, we can decide in which half space each such new edges lie.

Old Vertex: For each old vertex v_o lying on plane P, we transfer the edges connected to v_o to the half space in which their other vertex has been decided to lie in. By transferring we mean that we connect those edge to the copy of the vertex v_o on the corresponding cross-sectional graph. The edges connected to v_o which have been decided to be on plane P are transferred by procedure as described before. Finally, from $Q_\ell(Q_r)$, we create the face of $Q_\ell(Q_r)$ by creating the tree structures for the subchains in $Q_\ell(Q_r)$ and keep them associated with their edges. Splitting each face which are cut by the plane P effectively split the solid S into separate pieces.

In the method without robustness we visit only the vertices on the boundaries of $Q_\ell(Q_r)$ and for each vertex we spend constant time for setting relevant pointers and additional time for splitting and insertion operations in the trees corresponding to subchains in the faces. The latter is logarithmic in the number of vertices contained in the subchain. Hence, the separation takes $O\left(p' + \sum_{i=1}^{h}\ log\ p_i\right)$ time where p' is the number of vertices in $GP_\ell(GP_r)$ and h is the total number of subchains contained in the faces intersected by the notch plane P. p_i is the number of vertices in the i-th such subchain. Note that p' is also the number of edges of S intersected by P. This yields

Lemma 5.1. A polyhedron S of genus 0, having N notches can be partitioned robustly with a cut in (i) $O(t + N \log N)$ time using geometric reasoning for robust computations (ii) $O\left(\sum_{i=1}^{h}(\log p_i) + N \log N +\right.$ time without robustness. In both cases space complexity is $O(t)$, where t is the number of edges of S, p' being the number of edges of S intersected by the plane P supporting the cut, h being the total number of subchains in all the faces intersected by P, p_i being the number of vertices in the i-th such subchain,p' being the number of vertices on the cross-sectional graphs.

We can generalize the above result for a polyhedron of arbitrary genus. For this, as described in [6], we have to handle the situation when the cut does not separate S into two pieces, but only creates two new faces supporting the cut at the same geometric location. The method of handling this case is described in [3].

Lemma 5.2. Let $S_1, S_2, ..., S_k$ be the polyhedra in the current decomposition which contains a subnotch of g to be resolved, and let v_i' be the total number of vertices in the cross-sectional graphs resulted from intersection of S_i with a notch plane P, then since any notch can be intersected by at most $(N-1)$ notches, we have $k = O(N)$ and $v' = \sum_{i=1}^{k} v_i' = O(n + N^2)$, where v' is the total number of vertices on all the cross-sectional graphs of $S_1, S_2, ..., S_k$.

Proof: See [3] for details.

♣

Lemma 5.3: The total number of edges in the final decomposition of P with N notches is $O(n\ N + N^3)$.

Proof: Total number of edges in the final decomposition consists of newly generated edges by the polygon-cuts, and the edges of S which are not intersected by any notch plane. Now since the total number vertices in all the cross-sectional graphs of a partial decomposition is $O(n + N^2)$ as proved in Lemma 5.2, the total number of newly generated edges by each notch plane is $O(n + N^2)$. Thus N notch planes generate $O(n\ N + N^3)$ new edges. Hence, the total number of edges in the final decomposition is $O(n\ N + N^3 + n)$ $= O(n\ N + N^3)$ ♣

Theorem 5.1: A polyhedron S of arbitrary genus having N notches and n edges can be decomposed robustly into $O(N^2)$ convex parts in (i) $O(nN^2 + N^4)$ time using geometric reasoning for robustness, (ii) $O((nN + N^3) log N)$ time without robustness. Both methods require $O(nN + N^3)$ space.

Proof: *Worst-Case Time Analysis*: At a generic instance of the algorithm, let $S_1, S_2, ..., S_k$ be the k distinct (non-convex) polyhedra in the current decomposition, which contains the subnotches of a notch g which we are going to remove.Let S_i have t_i edges and p_i' be the number of edges in S_i intersected by the notch plane. Let t be the total number of edges in all polyhedra $S_1, S_2, ..., S_k$.

(i) *Method using geometric reasoning for robustness*: Using Lemma 5.1, we can say the time $\Im$ to remove the notch g is given by

$$\Im = O(\sum_{i=1}^{k}(t_i + N_i \log N_i)) = O(t + N^2 \log N) = O(nN + N^3 + N^2 \log N) = O(nN + N^3)$$

To carry out removal of N notches we need $O(nN^2 + N^4)$ time.

(ii) *Method without robustness*: Time complexity $\Im$ of polyhedron decomposition without robustness is given by

$$\Im = O((nN + N^3) \log N)$$

For further details see [3].

Space Analysis: In Lemma 5.3, we prove that the total number of edges in the final decomposition of S is $O(n\ N + N^3)$. Since, t = $O(n\ N + N^3)$, the space complexity of polyhedral decomposition is $O(n\ N + N^3)$. ♣

Decomposition into Tetrahedra: Each convex piece with t edges can be triangulated into tetrahedra as follows. First we triangulate each convex face. Then creating edges from a point inside the convex piece to all other vertices and subsequent splitting of the polyhedra about these edges, produces the desired tetrahedral pieces. This operation takes at most $O(t)$ time for each convex piece. Hence, triangulation of all pieces takes $O(n\ N + N^3)$ time.

6 Conclusion

We have implemented our robust polyhedral decomposition algorithm in Common Lisp on a Symbolics 3650. The numerical computations are all in C, callable from Lisp. A simple example is shown in Figure 6.1. The experimental results have been very satisfying.

Our next goal is to develop an efficient approximation algorithm for the decomposition of a polyhedron into a fixed number k of approximately equal sized sub-polyhedra. This decomposition yields a straightforward mapping of a sequential operation (say, finite-element analysis) onto k separate processors, with each processor analyzing a sub-polyhedron in parallel. Each processor, in turn may decompose its sub-polyhedron into convex or tetrahedral pieces, for efficient domain manipulation.

References

[1] Bajaj, C., (1989) "Geometric Modeling with Algebraic Surfaces", *The Mathematics of Surfaces III*, edited by D. Handscomb, Oxford University Press, to appear.

[2] Bajaj, C., Dyksen, W., Hoffmann, C., Houstis, E., Korb, T., and Rice, J., (1988) "Computing About Physical Objects", *Proc. of the 12th IMACS World Congress*, Paris, 642 - 645.

[3] Bajaj, C., and Dey, T., (1988) "Robust Decompositions of Polyhedra", Computer Science Technical Report, Purdue University, CER-88-44.

[4] Bajaj, C., and Dey, T., (1989) "Robust Computation of Polygon Nesting" *Proc. Intl. Workshop on Discrete Algorithms and Complexity*, Fukuoka, Japan, to appear.

[5] Chazelle, B., (1980), "Computational Geometry and Convexity", *Ph.D. Thesis*, CMU-CS-80-150, Computer Science, Carnegie-Mellon University.

[6] Chazelle, B., (1984), "Convex Partitions of Polyhedra: A Lower Bound and Worst-case Optimal Algorithm", *SIAM J. on Computing*, Vol. 13, No. 3, pp. 488–507.

[7] Chazelle, B., and Palios, L., (1989), "Triangulating a Non-convex Polytope" *Proc. of the 5th ACM Symposium on Computational Geometry*, Saarbrucken, West Germany,

[8] Dobkin, D., and Silver, D., (1988), "Recipes for Geometry and Numerical Analysis", *Proc. of the Fourth ACM Symposium on Computational Geometry*, Urbana, Illinois, 93 - 105.

[9] Edelsbrunner, H., (1987), "Algorithms in Combinatorial Geometry", Springer Verlag.

[10] Edelsbrunner, H., and Mucke, P., (1988), "Simulation of Simplicity: A Technique to Cope with Degenerate Cases in Geometric Algorithms" *Proc. of the Fourth ACM Symposium on Computational Geometry*, Urbana, Illinois, 118-133.

[11] Edelsbrunner, H., and Guibas, L., (1989) "Topologically Sweeping an Arrangement", *J. of Computer and System Sciences*, 38, 165 - 194.

[12] Fortune, S., (1989) "Stable Maintenance of Point-set Triangulations in Two Dimensions", Manuscript.

[13] Greene, D., and Yao, F., (1986), "Finite-Resolution Computational Geometry" *Proc. 27th IEEE Symposium on Foundations of Computer Science*, Toronto, Canada, 143-152.

[14] Guibas, L., Salesin, D., and Stolfi, J., (1989) "Building Robust Algorithms from Imprecise Computations", *Proc. 1989 ACM Symposium on Computational Geometry*, Saarbuchen, West Germany, 208-217.

[15] Hoffmann, C., Hopcroft, J., and Karasick, M., (1987), "Robust Set Operations on Polyhedral Solids", Dept. of Computer Science, Cornell University, Technical Report 87-875.

[16] Hoffmann, K., Mehlhorn, K., Rosenstiehl, P., and Tarjan, R., (1986), "Sorting Jordan Sequences in Linear Time using Level Linked Search Trees", *Information and Control*, 68, 170 - 184.

[17] Karasick, M., (1988) "On the Representation and Manipulation of Rigid Solids", Ph.D. Thesis, McGill University.

[18] Lingas, A., (1982), "The Power of Non-Rectilinear Holes", *Proc. 9th Intl. Colloquium on Automata, Languages and Programming*, Lecture Notes in Computer Science, Springer Verlag, 369 - 383.

[19] Milenkovic, V., (1988), "Verifiable Implementations of Geometric Algorithms Using Finite Precision Arithmetic", Ph.D. Thesis, CMU Tech. Report CS-88-168, Carnegie Mellon Univ., Pittsburgh.

[20] O'Rourke, J., and Supowit, K., (1983), "Some NP-hard Polygon Decomposition Problems", *IEEE Trans. Inform. Theory*, 29, 181 - 190.

[21] Ottmann, T., Thiemt, G., and Ullrich, C., (1987), "Numerical Stability of Geometric Algorithms", *Proc. of the Third ACM Symposium on Computational Geometry*, Waterloo, Canada, 119-125.

[22] Rupert, J., and Seidel, R., (1989) "On the Difficulty of Tetrahedralizing Three Dimensional Non-convex Polyhedra", *Proc. of the Fifth ACM Symposium on Computational Geometry*, Saarbrucken, West Germany, to appear.

[23] Segal, M., and Sequin, C., (1985), "Consistent Calculations for Solids Modelling", *Proc. of the First ACM Symposium on Computational Geometry*, 29 - 38.

[24] Sugihara, K., (1988), "A Simple Method of Avoiding Numerical errors and Degeneracy in Voronoi diagram Constructions", Research Memorandum RMI 88-14, Department of Mathematical Engineering and Instrumentation Physics, Tokyo University.

[25] Sugihara, K., and Iri, M., (1989), "A Solid Modeling System Free from Topological Consistency", Research Memorandum RMI 89-3, Department of Mathematical Engineering and Instrumentation Physics, Tokyo University.

[26] Yap, C., (1988) "A Geometric Consistency Theorem for a Symbolic Perturbation Theorem" *Proc. of the Fourth ACM Symposium on Computational Geometry*, Urbana, Illinois, 134-142.

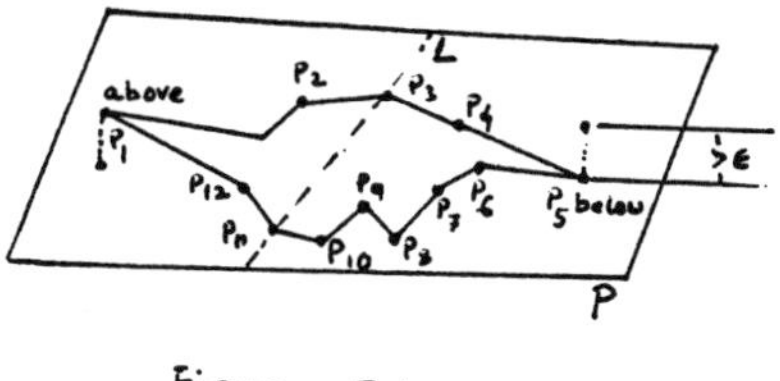

Figure 3.1

$P_2, \dots, P_4$ AND $P_6, \dots, P_{12}$ ARE maybe on vertices.
P_4 and $P_6, \dots, P_{10}$ gets classification of P_5.
P_2, P_{12} gets classification of P_1.

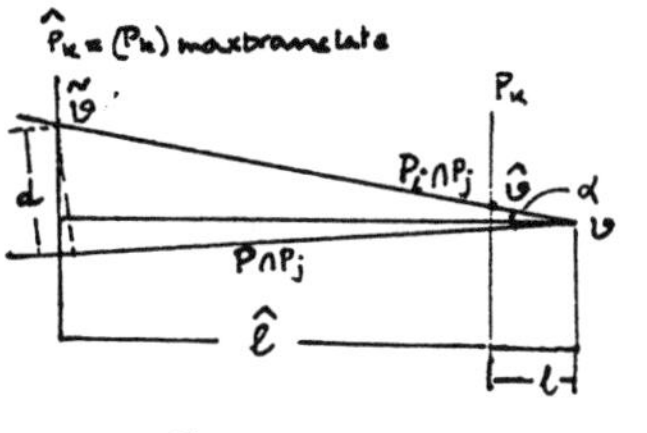

Figure 3.2

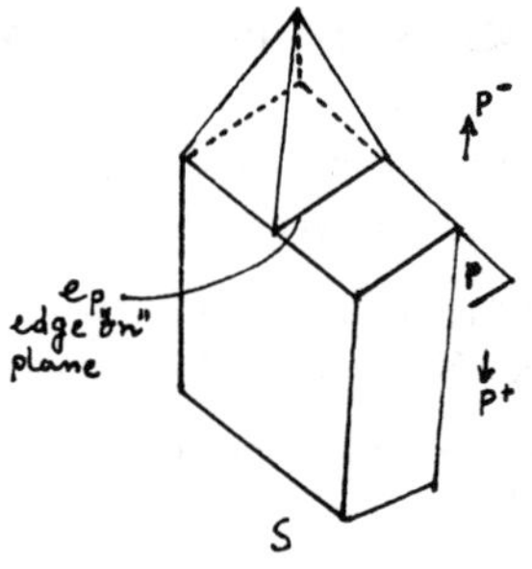

Figure 5.1 (a)

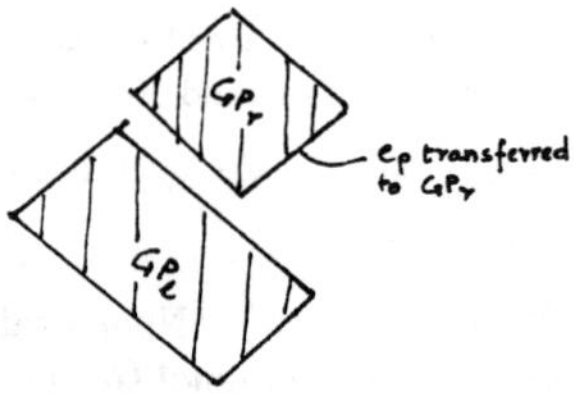

Figure 5.1 (b)

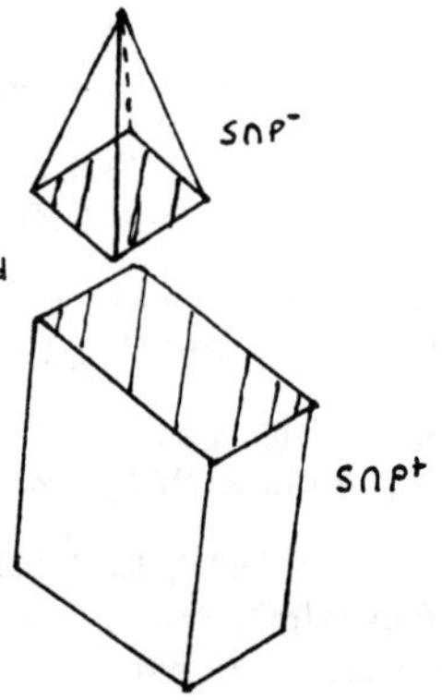

Figure 5.1 (c)

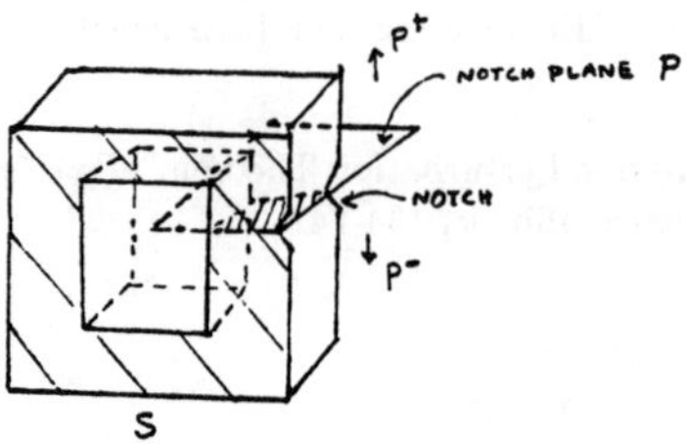

FIGURE 5.2 (a)

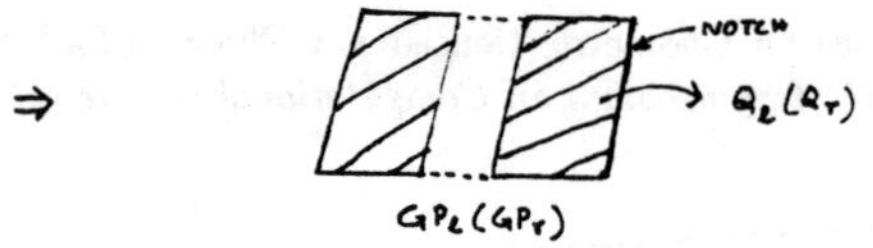

FIGURE 5.2 (b)

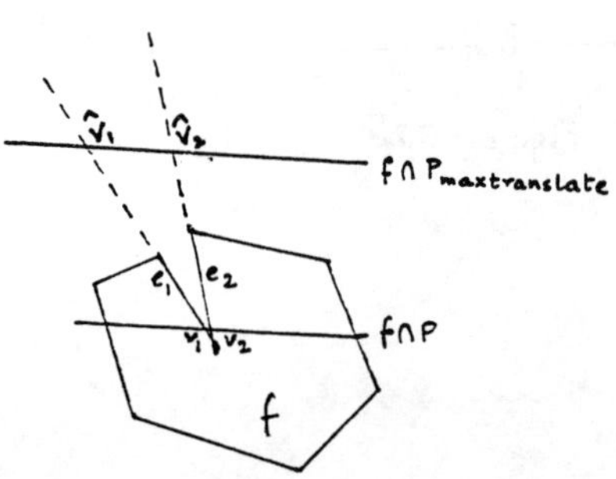

FIGURE 5.3

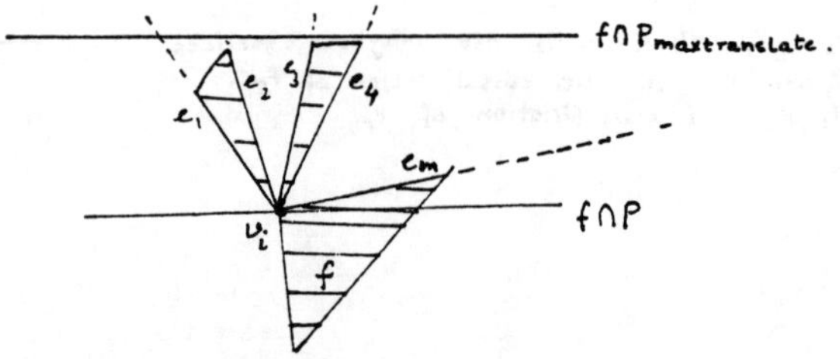

FIGURE 5.4

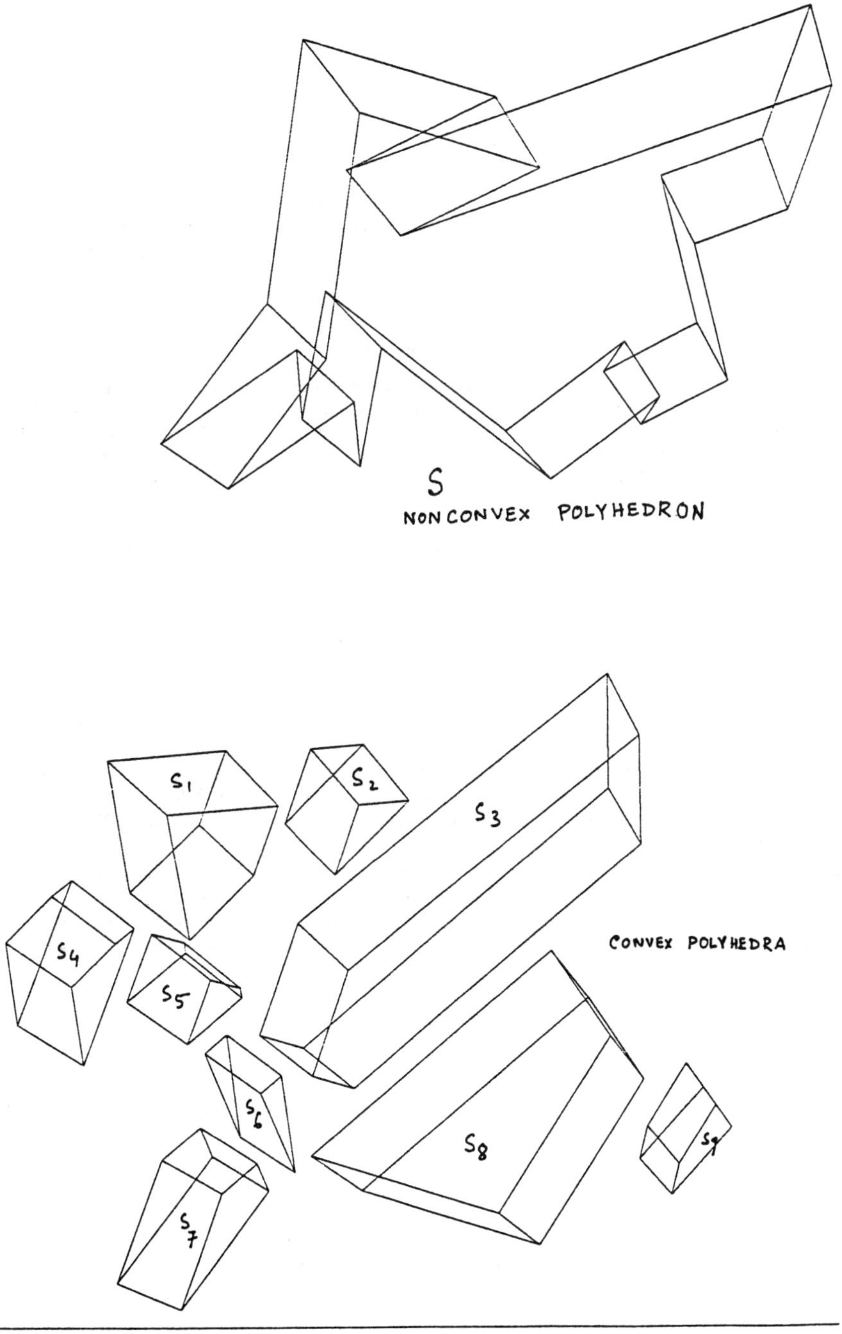

Figure 6.1
ROBUST POLYHEDRAL DECOMPOSITION

GATE MATRIX LAYOUT REVISITED:

ALGORITHMIC PERFORMANCE AND PROBABILISTIC ANALYSIS [†]

Sajal K. Das
Department of Computer Science
University of North Texas
Denton, TX 76203, U.S.A.

Narsingh Deo and Sushil Prasad
Department of Computer Science
University of Central Florida
Orlando, FL 32816, U.S.A.

ABSTRACT

We consider the gate matrix layout problem for VLSI design, and improve the time and space complexities of an existing dynamic programming algorithm for its exact solution. Experimental study indicates the requirement of enormous computation time for exact solutions of even small size matrices. We derive an expression for the expected number of tracks required to layout in gate matrix style based on a probabilistic model. A local search approximation algorithm is studied experimentally and found to perform reasonably well on average.

Index Terms: Approximation algorithms, dynamic programming, gate matrix layout, probabilistic analysis, VLSI circuits.

1. INTRODUCTION

Gate matrix style is a systematic approach to CMOS circuit layout [9]. A polysilicon stripe is assigned to each distinct transistor gate and to each output terminal of a CMOS circuit. The set of these poly-stripes, referred to as *gate lines* (or simply gates), form the columns of the *gate matrix*. The columns laid down as equally spaced poly-stripes serve as transistor gates when diffusion areas are placed on each side of the stripe. They also serve as conductors which connect the gates of each complementary pair of transistors. Transistors are connected by segments of metal lines, referred to as *nets,* which are placed along the rows of the gate matrix. For a detailed description of the layout of CMOS circuits in gate matrix style, refer to [2, 9, 16].

Formally, an instance of the gate matrix layout problem (GMLP) consists of a set of nets (rows) $N = \{1, \ldots, m\}$ and a set of gates (columns) $S = \{1, \ldots, n\}$ and their interconnections. A solution to GMLP is a permutation of the columns which minimizes the number of tracks (and hence the area) required to layout the circuit. For illustration, consider three nets connected to four gates in a gate matrix as follows.

Gates:	1	2	3	4
Net 1:	1	0	1	0
Net 2:	0	1	0	1
Net 3:	0	0	1	1

where a matrix-element is 1 if and only if net i is incident on gate j, otherwise it is zero. The layout apparently requires three tracks, as depicted by the left-hand side of the following diagram.

```
Gates:     1   2   3   4          Gates:      2   4   3   1

              Net 1                           Net 2   Net 1
track 1    x---------x            track 1     x----x  x----x

                  Net 2                           Net 3
track 2        x----------x       track 2         x----x

                     Net 3
track 3            x-----x
```

† This work was supported by grants from University of North Texas and U.S. Naval Training Systems Center.

However, two tracks are sufficient if columns are permuted, as shown on the right-hand side of the preceding diagram. In this case, nets 1 and 2 can be laid out on a single track.

It is known that GMLP is an NP-complete problem [6], and various approaches have been applied to solve it. For example, it can be formulated as the chromatic number of an interval graph [10, 11], which in turn is equal to the size of the maximum clique [4]. Several approximation algorithms and a few limited experiments have been reported in [7, 8, 10, 14-16]. Wing [14] has proposed an algorithm to reconstruct the dominant clique of a connection graph, which is obtained from the given net list. Since, finding all the dominant cliques is NP-complete [3], the method is less attractive from a practical point of view. As demonstrated by Deo et al. [2], any greedy or on-line algorithm for GMLP requires chip area unbounded by any constant multiplied by the optimum. Moreover, they have proved that unless P = NP, there exists no polynomial-time absolute approximation algorithm [5, 13] for this problem.

In this paper, we are interested in the expected performance of algorithms for GMLP. Although we undertake an experimental approach, analytic methods are also developed to predict and aid the experimentation. A dynamic programming formulation described in [2] is improved and implemented. Exact solutions of instances with 15 and 16 columns and 20 rows are computed in about 17 and 47 minutes, respectively, on IBM 3090. (The cases with 17 and 18 columns are expected to take about two and six hours, respectively, on the same machine.) Since computing an optimal solution in a reasonable time is unrealistic for problem instances of large size, it is difficult to evaluate the performance (namely, the goodness factor) of approximation algorithms due to the lack of a basis for comparing the average number of tracks computed by them. For this purpose, we take recourse to probabilistic method, and derive an expression for the expected number of tracks required. Although this expression leads to an approximate calculation, its results closely follow our empirical observations. Experimental study of a local search approximation algorithm (which finds a local minimal by transposition of a pair of columns) shows that it performs reasonably well on an average as compared to our probabilistic calculations.

The rest of the paper is organized as follows. Section 2 briefly sketches the dynamic programming formulation and its implementation. Probabilistic model and the derivation of an expression for the expected number of tracks is presented in Section 3, while Section 4 deals with a local search approximation algorithm. The final section concludes the paper and discusses future work.

2. DYNAMIC PROGRAMMING FORMULATION

A dynamic programming formulation for GMLP is presented in [2]. This method finds an exact solution requiring $O(n^2 2^n)$ time and $O(n\ 2^n)$ space, where n is the number of gates. Here we outline a slightly modified version that reduces both time and space complexities by a factor of n. Let us first introduce a few terminology.

Given a permutation of columns, a gate matrix is said to satisfy **consecutive 1's** property if its rows have all of their 1's consecutively [1, 4]. When this property holds, it can be easily verified that the minimum number of tracks required is given by the largest **column-sum** (i.e., the sum of all 1's in a column) of the gate matrix. But, in general, consecutive 1's property may not hold for a given permutation of columns. (In fact, it might well be possible that the gate matrix does not have this property for any permutation.) However, even when this property does not hold for a permutation, the number of tracks required can still be calculated as the largest column-sum after substituting zeros with 1's in the gate matrix, wherever necessary to satisfy consecutive 1's property. The zeros which are treated as 1's to satisfy consecutive 1's property for a given permutation of columns are referred to as **fill-ins.** In other words, zeros in a row which have 1's on their left and right are called fill-ins. For example, in the following permutation, fill-ins are indicated by asterisks which are otherwise zeros.

columns:	1	2	3	4	5
row 1:	1	*	*	1	0
row 2:	0	1	1	1	1
row 3:	0	0	0	1	0
row 4:	0	1	*	*	1

Counting fill-ins, the largest column-sum is four which is the number of tracks required to layout this permutation. In this example, a column α, for $2 \leq \alpha \leq 4$, has a fill-in in row i if the ith net is not incident on column α but is incident on at least one column to the left and at least one column to the right of α. For example, column 2 has a fill-in in row 1 because the net 1 is incident on columns 1 and 4, and column 2 has a zero in row 1. Similarly, column 3 has two fill-ins and column 4 has one. Column 2 will continue to have a fill-in in row 1 even if the permutation is changed to (1 2 3 5 4). That is, fill-ins in a column are decided only by the sets of columns to its left and to its right and not by different permutations of columns within these two sets. We use this idea later in this section to compute the number of number of fill-ins in a given column.

A solution based on the dynamic programming strategy usually involves computing partial solutions for different smaller subsets of a problem and gradually building solutions for larger subsets from these subsolutions. Given a set of columns $S = \{1, 2, \ldots, n\}$, our goal is to find a permutation which requires the least number of tracks, $T(S)$. For $S_1 \subseteq S$ and $\alpha \in S_1$, let $C(S_1, \alpha)$ denote the least number of tracks required to lay all the columns in S_1 such that α is the last column and the remaining columns in $S - S_1$ are laid to the right of α. (Actually, $C(S_1, \alpha)$ depends on S also but for brevity we have dropped S here.) The permutation corresponding to $C(S_1, \alpha)$ is as follows.

columns: $S_1 - \{\alpha\}$ $\quad\alpha\quad$ $S - S_1$

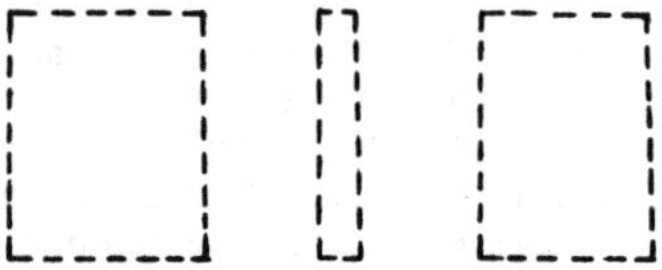

The placement of $S - S_1$ to the right of α only determines the fill-ins in the columns of S_1. Once the fill-ins are decided, $C(S_1, \alpha)$ is given by the least of the largest column-sums of all the permutations of columns in S_1 with α as the last column. With this definition, the minimum number of tracks to lay all the gates in S is given as $T(S) = \min\{C(S, \alpha) \mid \alpha \in S\}$. For detailed illustrative examples, refer to [2, 12].

Let $\bar{\alpha}$ denote the column α and $|\bar{\alpha}|$ be the column-sum of $\bar{\alpha}$. As a boundary condition, $C(\{\alpha\},\alpha) = |\bar{\alpha}|$ for $\alpha \in S$. Given a permutation of columns for $C(S_1, \alpha)$, for $S_1 \subseteq S$ and $\alpha \in S_1$, the number of fill-ins in $\bar{\alpha}$ is given by the column-sum of a column function $\bar{F}(S_1, \alpha)$ such that its ith element,

$$\bar{F}_i(S_1, \alpha) = \begin{cases} 1, & \text{if the } i\text{th net is incident on at least one column in} \\ & S_1 - \{\alpha\} \text{and at least one column in } S - S_1 \text{ and } \alpha_i = 0, \\ 0, & \text{otherwise.} \end{cases}$$

In general, for $S_1 \subseteq S$, $\alpha \in S_1$ and $|S_1| > 1$,

$$C(S_1, \alpha) = \max \left[\min_{\beta \in S_1 - \{\alpha\}} C(S_1 - \{\alpha\}, \beta), (|\bar{\alpha}| + |\bar{F}(S_1, \alpha)|) \right] \quad (1)$$

This is the expression we were looking for.

The permutation corresponding to the minimum number of tracks, $T(S)$, can be obtained by storing the values of α corresponding to each $\min\{C(S_1, \alpha) \mid \alpha \in S_1\}$.

2.1 Time and Space Complexity

For a set S of gates, $C(S_1, \alpha)$ must be calculated for each $S_1 \subseteq S$ and for each $\alpha \in S_1$. However, for a given subset S_1, we only need to store $\min\{C(S_1, \alpha) \mid \alpha \in S_1\}$ because the larger values of $C(S_1, \alpha)$ are not used in Expression (1). Therefore, evaluation of each of $C(S_1, \alpha)$ requires only one comparison since $\min\{C(S_1 - \{\alpha\},\beta) \mid \beta \in S_1 - \{\alpha\}\}$ is available from earlier calculations. Thus, for a subset S_1, we need to calculate $|S_1|$ number of $C(S_1, \alpha)$ each requiring a single comparison, and $\min\{C(S_1, \alpha) \mid \alpha \in S_1\}$ needs to be evaluated and stored requiring $|S_1|$ comparisons. The total number of comparisons for each $S_1 \subseteq S$ is, therefore, $2|S_1| - 1$. Note that this applies only to subsets of size ≥ 2. Thus, the total number of comparisons required to find the minimum number of tracks using our dynamic programming formulation is,

$$\sum_{i=2}^{n} \binom{n}{i} (2i - 1) = O(n2^n).$$

Assuming that the storage required for each of $\min\{C(S_1, \alpha) \mid \alpha \in S_1\}$ is one location, the total space requirement is $\sum_{i=1}^{n-1} \binom{n}{i} = O(2^n)$.

This clearly shows that we reduce the complexity of the dynamic programming algorithm by a factor of n as compared to that in [2].

2.2 Algorithm

The formulation in Section 2.1 has been implemented in Pascal on IBM 3090. The algorithm is described here for a gate matrix of m rows and n columns. (The detailed program is included in [12].)

for i := 1 **to** n **do**
  for j := 1 **to** $\binom{n}{i}$ **do**
  begin
    Let S_1 be the jth subset of $\{1, \ldots, n\}$ of size i; /* Assuming some order on the subsets */

    min := m; /* initialization for $\min\{C(S_1, \alpha) \mid \alpha \in S_1\}$ */
    for each $\alpha \in S_1$ **do**
      begin
        if $i = 1$ **then** $C(S_1, \alpha) := |\bar{\alpha}|$
        else $C(S_1, \alpha) := \max \left[\min_{\beta \in S_1 - \{\alpha\}} C(S_1 - \{\alpha\}, \beta), (|\bar{F}(S_1, \alpha)| + |\bar{\alpha}|) \right]$;
        if min > $C(S_1, \alpha)$ **then** min := $C(S_1, \alpha)$;
      end;
    store min **as** $\min\{C(S_1, \alpha) \mid \alpha \in S_1\}$;
  end;
  report $\min\{C(\{1, 2, \ldots, n\}, \alpha) \mid \alpha \in \{1, 2, \ldots, n\}\}$;

2.3 Empirical Results

For all experiments in this paper, we have considered randomly-generated gate matrices, assuming an uniform distribution of pseudo-random numbers. Let $T_d(n, m, p)$ be the average time for computing an exact solution with dynamic programming approach, which is a function of three independent variables – the number n of columns, the number m of rows, and the sparsity p of the gate matrix. The sparsity gives the probability that an entry in the gate matrix is 0 and it is independent of any other entry in the matrix. In our experiments, one of these three parameters was varied while the others were kept constant.

Figure 1 shows a least-square regression fit for $\log_e(T_d)$ against n. Sparsity has been chosen to be 0.95 because this value seems to be closer to reality. As expected, the growth of T_d with n is exponential. The case with $n = 16$ and $m = 20$ required about 47 minutes and $n = 17$ is expected to take more than two hours. The curves for experimental results are of the form

$$\begin{aligned} \log_e(T_d(n, 10, 0.95)) &\approx 0.79n + 6.36 \\ \log_e(T_d(n, 15, 0.95)) &\approx 1.01n + 5.48 \\ \log_e(T_d(n, 20, 0.95)) &\approx 1.00n + 5.76 \end{aligned} \qquad (2)$$

Figure 2 shows a plot for T_d with varying number of rows. The curves are linear, and they have the form

$$\begin{aligned} T_d(4, m, 0.95) &\approx 0.09m + 0.11 \text{ millisecs} \\ T_d(5, m, 0.95) &\approx 0.27m + 0.29 \text{ millisecs} \\ T_d(6, m, 0.95) &\approx 0.68m + 0.79 \text{ millisecs.} \end{aligned} \qquad (3)$$

Figure 3 is a plot for T_d versus sparsity p. The computation time is expected to be low when the gate matrix is dense, due to savings in time for computing the function $\bar{F}$, while the actual number of comparisons remains the same.

3. PROBABILISTIC MODEL

As is clear from the discussion in the preceding section, no exhaustive-enumeration technique can be of much practical significance for large gate matrix layout problems. Therefore, the average-case behavior of approximation algorithms needs to be studied which includes the time complexity as well as average number of tracks obtained. One of the problems that arises is that of evaluating the goodness of the approximate solutions obtained by these heuristics due to the lack of any reasonable method of computing the optimal number of tracks. Wing [14] has used the largest column-sum without fill-ins as a lower bound, and the highest column-sum with fill-ins (for an arbitrary permutation of gates) as an upper bound on the number of tracks. However, these bounds may not be tight enough. A better approach would be to analytically calculate the expected number of tracks required for a gate matrix of a given size and sparsity, and then use the expected value to compare with the average number of tracks obtained by different approximation algorithms.

Before deriving an expected number of tracks required for a gate matrix layout having n columns, m rows and sparsity p, we need to calculate the probability U that any two rows i and j, each of length n, cannot be merged – that is, the two rows cannot be laid on the same track. The probability U is a function of n and p. We first calculate $\overline{U}$, which is the probability that any two rows i and j, each of length n, can be merged (and hence can be laid on a single track). Then, U is given as $1 - \overline{U}$. The event that "rows i and j can be merged" occurs when either of the following $2n + 1$ mutually exclusive events occur. We count columns from left to right.

event 0: rows i and j have all zeros.

For $1 \le l \le n - 1$,

event l: row i has a net till lth column, and row j has all zeros till lth column

columns:	1	2	...	$l-1$	l	$l+1$	...	n
row i :	x	x	...	x	1	0	...	0
row j :	0	0	...	0	0	x	...	x

where x denotes 0 or 1.

event n: row i has a net till nth column and j has all zeros

columns:	1	...	$n-1$	n
row i :	x	...	x	1
row j :	0	...	0	0

For $1 \le l \le n - 1$,

event $n + l$: row j has a net till lth column, and row i has all zeros till lth column

columns:	1	2	...	$l-1$	l	$l+1$	...	n
row i :	0	0	...	0	0	x	...	x
row j :	x	x	...	x	1	0	...	0

event $2n$: row j has a net till nth column and i has all zeros

columns:	1	...	$n-1$	n
row i :	0	...	0	0
row j :	x	...	x	1

It can be easily verified that all of the preceding $2n + 1$ events are mutually exclusive. Moreover, they collectively exhaust all possibilities by which rows i and j can be merged. Now, we calculate the probability $\overline{U}$ as follows.

$\overline{U} = \sum_{k=0}^{2n}$ Pr(event k), where Pr(event k) gives the probability that event k, for $0 \le k \le 2n$, occurs.

Pr(event 0) = Pr(rows i and j have all zeros) $= p^{2n}$,

Pr(event 1) = Pr(row i has a 1 and j has a zero in column 1, and i has zeros everywhere else)

$$= (qp)\,(p^{n-1}) = qp^n, \quad \text{where } q = 1 - p.$$

Pr(event 2) = Pr(row i has a 1 in column 2 and zeros in columns 3 through n, and j has zeros in columns 1 and 2)

$$= (qp^{n-2})\,(p^2) = qp^n,$$

. . .

Pr(event l) = Pr(row i has a 1 in column l and zeros in columns $l+1$ through n and j has zeros in columns 1 through l)

$$= (qp^{n-l})\,(p^l) = qp^n.$$

Similarly, the probability of occurrence of an event k, $1 \le k \le 2n$, is qp^n. Therefore,

$$\overline{U} = \Pr(\text{rows } i \text{ and } j \text{ can be merged}) = p^{2n} + 2n(qp^n) = p^{2n} + 2nqp^n,$$

which yields $U = \Pr(\text{rows } i \text{ and } j \text{ cannot be merged}) = 1 - \overline{U}$

$$= 1 - p^{2n} - 2nqp^n = 1 - p^n(p^n + 2nq) = 1 - p^n(p^n + 2n - 2np), \quad \text{since } q = 1 - p.$$

It can be verified that $\lim_{p \to 1} U = 0$, $\lim_{p \to 0} U = 1$, and $\lim_{n \to \infty} U = 1$ for $p \neq 1$.

Thus, the probability U decreases monotonically with sparsity p with its maximum at $p = 0$ and minimum at $p = 1$.

For further analysis, we make a simplifying assumption as follows. The event that row i cannot be merged into row j is independent of the event that row i cannot be merged into row k and the event that row j cannot be merged into row k, where $i \neq j \neq k$. This allows us to calculate the probability that any three rows i, j, and k cannot be directly merged into each other. This probability is $U^{\binom{3}{2}} = U^3$, which generalizes to $U^{\binom{k}{2}}$ for any k such rows, where $k \ge 2$. Although this assumption yields an approximate result, the error reduces as the gate matrix becomes increasingly sparse or dense (so that $U \to 0$ or $U \to 1$, respectively) or as the number n of columns becomes large ($U \to 1$). Then, the probability that at least one track is required is given by

$\Pr(\ge 1 \text{ track}) = \Pr(\text{at least one entry in the gate matrix is a } 1) = 1 - p^{mn}$, and

$\Pr(\ge 2 \text{ tracks}) = \Pr(\text{there exists at least one pair of rows that cannot be merged})$

$$= \binom{\binom{m}{2}}{1} U - \binom{\binom{m}{2}}{2} U^2 + \binom{\binom{m}{2}}{3} U^3 - \cdots + (-1)^{\binom{m}{2}+1} \binom{\binom{m}{2}}{\binom{m}{2}} U^{\binom{m}{2}}$$

$$= 1 - \left[1 - U^{\binom{2}{2}}\right]^{\binom{m}{2}}.$$

Similarly,

$\Pr(\ge k \text{ tracks}) = \Pr(\text{there exists at least one set of } k \text{ rows which cannot be merged into one another})$

$$= 1 - \left[1 - U^{\binom{k}{2}}\right]^{\binom{m}{k}}$$

Therefore, using the principle of inclusion and exclusion, the probability that a gate matrix requires 0 tracks, 1 track, 2 tracks, etc. is

$$\Pr(0 \text{ tracks required}) = p^{mn}$$

$$\Pr(1 \text{ track required}) = \Pr(\geq 1 \text{ tracks}) - \Pr(\geq 2 \text{ tracks}) = \left[1 - U\right]^{\binom{m}{2}} - p^{mn}$$

$$\Pr(2 \text{ tracks required}) = \Pr(\geq 2 \text{ tracks}) - \Pr(\geq 3 \text{ tracks}) = \left[1 - U^{\binom{3}{2}}\right]^{\binom{m}{3}} - \left[1 - U\right]^{\binom{m}{2}}$$

. . .

$$\Pr(k \text{ tracks required}) = \left[1 - U^{\binom{k+1}{2}}\right]^{\binom{m}{k+1}} - \left[1 - U^{\binom{k}{2}}\right]^{\binom{m}{k}}, \text{ for } 3 \leq k \leq m.$$

Now we are ready to calculate the expected number of tracks $E(n, m, p)$ required to lay out a gate matrix with parameters m, n, and p. The expression is

$$E(n, m, p) = \sum_{k=1}^{m} k * \Pr(k \text{ tracks required})$$

$$= \Pr(1 \text{ track required}) + \sum_{k=2}^{m} k * \Pr(k \text{ tracks required})$$

$$= \left[\left[1 - U\right]^{\binom{m}{2}} - p^{mn}\right] + 2\left[\left[1 - U^{\binom{3}{2}}\right]^{\binom{m}{3}} - \left[1 - U\right]^{\binom{m}{2}}\right]$$

$$+ 3\left[\left[1 - U^{\binom{4}{2}}\right]^{\binom{m}{4}} - \left[1 - U^{\binom{3}{2}}\right]^{\binom{m}{3}}\right]$$

$$+ \ldots$$

$$+ m\left[\left[1 - U^{\binom{m+1}{2}}\right]^{\binom{m}{m+1}} - \left[1 - U^{\binom{m}{2}}\right]^{\binom{m}{m}}\right]$$

$$= m - p^{mn} - \left[1 - U\right]^{\binom{m}{2}} - \left[1 - U^{\binom{3}{2}}\right]^{\binom{m}{3}} - \ldots - \left[1 - U^{\binom{m}{2}}\right]^{\binom{m}{m}}$$

$$= m - p^{mn} - \sum_{k=2}^{m} \left[1 - U^{\binom{k}{2}}\right]^{\binom{m}{k}} \qquad (4)$$

Figure 4 shows a comparison between experimentally obtained average number of tracks and that calculated from Expression (4) with sparsity varying. They compare well when sparsity is either low or high while follow each other closely in the middle. As n becomes large, $U \rightarrow 1$ so that Expression (4) gives increasingly accurate results for $E(n, m, p)$. Figures 5 and 6 show the comparison with varying columns and rows, respectively.

4. A LOCAL SEARCH HEURISTIC

Several approximation algorithms for gate matrix layout have been proposed in the literature [7, 8, 10, 14-16]. However, only a few of them have been tested experimentally with a view to their average-case behavior. Existing experimental results are often limited to only a few data samples procured from the field-cases. Here, we have chosen to consider randomly-generated data for the gate matrix with varying sparsity. This approach is more suitable for comparison of different approximation algorithms and for easy verifiability of results.

A local search heuristic with transposition of column-pairs, which gives a local optimal, was implemented on IBM 3090. The search proceeds as follows. We start with an arbitrary permutation of columns and compute the number of tracks required for all the $n(n-1)/2$ permutations obtained by exchanging a pair of columns. If any of the $n(n-1)/2$ permutations require fewer tracks than the original, we choose the permutation with minimum number of tracks and repeat the procedure; otherwise report the original permutation as the optimal. The algorithm is described in the following.

4.1 Algorithm

```
Let π be an arbitrary initial permutation of columns.
optimal := tracks(π); /* initialization */
/* number of tracks is the largest column-sum after appropriate fill-ins */

stoplooping := false; /* loop control variable */
repeat
  min := m;
  for i := 1 to n do
    for j := i+1 to n do
      begin
        Let π' be the same permutation as π
              but with ith and jth columns interchanged.
        if min > tracks(π')
            then min := tracks(π'); π_min := π';
      end;
    if optimal > min
      then optimal := min; π := π_min else stoplooping := true
until stoplooping;
report optimal.
```

The **repeat-until** loop can be executed a maximum of m times in the worst-case with $n(n-1)/2$ permutations to check each time. Therefore, the worst-case time complexity of local search heuristic is $O(mn(n-1)/2)$. The detailed program is provided in [12].

4.2 Empirical Results

All the data presented in this subsection have been collected over 30 samples each. Let $T_l(n, m, p)$ be the average computation time of the local search algorithm. Figures 7 and 8 show the plots for mean CPU time required against the number of columns and rows, respectively. The curves have the following forms

$$
\begin{aligned}
T_l(n, 15, 0.95) &\approx 0.62n^2 - 12.00n + 55.17 \text{ millisecs} \\
T_l(n, 20, 0.95) &\approx 0.98n^2 - 19.47n + 88.55 \text{ millisecs} \\
T_l(10, m, 0.95) &\approx 0.002m^2 + 0.37m - 0.04 \text{ millisecs} \\
T_l(15, m, 0.95) &\approx 0.009m^2 + 1.77m - 2.99 \text{ millisecs} \\
T_l(20, m, 0.95) &\approx 0.046m^2 + 4.10m - 1.34 \text{ millisecs.}
\end{aligned}
\tag{5}
$$

Figure 9 shows the plot for $T_l(15, 20, p)$ which has an unsymmetrical shape with maxima around $p = 0.9$. When the sparsity is low, the local search does not find any new permutation requiring fewer tracks than the original permutation. Therefore, the search terminates with the first permutation itself. This process continues until sparsity becomes 0.7, as depicted in Figure 9. After this, as the gate matrix becomes further sparse, the local search continues until increasingly deep level into the solution space. But, again, when the gate matrix becomes too sparse, a process similar to that with dense gate matrix starts and the depth of the search starts decreasing.

Figure 10 shows a comparison between the average number of tracks obtained by the local search and the expected number of tracks (as computed using Expression (4)) with varying number of columns. On the average, the local search finds a permutation with tracks differing from the expected number of tracks just by one. This is an extremely good performance. Figures 11 and 12 show the comparison with varying number of rows and sparsity of the gate matrix, respectively.

5. CONCLUSION

In this paper, we have studied the gate matrix layout problem both analytically and experimentally. An improved version of an existing dynamic programming formulation is presented. An expression for the expected number of tracks required to layout in gate matrix style is also derived. The dynamic programming algorithm and a local search approximation algorithm are studied experimentally.

Expression (4) for the expected number of tracks for the gate matrix layout provides an useful estimate for evaluating approximation algorithms. However, due to assumptions made during its derivation, it is only a rough estimate. For an exact estimate, we have derived a new expression, which will be reported in a future paper.

From our experiments, we conclude that the local search could be an effective approximation algorithm for the gate matrix layout problem. A meaningful comparison of its performance with other reported experiments in [7, 10, 16] is not possible, firstly, because their test data was not randomly generated and, secondly, because of their limited number of data samples. An extensive experimentation of other existing approximation algorithms on a common basis is needed before we make an attempt at a fair comparison.

The fact that the exact solution for the layout problem through dynamic programming for at most 8 columns is computed in less than a second can be utilized to implement a hybrid divide-and-conquer approximation algorithm, in which a large problem could be divided into sets of $x \leq 8$ columns each, then solved through dynamic programming and finally combined. It is not yet clear what is the best way out of several possible ways of combining subsolutions. An empirical study is required to evaluate them and determine the average-case behavior of such a hybrid algorithm.

REFERENCES

[1] Booth, K. S. and G. S. Leuker, "Testing for the Consecutive Ones Property, Interval Graphs and Graph Planarity Using PQ-Tree Algorithms," *J. Comput. Syst. Sci.*, Vol. 13, pp. 335-79, 1976.

[2] Deo, N., M. S. Krishnamoorthy, and M. A. Langston, "Exact and Approximate Solutions for the Gate Matrix Layout Problem," *IEEE Trans. Computer-Aided Design*, Vol. CAD-6, No. 1, pp. 79-84, Jan. 1987.

[3] Garey, M. R. and D. S. Johnson, *Computers and Intractability: A Guide to the Theory of NP-Completeness*, W. H. Freeman and Co., San Francisco, California, 1979.

[4] Golumbic, M. C., *Algorithmic Graph Theory and Perfect Graphs*, Academic Press, New York, 1976.

[5] Horowitz, E. and S. Sahni, *Fundamentals of Computer Algorithms*, Computer Science Press, Rockville, Maryland, 1978.

[6] Kashiwabara, T. and T. Fujisawa, "An NP-Complete Problem on Interval Graph," *Proc. IEEE Int. Symp. Circuits and Systems*, pp. 82-83, 1979.

[7] Leong, H. W., "A New Algorithm for Gate Matrix Layout," *Proc. IEEE Int. Conf. Computer-Aided Design*, Nov. 1986.

[8] Li, J. T., "Algorithms for Gate Matrix Layout," *Proc. IEEE Int. Symp. Circuits and Systems*, pp. 1013-16, 1983.

[9] Lopez, A. D. and H. F. S. Law, "A Dense Gate Matrix Layout Method for MOS VLSI," *IEEE Trans. Electron Devices*, pp. 1671-75, Aug. 1980.

[10] Ohtsuki, T., H. Mori, E. S. Kuh, T. Kashiwabara, and T. Fujisawa, "One-Dimensional Logic Gate Assignment and Interval Graphs," *IEEE Trans. Circuits and Systems*, Vol CAS-26, No. 9, pp. 675-84, Sept. 1979.

[11] Ohtsuki, T., H. Mori, T. Kashiwabara, and T. Fujisawa, "On Minimal Augmentation to a Graph to Obtain an Interval Graph," *J. Comput. Syst. Sci.*, pp. 60-97, Feb. 1981.

[12] Prasad, S., *Gate Matrix Layout: Expected-Case Analysis and Performance of Algorithms*, M. S. Thesis, Dept. Comput. Sci., Washington State Univ., Pullman, WA, Aug. 1986.

[13] Reingold, E. M., J. Nievergelt, and N. Deo, *Combinatorial Algorithms: Theory and Practice*, Prentice-Hall, Englewood Cliffs, New Jersey, 1977.

[14] Wing, O., "Automated Gate Matrix Layout," *Proc. IEEE Int. Symp. Circuits and Systems*, Rome, Italy, pp. 681-85, 1982.

[15] Wing, O., "Interval-Graph-Based Circuit Layout," *Proc. IEEE Int. Conf. Computer-Aided Design*, pp. 84-85, 1983.

[16] Wing, O., S. Huang, and R. Wang, "Gate Matrix Layout," *IEEE Trans. Computer-Aided Design*, Vol. CAD-4, No. 3, pp. 220-31, July 1985.

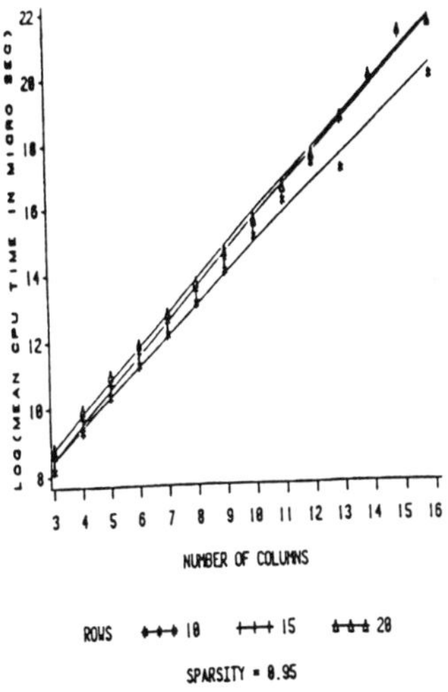

Figure 1. T_d vs. n

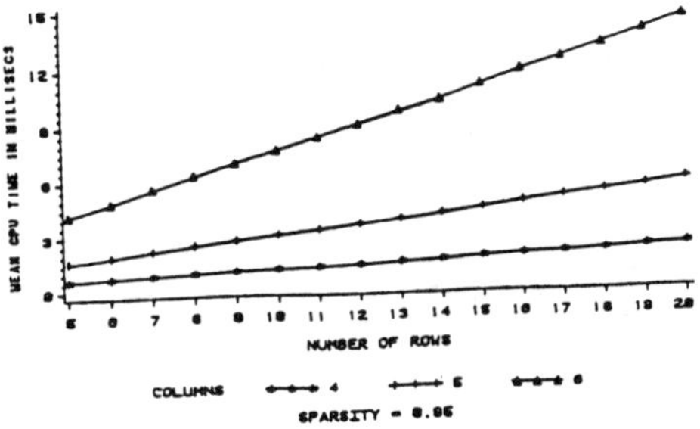

Figure 2. T_d vs. m

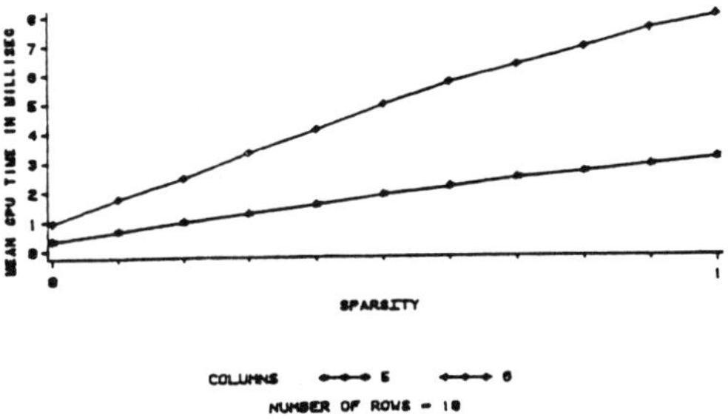

Figure 3. T_d vs. p

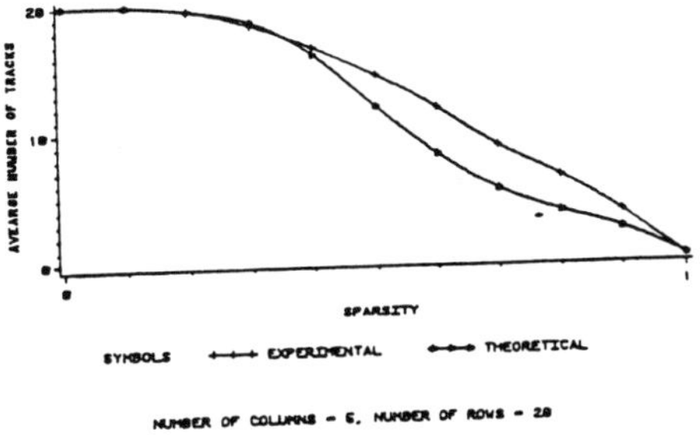

Figure 4. E vs. p

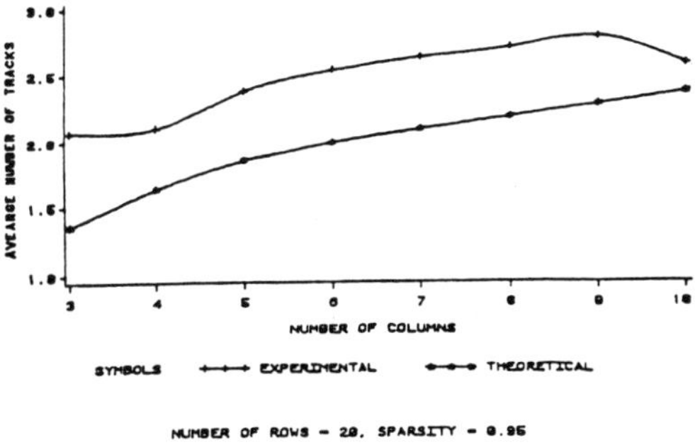

Figure 5. E vs. n

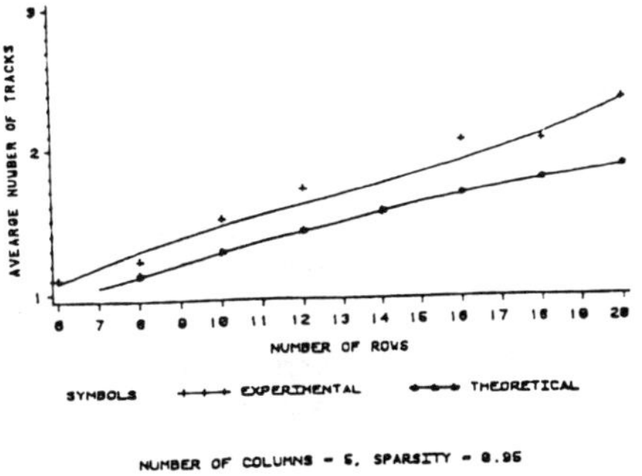

Figure 6. E vs. m

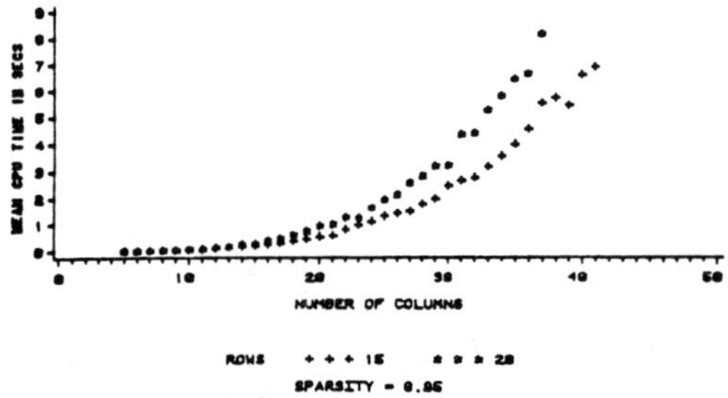

Figure 7. T_l vs. n

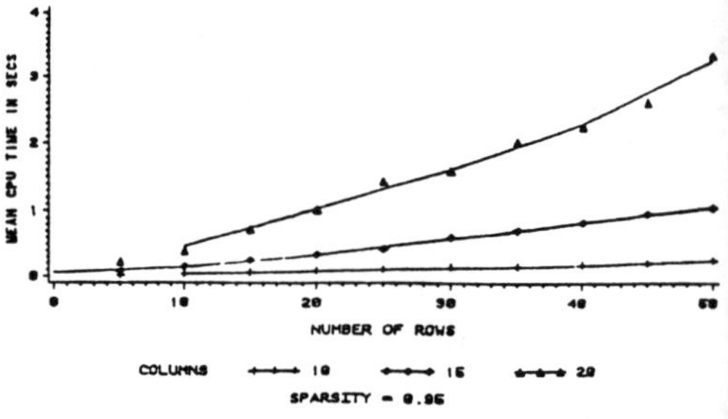

Figure 8. T_l vs. m

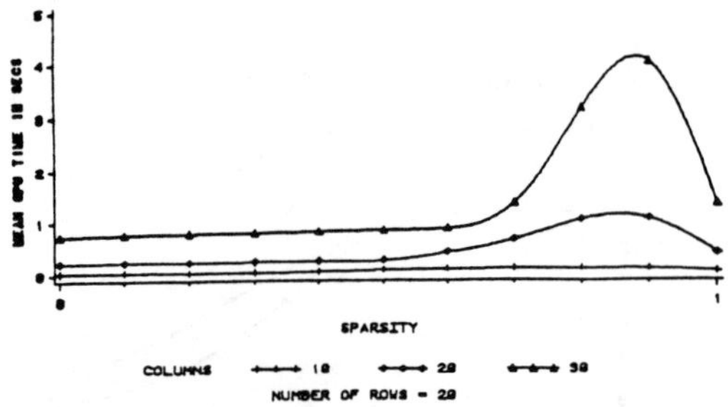

Figure 9. T_l vs. p

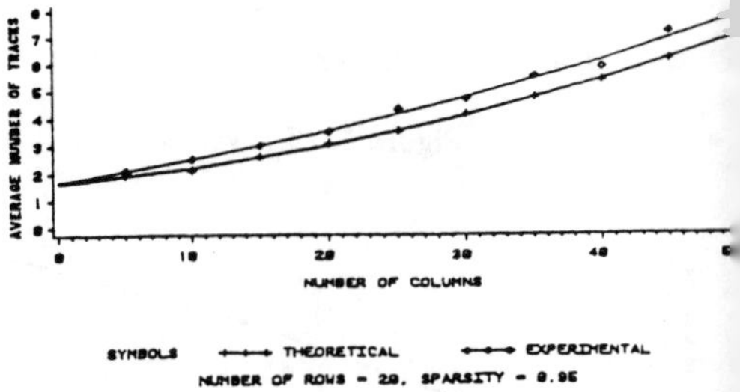

Figure 10. Expected performance of local search with varying n

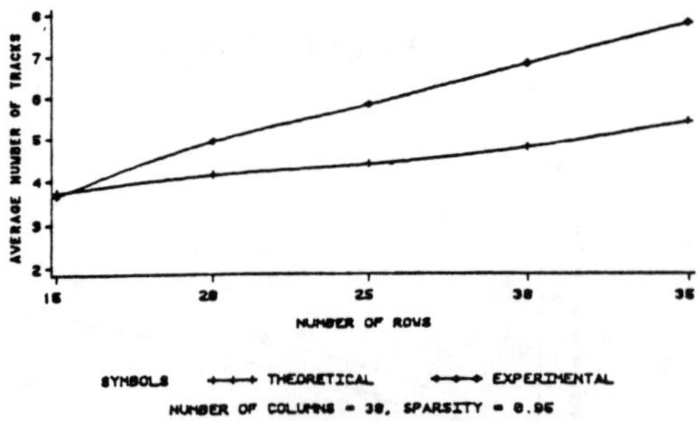

Figure 11. Expected performance of local search with varying m

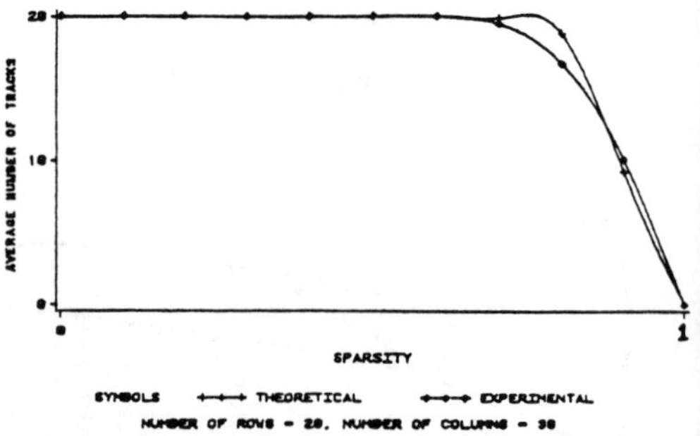

Figure 12. Expected performance of local search with varying p

Parallel Parsing on a One-way Linear Array of Finite-state Machines*

(Extended Abstract)

Oscar H. Ibarra, Tao Jiang† and Hui Wang

Department of Computer Science
University of Minnesota
Minneapolis, MN 55455, USA

Abstract

Efficient parallel algorithms for some parsing problems are presented. These problems include the parsing of linear context-free languages, languages accepted by nondeterministic one-counter automata, and transductions defined by a special class of two-tape nondeterministic finite-state transducers. The model of parallel computation is a one-way linear array of identical finite-state machines. The data movement in the array is one-way, from left to right. For inputs of length n, the array uses n nodes, but the design of the node (finite-state machine) is independent of n. Our algorithms can actually produce a parse, i.e., a sequence of rules (moves) that generates (accepts) an input, in linear time. When only a no/yes answer is required, the parsing problem becomes a recognition problem. The best serial (RAM) algorithms for the corresponding recognition problems take $O(n^2/\log^2 n)$ time and space. Previous parallel algorithms for the recognition problems run in linear time on a one-way linear array of finite-state machines.

1. Introduction

The main motivation for this paper comes from the following problem: Given a grammar (acceptor) G, develop an efficient algorithm which for any input x outputs "no" if G does not generate (accept) x; otherwise, the algorithm outputs a parse, i.e., a sequence of rules (moves) that generates (accepts) x. We call this a "parsing" problem. If we only require the algorithm to output "no" or "yes" (instead of a parse), then we have a "recognition" problem. In general, parsing is more difficult than recognition.

It is well known that parsing of context-free languages (CFL's) can be implemented on a multitape Turing machine (actually a transducer which can output at most one symbol per move) in $O(n^3)$ time and $O(n^2)$ space [YO67]. Here, we consider two important subclasses of context-free languages: linear context-free languages (LCFL's) and languages accepted by nondeterministic one-counter automata. It was shown in [GR76] that recognition of LCFL's can be done on a multitape Turing machine in $O(n^2)$ time and $O(n)$ space, but that parsing takes $O(n^2)$ time and $O(n^2)$ space. The reason for the extra space needed in parsing is that in the dynamic programming method for generating a parse, the $O(n^2)$ entries of a two-dimensional recognition matrix (which is constructed to determine if the string is generated by the grammar) are needed to recover a parse. The recognition matrix is evaluated row by row, and each row is dependent only on the previous row. Since for recognition, only the last row is needed, the space

* This research was supported in part by NSF Grants DCR-8420935 and DCR-8604603.

† Current address: Department of Computer Science and Systems, McMaster University, Hamilton, Ontario, Canada L8S 4K1

used for the computation is only O(n). It was left unanswered in [GR76] whether the space requirement of $O(n^2)$ for parsing can be reduced (without increasing the time). We show that this can be done. In fact, we show that parsing of LCFL's can be done on a *single-tape* Turing machine (*without* a separate read-only input tape) in $O(n^2)$ time and O(n) space. The same result applies to parsing of nondeterministic pushdown automata which make only one-turn on their pushdown stack. We also look at nondeterministic one-counter automata (1-NCA's). (These are pushdown automata with unary stack alphabet.) It is known that recognition can be done on a single-tape Turing machine in $O(n^2)$ time and O(n) space [GR76]. We show that the same time and space bounds hold for parsing. The proof in this case is slightly more complicated because these machines have counters which not only use unbounded memory but also make unbounded number of counter turns. We also consider the parsing problems for other devices such as two-tape (or two-head) nondeterministic finite-state transducers and show that they too can be solved on a single-tape Turing machine in $O(n^2)$ time and O(n) space.

Our results are actually stronger. Define a one-way linear iterative array (OLIA, for short) as a finite one-dimensional array of identical finite-state machines (nodes) in which information is allowed to move only in one direction - from left to right. For an input sequence of length n, the array uses n nodes which are initially set to the quiescent state. The design of the node is independent of n. The serial input is applied to the leftmost node and the serial output is observed from the rightmost node. Arrays which allow only one-way communication have nice properties with respect to, e.g., problem decomposition and fault-tolerance [KU84,SA87]. Clearly, an OLIA operating in linear time can be simulated by a single-tape Turing machine in $O(n^2)$ time and O(n) space. In this paper, we show that the parsing problems mentioned above can be implemented on an OLIA in linear time. The main proof technique is a divide-and-conquer (recursive) strategy, which we show can be implemented on an OLIA. As far as we know, this is the first paper that exhibits an implementation of recursion on a (one-way or two-way) linear array.

The paper is organized as follows. Section 2 formally defines the OLIA. Section 3 presents a linear-time algorithm (on an OLIA) for the parsing of transductions defined by discrete two-tape nondeterministic finite-state transducers (2-TNFT's). Discrete 2-TNFT's were introduced in [VA82] as generalizations of two-tape (or two-head) finite automata. They have applications in the study of parallel processes [VA82]. An interesting corollary is that parsing of discrete 2-TNFT transductions can be done on a single-tape Turing machine in quadratic time and linear space. Section 4 shows that the LCFL parsing problem can be recast in terms of the parsing of discrete 2-TNFT transductions. It follows that LCFL parsing can be implemented on an OLIA in O(n) time, and hence also on a single-tape Turing machine in $O(n^2)$ time and O(n) space. Section 5 considers the parsing problem for 1-NCA's and shows that this problem can also be solved on an OLIA in O(n) time.

2. One-way Linear Iterative Array

A one-way linear iterative array (OLIA) consists of an array of nodes with serial input/output and one-way communication between nodes. Each node is a finite-state machine. The array has n identical nodes for inputs of length n. The nodes operate synchronously at discrete time steps by means of a common clock. The input $a_1a_2 \cdots a_n\$$ is fed serially to the leftmost node, while the serial output $b_1b_2 \cdots b_k\$$ is observed from the rightmost node. The a_i's (b_i's) are symbols from some fixed finite input (output) alphabet. Both input and output sequences are terminated by a special delimiter \$. (We assume that \$ is not in the input and ouput alphabets.) The leftmost node receives a_i, $1 \leq i \leq n$, at time i-1, and \$ after time n-1. Hence, unlike the a_i's, \$ is not "consumed" when read by the OLIA, and is always available for rereading. The state and output of a node at time t are functions of its state and the state of its left neighbor (or the input in the case of the leftmost node) at time t-1. Thus, $S_i^{t+1} = f(S_{i-1}^t, S_i^t)$ and $O_i^{t+1} = g(S_{i-1}^t, S_i^t)$ for some functions f and g, where S_i^t and O_i^t denote the state and output of the i-th node at time t. We assume that $S_0^t = a_{t+1}$ for $0 \leq t < n$ and $S_0^t = \$$ for $t \geq n$. We require that $S_i^0 = q_0$ (the quiescent state), $O_i^0 = \lambda$ (representing blank), $f(q_0,q_0) = q_0$, and $g(q_0,q_0) = \lambda$. (Thus, at time 0, each node is in the quiescent state q_0, with its output set to λ. It remains in state q_0 with output λ until its left neighbor enters a non-quiescent state.) The serial output $b_1 \cdots b_k\$$ is observed from the rightmost node starting at time n. Thus, the outputs at times 1, 2, . . ., n-1, which are λ's, are not included in $b_1 \cdots b_k\$$. The OLIA has time complexity T(n) on input $a_1 \cdots a_n\$$ if it outputs \$ after at most T(n) time. Clearly, $T(n) \geq 2n$.

3. Parsing of Discrete 2-TNFT Transductions

A two-tape nondeterministic finite-state transducer (2-TNFT) $M = (Q,\Sigma,\Delta,\delta,q_0,F)$ is a nondeterministic finite automaton with 2 one-way input tapes (one head per tape) and 1 one-way output tape, where

Q is the state set,
Σ is the input alphabet,
Δ is the output alphabet,
$\delta : Q\times(\Sigma\cup\epsilon)\times(\Sigma\cup\epsilon) \rightarrow 2^{Q\times\Delta^*}$ is the set of *moves*,
q_0 is the initial state,
$F \subseteq Q$ is the set of accepting states.

The move $(q,a,b) \rightarrow (p,c)$ means: if M is in state q with the two input heads reading a and b respectively, $a,b \in \Sigma\cup\{\epsilon\}$, then M changes its state to p, input head 1 moves $|a|$ cells to the right, input head 2 moves $|b|$ cells to the right, and M outputs string c. We assume without loss of generality that at least one input head moves to the right every step. Note that, if a (b) is ϵ, then input head 1 (or head 2, respectively) is stationary. M defines a set of transductions $T(M) = \{ (x_1,x_2,y) \mid$ M on input (x_1,x_2) can output y and enter an accepting state $\}$. M is called ***discrete*** if it outputs exactly one symbol whenever one of the two input heads moves to the right [VA82]. When the two input heads move to the right at the same time, M outputs two symbols. Hence, if (x_1,x_2,y) is in T(M), then $|y| = |x_1|+|x_2|$. The transductions defined by a discrete 2-TNFT are called discrete 2-TNFT transductions. For simplicity, we only consider transductions that satisfy $|y| = |x_1|+|x_2|$.

Let M be a fixed 2-TNFT and $t = (x_1,x_2,y)$ be a transduction in T(M). A ***parse*** of t is a sequence of moves that takes M on input (x_1,x_2) to an accepting state with output y. The 2-TNFT transduction parsing problem is stated as follows: Given a transduction $t = (x_1,x_2,y)$, output a parse of t if $t \in T(M)$, "no" otherwise.

Discrete 2-TNFT transductions are quite useful. They have applications in, e.g., parallel processes [VA82]. In Section 5, we will show that the LCFL parsing problem can be recast in terms of the parsing of discrete 2-TNFT transductions. It was shown in [VA82] that discrete 2-TNFT transductions can be recognized on a RAM in $O((n+m)^2/\log(n+m))$ time and space, where n and m are the lengths of x_1 and x_2. The time and space were improved to $O((n+m)^2/\log^2(n+m))$ in [IB84]. A linear time OLIA algorithm for recognizing discrete 2-TNFT transductions was given in [IB87]. We will show that discrete 2-TNFT transductions can be parsed on an OLIA in O(n) time.

Let $M = (Q,\Sigma,\Delta,\delta,p_0,F)$ be a fixed discrete 2-TNFT. Let $t = (x_1,x_2,y) = (a_1 \cdots a_n,b_1 \cdots b_m,c_1 \cdots c_{n+m})$ be a transduction. We can check if t is in T(M) as follows [VA82, IB87]. Denote the configuration when M is in state q and input heads 1 and 2 are at positions i and j (i.e., after reading $a_1 \cdots a_i$ and $b_1 \cdots b_j$), respectively, by (q,i,j), where $q \in Q$, $0 \leq i \leq n$, and $0 \leq j \leq m$. The initial configuration is $(q_0,0,0)$. Construct an $(n+1)\times(m+1)$ matrix H such that $H(i,j) = \{q \mid$ M can enter (q,i,j) and output $c_1 \cdots c_{i+j}\}$, $0 \leq i \leq n$ and $0 \leq j \leq m$. Hence, (x_1,x_2,y) is in T(M) if and only if H(n,m) contains an accepting state. The matrix H is called the ***recognition matrix*** of M on transduction (x_1,x_2,y). Matrix H can be evaluated using the following recurrences:

$H(0,0) = \{q_0\};$

$H(0,j) = \{q \mid \exists p \text{ in } H(1,j\text{-}1) \text{ such that } (p,\epsilon,b_j) \rightarrow (q,c_j) \text{ is in } \delta\},\ 0<j\leq m;$

$H(i,0) = \{q \mid \exists p \text{ in } H(i\text{-}1,1) \text{ such that } (p,a_i,\epsilon) \rightarrow (q,c_i) \text{ is in } \delta\},\ 0<i\leq n;$

$$\begin{aligned} H(i,j) = &\{q \mid \exists p \text{ in } H(i\text{-}1,j) \text{ such that } (p,a_i,\epsilon) \rightarrow (q,c_{i+j}) \text{ is in } \delta\} \\ &\cup \{q \mid \exists p \text{ in } H(i,j\text{-}1) \text{ such that } (p,\epsilon,b_j) \rightarrow (q,c_{i+j}) \text{ is in } \delta\} \\ &\cup \{q \mid \exists p \text{ in } H(i\text{-}1,j\text{-}1) \text{ such that } (p,a_i,b_j) \rightarrow (q,c_{i+j-1}c_{i+j}) \text{ is in } \delta\}, \\ &0<i\leq n,\ 0<j\leq m. \end{aligned}$$

The recognition matrix H can be evaluated row by row (or column by column), starting from the first row (or the first column). Clearly, row (or column) i+1 only depends on row (or column) i. Given row (or column) i, the entries in row (or column) i+1 can be easily obtained one by one, starting from H(i+1,0) (or H(0,i+1)), using the recurrence equations.

We shall show how to parse the transductions defined by M on an OLIA in O(n+m) time. First, we present a serial (RAM) algorithm that can parse a transduction in O(nm) time and O(n+m) space. The basic idea behind the algorithm is divide-and-conquer. A similar technique was used in [HI75] for solving the longest common subsequence problem.

Without loss of generality, we assume the discrete 2-TNFT M has only one accepting state, i.e., F = {f}. We will denote the "reverse" of M by M^R, i.e., $M^R = (Q,\Sigma,\Delta,\delta^R,f,\{q_0\})$, where $\delta^R = \{ (q,a,b) \rightarrow (p,c) \mid (p,a,b) \rightarrow (q,c) \text{ in } \delta \}$. For any q,p in Q, let $M_{q,p} = (Q,\Sigma,\Delta,\delta,q,\{p\})$ and $M^R_{q,p} = (Q,\Sigma,\Delta,\delta^R,q,\{p\})$. Let lastrow(H,q,$x_1$,$x_2$,y) (lastrow($H^R$,q,$x_1$,$x_2$,y)) denote the function that returns the last row of the recognition matrix H of $M_{q,f}$ (M^R_{q,q_0}, respectively) on transduction (x_1,x_2,y) and lastcolumn(H,q,x_1,x_2,y) (lastcolumn(H^R,q,x_1,x_2,y)) denote the function that returns the last column of the recognition matrix H of $M_{q,f}$ (M^R_{q,q_0}, respectively) on (x_1,x_2,y). Note that, the recognition matrix of a 2-TNFT on a transduction does not depend on the accepting states of the 2-TNFT. It is easy to see that these functions can be computed in O(nm) time and O(n+m) space, where $n = |x_1|$ and $m = |x_2|$. The following algorithm can parse a transduction in O(nm) time and O(n+m) space. A call TPARSE(q,p,x_1,x_2,y,S) to the algorithm will find a parse, with respect to $M_{q,p}$, of the transduction (x_1,x_2,y). The parse will be stored in S. In particular, TPARSE(q_0,f,x_1,x_2,y,S) gives a parse (with respect to M) of transduction (x_1,x_2,y).

Algorithm TPARSE(q,p,x_1,x_2,y,S);
{ Let $x_1 = a_1 \cdots a_n$, $x_2 = b_1 \cdots b_m$, and $y = c_1 \cdots c_{n+m}$.
For convenience, we assume n+m > 0 }
1. { If n,m ≤ 1 then solve the problem directly }
if n = 1 and m = 0 **then**
  if $(q,a_1,\epsilon) \rightarrow (p,c_1)$ is in δ **then** S := $(q,a_1,\epsilon) \rightarrow (p,c_1)$
  else S := "no"
elseif n = 0 and m = 1 **then**
  if $(q,\epsilon,b_1) \rightarrow (p,c_1)$ is in δ **then** S := $(q,\epsilon,b_1) \rightarrow (p,c_1)$
  else S := "no"
elseif n = 1 and m = 1 **then**
  if $(q,a_1,b_1) \rightarrow (p,c_1c_2)$ is in δ **then** S := $(q,a_1,b_1) \rightarrow (p,c_1c_2)$
  elseif ∃u ∈ Q such that $(q,a_1,\epsilon) \rightarrow (u,c_1)$ and $(u,\epsilon,b_1) \rightarrow (p,c_2)$ are in δ **then**
    S := $(q,a_1,\epsilon) \rightarrow (u,c_1)$, $(u,\epsilon,b_1) \rightarrow (p,c_2)$
  elseif ∃u ∈ Q such that $(q,\epsilon,b_1) \rightarrow (u,c_1)$ and $(u,a_1,\epsilon) \rightarrow (p,c_2)$ are in δ **then**
    S := $(q,\epsilon,b_1) \rightarrow (u,c_1)$, $(u,a_1,\epsilon) \rightarrow (p,c_2)$
  else S := "no"

```
2.      else  { Split the problem }
2.1.       if n ≥ m then
2.1.1.        i := ⌈n/2⌉;
              row1 := lastrow(H,q,a1...ai,b1...bm,c1...ci+m);
              row2 := lastrow(H^R,p,an...ai+1,bm...b1,cn+m...ci+1);
2.1.2.        { Find a j such that ∃u ∈ Q, (a1...ai,b1...bj,c1...ci+j) is in T(Mq,u)
                and (ai+1...an,bj+1...bm,ci+j+1...cn+m is in T(Mu,p) }
              j := 0;
              while row1(j) ∩ row2(m−j) = ∅ do
                 j := j+1;
              end;
              if j > m then S := "no"; return endif
              u := an arbitrary state in row1(j) ∩ row2(m−j)
2.2.       else  { n < m }
2.2.1.        j := ⌈m/2⌉;
              column1 := lastcolumn(H,q,a1...an,b1...bj,c1...cn+j);
              column2 := lastcolumn(H^R,p,an...a1,bm...bj+1,cn+m...cj+1);
2.2.2.        { Find an i such that ∃u ∈ Q, (a1...ai,b1...bj,c1...ci+j) is in T(Mq,u)
                and (ai+1...an,bj+1...bm,ci+j+1...cn+m is in T(Mu,p) }
              i := 0;
              while column1(i) ∩ column2(n−i) = ∅ do
                 i := i+1;
              end;
              if i > n then S := "no"; return endif
              u := an arbitrary state in column1(i) ∩ column2(n−i)
           endif;
3.         { Solve simpler problems }
           call parse(q,u,a1...ai,b1...bj,c1...ci+j,S1);
           call parse(u,p,ai+1...an,bj+1...bm,ci+j+1...cn+m,S2);
4.         S := S1, S2
        endif
     end.
```

Algorithm TPARSE works as follows. To find a parse, with respect to $M_{q,p}$, of a transduction (x_1,x_2,y), TPARSE first checks if the lengths of both x_1 and x_2 are ≤ 1. If yes, it finds a parse of (x_1,x_2,y) directly. Otherwise it divides the transduction into two smaller transductions and finds a parse, with respect to some 2-TNFT, for each of them. Clearly, the space complexity of TPARSE is $O(n+m)$ and the time complexity of TPARSE $= O(nm)+O(nm/2)+O(nm/4)+... = O(nm)$.

Implementation of the above algorithm on an OLIA yields the following theorem.

Theorem 1. Parsing of discrete 2-TNFT transductions can be done on an OLIA in linear time.

Proof. The OLIA implementation is quite involved and omitted here. It will be given in the full paper. □

Corollary 1. Parsing of discrete 2-TNFT transductions can be done on a single-tape Turing machine in quadratic time and linear space.

As an application, we show that the string shuffling problem [VA82] can be solved on an OLIA in linear time. The problem is defined as follows: given three strings x,y and z (over alphabet Σ), determine if z is a shuffle of x and y and if so, find one such shuffle (i.e., how z can be obtained as a shuffle of x and y). It was shown in [VA82] that the set $L = \{(x,y,z) \mid z \text{ is a shuffle of } x \text{ and } y\}$ can be recognized on a RAM in $O((n+m)^2/\log(n+m))$ time, where n and m are the lengths of x and y. [IB87] showed that the set L can be recognized on an OLIA in linear time. The string shuffling problem (which is more than just recognition of L) can be restated as a discrete 2-TNFT transduction parsing problem. Define a discrete 2-TNFT $M = (\{q_0\},\Sigma,\Sigma,\delta,q_0,\{q_0\})$, where $\delta = \{(q_0,a,\epsilon) \rightarrow (q_0,a) \mid a \in \Sigma\} \cup \{(q_0,\epsilon,a) \rightarrow (q_0,a) \mid a \in \Sigma\}$.

It is easy to see that $T(M) = L$. Hence, given strings x, y and z, a parse of the transduction (x,y,z) tells us how z can be obtained as a shuffle of x and y.

Corollary 2. The string shuffling problem can be solved on an OLIA in linear time.

One can define a two-head nondeterministic finite-state transducer (2-HNFT) as a nondeterministic finite automaton with 2 independent heads on a single one-way input tape and 1 one-way output tape. A two-tape (two-head) nondeterministic finite-automaton is a 2-TNFT (2-HNFT) without an output tape.

Corollary 3. The parsing problem for 2-HNFT's, two-tape nondeterministic finite automata, and two-head nondeterministic finite automata are solvable on an OLIA in linear time.

4. Parsing of LCFL's

An important subclass of context-free languages (CFL's) is the class of linear context-free languages (LCFL's). A context-free grammar $G = (V,\Sigma,P,S)$ is a linear context-free grammar (LCFG) if each rule in P is of the form $A \rightarrow uBv$ or $A \rightarrow u$, where $A,B \in V$ and $u,v \in \Sigma^*$. (V is the set of nonterminals, Σ is the set of terminal symbols, P is the set of rules, and S is the starting nonterminal.) The language generated by an LCFG is called an LCFL. Let $G = (V,\Sigma,P,S)$ be an LCFG. G is in *normal* form if the rules in P are of the form $A \rightarrow aB$, $A \rightarrow Ba$ or $A \rightarrow a$, where $a \in \Sigma$ (i.e., a is a single terminal symbol). It is easy to transform any LCFG which does not generate ϵ to one in normal form. Thus, without loss of generality, we will only consider normal LCFG's. Let x be a string in L(G). A parse of x is a sequence of rules that derives x from S. The definition of the parsing problem for LCFL's is straightforward.

A RAM algorithm for LCFL recognition running in $O(n^2)$ time and $O(n)$ space was given in [GR76], but the question of whether or not a parse can be found in the same time and space was left unanswered, where n is the length of x. The time for LCFL recognition was improved to $O(n^2/\log^2 n)$ in [IB84]. It was also shown in [CU84] that LCFL recognition can be done on an OLIA in O(n) time. Here, we show that parsing of LCFL's can be done on an OLIA in O(n) time.

Interestingly, the LCFL parsing problem can be recast in terms of the parsing of discrete 2-TNFT transductions. Let $G = \langle V,\Sigma,P,S\rangle$ be a normal LCFG. Define a discrete 2-TNFT $M = (Q,\Sigma,\Delta,\delta,S,\{f\})$ as follows:

$$
\begin{aligned}
&Q = V \cup \{f\} \ (f \notin V \text{ is a new symbol}),\\
&\Delta = \{0,1\},\\
&\delta = \{\ (A,a,\epsilon) \rightarrow (B,0) \mid A \rightarrow aB \in P\ \}\\
&\qquad \cup \{\ (A,\epsilon,a) \rightarrow (B,0) \mid A \rightarrow Ba \in P\ \}\\
&\qquad \cup \{\ (A,a,\epsilon) \rightarrow (f,0) \mid A \rightarrow a \in P\ \}\\
&\qquad \cup \{\ (f,a,\epsilon) \rightarrow (f,1) \mid a \in \Sigma\ \}\\
&\qquad \cup \{\ (f,\epsilon,a) \rightarrow (f,1) \mid a \in \Sigma\ \}.
\end{aligned}
$$

Note that, in a computation, exactly one input head of M moves per step. Clearly, for any string x, x is in L(G) if and only if the transduction $(x,x^R,0^{|x|}1^{|x|})$ is in T(M). (x^R denotes the reverse of x.) Suppose x is a string in L(G). Let $W = w_1,w_2, \cdots ,w_{2n}$ be a parse of transduction $(x,x^R,0^{|x|}1^{|x|})$, where $n = |x|$, $w_i = (q_i,a_i,b_i) \rightarrow (q_{i+1},0)$, $1 \leq i \leq n$, $q_1 = S$, $q_{n+1} = f$, and $w_i = (f,a_i,b_i) \rightarrow (f,1)$, $n+1 \leq i \leq 2n$. Define $r_i = q_i \rightarrow a_i q_{i+1}$ if $a_i \neq \epsilon$, $q_i \rightarrow q_{i+1} b_i$ if $b_i \neq \epsilon$, $1 \leq i \leq n-1$, and $r_n = q_n \rightarrow a_n$. Then, it is easy to see that $R = r_1,r_2, \cdots ,r_n$ is a parse of string x. Hence,

Corollary 4. LCFL's can be parsed on an OLIA in linear time.

The following corollary improves the result in [GR76].

Corollary 5. LCFL's can be parsed on a single-tape Turing machine in $O(n^2)$ time and O(n) space.

5. Parsing of 1-NCA Languages

Another important subclass of CFL's is the class of languages accepted by nondeterministic one-counter automata (1-NCA's). A 1-NCA is a nondeterministic finite automaton with a one-way input tape and a counter. A 1-NCA M is denoted by a 5-tuple (Q,Σ,δ,q_0,F), where Q is the state set, Σ is the input alphabet, $\delta : Q\times(\Sigma\cup\epsilon)\times\{0,1\} \rightarrow 2^{Q\times\{-1,0,1\}}$ is the set of moves, q_0 is the initial state, and $F \subseteq Q$ is the set of accepting states. The move $(q,a,e) \rightarrow (p,d)$ means: if M is in state q with input head reading a (in $\Sigma\cup\epsilon$) and counter status e (0 for empty counter, 1 otherwise), M changes its state to p, input head moves one cell to the right, and adds value d to the counter. (Note that, M is not allowed to decrement an empty counter.) The language accepted by M, denoted by L(M), is $\{x \mid x \in \Sigma^*$ and M on input x can enter an accepting state$\}$. It has been shown in [GI74] that 1-NCA's are equivalent to real-time 1-NCA's. Thus, without loss of generality, we assume that M advances its input head on each atomic move and accepts with the counter empty [GI74]. Again, we assume that F contains only one accepting state f. Let x be a string. A parse of x (with respect to M) is a sequence of moves that takes M on input x to the accepting state f with the counter empty. Note that, in an accepting computation, the counter value of M is always $\leq n/2$.

It was shown in [GR75] that 1-NCA languages can be recognized on a RAM in $O(n^2)$ time, where n is the length of x. Again, the time was improved to $O(n^2/\log^2 n)$ in [IB84]. It was shown in [IB86] that the recognition of 1-NCA languages can be done on an OLIA in O(n) time. Using the techniques given in Section 4, we can show that 1-NCA languages can be parsed on an OLIA in O(n) time.

Let $M = (Q,\Sigma,\delta,q_0,\{f\})$ be a fixed 1-NCA. Let q_1,q_2 be any two states in Q and c_1,c_2 be nonnegative integers. Define a generalized 1-NCA M_{q_1,c_1,q_2,c_2} (a variation of M) as follows. The state set and move function of M_{q_1,c_1,q_2,c_2} are Q and δ, respectively. Given any input, M_{q_1,c_1,q_2,c_2} starts the computation with state q_1 and counter value c_1. An input x is accepted by M_{q_1,c_1,q_2,c_2} if M_{q_1,c_1,q_2,c_2} can enter state q_2 and counter value c_2 after reading x. We can check if a string $x = a_1 \cdots a_n$ is accepted by M_{q_1,c_1,q_2,c_2} as follows. Since M_{q_1,c_1,q_2,c_2} can decrement (or increment) the counter by at most n during an accepting computation on input x, we assume $|c_2-c_1| \leq n$. Let $b_1 = \max\{0,\lceil(c_1+c_2-n)/2\rceil\}$ and $b_2 = \lfloor(c_1+c_2+n)/2\rfloor$. Construct an $(n+1)\times(b_2-b_1+1)$ matrix E such that $E(i,j) = \{q \mid M_{q_1,c_1,q_2,c_2}$ can enter state q with counter value j after reading $a_1 \cdots a_i\}$, $0 \leq i \leq n$ and $b_1 \leq j \leq b_2$. Thus, x is accepted by M_{q_1,c_1,q_2,c_2} if and only if $E(n,c_2)$ contains the state q_2. E is called the recognition matrix of M_{q_1,c_1,q_2,c_2} on x. The recognition matrix E can be evaluated using the following recurrences [GR75, IB84]. For any nonnegative integer c, let pos(c) = 1 if c > 0, 0 if c = 0.

$$E(0,c_1) = \{q_1\},$$
$$E(0,j) = \emptyset,\ b_1 \leq j \leq b_2,\ j \neq c_1,$$
$$\begin{aligned} E(i,j) = & \{q \mid j > b_1 \text{ and } \exists p \text{ in } E(i-1,j-1) \text{ such that } (p,a_i,pos(j-1)) \rightarrow (q,1) \text{ is in } \delta\}, \\ & \cup \{q \mid \exists p \text{ in } E(i-1,j) \text{ such that } (p,a_i,pos(j)) \rightarrow (q,0) \text{ is in } \delta\} \\ & \cup \{q \mid j < b_2 \text{ and } \exists p \text{ in } E(i-1,j+1) \text{ such that } (p,a_i,1) \rightarrow (q,-1) \text{ is in } \delta\} \\ & 1 \leq i \leq n,\ b_1 \leq j \leq b_2. \end{aligned}$$

Clearly, the matrix E can be evaluated row by row, starting from the first row.

Before we can describe the parsing algorithm, we need to define another matrix E^R. Define $E^R(i,j) = \{q \mid$ starting from state q and counter value j, M_{q_1,c_1,q_2,c_2} can reach state q_2 with counter value c_2 after reading $a_i \cdots a_1\}$, $0 \leq i \leq n$, $b_1 \leq j \leq b_2$. E^R is called the *reverse recognition matrix* of M_{q_1,c_1,q_2,c_2} on x^R. Matrix E^R can be computed according to the following recurrences.

$E^R(0,c_2) = \{q_2\},$

$E^R(0,j) = \emptyset,\ b_1 \leq j \leq b_2,\ j \neq c_2,$

$E^R(i,j) = \{q \mid j > b_1 \text{ and } \exists p \text{ in } E^R(i\text{-}1,j\text{-}1) \text{ such that } (q,a_i,1) \rightarrow (p,-1) \text{ is in } \delta\},$

$\quad \cup \{q \mid \exists p \text{ in } E^R(i\text{-}1,j) \text{ such that } (q,a_i,pos(j)) \rightarrow (p,0) \text{ is in } \delta\}$

$\quad \cup \{q \mid j < b_2 \text{ and } \exists p \text{ in } E^R(i\text{-}1,j+1) \text{ such that } (q,a_i,pos(j)) \rightarrow (p,1) \text{ is in } \delta\}$

$\quad 1 \leq i \leq n,\ b_1 \leq j \leq b_2.$

Let lastrow(E,q_1,c_1,x) (lastrow(E^R,q_2,c_2,x^R)) denote the function that returns the last row of recognition matrix E (or the reverse recognition matrix E^R, respectively) of M_{q_1,c_1,q_2,c_2} on string x. Clearly, the function lastrow can be computed on a RAM in $O(n^2)$ time and $O(n)$ space.

We present a RAM algorithm CPARSE for parsing L(M). The call CPARSE(q_1,c_1,q_2,c_2,x,S) to the algorithm gives a parse (with respect to M_{q_1,c_1,q_2,c_2}) of string x. The parse will be stored in S. A parse (with respect to M) of the input string x can be found by calling CPARSE$(q_0,0,f,0,x,S)$.

```
      Algorithm CPARSE(q1,c1,q2,c2,x,S);
        { Let x = a1 ··· an. For simplicity, assume n > 0.
          b1 and b2 are defined as in the above discussion }
1.      { If n = 1 then solve the problem directly }
        if n = 1 then
          if (q1,a1,pos(c1)) → (q2,c2−c1) ∈ δ then S := (q1,a1,pos(c1)) → (q2,c2−c1)
          else S := "no"
2.      else  { Split the problem }
2.1.      i := ⌈n/2⌉;
          row1 := lastrow(E,q1,c1,a1...ai);
          row2 := lastrow(E^R,q2,c2,an...ai+1);
2.1.1.    { Find a j such that ∃p ∈ Q, p ∈ row1(j) ∩ row2(j)}
          j := b1;
          while row1(j) ∩ row2(j) = ∅ do
            j := j+1
          end;
          if j > b2 then S := "no" ; return
          else p := an arbitrary state in row1(j) ∩ row2(j);
3.        { Solve simpler problems }
          call CPARSE(q1,c1,p,j,a1...ai,S1);
          call CPARSE(p,j,q2,c2,ai+1...an,S2);
4.        S := S1, S2
        endif
      end.
```

It is easy to see that the space complexity of CPARSE is $O(n)$ and the time complexity of CPARSE is $O(n^2)$.

There is a problem that hinders the implementation of Algorithm CPARSE on an OLIA. Let $x = a_1 \cdots a_n$ be an input to M. During a computation on x, the value of M's counter may be of the same magnitude as n. Since each node of the OLIA can only hold a finite amount of information, it needs $O(\log n)$ nodes to hold a counter value. When CPARSE$(q_0,0,f,0,x,S)$ is called, the input string x will eventually be divided into $O(n)$ substrings and the (parsing) problem will be split into $O(n)$ subproblems. For each subproblem, it takes at least $O(\log n)$ nodes to store the initial and final counter values. Thus, an OLIA would need $O(n \log n)$ nodes to execute CPARSE on input x. Since an OLIA can only have n nodes for inputs of length n, it is impossible to implement Algorithm CPARSE on an OLIA. This problem can be resolved by relativizing the counter values as follows. Let $x_1 = a_s \cdots a_t$ be a substring of x and $m = t-s+1$. Suppose that the counter value before reading a_s (after reading a_t) is c_1 (c_2,

References

[CU84] Culik II, K., J. Gruska, and A. Salomaa, Systolic trellis automata, *Internat. J. Comput. Math.* 16-1, (1984), pp. 3-22.

[GI74] Ginsburg, S. and G. Rose, The equivalence of stack counter accepters and quasi-realtime acceptors, *J. of Computer and System Sciences* 8, (1974), pp. 243-269.

[GR75] Greibach, S., A note on the recognition of one counter languages, *R.A.I.R.O.*, (1975), pp. 5-12.

[GR76] Graham, S. and M. Harrison, Parsing of general context-free languages, *Advances in Computers*, 14, Academic Press, NY, (1976), pp. 77-185.

[HI75] Hirschberg, D., A linear space algorithm for computing maximal common sequences, *Communication of ACM* 18-6, (1975), pp. 341-343.

[IB84] Ibarra, O., M. Palis, and J. Chang, On efficient recognition of transductions and relations, *Theoretical Computer Science* 39, (1984), pp. 89-106.

[IB85] Ibarra, O., M. Palis, and S. Kim, Some results concerning linear iterative (systolic) arrays, *Journal of Parallel and Distributed Computing* 2, (1985), pp. 182-218.

[IB86] Ibarra, O., S. Kim, and M. Palis, Designing systolic algorithms using sequential machines, *IEEE Trans. on Comput.* 35-6, (1986), pp. 531-542.

[IB87] Ibarra, O. and M. Palis, VLSI algorithms for solving recurrence equations and applications, *IEEE Trans. on Acoust., Speech, and Signal Process.* 35-7, (1987), pp. 1046-1064.

[KU84] Kung, H. and M. Lam, Fault-tolerance and two level pipelining in VLSI systolic arrays, *Proc. 1984 Conference on Advanced Research in VLSI,* M.I.T, (ed. Paul Penfield, Jr.), pp. 74-83.

[SA87] Savage, C. and M. Stallmann, Decomposability and fault-tolerance in one-dimensional array algorithms, (1987), in preparation.

[VA82] Van Leeuwen, J. and M. Nivat, Efficient recognition of rational relations, *Inform. Processing Lett.*, 14, (1982), pp. 34-38.

[YO67] Younger, D., Recognition and parsing of context-free languages in time n^3, *Information and Control* 10, (1967), 189-208.

respectively). If $c_1+c_2 > m$, then the counter is always nonempty when the input head is reading a symbol of x_1. Thus, we have the following relativization process. Let c_1 and c_2 be the initial and final counter values of a subproblem. Without loss of generality, assume $|c_2-c_1| \leq m$. If $c_1+c_2 \leq m+2$, then c_1 and c_2 should remain unchanged and do not have to be relativized. Otherwise, let $d = \lceil (c_1+c_2-m)/2 \rceil$, $c_1 = c_1-d+1$, and $c_2 = c_2-d+1$. Clearly, the relativized counter values will be less than or equal to m+1 and can easily be stored using O(m) cells. Note that, now $b_1 = \max \{0, \lceil (c_1+c_2-m)/2 \rceil\} = 1$ and $b_2 = \lfloor (c_1+c_2+m)/2 \rfloor = m+1$. The above discussion results in the following algorithm which can be implemented on an OLIA.

```
     Algorithm PCPARSE(q1,c1,q2,c2,x,S);
        { Let x = a1 ··· an. For simplicity, assume n > 0.
          b1 and b2 are defined the same as before }
1.      { If n = 1 then solve the problem directly }
        if n = 1 then
           if (q1,a1,pos(c1)) → (q2,c2-c1) ∈ δ then S := (q1,a1,pos(c1)) → (q2,c2-c1)
           else S := "no"
2.      else
2.1.       {Relativize counter values }
           d = ⌈(c1+c2-m)/2⌉;
           c1 = c1-d+1; c2 = c2-d+1;
2.2.       { Split the problem }
           i := ⌈n/2⌉;
           row1 := lastrow(E,q1,c1,a1...ai);
           row2 := lastrow(E^R,q2,c2,an...ai+1);
2.3.       { Find a j such that ∃p ∈ Q, p ∈ row1(j) ∩ row2(j)}
           j := b1;
           while row1(j) ∩ row2(j) = ∅ do
              j := j+1
           end;
           if j > b2 then S := "no" ; return
           else p := an arbitrary state in row1(j) ∩ row2(j);
3.         { Solve simpler problems }
           call PCPARSE(q1,c1,p,j1,a1...ai,S1);
           call PCPARSE(p,j2,q2,c2,ai+1...an,S2);
4.         S := S1, S2
        endif
     end.
```

Theorem 2. Parsing of 1-NCA languages can be done on an OLIA in linear time.

Proof. The OLIA implementation is quite involved and omitted here. It will be given in the full paper. □

Corollary 6. 1-NCA languages can be parsed on a single-tape Turing machine in $O(n^2)$ time and O(n) space.

6. Conclusion

We have shown that the following problems can be solved on an OLIA in linear time: 1) parsing of discrete 2-TNFT transductions, 2) parsing of LCFL's, 3) parsing of 1-NCA languages, and 4) string shuffling problem. For these problems, we were interested in not only the membership but also a parse.

Energy-Time Trade-offs in VLSI Computations

AKHILESH TYAGI
Department of Computer Science
University of North Carolina
Chapel Hill, NC 27599-3175

ABSTRACT

We show a lower bound of $\Omega(I^2(n))$ on the energy-time product ET for a function with the information complexity $I(n)$ both in uniswitch and multiswitch energy models. However the multiswitch circuits can be shown to be more energy efficient than the uniswitch circuits. We show a lower bound of $\Omega(I^2(n))$ on the uniswitch energy and a lower bound of $\Omega(I^{3/2}(n))$ on the multiswitch energy. The matching upper bounds can be shown to exist for several functions.

1 Overview

The *area, energy* and *time* are three fundamental resources in a VLSI computation. The relationship between area and time has been explored extensively starting with the pioneering work of Thompson [Tho79] and Brent & Kung [BK80]. However, *energy* did not receive much attention until recently. The following is a chronological overview of the related research with energy as a complexity measure. Mead [Chapter 9, [MC80]] considers the possibility of using *energy* as the fundamental measure of the computational complexity. Thompson [Tho80] takes it a step further and demonstrates some lower bounds on the energy requirements of some functions such as DFT. However, his model of energy consumption is not realistic. He charges a unit of energy for every wire for every time unit. Hence his view of energy consumption is equivalent to the area-time product AT. Kissin [Kis82] remedies the situation by providing a model of *switching* energy. About the same time, Lengauer and Mehlhorn [LM81] showed that the switching energy of transitive functions is $\Omega(n^2)$ if $AP^2 = O(n^2)$ where P is the period of a pipelined computation. Snyder and Tyagi [ST86] derive a similar result for the average case energy consumption. Kissin ([Kis85] and [Kis87]) develops several techniques to build energy-efficient circuits for monotonic circuits. Tyagi [Tya88] shows that the average energy-time product ET for a function with information complexity of $I(n)$ is $\Omega\left(\frac{I^2(n)}{\log n}\right)$. For information-optimal computations, energy and time trade according to $ET = \Theta(I^2(n))$. At the same time, Aggarwal, Chandra and Raghavan [ACR88] derived a lower bound of $\Omega(n^2)$ on the worst case uniswitch energy of shifting using a novel cutting method. Tyagi [Tya88] shows a lower bound of $\Omega(n^{4/3})$ on the average multiswitch energy of transitive functions.

In this paper, we extend the results of Aggarwal et. al. [ACR88] and Tyagi [Tya88] by using a generalized version of the cutting method of [ACR88] and information-theoretic techniques of [Tya88]. In particular, we show that the worst case energy-time product $ET = \Omega(I^2(n))$. Note that Aggarwal et. al. [ACR88] result applies only to the functions with $\Omega(n)$ output bits. Additionally, their result is good only for the uniswitch energy model (Every wire can switch at most once.). Our result holds for both uniswitch and multiswitch cases. It is worth noting that our multiswitch model [Tya88] is more general than the one used by Kissin [Kis87] and Aggarwal et. al. [ACR88]. We allow for cyclic circuits and hence the multiple switching of a wire can be the property of an algorithm for transmitting large amount of information. While Kissin and Aggarwal et. al. consider only acyclic circuits and multiple switching of a wire is due to race conditions rather than being an algorithmic feature. Hence our energy-time trade-off result demonstrates a fundamental trade-off for VLSI computation. It is not a by-product of our assumptions. In a similar vein, the worst case uniswitch energy is shown to be $\Omega(I^2(n))$. For the multiswitch case, the worst case energy is $\Omega(I^{3/2}(n))$. Both uniswitch and multiswitch lower bounds have matching upper bounds for a transitive function – shifting. Note that no other lower bound techniques for the multiswitch energy case are known.

We also show that the average switching energy-time product E_aT of a function is $\Omega(I_aH_f)$, where I_a is the average information complexity of f. H_f is the entropy of the given function. It quantizes the evenness of the distribution of the output values with respect to the input values. For a transitive function: shifting, the average energy-time product is shown to be $\Omega(n^2)$.

The physics of computation [BL85] has long been concerned with the question if there is some minimum energy required to perform a basic step of computation. They show that the laws of both classical and quantum-mechanical physics do not impose a lower bound on energy. In fact there is an energy-time trade-off in all the physically ideal models they consider. Seitz et al [SFM*85] demonstrate that slowing down the clock in an elementary nMOS driver can reduce the energy consumption arbitrarily. They also conjecture that there might be a similar trade-off at the function level. Our trade-off result validates that conjecture.

Energy-time trade-off implies that a computation can be speeded up only at a cost of additional energy and that drives up the power even higher (power is the rate of energy consumption). This energy is lost in the resistances of the transistors in the form of heat. The cooling of VLSI chips to dissipate the heat generated due to power consumption has long been a major engineering problem. Increased integration levels will only enhance the problem, if one believes Mead and Conway's premise [MC80] that the supply voltage will not scale beyond a point. Three dimensional technology will be more susceptible to this problem since the surface area does not grow as fast as the volume. Thus an analysis of energy complexity and its relationship with other resources pays off in avoiding excessive heat generation on chip. Besides, savings in energy (a precious resource) is a desirable characteristic of a VLSI algorithm.

This paper is organized as follows. In Section 2, we introduce the energy model. Section 3 contains the energy-time trade-off results for both the worst case and average case switching energy. The lower bounds on the energy in uniswitch and multiswitch models are also derived. We show matching upper bounds for shifting in Section 4.

2 Model

The model of VLSI computation is essentially the same as the one described by Thompson [Tho79]. A computation is abstracted as a communication graph. A communication graph is very much like a flow graph with the primitives being some basic operators that are realizable as electrical devices. Two communicating nodes are adjacent in this graph. A layout can be viewed as a convex embedding of the communication graph in a Cartesian grid. Each grid point can either have a processor or a wire passing through. A wire cannot go through a grid point with a processor unless it is a terminal of the processor at that grid point. The number of layers is limited to some constant γ. Thus both the fanin and fanout are bounded by 4γ. Wires have unit width and bandwidth and processors have unit area. The initial data values are localized to some constant area, to preclude an encoding of the results. The input words are read at the designated nodes called input ports. The input is synchronous and each input bit is available only once. the input and output conventions are where-determinate but need not be when-determinate.

The following is an enhancement of this model to account for energy. It is more or less similar to the model proposed by Kissin [Kis82], [Kis85] except for the multiswitch energy case. We assume that whenever a wire of length l changes state, it consumes $\Theta(l)$ switching energy. We do not account for the switching energy consumed by the processors. This is in accordance with the widely held belief that the wires take up most of the area in a VLSI layout and therefore dominate in the performance analysis. Since we are working with the lower bounds on switching energy, energy consumption of the wires definitely provides a lower bound on the total energy consumed.

We distinguish between the following two cases. When a wire can switch at most once during a computation, it is a Uniswitch computation. It was named Uniswitch Model (USM) by Kissin [Kis82]. In contrast, if a wire is allowed to switch any number of times, we get the Multiswitch model (MSM). We denote a circuit $C(V, W)$ as a graph, where V is the set of nodes and W is the set of edges or wires in $V \times V$. Notice that a circuit is allowed to be cyclic.

Definition 1 *A circuit $C(V, W)$ is said to be in state $s : V \cup W \longrightarrow \{0,1\}$, if s is consistent according to* *the following conditions.*

- *For an input node x_i, $s(x_i)$ is consistent with the input $x_0x_1 \dots x_{n-1}$. For an input wire $w = (x_i, y)$, $s(w)$ must equal $s(x_i)$.*
- *Non input nodes and edges have the values consistent with the input values and the labels of the nodes. For example, for a node, v, labeled by $\wedge$ with state of input wires $s(w_1) = 1, s(w_2) = 1$, $s(v)$ must equal 1.*

Definition 2 *A wire w (node v) is said to have switched from state s_0 to state s_1 if $s_0(w) \neq s_1(w)$ ($s_0(v) \neq s_1(v)$).*

We define a measure of energy consumption for a circuit. When a circuit C is subjected to an input $\vec{x}$, let wire w_i switch k_i times before the circuit is settled. Let l_i be the length of the wire w_i in the circuit C's embedding in a grid. Then the energy consumption for circuit C, $E_W(C, s, \vec{x})$ in state s with $\vec{x}$ as the input is defined to be $u \times \sum_{w_i \in W} k_i \times l_i$. For the Uniswitch model $k_i \leq 1$. We will distinguish between worst case energy consumption and average case energy consumption.

Definition 3 *The worst case energy consumption for a circuit C, $E_w(C)$, is defined to be $max_{s,\vec{x}}$ $E_W(C, s, \vec{x})$, where the maximum is taken over all (state, input vector) pairs.*

The average case energy consumption is defined in a similar way. It is the average of switching energy consumed for all possible initial state, next input vector combinations.

Definition 4 *The average case energy consumption for a circuit C is defined to be its energy consumption averaged over all initial states and all input vectors. Thus $E_a(C) = \sum_{s,\vec{x}} E_W(C, s, \vec{x}) /$ $(|S_i|\,|I|)$, where S_i is the set of initial states and I is the set of input vectors.*

For further details of this model, the reader is referred to either of the theses [Kis87], [Tya88] or to Kissin's papers [Kis82], [Kis85].

3 Energy Time Trade-off

Let a given circuit $C(V,W)$ compute a function $y_m y_{m-1} \cdots y_1 = f(x_n x_{n-1} \cdots x_1)$. The information complexity of this function, $I(n)$, is the minimum number of bits exchanged between any two equal sized partitions of the input bits. We use I to denote $I(n)$. Many results in the following apply to the transitive functions as defined by Vuillemin [Vui83]. Many commonly occuring functions such as shifting, multiplication and DFT are transitive since they embed a computation of a transitive permutation group. The information complexity of the transitive functions is known to be $\Omega(n)$.

The main difficulty in proving lower bounds on energy consumption arise from the following perspective. I bits need to be sent across a bisection. But nothing prohibits the chip from increasing the number of bits to $\omega(I)$ and hence reduce the switching. An extreme scenario expands the information exponentially. For instance, a chip could transmit 2^k-bit long strings to convey k information bits. Only the strings from $\{0^*10^*\} \cap \{0,1\}^{2^k}$ (strings of length 2^k with only one 1) are used to transmit the information. The string $0^{i-1}10^{2^k-i}$ conveys the ith event. Note that the switching in such a string is limited to only two, at the borders of the bit 1.

Let us consider the worst case switching energy first.

3.1 Worst Case Switching Energy

The strategy for the proof is as follows. We cut the given chip in a certain way so that there are two widely separated sections of the chip containing a high number of input bits ($n/c >$) each. By the results in Yao [Yao79] and Ja'Ja', Kumar [JK84], these sections exchange at least I bits, where I is $\Omega(n)$ for transitive functions. A cut is a bounding box around these input bit regions. The techniques in Tyagi [Tya88] provide a lower bound on the switching energy consumed at such a cut. This energy is summed over several such cuts. Since the uniswitch energy case is simpler, let us prove it first.

Uniswitch Energy:

We first prove a generalized version of Aggarwal et. al. [ACR88] cutting lemma (Lemma 2.3). In the following ω is the minimal bisection width of the given circuit $C = (V, W)$ as defined in Thompson [Tho79]. Note that C has n input ports due to uniswitch assumption.

Lemma 1 *Let $C = (V, W)$ compute f as described above. There exist two sets of input ports I_1 and I_2 with $|I_1|, |I_2| \geq n/d$ for a constant d. Let R_{I_1} and R_{I_2} denote the smallest rectangles containing I_1 and I_2 respectively. Let h (v) be the horizontal (vertical) distance between R_{I_1} and R_{I_2}. Then one of the following statements holds true for a constant e.*

1. *$h \geq \omega/d$ and the height of either R_{I_1} or R_{I_2} is at most ω/e.*
2. *$v \geq \omega/d$ and the width of either R_{I_1} or R_{I_2} is at most ω/e.*
3. *Both $h, v \geq \omega/d$.*

PROOF OMITTED.

Now we can state a theorem similar to Theorem 2.5 in Aggarwal et. al. [ACR88] that holds for functions with any number of bits. We use the result [Tya88] (Lemma 3.6, Page 44 also stated in Appendix A) that $\Omega\left(\frac{n}{\log(m/n)}\right)$ average switching energy is required to transmit n bits of information using $m > n$ bits.

Theorem 1 *A VLSI computation of a function f with information complexity I has an energy-time product $ET = \Omega(I^2/\log(n/I))$. The uniswitch energy consumption is also $\Omega(I^2/\log(n/I))$. Hence the ET product and the switching energy of transitive functions are $\Omega(n^2)$.*

PROOF OMITTED.

Multiswitch Energy:

In the multiswitch model, the principal difficulties are as follows. An input port can be used to read many input bits. A wire can be used to multiplex many information bits. In the uniswitch case, a wire carries at most one bit. On the other extreme, a wire can be kept busy all the time. Or to make things even more complicated, a hand-shaking protocol might induce a few periods of activity on a wire. Thus the expansion of information to reduce switching still remains an adversarial technique.

We first prove a new cutting lemma.

Lemma 2 *Let $C = (V, W)$ compute f as described above. Let us assume that no input port reads more then $n/71$ input bits. There exist two sets of input ports I_1 and I_2 such that I_1 and I_2 each read at least $n/71$ input bits. Let R_{I_1} and R_{I_2} denote the smallest rectangles containing I_1 and I_2 respectively. Let p_1 (p_2) be the perimeter of R_{I_1} (R_{I_2}). Let h (v) be the horizontal (vertical) distance between R_{I_1} and R_{I_2}. Then one of the following statements holds true.*

1. *$h \geq \min(p_1/4, p_2/4)$.*
2. *$v \geq \min(p_1/4, p_2/4)$.*

PROOF SKETCH: Since no input port reads more than $n/71$ input bits, we can find a vertical line V bisecting the chip into two halves such that each half reads at least $n/3$ input bits. The argument for it is similar to that in Ullman [[Ull84] , page 49]. Let us concentrate on the right-hand side of V. Once again, we can find a horizontal line H that cuts the right-hand side of V into two parts such that each part reads at least $n/9$ input bits. The left-hand side of V is also cut into two parts by the line H. At least one of these parts reads $n/6$ input bits. Without loss of generality (WLOG), let the bottom part read at least $n/6$ input bits. Let R_{I_1} and R_{I_2} be the smallest rectangles containing the input ports in the bottom-left and top-right quadrants respectively, as shown in Figure 1.

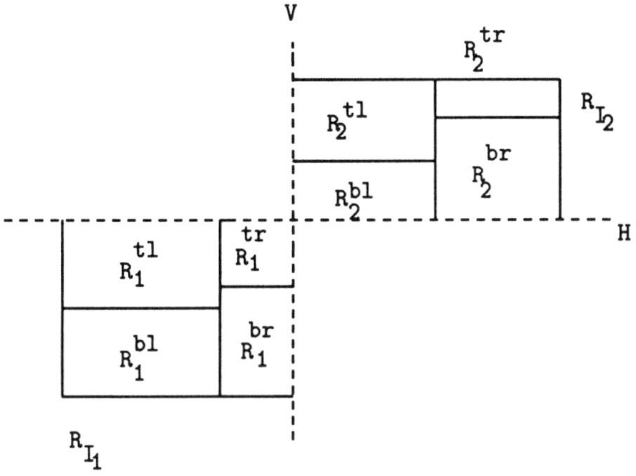

Figure 1: An Illustration of the Cutting Method

Now cut both R_{I_1} and R_{I_2} first vertically and then horizontally as before. This gives rise to four rectangles R_1^{tl}, R_1^{tr}, R_1^{bl} and R_1^{br} each reading at least $n/54$ input bits. We also get R_2^{tl}, R_2^{tr}, R_2^{bl} and R_2^{br} each reading at least $n/71$ input bits. Let R_1^{tl}, R_1^{tr}, R_1^{bl}, R_1^{br}, R_2^{tl}, R_2^{tr}, R_2^{bl} and R_2^{br} have perimeter p_1^{tl}, p_1^{tr}, p_1^{bl}, p_1^{br}, p_2^{tl}, p_2^{tr}, p_2^{bl} and p_2^{br} respectively. Without loss of generality, let a rectangle in R_{I_1} have the smallest perimeter. Let this rectangle be R_1^{tr} with the smallest perimeter $p = p_1^{tr}$. Since we will be separating this rectangle from one of the rectangles in R_{I_2}, any other rectangle in R_{I_1} can only have a larger separation. Consider the rectangle R_2^{bl}. It has perimeter $p_2^{bl} \geq p$. Then either its width $w \geq p/4$ or its height $h \geq p/4$. If the width of R_2^{bl} is at least $p/4$ then R_2^{br} is horizontally separated from R_1^{tr} by at least $p/4$ where the perimeter of R_1^{tr} is p. Otherwise R_2^{tl} is vertically separated from R_1^{tr} by at least $p/4$.

All the other cases follow the same line of reasoning. □

Now we are ready to prove a lower bound on the ET product. Note that since the multiswitch energy is no greater than the uniswitch energy, the following is a stronger lower bound on the ET product than the one provided by Theorem 1.

Theorem 2 *A VLSI computation of a function f with information complexity I has an energy-time product $ET = \Omega(I^2)$. Hence the ET product of transitive functions is $\Omega(n^2)$.*

PROOF SKETCH: Let us assume that no input port reads more than $n/71$ input bits. Otherwise, T is at least $n/71$ and E is at least $n/142$ giving an $\Omega(n^2)$ lower bound on ET in a trivial way.

Otherwise, let us use Lemma 2 to derive two rectangles R_{I_1} and R_{I_2} satisfying the following conditions. The input ports in R_{I_1} and R_{I_2} each read at least $n/71$ input bits. Their horizontal or vertical separation is at least $\min(p_1/4, p_2/4)$ where p_1 and p_2 are their respective perimeters. Without loss of generality, let this separation be $p_1/4$. We build $p_1/4$ new bisections in the following way. Let $W(0)$ be the set of all the horizontal or vertical unit length wire segments crossing the perimeter of R_{I_1}. Let $W(i)$ be defined recursively as the set of unit length wires adjacent to the wires in $W(i-1)$ and not in $W(0), \ldots, W(i-1)$ and not inside R_{I_1}. These are the rings around R_{I_1} as shown in Figure 2. Let us consider the rings

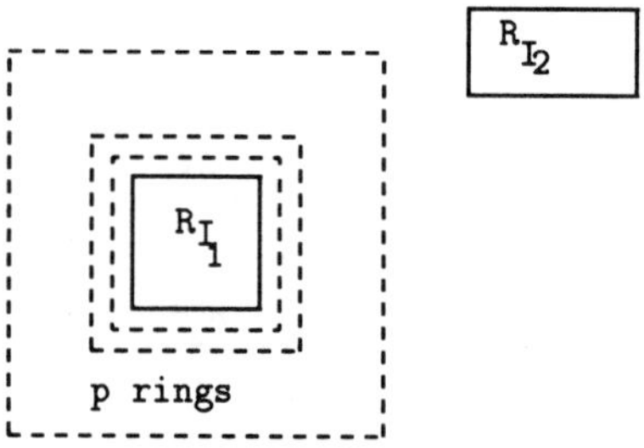

Figure 2: The Rings Used in ET Lower Bound

$W(0), W(1), \ldots W((p_1/d)-1)$. Note that $W(0)$ contains at most $2p_1$ wires. It can also be shown that the number of wires in $W((p_1/d)-1)$, $|W((p_1/d)-1)| \leq 16p_1$. If the computation takes time T, then the total number of bits transmitted across a ring, m, can't exceed $16p_1T$. If the majority of the output bits are generated inside a ring $W(i)$, then the information about the input bits read in R_{I_2} needs to come into the ring. Otherwise, the information about the input bits read inside the ring needs to go out. In either case, since R_{I_1} and R_{I_2} read at least $n/71$ input bits, the number of information bits required is $\Omega(I)$. Hence the energy consumption at a ring $W(i)$ is $\Omega\left(\frac{I}{\log(16p_1T/I)}\right)$ by Lemma 8 in Appendix A. Summed up over $p_1/4$ rings, the energy E is $\Omega\left(\frac{Ip_1}{\log(p_1T/I)}\right)$. Then the ET product is $\Omega\left(\frac{Ip_1T}{\log(p_1T/I)}\right)$. Note that for the correctness of the computation, $p_1T \geq I$. Also observe that for $p_1T > I$, $\frac{p_1T}{\log(p_1T/I)} > I$. This implies that $ET = \Omega(I^2)$. □

To show a lower bound on the multiswitch energy of transitive functions, we need a lemma similar to Paterson, Ruzzo, Snyder [PRS81]. This lemma shows that no matter how you pack the input ports and output ports together, the average distance an input bit has to travel is $\Omega(\sqrt{n})$.

Lemma 3 *The average distance between a set of n nodes in a VLSI layout is $\Omega(\sqrt{n})$.*

Proof Omitted.

Another lemma based on Baudet's ideas [Bau81] claims that even if an input port reads many input bits, these bits would have to be remembered before an output bit can be produced for a transitive function. Thus before any output bit can be generated, the information about all the n input bits should either be stored on the chip or should be read at that time.

Lemma 4 (**Baudet 1981**) *For a transitive function computation, let the first output bit be generated at time t_k. Let the number of bits stored on the chip by computations until t_{k-1} be denoted by s_k. Let the number of input bits read at time t_k be n_k. Then for a transitive function of degree n, $s_k + n_k \geq n$.*

Proof Omitted.

Now let us prove a lower bound on the multiswitch energy.

Theorem 3 *The multiswitch energy of a transitive function is $\Omega(n^{3/2})$.*

PROOF: Lemma 4 says that right before the first output bit is generated, there are at least n nodes on the chip that contain the input bits (in encoded or un-encoded form). Let us use Lemma 2 to bisect these n nodes to derive two rectangles R_{I_1} and R_{I_2} each containing at least $n/71$ of these nodes. Let R_{I_1} have the smaller perimeter of the two rectangles equal to p. Note that due to Lemma 3, p is $\Omega\left(\sqrt{n}\right)$. Additionally, R_{I_1} has either a vertical or horizontal separation of $p/4$ from R_{I_2}.

As in Theorem 2, let $W(0)$ be the set of unit length wire segments crossing the perimeter of R_{I_1}. We can similarly define $p/4$ rings $W(1)$ through $W(p/4)$. Notice that each ring has at most $16p$ wires. At least n bits of information cross each of these rings. Then the energy consumed at each ring is $\Omega\left(\frac{n}{\log(16pT/n)}\right)$. Summing it over $p = \Omega(\sqrt{n})$ rings gives a total energy consumption of $\Omega\left(\frac{n^{3/2}}{\log(16pT/n)}\right)$. If the number of bits crossing each ring $n \leq m \leq 16pT$ is $O(n)$ then this gives us an $\Omega(n^{3/2})$ lower bound.

Otherwise $n < m \leq 16pT$. This implies that the n bits inside a ring are being encoded into m bits. In this case, we estimate the energy required for the encoding. We will observe the encoded bits coming out at the periphery of R_{I_1} at every time slot from t_0 through t_T. An information bit y_{lt} appearing at the lth wire in $W(0)$ is said to *depend* on the input bit x_i if there exists a binary assignmnet to the other input bits such that changing the value of x_i at time t switches y_{lt} at time t. The set of m information bits can be partitioned into n disjoint sets Y_1 through Y_n such that the information bits in Y_i depend on x_i. Note that an information bit can depend on more than one input bit. In such a case, we assign it to one of the sets Y_i arbitrarily. This does not make any difference to the lower bound we derive later. Let the cardinality of Y_i be m_i. Note that $m = \sum_{i=1}^{n} m_i$. Let Y_{ij} contain m_{ij} information bits out of m_i information bits from Y_i generated at time t_j. Note that $m = \sum_{i=1}^{n}\sum_{j=0}^{T} m_{ij}$ and $Y_i = \bigcup_{j=0}^{T} Y_{ij}$.

How much switching energy is consumed at time t_j? Let us observe the input bit x_i and the information bits in Y_{ij}. By Lemma 3 the average distance of a path from x_i to any of the m_{ij} wires in $W(0)$ carrying the information bits in Y_{ij} is $\Omega(\sqrt{m_{ij}})$. Note that $\Omega(n/\log(m/n))$ of these information bits switch. Hence the switching energy at time t_j is $\Omega\left(\frac{n}{\log(m/n)}\sum_{i=1}^{n}\sqrt{m_{ij}}\right)$. Note that for two non-negative numbers x and y, $\sqrt{x+y} \leq \sqrt{x} + \sqrt{y}$. Then the lower bound on the energy at time t_j is $\Omega\left(\frac{n}{\log(m/n)}\sqrt{\sum_{i=1}^{n} m_{ij}}\right)$. Let us sum this energy over time t_0 through t_T. Then the total energy is $\Omega\left(\frac{n}{\log(m/n)}\sqrt{\sum_{j=0}^{T}\sum_{i=1}^{n} m_{ij}}\right)$ which is $\Omega\left(\frac{n\sqrt{m}}{\log(m/n)}\right)$. For $m \geq n$ this expression is minimized at $m = n$ to $\Omega(n^{3/2})$. □

We will show matching upper bounds for *shifting*. Let us first consider the average energy case.

3.2 Average Case Switching Energy

Estimating the average case switching energy is all the more important for VLSI circuits. A high average level of current flow gives rise to *metal-migration* [MC80] problems. All the proofs for the average-case analysis follow the same reasoning as the ones for the worst case switching energy with two crucial differences. *One:* we have good lower bounds on the worst case information complexity of many functions due to [Yao79] and [JK84]. What can be said about the average case information complexity? We prove that all the lower bounds on the information complexity derived by Yao and Ja'Ja' & Kumar are valid for the average case as well. *Two:* the lower bound on the energy required to transmit n bits of information using $m > n$ bits (by Lengauer, Mehlhorn [LM81] and Tyagi [Tya88]) assume that all the 2^n information strings are equally likely. We show it not to be the case. We first deal with the average information complexity bounds.

Recall from Yao [Yao79] that the worst case communication complexity is given by the minimum value of the communication complexity $c(p)$ over all the protocols p. For a two-way protocol, Yao defines the *2-way communication complexity* to be $C(f, A \Leftrightarrow B) = \min_p\{c(p) \mid \text{the protocol } p \text{ computes function } f\}$. In the same vein, we define the *average communication complexity* $c_a(p)$ for a protocol p to be the average number of bits exchanged in computing f under the protocol p. We define the average communication complexity of a function f, $C_a(f, A \Leftrightarrow B) = \min_p\{c_a(p) \mid \text{the protocol } p \text{ computes function } f\}$. The following lemma provides a technique for deriving a lower bound on the average communication complexity. For the definitions of the *decomposition number* $d(f)$, a monochromatic rectangle and a rectangle decomposition, the reader is referred to either Yao [Yao79] or Ja'Ja', Kumar [JK84].

Lemma 5 *For a function $f = \{f_1, f_2, \ldots, f_m\}$ the average communication complexity $C_a(f; A \Leftrightarrow B) \geq \log d(f)$.*

Proof omitted.

Theorem 2.1 in [JK84] states that the worst case communication complexity $C(f; A \Leftrightarrow B) \geq \log d(f)$. Thus, again, deriving a lower bound of $h(n)$ on $C(f; A \Leftrightarrow B)$ essentially involves finding an A or B monochromatic rectangle decomposition of size $2^{h(n)}$. By Lemma 5, it also implies a lower bound of $h(n)$ on $C_a(f; A \Leftrightarrow B)$. Thus all the known lower bounds on the worst case communication $C(f; A \Leftrightarrow B)$ constitute a lower bound on $C_a(f; A \Leftrightarrow B)$ as well.

The other concern we have to address has to do with the average alternation in a set of binary strings. We prove in Appendix A, Lemma 8 that transmitting n bits of information with m bits requires $\Omega\left(\frac{n}{\log(m/n)}\right)$ energy. Recall that the average switching energy is derived by averaging over all initial state and all input vector pairs. Since every leaf in the protocol decision tree for the circuit C is reachable from the root, cycling through all the input values must take the computation to all the leaves. Each leaf can be associated with one information bit string. Thus averaging over all the input values is equivalent to averaging over all the information bit strings. A uniform distribution of the information strings or the output words gives rise to the analysis in Appendix A. Thus we first need a notion of skew of a given function with respect to the distribution of its output values.

Let I be the set of information strings that need to be transmitted across any bisection of the input bits for a given function. Let n_x be the number of input values that give rise to the information string x. Then we define *information entropy* of a function f as follows.

Definition 5 *The information entropy of a function f with the set of information strings I, $H_{f,I}$ is $\sum_{x\in I} \frac{n_x}{2^n} \log\left(\frac{2^n}{n_x}\right)$.*

A quantity that is easier to measure is the *entropy* of a function. The *entropy* of a function H_f measures the evenness of the distribution of the output values.

Definition 6 *Let n_y be the number of input values that give rise to the output value y. Then the entropy of f H_f is $\sum_{y\in O} \frac{n_y}{2^n} \log\left(\frac{2^n}{n_y}\right)$.*

Note that a lower bound on the entropy of a function is also a lower bound on the information entropy as well but not vice versa. This is because there are Boolean functions as shown in Sipser, Papadimitriou [PS82] whose entropy is constant but the information entropy is $\Omega(n)$.

Now Lemma 8 can be modified as follows.

Lemma 6 *Let k' and k be two positive integers such that $k' \geq k$. The average number of alternations in transmitting a k' bit encoding of k information bits, $A(k', k) = \Omega(H_f/4\log(k'/H_f))$.*

Now the *ET* trade-off for the average case energy can be bounded.

Theorem 4 *A VLSI computation of a function f with information compexity I and entropy H_f has an average energy-time product $E_aT = \Omega(IH_f)$.*

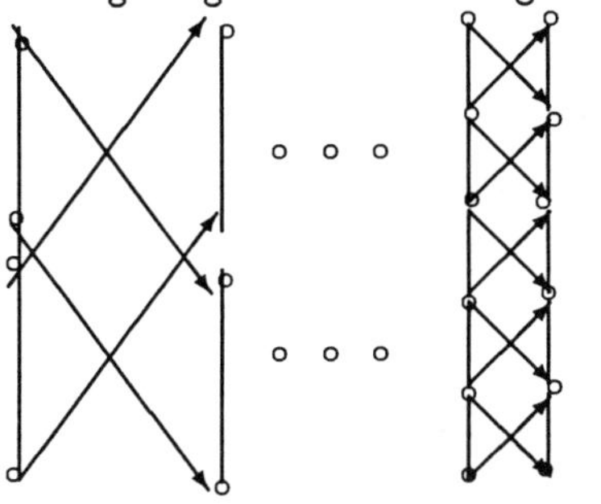

Figure 3: A Barrel Shifter

Entropy of Shifting

Shifting has a very even distribution of the input values to the output values. It is an injective function. Hence the entropy of shifting is n. Theorem 4 then implies that shifting has an average energy-time product of $\Omega(n^2)$.

4 Upper Bounds

A barrel shifter, as shown in Figure 3 can be implemented in area $O(n^2)$ and it takes time $O(\log n)$ to shift one set of data, as described in Ullman [Ull84]. For each of the $\log n$ bits in the control input (shift value) there is a stage in the barrel shifter. The ith stage shifts the data bits by 2^{i-1} bit positions. Thus, in general, the wires corresponding to the ith stage, for $1 \leq i \leq \log n$, have a length of $\Theta(2^{(i-1)})$. The wires for the stage corresponding to the most significant bit (a shift by $n/2$) have length $\Theta(n/2)$. On average, half of the wires at each stage switch. Then the average energy consumption for this circuit is $\Theta(A)$, which is $O(n^2)$. T being $O(\log n)$ gives an upper bound of $O(n^2 \log n)$ on ET product for shifting. Compare it with the lower bound of $\Omega(n^2)$.

Another shifter, as described in Ullman [[Ull84], page 69], has a lower ET product. It is illustrated in Figure 4. The n bits to be shifted are stored along a $\sqrt{n} \times \sqrt{n}$ array. We number the rows bottom-up from 1 to $\sqrt{n}$ and columns left-right from 1 to $\sqrt{n}$. The least significant input bit x_1 is stored at $(1,1)$ position, $x_{\sqrt{n}}$ at $(\sqrt{n}, 1)$, $x_{\sqrt{n}+1}$ at $(1,2)$, and x_n at $(\sqrt{n}, \sqrt{n})$. The first half control bits $c_{\log n} \ldots c_{(\log n)/2+1}$ specify the horizontal shift amount and the least significant half bits specify the vertical shift amount. It takes area $\sqrt{n} \times \sqrt{n}$ and time $O(\sqrt{n})$. For each horizontal shift through a column, half of $\sqrt{n}$ bits are expected to switch, which switches half the area. The expected shift amount is $\sqrt{n}$, giving rise to $O(n^{3/2})$ average switching energy for both horizontal and vertical shifting. The time taken is $O(\sqrt{n})$. Thus we have an ET product of $O(n^2)$ which matches the lower bound. Interestingly, this circuit is also AT^2 optimal.

ACKNOWLEDGEMENTS: It is a pleasure to acknowledge many stimulating discussions with Larry Snyder & Larry Ruzzo of Washington and Martine Schlag of U. C. Santa Cruz and J. Nievergelt & David Plaisted of UNC. I am grateful to Alok Aggarwal of IBM Yorktown for pointing out a bug in one of my earlier proofs. This work was supported in part by NSF Grant #MIP-8806169.

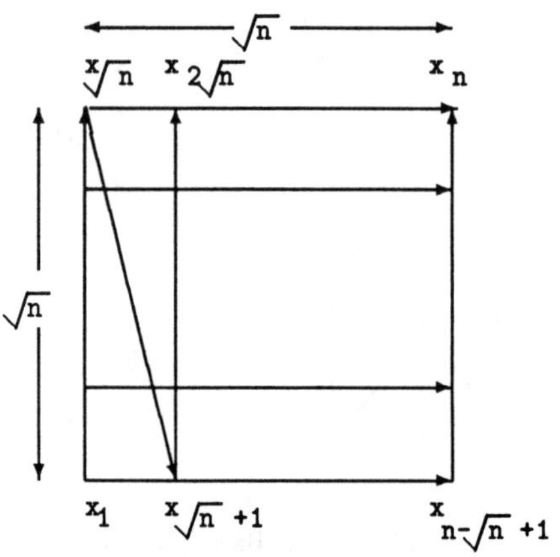

Figure 4: A Shifter with $ET\ O(n^2)$

References

[ACR88] A. Aggarwal, A. K. Chandra, and P. Raghavan. Energy Consumption in VLSI Circuits. In *ACM Symposium on Theory of Computing*, pages 205–216, ACM-SIGACT, 1988.

[Bau81] G. M. Baudet. On the Area Required by VLSI Circuits. In *Proceedings of CMU Conference on VLSI*, pages 100–107, CMU, Computer Science Press, 1981.

[BK80] R.P. Brent and H.T. Kung. The Chip Complexity of Binary Arithmetic. In *ACM Symposium on Theory of Computing*, ACM-SIGACT, 1980.

[BL85] R. Bennett and R. Landauer. Fundamental Physical Limits of Computation. *Scientific American*, July 1985.

[JK84] J. Ja'Ja' and V.K. Kumar. Information Transfer in Distributed Computing with Applications to VLSI. *Journal of the ACM*, January 1984.

[Kis82] G. Kissin. Measuring Energy Consumption in VLSI Circuits: a Foundation. In *ACM Symposium on Theory of Computing*, ACM-SIGACT, 1982.

[Kis85] G. Kissin. Functional Bounds on Switching Theory. In *Chapel Hill Conference on VLSI*, U.N.C., Chapel Hill, Computer Science Press, 1985.

[Kis87] G. Kissin. *Measuring Energy Consumption in VLSI Circuits.* PhD thesis, Department of Computer Science, University of Toronto, Toronto, 1987.

[LM81] T. Lengauer and K. Mehlhorn. On the Complexity of VLSI Computations. In *Proceedings of CMU Conference on VLSI*, CMU, Computer Science Press, 1981.

[MC80] C. Mead and L. Conway. *Introduction to VLSI Systems.* Addison-Wesley, Reading, Mass., 1980.

[PRS81] M. S. Paterson, W. L. Ruzzo, and L. Snyder. Bounds on Minimax Edge Length for Complete Binary Trees. In *ACM Symposium on Theory of Computing*, ACM-SIGACT, 1981.

[PS82] C. Papadimitriou and M. Sipser. Communication Complexity. In *ACM Symposium on Theory of Computing*, ACM-SIGACT, 1982.

[SFM*85] C. L. Seitz, A. H. Frey, S. Mattisson, S. D. Rabin, D. A. Speck, and Van de Snepscheut J. Hot-Clock nMOS. In *Chapel Hill Conference on VLSI*, U.N.C., Chapel Hill, Computer Science Press, 1985.

[ST86] L. Snyder and A. Tyagi. *The Energy Complexity of Transitive Functions.* Technical Report TRCS-86-09-07, Dept. of Computer Science, University of Washington, Seattle, 1986. A preliminary version appears in the Proceedings of the Twenty-fourth Annual Allerton Conference on Communication, Control and Computing, 1986.

[Tho79] C.D. Thompson. Area-Time Complexity for VLSI. In *ACM Symposium on Theory of Computing*, ACM-SIGACT, 1979.

[Tho80] C. D. Thompson. *A Complexity Theory for VLSI.* PhD thesis, Department of Computer Science, Carnegie-Mellon University, Pittsburgh, 1980.

[Tya88] A. Tyagi. *The Role of Energy in VLSI Computations.* PhD thesis, Department of Computer Science, University of Washington, Seattle, 1988. Available as UWCS Technical Report Number 88-06-05.

[Ull84] J.D. Ullman. *Computational Aspects of VLSI.* Computer Science Press, Rockville, Md., 1984.

[Vui83] J. Vuillemin. A Combinatorial Limit to the Computing Power of VLSI Circuits. *IEEE Transactions on Computers*, 294–300, March 1983.

[Yao79] A.C. Yao. Some Complexity Questions Related to Distributed Computing. In *ACM Symposium on Theory of Computing*, ACM-SIGACT, 1979.

A Lower Bounds on Average Alternation

Note that the number of alternating zero-one blocks in a binary string is a measure of the switching induced in transmitting that string. The objective in this section is to prove some lower bounds on the average number of alternating zero and one blocks in a string chosen in one of the following ways. We show that when k bits are used to convey k information bits, the average number of alternating zero and one blocks is $\Omega(k)$. The other way is to encode k information bits by $k' > k$ bits. Then the average number of zero and one blocks in such a $k'-$ bit string is $\Omega(k/\log(k'/k))$.

The following notation is helpful in the proofs that follow. We say that in a bit sequence $a_1, a_2, \ldots, a_l$, there is an *alternation* at position j if $a_j \neq a_{j+1}$ for $1 \leq j \leq l-1$. Let δ_j be 1 if $a_j \neq a_{j+1}$ and 0 otherwise. Then the *total alternation* for a l-bit sequence is given by $\sum_{j=1}^{l-1} \delta_j$. The following lemma shows that, on average, a k bit sequence has about $k/2$ bit alternations. This is true if each of the 2^k k-bit sequences can be picked with equal probability.

Lemma 7 *Let $k > 1$ be a positive integer. The average alternation $A(k)$ for a k-bit sequence from the set $\{0,1\}^k$ is $(k-1)/2$.*

Lemma 7 assures us that the average number of alternations in transmitting k bits at a bisection, $A(k)$, is $\Omega(k)$, if the computation is using exactly k bits to transfer k information bits. We refer to this type of computation as *information-optimal* computation. An information-optimal computation has a *uniform* distribution of the k-bit crossing sequences. But, as shown in Section 3, information expansion can lead to a skewed distribution of information strings and hence to a lower switching. The next lemma (proved in [Tya88]) addresses this question of average alternation under information-expansion.

Lemma 8 *Let k' and k be two positive integers such that $k' \geq k$. The average number of alternations in transmitting a k' bit encoding of k information bits, $A(k', k) = \Omega(k/4\log(k'/k))$.*

Time and Real-time in Programs

*Mathai Joseph**
University of Warwick

EXTENDED ABSTRACT

1 Introduction

Designing correct real-time programs has been seen as a significant problem for many years. Work on the description and analysis of such programs has usually followed one of two paths: the study of formal specification, the design of language constructs and the construction of semantic models, or performance analysis using scheduling theory to determine the timing properties of programs in relation to their use of computational resources. These two views address different problems, correctness and performance, which are normally considered independently. But in a real-time system, correctness and performance are closely related and it is as incorrect for a real-time program to produce a result which deviates from its specification as it is for it produce the right result at the wrong time.

The difference in these views is of course a consequence of using different analytical methods and theories so it may be argued that the problem of designing real-time programs is merely one of using the right tools. However, there are results from scheduling theory that must have some bearing on correctness: for example, Mok [12] has shown that the problem of scheduling certain classes of processes to ensure mutual exclusion is NP-hard. Similarly, given a functionally correct real-time program, the problem of transforming it to use the minimum number of processors that will allow it to satisfy its real-time constraints is NP-complete.

A link between the two views can be established if it is recognized that scheduling is concerned with the allocation of a limited set of resources (e.g. processors, memory) to computations with competing demands, while most studies of correctness assume, often unrealistically, that a program has all the resources needed for its uninterrupted execution. But there are other important issues that must be resolved before real-time program design can be given a sound basis. The representation of time in the semantics is one such issue, as is the question of how the timing requirements in a program specification can be refined along with the functional properties.

---

*Address for correspondence: Department of Computer Science, University of Warwick, Coventry CV4 7AL, U.K. This work was supported by research grants GR/D 73881 and GR/F 35418 from the Science and Engineering Research Council.

In this paper, we discuss some of these problems and emphasize the need for developing a sound *theory* and a *method* for the design of real-time programs.

2 Time

Consider the execution of a distributed program in which each process can read a 'local' value of time, represented as a real number. Let the local time of each process be measured in the same units, start with value 0 when the process begins execution, and have the usual properties of increasing monotonically and uniformly. In such a program, *Clock* is an alarm-clock-like process which loops waiting for its local time to equal the successive values taken by its variable *Tick*. Assume that the time taken to execute a command is suitably small when compared to the waiting time of this process.

$$Clock :: Tick := 1; *[when\ Tick = Localtime_1\ do\ Tick := Tick + 1]$$

X is a similar process, but the waiting time of its loop is halved for each successive iteration.

$$X :: Halftime := 1; Inc := Halftime/2;$$
$$*[when\ Halftime = Localtime_2\ do\ Halftime, Inc := Halftime + Inc, Inc/2]$$

In the parallel composition $Clock \| X$, what is the value of *Halftime* when $Tick = 2$? Will the value of *Tick ever* become 2 ?

If we make the common assumption that independent actions in different processes in a distributed program can occur arbitrarily close together in time, then although computations are 'discrete', the time of their execution must be represented as some dense domain. But it must also be assumed that there is a lower bound to the execution time of any instruction, for if this is not the case, in the program above *Halftime* will approach but never become 2 (rather like a computational equivalent of Zeno's paradox of Achilles and the tortoise). On the other hand, if there *is* a fixed lower bound to the execution time of any command, it can be assumed without much loss of precision that the execution times of all commands are multiples of this (or some other) amount and the time can be expressed in natural numbers; in this case, the value of *Inc* will eventually become smaller than the lower bound. How then is a choice made between representing time by a dense or a discrete domain ?

There is therefore a question of how to relate discrete computational actions, which by their nature have granularity, with well-established physical theories of continuous time. However, similar problems have been studied before and Whitrow [17] describes how from the work of Russell [14] and Walker [16] it is possible to obtain a continuous time domain from an appropriate definition of instants of time. A crucial aspect of this work is that time is defined *in terms of* actions, not conversely; this contrasts with the view so far taken in computational models, where actions are laid out in some order over a pre-ordained domain of time.

3 Time from Actions

Assume that an execution of a program consists of a set of *actions*; an action can be considered as the execution of a terminating command in a program and so some actions may be performed sequentially and some in parallel. Let *ACT* be the set of all actions.

An action *a precedes* another action *b* ($a \prec b$) if *b* does not start before *a* terminates (but the beginning of *b* may coincide with the termination of *a*). Two actions *a* and *b* *overlap* if *a* does not precede *b* and *b* does not precede *a*. The relation '$\prec$' on *ACT* is *irreflexive* and *antisymmetric*. It is also assumed to satisfy the following condition:

$$\forall a, b, c, d \in ACT : (a \prec b \wedge b \sim c \wedge c \prec d) \Rightarrow (a \prec d)$$

where '$\sim$' (*overlaps*) is a relation on *ACT* defined by

$$\forall a, b \in ACT : a \sim b \Leftrightarrow \neg(a \prec b) \wedge \neg(b \prec a)$$

There are other conditions that can be placed over the set of actions, e.g. it may be assumed that this condition applies over disjoint subsets of *ACT* but not over the whole set *ACT*. However, for this paper we shall assume for simplicity that this condition holds over *ACT*.

For $A \subseteq ACT$, define

$$After(A) = \begin{cases} ACT & \text{if } A = \emptyset \\ \bigcap_{a \in A} After(a) & \text{otherwise} \end{cases}$$

$$Before(A) = \begin{cases} ACT & \text{if } A = \emptyset \\ \bigcap_{a \in A} Before(a) & \text{otherwise} \end{cases}$$

Let '$\dashv$' and '$\vdash$' denote the relations 'right-aligned' and 'left-aligned' respectively. Action *a* is right-aligned with action *b* (i.e. $a \dashv b$) if *a* terminates no later than *b* and *b* terminates no later than *a*. Formally,

$$a \dashv b \Leftrightarrow a \notin After(b) \wedge b \notin After(a)$$

Similarly,

$$a \vdash b \Leftrightarrow a \notin Before(b) \wedge b \notin Before(a)$$

The precedence relation over actions, and the property of overlapping, suggests that each action has some 'duration'. Informally, two actions can be said to overlap if their durations overlap. Relations between actions can be used to introduce the idea of an instant.

An *instant* of time can be considered as a durationless point in the time domain; it is defined as a set-theoretic 'cut' in *ACT*. Formally, $\{A, B\}$ is a $\prec$-cut if

$$A \neq \emptyset \wedge B \neq \emptyset \wedge A \lhd B$$

$$\wedge \forall c \in ACT : (\forall b \in B : c \prec b) \Rightarrow c \in A$$
$$\wedge \forall c \in ACT : (\forall a \in A : a \prec c) \Rightarrow c \in B$$

and (A, B) is then an *instant*.

The set *T* of instants is isomorphic with the set of real numbers if it satisfies the standard axioms for real numbers([1,17]).

4 Actions and Computations

At one level, the relation between an action and a computation can be simply defined: an action is an execution of a finite (i.e. terminating) program command. If the time associated with computation is to be in the real domain, then the actions derived from computations must be capable of producing a set of instants which is dense.

To examine how program actions can result in a dense set of instants it is necessary to consider denseness in sets of actions. Let A be a set of actions. For any $a, b \in A$ such that $b \in After(a)$, let the set $A[a, b]$ consist of all actions of A that do not terminate before a or after b. i.e.

$$A[a,b] \triangleq \{c \in A \mid a \notin After(c) \land c \notin After(b)\}$$

The set $A[a, b]$ is an *interval* of A. When no confusion arises, we shall omit the prefix 'A' from the notation $A[a, b]$ for intervals.

A set A of actions is *$\sim$-dense* (or overlap-dense) in $A[a, b]$ *iff* for any action $c \notin A$ which lies in the interval $(A \cup \{c\})[a, b]$, there is some action $d \in A$ which does not terminate after c and c does not terminate after d.

$$\forall c \notin A : (c \in (A \cup \{c\})[a,b]) \Rightarrow (\exists d \in A[a,b] : c \dashv d)$$

Assumption 1: Fixed Command Execution
The execution of a command is modelled by exactly one action which bears a fixed relation to all other actions in the program.

This is the simplest assumption that can be made about the execution of a command and it corresponds to the assumption that each command has a fixed execution time. Since in any program of finite size, there can be only a finite number of commands executing at any instant there can only a be a finite number of actions overlapping) at any instant. From *Assumption 1* it follows that the set of actions in any single program execution is not $\sim$-dense.

In any single execution of a program, an action represents one finite execution of a program command. Due to the physical processes involved (e.g. gates with variable delays, buses with variable transmission times, etc.), each such execution is just one of a set of possible executions and it is not possible to determine *a priori* which of these executions will occur. A model of computation must consider *all* possible executions of a program.

Lemma 1 *A set A of actions is $\sim$-dense in $[a, b]$ only if for all x, x' in $[a, b]$ for which $x' \in After(x)$, there is some $x'' \in A$ for which*

$$x'' \in After(x) \land x' \in After(x'')$$

For any command C executed in isolation, i.e. not in composition with any other command, let $ACT(C)$ denote the set of all actions of C. Assume that, in any context of execution, C has an *earliest* action c_{min} and a *latest* action c_{max}, where

$$ACT(C) \cap Before(c_{min}) = \emptyset$$
$$\land [\forall b \in ACT(C) : c_{min} \notin After(b)]$$

and

$$ACT(C) \cap After(c_{max}) = \emptyset$$
$$\wedge\ [\forall b \in ACT(C) : c_{max} \notin Before(b)]$$

For any two commands C and D, let c_{min} in $ACT(C)$ be left-aligned with d_{min} in $ACT(D)$.

Assumption 1a: Denseness in Execution of Primitive Commands
For any primitive command C, the actions in $ACT(C)$ are left-aligned and the termination point of these actions is densely dispersed, i.e. for any primitive command C, $ACT(C)$ is $\sim$-dense in the interval $[c_{min}, c_{max}]$.

Although $ACT(C)$ is $\sim$-dense by assumption, in isolation it produces just one instant. More instants can be produced *iff* one or more actions of the command precede some other actions. Such a precedence relation on actions is obtained through the sequential composition of commands.

In the sequential composition $C_1; C_2$ the starting and termination points of any action in $ACT(C_2)$ must be shifted, or delayed, by the same amount. For a command C, let $Shifted(C)$ be the set of all actions generated by all possible ways of shifting the actions in $ACT(C)$.

Assumption 2: Sequential Composition
Let C_1 and C_2 be two commands and C the sequential composition $C_1; C_2$. If $Shifted(C_2, C_1)$ is the maximal subset of $Shifted(C_2)$ in which the starting point of any action coincides with the termination point of some action in $ACT(C_1)$, then

$$ACT(C) = ACT(C_1) \cup Shifted(C_2, C_1)$$

Thus, sequential composition does not introduce any 'holes' between the execution of its constituent commands and one action starts immediately after the termination of the previous action. This provides an important result — if the set of actions of an infinite sequential composition is $\sim$-dense, then the condition of denseness is satisfied.

Lemma 2 *Let a set A of actions be $\sim$-dense in the intervals $[a, b]$ and $[c, d]$ where $c \in After(a)$; if A does not contain any action e for which*

$$e \in After(b) \wedge c \in After(e)$$

then A is $\sim$-dense in $[a, d]$ iff *$c \notin After(b)$.*

To show that the set of actions of an infinite sequential composition is $\sim$-dense everywhere, consider the *termination dispersion* of a terminating command C. This is a measure of the distance between the earliest and the latest termination points of the executions of C. Assuming that intuitive meaning of the *length* or duration of an action, for any primitive command E, let $min(E)$ and $max(E)$ be the lengths of the actions e_{min} and e_{max} respectively. The termination dispersion τ_C of C is

a) $(max(C) - min(C))$ if C is a primitive command, and

b) $\tau_{C_1} + ((max(C_2) - min(C_2))$ if C is the sequential composition $C_1; C_2$ and C_2 is a primitive command.

Let $C^{(i,n)}$ be the sequential composition $C_i; C_{i+1}; \ldots; C_n$, $i \leq n$. The set $ACT(C^{(1,n)})$ is *$\sim$-dense from C_i onwards* if, for any $b \in After(c_{i_{min}})$, $ACT(C^{(1,n)})$ is $\sim$-dense in $[c_{i_{min}}, b]$.

Theorem 1 *Let C be the infinite sequential composition*

$$C_1; C_2; \ldots; C_i; \ldots$$

where each C_i is a terminating primitive command; then there is some finite k such that $ACT(C)$ is $\sim$-dense from C_k onwards.

Theorem 2 *If D is a primitive command such that $\tau_D \geq min(E)$ for any primitive command E then, for any command D', $ACT(D; D')$ is everywhere $\sim$-dense.*

Assumption 3: Parallel Composition
Let C be the parallel composition $C_1 \| C_2$; then

$$ACT(C) = ACT(C_1) \cup ACT(C_2)$$

If a set A of actions is $\sim$-dense in an interval $[a,b]$ then, for any $c \notin A$, the set $A \cup \{c\}$ is $\sim$-dense in the interval $(A \cup \{c\})[a,b]$. So the set of possible executions of $C_1 \| C_2$ is $\sim$-dense wherever the sets of possible executions of C_1 and C_2 are $\sim$-dense. This parallel composition rule models the case where the first commands of all parallel components begins execution simultaneously. Let this be *Assumption 0*. An alternative is to assume that the starting points of the first commands in the parallel components can be delayed arbitrarily within a limit; let this be *Assumption 0a*. The effect of making this assumption is similar to that obtained by adding to the start of each C_i $(i = 1, 2)$ a primitive command E_i for which

$$min(E_i) = 0 \wedge \tau_{E_i} > 0$$

Let M be the longest of the lengths of the earliest actions of the primitive commands. Let $maxdelay(C)$ be the greater of τ_{E_1} and τ_{E_2}. From Theorem 2, if $maxdelay(C) \geq M$, then $ACT(C)$ is everywhere $\sim$-dense. Thus, a sufficient condition for the set of actions obtained by sequential and parallel composition to be everywhere $\sim$-dense is that either the termination dispersion of a primitive command or the delay in the starting of a parallel component is greater than or equal to M.

Components of a program executed in parallel usually communicate with each other by sending messages. With *synchronous* communication, a message is transferred by executing the sending command and the receiving command simultaneously. Such communication is consistent with Assumption 3. But if the communication is *asynchronous*, there may be an arbitrary delay between the despatch of a message and its receipt. If $C!$ is a sending command and $C?$ its matching receiving command, then with asynchronous communication the possible executions of $C?$ will span an interval $[c_{min}?, c_{max}?]$. Let this be *Assumption 4*. As was shown for sequential composition, it can be shown that after a finite number k of communications, the set of actions is everywhere $\sim$-dense.

4.1 Range of Execution Models

There are, of course, many different assumptions that can be made to relate computation with time. The assumptions chosen above are fairly basic and it has been shown how they lead to denseness in the set of possible executions of actions, and thereby to time represented by a dense domain. However, whether the dense domain should consist of all the reals, the computable reals, the rationals or an arbitrary dense domain is a more difficult question, and one for which the answers depend on further assumptions. Moreover, the results mentioned here have been derived under the assumption of strict precedence of actions, which leads to a total order over instants of time. More generally, however, there is a partial order over actions and further assumptions are needed to derive a domain of time which is consistent with possible causality relations over actions (cf Lamport [9],[8]).

5 Semantics

There are different views on how the semantics of real-time programs should model time and the availability of resources. In synchronous deterministic languages such as ESTEREL [3], the execution times of the real-time system are considered to be insignificant when compared to the time constants of the external events, so the resources of the system are effectively assumed to be infinite. Other semantic models [5,13] assume that the system has the maximum resources needed to execute a program and that, for example, every parallel process is able to execute when it is not waiting to communicate with another process (or the external world).

However, a crucial aspect of the 'real-ness' of many real-time systems is that they have a limited set of computational resources such as processors, memory, channels, etc. whose use must be scheduled appropriately for the real-time program to meet its deadlines. In these cases, the real-time program must be seen as a concurrent program which is executed on a system with limited resources and it is necessary for these limitations to be represented in the associated semantic models.

The execution time of a command depends on the availability of resources such as processors, memory, communication channels etc. Assume that here are bounds, $Lower(C)$ and $Upper(C)$ (which is the maximal requirement), to the resources needed for any command C.

Let us call a command C' the *functional equivalent* of C if they use the same variables and if each behaviour of C is a possible behaviour of C' (but possibly with different times). For example, if C is an assignment command then C' is the same assignment command but executed at different times due to the limited availability of resources. The semantics $\Gamma(C)$ of a command C is a set of quadruples $< R, C', F, W >$, where F is a behaviour of C, W is the set of (command,wait) pairs associated with F, R is a description of the resource availability and C' is a functional equivalent of C for which R is the upper bound of the resource requirement. If C is a primitive command, then $Lower(C)$ and $Upper(C)$ are the same, and C' is C. The set W may be nonempty even for a primitive command if its termination depends on cooperation from other commands.

5.1 Combinators and limited resources

Individual commands in a program are composed together using combinators. For example, in the sequential composition $C_1; C_2$ the combinator ';' composes the two commands C_1 and C_2 while in the parallel composition $C_1 \| C_2 \| \ldots \| C_n$, the n individual commands $C_1 \ldots C_n$ are composed using the parallel combinator $\|$.

Let $\diamond$ be an n-ary combinator and

$$C \triangleq C_1 \diamond \cdots \diamond C_n$$

The *R-semantics* of C is obtained by combining

$$< R_i, C_i', F_i, W_i > \in \Gamma(C_i)$$

for $i \in [1, n]$, such that the F_i's are consistent with respect to $\diamond$ and an execution of C with R can be obtained by executing C_1 with R_1, C_2 with R_2, and so on.

Consider the case of the parallel composition combinator. A limited processor behaviour of a parallel command can be obtained from the limited processor behaviours of its constituent commands. Let each constituent command be partitioned so that if a sub-component does not contain processes its variables are in the same element of the partition, while if it has nested processes each such process is assigned to a different element of the partition.

Given such a partitioning, let $\pi_1 \triangleq \{X_1, \ldots, X_p\}$ be the p-partition of a command c_1 and $\pi_2 \triangleq \{Y_1, \ldots, Y_q\}$ the q-partition of a command c_2. Then the k-combination of π_1 and π_2, written $\pi_1 \oplus_k \pi_2$, is defined if $p + q \geq k$ and is a set of k-partitions, each of the form $\{Z_1, \ldots, Z_k\}$ where $Z_i \in \pi_1 \cup \pi_2$ or Z_i is the union of two or more elements of $\pi_1 \cup \pi_2$.

Obviously, if $p + q = k$, then for example $\pi_1 \oplus_k \pi_2 \; = \; \pi_1 \cup \pi_2$.

It is usual to take the specific case of the processors when considering resource limitations but the approach can readily be generalized to any resource whose requirement can be determined from the syntax of a command. Limited processor semantics of several other combinators have been defined [7] and further details are available elsewhere [4].

6 Implementation

The specification of a real-time program will define its functional properties and the time constraints that must be satisfied by its implementation. If the normal design strategy of implementation by refinement is followed, both of these requirements will need to appear in the specification of smaller units. But while the functional properties may be decomposed using a standard method, there is no obvious way in which the timing constraints can similarly be decomposed. And the closer a design gets to an implementation, the harder it is to consider the functional and timing requirements of a design simultaneously. Moreover, both of these requirements will need to be examined afresh after every program modification.

Suppose that the functional specifications are used to refine the design into successively smaller units; during this refinement, no attempt is made to tailor the design to ensure that the timing properties will be satisfied. Instead, it is merely assumed that the program is implemented with *sufficient* computing resources (i.e. processors of adequate speed, enough memory, etc.) for all the timing constraints to be met. Let this be called the *maximum resource implementation.* If the functional specification and the design refinement are correct, then such an implementation must exist.

The next stage of the design is to transform the maximum resource implementation into an implementation on a specific system. Such transformations will not in general be unique and may not always be possible, for example if the system lacks the resources needed to satisfy the time constraints of the specification.

Assume that in the maximum resource implementation, each process is implemented on a separate processor [15]; normally, the processors will not be fully utilised. We may then determine if two processes can be combined to execute on a single processor so that each process still meets its timing constraints. This will allow the number of processors needed for the implementation to be reduced by one. The procedure can be repeated until the number of processors (or, in general, the size of any other resource) is reduced until it is equal to that available in the system, or until no further reduction is possible if the timing constraints for each process are to be satisfied. The method is in some ways similar to the implementation technique called "process inversion" which is used in Jackson System Development [6] though there no particular attention is paid to the execution times of processes. The question of finding an *optimal* implementation (i.e. one using the fewest resources) is in general NP-complete. The procedure merely enables the amount of resource needed for a particular program to be reduced by combining processes to share resources. The choice of processes to be combined is left to the designer, so there may be cases where more reduction is possible using a different choice.

7 Program Transformation

In the class of programs we shall initially consider, there is one important constraint: each communication command must match syntactically with exactly one communication statement in another process. There is then no distinction between syntactic and semantic matching [2] but note that this still allows processes to have nondeterministic behaviours. The restriction enables programs to be statically analyzed.

The real-time constraints of the problem are specified as deadlines, or as timed input-output relations. Assume that all the input devices and some output devices are cyclic. (Any devices which receive outputs produced as responses to inputs and which can accept successive outputs with some minimum interval can also be considered cyclic in the worst-case). The deadlines for level $L1$ input processes and output processes come from the characteristics of their associated devices and can be converted into deadlines over the execution of the communication commands within these processes. The deadlines for level $L2$ processes can then be derived from these deadlines, and will once again translate into deadlines over communication commands.

Informally, the system's real-time requirement can then be defined briefly as (i) receive all inputs, (ii) send outputs at regular intervals to cyclic output devices, and (iii) send outputs within deadlines to acyclic output devices. The worst case load on the system from a single device arises when successive inputs from the device arrive with the minimum separation time. The worst case load on the system as a whole arises when all the input devices produce their individual worst case loads and the first inputs from all processes arrive simultaneously [10].

Example: In the following program, inputs from two devices are received by processes $P1$ and $P2$, and outputs are sent to a device by process $P3$. Processes $P1$, $P2$ and $P3$ are level 1 processes. Process $P4$ is a level 2 process which receives inputs from processes $P1$ and $P2$ and then produces an output for process $P3$. The deadline for process $P1$ is specified by requiring that the statement Receive(x) be executed every d_1 units. Similarly, d_2 and d_3 specify deadlines for processes $P2$ and $P3$. So in the program, each deadline is the maximum time between successive iterations of the loop.

```
P1 :: Init1;
      *[d1 : Receive(x); P4 ! x ]

P2 :: Init2;
      *[d2 : Receive(y); P4 ! y ]

P3 :: Init3;
      *[d3 : P4 ? z; Send(z)]

P4 :: Init4;
      *[ P1 ? x → P2 ? y; P3 ! f(x,y)
         □
         P2 ? y → P1 ? x; P3 ! f(x,y)]
```

In a maximum resource implementation of this program, there will be four processors for the four processes P_1 to P_4 and we assume that such an implementation will meet the deadlines. Other implementations of this program which meet the deadlines may also be possible and so, for example it is possible to ask under what conditions the program can be implemented on fewer than four processors and still meet all its deadlines.

Let a real-time program P consist of n processes $P_1, P_2, \dots, P_n$. Assume that the processes are *cyclic*, i.e. that each process contains a loop which is executed forever. The structure of process P_i can be represented as a sequence of commands

$$P_i :: C_1, C_2, \dots, C_{j-1}, \{C_j, \dots, C_k\}^*$$

where $Init(P_i) = C_1, C_2, \dots, C_{j-1}$ is the initialisation section and $Cycle(P_i) = C_j, \dots, C_k$ is the loop. For convenience we will at times consider $Init(P_i)$ and $Cycle(P_i)$ to be sets in which each command C_i is unique.

Let $Prec(C)$ be the set of sequential commands which are the *immediate* predecessors of C in all possible executions: in any execution, if C is not the first command in the program then exactly one of the commands in $Prec(C)$ will be executed immediately before C. Similarly, let $Post(C)$ be the set of sequential commands which are the *immediate* successors of C in all possible executions.

A *feasible* schedule is a schedule which is *proper*, i.e. each command is executed in the right order, and which always meets its deadlines. If d_{ij} is the deadline for command $F(c_{ij})$, then it is the deadline for each execution of c_{ij}.

Assume initially that all communication between processes is synchronous and let $Match(C_1, C_2)$ be a predicate which is true if C_1 and C_2 are syntactically matching communications in different processes. $Pred(C)$, the set of all commands that may immediately precede C, can then be defined as

$$Pred(C) = \{C_1 \mid C_1 \in Prec(C_2) \wedge Match(C, C_2)\} \cup \{C_1 \mid C_1 \in Prec(C)\}$$

For a different communication mechanism, e.g. asynchronous communication, the definition of $Pred$ must be changed appropriately.

In the transformations, a common operation is to merge two processor sequences into one sequence, for execution on a single processor. Typically, such a merge will require some shifting in time of the elements of one or both sequences, and the communication dependencies between schedules may then cause shifts of the elements of other sequences. There may be more than one way in which one processor sequence is merged into another, so the merge will in general require nondeterministic choices. Let each process have a unique identifier and for any schedule S_k let the set of identifiers for the processes in the schedule be $Ids(S_k) = \{x \mid \exists y \in S_k : Process(y) = x\}$. Then the merge of sequences S_i, S_j in a schedule $< S_1, \ldots, S_n >$ is represented by

$$SeqMerge(< S_1, \ldots, S_n >, Ids(S_i) \cup Ids(S_j))$$

Informally, $SeqMerge(< S_1, \ldots, S_n >, Ids(S_i) \cup Ids(S_j))$ is a set of schedules in each of which the e-commands executed on the original S_i and S_j are merged into a single sequence.

A reduced implementation is produced by transforming a feasible schedule into another feasible schedule for a system with fewer resources. In general, this would mean starting with the maximum resource implementation, since that can be defined directly from the program and the characteristics of the real-time environment. A transformation is *valid* if, given a feasible schedule, it produces a new feasible schedule.

7.1 Transformations and target architectures

A valid transformation converts a feasible schedule into another feasible schedule. The transformations should not be viewed as depending on either the components or the structure of the target architecture. Rather, transformations are like functions which operate on *schedules*: it is the choice of transformation which is dictated by the target architecture. Schedule transformations can be shown to be commutative and associative. Hence the order of application of transformations can be ignored and a particular reduced implementation can be obtained by choosing the appropriate transformations in any order.

Theorem 3 (Commutativity): *If SC is the schedule* $< S_1, \ldots, S_n >$ *with* $n \geq 2$ *then*

$$SeqMerge(SC, Ids(S_i) \cup Ids(S_j)) = SeqMerge(SC, Ids(S_j) \cup Ids(S_i))$$

Theorem 4 (Associativity): *If SC is the schedule* $< S_1, \ldots, S_n >$ *with* $n \geq 3$ *then*
$$SeqMerge(SeqMerge(SC, Ids(S_i) \cup Ids(S_j)), Ids(S_i) \cup Ids(S_j) \cup Ids(S_k)) =$$
$$SeqMerge(SeqMerge(SC, Ids(S_j) \cup Ids(S_k)), Ids(S_i) \cup Ids(S_j) \cup Ids(S_k)) \quad (1)$$

The use of *SeqMerge* allows the problem of scheduling to be considered *compositionally* and many interesting scheduling methods can be constructed in this way. Not all these compositions are commutative and associative but many useful methods are, for example, pre-emptive scheduling using fixed priorities. More details can be found elsewhere [11].

8 Conclusions

There a several interesting and important problems in the study of real-time programs, of which just a few have been described here. The area is significant both because of the need for a sound theory and because the implementation of such systems is often in safety-critical applications.

9 Acknowledgements

The work described here is the outcome of collaboration over several years with Asis Goswami at the University of Warwick and with Abha Moitra, now at GE Research in Schenectady. My thanks to both of them.

References

[1] A. Abian. *The Theory of Sets and Transfinite Arithmetic.* W.B. Saunders Company, Philadelphia and London, 1965.

[2] K.R. Apt, N. Francez, and W.-P. de Roever. A proof system for Communicating Sequential Processes. *ACM Transactions on Programming Languages and Systems*, 2(3):359–384, 1980.

[3] G. Berry, P. Couronne, and G. Gonthier. *Synchronous Programming of Reactive Systems: An Introduction to ESTEREL.* Technical Report 647, INRIA, Sophia Antipolis, 1987.

[4] A. Goswami and M. Joseph. A semantic model for the specification of real-time processes. In *CONCURRENCY 88, Lecture Notes in Computer Science 335*, pages 292–306, Springer-Verlag, Heidelberg, 1988.

[5] J. Hooman. A compositional proof theory for real-time distributed message passing. In *Lecture Notes in Computer Science 259*, pages 315–332, Springer-Verlag, Heidelberg, 1987.

[6] M. Jackson. *System Development.* Prentice-Hall International, 1983.

[7] M. Joseph and A. Goswami. What's 'real' about real-time systems? In *Proceedings of the 9th IEEE Real-Time Systems Symposium*, pages 78–85, Huntsville, Alabama, 1988.

[8] L. Lamport. On interprocess communication: part I: basic formalism. *Distributed Computing*, 1:77–85, 1986.

[9] L. Lamport. Time, clocks, and the ordering of events in a distributed system. *Communications of the ACM*, 21(7):558–565, 1978.

[10] C.L. Liu and J.W. Layland. Scheduling algorithms for multiprocessing in a hard real-time environment. *Journal of the ACM*, 20:46–61, 1973.

[11] A. Moitra and M. Joseph. Implementing real-time systems by transformation. In *Proceedings of the Real-Time Workshop, University of York*, Elsevier, (to appear), 1989.

[12] A.K. Mok. *Fundamental Design Problems Of Distributed Systems for the Hard Real-Time Environment.* Technical Report MIT/LCS/TR-297, Massachusetts Institute of Technology, 1983.

[13] G.M. Reed and A.W. Roscoe. A timed model for Communicating Sequential Processes. In *Lecture Notes in Computer Science 226*, pages 314–323, Springer-Verlag, Heidelberg, 1986.

[14] B. Russell. On order in time. In *Proceedings of the Cambridge Philosophical Society, vol. 32*, pages 216–228, 1936.

[15] A. Salwicki and T. Müldner. On the algorithmic properties of concurrent programs. In *Lecture Notes in Computer Science 125*, pages 169–197, Springer-Verlag, Heidelberg, 1981.

[16] A.G. Walker. Durées et instants. *Revue Scientifique*, 85:131–134, 1947.

[17] G.J. Whitrow. *The Natural Philosophy of Time.* Clarendon Press, Oxford, 1980.

A Proof System for Communicating Processes with Value-passing (Extended Abstract)

M. Hennessy
University of Sussex

Abstract: A proof system for a version of CCS with value-passing is proposed in which the reasoning about data is factored out from that about the structure of processes. The system is sound and complete with respect to a denotational semantics based on Acceptance Trees.

1 Introduction

In the pioneering publications, [Mil 80], [Hoa 85], both CCS and CSP were presented as languages for describing concurrent processes which transmit data between each other. In much of the subsequent research in this area data transmission has not received much attention. Instead so-called "pure" versions of these languages have been studied extensively and a general notion of "process algebras" has emerged. These are a variety of process description languages which are expressed in terms of sets of combinators for constructing processes which synchronise on channels rather than transmit data. Semantic theories for process algebras, and their associated proof systems, are now fairly well established and it therefore seems appropriate to turn our attention once more to the more general form of processes which may transmit values.

In a companion paper, [HI 89], we have presented a denotational model for such a language and shown that it is fully-abstract with respect to a natural behavioural notion based on testing. The language studied is essentially the original value-passing version of CCS, except that the troublesome τ is replaced by versions of the internal and external choices operators from TCSP.

The process expression

$$c?x.p$$

is meant to denote a process which can input an arbitrary value, v, and then proceed to act like the process $p[v/x]$. The behaviour of this latter process will vary as the particular value input, v, varies. There is a matching output process expression

$$c!e.p$$

which denotes a process which outputs the value of the expression e along the channel c and then acts like p. In the denotational model the input expression $c?x.p$ is represented "functionally", roughly speaking, as a function mapping data-values to semantic objects. However, this function is itself a semantic object and so the domain used is actually the solution of a recursive equation.

From this very brief glance at the model in [HI 89] it should be apparent that our interpretation of

$$c?x.p$$

is very different from that advocated in [Mil 89], where it is interpreted as an infinite choice

$$\sum\{p[v/x] | v \in \mathit{Values}\}.$$

The extension of the syntax to include an infinite choice operator is very convenient descriptively but the mathematical foundations are immediately more complicated. For example, one has to accept unbounded nondeterminism and the lack of any adequate *cpo*-based interpretation. On the other hand, with our "functional" approach we stay within the realm of traditional denotational semantics; our model is a well-behaved algebraic cpo which supports the standard proof techniques. Indeed, in [HI 89] we give a sound and complete proof system based on equational reasoning and a powerful form of induction for recursively defined processes. It is essentially obtained from that for the pure process algebra in [He 88] by adding the ω-data-rule

$$\frac{\forall v \in \mathit{Values}, p[v/x] \leq q[v/x]}{c?x.p \leq c?x.q}$$

This completeness result is only of theoretical interest as the presence of this ω-rule makes the proof system unusable. The aim of this paper is to propose a different proof system, which is still sound and complete, but which is at the same time realistic and, we hope, useful.

In a certain technical sense we are irrevocably doomed. Even the pure language, without data-transmission, is Turing-powerful (see [Mil 89]) and therefore no effective complete proof-system can exist. Nevertheless, we wish to propose a system within which we have powerful methods for reasoning about value-passing processes; and which is such that if we add sufficiently powerful inductive methods for handling recursively defined processes would become complete (and therefore ineffective). The main idea is to separate as much as possible reasoning about the data from reasoning about process behaviour. So in the system we derive statements of the form

$$\mathit{Ass} \vdash p \leq q$$

Here *Ass* is a list of assumptions about data-expressions and this statement means that whenever these assumptions are true then the process p is semantically less than or equal to the process q . A simple rule, for handling output processes, from our proof system is:

$$\frac{\mathit{Ass}, e_1 = e_2 \vdash p \leq q}{\mathit{Ass}, e_1 = e_2 \vdash c!e_1.p \leq c!e_2.q}$$

Intuitively this means that if on the assumption that $e_1 = e_2$ we can prove that p is less than or equal to q , then we can deduce, from the same assumptions that $c!e_1.p$ is also less than or equal to $c!e_2.p$. The rule for input expressions is

$$\frac{Ass \vdash p \leq q}{Ass \vdash c?x.p \leq c?x.q}$$

provided x does not occur in the assumptions Ass.

The methods used to prove the validity of the assumptions about data will depend on the type of data involved. In general we may think of entirely separate proof systems for handling the reasoning on data. This subsidiary proof system would be used or called by the main proof system. For example, if in this subsidiary system we could derive

$$Ass \vdash_{data} e_1 \leq e_2$$

then, after an application of the above output rule, we could conclude

$$Ass \vdash c!e_1.p \leq c!e_2.q.$$

Unfortunately the interaction between the main and subsidiary proof systems will be quite complex. But this should not be surprising as the behaviour of a process depends on the data it receives and therefore the structure of a particular proof will depend on properties of the data-expressions involved. The most general form of interaction will be in the "cut-rule":

$$\frac{\begin{array}{c} Ass_1 \vdash p \leq q, Ass_2 \vdash p \leq q \\ Ass \vdash_{data} Ass_1 \vee Ass_2 \end{array}}{Ass \vdash p \leq q}$$

We do not wish to get involved in designing particular proof systems for particular data domains. Instead we wish to design the main proof system, outlined above, on the assumption that these subsidiary proof systems exist. One way of factoring out these issues is to incorporate semantic statements about data into the rules. So instead of using the proof-theoretic statements

$$Ass \vdash_{data} e_1 = e_2$$

$$Ass \vdash_{data} Ass_1 \vee Ass_2$$

in the proof rules of the main proof system we use the corresponding semantic statements

$$Ass \models e_1 = e_2$$

$$Ass \models Ass_1 \vee Ass_2$$

This allows us to investigate the main proof system which now assumes that there are subsidiary proof systems sufficiently powerful to answer arbitrary questions about data expressions. In this setting a completeness result will, in fact, be a relative completeness result - relative to an oracle about the data expressions. Nevertheless, we believe the system will be useful because in an actual implementation this reliance on an oracle would be replaced by the ability to call subsidiary and independent proof systems.

This extended abstract is outlined as follows. In the next section we define the syntax of the process language. This is a "value-passing" version of the language studied in [He 88], which contains a mixture of CCS and CSP. It is followed by an exposition of the proof system and two examples of its use. In the complete version of the paper, available from the University of Sussex as a technical report, the proof system augmented by a powerful form of induction to handle recursively defined processes is shown to be both sound and complete with respect to the denotational model of [HI 89].

2 The Language

We avoid specific details of the language for expressing data by assuming some predefined category of expressions *Exp*, ranged over by e. This should include, at least, a set of values *Val*, ranged over by v, and a set of variables, *Var*, ranged over by x, and it should be equipped with a reasonable notion of substitution, denoted by $e[e'/x]$. In examples we will use the data-type *Natural numbers* with constants $0, 1, ..$ and function symbols $+, -$ etc. We will also assume the syntactic category of boolean expressions, *BExp*, ranged over by *be* . Here the only values are T and F and the set of boolean variables, denoted by $BVar$, is ranged over by bx.

The set of process-expressions in the language is given by the BNF-definition

$$\begin{array}{lcl} t & ::= & op(t_1, \ldots, t_k), op \in \Sigma_k \mid P \mid pre.t \mid recP.t \\ & & \mid (be \longrightarrow t, t) \\ pre & ::= & c!e \mid c?x \end{array}$$

for a specific set of operator symbols Σ. Here P ranges over a predefined set of process names *PN* and c over a predefined set of channel names *Chan*. The allowed operators are

$\Sigma_0 - \{Nil, \Omega\}$

$\Sigma_1 - \{\backslash C$ where $C \subseteq Chan, [R]$ where R is a finite permutation of $Chan$ }

$\Sigma_2 - \{+, \oplus, |\}$

Those familiar with CCS or CSP will recognise most of these operators. *Nil* is the empty or deadlocked process; Ω is the divergent process; | is parallel composition while + and $\oplus$ are two choice operators, external and internal choice. The operator $\backslash C$ is channel restriction and $[R]$ channel renaming. Input and output of values is represented by the prefixes $c?x$ and $c!e$ respectively. In later sections we will use S to denote the set of operators $\{+, \oplus, |, \backslash C, [R]\}$; these will be interpreted in the denotational model as strict functions.

In process terms we now have two kinds of variables, process-variables, which may be bound by $recP.-$, and data-variables, which may be bound by $c?x.-$. So, for each kind of variable we have free and bound occurrences with each of which is associated a notion of substitution. For process variables this is defined as usual while for data variables the substitution of data expressions for data variables in data expressions, already assumed to exist, is generalised to the substitution of data expressions for data variables in process expressions in the obvious homomorphic manner. We use $FDVar(t)$ to denote the set of free data variables in t while $BDVar(t)$ denotes the set of bound data variables. Unlike in [HI 89] we will make much use of terms with open occurrences of data variables. Consequently we now let *VPL* (Value Passing Language) denote all terms described by the above BNF definition; it is ranged over by meta-variables such as t, u, t', u' etc. However we are primarily interested in terms with no free occurrences of process variables which we call *closed* terms although they may have free occurrences of data variables.

3 The Proof System

The proof system is based on equational transformations plus induction for recursively defined processes. But this must be augmented to handle data-values. As explained in the introduction, we wish to factor out as much as possible those parts of proofs concerned with the space of data-values and therefore some of the rules will appeal to the semantic interpretation of data expressions. We will derive statements of the form

$$Ass \vdash t \leq u$$

where *Ass* is a possibly empty list of assumptions about data expressions, each of the form $e = e'$, $be = be'$, $e \neq e'$ or $be \neq be'$. The intention is such that, whenever we derive such a statement, then for every value environment σ, if $\sigma(Ass)$ is true then $\mathcal{V}[\![t]\!]\sigma \leq \mathcal{V}[\![t]\!]\sigma$. By $\sigma(Ass)$ being true we mean that $\sigma(e) = \sigma(e')$ and $\sigma(be) = \sigma(be')$ for every $e = e'$ and $be = be'$ in *Ass* and $\sigma(e) \neq \sigma(e')$ and $\sigma(be) \neq \sigma(be')$ for every $e \neq e'$ and $be \neq be'$ in *Ass*. The basic system is given in Figure 1 the first part of which is taken directly from [HI 89]. Many of the rules involve $t = u$ rather than $t \leq u$. However the former may be viewed as a shorthand for both $t \leq u$ and $u \leq t$, i.e. representing identity in the model. In rule IV ρ is meant to denote an arbitrary syntactic substitution, i.e a mapping from process names to terms. The equations used in the same rule are those necessary to characterise the model AT^v. For completeness sake these equations, again taken from [HI 89], are given in the Figures 3, 4 and 5, although the interleaving law is changed slightly so as to apply to terms with open occurrences of data variables. As usual in this rule $comms(X,Y)$ is true if X and Y can communicate, i.e. for some $i \in I$ and some $j \in J$ pre_i and pre_j are complementary. The more interesting rules are those to do with data values. The output rule is easily understood: if $t \leq u$ follows from a set of assumptions, then $c!e.t \leq c!e'.u$ also follows, provided $e = e'$ is included in the assumptions. The input rule is similar except we do not augment the assumption list. However, we do have to ensure that the proof of $t \leq u$ does not depend on any particular assumptions about the variable x. So we have the side condition that x should not appear in the list of assumptions. The reasoning about data has significant impact on the reasoning about processes by virtue of the final three rules. The final rule, Contradiction, is self-explanatory: from a contradiction any statement may be derived. The rule of consequence is also straightforward: the set of assumptions may always be strengthened. Finally, the cut rule allows a proof to proceed by case analysis on the assumptions made about the data values. These last two rules will be the greatest obstacles to the automatic or semi-automatic generation of proofs. The less they are used the more the structure of the proof will be governed by the structure of the processes being investigated.

The rules for *If*-expressions are given in Figure 2. The first says that it distributes over the strict function symbols from S. The second simply says that the semantic inequality is preserved by it while the third gives a method for handling $(be \longrightarrow \ldots, \ldots)$ expressions by case analysis. For example, if we can deduce $t \leq r$ under the extra assumption that $be = true$ and that $u \leq r$ under the extra assumption $be = false$, then we can conclude from no extra assumptions that $(be \longrightarrow t, u) \leq r$.

4 Examples

We now give two example proofs about simple processes. The objective is not to derive significant results; rather we wish to show how the system works. However, even to prove the most trivial theorems the system needs to be augmented with some form of induction, otherwise there would be very little one could do with recursively defined processes. We

I
$$\frac{}{\vdash t \leq t} \qquad \frac{\vdash t \leq u,\ u \leq v}{\vdash t \leq v}$$

II
$$\frac{\vdash t_i \leq u_i}{\vdash op(\underline{t}) \leq op(\underline{u})} \quad \text{for every } op \in \sum$$

III
$$\frac{\vdash \quad t \leq u}{\vdash recP.t \leq recP.u} \qquad \frac{}{\vdash recP.t = t[recP.t/P]}$$

IV
$$\frac{\vdash t \leq u}{\vdash t\rho \leq u\rho} \qquad \frac{}{\vdash t \leq u} \quad \text{for every equation } t \leq u$$

V
$$\frac{}{\vdash c?x.t = c?y.t[y/x]} \quad \text{if } y \text{ does not occur free in } t$$

Output
$$\frac{Ass, e = e' \vdash t \leq u}{Ass, e = e' \vdash c!e.t \leq c!e'.u}$$

Input
$$\frac{Ass \vdash t \leq u}{Ass \vdash c?x.t \leq c?x.u} \quad \text{if } x \text{ does not appear in } Ass$$

Consequence
$$\frac{\begin{array}{c} Ass \vdash t \leq u \\ \models Ass' \rightarrow Ass \end{array}}{Ass' \vdash t \leq u}$$

Cut
$$\frac{\begin{array}{c} Ass_1 \vdash t \leq u,\ Ass_2 \vdash t \leq u \\ \models Ass \rightarrow Ass_1 \vee Ass_2 \end{array}}{Ass \vdash t \leq u}$$

Contradiction
$$\frac{}{false = true \vdash t \leq u}$$

Figure 1: The Basic Proof System

If1 $$\frac{}{\vdash op((be \longrightarrow t,u),r) = be \longrightarrow op(t,r), op(u,r)}$$

$$\frac{}{\vdash op(r,(be \longrightarrow t,u)) = (be \longrightarrow op(r,t), op(r,u))}$$

for every $op \in \{|, +, \oplus\}$

$$\frac{}{\vdash (be \longrightarrow t,u)[R] = be \longrightarrow t[R], u[R]}$$

$$\frac{}{\vdash (be \longrightarrow t,u) \setminus C = (be \longrightarrow t \setminus C, u \setminus C)}$$

If2 $$\frac{\vdash t \leq u}{\vdash (be \longrightarrow t,r) \leq (be \longrightarrow u,r)}$$

$$\frac{\vdash t \leq u}{\vdash (be \longrightarrow r,t) \leq (be \longrightarrow r,u)}$$

If3 $$\frac{\begin{array}{c} Ass, be = true \vdash t \leq r \\ Ass, be = false \vdash u \leq r \end{array}}{Ass \vdash (be \longrightarrow t,u) \leq r}$$

$$\frac{\begin{array}{c} Ass, be = true \vdash r \leq t \\ Ass, be = false \vdash r \leq u \end{array}}{Ass \vdash r \leq (be \longrightarrow t,u)}$$

Figure 2: Rules for $(be \longrightarrow \ldots, \ldots)$

$$
\begin{aligned}
X \oplus (Y \oplus Z) &= (X \oplus Y) \oplus Z \\
X \oplus Y &= Y \oplus X \\
X \oplus X &= X \\
X + (Y + Z) &= (X + Y) + Z \\
X + Y &= Y + X \\
X + X &= X \\
X + NIL &= X \\
pre.X + pre.Y &= pre.(X \oplus Y) \\
c?x.X + c?x.Y &= c?x.X \oplus c?x.Y \\
c!e.X + c!e'.Y &= c!e.X \oplus c!e'.Y \\
X + (Y \oplus Z) &= (X + Y) \oplus (X + Z) \\
X \oplus (Y + Z) &= (X \oplus Y) + (X \oplus Z) \\
X \oplus Y &\leq X \\
X + \Omega &\leq \Omega \\
\Omega &\leq X
\end{aligned}
$$

Figure 3: Basic Equations

$$
\begin{aligned}
(X + Y) \setminus C &= X \setminus C + Y \setminus C \\
(X + Y)[R] &= X[R] + Y[R] \\
(X \oplus Y) \setminus C &= X \setminus C \oplus Y \setminus C \\
(X \oplus Y)[R] &= X[R] \oplus Y[R] \\
(pre.X) \setminus C &= \begin{cases} pre.(X \setminus C) & \text{if } chan(pre) \notin C \\ Nil & \text{otherwise} \end{cases} \\
(pre.X)[R] &= R(pre).(x[R]) \\
Nil \setminus C &= Nil \\
Nil[R] &= Nil \\
\Omega \setminus C &= \Omega \\
\Omega[R] &= \Omega \\
(X \oplus Y) \mid Z &= X \mid Z \oplus Y \mid Z \\
X \mid (Y \oplus Z) &= X \mid Y \oplus X \mid Z \\
Nil \mid P &= P \mid Nil = P \\
X \mid (Y + \Omega) &= (X + \Omega) \mid Y = \Omega
\end{aligned}
$$

Figure 4: More Equations

Let X, Y denote $\sum\{pre_i.X_i, i \in I\}, \sum\{pre_j.Y_j, j \in J\}$, where $FDVar(X) \cap BDVar(Y) = FDVar(Y) \cap BDVar(X) = \emptyset$. Then

$$X \mid Y = \begin{cases} ext(X,Y) & \text{if } comms(X,Y) = false \\ (ext(X,Y) + int(X,Y)) \oplus int(X,Y) & \text{otherwise} \end{cases}$$

where

$$ext(X,Y) = \sum\{pre_i.(X_i \mid Y),\ i \in I\} + \sum\{pre_j.(X \mid Y_j),\ j \in J\}$$
$$int(X,Y) = \textstyle\sum \{X_i[e/x] \mid Y_j,\ pre_i = c?x,\ pre_j = c!e\}$$
$$\oplus \textstyle\sum \{X_i[e/y] \mid Y_j,\ pre_i = c!e,\ pre_j = c?y\}$$

Figure 5: Interleaving Law

otherwise there would be very little one could do with recursively defined processes. We choose to use a very simple form of induction, namely *Unique Fixpoint Induction*

$$\frac{\vdash t = u[t/P]}{\vdash t = recP.u}$$

It is well-known that this rule is only sound for so-called "guarded processes" but here we will ignore this issue; all processes we examine will be guarded. As a first example, consider the two processes:

$$recP.in?x.(even(x) \longrightarrow b!(2 * x).a?z.P, P)$$

and

$$recQ.b?x.(div(3,x) \longrightarrow out!(3 * x).a!0.Q, a!0.Q)$$

For convenience let us refer to these as P, Q respectively, although this does involve an abuse of notation. Then let I denote the term

$$(P|Q) \setminus \{a, b\}$$

and by the same abuse of notation let S denote

$$recS.in?x.(div(6,x) \longrightarrow out!(6 * x).S, S)$$

We show how to derive

$$\vdash S = I.$$

We do not give a formal proof of this statement in the proof system, i.e. a sequence of applications of the proof rules from the previous section; this would be too boring and uninformative. Instead we show informally, in a goal-directed manner, how such a formal proof could be constructed. For pure process algebras there is a fairly standard "tactic" which may be applied in order to generate such proofs and which works (with minor adjustments) in a large number of cases. Here we show that more or less the same tactic is applicable; the only difference is that the evolution of the tactic is periodically influenced by a case analysis of the data.

The term S is a recursive definition and in order to show $\vdash S = I$ we therefore use an instance of Unique Fixpoint Induction. So it is sufficient to derive

$$\vdash I = (in?x.div(6,x) \longrightarrow out!(6 * x).I, I) \tag{1}$$

In order to derive this statement we try to apply the standard strategy, namely, expand out all recursive definitions in I, apply the interleaving law and then the restriction laws. Expanding out the recursive definitions we obtain

$$\vdash I = (in?x.P_1|b?x.Q_1) \setminus \{a,b\}$$

where P_1, Q_1 denote the *If*-statements in the bodies of P, Q respectively. An application of the interleaving law gives

$$\vdash I = (in?x.(P_1|b?x.Q_1) + b?x.(in?x.P_1|Q_1)) \setminus \{a,b\}$$

and the restriction laws

$$\vdash I = in?x.((P_1|b?x.Q_1) \setminus \{a,b\}.$$

So, in order to prove equation(1), it is now sufficient to show

$$\vdash (div(6,x) \longrightarrow out!(6*x).I, I) = (P_1|Q) \setminus \{a,b\}$$

for then we may apply the input rule. At this point we call on the rule If3. In order to apply it we need to establish two results:

$$div(6,x) = true \vdash out!(6*x).I = (P_1|Q) \setminus \{a,b\} \qquad (2)$$

and

$$div(6,x) = false \vdash I = (P_1|Q) \setminus \{a,b\}. \qquad (3)$$

Let us first consider (2). By using the fact that $|$ and $\setminus C$ distributes through If-statements (see the rule If1) we obtain :

$$\vdash (P_1|Q) \setminus \{a,b\} = (even(x) \longrightarrow (P_t|Q) \setminus \{a,b\}, (P|Q) \setminus \{a,b\})$$

where P_t denotes the true branch in the *If*-expression in the body of P, $b!(2*x).a?z.P$. So equation (2) may be proved with another instance of the rule If3 if we can derive

$$even(x) = true, div(6,x) = true \vdash out!(6*x).I = (P_t|Q) \setminus \{a,b\}$$

and

$$even(x) = false, div(6,x) = true \vdash out!(6*x).I = (P|Q) \setminus \{a,b\}.$$

The latter is easily established since there are contradictory assumptions. The contradiction rule gives

$$true = false \vdash out!(6*x).I = (P|Q) \setminus \{a,b\}$$

and since

$$even(x) = false, div(6,x) = true \models true = false$$

we may apply the rule of consequence. So we are left with the former statement to establish. We apply the standard strategy to $(P_t|Q) \setminus \{a,b\}$. In this case this means expand the definition of Q, apply the interleaving law and then apply the restriction laws. The result is

$$\vdash (P_t|Q) \setminus \{a,b\} = (a?z.P|Q_1) \setminus \{a,b\}$$

where Q_1 is $(div(3, 2*x) \longrightarrow Q_t, Q_f)$ and where Q_t, Q_f are $out!(3*2*x).a!0.Q$ and $a!0.Q$ respectively. Note the presence of $2*x$ rather than simply x in this expression. Once more we apply the distributivity of $|$ and $\backslash C$ through $(be \longrightarrow \ldots, \ldots)$ and therefore we are left with establishing

$$even(x) = true, div(6,x) = true$$
$$\vdash out!(6*x).I = (div(3,2*x) \longrightarrow (a?z.P|Q_t) \setminus \{a,b\}, (a?z.P|Q_f) \setminus \{a,b\}).$$

Once more we need to apply the rule If3 and therefore we must establish the two statements

$$even(x) = true, \quad div\ (6,x) = true, \quad div\ (3, 2*x) = true$$
$$\vdash out!(6*x).I = (a?z.P|Q_t) \setminus \{a,b\}$$

and

$$even(x) = true, \quad div\ (6,x) = true, \quad div\ (3, 2*x) = false$$
$$\vdash out!(6*x).I = (a?z.P|Q_f) \setminus \{a,b\}$$

As before, the latter contains contradictory assumptions and therefore may be derived from the contradiction and consequence rules and so we concentrate on the former. The standard strategy gives

$$\vdash (a?z.P|Q_t) \setminus \{a,b\} = out!(3*2*x).((a?z.P|a!0.Q) \setminus \{a,b\}).$$

Another application of the strategy gives

$$\vdash (a?z.P|a!0.Q) \setminus \{a,b\} = I$$

and an application of the output rule then gives

$$6*x = 3*2*x \vdash out!(6*x).I = (a?z.P|Q_t) \setminus \{a,b\}.$$

However $\models 6*x = 3*2*x$ and therefore the rule of consequence gives

$$\vdash out!(6*x).I = (a?z.P|Q_t)\{a,b\}$$

and a final application of the same rule gives the required

$$even(x) = true, \quad div\ (6,x) = true, \quad div\ (3, 2*x) = true$$
$$\vdash out!(6*x).I = (a?z.P|Q_t) \setminus \{a,b\}$$

This completes the proof of equation (2) above or, more accurately, shows how a proof of equation (2) may be found. To establish the overall result it is also necessary to prove equation (3). This proceeds in much the same manner. It can be reduced to proving the two statements

$$div(6,x) = false, even(x) = true \vdash I = (P_t|Q) \setminus \{a,b\}$$

and

$$div(6,x) = false, even(x) = false \vdash I = (P|Q) \setminus \{a,b\}.$$

The second is obvious while the same strategies as above may be applied to $(P_t|Q) \setminus \{a,b\}$, as before to reduce it to the two statements

$$div(6,x) = false, even(x) = true, \quad div\ (3, 2*x) = true$$
$$\vdash I = (a?z.P|Q_t) \setminus \{a,b\}$$

$$div\ (6,x) = false, even(x) = true, div(3, 2*x) = false$$
$$\vdash I = (a?z.P|Q_f) \setminus \{a,b\}$$

The first of these involves contradictory assumptions and therefore may be derived in the usual way from the rules of contradiction and consequence. The second, on the other hand, may be derived by one more application of the standard strategy, without appeal to the assumptions.

We finish with a very simple example whose only purpose is to show the need for the cut rule. We show how to derive

$$x \leq 1, 0 \leq x \vdash c!(x-1).Nil \oplus c!1.Nil \quad \leq \quad c!x.Nil.$$

This may seem a little artificial but it arises naturally when proving, for example, the equivalence between the two processes

$$x \leq 1 \longrightarrow (x < 0 \longrightarrow c!x.Nil, c!(x-1).Nil \oplus c!1.Nil), c!x.Nil$$

and

$$c!x.Nil.$$

There are only two possible values for x which satisfy the assumptions, 0 and 1. When $x = 0$ the process $c!(x-1).Nil \oplus c!1.Nil$ and $c!x.Nil$ are related because $x = 0 \models x = (x-1)$ - in the natural numbers the predecessor of 0 is 0 - and therefore we can derive

$$x = 0 \vdash c!(x-1).Nil \leq c!x.Nil$$

using the output rule and the rule of consequence. Then using the equation

$$X \oplus Y \leq X$$

we obtain

$$x = 0 \vdash c!(x-1).Nil \oplus c!1.Nil \leq c!x.Nil.$$

On the other hand, when $x = 1$ the reasoning is different. In this case $x = 1 \models x = 1$ and therefore we may use the output rule to derive

$$x = 1 \vdash c!1.Nil \leq c!x.Nil$$

and then the equation

$$X \oplus Y \leq Y$$

to obtain

$$x = 1 \vdash c!(x-1).Nil \oplus c!1.Nil \quad \leq \quad c!x.Nil.$$

So the two different possible values for x require different proofs. However, these may now be pulled together using the cut rule because

$$x \leq 1, 0 \leq x \models x = 0 \vee x = 1.$$

The application gives the required result:

$$x \leq 1, 0 \leq x \models c!(x-1).Nil \oplus c!1.Nil \quad \leq \quad c!x.Nil.$$

CONCLUSION

In this paper we have designed a new style of proof system for an extension of process algebras in which value-passing is accommodated. The central idea is to try to dissociate the reasoning about the data as much as possible from the reasoning about the processes with the result that the new proof system may be viewed as an extension of the well-known proof methods for "pure" process algebras based on equational transformations and induction. Of course this dissociation is not possible in general as the behaviour of a process will often depend on the data it receives. Nevertheless our new proof system sets up a clear framework within which the interaction between two different proof domains, that associated with data and that associated with the processes themselves, can be easily managed. Indeed we hope that it forms the basis of a practical proof environment the central component of which is the basic proof system outlined in section 3. In addition the user would have access to a range of auxiliary independent proof systems for establishing facts about the data-domain. Then in the central system when one needs to apply a rule which requires knowledge of the data domain, such as the rule of consequence, a call would be made to an auxiliary proof system to establish the required facts about the data expressions. In other words in a practical proof system the rules which appeal to the semantics of the data-domain, those which use $\models$, would be implemented by calls to appropriate independent proof systems. The design of such a proof environment is a major and exciting challenge.

There is very little work in the existing literature on the subject of process algebras and value-passing. The equational proof systems for pure process algebras on which our system is based are well established and standard references are [Hoa 85] and [Mil 89]. In the latter a value-passing process algebra is reduced to a pure calculus augmented by an infinite choice operator. This has already been discussed in the Introduction. The only other extension of these techniques to value-passing in the literature of which I am aware is in [RH 88]. Here they extend the equational system for CSP to a subset of OCCAM. The resulting system is quite different from ours in that it consists of a large number of equational identities. Nevertheless these are shown to be complete in some sense and the authors advocate as a proof technique the reduction of programs to a standard or normal form. Also OCCAM is quite different from our language. It is imperative rather than applicative in that the programs act on a store. Proof systems for these kinds of languages, based on the original version of CSP, [Hoa 78], have been developed by a large number of researchers. By and large these languages are viewed as extensions of Dijkstra's guarded command language, [Dijk 76], and the associated proof systems are extensions of Hoare Logics, originally designed for sequential programming languages but subsequently extended to Dijkstra's language. A good survey of this area of research may be found in [Apt 85].

Acknowledgements The research reported here was partially funded by SERC. The author would also like to thank F. Williams for help in producing the document.

References

[Apt 85] Apt, K. "Proving Correctness of CSP Programs - A tutorial" *Proceedings of IFIP Workshop on Protocol Specification, Testing and Verification V*, M. Diaz, ed., pp. 73-84. North-Holland, Amsterdam, 1986.

[Bri 86] Brinksma, E. "A Tutorial on LOTOS." *Proceedings of Control Flow and Data Flow: Concepts of Distributed Programming* NATO ASI Series, Vol F14, edited by M.Broy, Springer-Verlag, 1985.

[Dijk 76] Dijkstra, E.W., *A discipline of Programming* Prentice Hall, Englewood Cliffs, 1976.

[DNH 84] DeNicola, R. and M. Hennessy. "Testing Equivalences for Processes." *Theoretical Computer Science*, 24, 1984, pp. 83-113.

[Gue 81] Guessarian, I., "Algebraic Semantics", *Springer-Verlag Lecture Notes in Computer Science*, vol.99, 1981.

[HP 80] Hennessy, M. and Plotkin, G., "A Term Model for CCS", *Springer-Verlag Lecture Notes in Computer Science*, vol.88, 1980.

[He 85] Hennessy, M. "Acceptance Trees." *Journal of the ACM*, v. 32, n. 4, October 1985, pp. 896-928.

[He 88] Hennessy, M. *Algebraic Theory of Processes.* MIT Press, Cambridge, 1988.

[HI 89] Hennessy, M and Ingolfsdottir, A. " A Theory of Communicating Processes with Value-passing" University of Sussex Technical Report No 3/89, 1989.

[Hoa 85] Hoare, C.A.R. *Communicating Sequential Processes.* Prentice-Hall International, London, 1985.

[Hoa 78] Hoare, C.A.R. "Communicating Sequential Processes" *Communications of ACM* , 21, no 8, pp. 666-677, 1978.

[RH 88] Hoare, C.A.R. and Roscoe, A.W., "The Laws of Occam" PRG Monograph, Oxford University, 1986. (Also published in *Theoretical Computer Science*)

[In 84] Inmos Ltd., *The Occam Programming Manual*, Prentice-Hall, London, 1984.

[Miln 88] Milne, R., "Concurrency Models and Axioms", RAISE/STC/REM/6/V2, STC Technology Ltd., 1988.

[Mil 80] Milner, R. *A Calculus of Communicating Systems*, Lecture Notes in Computer Science 92. Springer-Verlag, Berlin, 1980.

[Mil 89] Milner, R., *Calculus for Communication and Concurrency*, Prentice-Hall, London 1989.

[Plo 81] Plotkin, G., "Lecture Notes in Domain Theory", University of Edinburgh, 1981.

[Ros 87] Roscoe, A.W., "Denotational Semantics for Occam", PRG Monograph, Oxford University, 1988.

[Smt 86] Schmidt, D., *Denotational Semantics*, Allen and Bacon, 1986.

[SP 82] Smyth, M. and Plotkin, G., "The Category-Theoretic Solution of Recursive Domain Equations", *SIAM Journal on Computing*, vol.11, No.4, 1982.